THE PERSECUTION OF THE CATHOLIC CHURCH IN THE THIRD REICH: FACTS AND DOCUMENTS

THE PERSECUTION OF THE CATHOLIC CHURCH IN THE THIRD REICH

FACTS AND DOCUMENTS
TRANSLATED FROM THE GERMAN

PELICAN PUBLISHING COMPANY
Gretna 2003

Manufactured in the United States of America
Published by Pelican Publishing Company, Inc.
1000 Burmaster Street, Gretna, Louisiana 70053

TRANSLATOR'S FOREWORD

THIS book is a translation, direct from the German manuscript, of the work of one who has observed closely and recorded faithfully every phase of the relations between the Catholic Church and National Socialism. The sub-title, "Facts and Documents," describes its contents and its scope. It is not a formal historical study. The evidence is not elaborated, still less manipulated, to give plausibility to a thesis. But it *is* an exhaustive and orderly presentation of the evidence, a sober record of fact which never for a moment leaves the final verdict in doubt.

That verdict is that the word "persecution" is applicable in its most exact sense to the treatment meted out by the National Socialists to the Catholic Church in Germany. There are many, including some Catholics, whose minds have been dulled and anæsthetised into universal scepticism by that wholesale distortion of truth which is synonymous with propaganda of a certain type. Unless the facts are made to stare them in the face, they are apt to pooh-pooh the assertion that there is a genuine persecution of the Church in Germany. It is the function of this book to present them with the facts in that inexorable way. Hence the general arrangement and method of the work, which is prodigal of facts, documents and circumstantial detail but economical in those large synoptic developments which belong to the writing of history as a literary art. Nevertheless the facts and documents are set forth in a connected narrative sufficient to render them intelligible in their proper setting.

Much use has been made of the Pastoral Letters of the German Bishops, for they are evidence of the first rank for the authenticity of the facts which they narrate: any inaccuracy in matters of fact would have been challenged immediately. The large number of these Pastorals will occasion no surprise if it be remembered that, with the Catholic Press effectively muzzled, they were the sole means of bringing home to Catholics the realities of the religious situation.

As for the identity of the author, for obvious reasons he must remain anonymous. National Socialism has a short way with those who bear witness against it. In any case, the truth of the evidence here presented is so compelling that the publication of the author's name would neither enhance nor diminish its authority.

Our thanks are due to the Catholic Truth Society for permission to use its translation of the Papal Encyclical *Mit brennender Sorge* and to the *Universe* for the account of the closing of the " Canisianum."

PREFACE

THIS is no polemical work; it is intended merely to provide a factual report of the National Socialist persecution of the Church in Germany. This report will be simple and comprehensive—simple, since the facts speak for themselves; and comprehensive, since the persecution itself is all-embracing, carried through in season and out of season and with full deliberation. It is not a mere episode or a temporary tactical method, but an essential element of National Socialism, something systematic and calculated. The intention of the book is to make this clear to right-minded men. But it is our purpose to achieve this without engaging in polemics; a plain, yet full account of the actual facts will make the matter clear enough.

It appears to us of the utmost importance that such a report should be made available. Propaganda, carried out with typical German thoroughness and organising ability, has succeeded in clouding over this issue of religious persecution (and many questions besides) in such a way that for the most part it is impossible to get at the facts or know the truth.

The system which is so fond of lightning strokes in all that it undertakes, and boasts of launching its relentless attacks " into the very gates of the enemy," is cautious and wary to a degree in the measures taken against the Church. Whatever happens, there is the desire to avoid giving the impression of fundamental enmity towards the Church. For this reason the Church's positions are not all attacked at once, but step by step after the most careful and painstaking preparation of public opinion. It is in this way that even the most radical measures are put into operation; recourse is had to petty subterfuges and trifling mitigations are offered to mollify the public and cloud the situation: the measures will be ascribed to " the mistake of some subordinate," a few exemptions will be granted, and at least a show will be made of withdrawing noxious regulations temporarily. Above all the effort is made to allay public disquiet by constantly repeated assurances that there is no question at all of any intention to institute a persecution against the Church. Year after year, up to the present day, the National Socialist press and the leading personalities of the movement are never tired of proclaiming that the new State is to be built up " on a basis of positive Christianity," that all that is being done is to " purge and free the Church and Religion from politics," and so on. Woe to the parish priest in his pulpit, or the writer in his parish magazine, who hazards the faintest suggestion that the Church is oppressed in Germany today; such "dissemination of atrocity fables" would at once be rewarded by a sentence of imprisonment. In 1938 a booklet was issued by the central press of the NSDAP (German National Socialist Workers' Party) bearing the title, "Political Catholicism's Great Falsehood"; the text, statistics and pictures purported to show the flourishing nature of Catholic life in the Third Reich, and culminated in the indignant query: "How can they speak of a persecution of the Church?" The enormous resources of the National Socialist propaganda with its army of agents, correspondents of the DNB (Official German News Agency), and its paid propagandists with huge sums of money at their disposal, ensure that even in the most distant countries the cry shall resound: "In the Third Reich there is no persecution of the Church."[1]

This makes it all the more necessary to expose by a clear and comprehensive account of the facts the real intentions and the true character of the ecclesiastico-political measures adopted by National Socialism. With this in mind it will be our earnest endeavour to lay before the reader nothing but **reliable** material. It will, however, be readily understood that the very method used by National Socialism in its fight against the Church has placed enormous difficulties in the way of collecting and confirming the information we are here offering. To this must be added the terror which reigns in Germany today, and the cowed and intimidated attitude of the Catholic section of its population. In spite of all this we have spared ourselves no trouble in the way of journeys, enquiries, interviews and reading in order that, as far as possible, full documentation and reference should be given for the facts which we are to narrate, so that they may be checked by anybody. In cases where documentary evidence is lacking, our statements are based on information from entirely trustworthy persons, often in the form of sworn declarations. There can be no doubt that when once the National Socialist régime has been cleared away, almost every Catholic family and every Catholic presbytery will be able to relate dozens of cases similar to those which are given in this book. Whoever is still unbiassed enough to be able to discern the truth and recognise it will find it in this factual report.

We purposely limit ourselves here to a treatment of the persecution of the Catholic Church. The battle in defence of the Evangelical Church, conducted in some parts in a manner truly heroic—particularly by the body known as the "Confessional Church"—deserves a separate treatment.

[1] *Cf.* the repeated asseverations and passionate protestations in *Das Schwarze Korps*, February 25th, 1937, p. 3; April 29th, 1937, p. 1; June 3rd, 1937, p. 9 *sqq.* (illustrated); June 10th, 1937, p. 1 *sqq.*; August 18th, 1938, p. 2, etc.

CONTENTS

	PAGE
TRANSLATOR'S FOREWORD	v
PREFACE	vii

PART ONE

AUTHENTIC TESTIMONIES TO THE FACT OF A PERSECUTION OF THE CHURCH IN GERMANY

CHAPTER
I. EVIDENCE FROM THE VATICAN	1
II. EVIDENCE FROM THE GERMAN HIERARCHY	13

PART TWO

THE GOVERNMENT OF THE THIRD REICH AND THE CHURCH

I. OFFICIAL ACTION AGAINST THE CHURCH'S GOVERNMENT AND ADMINISTRATION	41
II. INTERFERENCE WITH THE TEACHING OF THE CHURCH	59
III. THE CHURCH IS EXCLUDED FROM THE WORK OF EDUCATION: I. THE DESTRUCTION OF THE CATHOLIC YOUTH ASSOCIATIONS	82
IV. THE CHURCH IS EXCLUDED FROM THE WORK OF EDUCATION: II. THE DESTRUCTION OF THE CATHOLIC SECONDARY SCHOOLS	115
V. THE CHURCH IS EXCLUDED FROM THE WORK OF EDUCATION: III. THE DESTRUCTION OF THE CATHOLIC ELEMENTARY SCHOOLS	143
VI. THE CHURCH IS EXCLUDED FROM THE WORK OF EDUCATION: IV. RELIGIOUS INSTRUCTION	163
VII. THE OBSTRUCTION OF THE CHURCH'S PASTORAL WORK: I. THE DESTRUCTION OF CATHOLIC ORGANISATIONS FOR ADULTS	187
VIII. THE OBSTRUCTION OF THE CHURCH'S PASTORAL WORK: II. SUNDRY APOSTOLIC WORKS	206
IX. THE REFUSAL OF LEGAL PROTECTION FOR THE CATHOLIC CHURCH	234
X. ATTACKS ON THE HONOUR OF THE CHURCH	263
XI. THE CURRENCY TRIALS AND THE "IMMORALITY" TRIALS	295

PART THREE

THE NATIONAL SOCIALIST PARTY AND THE CHURCH

I. THE PARTY ORGANISATIONS AND THEIR PUBLICATIONS	329
II. OCCUPATIONAL ORGANISATIONS AND THEIR PUBLICATIONS	353

CONTENTS

CHAPTER	PAGE
III. ORGANISATIONS FOR YOUTH AND THEIR PUBLICATIONS	370
IV. OFFICIAL SUPPORT LENT TO OTHER ATTACKS ON THE CHURCH	395
V. ATTACKS ON THE CHURCH AND HER REPRESENTATIVES	414
VI. ATTACKS ON CATHOLIC FAITH AND PRACTICES	437
VII. THE NEW MORALITY	457
VIII. THE *ersatz* RELIGION	479
CONCLUSION	513
APPENDIX I.: CONCORDAT BETWEEN THE HOLY SEE AND THE GERMAN REICH	516
APPENDIX II.: THE PAPAL ENCYCLICAL *Mit brennender Sorge*	523
APPENDIX III.: SERMON PREACHED BY CARDINAL FAULHABER TO THE MEN'S SODALITY IN ST. MICHAEL'S, MUNICH, ON SUNDAY, JULY 4TH, 1937	538
APPENDIX IV.: DIOCESAN REPORTS ON THE DESECRATION OF CRUCIFIXES, ETC.	544
APPENDIX V.: NATIONAL SOCIALIST ORGANISATIONS	550
INDEX	553

LIST OF ILLUSTRATIONS

	FACING PAGE
SEVEN MILLIARD REICHSMARKS CHURCH TAXES	52
"FEED MY—LAMBS"	53
THE POLICE STATION AT ESSEN	104
THE VATICAN SOLVES THE RACIAL QUESTION	105
THE CROSSED ADDER	202
FAULHABER AND MOSCOW	203
THE TWO REDS	278
CATHOLIC RELIGIOUS HOUSES	279
CATHOLIC FASHIONS	338
FOUND OUT AT LAST	339
PRIGS AND HUMBUGS	380
THE CARDINAL'S JOURNEY TO FRANCE	381
THE CONFESSIONAL	442
GERMAN CHRISTMAS	443
NEO-PAGAN "CHRISTMAS"	488
NAZI DEMAGOGY	489

PART ONE
AUTHENTIC TESTIMONIES TO THE FACT OF A PERSECUTION OF THE CHURCH IN GERMANY

CHAPTER I
EVIDENCE FROM THE VATICAN

IN the years following the conclusion of the Great War, papal policy was characterised by a number of Concordats with European states, of which three were made with German states—with Bavaria in 1924, with Prussia in 1929 and with Baden in 1932—and a fourth, the most important, with the new Germany of the Third Reich in July, 1933.[1] Negotiations for this last Concordat were undertaken " at the request of the German Government,"[2] which was anxious for it for reasons of external prestige and internal policy, but it was " in spite of many serious misgivings "[2] that the Holy See finally decided to give its consent. Nevertheless, all questions of importance, as free communication between Rome and the local ecclesiastical authorities, freedom of the Catholic press, of Catholic education, of Catholic Action in charitable, professional and youth organisations, etc., were dealt with and their basic principles formulated and agreed upon. After the conclusion of the Concordat, it should then have been possible to look forward to a period of peace and harmony between Church and State in the Third Reich. Unfortunately it was not so, as is proved by the clear declarations of the Vatican. There was already in evidence that will to annihilate, of which Pius XI was later to write so trenchantly.

But it is not our purpose to reproduce all the Vatican's declarations relating to the persecution of the Church in Germany: we wish rather to draw attention to the continual series of Roman protests against breaches of the Concordat by the German Government. In the very month in which the treaty was signed, the Vatican journal *L'Osservatore Romano*[3] found it necessary to raise its voice against false interpretations of the text of the Concordat, made in favour of the State authority. Then in October, 1933, the Holy Father, Pius XI, gave an address to a pilgrimage of the German Catholic Young Men's

---
[1] The full text will be found in Appendix I.   [2] *Mit brennender Sorge*.
[3] July 26th and 27th, 1933.

Association, which showed his very deep anxiety about religious developments in Germany. His actual words on that occasion were:

> German Catholic Youth! German — Catholic — Youth: three words and each one of them a reason for a specially hearty welcome. You feel that it is so, especially at this time, in this hour which is so historic for Germany, and not merely so historic, but *so hard*. You understand Us. By temperament and desire We are optimistic. And so, difficult and hard as this hour undoubtedly is, We are constrained to say that great hopes are reposed in you. The future lies in the hands of God. It would be much worse if we men were able to take the future into our own hands and shape it for ourselves. We must lay up great hopes in our hearts. But, beloved sons, our hopes cannot exclude every danger. You know that We are filled with the deepest anxiety and real alarm about the youth of Germany, and entertain fears with regard to religion in Germany.

On the occasion of this pilgrimage Cardinal Pacelli, the Secretary of State, took the opportunity of addressing the Catholic Youth Societies at an audience, when he said to them:

> In these apartments in which I now receive you, there was signed a short time ago the Concordat, in which the Father of Christendom, in his love and solicitude, took thought for you expressly, and brought into effect measures of State protection which should ensure for you and your societies room to live in and a field of activity in which to work. May Christ the King, Whose feast you celebrated yesterday at Santa Croce, hold His protecting hand over all that important work of peace which was then agreed upon in an hour of mutual understanding between Church and State. May He bring it about that the magnanimous intentions, which inspired both parties to the Concordat at the time, be more and more shared by all—to the well-being of the nation, to the safeguarding of its harmony and its strength. May He Who commands the wind and the waves stem the rising tide that is flooding in from the most diverse quarters to destroy the work of peace, in opposition to the will of the supreme authority in Germany as expressed at the conclusion of the Concordat.

At Easter, 1934, the Holy Father sent a personal greeting to the Catholic Youth of Germany, from which we give the following extracts:

> To the Catholic Youth Associations of Germany. . . . With deep sympathy and with great satisfaction We accept the expressions of filial devotion to the Vicar of Christ and of unswerving loyalty to Holy Church which you have communicated to Us. With deep sympathy, We say, since you are in the forefront of those who have already made sacrifices for your religious ideals and continue to make them daily: with great satisfaction for the courageous witness you have borne, and the truly supernatural spirit which inspires you. In spite of all the hardships through which Providence is leading you, and in defiance of a propaganda both of allurement and of pressure in favour of a new way of life which leads away from Christ to paganism, you have not forsaken the love and fidelity which you have sworn to Our Saviour and His Church. For this very reason you remain more constant than ever to your nation and Fatherland, which you still wish to serve, as in days gone by, in closest union and forgetfulness of self. Our pastoral care and responsibility has impelled Us to keep in constant touch with the situation of the Catholic Youth of Germany, and that is also, We know, the great care and anxiety of your bishops. Your Associations may in any case rest assured that their interests are Our interests also. With fatherly love We lead you to the foot of the Cross, whose symbol shines

forth on your banners, and impart to you from Our heart, as a source of strength and inviolable devotion to the Faith, the Apostolic Blessing which you request. From the Vatican, Easter, 1934. Pius P.P. XI.

A few days later Pope Pius XI received in special audience about 200 members of the *Neudeutschland* organisation and nearly 100 members of the *Sturmschar* (élite) of the Catholic Young Men's Association, and gave them an address from which the following is taken:

We know—to Our misfortune We know and know too how few are **able** to know—what a painful hour this is for you, dear sons, for the whole of Germany, for Catholic Germany especially, and even more especially for you, *Neudeutschland*, for you, Catholic young men, Catholic Youth. Day after day news is coming in to us, and, alas, it is not good news. And yet we do not abandon hope in a better, finer future, as the saying is in Germany today. It will come, perhaps even soon. We must never lose our confidence, for that would be to wrong divine Providence. Providence will intervene, and will be on our side so far as we do not wish to be against it or deprived of it. . . . We know that so many, so very many have already suffered so much. We know that so many from these splendid ranks of yours, from the *Sturmschar*, from *Neudeutschland* and from the Young Men's Association in general have already given proof of heroic courage and truly martyr-like faith and loyalty. And We, beloved sons, We congratulate you. We congratulate you on the good, generous resolutions you have made for the future. We congratulate you also for all that you have already had to suffer, and perhaps still have to suffer. For, beloved sons, the hour has come when each one must call to mind that splendid and glorious truth, those proud words of the first days of our Redemption, when the Apostles were glad and went forth rejoicing that they had been found worthy *pro nomine Iesu contumeliam pati*—to suffer something for the name of Jesus. To all your comrades and your friends give Our greeting, give them Our congratulations and Our blessing. Tell all of them what We now say to you—that We shall do everything, everything that lies in Our power to take true care of them, and, if necessary, to protect them. We know that you will defend the holy Catholic Faith, live it and honour it, and that you will bring honour to the Catholic Faith in Germany. We see that you are fighting a good and glorious fight for Us, for the honour of the Church and the honour of God. Beloved sons, We shall fight; wherever it is possible, We Ourselves shall fight for you. Tell that to everyone. Also, alas, We know that negotiation often necessitates a renunciation of action. Whatever it costs us, of this you may be sure—We shall always speak the truth and defend the truth, and with it your rights, which are the rights of conscience, the rights of the Catholic Faith, the rights of God's honour. These rights We shall ever defend. . . .

The hour has come, and has already been long upon us, when in Germany especially it is not enough to say " Christian life, Christian doctrine." We must say " Christian-Catholic life, Christian-Catholic doctrine." For what remains of Christianity, of real Christianity without Catholicism, without also the Catholic Church, without Catholic doctrine, without Catholic life ? Nothing, or almost nothing. Or better, in the end, one can and must say—not merely a false Christianity but a true paganism.

(*Easter Tuesday*, 1934.)

The Secretary of State, Cardinal Pacelli, in a message sent by him to Cardinal Schulte of Cologne on the occasion of the twenty-fifth anniversary of the latter's episcopal consecration, speaks very clearly about the persecution of the Church in Germany. We give the following extract from the message, which is dated March 12th, 1935:

> When, however, false prophets arise, proclaiming themselves with satanic pride to be the bearers of a new faith and a new gospel that is not the Gospel of Christ; when violent and irreverent hands are raised against that sacred heritage which the all-holy God has given and revealed to us in the religion of Jesus Christ as a supernatural and all-sufficient treasure of faith and of life; when the custodian of the true Faith, the Church, and her supreme head, the Pope, are subjected to unheard-of attacks; when the lying attempt is made to conjure up a conflict between loyalty to the Church of Christ and loyalty to the earthly fatherland, such as does not and cannot exist so long as every earthly power is aware of its own subordination under the royal sceptre of the Son of God—then indeed has the hour struck in which the bishop who is a true pastor and no hireling must, in virtue of his office and of the sworn fidelity which has bound him to the souls entrusted to him since the day of his consecration, lift up his voice and with inflexible courage repeat the words spoken by the Apostles before the Council: " If it be just in the sight of God, to hear you rather than God, judge ye."[1] To those who find it difficult to accept such a declaration of the pastoral office may be given the answer made by St. Ambrose to a wrathful magnate of his own time: " Until now thou hast never been faced by a bishop !" . . . And if such an answer should lead to enmity and slander, to suspicions and persecutions on the part of those who are unable to appreciate an attitude like that of a St. Ambrose towards the temporal power, the pure intention, the manly courage, the sacred duty and necessity of his action, then the redoubled love, the increased devotion, the unswerving loyalty and willingness of his faithful people will compensate the confessor-bishop for the misunderstandings and misrepresentations of those who stand without the fold. Whether the bishop who fulfils his apostolic duty of making known the truth and exposing those who in the stubborn blindness of their neo-paganism would erase the Cross of Christ from the Credo of their people contributes to the true exaltation and real greatness of his country and nation—that will fortunately be decided by the Eternal God Himself and not by the transitory and self-seeking passions of the day. . . . The struggles and sufferings of the present may cloud the brows of the faithful, but never their souls. Both the enticements and the menaces of things temporal lose their power over him whose soul is living in harmony with the Eternal. " Thou hast conquered, O Galilean "—this saying of a neo-pagan in the past will be echoed in due time by his followers of today. May this conviction hearten the faithful Catholics of the Archdiocese and of all Germany, when from the bells of Cologne Cathedral the joyous message of the Bishop's Jubilee rings out over the fields and hills of the Rhineland.

On Easter Monday, April 22nd, 1935, the Holy Father received in solemn audience a representative group of the Catholic Youth Associations of Germany, numbering nearly 2,000 persons. We reproduce here some of his words on that occasion:

> You love your great Fatherland. You wish to serve it in loyalty and love and it should be so, beloved sons. For you know well that We also love Germany and Our German sons; indeed, we can say that We love the whole world, and Our love goes forth both to those that are near and those who are far away. We rejoice in the very depths of Our heart at what you have so often told us and have confirmed. We say confirmed, for we were already aware, We were already convinced, that you are the representatives of the whole of German Catholic Youth, which you represent at this moment which is so special, so important, a time so troubled, a time also so painful

---

[1] Acts iv, 19.

for Us—this Youth which is the best reserve for the resistance and stability of Christian and Catholic life in Germany. For, beloved sons, difficult hours are coming, and they may be as difficult in the future as they are at present. Difficult hours may even come continuously. All may become doubtful—all may perhaps be endangered. But, beloved sons, one thing is certain, yes, quite certain and beyond all doubt—Almighty God in His goodness will be with us, and not against us. The risen Redeemer says to us all, and to you particularly, what He said to the fearful and perplexed Apostles: " Doubt not, neither be afraid; for I am with you always."

On May 6th the Pope once again took the opportunity of addressing a German pilgrimage. He spoke with some sharpness about the measures which the German Government had taken against the young people who had so recently visited him.[1]

Almost daily We receive reports which show how loyal Catholics in Germany are persecuted and hindered from the exercise of their Faith. In the name of so-called positive Christianity efforts are being made to de-Christianise Germany and lead her back to barbarous paganism. We hope that you, who have made this pilgrimage to Rome and to the Vatican, will be better received and better treated on your return home than were those devoted and upright young people who, loyal to the Church and the Fatherland, recently came here on a visit to their common Father. We hold them up with honour and commendation to the whole Catholic and civilised world. Unfortunately We cannot do the same—indeed We must do the very opposite—to those who were responsible for the reception and the treatment We have mentioned.

In July, 1935, the *Osservatore Romano* found it necessary once again to voice its opposition to the utterances of men in the most responsible positions in Germany, such as Göring and Frick.

The year 1936 brought with it a new and heightened tension between the Vatican and National Socialism. On the occasion of the opening of the International Catholic Press Exhibition, the Pope for the first time placed Russian Bolshevism and National Socialism in juxtaposition. He deemed it necessary to point out that Russia and Germany were unable to be represented at this exhibition, and, after he had first commented on Russia's absence, went on to deal with that of Germany in the following words: " The second absentee is Germany, since in that country, contrary to all justice and truth, by means of an artificial and intentional confusion between religion and politics, the very existence of a Catholic Press is contested."

When in the same year 1936 the Pope made some observations about the Spanish Civil War, he did not fail to make a reference to Germany and to rebut the pretensions of the Third Reich to be the only agency combating Bolshevism. Here are some of his remarks:

How can the Catholic Church do other than complain, protest and pray, when she sees that at every step she takes in her approach to the family, to youth, to the people, that is to those very quarters . . . that have most need of her, she meets with contradictions and difficulties ? How can the Church act otherwise when the Catholic Press is fettered, ever more and more restricted and suspected, that Press whose office it is to broadcast the basic

---

[1] Audience of April 22nd, 1935. *Cf.* p. 105.

doctrines of genuine Christianity, and to defend those convictions which the Catholic Church, as the exclusive guardian of Christianity genuine and entire, alone possesses and teaches ? And meanwhile every freedom and favour, or at least complete tolerance, is conceded to organs of the Press whose intention it seems to be to confuse the issue, to falsify the facts and publicly to discredit the Church, her interests, her members and her organisation; so that finally, instead of genuine and authentic Christianity, new-fangled christianities and new-fangled religions are promulgated.

Cardinal Pacelli, the Secretary of State, in a speech of welcome to the International Congress of the Catholic Press in the autumn of 1936, also complained of the suppression of Catholic papers in Germany.

We cast a troubled glance towards Germany. We feel deep and sincere regret that no official representatives of the German Catholic Press have appeared at this Congress. After the last Pastoral of the German bishops it is incomprehensible that the Catholic Press in Germany should be intimidated, strangled and obstructed in its apostolate and its struggle against Bolshevism. We are forced almost to suppose that it is the deliberate intention to doom the Catholic Press of Germany to extinction. All the more warmly do we greet the German-speaking Press in the representative of Austria. . . . Two thousand years of relationship between Christianity and the Germans assure us that the bonds can never be broken which bind the German peoples so closely to Christianity and to the Latin cross.

In his Christmas allocution of 1936 the Pope raised his voice in warning with reference to the atrocities in Spain: such events ought to open the eyes of Europe and of the whole world to the fate which would be theirs unless they adopted effective counter-measures.

But among those who proclaim themselves as the defenders of order against the spread of Godless Communism, and who even pretend to leadership in this matter, it gives Us pain to see no small number of persons who allow themselves to be led by false and disastrous principles in the choice of their methods and the discrimination of their opponents. For those who seek to destroy and extinguish faith in God and divine revelation in the hearts of men, and especially in the hearts of Youth, who have the audacity to represent the Church, the guardian of the divine promises and the divinely appointed teacher of the nations, as a declared enemy of the good estate and progress of the nation, do not contribute to the shaping of a better future for mankind or, consequently, for their own country. Rather do they destroy that which is the most effective and most decisive means of protection against the very evil which is feared, and, consciously or otherwise, work hand in hand with the very enemy they think, or at least claim, to combat.

It would be impossible to express more clearly the inability of National Socialism to form a rampart against Bolshevism.

On the occasion of the anniversary of the Pope's coronation in 1937, Cardinal Faulhaber of Munich delivered a sermon in which he dealt with breaches of the Concordat on the part of the German Reich. This caused the German Government to raise a protest at Rome. The pulpit, they urged, was not the place in which to indulge in interpretations of treaties and agreements. Should the necessity for political discussion arise, it should be conducted through diplomatic and political channels. Commenting on this, the *Osservatore Romano* pointed out that the Vatican had been employing the diplomatic approach for long enough already, but always without result. Actually the time had gradually become ripe for a solemn protest by Rome, branding the attitude of the German Government as contradictory to the terms of the Concordat and inimical to the Church. This was done by means of the Papal Encyclical of March 14th, 1937, on the state of the Catholic Church in the German Reich.[1] It is, in fact, in its own way a companion piece to the Concordat concluded four years earlier, and gives illuminating answers to the questions we might well raise as to the German interpretation of such expressions as " good faith," " promises," " word of honour," etc. It analyses the fundamental errors that are at the root of National Socialist opposition to the Church, insisting on a Christian conception of God, the recognition of the Divinity of Christ and all that that entails, the position of the Church and of the Papacy and the part they must play by divine institution in teaching men about God, Christ and the moral order, which last can be founded securely on the Christian Faith alone, and ends with words of exhortation and encouragement to Youth, to priests and the laity.

What the Encyclical makes clear to the eyes of all, receives further confirmation from later utterances of the Pope. Thus, on June 9th, 1937, he told German pilgrims from the Reich that the times were not merely difficult, but deplorable; indeed, they were so bad, so menacing and so painful as to call for the loudest protests.

The Holy Father expressed himself in a similar way on the war against the Church in the Third Reich on June 16th, 1937, to a group of newly ordained priests from the German College and other Germans on pilgrimage to Rome. In the first instance the Pope directed his words to the new German priests who were shortly to leave Rome and return to their homeland. The theological training and priestly formation they had received in the Eternal City would prove a great and invaluable support to them in the difficult apostolate which awaited the priest in Germany today, in the midst of a blind and furious war against the Church of Christ. Addressing the German pilgrims, the Pope also referred to the hard and painful position of the Church in Germany. One may, declared Pius XI, speak of a **persecution** of the Church; for today believing Catholics were being persecuted for their love of Christ by persons who represented themselves as adherents of positive Christianity. But the Catholic Church alone is the bearer of redemption and the guardian of the glorious heritage of truth.

Some months later the Holy Father, at an audience of 200 pilgrims from Germany, said that the visit of so many of his sons was a consolation to his fatherly heart, especially since they came from Germany, *whence such deeply sorrowful news arrived every day.* The holy Father expressed his firm confidence that the splendid German Catholics

---

[1] The text of the Encyclical will be found in full in Appendix II.

would know how to hold fast to the ancient Faith of their glorious forbears. In the same strain he said on another occasion:

> We have a specially warm greeting for you who come from Germany, from a land which is so near to Our heart, and which nevertheless for some time past has seemed in many ways to wish to estrange itself from the house of its Father. We can only do what lies within our power, cost what it may. We have confidence in you, and in all the good Catholics of Germany, and know that you will remain true to Holy Church.

In the month of October, 1937, appeared the Papal Encyclical on the Holy Rosary. At the conclusion of this document the Pope re-echoes the protests of the Hierarchy and faithful of the Polish nation, who honour Mary in a special way as their heavenly Queen, against the insults offered to the most holy Virgin with impunity in the press of another country (Germany is referred to—*Editor's note*) and unites himself to those in Poland who were offering reparation to Our Lady for these insults.

At the nomination of five new Cardinals on December 13th, 1937, Pius XI made a long allocution, in the course of which he touched on the position of the Church in Germany. He said: " If we turn our gaze upon Europe, we see with no little disquiet the godless and cruel proceedings in Russian territory, and measures taken in Germany which constitute a great danger to Christian life."

In his Christmas allocution of 1937 the Pope, with a severity he had not hitherto employed, pilloried the persecution of the Church in Germany. " For some time past," he said, " facts have been misrepresented, made the subject of lies and distortion. This applies particularly to a fact that is as great in its geographical extension as in its moral gravity and seriousness." It was to the very grievous and painful fact of the *religious persecution in Germany that the Holy Father wished to refer*; for, as he said himself, " *we wish to call things by their right names.*"

> It shall not be said of Us, in the words of an ancient historian, that We have forgotten the real names of things. No, thank God, We have not forgotten how to describe things as they truly are, and We intend to do so. In Germany there exists in very truth a religious persecution. For a considerable time efforts have been made to make men believe that there was no persecution. But it is known that there is such a persecution and that it is a heavy one. Indeed, seldom has there been a persecution so heavy, so terrifying, so grievous and lamentable in its far-reaching effects. It is a persecution that spares neither force nor oppression nor threats, nor even the subterfuge of intrigue and the fabrication of false facts.

The Pope said that he had stressed this matter in order to show that he was well informed. . . . Nearly every German knew, it had been repeated so often elsewhere, that the Holy Father had been a great friend of Germany and remained so. There was scarcely any other country that His Holiness knew better than Germany, a country that is so outstanding and representative for learning, talent, culture and science. " Yours are the legions the Pope has admired, not only because you come to visit him in your pilgrimage, but also because he came to know you in your homeland, in your libraries, in your great institutions, in your mighty cities." But sad, doubly sad was that which was done in this country against the truth—a truth which did not merely concern the Holy Father personally, for that were the least of evils, but a truth which lay near to his heart, the most cherished object of his thoughts and affections—the Catholic hierarchy, the Catholic religion, the holy Church of God whose supreme governance had been entrusted to him. It was maintained that the Catholic religion was no longer Catholic but political. This served as a pretext for persecution, as though there were really no persecution, but only measures taken, so to speak, in defence of proper civil order. It was in just this way that they accused Christ before Pilate—as a political disturber, a usurper, a plotter against the temporal power, an enemy of the Emperor. To Pilate's question Christ made answer: " My kingdom is not of this world." The Holy Father proclaimed to the whole world:

> We do not engage in politics. Quite the contrary, indeed; for if We were engaged in politics, Our people—and We have one people throughout the entire world—Our faithful sons would come to Our help. . . . None of these sons of Ours, scattered as they are over the whole face of the earth, believes that We are engaged in politics, but they can all see and testify again and again that it is religion with which We are concerned, and nothing else. Certainly it must be maintained that the ordinary citizen must conduct the affairs of his own life in accordance with the laws of God. Is that religion or is it politics ? Certainly not politics ! But We wish that in everyday life, both individual and social, consideration should be given to the rights of God, which are also the rights of souls. That is what We have done, and that alone: those who think and say otherwise, offend against the truth.

It is a source of great pain to the Holy Father that the accusation should be made again and again, that religion is being misused for political aims. He feels it keenly that such a calumny, to give it its right name, should be brought against his brethren in the Episcopate, against authoritative members of the Sacred College, against so many priests and so many of the faithful who are occupied with nothing else but the observance of God's commandments, the teaching of the divine law, and the works of Christian charity. This was known to all: all who had a mind to see, could see that he was concerned with religion and not with politics. His brethren the clergy and the faithful who are suffering so sorely under this persecution might be assured that he was well aware of this tribulation, that he suffered with them, and that his greatest pain was to see them so tormented.

In the year 1938 Austria was incorporated into the German Reich. A statement issued at that time by the Austrian bishops, making known their attitude to National Socialism, occasioned the appearance in the *Osservatore Romano*[1] of an explanation in the following words:

> With reference to the various and often tendentious interpretations of the well-known declaration of the Austrian bishops—even from quarters from

[1] April 2nd, 1938.

which this was scarcely to be expected—we are authorised to make the following statement for the sole purpose of establishing the facts, and without any regard for extrinsic considerations or questions of a political nature. The above-mentioned declaration was drawn up and signed without any sort of previous agreement or any sort of subsequent approval on the part of the Holy See, and with the sole responsibility of the Austrian episcopate.

And later, when Cardinal Innitzer came to Rome from Vienna, he made the following declaration in the name of the whole Austrian episcopate:

1. The solemn declaration made by the Austrian episcopate on March 18th was, of course, not an approbation of anything incompatible with the laws of God and the liberty of the Catholic Church. This declaration must not be regarded by the State or by the Party as binding in conscience, and it must not be used for propaganda purposes.
2. For the future, the Austrian bishops demand:
> (*a*) That no change should be made in any question concerning the Concordat with Austria without the previous consent of the Holy See.
> (*b*) That, in particular, the application of all regulations concerning schools, education and youth training should be in accordance with the natural rights of parents and of the religious and moral training of the Catholic youth, according to the rules of the Catholic Church.
> (*c*) That all propaganda against religion and the Church shall be prohibited.
> (*d*) That the rights of Catholics, the Catholic Faith and Christian principles, in all aspects of human life, must be proclaimed, defended and practised by all the means open to modern civilisation.

THEODOR CARD. INNITZER,
in the name of the whole Austrian Episcopate.

ROME, *April 6th*, 1938.[1]

All will remember also the sensational broadcast in German from the Vatican Radio on April 1st, 1938, on Political Catholicism, which, although not strictly official, as the *Osservatore* reported, would not be disowned by any official ecclesiastical authority so far as its contents and the reasons for those contents were concerned.

On April 13th, 1938, the Sacred Congregation for Seminaries and Universities issued instructions for combating the false doctrines of modern Racialism. The document is addressed to Cardinal Baudrillart, and opens with the following words:

Your Eminence ! Last year, on the vigil of Our Lord's Nativity, our august Pontiff and gloriously reigning Pope, in his allocution to the Cardinals and Prelates of the Roman Curia, referred in grave and sorrowful terms to the grievous persecution of the Catholic Church in Germany. It was a cause of the greatest pain to the heart of the Holy Father that shameless calumnies were scattered by way of excuse for such great injustice, and that highly dangerous doctrines were spread and broadcast, doctrines that falsely pretend to be scientific, bringing minds into the greatest confusion and seeking to uproot true religion. In view of this state of affairs the

---

[1] *Osservatore Romano*, April 7th, 1938.

Sacred Congregation of Studies urges the universities and Catholic faculties to direct all their resources and industry to the defence of the truth against the inroads of this error. Those who are teaching in centres of higher studies must mobilise all the means at their command in biology, historical scholarship, philosophy, apologetics, legal and moral science, and thus forge the weapons with which to rebut in a decisive and expert manner the following *altogether untenable and erroneous doctrines*. . . .

When Hitler came to Rome in the spring of 1938, the Vatican newspaper, the *Osservatore Romano*, made no allusion to that event. But the Pope, in an audience given at this time at Castel Gandolfo, said:

Sad events are taking place, very sad, both at a distance and also near at hand; yes, saddening events indeed, and among them one may well mention the fact that on the feast day of the Holy Cross there is openly borne the badge of another cross, which is not the Cross of Christ. I shall have said enough if I tell you how necessary it is to pray, to pray very, very fervently, that God's mercy may not be wanting.

Monasteries, convents, religious houses and ecclesiastical colleges were at this time strictly forbidden to fly the Swastika flag.

In the course of the summer of 1938 the Pope on various occasions spoke of the errors of exaggerated nationalism. Thus in mid July[1] he spoke of his intention to issue a comprehensive Brief on this subject; and again a few days later (July 23rd), when he began by quoting the Italian proverb that " the tongue must always return to the tooth that is aching," he went on to say that in much the same way he himself must come back again and again to this question of nationalism which caused him so much anxiety. For it could be truly said that an article of the Creed itself, " I believe in the Catholic Church," had been relegated to oblivion. " Catholic " means universal, world-wide—not racial, not nationalistic, not separatist; Catholic Action (it was to the representatives of Catholic Action that he was speaking) must be catholic in just this sense, and be filled with just this spirit; for there is something which is to a certain extent greater and better than the Faith itself, and that is the *spirit* of the Faith; just as there is unfortunately something much worse than this or that formula of Racialism or Nationalism—namely, the spirit which inspires them. One was forced to give utterance to the fact that there was something especially detestable about this spirit of separation and exaggerated nationalism, which, precisely because it is not Christian and religious, goes so far that it is no longer even human.

Pius XI showed the white heat of his indignation over the persecution of the Church in Germany in an audience which he gave to the members of the Congress of Christian Archæology. On this occasion he declared: " In certain neighbouring countries events of a challenging nature are taking place. You will remember the persecutions of Julian the Apostate, which were not only very bloody and woeful, but extraordinarily cunning as well; and there comes to mind also the despicable act of the apostle Judas, who betrayed his Master." Pius XI was

[1] *Osservatore Romano*, July 17th, 1938.

there alluding to a certain speech made not long before, of whose official character it was impossible to doubt. The Pope added:

> These persecutions in Germany and in Austria are carried out with an audacity that is truly unique, and they are being constantly intensified in their methods and their severity. We learn this from witnesses whom we have had before Our own eyes. This persecution affects the Pope very deeply, and his grief and anxiety are immeasurable. And this, not only in so far as he is the Head of faithful Christendom as Pope, but also because as a man he sees human dignity betrayed so basely, just as it was by Julian the Apostate and Judas Iscariot; for this persecution extends even to the least layman.

Finally, Pius XI declared emphatically and energetically that it was a lie if anyone said that the Church mixes in politics. " Our politics," he repeated, " are those of the common good, the application of all resources to secure that common good. That is the kind of politics in which We have always been active and in which We shall continue to be active in the future so long as God gives us the opportunity, the strength and the grace."[1]

With this we conclude the evidence for a religious persecution in Germany from the Vatican, and principally from the mouth of Pius XI. The views of his successor, Pius XII, are no different, though the desire not to shut the door on the possibility of yet another understanding with the enemy, and the necessity of avoiding any pretext for fresh misrepresentations—and such pretexts are ready enough to hand in war-time—impose the greatest restraint upon him. It was not for nothing that we include in the foregoing his utterances on the position of religion in Germany delivered when he was Secretary of State. It is unnecessary to show how near Germany lies to the heart of the present Pope, since he has so often expressed it himself. German Youth, however, is an object of his special solicitude, as he said to German pilgrims in an audience at the beginning of September, 1938: " We pray that Mary will spread her mantle wide over German Youth, so that their souls shall suffer no damage."

[1] *La Croix*, October 22nd, 1938.

CHAPTER II

EVIDENCE FROM THE GERMAN HIERARCHY

It has frequently been said and, doubtless, more often thought that the German Hierarchy has shown a certain slackness, if not even cowardice, in its opposition to the attacks on the Church on the part of the Government of the Third Reich. Others have thought (and said) that, beguiled perhaps by their own patriotism, the bishops have been altogether too yielding to the State's demands. Many, however, of the individuals who air their views so freely in this sense probably are not aware that National Socialism was opposed by the Church in Germany, even before it came into full power, and even to the extent of refusing the Sacraments to its adherents, and that its fears were allayed, it is too much to say removed, by the signing of the Concordat and the solemn promises given by the highest authorities in the new State.

As soon, however, as National Socialism began to drop its disguise and to show its true colours, the bishops one after another and then all together began in their turn to protest and to warn their flocks. But they were faced with a difficult and delicate situation. On the one hand they could not remain silent and let the faithful be utterly deceived, and on the other they did not wish to ruin any chance there might have been of preserving at any rate the greater part of the Concordat as a working proposition. In any case, as soon as the Third Reich had got into its swing with its Gestapo and press censorship and the like, there was little chance that their protests would ever reach the world outside Germany. That is, in part, the reason why harsh judgments are passed on the Hierarchy, and that is, at least, one reason why we should here include a few of their words of protest, to prove to the world that from the beginning they were not hoodwinked and that they did not fail in their pastoral duties.

As early as April, 1933, these words were used in a manifesto signed by the Bishops of the Ecclesiastical Province of the Upper Rhine and their Metropolitan, Archbishop Konrad Gröber of Freiburg-im-Breisgau:

> We deplore everything which detracts from the good reputation of our nation and Fatherland, and which presents, both to the minds of our own people and to those of neighbouring nations, the appearance of cruelty and injustice: this is true of the practice, unfortunately increasing, of removing loyal citizens and men of industry and merit from the positions they have hitherto occupied.

14 EVIDENCE FROM THE GERMAN HIERARCHY

In May, 1933, the Bavarian bishops issued to their flocks a call to national co-operation. It was, however, only with difficulty that they could conceal the misgivings caused by the attitude of the National Socialist party in spite of the Führer's assurances. This important document says:

> Just as harmonious co-operation between Church and State is necessary and beneficial, so disastrous effects follow, as history teaches us, when the State abuses its power in order to interfere with the life of the Church, when Church and State are fused together, or when the Church is degraded to the status of a servant of the State.

It continues later:

> We hope that the Reich Government does not approve of the efforts and proceedings of those who on principle apply a different legal standard, or seek to employ the word " uniformity " (*Gleichschaltung*) in a manner which is in conflict with the assurances given by the Chancellor of the Reich.

And speaking of youth, the document continues:

> The rights and duties of parents with regard to the spiritual, religious and moral training of their children ought not to be impeded and even pared down and curtailed by measures taken by educational authorities or the State. . . . On no account can we ever agree to universal [*i.e.*, undenominational] elementary schools of whatever form.

After the bishops had spoken of the importance of the Catholic Youth Associations, they referred pointedly to the interference of the State with the Catholic Press:

> We are no advocates of a form of criticism which combats and discounts all State authority, which conceives it to be its task to agitate and to undermine, which stirs up the nation and seduces it, and indeed makes its living out of agitation and unrest. But there is no reason why such abuses should lead to a complete suppression of free opinion and free expression, especially in the daily press. . . . In common with the other German bishops we have made representations to the Reich Government on behalf of those men who, in the stormy times of transition, were removed from their posts, although they have always fulfilled their duty and have served the Fatherland to the best of their ability.

A great deal may be read into the concluding sentence of this document: " No one may hang back from the great work of reconstruction, but no one should be repulsed from participation in it."

In a decree of July, 1933, Bishop Matthias Ehrenfried of Würzburg admonished the clergy of Lower Franconia to observe due subordination towards the lawful national Government, and urged them to engage in a positive presentation of the truths of the Faith.

> Under present conditions it is possible that subordinate officials might initiate wrongful and interfering measures, which might militate against our co-operation with the national movement and disturb our sympathetic attitude towards it. It is not, however, the duty of the individual priest to judge of such matters or to redress them. . . . In so far as necessity arises, such questions will be dealt with by higher ecclesiastical authority.

The new condition of things very soon involved considerable difficulties for Catholic theological students. The Cardinal of Breslau, in consequence, with holy earnestness warns those responsible (July, 1933):

> The episcopate does not abandon the hope of coming to some agreement regarding matters particularly affecting theological training, especially with those who are able to appreciate the fact that the blessings attached to pastoral activity must spring from the interior life. . . .

As the months went by, the anxiety of the bishops was unfortunately not diminished. It was " grievous and gnawing anxiety," to use his own expression, that haunted Cardinal Bertram as he travelled on his *ad limina* visit to the Father of Christendom in October, 1933. He described this anxiety later in a Letter. It was anxiety about Catholic organisations, the freedom of Catholic works of charity, Catholic Youth, the freedom of the Catholic Press, Catholic Action and, not least, about the fate of many good Catholics who now had so much to suffer because of their former political opinions.

> There is yet another very heavy and serious anxiety which afflicts many thousands of loyal Catholic Christians. I refer to the anxiety that is felt on behalf of those who, under the former system of party government, followed those leaders whose aim it was as a matter of religious duty to combat Marxism and Bolshevism in a manner appropriate to the form of government then obtaining. These men, who did their best for the nation and the State, for religion and the Church, in dutiful obedience to those who were in authority at the time, are today no less ready to serve the new State loyally and uprightly for the nation's good, and to employ all their power and resources in the common task of rehabilitation in honourable harmony with the present Government. Far be it from us to seek exemption for cases which really deserve punishment from the processes of an incorruptible justice which treats both friend and foe with an equal measure and admits of no arbitrary exceptions. Our word of pastoral sympathy refers to those numerous men and women of irreproachable character whose intentions were, and still are, good and loyal. If such folk in very great numbers have suffered severely and are still suffering, the Church, and especially the Holy Father, have a warm sympathy for them. If opportunity offers of alleviating their hard lot, it becomes a manifest and grave Christian duty to take it. The bishops have not been inactive in fulfilling this duty. But we urgently request authoritative quarters in the Reich and State to make an earnest, benevolent and early revision of the harsh measures which have been put into operation.

In the summer of 1934 Bishop Kaller of Ermland at a pilgrimage to Dietrichswalde made some sharp comments on the attacks on the Church that were being made in Germany.

> We declare with sorrow that during the last year or two movements and currents of opinion have appeared and grown stronger in our Fatherland which are directed against the fundamental truths of the Catholic Church, and aim at setting up a new religion—a German national church founded on the myth of blood and race.

At the celebration of the feast of Christ the King in the *Stadthalle* of Coblenz, Bishop Bornewasser of Trier spoke in a similar way:

> Our Catholic people are acutely aware of the tremendous dangers that threaten the life of the Faith and the existence of the Church from the neo-pagan movement in Germany.

It is Catholic Youth which is above all else a cause of anxiety to the bishops.

I cannot conceal the fact that I was greatly shocked and troubled by something which I read a few days ago on this subject. On the 5th of November it was stated in Berlin: " Rosenberg's way is the way for German Youth." ... There is still another thing which causes great anxiety to your bishop and the faithful teachers of Catholic Youth. At the meeting of philologists and educationalists in Trier a few weeks ago it was said: " We German teachers will build around our Youth a wall with the inscription, ' Theological hatred and theological sophistry not admitted to German Youth.' " After the bishop had protested against these offensive utterances and against slanderous attacks on the Church and the Papacy in general, he concluded: " Of what do we Catholics in Germany stand in need in the midst of this unrestrained conflict against Christianity and the Church ? We need gratitude (for the grace of the Catholic Faith), confidence and loyalty ! . . . *Non prævalebunt !* The gates of Hell shall not prevail against the Church. The Cæsars on the throne of ancient pagan Rome could not prevail, and the prophets of the new paganism in Germany will fail likewise."

Bishop Wilhelm Berning of Osnabrück expressed himself with equal clearness about the war on the Church in Germany in a sermon on New Year's Eve:

Our Faith is not built on sagas and myths, but on the infallible revelation of God. . . . What then can it mean when a war of extermination is undertaken against this Christian faith in God, when it is sought to tear it out of the hearts of the young in order to substitute for it a new, a Germanic belief in God?

In a Pastoral issued early in 1935 Bishop Matthias Ehrenfried of Würzburg discusses the notion of " positive Christianity," which is so much misused and misinterpreted. It may well be that the new State has taken its stand on the basis of positive Christianity and assured both Catholic and Protestant of its protection; but in contrast to this the whole country is flooded with weeklies, monthlies, books and pamphlets in which Christianity is attacked and rejected. In conclusion the bishop warns the Catholics of Germany not to be deluded by the idea that after all the Church had managed at other times and places to carry on without Catholic associations and schools. It is true that the Church survived the ages of persecution and the stifling atmosphere of her refuge in the catacombs, but that was a time of emergency for the Church, when she enjoyed scarcely even the bare necessities of existence. " Do you want only the rights of bare necessity, or do you want full rights for your Church ? Bestir yourselves and defend the full rights of your Mother the Church !"

In his Lenten Pastoral, Cardinal Schulte of Cologne praises the faithful " for the inflexible determination by reason of which the continual outrages against your most sacred feelings and beliefs are used by you as an opportunity of publicly demonstrating your uncompromising Catholic loyalty."

On the feast of SS. Peter and Paul the Archbishop of Freiburg issued a Pastoral which concluded with these words:

Come what may, we are resolved and fear nothing. Especially on this feast of the holy Princes of the Apostles, Peter and Paul, Catholic Germany will lovingly turn her thoughts towards the tomb of the Apostles which has been so vilified and abused, and raise her hand to swear fidelity anew.

It was in stirring words that the new Bishop of Berlin, Count von Preysing, took leave of the Episcopal Theological and Philosophical College of Eichstätt. His call to the episcopal throne in the capital city of the Reich is for him " a disposition of Divine Providence itself," of which he can say with the apostle Paul: What lies before me I know not, but perils threaten and will continue to threaten.

There can be no possible doubt that we Christians are engaged in a hard fight. The new religion of blood has declared war upon us; their battle-cries range from a cold rejection of Christian doctrine to an exacerbation full of hate. They seek for allies wherever they can find them. A regular barrage of contentions, culled both from history and from contemporary sources, thunders down upon us. The aim of this struggle in which we are now engaged is to drive Christianity out of our Fatherland.

The days were already numbered, in which it would still be possible to propagate Christian doctrine in Germany. Above all the enemy wished to rob the Church of her schools. If she is despoiled of her children Christianity can safely be left to her fate.

The combined Pastoral of the bishops assembled at Fulda had been awaited with eager suspense. It appeared on August 20th, 1935—a witness to the watchful care but growing anxiety of the German bishops.

It is in a very grave and decisive hour that the bishops, by means of this Pastoral, address the Catholics of Germany. . . . From the tomb of St. Boniface there came forth to us bishops the injunction to send a pastoral message to German Catholics, to clergy and layfolk alike, in order to strengthen your souls against the propaganda of a new paganism. . . . *The number of the enemies of the Christian Faith and the Catholic Church has become legion.* Youthful individuals, who are either unacquainted with the Catechism of Christian Doctrine or have but superficial acquaintance with it, feel themselves called to sit in judgement upon all things Catholic. Men and women who have never experienced the beauty of our liturgy or the peace of soul that follows Holy Communion busy themselves with all possible means of propaganda, calling on men to leave the Church and apostatise from Christianity. Writers who have never studied Church history and Church law from unbiased sources confuse the minds of the uncritical with high-sounding words. The Holy Scriptures of the Old Testament, and even more the Gospels and the Epistles of St. Paul, are no longer to count for anything. Jesus Christ, Our Lord and Saviour, is no longer to be the Way, the Truth and the Life; all connection with the Primacy set up by Christ Himself is to be broken, and in its place a so-called " Rome-free " National Church is to be set up.

Among themselves, these deadly enemies of Christianity are split up by mutually opposing aims and contradictions into a multitude of groups, like the peoples at the Tower of Babel. On one point alone are they united—namely, that *it is no longer a question of attacking individual dogmas or beliefs* as in former religious conflicts, but *it is the whole essence and basis of Christianity which must be overthrown. In carrying out their war of annihilation they are agreed that it is principally against Rome and the Roman Catholic Faith that their attacks must be directed.* . . .

The freedom of the Press, as we observe with the deepest distress, is so much restricted that the formerly Catholic papers may no longer publish religious articles, and are sometimes forced to accept articles which are an outrage to Catholic readers. . . .

We condemn all offences against the just laws of the State. But we condemn also, with the Gospels, that pharisaical arrogance which only casts stones at other men, which does not perceive the beam in its own eye, which covers the doings of its own associates with the mantle of silence, and cries the doings of other men from the house-tops. We rise in condemnation when a double measure of justice is applied, and when the offences of individual Catholics are imputed to the whole body of German Catholics as such. . . .

The new slogan of " political Catholicism," the reproach that Catholics concern themselves too much with State and political affairs, can only impress those who are lacking in judgement. It can only impress those who do not ask themselves why it is that there is so much talk about the servants of religion who are represented as intruding into the political sphere, while so little is said of politicians who intrude into the sphere of religion and of the Church. . . . To suppress the " Confessions " in public life is to suppress Christianity in public life and, if this measure be carried into effect, stand fast in the Faith. . . .

For these reasons the Conference of Bishops has sent a memorandum to the Führer and Chancellor of the Reich, and has called his attention to the dangers arising from the misuse of the new slogans, and to other restrictions on the liberty of the Church and oppressions of the Christian conscience. . . .

Catholics of Germany ! In recent years you have often asked, " Must we Catholics then approve of everything in our own Fatherland ? Ought we to be reviled as traitors to our country and our people, seeing that we spilt our blood so freely for Germany in the World War ?" . . . Catholics are instigating no revolt, nor are they offering violent resistance or employing force. That is so well known that at all times those who wish to gain an easy victory attack precisely Catholics. We are not anxious about our Church. But we are in the greatest anxiety for our nation and our Fatherland.

At the Conference of Bishops at Fulda it was decided to issue a separate message, in some form or other, to the priesthood. In the document of August 24th, 1935, we read:

In a special memorandum sent to the Führer and Chancellor of the Reich we have drawn attention to the concerted agitation against the clergy which is going on at present, and have called for greater respect and protection for the clergy in accordance with the Reich Concordat. For when denunciators are believed without the cleric being able to justify himself; when almost daily in the papers and the streets the clergy are insulted, even by immature youths, with opprobrious epithets which we cannot reproduce here, then, consciously or unconsciously, the right atmosphere is set up for a *Kulturkampf*.

And towards the end of the letter the Cardinal again repeats:

It is sad enough, in all conscience, when an unrestrained Press, and even organs of the Press designed for the young, are allowed to drag in the mud the celibacy of the clergy, the confessional, the veneration of relics and nearly all the dogmas of the Church, without Article 5 of the Concordat affording any protection to the reputation and persons of the clergy.

In the late autumn of 1935 Archbishop Gröber of Freiburg sent a circular letter to his clergy, in which, among other things, he said:

In the name of the rights of the individual . . . we must deplore the public indictment and defamation of honourable men without opportunity being given them of justifying and protecting themselves. We deplore further the fact that " protective arrests," that differ in nothing from penalties inflicted for crime, can be imposed without judicial trial and judgement, or any possibility of legal recourse. We deplore the dismissal of, or the failure to appoint, officials and employees *for the sole reason that they are Catholics true to their convictions*, and will not allow their consciences to be overcome by violence. We regard it as deplorable that those whose conscience forbids them to agree with a State law should for that reason alone be reckoned as a national pest or as guilty of high treason. They reproach us Catholics with placarding the *Kulturkampf* and publishing it abroad . . . but unfortunately we are unable to overlook *facts*, which without any assistance from us spread abroad into foreign countries a picture of the position of the Church in Germany which gives the impression of a very fierce *Kulturkampf*.

In 1936 we come to a period in which the main assault on the most important Catholic positions was carried out. Small wonder, then, if the religious perils with which the faithful were afflicted, find their echo in the utterances of the bishops.

Even in the early days of January, the German bishops assembled at Fulda once more address the faithful and refer to the dangers that menace them:

> For this reason, even at the present moment, which many regard as a turning point not only in the political but also in the religious sphere, we have issued warnings and exhortations over and over again, especially after our meetings at Fulda, and have left nothing undone to save the German people from a *Kulturkampf*. But in spite of all, the struggle does not appear to be dying down, but rather to rage with growing intensity round the souls of the German people.

On February 9th, 1936, Bishop Galen of Münster made a speech at Xanten which has become famous:

> See how Holy Church, the Pope, the bishops, priests and Religious, see how the loyal children of the Church today in Germany are insulted, reviled and derided publicly and with impunity. How many Catholics, priests and laymen, have been attacked and insulted in the papers and at public meetings, driven out of their professions and positions, and imprisoned and ill-treated without judicial sentence being passed ! . . . *There are fresh graves in German soil in which are lying the ashes of those whom the Catholic people regard as martyrs for the Faith, since their lives gave witness to their most dutiful and loyal devotion to God and the Fatherland, to the nation and the Church, while the dark secrecy which surrounds their deaths is most carefully preserved.* And what a heavy load is that conflict of conscience which so many officials and employees, parents and teachers have to sustain, who are forced into the position of having to choose between their loyalty to God and their Christian conscience, on the one hand, and on the other the good pleasure and favour of those from whom their positions and their livelihood itself depend.

Naturally enough, the conflict with the opponents of our Faith had a great deal of space devoted to it in the Lenten Pastorals of the bishops. We quote only the following examples. Cardinal Bertram of Breslau:

> From all parts of this extensive Archdiocese we know that thousands and thousands of our people are being subjected to temptations against their

loyalty to the Church. It could not be otherwise in view of the enormous scale on which anti-religious ideas and writings are being propagated. But remember: no cross, no crown.

In the same Pastoral the Cardinal had already said:

How many hundreds of thousands of books and pamphlets against Christianity, against the Catholic Church, against the foundations of belief in God, have been distributed in all districts, *not excepting the tiniest village.*

Similarly Bishop Kaller of Ermland:

Our hearts are filled with sorrow; we live in the midst of peril and anxiety. We tremble for the maintenance of our Faith in its purity. We tremble for the welfare of the Church in our Fatherland. We tremble for the welfare of our children and our growing youth. We tremble for the welfare of the German nation itself.

In the midst of all these dangers the anxious bishop turns to the Divine Helper in the tabernacle, and expresses the wish that His divine assistance should be implored by the perpetual adoration of the whole diocese.

There are special motives nowadays which urge us to honour our Divine Saviour in the Most Holy Sacrament. They seek to drive Him from His throne. They seek to annihilate His Holy Church. They are trying to eradicate Christianity itself. . . . O Lord . . . the more they seek to reject Thee . . . so much the more do we wish to love Thee.

In a most courageous sermon in Buer on Sunday, March 22nd, 1936, a week before the General Election, Bishop Galen of Münster made known to all what he would like to write to the Führer on his voting slip:

Is the Führer and Chancellor of the Reich aware of the spiritual distress of countless German men and women whose consciences are oppressed, whose Faith is slandered, whose rights are encroached upon and whose honour is injured? Does he know of the insults and the base insinuations against Christianity and the Holy Catholic Church to which he himself belongs by baptism, against her divinely appointed head, the Pope, against bishops and priests, against Catholic organisations and societies, which are printed and propagated in Germany, and are forced and thrust upon audiences at meetings and training courses? I can scarcely believe that he knows all this, or is aware of the frightful danger of this fiery war against the Faith that has been set ablaze. . . . Does the Führer know that men belonging to the Movement are themselves directing this war on Christianity and fanning the flames of conflict in speeches, and in publications issued and recommended by official quarters in the Party? Is he aware that this onslaught against Christianity and our most sacred religious convictions is even carried on by the agency of meetings, technical journals, and professional periodicals which are obligatory for the various professions concerned? Does he know that, even in the publications issued by the Supreme Command of the Hitler Youth, Christianity is made contemptible as being alien to the German nature and an enemy of the German race, so that our young people are actually given instruction in disloyalty to God, to Christ and to His Church? Does our Führer and Reich Chancellor know all that? How can Christian parents with a good conscience allow their children to take part in the Land Year, labour camps, Hitler Youth meetings and training courses, when they know that the religious guidance and instruction, which is so necessary for the young, is lacking; or when they even have good cause to fear, by repeated experience and reports, that perhaps mistrust, and indeed hatred, of Christianity and the Church will be preached to those who take part in such gatherings!

It was in significant terms that Bishop Rackl of Eichstätt addressed his young people on Trinity Sunday of 1936:

We are at the moment in the midst of a fearful clash of ideas and aims. Last year it was solemnly announced that the political revolution was over, and that the ideological revolution (*Weltanschauung*) was to begin. And after all, *Weltanschauung* is nothing else than religion; for the very word *Weltanschauung* means " the way in which we look at the world." Do I look upon the world with the eyes of a mortal destined soon to pass away, or with the eyes of one whose destiny it is to live for ever, when the world itself and all its vanities shall have disappeared?

The same prelate had expressed himself in a very similar way in Ingolstadt on May 24th, 1936:

We live in dreadfully threatening times, and most men have not yet realised that an effort is being made to undermine the very foundations of the Holy Catholic Church. . . . Last year the slogan was given out: " The political revolution is over; it is an ideological revolution which is now beginning." . . . It is consequently no longer a question of politics but one of *Weltanschauung*, of outlook, of opinion, of conviction. . . . It is, indeed, laid down in the Concordat that the Catholic Church should enjoy full freedom, but you all know that this is unfortunately not the case. . . . The most dangerous aspect of all is that they do not admit that they are attacking religion, but pretend that their quarrel is merely with the " denominational " associations.

We come now to the Fulda Pastoral of 1936.

As was the case in the manifold anxieties of last year, so again this year, at the conclusion of our Plenary Conference we have sent an exhaustive Memorandum to the Führer and Reich Chancellor. In that Memorandum, with a sense of genuine national solidarity and Christian loyalty, but also with German honesty and candour, we have drawn attention to the increasingly grievous disturbances and curtailments of religious and ecclesiastical life, to all the undeserved generalisations and grave accusations, to all the injuries offered to the Holy Father, bishops, priests and Religious. May it be granted to us this year not merely to make known to our Catholic people, anxious at heart just as we are, the contents of this comprehensive Memorandum of ours, but also to announce to them the actual removal of the abuses complained of.

The summary of the attack on the Catholic Church, given at the end of the Pastoral, is very effective:

Beloved Diocesans! With these incontestable considerations in mind, we German bishops are less than ever able to understand why it is that in our Fatherland and amongst our people the sphere of influence of Christianity and of the Church is subjected to ever-increasing restrictions, and in the last resort is limited merely to activities that can be carried out on actual church premises. We cannot understand why it is that the activities of our Catholic societies, which have been attended with such blessings in the past, should be obstructed, and the further existence of those societies themselves brought into question. We cannot comprehend why it is that those who are members of Party organisations are forbidden [on the score of reprobating "double membership"] to retain their membership of any Church society, right down to the Young Women's Sodalities inclusive; and that here and there threats are made to deprive honest fathers and their dependants of their daily bread, unless they break off all connection with the Catholic societies of which they have been hitherto members. We fail to understand why it is that the gentle and benevolent arm of *Caritas*[1] should be shortened more and more, and the Catholic Sisters driven away from the sick-beds and the orphanages. We cannot understand why the Catholic Press is estricted to purely ecclesiastical and religious matters by decrees which give the people the impression that what is really aimed at is the complete suppression of the Catholic Press. We cannot understand why our growing German Youth is so frequently withdrawn from Christian influences in order to be inoculated with ideas which are destructive of their faith in Christ, or by mixed " interdenominational " relationships to deprive them of the vital force of their Catholic convictions. We cannot understand why in certain German territories it is sought to eliminate the confessional (denominational) schools and the private Catholic schools, or their elimination is effected by means of a " popular vote," although the German Concordat guarantees the maintenance and erection of such schools, or at least, in the case of private schools, their due authorisation and the right of Religious Orders and Congregations to conduct them. . . .

Bishop Michael Rackl of Eichstätt was remarkably outspoken in a sermon preached at Buchsheim on September 29th, 1936: " The agitation against the Catholic Church often assumes a form which *goes far beyond that to which we are accustomed in Russia.*"

Bishop Buchberger of Regensburg also pillories the injustice of the attack on the Church which has blazed up: " A violent attack is raging, especially against the Catholic Church. To be Catholic and to live in Catholic fashion is for many equivalent to being un-German. And this after the World War, in which none fulfilled their duty to the Fatherland more loyally than the Catholics." Later the same prelate repeated: " No matter where we look, there rages on all sides a violent assault upon our Faith, by the spoken word and in the press, openly and in secret." (Sermon in Regensburg Cathedral, towards the end of 1936.)

The religious difficulties of 1936 brought both the Bavarian bishops and the entire German episcopate again into the arena before that troubled year drew to a close. The Bavarian Pastoral points out that the attempts which are being made in certain circles to expand the doctrines of National Socialism into a *Weltanschauung* whose encroachments upon the religious sphere were deep and revolutionary were assuming more and more the character of *an intense and purposeful assault on the Christian Faith and the Catholic Church*. But the following words especially reveal the magnitude of the danger: " We must, however, request that it no longer be put about among young folk and the people in general, that after the overthrow of Bolshevism, Public Enemy No. 1, the next on the list is the Catholic Church as Public Enemy No. 2."

And lastly, let us refer to Cardinal Faulhaber's sermon at Munich on New Year's Eve, 1936. The Cardinal is oppressed with two great

---

[1] The principal German Catholic charitable organisation.—*Translator's note.*

anxieties—the overthrow of Bolshevism, and the protection of Christianity from enemies within the gates. With regard to the second he says:

> Propaganda has been set on foot, whose aim it is with all possible resources, and by means of economic pressure, to de-Christianise the life of our nation, and to drive as many as possible to leave the Church. This propaganda is applied particularly to officials and those holding leading positions in the movement, together with those whose professions or occupations are economically dependent thereon. The hour has come of which Christ spoke: " Satan hath desired to have you that he may sift you like wheat " (Luke xxii, 31).

In 1937 the great assault on all Catholic positions is carried further. Many episcopal declarations deal with particular spheres of the Church's life, such as youth, schools, etc., which will be dealt with in greater detail elsewhere. The general character of the war of annihilation against the Church is, if possible, even clearer than before. From this abundance of material we can offer only a small selection here.

In a New Year Pastoral at the beginning of 1937, Archbishop Gröber of Freiburg summarises the grounds of complaint of the German Catholics against their persecutors.

> "Unfortunately . . . I repeat, unfortunately, the past year has also brought troubles of a religious and ecclesiastical nature in our own Fatherland to a head. He must be completely out of touch with reality, or blind or deaf or deluded in some way, who would venture to maintain that peace reigns in the Church everywhere in Germany, and that Christianity and the Catholic Church everywhere enjoy equal respect, freedom and liberty of action with their opponents. On the contrary, in these last few months we cannot but perceive ever more clearly, with the greatest grief and deepest concern, that the enmity towards our Church and towards Christianity in general has greatly increased, both in its extension and in the intensity of its hatred. These unassailable and demonstrable facts are in no wise altered by certain pacifying words and conciliatory measures of the last few weeks, since from the fundamental attitude of our adversaries we clearly recognise the whole aim and object of this religious struggle, and reckon these occasional days of rest merely as pauses in the battle or short-lived armistices, and not as a dying away of the conflict or an end to the clash of arms and the beginning of peace and prosperity. Moreover, the protagonists of this new *Kulturkampf* carry on their activities with increasing openness and diminishing prudence, and are disclosing their ultimate aims with ever greater clearness and boldness: they even reveal to their hearers and readers on certain occasions the actual date by which they hope to achieve a decisive and lasting victory over Christianity and the Church. In this very year whose dawn we are greeting with Christian courage and hope it is expected in certain quarters, according to reliable reports, that the anti-Christian forces will gather together all their resources for a general attack on a wide front." Then the bishop brings up questions " which each of us has indeed already put to himself over and over again, but which at this moment, on the first day of the year, seem to become welded together into a chain, as it were—a chain which we would fain cast off as an unworthy yoke of slavery. . . . Is the Catholic Church . . . to be repeatedly (if sometimes covertly) branded as Public Enemy No. 2, and treated as the sworn associate of Bolshevism ? . . . Is the German nation as a whole to be prepared for a possible conflict with godless world-Bolshevism, which might—though God forbid it should—be forced upon us from outside, by concealing the essential and irreconcilable contradiction between the basic principles of religion and those of Russian

atheism ? Are we preparing wisely for such an eventuality when the deification of Man and of the Nation, and the denial of the immortality of the human soul, bring us perilously near to a cultural hand-shake with Communism itself ? Is the spirit of Julian the Apostate, whose foolhardiness brought such swift retribution, to gain an unholy victory here in Germany ? Is that spirit to prevail, which seeks by means of restriction, oppression and defamation to destroy in a few years all that hundreds of generations of Christian Germans have reverenced and held sacred, and all that by the inspiration of their Christian faith they have achieved for their country and their people in culture, art and science ? . . . Is the agitation for abandoning Church membership, which, as we hear to our bitter sorrow, is not unpleasing to certain quarters, and is indeed actively and expressly supported by example and recommendation and even by precept or thinly-veiled threats —is all this, I ask, to give the lie in irresponsible fashion to the solemnly pledged word of our Führer that he would not encroach in the slightest degree on either of the denominations ?"[1]

Bishop Kaller of Ermland is no less outspoken in his Pastoral at the end of January, 1937.

Never before has our German Fatherland been the arena for a struggle against the existence of our Christian heritage so embittered as that which is raging today. . . . Yes, we are at war; and no Concordat, no solemn profession of positive Christianity on the part of the Führer is able to protect us against the fanaticism of the enemies of Christ. . . . Certain papers have only to give the word, and all the rest plunge into the fight against Christianity and the Church, and labour for the de-Christianisation and ruin of the Catholic Church in Germany. . . . Have we deserved all this, have we deserved to be attacked in this way ? The true Catholic, who is Catholic to the very core, may well be seized with a righteous anger as he considers this question.

In his sermon on the anniversary of the Pope's Coronation,[2] Cardinal Faulhaber said with reference to violations of the Concordat:

The correspondence of bishops is confiscated, priests are arrested, Church property is seized, religious and Catholic teachers are dismissed, processions are forbidden, and high ecclesiastical dignitaries are assailed by a flood of calumnies. The Concordat which was made between the Catholic Church and Germany in 1933 cannot be broken or violated without coming into conflict with honour. Today, the whole world is saying that the Concordat was only signed in order to gain time and power, so that later, when the way was at last free, any sort of influence exercised by the Church could be eradicated.

At the beginning of the summer of 1937, Bishop Galen of Münster preached a striking sermon of nearly two hours' duration on the manifold violations of the Concordat. He referred to the illegal dissolution of Church organisations and confiscation of their property; expulsion of the Sisters of Mercy from the schools, hospitals and other charitable institutions; suppression of denominational schools; restriction of religious instruction; veto on visitation of schools by Church authorities; expulsion of Catholic teachers from denominational schools, etc.

All that, and much else that is in contradiction to the Concordat with the Reich, is known to all of us. . . . And the Pope knows it too ! Should he therefore remain silent ? . . .[3]

[1] *I.e.*, Catholic or Protestant.—*Translator's note.*   [2] *Cf.* p. 6.
[3] This is a reference to the Encyclical *Mit brennender Sorge* of March, 1937.

And now, in a letter to the German bishops of March 23rd, 1937, the Reich Minister for Ecclesiastical Affairs declares: " The Papal Encyclical is in gross contradiction to the spirit of the Concordat. The Concordat with the Reich does not give any warrant for procedure of this kind. Consequently, in accordance with Article 16 of the Concordat of July 20th, 1933, the bishops and other ordinaries are forbidden to print or duplicate or distribute the Encyclical in any form."

After Bishop Galen had announced the contents of this letter, he gave a description of the unheard-of measures of revenge which the Government had adopted because of the distribution of the Papal Encyclical, and also other instances of the bludgeoning of the Catholic Press by State agencies. The bishop was able to refer to the fact that threats had already been made to confiscate all typewriters and duplicating machines in ecclesiastical possession.

A little later, in July, 1937, Cardinal Faulhaber, in a sermon in Munich, occasioned by the arrest of Father Rupert Mayer, S.J.,[1] made a relentless exposure of the ultimate aims of the fight against the Church. Bishop Preysing of Berlin expressed himself with similar clearness in a sermon at the beginning of autumn, 1937.

The faithful shall hear from the lips of their bishop that the powers of darkness are at work to destroy the Kingdom of God on German soil. For the most part you are able to perceive for yourselves the form which this great struggle is taking, the fight between faith and infidelity, between Christianity and anti-Christianity. But our opponents do not everywhere fight with the visor open. It is consequently my sacred duty to tell you what are the true issues of the battle and what are not.

Then the bishop showed in detail how it was not State authority or peace between the denominations that was in question, but God, Christ and the Church.

My beloved diocesans ! What moves me particularly to address you today is the fact that the fight has broken out in a form hitherto unknown, especially in articles in the press and caricatures directed against the truths of faith and morality, against the Church, Pope, bishops, priests and faithful. This campaign is being conducted not merely by journals which have long been known as open opponents of Christianity; no, Party organs with the very widest circulation, directed and recommended by those in leading positions, are in the forefront of the battle, which is being carried on with all available weapons, even with poisoned weapons—with insult, scorn, mockery, *falsehood and misrepresentation.*

On the occasion of a pilgrimage of men to Weingarten on October 10th, 1937, Bishop Sproll of Rottenburg addressed his audience with such effect that he had continually to beg for silence from clapping and loud bursts of applause. Speaking of the Papal Encyclical on the Holy Rosary, which was confiscated in Germany because it dared to criticise National Socialism, he mercilessly exposed the methods of the enemy in the educational struggle, producing documentary evidence that the solemn undertaking with regard to teachers of religion had been violated, and urging that consequently the National

---

[1] Father Rupert Mayer is a popular Munich preacher. Details of his arrest are given on p. 67, and in the sermon here referred to, which is given in full in Appendix III.

Socialist Press should no longer receive credence. "That is a lie," rang out again and again from the pulpit, as the bishop gave one example after another of misrepresentation of truth, and finally countered the tactics of the infamous "Immorality" trials.

At about the same time Cardinal Bertram of Breslau addressed a stirring Pastoral to his archdiocese, recommending the recital of the Rosary.

The harder the times become, the more confidently do Christians turn their gaze upon the picture of Christ on Calvary and upon His Holy Mother. . . . All over Europe in these days, with blasphemous rashness and fury, a fight is being carried on against the God-Man, our Redeemer. Faith in Christ and Christianity is being everywhere represented as obsolete and worthless, as unworthy of a German. Moreover, the Church itself is attacked by those who maintain that she is the enemy of our nationality. Step by step our youth is being estranged from the Church. Havoc is being wrought in the religious thought of our children. The more the priest is excluded from the work of education, the more rapidly does youth lose its hold on the true Faith, religious life, and joyful devotion to the Catholic Church. . . . Now the Rosary is a prayer which, like a golden chain, binds together and unites all sorts and conditions of men, from the youngest child to the Vicar of Christ on the Throne of St. Peter. . . . Whenever the Christian feels depressed as he gazes forward into a future that looks so gloomy, the recitation of the Rosary will again strengthen his confidence in God. While our enemies are already pricking up their ears to hear the death-knell of the Catholic Church sound in Germany, the Rosary gives us joyful presage of the future resurrection. . . . In many courses of instruction nowadays a secret war is being waged against Christ and Christianity. . . . In thousands and thousands of cases our faith is affronted and insulted with impunity, nor is the sacred person of our Redeemer Himself spared.

Towards the end of November, 1937, Bishop Galen of Münster gave a sermon in which he laid bare all the sorrow with which his soul was afflicted over the course of events in Germany, especially in regard to the youth question.[1]

In December of the same year Bishop Galen spoke out once again, to rebut the reproach that "Christian" meant nothing more than "un-German," or "foreign to the German nature."

Truly, a holy anger seizes me, a holy anger must fill each one of you, and indeed every honourable German man, when day after day he has to read such insults and abuse of his fathers and ancestors, and must let it pass unchallenged. . . . We will not permit our heroes and our saints, our forbears and ancestors, our fathers and mothers to be insulted. (Speech at Vreden in Westphalia.)

In December, 1937, a Pastoral was read in German Catholic churches that was ascribed by many to Bishop Preysing of Berlin personally. It is a monument of episcopal and apostolic candour. In it we read:

One says nothing more than the truth with regard to the position in which the true Christians of our Fatherland now find themselves, if one declares that the loyal Catholic in Germany is an outlaw. . . .

The true Christian, declared the Pastoral, would never agree to a dictatorship over men's consciences. Force and power, it is true.

---
[1] Extracts from this sermon will be found on pp. 111, 165, 167.

gained easy victories in the fight against Christianity, but it was a deadly menace to the unity of the German people when that section of the population which was Christian-minded was deprived of freedom of conscience and freedom of faith. The bishops would welcome the hour of peace, but not a peace at any price. "We should be hirelings, were we to buy peace at the price of a betrayal of the All-Holiest." This Pastoral was read in Berlin on December 5th.

Lastly, we must mention a Pastoral of Bishop Bornewasser of Trier, written at the end of 1937, in which he sharply criticises the injustices which had been visited on the Catholic schools.[1]

The assault, however, on all things Catholic carries on unchecked. The only new feature is a clearer avowal of the will to annihilate on the part of the enemy, which is countered on the part of the bishops by an increased confidence in the final victory of the Church.

At the beginning of February, 1938, Cardinal Faulhaber of Munich delivered a moving sermon, from which we reproduce the following:

> The worst form of spoliation which can be inflicted on a nation is to rob it of its faith in God. Woe to the country in which youth and the family have been robbed of God ! . . . We shudder when in German newspapers on almost every page we read frightful blasphemies. We see in spirit how the Angel of the Apocalypse stands ready to pour out the vial of God's wrath upon the earth. But we know also that God counts up the just before He punishes, and that for the sake of the just the days of trial shall be shortened. . . . Each of us is responsible for the fate of his people. . . .
>
> Here and there it is maintained that religion is falling to pieces, and that in the near future the churches will be empty. That is untrue. In spite of all the persecution and oppression the religious life does not die. Dangers, threats, reprisals and persecution cannot break the faith that is founded on the certainty that God will triumph over all His enemies. The heroic courage of the faithful is rooted above all else in unshakable trust in God, who will not desert His Church.

In the course of his speech, Cardinal Faulhaber had also said: "Next year the State subsidy for priests will be curtailed or even completely withdrawn." And yet, in spite of this, he reported, young men were continually offering themselves as candidates for the priesthood, and the same applied to young women wishing to become nuns.

As if with one voice, the Lenten Pastorals of 1938 protest against the religious persecution. Bishop Galen of Münster rebuts the reproach that Catholics are being persecuted because of their abuse of religion, and even because of the secret aims of Rome in the secular political sphere, which are contrary to the political aims of the Government. Later in the Pastoral we read:

> In the last few months the National Socialist Party speakers have frequently called upon the Church to confine herself to the next life, and to leave this life to the National Socialist State to deal with. . . . Indeed, a highly-placed and influential Party speaker of National Socialism openly declared a few months back that *Christianity no longer had any significance for the present and future of the German nation* ! Truly, when such opinions are openly

---

[1] An extract from this Pastoral will be found on p. 160.

expressed in Germany and even urged by individuals in positions of authority, it must be admitted that the Holy Father did but express the sad truth when He spoke in the spring of " a war of extermination against the Church," and at Christmas of " a religious persecution in Germany."

It will rend your hearts when you see how the faith and salvation of your children are menaced, and how loyalty to Christ and his Church claims victim after victim. (Cardinal Schulte of Cologne.)

It is for the sake of Christ that this tribulation has come upon the Catholics of Germany. For Christ's sake Catholic men and women have had to pass through times of sorrowful anxiety, Catholic parents have had to wrestle for the souls of their children, Catholic young men and women have been derided and ridiculed. (Auxiliary Bishop Sträter of Aachen.)

The Lenten Pastoral of the Bishop of Berlin, Count von Preysing, says: " Even the condemnation of Jesus by Pontius Pilate was made ' for political reasons.' " The bishop went on to point out that still more difficult days lay ahead for the Church, and called upon the faithful to meet them in a spirit of loyalty to their religion, setting before their eyes the coming triumph of Christ, which would also be the triumph of His Church.

Archbishop Gröber of Freiburg spoke in a similar sense: When it was declared a few years ago that Marxism was dead, this gave rise to the hope that the de-Christianisation of the German people would also cease. " We have been deceived," said the Archbishop. The second part of his Pastoral was concerned with the pretexts " which are thrown at the people like missiles, in order to wage war against Christ." Others again say that Christ has emptied this life of all its value for the German, and fixed his gaze exclusively on the life to come. The first part of this statement is untrue, and with regard to the second " many today in this valley of tears are laughing too early."

" For many the hour has now come, when they have to decide whether they will confess Christ or not, whether they will fight for Him or against Him. . . . Fear not! the sun of Christianity will still be shining forth, long after those who are now trying to extinguish it among our people have turned to dust and ashes, and their names have been forgotten," wrote Bishop Berning of Osnabrück, whose Pastoral concludes with the striking words: " Today, the whole world is in a ferment. Men are struggling for a new culture and a new humanity. There is no question here of isolated points of doctrine; today the most decisive factors of all are in the melting-pot."

Bishop Landersdorfer of Passau drew attention to the fact that in every persecution of the Church, attempts were made to strike the Pastor that the sheep might be dispersed. With us they are trying to effect a " moral extermination " of the Pastors, and to destroy their influence over the Christian population to the greatest extent possible. They are driven out of public life, and even in the church itself their every step is supervised and spied upon in a most unworthy manner. The bishop then deals in a striking manner with the triple priesthood which the Church of God contains: the ordained or ministerial priesthood, the priesthood of the laity and the priesthood of the family. " Today the Church is in the midst of a fierce battle, in which she is contending for the very existence of Christianity."

The Pastoral of Bishop Sproll of Rottenberg is characterised by clarity and confidence in the future.

What is to become of our German Fatherland when, in spite of all the declarations of freedom of conscience that have been made, in spite of all the official assurances, in spite of the Concordat, so many voices proclaim that Christianity, Cross and Church must be eradicated ?—when the fight against all that is good and sacred to us Catholics is waged in the open light of day and with brutal ruthlessness ?—when Catholic religious instruction is countered and nullified by instruction in a new and anti-Christian outlook ? ... Be proud of your Church in these days. It is utterly false, though you will often hear it said, that the Catholic Church is now engaged on her last death-struggle, and that we need only await the ringing of her knell. . . . Do not be afraid ! This tempest will pass away, just as so many others have done, which beat against the Church in times gone by. Fear not ! Have courage, be confident and steadfast. . . . Through the conflict, on to victory ! Even the most mighty opponents of the Church must come to die, but the Church lives on. And so we, too, will be unscathed if we stand fast to the Church in our hearts and with our words, and show our inviolable fidelity to her in our lives and actions. Fearless and faithful !

Cardinal Bertram of Breslau appealed for " days of recollection " to be followed by the faithful, and went on:

Wherever we go we see and we hear a daily flood of attacks and insinuations, of errors and lies, of misrepresentations and calumnies against all that we hold sacred. They even employ economic pressure against practising Christians who are in dependent positions, in order to force them into apostasy. The assault is directed against the Catholic Church in particular, since in spite of all attacks she stands firm and, with the same courage that she taught the martyrs, defends the truths that Christ has hidden in the bosom of His Spouse—that is, in the heart of His Church.

Here we may add, since it breathes the same spirit, what was said by Cardinal Faulhaber of Munich in a speech given at about the same time. Among other things, the Cardinal dealt with the accusation that the Church was pursuing political aims. Any policeman, he said, could decide what was or was not " political Catholicism," while the Pope and the bishops were excluded from any discussion of the matter. We had to be careful not to fall into the mistake of believing that, after 1,000 years of Christian tradition, any future was possible for Germany without Christianity. The Cardinal was convinced that the nation would not accept Rosenberg's " Myth " in place of the Gospel, or take a stone instead of bread.

After his return from a visit to the Holy Father, Bishop Albert Stohr of Mainz sent out a Pastoral to his people (April, 1938), in which he said that after the Papal Encyclical *Mit brennender Sorge*, Catholics had hoped for an improvement of the position. But peace was not yet. On the contrary ! A regular flood of calumnies, insults and derision broke out against the Church. From this time on, the position of the Church grew worse from week to week and from day to day, while the anxiety of the bishops grew ever deeper. Here the bishop enumerated the constant and grievous violations of the Concordat. The freedom of religious instruction, which was guaranteed to the Church, was disregarded. The printing of the Papal Encyclical was treated as a crime against the State, and twelve Catholic printing-presses were confiscated. The publication of Pastorals was forbidden. The Church Press was suppressed, although it was conducted exclusively in the interests of truth and of the Church, while anti-Christian journals could write against Church and religion without hindrance. Two important Encyclicals of the Holy Father, that namely on Godless Communism and that on the Holy Rosary, could not be brought to the notice of the faithful. Religious instruction was suppressed, or entrusted to unbelieving individuals; priests were kept out of the schools. The official magazine of the National Socialist teachers contained instructions that were in open contradiction to Christian doctrine. It was publicly demanded of the Catholic clergy that they should no longer speak of the Creation according to the account given of it in Holy Scripture, nor of Original Sin, nor of Redemption. The bishops had found it necessary to call upon the faithful to keep their children away from religious instruction in the National Socialist community schools, since their faith was endangered thereby. The State had now obliged all children to be present at these instructions, which, though they bore the name of " religious instructions," were used for the propagation of false doctrine in the religious sphere. The fight against the Catholic schools was a violation of the Concordat, and an infringement of the rights of parents. The urgent complaints of the bishops had produced no result. On the contrary, outrage and persecution increased. Various utterances of the Reichsminister for Ecclesiastical Affairs had confirmed the fact that it was the endeavour of the State to curtail the liberty of the Church.

On School and Educational Sunday (May, 1938), the German bishops issued a Pastoral, in which it was emphasised that it was an obligation of conscience to secure the religious instruction of children. " Unfortunately, religious instruction as it is given in the schools nowadays is, for the most part, insufficient." If Church and parents worked together, we might hope that in spite of the many difficulties of the present time, the souls of the children " might be protected from the blight of the night frost, and day by day unfold themselves in unspoiled beauty."

Undoubtedly the most important document of the year regarding the persecution of the Church in Germany is the Combined Pastoral of the bishops at Fulda, issued on August 19th, 1938. Unfortunately it is impossible to reproduce the full text here. The introduction to the document by itself gives one a good deal of insight into the conditions obtaining.

When we German bishops from the tomb of St. Boniface address a Joint Pastoral to our diocesans, we are first of all demonstrating our spiritual unity in Christ, Whose Mystical Body imparts the most intimate unity to all Its members. . . . We send a hearty and fraternal greeting to the most reverend episcopate and to all our comrades in the faith in the lands that were formerly Austrian. Unfortunately it is one and the same religious war that is being waged openly and secretly on both sides of the former frontiers, it is the same aim which our enemies pursue both on this side of those frontiers and beyond them, and they are using the same weapons and the same methods of warfare. . . . We German Catholic bishops have already in earlier Pastorals dealt with this struggle which has been forced upon us. And again today, from repeated experiences, we have to place it on record that these attacks have not moderated or become more bearable, but have grown fiercer and are being pressed with greater enmity than ever, though it is also true that our enemies' aims have now become more evident.

They are trying to restrict us on every side, to bleed our Catholic life to death. Yea, more; they aim at the complete overthrow of the Catholic Church on German soil, and even at the entire elimination of Christianity of whatever sort, and the introduction in its place of a form of belief which is utterly alien to the true faith in God and belief in a future life.

Now that even further restrictions on Catholic life have been introduced, thousands of German Catholics in their religious extremity are asking themselves the question whether, in spite of their good citizenship and loyalty to the State, they are any longer considered to have the same rights as their fellow-citizens, whether they are to be condemned without a hearing, without credence given to them, and without any possibility of either defence or compensation. When with incomprehensible arrogance it is even demanded of a German bishop that he should leave his diocese, and when, after his return in the ordinary course of his duty, he is continually harassed by commotions, tumults and deeds of violence directed against him, without any official action being taken to protect him, then the Catholic population can scarcely rid themselves of the fear that at no distant date we bishops in general will be handed over in a similar manner to the rabble deliberately incited for the purpose. To our deepest sorrow we have even been forced to observe that the personal honour of the Holy Father has been attacked in a grievously injurious manner. . . . But that is precisely what they are striving for in so many quarters at present, and always without check by anybody—the complete annihilation of the Catholic Faith in Germany. Let it not be objected that this is only a baseless fear, or even a calumnious accusation inspired by a lack of nationalistic sentiment. Men of standing and authority have themselves announced with the greatest publicity that their ideological aim is none other than the destruction of German Catholicism. Nor can it be urged against this that, after all, no hindrance is placed in the way of holding Catholic church services. On the whole that is still the case. In actual fact, however, it is in this direction that constant efforts are being made, notably by the endeavour to engender in youth and in those in the various camps a distaste for going to church and by putting difficulty in the way of their going to church, also by representing " denominationalism " as destructive of the unity of the nation, and striving to drive everything ecclesiastical out of the public gaze. There has thus been allotted to us a life like that in the catacombs, which is to be the beginning of the end. As a foundation for all this, and by way of justification, everything that is noble and sacred in the history of our Church (and this applies also to instructional methods in the schools) is passed over or suppressed or misrepresented in the interests of racialism, while all that is bad and blameworthy is brought out in the full light of day and exaggerated, with complete disregard for scientific or natural justice. Have we then to admit that those who are now defenceless and silent in the grave have a lesser claim to justice and truth than the living who can defend themselves ? For the purposes of this " historical " propaganda they even welcome books and documents, publish them and recommend them, which have been condemned both by German scholars and by all well-read and objectively-thinking German men. In contrast to all this, Catholic books and publications are frequently subjected to the most stringent supervision, which goes so far as prohibition, seizure and destruction. At the same time, constantly and everywhere, often by the employment of most questionable methods and agents, they set themselves to ferret out any moral lapses on the part of clergy or religious, represent them in a one-sided way, and constantly rake up judicial processes that are long since past. Meanwhile the Church is reproached with having secret relations, both personal and political, with Russian Bolshevism. . . . Even every word of friendship addressed to other States and peoples by the Supreme Head of our Church, or attitudes and actions of his dictated by political courtesy and convention or by the religious conditions of the time, is regarded as an unfriendly act towards Germany and even as a tacit alliance with her enemies. Within our German frontiers a movement for giving up Church membership has been set on foot and supported, and loyal Catholic officials, employees and workmen, together with Catholic students at the Universities and Technical High Schools, have been threatened with economic pressure, and these threats have even been put harshly into actual execution. In marriage legislation, a basic concept of the matter is defended which we cannot accept without making a combined and solemn protest. Among the motives advanced in support of the legislation respecting the making of testamentary dispositions, mention was even made of the covetous legacy-hunting of the clergy, which constituted a shameful exploitation of the death-bed. . . . Now if it be suggested that much of that of which we have been complaining and which we have had to endure has been brought on by ourselves as a reaction and protective measure by the State, because we German bishops and Catholics have not adopted an unexceptionable attitude towards the new Reich, our answer is as follows: We German bishops have repeatedly, and in the most unequivocal and genuine manner, professed our loyalty to the nation and the Fatherland even in its new form, and have carried out our duties of citizenship conscientiously. But we have to add in all candour, and the development of the Movement in its ideological aspect seems to make the matter ever clearer, that those in leading circles simply do not wish for a genuine and lasting agreement with us and with the Catholic Church. Either such agreement is excluded *a priori* by basic incompatibilities in the Movement as such, or else, as events have developed, the upper hand has been gained by those who are seeking the Church's ruin and not peace or a working understanding between Church and State. But let it be made clear once and for all, that we German bishops will never buy favour or even merely tolerance and freedom from molestation at the price either of the mutilation of our religious heritage of faith, or of the surrender of Church rights, or of detriment to our personal courage and character. . . . Once again unequivocal announcements have demonstrated that the fight is being waged, not against the Church alone, but against Christianity as such. The rejection of the Old Testament was already a step in this direction. Now Christianity is represented as an ancient fossilised remnant from an epoch that has passed, impotent and utterly devoid of present value. Quite apart from that, on the ground of racial and " blood " theories, it is maintained that the personality and the life of Jesus Christ are alien to the German nature, as are also the main points of the faith He taught—this applies specially to the doctrines of Original Sin, Redemption, reward and punishment after death, which are all superstitions from the Near East, forced upon the Germanic tribes when they were perfidiously invaded. Led by opinions like these, especially in certain districts, young people had been led to banish the Cross, as the symbol of the Christian religion, from all positions in public, and even to destroy crucifixes (with complete indifference to their importance as outstanding works of art) to the bitter grief of Christian people. . . . In certain circles among our opponents—how it grieves even to speak of such things—the convinced believer in Christ, who " obeys God rather than men," may even be driven out of the community, or stigmatised as " politically unreliable," with all the painful consequences that result therefrom. It is then an uncommonly distressing and contradictory picture-While Catholic Spain is fighting with the most heroic constancy as the unconquerable enemy of the Bolshevistic Antichrist, while Christians and Catholics in Germany do their duty as citizens and soldiers in conscientious loyalty and, for the sake of the community at large, patiently pass over and forget the injuries and sufferings inflicted on them so continually, not a few among the German people are trying to undermine the Christian Faith as the enemy of the people, and with purposeful, relentless destruction to annihilate it entirely. . . . Are they really so deluded and so blinded that they can promise themselves that the bright rays of Christianity are destined soon to be extinguished in the German nation by means of dictatorial edicts and acts of violence ? Just as was done to the Holiest One of all, Who said, " I am the Way, the Truth and the Life," they can take Christian truth prisoner, scourge her, hand her over to the civil power, crown her with the thorns of calumny, condemn her to death and crucify her on a Germany Calvary. But for her, short indeed will be the silence of the grave, and she will rise again and gaze in triumph at the tomb men dug for her and sealed over her, and at the silent graves of her enemies, closed for ever. . . . When we German bishops with apostolic courage and in the public light of day demand that a stop should at last be put to this war on Christianity, we do this no less in the interests of our Fatherland and our people than in the interests of our Faith. . . . They seek to banish the Christian God, and to set up a " German God " in His place. Is this " God " a different God from the God of the other nations ?

If he is, then there are as many " Gods " as there are races and peoples, which is as much as to say that none of them are " Gods " at all, since the true God is necessarily unique. . . . It has now been announced, and on an official occasion, that the German will not accept a " Creator-God." In that case, the German is turning this passing world into something eternal, and in so far as the one and only true God is rejected he can understand by the word " God " at most some manifestation of the racial soul. Such a " God " as this has no meaning. . . . If the Christian concept of God be abandoned, there at once arise doubts and even complete denials of a life after death and of responsibility to an ultimate moral authority. . . . It is for this reason that we hear so much nowadays about a life belonging exclusively to the present, a present to which each German is bound to devote his entire service, since belief in a life to come, and the longing and striving for this future life, deprive our earthly life of all its value, stigmatise it as a valley of tears, trouble the individual with the fear of death, and hinder the full exploitation of his powers in the service of nation and Fatherland. But all this is a hackneyed theme, sung to much the same old tune as we used to hear in the times of godless Marxism. These are the doctrines of sheer hedonism, either in the form of coarse libertinism or with a thin veneer of culture to conceal its ugliness, but they do not suffice to supply motives for a life lived earnestly in a manner befitting the dignity of a man. There are times when something more than mere enjoyment is required as a source of power and action. Or is Germany perhaps specially insured against the onslaught of the horsemen of the Apocalypse ? . . . Conscious therefore of our responsibility, we raise our voices in loud protest against this exclusive preoccupation with this life and the denial of the soul's immortality after death; and this we do in order to protect our German people from such fatal errors and to save it from ruin. Once again we repeat: We are not fighting against the State and the people, but for them, and consequently against all those whom, with the courage proper to our apostolic office, we must denounce as enemies of our nation. For this we shall be misrepresented and reviled. . . . We call on you to make profession of your faith, as we have of ours. . . . It fills us with sorrow to know how terribly hard this profession will be for not a few of our countrymen. We therefore appeal for aid to Catholic solidarity, so that no single brother of ours shall be reduced to hunger and destitution because of his faith. We appeal to you not to murmur and not to be despondent. " Why are you fearful, O ye of little faith ?" (Matt. viii, 26). This is not the first storm that has burst over the Church in Germany, and it will not be the last. The more we are oppressed by man, the nearer God is to us.

Of the further pronouncements of the bishops in the year 1938 let us content ourselves with mentioning a sermon of Cardinal Faulhaber in Munich on November 6th, in which he complains of the Nazi fashion of stigmatising as " traitors to the nation " all those who wish to remain in harmony with the Church; and also the outspoken discourse given by Archbishop Gröber of Freiburg in December, 1938, to a large concourse of the faithful at Constance. Probably, said the bishop among other things, hard times still lay ahead in the future for the faithful of Germany. Various incontestable facts and signs showed that forces were at work to destroy Christianity. So far, however, these forces had produced the contrary effect. Never had the sense of Catholicity and the Faith shown up so clearly as it had in these recent times. The de-Christianisation of the schools was being constantly carried through. But just as a Nero and other potentates had been unable to destroy Christianity, so also those in power today would fail. For the rest, Bishop Gröber rebutted the accusation that the German bishops and the Catholic people were traitors to the German nation.

In 1939 the persecution carried on along the lines already laid down. The opposing fronts now stand out clearly. The German episcopate again calls upon the Catholic population in their long-drawn-out religious trial to remain loyal to the Faith, and to proclaim it heroically in spite of all difficulties.

On the Feast of the Holy Family, Bishop Galen of Münster issued a special Pastoral to Catholic parents, in the course of which he said:

Today more than ever, when the school cannot or may not any longer co-operate in the religious education of the children, a special responsibility rests upon the Catholic family for the maintenance and care of religious life.

From the same prelate's Lenten Pastoral of 1939 we take the following:

Those who place the Race or the Nation or the State . . . outside this earthly scale of values, who take these factors as the supreme norm of all things, even of things religious, and deify them with a divine cultus, are distorting and falsifying the divinely created and divinely ordained order of things. . . . Only superficial minds can fall into the error of speaking of a national God or of a national religion. . . . The personal immortality of the human soul is being denied. As a substitute for this, they offer us in high-sounding phrases a so-called " eternity " in the form of a chain of succession between forbears and offspring. . . . Whoever uses the word immortality to mean only collective survival in the continuity of one's own people for an undetermined length of time in the future perverts and falsifies one of the fundamental verities of the Christian faith. . . .[1] Those who dare to demand obedience to commands and ordinances that are in opposition to the holy will of God misuse their power and forfeit the right to require obedience. In such cases it would be our duty to withstand the authority thus abused, in accordance with the example set by the holy Apostles. . . . For this reason we cannot accept a totalitarian demand to follow other doctrines or pursue purely earthly aims.

[1] Quoted from the Encyclical *Mit brennender Sorge*.

In his Lenten Pastoral, Bishop Stohr of Mainz wrote:

The deepest roots of the religious distress of our times are to be found in the fact that people are acting as if man himself, and not God, were the highest consideration of all. Man is manufacturing his own " God " for himself, to fit in with his own requirements and fancies—and then actually calls upon others to do reverence to this pitiable product of human hands. In this way God is deprived of all dignity and robbed of all power; it is no longer He, but man who sits upon the throne. . . . They would like a God built on the human model, a " Friend-God," such as the ancient Germanic tribes loved; a God before whom one does not kneel, but stands; a God from whom one need not keep at a distance. . . . We believe in God the Father Almighty. We will not allow ourselves to be robbed of this faith, or of the heritage which it enshrines for us, by anything at all. Nothing shall rob us of it, not even the siren-songs of the new prophets, not even the hint that it might perhaps be of advantage to us if we ceased to belong to the Church.

Bishop Stohr also dwelt on the paramount importance of the family in times like these.

A vivid picture of the religious persecution is given in the Lenten Pastoral of Bishop Ehrenfried of Würzburg:

In these days you stand less in need of instruction than of encouragement and consolation. . . . Today many are mistaken in their idea of the true God. In many circles they ridicule the idea of a God Who does not belong to this world, but stands outside His own creation. They want a new God, in and with the world; in fact, a worldly God. Others base their dislike of the Christian Faith on quite different reasons. They treat our Faith as something Jewish. . . . There is one special danger to our Faith that we ought clearly to recognise as such. I refer to the deliberately planned propaganda against Christianity which is being carried out by word of mouth and in the Press. This danger is all the more considerable, since we are here carrying on an unequal struggle. Our means of protection are limited to that which can be said on Church premises or printed in journals of a purely religious character. The use of the general Press or of public meetings in order to vindicate ourselves is at present impossible. They carefully avoid a straight and open contest in this battle of ideas. But gradually these very tactics of the forces of unbelief defeat their own ends. People no longer have entire confidence in the truth of what is published. In the face of this loud-mouthed propaganda you should maintain a dignified composure, and turn your backs upon it as unworthy of your attention. It is true that there are many who derive confidence in their written and spoken attacks from the conventional silence of the great mass of people. They think they see agreement and acquiescence therein, and are already dreaming of a break-up of the Christian Faith. But they delude themselves. There is also a silence, not of agreement, but of impotence, when free discussion and refutation of such speeches and writings is made impossible. There is, moreover, a silence of prudence, which is maintained towards those who are impervious to the truth. Indeed, there is even a silence of interior rejection; and it is all too easy to forget that general silence may but cover general disapproval. . . . Today, all who are loyal to the Church must be carriers of the Cross. You know and feel yourselves how extensive are the hosts which have ranged themselves against the Roman Church. This is often done under the pretext that the fight is directed, not against religion, not against religious Catholicism, but against political Catholicism. But it is easy to recognise that this distinction is an arbitrary one. It has no sure basis in fact. For those who think in this way, it is quite natural and consistent that the religious rights and activities of the Church should be swept aside—they simply say that all these are of a political nature. . . .

A favourite method in the war against the Church is the intimidation of the masses. Their sympathies and dispositions are branded as un-German. By this means the timid are unnerved in their Catholic life. They begin to tremble for their reputations and their positions. They no longer dare to attend Holy Mass when there is an obligation to do so, and do not venture to take part in Church processions. With St. Paul I should like to cry out to these faint-hearted ones: " Watch ye, stand fast in the faith, do manfully, and be strengthened " (1 Cor. xvi, 13). . . . Every day of our lives we need the blessing of the Cross. I therefore regard it as barbarous and inhuman when many cry: Away with the Cross from our houses and our fields ! I regard it as an altogether atrocious thing when deluded and maddened individuals violate and destroy our ancient and venerated roadside shrines, pictures of Our Blessed Lady and crucifixes, as we have had to deplore repeatedly in our diocese in recent times.

Archbishop Gröber of Freiburg speaks in his Lenten Pastoral of the war against the Person of Christ: " It can unfortunately no longer be doubted, that in Germany also Jesus Christ is being more and more misunderstood and misrepresented. The proofs of this are too many to admit of doubt !" Even that which is human in Christ is not allowed to have any value today, since it is spoiled and rendered repulsive by that which is Jewish in him. It is vain to attempt to stamp Christ as an Aryan. According to His human nature, Christ grew from Jewish stock, though only on His Mother's side, since He was conceived of the Holy Ghost. The modern enemies of Christ smile at this mystery, " for they simply deny outright everything of a miraculous or supernatural nature, and at most speak of miracles which, in our view, are perhaps striking achievements of man, but which are no miracles in the true sense of the word." This new hatred of Christ itself has recourse today to hate-inspired and obscene passages from the Jewish Talmud. Catholics raise a solemn protest against such nauseating attacks. But as a matter of fact all this talk about the Jewish origin of Our Lord and the monstrous insults offered to His Virgin Mother are but a thinly veiled pretext. For even if Jesus had not been a Jew, they would reject Him, since their pride makes the idea of a Redeemer repellent to them.

From other episcopal utterances on the Church situation belonging to this period, we select the courageous sermon which Archbishop Gröber of Freiburg delivered on the Feast of St. Fridolin (March, 1939) at Säckingen.

We know the battles that we have to fight. Today, the fight rages around one point alone: Either a true Christ or an Antichrist. The world of today is a world that wishes to deify itself and which will give no peace to Christianity. . . . The fight is a fierce one, but fight it we shall; we are no longer asleep and our enemies shall know it. . . . I know that our enemy is not minded to conclude a lasting peace with the Holy See. Christianity, they say, is something which has grown old and obsolete, and we cannot make a pact with it. And so there is war. In this fight the bishop will prove himself to be a shepherd and no hireling ! For this fight we arm ourselves, not with a revolver, but with the power of the Spirit. It is not enough merely to say that you are a Catholic; you must also live in accordance with the fundamental laws of your Faith. We do not need crowds; we only need a few hundred thousand practising Catholic men, and then we shall gain the victory. The enemy is counting on our weakness and faintheartedness, therefore the Catholic must today before all things show character. To be a Christian and a Catholic demands readiness for sacrifice. We are asking for nothing that is inequitable; we ask only for justice. We wish to give the State what the State requires of us. . . . But we do want the rights of freedom, and we do ask that justice should be exercised in our regard. We pay our taxes as well as other people.

The same prelate also composed a moving prayer for loyalty to the Faith, which was to be recited regularly at the May Devotions in the churches. We make the following extract from it:

Many, O Divine Lord, turn away from Thee, as if Thou wert a light that is waning or already extinguished, or a conquered King without a people, or an intruding stranger in the land, or even a dangerous and outlawed enemy. Forgive, O Lord, in Thine infinite mercy, all those who indeed still cleave to Thee in the secret of their hearts, but do not confess Thee openly. Have mercy also on those, who were once Thy friends and companions at Thy table, but who now consort with Thine archenemies and with the Scribes and Pharisees cry " Crucify Him." Restrain all those who estrange our youth from Thee, the Divine Friend of children, and let Thy warning words about scandal to little ones burn deep into their consciences. . . . But we, O Lord, we believe unshakeably in Thee, and will serve Thee in loyalty and self-sacrifice and fight with Thee unto death. The world may strike us with all its might and power. But these will be like the blows of a hammer forging us and hardening us like inflexible steel. And when men calumniate and dishonour us, may Thy voice sound in our ears through all the tumult of hate: " Blessed are ye when men shall revile you. . . ." Thou knowest, O God of Wisdom, the hour in which Thy divine word shall still the storm of oppression. Still as of yore Thou askest with royal dignity: " Will you also go away ?" for Thou dost not force or bind any man. . . . But we answer with Peter . . . with the same sacred vow: " O Lord, to whom shall we go ? Thou hast the words of eternal life."

Finally, we quote a passage from the Pentecost message of the Archbishop of Freiburg, which refers to the opportunity of a profession of faith given by the Feast of Corpus Christi. " With the ever-increasing cleavage of opinions, this feast has acquired a new significance, since the attitude of Catholics to the procession has almost become a recognised test of the Catholic Faith." The Archbishop rejects the suggestion that the procession is a " demonstration of political Catholicism." It was, rather, a piece of heroism, which had already often brought Christians to the verge of martyrdom. " The German nation may well rejoice at the fact that Christian characters are on the increase, who place the service of God and their religious convictions higher than the contempt and disadvantages with which these are perhaps rewarded."

It will perhaps be of interest and utility to refer to the manifesto, in which the Austrian bishops expressed to the German episcopate their sorrow at the persecution to which the Church in Germany was being subjected. We reproduce the text as it appeared in the *Reichspost* of December 6th, 1937. This was, of course, just shortly before the Anschluss with Germany.

VIENNA, *December 6th.*

The Austrian episcopate in the last Conference of Bishops held in Vienna issued the following Manifesto to the bishops of the German Reich; this Manifesto has already been published in the *Osservatore Romano* on December 3rd:

At this present time of grievous oppression for the sake of the Catholic Faith, which the clergy and Catholic faithful are suffering in the German Reich, we bishops of Austria, being now gathered together for our yearly conference, feel constrained to express our innermost sympathy and to say how greatly we are distressed by what is happening in Germany, where the State applies all its might—which in the course of the last few years has been growing ever more extensive—to a continual and carefully worked-out attack on religion, which leaves nothing undone to effect the suppression and even complete elimination of the Christian Faith, and especially of the Catholic Church, in the Reich. So fierce is this attack that any attempt at active defence against it is at once avenged with new penalties and persecutions. But however great may be the arrogance of these destructive forces, and however thoroughly they carry their programme through, their efforts cannot have any lasting effect, and we cannot doubt that in spite of all the Catholic Church in the German Reich will be preserved. . . . In times like these, with great confidence we unite our prayers with yours, and we exhort our faithful people also to pray fervently for your intentions and necessities, which are also ours. . . . Moreover, we are also united closely to you in this fateful hour by another tie, since many are now actively attempting to bring about in our country also a state of affairs similar to that which you have to bewail in Germany, thus assisting the forces of godlessness to a final victory. We are confident, however, that these attempts will be in vain, and that we shall still be able to furnish help and consolation to you. Though it is a stormy sea which is tossing the Barque of Peter so violently, yet that very sea supports it, and the ship will not sink, however great be the efforts of those who seek for its destruction. In common with you, we cherish the hope that the greater the hatred which seeks to shatter it, by so much the greater will be the measure of success vouchsafed to the Catholic Church in the end. That is what we wanted to tell you, our brethren in the Faith, in these sorrowful times, you, the confessors of Christ, who are suffering persecution for His sake. You have a special right to a blessing from Christ that shall be all the greater for the heavy load of oppression that weighs upon you, and when the prospects of human protection seem darkest the help of God will manifest itself most powerfully. . . .

Things turned out very differently from what it was still possible at that time for the Austrian bishops to hope. In spite of all assurances to the contrary, religious persecution followed in the very footsteps of the political Anschluss. In this connection we have already heard the authoritative words of the German bishops.[1]

But the Austrian bishops themselves soon found that they had to join their voices to the complaints of their episcopal brethren in the old Reich. It will suffice to refer to the Common Austrian Pastoral of August 19th, 1938. The first part of this document dealt with the state of affairs brought about by the State law of July 6th, which introduced compulsory civil marriage. A clear and sharp contrast was drawn between the Catholic concept and the debased Nazi idea of marriage. The second part of the Pastoral concerned the withdrawal of recognition from the Catholic private schools in Austria.

[1] *Cf.* p. 30.

In this regard, distressing occurrences of recent times force us to address a frank message to the faithful of our dioceses. By means of various enactments, recognition and public rights were withdrawn from ecclesiastical colleges, and in many cases the opening of the lowest class was forbidden. In this way the private secondary schools in which future candidates for the priesthood receive their preparatory formation, and the private establishments managed by Sisters and Brothers belonging to religious Orders and Congregations, were hard hit, and in fact condemned to extinction. Thus, by means of these ordinances a large number of religious Sisters and Brothers were deprived of the bread they had honourably earned, and many old teachers belonging to these Orders and Congregations, who had retired and are no longer fit for work, but shared the livelihood earned by their younger colleagues, have been condemned to spend their declining years in anxiety and want. The episcopal Ordinaries have raised a protest against these ordinances in the proper quarter. . . . That training in citizenship and love of country was not neglected in these schools is proved by the fact that men and women have been educated by the religious teachers in these institutions, whose self-sacrificing devotion to the community and the Fatherland is universally recognised and highly valued by their fellow-citizens. We do not hesitate to thank these teachers and educators from the ranks of the Orders and Congregations of men and women in the name of the whole Catholic population, and we hope that this may bring them some consolation in this hour of grievous trouble.[1] . . . Catholic parents ! Since under the present circumstances you are deprived of so many helps in the education of your children, a greater burden and a greater responsibility than ever rests upon your shoulders. But do not waver ! . . . In Holy Communion, especially in family Communion, the work of the parents, the care of the father and the love of the mother, will receive ever new blessings, so that nothing will be able to disturb your family happiness or deprive the life of your children of its joy. Every epoch has its own special tasks; the present time brings to you a great task indeed in the maintenance of the genuine Catholic spirit in the family and among your children. The greater the task, the greater is the grace which God in His goodness places at our disposal.

*　　　*　　　*　　　*　　　*

We have given this selection from episcopal Pastorals, partly, as was said before, in defence of the German Hierarchy, but chiefly because they should be put on record in any detailed account of the relations between the Catholic Church in Germany and the German State. In the two following Parts, which deal with the relations in detail, we shall have occasion to offer further excerpts, but only when they directly concern the immediate topic under review and so, unless a place had been found for the more general utterances of the German episcopate, they would have had to be omitted, which would have deprived Catholics outside Germany of some stirring reading, and at the same time impaired the completeness of this history. That is the *apologia* we offer, if an *apologia* be needed, for including them in this rather lengthy book.

[1] This part of the Pastoral is continued on p. 138.

PART TWO

THE GOVERNMENT OF THE THIRD REICH AND THE CHURCH

We have to deal here with a whole mass of anti-religious stratagems and devices, official ordinances, a flood of speeches and newspaper articles, influence exercised by moral and economic pressure, by threats, insinuations and persuasion—in a word, all the means of influencing public opinion at the disposal of the authorities in a modern civilised State are exploited directly or indirectly, covertly or openly, in the fight against the Church. It is not always easy to draw a distinction between official and unofficial measures, for it is well known that State and Party are in practice identified. It is our wish, however, as far as possible, to consider separately the official measures taken by the State authorities, in so far as these have an anti-religious character, and that is the scope of this Part.

What do these measures affect? They affect every single sphere and aspect of the Church's life. We shall deal with these various spheres in order under the following heads: Church Government and Administration; Propagation of the Church's Doctrine; Religious Instruction of Youth; Care of Souls; and, finally, Rights of the Church and the Protection of the Church's Honour.

CHAPTER I

OFFICIAL ACTION AGAINST THE CHURCH'S GOVERNMENT AND ADMINISTRATION

1. *Interference in Church Administration.*

DESPITE the guarantees legally established by the Concordat, in the course of the last year or so the headquarters of the Diocesan Administration (Ordinariates, as they are called in Germany) of almost every German Diocese have been forcibly entered by the police and searched, and the energetic protests of the bishops against this infringement of the Church's freedom have been ignored. The officials who conducted these searches examined all the documents in the diocesan archives, confidential or not, and the correspondence with the Holy See: in some cases documents were even taken away in lorries to the police offices for a closer scrutiny and only returned when that had been completed.

So far as we have been able to ascertain, action of this kind has been taken, in 1936 in the offices of the Diocesan Administration of Freiburg-im-Breisgau; in 1937 in Cologne, where some fifty officials of the Gestapo under the leadership of a detective-superintendent took temporary possession of the Administration buildings while they conducted their search, and also in the Vicariate-General in Aachen. In 1938, during the first few days after the Anschluss, a search was carried out in the " Ordinariates " of Vienna, Salzburg and Seckau, where Army Bishop and Prince Bishop Dr. Pawlikowski was kept under guard for several days by two SS-men, while the documents from his archives were taken to the Gestapo headquarters in motor lorries. Then on August 31st, 1938, there was a search at the Archiepiscopal Administration buildings in Munich, and another in Limburg on April 15th, 1939, in which not only were the archives of certain ecclesiastical foundations confiscated and carried away, but also the moneys belonging to them were seized.

Not dissimilar was the case of Mgr. Ehrenfried, Bishop of Würzburg. When he was travelling to Rome in November, 1938, he was held up at the German frontier and had to stand by while all his portmanteaux and documents were searched through, and photographic copies made of everything written in Latin. In the same way officials of the State Police and of the Party have frequently attempted to obtain from the clergy information regarding purely ecclesiastical matters, as, for example, about Church property, copies of the lists of members of Church Societies, lists of those who attended spiritual exercises and retreats, statistical details regarding charitable organisations, and the like, so that the diocesan authorities have had to warn their clergy repeatedly against giving such information under any circumstances whatsoever.[1]

To these infringements of the Concordat others were soon added. In the Diocesan Administration buildings in Berlin, the German bishops had set up an Information Bureau under the direction of Mgr. Dr. Banasch, the former Administrator of the Berlin diocese. This Bureau, whose function it was to provide the German bishops with a means for exchanging opinions and reports on purely internal Church affairs, was suddenly put under the control of the Gestapo in December, 1935, the whole of the papers were examined, and Mgr. Banasch was arrested. He did not succeed in obtaining his freedom again until the middle of March, 1936.

It should be mentioned further that by the violation of postal and telephonic secrecy, both in the old Reich and in the formerly Austrian territories, official communications between the various Church authorities were repeatedly subjected to control and obstruction by the State.

But that is not all, for representatives of the Church, besides being interfered with, were even banished arbitrarily by the Civil Power. After the well-known attack on his residence on July 18th, 1938, which we shall report in detail later,[2] Mgr. Dr. Sproll, the Bishop of Rottenburg, was expelled from Württemberg territory, a step which the official German News Agency justified on the grounds that " the bishop

---

[1] *Cf.*, *e.g.*, Vicar-General of Fulda, in *Kirchl. Amtsblatt*, January 10th, 1935.
[2] *Cf.* p. 255.

INTERFERENCE IN CHURCH ADMINISTRATION 43

was the only citizen of his locality who failed to participate in the election of April 10th," and for that reason " demonstrations by the indignant population had been made against him " on several occasions. A bishop " who grossly neglects his State and political duties " could not be tolerated.

We shall deal later with these " enraged crowds of people " from the reports of eye-witnesses. So far as the " gross neglect " of State and political duties is concerned, it must be said that the election of April 10th, 1938, was expressly announced as a *free* election, so that every citizen had the right either to vote or not to vote, to vote " Yes " or to vote " No." If Mgr. Sproll did not vote, then he simply made use of his right as a citizen; and it should be one of the State's essential duties to defend its citizens in the exercise of such a right against any and every attack, even against that of an " enraged mob." Moreover, as the *Osservatore Romano* rightly remarked at the time, the banishment of Mgr. Sproll amounted to a virtual removal from his office, a proceeding which was contrary to all the engagements entered into between State and Church.

A similar case is that of the bishop's Official in Vechta.[1] This official representative of the Bishop of Münster in that part of the Münster diocese which lies in the territory of Oldenburg, received instructions from the Gestapo by word of mouth on June 27th, 1938, that he was no longer permitted to remain in that territory. This prohibition was due no doubt to the fact that he had protested against the conversion of the denominational schools in Oldenburg into National Socialist community schools at the order of Minister Pauly. The following is the description of the case given by Mgr. Count von Galen, the Bishop of Münster, in a Pastoral which was read from the pulpits on July 31st, 1938:

> The episcopal Official in Vechta is the permanent representative of the Bishop of Münster and his Vicar-General for the Catholics in the territory of Oldenburg, and is recognised by the State Government as such. Without any communication being made to the bishop, his principal and superior, he was ordered to leave his official post, his home, and the territory of Oldenburg. Loyal to the duties of his office, Herr Official Vorwerk refused to leave, of his own free will and without the approval of the Bishop of Münster, the post which had been entrusted to him. He then at once informed me of these events in writing. When I received this report on June 28th I at once telegraphed to the Führer and Reich Chancellor Adolf Hitler, and requested that this order should be rescinded. I also sent telegraphic protests to the Minister for Ecclesiastical Affairs and to the State Police Headquarters in Berlin. The first reply I received came from Berlin on the evening of July 1st in the form of a letter from the Chief of the Reich Chancellery, Reichsminister Dr. Lammers, dated June 29th, in which the reception of my telegram to the Führer and Reich Chancellor was confirmed and a further communication was promised. In the meantime, however, the Gestapo had already taken proceedings by the use of force against Herr Official Vorwerk. On the evening of June 30th he was compelled by the police to leave Vechta and the territory of Oldenburg. Guarded

[1] *Translator's Note.*—An " Official " is a representative of the bishop in some particular part of his diocese, and has powers somewhat similar to those of a Vicar-General.

by two police officials he was brought to Münster by car, and set free on the Cathedral Square in Münster at half-past nine in the evening !

To the best of my knowledge this is the first time since the *Kulturkampf* of the last century that in Germany a high official of the Catholic Church has been removed by force from his post on account of representations regarding ecclesiastical affairs which he was in duty bound to make, and no account was taken of the fact that his official duties would thereby be hindered or rendered impossible.

In reply to my protest of June 28th, the Reichsminister for Ecclesiastical Affairs wrote on July 9th that the banishment of the Official was carried out because he had in an unjustifiable way stirred up agitation among the population. I felt that I was justified in replying to this that it was not the Official who had caused this agitation, but that all this excitement had rather been brought about by the illegal introduction of the National Socialist community school into Oldenburg; and that although it had been outwardly quelled by the measures adopted by the Gestapo, yet in the hearts of the Christian population these same measures had stirred it up to boiling point.

Once again on July 18th I complained of the action of the Gestapo to the Chief of the Reich Chancellery, and requested that opportunity should be given to the Official to defend himself before a non-Party tribunal against the accusations alleged against him as reasons for his banishment. This petition was unfortunately not granted. Under date July 24th, the Chief of the Reich Chancellery gave me a final rebuff. After this rejection of my complaint on the part of officials in close touch with the supreme direction (*Führung*) of the State I am forced to conclude that Herr Official Vorwerk will for the present be forcibly excluded from his official territory, and that we shall be constrained to direct ecclesiastical affairs and safeguard the interests of the Catholics of Oldenburg as best we may from a distance. But when my representations were rejected, I felt it to be my duty to let all the Catholics of the diocese of Münster know what has happened in these last few weeks.

This case of Mgr. Vorwerk was not the only one of its kind. Repeatedly the Catholic clergy were disciplined, by being banished from the local Government area where they had their place of residence, without, in most cases, any intimation being given to the bishop. The result was that on Sundays and feast-days no services could be held in the places concerned.

In April, 1937, for example, after a courageous sermon, in which he commented on a number of calumnies which had appeared in the Press, Father Kraus of the Cathedral parish in Eichstätt, was served with an order of expulsion. In his case, however, his diocesan bishop, Mgr. Rackl, openly proclaimed from the cathedral pulpit that he had given Fr. Kraus a formal order not to leave his parish and, so far as we know, the order of expulsion was not carried into effect.

2. *Arbitrary Disposal of Church Property.*

It was, however, not to be expected that a State which showed so little respect for persons attached to the Church would be more scrupulous in regard to its property. It is, for example, well known that before the Anschluss there was a project, approved by the Holy Father, of setting up a Catholic University in Salzburg. Money for this purpose had been collected with great difficulty over a number of

ARBITRARY DISPOSAL OF CHURCH PROPERTY 45

years and all this, to which every section of the population had contributed, was seized and confiscated shortly after the occupation of Austria.

Similarly, in most Austrian parishes what are called " parish homes " which are Church property (since they belong to the parish) had already been forcibly occupied by the Hitler Youth early in 1938 and so far we have heard nothing about their being given back.

But it is the monastic property which, under the Third Reich, has been the chief object of attack. In the Rhineland, for example, in 1939, the Franciscan Friary in Kelheim was closed. The " crime " of the friars was that they had been " living extravagantly," because thirty bottles of wine or cordial were found on the premises, as well as butter and fat given them as alms by the Catholic population of the district, and, to the horror of the police, some sixty packets of cigars or cigarettes. Besides, their pigs were being fed on potatoes and their chickens on corn and that is forbidden in the Third Reich. A not dissimilar case was that of Hadamar, where the Gestapo alleged they had discovered " shocking immorality " and that the Fathers and the pupils had indulged in " orgies."

In Austria especially the attacks on monastic institutions have been carried out with a particular ruthlessness. In the course of 1938, for example, by order of Reich Commissar Bürckel, the German Order of Knights was forbidden, and its property taken over by the State: in Eggenberg, near Graz, an important group of buildings, housing several different school divisions, was seized out of hand and the nuns who directed the school were thus robbed of their means of livelihood: the same thing happened to the teaching nuns at Mariazell who not only lost their school buildings but also their rest home, the " Marienheim " as it is called, which was given over to the German Girls' Union (BDM): the Benedictine foundation of St. Lamprecht was first occupied by SS detachments in autumn, 1938, and then later appropriated: the Franciscan friars in Salzburg, whose priory was on the first floor of a Government building which had been placed at their disposal, received in October, 1938, an order to vacate the rooms occupied by them: in the school and conventual buildings of the Cistercians of Mehrerau, a State home for youth and a business academy were installed.[1]

The following cases relating to the year 1939 deserve special mention: The Missions Institute of St. Ruprecht in Kreuzberg (Salzburg) was dissolved by the Nazi authorities and taken over by the Salzburg school foundation. According to the declaration of the Nazi Gauleiter Rainer this affair was to be regarded as a step for " rendering innocuous a rallying point of anti-German opinion "—a means, too, by which " goods extracted from the resources of the people have been restored to the people."

By order of the Nazi authorities, the three houses of the Society of

---

[1] This list of confiscations is supplemented in Chapter IV (p. 134 *seq.*), which treats of the closing of schools.

Christ the King in former Austrian territory were also closed and its property confiscated. This Society is a brotherhood formed in recent years which devotes itself especially to the cure and care of inebriates. In all its houses an atmosphere of fervent religious life had been created and the Society was known throughout the world especially for the pamphlets issuing from its press. The ground alleged for the closure was the " Law of Associations " which also furnished authority for " safeguarding " the property.

The case of the Society's motherhouse, a monumental building on one of the main streets of Graz, deserves special mention. For some months the Nazis had already been " lodging " in one of the storeys of this building. That, however, was not enough, for, after it had been ascertained that the statutes of the Society resembled those of a religious association rather than those of a monastic order, the relevant paragraph of the " Law of Associations " was invoked, and the Graz motherhouse was confiscated out of hand. The other two Austrian houses were of lesser importance.

In the same year the ancient Austrian abbeys of Göttweig, Admont, St. Lamprecht and Engelzell were finally appropriated and, by order of District Leader Bürckel, the whole of the leased-out property of the foundation of Klosterneuburg, near Vienna, was taken over by the Government. Since May, 1939, rents due from some 9,000 leaseholders have had to be paid to the State, with the result that this foundation, so well known to all German-speaking Catholics by its popular liturgical apostolate, has been deprived, without any kind of compensation, of a substantial part of its possessions.[1] There is, too, the " Feldkirchner Hof "—the hostel once run by the Sisters of the Holy Cross in Feldkirchen-bei-Klagenfurth—which was confiscated by order of the Gestapo and declared to be State property on the pretext that it had lent its aid to " endeavours hostile to the State and people."

At about the same time (May 20th, 1939) there took place the formal conversion of the Mission school of St. Ruprecht at Kreuzberg, near Bischofshofen (Salzburg), into a Nazi headquarters, when a number of anti-religious speeches were made, in which it was declared that " this was no educational establishment for missionaries, but a most pernicious hot-bed of open hostility to the State and people." In Salzburg, too, the regional authorities ordered the dissolution of the Sodality of St. Peter Claver in Maria-Sorg, near Lengfelden, and its property was seized by the State.

The summer of 1939 saw another ominous measure, when Dr. Frick, Reichsminister of the Interior, ordered a standing inventory to be kept of all Church foundations and funds in the Protectorate of Bohemia and Moravia. One cannot say yet what this portends, but the experiences we have already had lead us to fear that this order will be the precursor of high taxation and of further confiscation and plundering of Church goods.

[1] *Cf. Frankf. Zeitung*, No. 251, 1939.

ARBITRARY DISPOSAL OF CHURCH PROPERTY

The brutal methods employed in closing monastic institutions may be seen from the report, made by a Swiss business man, of the occupation of the Servite monastery in Innsbruck. The report, for whose accuracy the author expressly vouches, runs as follows:

> After a thorough search of the house had been made, all the members of the Order were ordered to the front hall near the door, where they all had to stand with their faces against the wall. They were informed that they would have to leave the house within three-quarters of an hour, and that they would be allowed to take small articles with them (in a small handbag). After three-quarters of an hour the Fathers and lay-brothers were again ranged with their faces to the wall in the front hall, and freed one by one at lengthy intervals of time. Nine of the Fathers, some of them belonging to distinguished families in Innsbruck, were arrested.
>
> Press reports alluding to " abominable moral depravity " referred to the misconduct of two gardener lads (day workers, not belonging to the monastery) with a lay-brother whose dismissal had already been decided upon. The citizens of Innsbruck who were arrested in connection with this affair were, without exception, those who witnessed the behaviour of the SS on the streets and had dared to murmur against them. Neither citizens nor Fathers were implicated in the affair at the monastery.
>
> While the Fathers were being evicted, from the house adjoining the monastery which had been confiscated by the Party and used as a depot, rifles and machine-guns were loaded into lorries drawn up at the monastery porch, in order to make it appear as if weapons had been found in the monastery.
>
> These are the facts and I can vouch for their accuracy. I am a Swiss.

Typical of the surreptitious methods so often employed is a case in Vienna in October, 1938. A State Commissar was sent to a certain monastery, on which the authorities had designs. Without this man's approval no action of any kind could be taken, while he himself possessed the fullest authority. In the short space of one week he completed the sale of the entire property, selling it bit by bit in accordance with the instructions which he had been given. In the newspapers there was just a short notice to say that the Order had disposed of its property by sale, though actually it did not receive one penny of the proceeds!

A great number of confiscations of Church property were carried out on the occasion of the closing of hundreds of convent schools and other schools conducted by the Orders and Congregations, of which we give details below. One particularly unpleasant case occurred in Straubing, in April, 1939, where the Mayor not only ordered the vacation of the schoolrooms and students' hostel of the Commercial School directed by the Ursulines but also took possession of a considerable number of the rooms in the enclosed part of the premises reserved to the nuns.

Besides the open spoliations exemplified in the above account there were other, more indirect, means by which many a monastic establishment was ruined. The mendicant Orders are a case in point. Possessing no property of their own, they were especially hard hit by the ministerial prohibition against begging and reduced to dire extremity: in order, therefore, to supply the most urgent of their necessities, special collections were announced in the churches.

But perhaps the greatest distress is to be found among the teaching nuns, who have been deprived by these governmental measures of all means of gaining a livelihood. Nor is it a question of a few destitute nuns here and there, for, according to an estimate arrived at by the editor of the important American paper *The Commonweal* after an extensive tour through Germany in 1939, there are at least 15,000 nuns without home or sustenance.

Catholic hospitals were also confiscated. A great sensation was caused by the closing of the one in Duisburg, which belonged to the parish of St. Joseph. This hospital was both extensive and up-to-date in its equipment, yet the Chief of Police, who was responsible for closing it, issued on May 11th, 1937, the following communication to the Press through the German News Agency:

> After a thorough enquiry into the management of the Hospital of St. Vincent, which is unable to guarantee in all cases of sickness the requisite medical treatment and which, according to medical opinion, was in one case the chief cause of a Duisburg woman's death, I find myself forced to order the immediate closing of this hospital.
>
> In the interests of the general public no further treatment of cases can be permitted in the Hospital of St. Vincent. Measures have been taken to secure proper hospital care for the cases at present in this hospital.

Without any previous announcement or negotiations, the management of the hospital was informed of the police order at 5 p.m. on May 11th, and the transfer of the nearly 400 patients was begun at 8 a.m. on the following day. A telegram from the Bishop of Münster to the President of the Düsseldorf Local Government, asking that at least an orderly procedure should be adopted, and that in the meantime the transport of cases to other institutions should be suspended, was in vain. The pretexts alleged by the Police President in the announcement which we have quoted above may be seen at their true value in the light of a communication read in the churches of Duisburg on May 12th, by order of Urban Dean Cuppers:

> The Hospital of St. Vincent has been closed, because in one case, which occurred eight months ago, we would not permit a certain operation to be performed on a woman, the sort of operation which we cannot allow to take place under our roof, because it is an offence against the law of God. The woman was consequently removed to another hospital at the suggestion of the doctor concerned, and died there. That is the reason why the hospital was closed. All other reasons which have been alleged are untrue.

Some months later it became known that the Reichsminister of the Interior had granted the petition which had been addressed to him. The hospital was opened once more, but closed again a few hours later by the Mayor of Duisburg, in his capacity as Director of the Health Department.

3. *The Closing of Theological Faculties*

It was in Austria that the policy of closing the Theological Faculties in the Universities was first put into operation. In 1938 the Theological Faculty in the University of Innsbruck was closed down, by order of the Minister of the Interior in Vienna. At the same time, sentence of death was pronounced on the Canisianum at Innsbruck, a large and well-appointed college that served as a hostel for the many foreign students attending lectures in the Theological Faculty, whose reputation for scholarship was such that the foreigners attending its lectures were far more numerous than the native students;[1] so that the destruction of this faculty was a severe blow, even from an economic point of view, for the whole of the Tyrol province. On January 6th, 1939, the *Universe* published a moving account of the closing of the Canisianum, written by an eye-witness, an American who had for some years been studying in Innsbruck. We reproduce this graphic report word for word:

American Student tells how Nazis scattered the Priests and Students of Jesuit Seminary

A " Priestless Tyrol " as Present for Herr Hitler

(By NCWC News Service)

BALTIMORE.

How Nazi Secret Police suppressed and occupied the Canisianum, the celebrated Jesuit seminary in Innsbruck, Austria, is described by an American student for the priesthood in a letter published.

Writing from Switzerland, he says that " the present Governor of the Tyrol is a particularly vicious man who has promised Hitler that on his next birthday he will present to him as a birthday present a Jewless and priestless Tyrol."

Until Wednesday, November 23rd, everything was quiet. Then suddenly the blow was struck.

Just before lunch on that fateful day the Hitler secret police arrived in the house and bluntly announced to the Rector that they were taking over the house immediately and that 30 rooms had to be vacated within 24 hours and the remainder of the building evacuated by December 17th.

No reasons whatever were given and all protests were useless.

The Rector called the whole community together and in a most stirring speech told us that our house had been suppressed. His words were most inspiring and he lived up to the very best traditions of the Society of Jesus in his perfect and complete acceptance of the will of God.

All-night Exposition

We had exposition of the Blessed Sacrament all night Wednesday night in thanksgiving to God for favours in the past and asking His protection for the future.

The next day we had our Thanksgiving Day banquet as planned in an inn about 25 miles from Innsbruck. We all knew it was our last outing together in the Tyrol, so we made the best of it and had great fun.

We returned to Canisianum at 8 o'clock that night to find the ground floor (30 rooms) already occupied by Hitler police. They had women in the building, were smoking cigars in the hall and generally making themselves at home.

All day Friday and Saturday we were busy packing. . . . Everybody helped everybody else, and by Saturday night the whole community were pretty well packed. . . .

Sunday, November 27th, was our last day in the Canisianum as a community, as the evacuation of the building began on Monday the 28th. . . .

In the summer semester of 1937 there were 269 foreign and 183 native students.

50 OFFICIAL ACTION AGAINST CHURCH'S GOVERNMENT

On Monday morning we were told to have all our baggage in the corridor outside of our rooms, as the police were going through the building all morning inspecting everything we were taking with us. We obeyed orders and spent the entire morning in the corridors while the police and customs men went through our luggage and sealed our boxes and trunks and bags. All afternoon we spent loading our things on trucks to be moved to Switzerland. . . .

Community Dwindled

When I first came to the Canisianum the community consisted of about 250 men. The number remained approximately the same during my second and third years (last year it was actually 235).

At the beginning of this year, due to the general unrest in Europe, persecutions, widespread dislike of the Hitler Government and other reasons, our community was considerably reduced in number. We began this year with 155 men, of whom about 65 were Germans and Austrians and 90 foreigners —Americans, English, Swiss, Hungarians, etc.

When the suppression took place it was announced that none of the Germans and Austrians would be allowed to leave the country. These men will either go to other seminaries in Germany (not run by Jesuits) or be forced temporarily to abandon their vocation and enter military service. Only the foreigners were moved to Switzerland. Eighty men were left. . . .

Passport Difficulties

The plan was to send 25 Monday night, 25 Tuesday night and 25 Friday night on the train for Milan. There they would change, hear Mass, have breakfast and proceed the following day to Sion. . . .

After supper on Monday night we had devotions and then went into the front hall to say good-bye to the first group leaving for Milan. Four of the Jesuit Fathers went with this group, including old Fr. Donat, who had lived in the Canisianum 35 years. He is 72 years old.

It was very sad, seeing these old men who had never done any harm in their lives turned out into the street. But they took their suppression in the same way all Jesuits have always taken their suppressions and were a great example to the rest of us.

On Tuesday morning 11 of us got up at 4 o'clock and walked 10 miles through the early morning to our favourite shrine at Alsam. We had Mass there for the last time. . . .

Tyrolese Want Them Back

Let me say here that the people of Innsbruck were sorry to see us go. . . . It was pathetic to see the line of poor old Tyrolese weeping in front of our door. They kissed our hands and said they would pray that we would soon be back.

Things are getting worse and worse in Innsbruck. The Jews are being murdered openly in the streets, and two nights before I left I could hear the agonising shrieks of Jews outside of my window as the Hitler secret police were amusing themselves by throwing the Jews in the river. Three of the poor devils were drowned.

Everyone expects that within the next few weeks there will be bloodshed among the clergy, and several people for this reason said they were relieved to see us go.

Our community, as I have said, will be much smaller—80 in all—37 Americans, 10 Englishmen, 10 Swiss, 10 Hungarians, 8 Italians, 2 Poles, 1 Frenchman, 1 Dutchman and 1 Japanese. Ten of the Jesuit Fathers from Innsbruck came with us.

Scarcely two months later the Theological Faculty in Salzburg met with the same fate. The pretext given was that the single faculties which have survived from the old University of Salzburg " have entirely lost their scientific and organic continuity," but in order to preserve the scientific importance of Salzburg as a seat of learning there would be installed, in place of the Theological Faculty, " an Institute of Natural Science of the very highest international rank." There followed, in May, 1939, the closing down of the Faculty of Theology in the University of Munich, where the Minister of Education, Dr. Rust, had appointed to the Catholic Theological Faculty two professors who were decisively rejected by Cardinal Faulhaber. The State authorities, however, after a protest had been made, refused to rescind the measures they had taken, and so the Cardinal forbade Catholic theological students to attend the lectures given by the two professors in question. By way of a reply to this Dr. Rust, the Minister of Education, in collaboration with the Minister for Ecclesiastical Affairs, Herr Kerrl, ordered the closing of the faculty, which had been further diminished in the meantime by the transfer of two of its professors to Würzburg. The Theological College in Freising was also prepared gradually for its final destruction by the removal of one professor after another. Early in 1939 the Theological Faculty in Graz was also closed.

The study of theology, even in places where it has not been brought to a complete standstill, does not proceed unhindered. Three of the professors, for example, proposed for the Theological Faculty in Freiburg were rejected by the Government and so their chairs remain vacant. The hostel for theological students in Salzburg, the " Rupertinum," was converted into a Nazi Girls' Home in the autumn of 1938, and by an official order of June 23rd of the following year the theological seminary of the diocese of Linz was confiscated, as the seminary buildings were to be used as barracks. In the same way the seminary of the diocese of Berlin at Hermsdorf was dissolved, since, after its removal to an old castle, the State approval necessary for the exercise of the teaching profession in Germany was not forthcoming.

The lesser seminaries, in which those who aspire to the priesthood study the Humanities before proceeding to higher studies in Philosophy and Theology, and which are in the strictest sense episcopal institutions, were without exception closed down throughout the whole of Austria, and were for the most part converted into State schools. The same fate befell the lesser seminary in Mariaschein immediately after the occupation of the Sudeten areas.

4. *Financial Difficulties*

A further encroachment on the Church's rights was made in 1937, when the Minister of the Interior, in collaboration with the Minister for Ecclesiastical Affairs, issued an order forbidding any public announcement of the names of those who had left the Church,[1] and

---

[1] *Translator's Note.*—In Germany, a Church Tax (*Kirchensteuer*) is payable by all those who are members of recognised denominations. To pay the Church Tax is therefore regarded in a way as a public profession of one's faith. Many who have grown lax, and no longer practise their religion, will shrink with horror at the idea of not paying their Church Tax, for

during recent years a large number of parish clergy have been subjected to disciplinary measures because they continued to read out from the pulpit the names of those who had left the Church.

As early as November 5th, 1934, an enactment was made, called the Reich Law of Collections, which laid down in paragraph 15 that Church collections must be confined to those taken up during divine service, and that any public collection for Church purposes required the approval of the civil authorities, which, as a matter of fact, was practically never granted. When, therefore, the permit granted to the Catholic Women's Organisations to collect money for the Church of Our Lady of Peace in Frankfurt-am-Main expired on September 1st, 1936, the request for an extension was absolutely refused, and so the Catholic Women's Organisations are unable to meet the debts of the church which they have founded.

In practice the measures adopted with regard to collections have even gone beyond the provisions of the ordinance referred to above. In one place in Bavaria, for example, money which had been contributed for the purpose of erecting Stations of the Cross was confiscated, although in this case there was no question of a public house-to-house collection, for the people had brought the money in person to the parish priest, after he had announced this collection from the pulpit. Another parish priest was fined, because during the service he had asked his parishioners to bring alms to the presbytery for the purchase of a new cope, the Public Prosecutor finding that this action was " a public collection in a room to which anyone had access." Another parish priest was punished, because in his parish magazine he had requested alms for the purchase of a statue of Our Lady.

These restrictions were made still more stringent by the order of April 5th, 1937, circulated by the Minister of the Interior, which made nearly all non-monetary alms—*i.e.*, gifts in kind or produce—impossible. We have an authentic report which shows the havoc wrought in one German diocese—namely, the Archdiocese of Freiburg-im-Breisgau—by these violations of rights which the Church has always enjoyed from the very earliest times:

Since the issue of the Law of Collections on November 5th, 1934, the following prohibitions have been made in favour of the Nazi collections for Public Welfare and Winter Relief Work:

The annual autumn Church collection of food has been forbidden since 1935. At first, in the years 1934 and 1935, the mendicant Orders were permitted to collect food, but this has now been strictly forbidden, since it is looked on as a public collection, and legal penalties have been inflicted in some cases. In the year 1937 the great public collection for the *Caritas* (National Organisation of Catholic Charities), which in Germany used to amount to nearly 33 million marks annually, could not be made. By way of compensation, some 600,000 marks have been granted to specially necessitous institutions by the " Winter Relief Work," but even so the *Caritas* has lost hundreds of thousands of marks through these restrictions,

---

this is regarded as the last step in formal apostasy. Those, however, who do wish to take this step have to make a formal declaration before a State official that they have left their Church and their names are then struck off the roll of those liable for payment of the tax.

SEVEN MILLIARD REICHSMARKS CHURCH TAXES.

Choir of Tax Accountants: " A Safe Stronghold our Gold is Still."

[*Das Schwarze Korps*, Dec. 2nd, 1937.

"Feed My—Lambs."

[*Das Schwarze Korps*, May 6th, 1937.

and the Church's other enterprises for raising funds have been greatly obstructed by divers prohibitions. Anything like public efforts to increase enrolment, film appeals, public meetings are forbidden. The annual " Petition Collection " at Christmastide, which has been conducted for years past by the Catholic Church Homes and Institutions, has not been allowed since 1937, with the consequence that, throughout the whole Reich, these institutions lose about 300,000 marks. The collections made by the clergy for the " first communicants " have, since 1935, been restricted to specific and limited circles (non-public collection).

Since the enactment of the Law of Collections of November 5th, 1934, some twenty-two parishes in the Archdiocese have had proceedings taken against them on account of their collecting activities. Sometimes these took the form of a police warning, sometimes the money collected was appropriated, and sometimes heavy penalties were inflicted on clergy and layfolk.

These restrictions have, of course, hit the parish clergy hard, so that, to try to make up some of the deficit caused by the prohibition of outdoor collections, extra ones have had to be made everywhere in the churches and in some places, in an endeavour to make ends meet, a local church tax, too, has been arranged with the parishioners.

In view of the hostile attitude of the Government towards the Church it might seem at first sight a matter of surprise that the Third Reich continues to pay the clergy their stipends. Why is it that these disbursements have not simply been cut off ? In the first place we may answer that such a measure is only a question of time, for Herr Kerrl, the Minister for Ecclesiastical Affairs, has already hinted quite clearly at the discontinuance of these payments in a speech which he made at Fulda on November 24th, 1937: " It is not the task of the National Socialist Government to provide for the maintenance of the Churches, but the task of the faithful. Although it has not yet been put into operation, this is nevertheless our definite aim." He made a similar declaration in an interview published by the German News Agency in December, 1937, saying that the idea of withdrawing all State contributions to the Churches was being seriously entertained.

But, by the side of that there is undoubtedly the desire to avoid giving foreign countries the impression that a *Kulturkampf* is in progress. The Reich Chancellor Adolf Hitler himself, in his speech of January 30th, 1939, dwelt with emphasis on the State financial provision for the Church, and quoted it as a proof that there was no intention on the part of the Third Reich to attack religion. A similar argument was advanced in a pamphlet " Political Catholicism's Great Falsehood,"[1] written by a certain Dieter Schwarz and zealously distributed by the Party, especially in foreign countries. In the fact that the cessation of the financial contributions to the Churches is apparently to be one of the last measures adopted in the Nazi campaign against religion, we see an example of the clever methods of camouflage which, as repeated experience shows, do not fail to impress foreign opinion.

[1] *Die grosse Lüge des politischen Katholizismus*, Zentralverlag der NSPAD, Franz Eher Nachf., 1938.

54 OFFICIAL ACTION AGAINST CHURCH'S GOVERNMENT

It is, however, by no means true that the State continues without restriction to pay its contributions to the Church. Let us give a few examples:

As early as April 18th, 1935, an announcement was made in the Press that the State subsidy to the Churches in Württemberg had, from April 1st onwards, been curtailed by a considerable amount. In May, 1936, the Bavarian bishops made a protest against the proposal that the State subvention to the Churches for the territory of Bavaria should be further decreased by some $4\frac{1}{2}$ millions of marks. Nevertheless at a Party Congress in Fürstenfeldbruck near Munich in 1937 Dr. Wagner, the Bavarian Minister of Education, declared that the Bavarian Government had decided to discontinue the voluntary subsidies to the two Christian Churches, and thus to decrease Church income by about 50 per cent.; the payments would not, however, be discontinued at once, but gradually in the course of the next three years.

Then on April 1st, 1938, the Bavarian Ministry of Education and Worship ordered the complete discontinuance of the State subsidies which had hitherto been made as a supplement to income derived from pastoral work. The Church was thus faced with an extremely grave financial position, for in some dioceses even as much as three-quarters of the salaries of the parish clergy had been derived hitherto from these State payments, and so, even when every other economy possible had been made (such as payments to local Church councils, disbursements for the general needs of the diocese, etc.), the total proceeds of the Church Taxes, both local and regional, did not suffice to cover the deficit caused by the decrease of the State subvention. It was therefore necessary to reduce the salaries of the clergy everywhere.

From May 1st, 1939, the pensions of retired clergy in the diocese of Münster had to be reduced by 15 per cent.

On the other hand, conventual and many other ecclesiastical institutions, which were formerly exempt from taxation as institutions of general public utility, have had to bear such a load of taxation during the last few years that they are gradually succumbing under the burden. The Church's missionary activity in non-German countries has also been denied any sort of exemption from taxation.

Isolated efforts were even made to tax payments made to the clergy as Mass-stipends, and for giving spiritual retreats, preaching missions, etc., on the plea that these receipts were liable to the business turnover tax. In one place in Bavaria, for example, individual men and women had collected stipends to have Masses said for their respective professional Guilds (Guild Masses). These stipends were then handed to the parish priest. Against every principle of equity the parish priest was then required by the authorities to contribute the sum of 20 RM. from these Mass-stipends to the Winter Relief Fund; otherwise he must expect to be denounced and subjected to heavy penalties.

In Austria the traditional financial arrangements of the Church were different from those in the old Reich. There were no Church

Taxes, but financial provision for church personnel and fabric was derived principally from the State and from the local parish councils. This arrangement was fundamentally modified by a regional law of May 1st, 1939, which at one blow cancelled all the obligations devolving upon the State, the funds and foundations managed by it, parish councils, education councils and public patrons,[1] to provide for the personnel and upkeep of the churches. In compensation, the Church received the right to levy a Church Tax, a form of contribution hitherto unknown in Austria. All members of the Church who are of age are liable to the tax, and should an individual leave the Church his liability to tax ceases three months after the first day of the month following his notification of leaving. For the levying of this tax the Church has to issue a Church Contributions Order, which has then to receive the approval of the State.

Moreover, at the beginning of every financial year the Church is obliged to furnish the State Auditor's Department with a statement which shows both the domestic expenditure it proposes to make from the income of its own property and the anticipated returns from the Church Tax. Not only has the State the right of inspection of Church administration at any time, but it may also demand at the end of the financial year an account of domestic expenditure and of the disposal of all funds, and is empowered to disallow specific items of domestic expenditure in such a way that such payments are ruled out at the time and for the future.

By means of this legislation the financial position of the Church is one of extreme constraint. She has to collect her funds from her own members in the form of a tax, but her right to make outgoing payments is dependent on the approval of the State Auditor. The sole compensation that the State offers for this right of auditing and vetoing expenditure is the recognition that the Church's claim to her taxes can be enforced in law.

About the same time the Reich Governor of the Sudeten District issued a decree which brought into force in the Sudetenland the Church Tax legislation obtaining in Austria since May 1st.[2] This gives the Roman Catholic, German Evangelical and Old Catholic Churches the right to levy " Church Contributions," and extinguishes the former obligations of the State, local councils, etc., towards the support of the clergy and the maintenance of church fabrics. As a result of this legislation, numerous parishes, priests and Church employees have been reduced to extreme want, so that the episcopate of the old Reich had to come to the rescue of the Sudeten Catholics by means of a general church collection in the summer of 1939.

---

[1] *Translator's Note.*—The privileges of " patrons " in Austria were in many respects similar to those enjoyed in some cases by the " lord of the manor " in England. To these privileges usually corresponded certain obligations respecting the upkeep of the church, or of a part of it.

[2] *Translator's Note.*—In 1803 the Ecclesiastical Principalities in the Holy Roman Empire were secularised. The States that took over their territories, Austria, Prussia, Bavaria, etc., undertook to pay from the interests on the properties seized certain sums to the ecclesiastical authorities to defray church expenses, which before had been met by the ecclesiastical sovereigns themselves. The law, therefore, under which the State makes these payments (*Kongrua*) to the Church was framed as a sort of compensation of the Church's just claims to the property of which she had been despoiled.

56 OFFICIAL ACTION AGAINST CHURCH'S GOVERNMENT

How deeply the financial legislation of the new State has cut into the economic foundations of Church life can be realised in the concrete from the example of the Archdiocese of Freiburg-im-Breisgau. In an authentic report drawn up by the " Ordinariate " of that diocese we read:

> The ultimate object of the present proceedings of the new State is to do away with all the privileges which the Church has hitherto enjoyed, even in the sphere of financial and property laws.
>
> In Baden since April 1st, 1935, the State contributions towards the stipends of the clergy of the recognised Churches have been completely discontinued. For the Catholic Church, these contributions amounted to 1,050,000 RM. annually from October 1st, 1924, to March 31st, 1931, and since then to 670,104 RM.
>
> Similarly, since 1936-37, the civil parish or commune councils in Baden have discontinued their contributions for Church purposes—they were not, however, under any legal obligation to make these contributions. The loss to the Church is estimated at 350,000-400,000 RM. Hence a large number of parishes have thus been forced to introduce local Church Taxes, in order to cover the expenses of divine service and the salaries of those employed in the churches, especially organists and sacristans.
>
> Moreover, other changes in the law of Church taxation have been planned and partly put into execution, making for a reduction to the bare minimum of those sources of income which are quite indispensable for the Church.
>
> In Hohenzollern, the proportion of Income Tax accounted as Church Tax was lowered by 1 per cent. for the financial year 1937 by the Prussian Ministry of State, and this involved a deficit of one-fifth of the total sum required.
>
> On the other hand, the clergy and the Churches have to bear a load of new taxation in favour of the public at large. Up to the age of sixty-five, for example, the Catholic clergy have to pay, in addition to the ordinary Income Tax, a very burdensome Bachelors' Tax out of their modest stipends.
>
> The exemptions from " lecture money " and various other university contributions, formerly enjoyed by the Catholic students of Theology in the University of Freiburg, have been reduced to a very small fraction (less than 10 per cent.), and this has meant a considerable increase in the expense of studying Catholic theology.
>
> The new Land Laws will involve the Catholic Church in Baden, as from April 1st, 1939, in an increased load of taxation amounting to about 150,000 RM. Moreover, the municipalities in Baden have recently added to the burdens borne by the parishes, an increase amounting to thousands of marks in the charges for water rates, collection of refuse, etc., in Catholic buildings.

The new agrarian policy is also extremely unfavourable to Church land-tenure, for the Church has to give up land and ground, especially for settlement schemes, but is not permitted to acquire any new agricultural property.

Moreover, as far as the future is concerned, the State has reserved to itself the power to make life economically impossible for any particular member of the clergy who may be obnoxious to the authorities because of his lack of enthusiasm for the Nazi programme and point of view. In the *Frankfurter Zeitung* of June 28th, 1938, for instance, an article on State subsidies to the Church, levying of Church Taxes, etc., contains the statement that such financial assistance can be counted on in the future only on the presupposition " that the Churches comply with what the legal enactments of the State and its maintenance of public order require." Hence, then, it is openly admitted that an attempt is being made to influence the inner convictions of clergy and laity by means of " bread-basket politics " or economic pressure. In other words, those of the clergy who show themselves amenable to the Nazi régime will be well paid, and will experience no difficulty about the State grants. The same threat was suggested in May, 1939, when there was renewed insistence on a former Ministerial Order, to the effect that " Payments of whatever kind to a clergyman newly appointed to an ecclesiastical post may only be approved and carried into effect when a declaration has been made to the Church authorities at the time of the appointment, that no objections will be raised against the said official on the part of the State authorities."

As regards Austria, the Ministry of the Interior in Vienna announced that the subsidies laid down in the *Kongrua* laws[1] for the stipends of the pastoral clergy and the salaries of professors in Theological Colleges may only be paid (according to a direction given by the Minister for Ecclesiastical Affairs) to such persons as " prove themselves worthy of such provision by the State." Regional authorities were instructed to withhold stipends, pensions and other payments from such of the clergy as " commit offences against the law and order of the State." Since May, 1939, therefore, all Church officials on taking up their appointments are obliged to obtain the agreement of the State if, in the words of the order, " they expect the emoluments of the office (*Kongrua*) to continue to be paid."

Another anti-ecclesiastical measure was the Reich Law of Wills and Testaments, enacted in the summer of 1938, which will undoubtedly afford opportunity to many to make decisions against the interests of the Church. The anti-religious intentions of the legislators are at once apparent in the reasons which they advance to justify this enactment:

It has sometimes happened that those who serve the interests of religion, forgetting their real duty, have influenced testators on their death-beds to make testamentary dispositions in favour of their own organisations, exploiting for this purpose the dying person's fear of punishment in the next life. Such conduct cannot be approved.

A will made under these conditions is, according to this new law, null and void. Discontented relatives will find in this paragraph of the law a useful ground for contesting the validity of any eleventh-hour wills or codicils in favour of religious societies, and should the date of such a will or codicil render recourse to this paragraph of the statute impossible, they may turn to another paragraph if they want to contest the validity of any bequest made to the Church. For according to this Statute, any will in general is null and void " in so far as, in gross contradiction to a sound national feeling, it fails to make that provision

[1] See note on p. 55.

for family and community which is incumbent on a testator who is aware of his responsibilities."

In conclusion, we wish to direct attention to a law which, although it makes no explicit mention of the Church, gives every prospect of having a disastrous effect on Church property. This is the law of December 19th, 1937, which extinguishes all third-party claims against those whose property is confiscated on the ground that they are enemies of the State. This law destroys, or at least seriously diminishes, the value of Church buildings as securities for loans, mortgages, and Catholic enterprises in general, for supposing that someone had lent money to, let us say, a printing business, which was then appropriated by the State (perhaps for printing the Papal Encyclical *Mit brennender Sorge*), he would lose his money in spite of the real security which had warranted the loan. The consequence will be that in future no credit will be extended to any institution that is in danger of being declared " inimical to the State " and so appropriated.

[1] *Reichsgesetzblatt*, No. 134, p. 1333.

CHAPTER II

INTERFERENCE WITH THE TEACHING OF THE CHURCH

1. *Encyclicals and Pastorals*

THE first paragraph of Article 4 of the Reich Concordat reads as follows:

> In its relations and correspondence with the bishops, clergy and other members of the Catholic Church in Germany, the Holy See enjoys full freedom. The same applies to the bishops and other diocesan officials in their dealings with the faithful in all matters belonging to their pastoral office.

With this, the freedom of teaching of the Pope and the bishops is juridically secured, but what degree of freedom is, in fact, allowed must be judged from incidents like the following:

On Palm Sunday, March 14th, 1937, in most of the parish churches of the Third Reich, the Papal Encyclical about the situation of the Catholic Church in Germany (*Mit brennender Sorge*) was read from the pulpits. Immediately the State proceeded to severe measure of retaliation. Twelve printing offices which had printed this Encyclical were closed without compensation; parish magazines and diocesan gazettes which had copied the wording of its text were banned for three months; all the copies which the police could get hold of were seized and people who had transcribed or even circulated it were arrested. Particularly characteristic incidents occurred in the village of Essen in Oldenburg, where seven Catholic girls, who had been taken into custody for distributing the Encyclical, were released only because of the threatening attitude of the inhabitants.

Nor are other Papal Encyclicals any longer allowed to be printed in Germany. Thus, for instance, the Encyclical on the Christian Education of Youth of December 31st, 1929, which was reprinted in Huber's printing establishment in Munich, was forbidden on March 3rd, 1937, on account of the passages about the denominational schools, and a calendar for Catholic parents published in 1935 was seized because some parts of the same Encyclical were quoted in it.

The reading and distribution of the Encyclical of Pius XII *Summi Pontificatus* of October 28th, 1939, in the Catholic churches was to be observed and notified by order of the Secret Police (Gestapo), the priests who had a share in it were to be reported and steps were to be taken by the police against the reproduction and distribution of the whole text.

60 INTERFERENCE WITH TEACHING OF THE CHURCH

The Catholic population of Germany has at all times been accustomed to receiving from the Episcopate directions and explanations concerning the more important religious questions of the day, and the means usually employed for this were Pastoral Letters published at regular intervals during the year, which, besides being read from the pulpit, were given also wide publicity in the daily papers. Since 1935, however, all this has changed, and now it is almost an essential characteristic of a Pastoral that it should have to be brought to the notice of Catholics illegally, and it is very rare that any part of it may be published in the various parish magazines, notwithstanding the fact that in no Pastoral issued by a German bishop since 1933 has a demand been made or a right claimed that was not already contained in the public law of the Reich Concordat.

In what follows we give a brief summary of the prohibitions and confiscations that have come to our knowledge.

On May 5th, 1935, a Pastoral Letter of the Prussian Episcopate was issued for what is called " Educational Sunday," dealing with Catholic principles of education and referring to the dangers that nowadays face the young in respect of religion and morals, but it was forbidden, and such parish magazines as had printed it were confiscated on the grounds that it contained " in several passages an intolerable criticism of the *Landjahr* organisation."[1] The Pastoral Letter of Mgr. Kaller, Bishop of Ermland, of July 21st, 1935, which treated of the great importance of the Catholic organisations and their present distress, was confiscated even before it was read.

The joint Pastoral Letter of the Bishops' Conference at Fulda of August 20th was read publicly on September 1st, 1935. It warned its hearers of the dangers to the Faith, complained about the restrictions set to the freedom of the Church, answered the commonly made charge of " political Catholicism," and spoke gravely of the loss of the Christian spirit in public life, the schools, etc. No sooner, however, was it read than it was everywhere confiscated, in the " Ordinariates," in printing establishments, bookshops, presbyteries, and it was even removed from the very credence tables of the churches by policemen, while Catholics who had helped to circulate it were in some places, as, for example, Munich, arrested.

In March, 1936, Germany was preparing for the Reichstag elections, and the Catholic bishops felt it incumbent on them to advise the faithful that a vote in the affirmative did not necessarily involve approval of the many restrictions that hampered the freedom of the Church. Their communications were, however, forbidden and characterised in the press by State officials, as, for example, by Chief of Police Heydrich,[2] as an attempt to paralyse the internal reconstruction of the State by the Führer.

The same fate befell the Common Pastoral of the German bishops, calling on Catholic young men to remain steadfast in their faith, which

---

[1] Comment of the DNB. *Cf., e.g., Germania*, May 5th, 1935.
[2] *Völkischer Beobachter*, No. 120, April 29th, 1936.

was not allowed to be published after it had been read on the second Sunday of May, 1936, and one issued by the Bavarian bishops, protesting against the suppression of the schools belonging to the religious Orders, which after it had been read on June 21st and 28th was then forbidden and confiscated.

Once again, on August 20th, 1936, the Bishops' Conference at Fulda issued a Pastoral, which was read in the churches at the end of the same month. At a time when the National Socialist Press was inveighing against them for their inactivity against Bolshevism, their Pastoral was seized, as soon as it was read, and confiscated at the printing presses, though it declared that the danger from Bolshevism in many other countries demanded peace and union in Germany, which was, nevertheless, made impossible by non-Christian propaganda, interference with ecclesiastical rights and the suppression of the Catholic Press. Another letter of theirs expressing uneasiness for the future of the denominational schools, which was read on September 20th of the same year, was not allowed to be published.

In the same way a Pastoral Letter of the Bavarian bishops was read on December 13th, 1936, but was not allowed to be printed, and one of the Bishop of Freiburg protesting against the spiteful and systematic attacks on the Church could not be printed because, according to Mgr. Gröber, the Gestapo insisted, " contrary to the Concordat," on censoring the *Diocesan Gazette*.

Till 1937, then, the bishops continued to try both by the spoken and the written word to perform their duty of instructing their flocks. Such, however, had been their experience that from that time on they gave up, for the most part, all attempts at printing and circulating their Letters, since that usually led to confiscation and acts of retaliation against their helpers. They were confirmed in their attitude by a letter from Church Minister Kerrl of October 4th, 1936, mentioned in a Pastoral of the Bishop of Münster of December 21st of the same year, which threatened any printing of Pastorals " with confiscation by the Gestapo or complete prohibition, as well as further measures on the part of the Reichsminister for Popular Education and Propaganda." Henceforth the Catholic bishops content themselves with having their Pastorals read, nor do they always succeed even in this, as the following incidents will show.

A Pastoral Letter of December 13th, 1936, of the Archbishop of Freiburg, describing the struggle to preserve the Crucifix in its old place in the schools of Oldenburg and a declaration of June 6th, 1937, from part of the German bishops to be read from the pulpits criticising the notorious speech of Göbbels about the immorality of Catholic priests were both forbidden and in large measure confiscated before they were read, and in the former case the *Diocesan Gazette* was seized at the offices of the Diocesan Administration.

A similar thing happened in the case of the Lenten Pastoral (January, 1937) of Mgr. Kaller, Bishop of Ermland, when the issue of the *Diocesan Gazette* that reprinted it (No. 2 of February 1st, 1937) was seized at Diocesan Headquarters and at the houses of the clergy, and in many places the confiscation took place during Mass itself by the police snatching the Letter out of the hands of the priest as he was in the course of reading it.

Again, on September 4th, 1938, the Pastoral of the Bavarian bishops protesting against the measures taken against the teachers and the teaching of religion and against the schools was confiscated and the names of such ecclesiastics as had publicly read the Letter were ascertained with a view to punishment.

Similarly the Pastoral Letter of the Bishops' Conference of Fulda of August 19th, 1938, was forbidden, and in the diocese of Rottenburg any parish priest who had read it out was fined 30 RM., while duplicating machines were seized from several of the "Ordinariates."

Protest was, however, useless. In a communication to his clergy of December 21st, 1936, the Bishop of Münster complained of a decree of the President of Westphalia

> by which religious instructors in secondary schools are forbidden, under threat of immediate dismissal from their posts, to publish in their Sunday-school services Pastoral Letters ordered by the bishops to be read in all the churches. Our protest against such an interference with Divine Service has up to now remained disregarded and unsuccessful.

The climax of brutal oppression of freedom in religious teaching reached in the prohibition of the " Truths of the Catechism,"[1] reveals two important aspects of the State's fight against the Church—namely, a determination to silence the plainest and most restrained protests in self-defence, and a hostility, based on ideological-metaphysical reasoning, that demands, even from the Church, an acknowledgment of State-promulgated dogmas. The Minister for Culture of Baden in a letter of January 27th, 1937, declared the " Truths of the Catechism "—with special reference to Questions 17, 23, 28 and 34, which are inserted here with their answers—to be " injurious to the State."

> *Question* 17.—What was the greatest honour of the Jewish people ?—The greatest honour of the Jewish people was that the Divine Saviour came forth from it. In *this* sense Christ says: " For salvation is of the Jews." (John iv, 22.)
>
> *Question* 23.—How is it that, in spite of this, grievous sins also occur in the Catholic Church ?—Grievous sins occur in the Catholic Church because many Catholic Christians do not listen to the Church and do not live with her. The offences of her own children are more painful to the Church and a greater hindrance to her growth than persecution by enemies of the Church. " It is impossible that scandals should not come: but woe to him through whom they come." (Luke xvii, 1.)
>
> *Question* 28.—What then is lacking to a man who has no humility ?—A man who has no humility lacks a love of truth and courage.
>
> *Question* 34.—Who alone has the ultimate right over our bodies and our health ?—God alone has the ultimate right over our bodies and our health.

---

[1] These " Truths of the Catechism," a book edited by the Bishops' Conference of Fulda, were explanations of Catholic doctrine in the light of modern problems and questions.

In a decree issued to the Education Committees of towns and rural areas and to Directors of Education of secondary, technical, commercial and private schools, the Minister declares that these questions with their corresponding answers render the employment of this book impossible for teaching and learning religious knowledge; its use or distribution is forbidden and the copies already issued to the pupils are to be returned and destroyed.

Printed sermons of bishops which did not flatter the State or which even hinted at the restriction of ecclesiastical rights suffered a fate similar to that of the Pastoral Letters and of the " Truths of the Catechism." The police headquarters in Munich on February 19th, 1936, confiscated the festival sermon in honour of the Pope, " The Casting of Stones against the Papal Throne," preached by Cardinal Faulhaber on the 9th, during the jubilee service. The reprinting of the sermon was also forbidden, but, as this was based on the prohibition of pamphlet propaganda, the Vicar-General of the diocese had the sermon on the Pope, together with one in honour of the silver jubilee of His Eminence as Bishop and the Jubilee Pastoral issued as a brochure. On the same day the police also banned the sale of Cardinal Faulhaber's New Year's Eve sermon of 1935 on " Christian Belief " on the pretext that it was a supplement of the *Diocesan Gazette*. Similarly the Regensburg Catholic Sunday paper was suspended in 1936 because it printed Bishop Mgr. Buchberger's sermon on " The Threat to Catholic Faith " which had been delivered at the end of a people's mission. Early in 1937 the second series of " The Sermons of the Cardinal of Munich "—including " Strength in Suffering and Strength in Action," " Christianity in the German People," " Parents' Rights and Parents' Duties "; and the third series—" The Reich Concordat, Yes or No ?"—were confiscated and destroyed by the police. The Cardinal's last All Souls' sermon, " Christian Burial or Pagan Cremation," was confiscated from the Diocesan Administration offices in Munich at the very time when a film to popularise cremation was being shown in many places in Bavaria without police intervention.

2. " *Abuse of the Pulpit* "

The resurrection of the Pulpit Paragraph, dating back to the *Kulturkampf* of the seventies, and the law of December 20th, 1934, inflicting penalties for all " malicious attacks on State and Party," are responsible for many arrests of Catholic preachers. As the sermon of the priest is the most fruitful and the most important channel through which religious truths are constantly brought to the notice of Christian people, it is small wonder that the penalties suffered by the conscientious and loyal Catholic clergy are far more numerous than the isolated cases that receive notice in the press would lead the public to believe. It must, too, be fully realised that the insistence on these disciplinary measures subjects the Catholic priest to the gravest conflicts of conscience. On the one hand he is, as a priest, in duty bound to preach the whole of Catholic truth, to explain to the faithful the principles laid down by ecclesiastical authorities, and to warn them against dangers to Faith and morals. On the other hand, as is proved by innumerable facts and made clear by these pages, the National Socialist State itself is pursuing a definitely anti-Christian course in its administration of education, the controlled press, the official party organisations and the new religious movements which it tolerates.

The majority of sermons in Germany are subjected to a close observation, as the bishops have repeatedly stated in public, for a whole army of Gestapo spies and agents report every passage, even every word, which can in any way be interpreted as an attack upon the State or the Party. It matters little that these informers, on account of their poor education, are unable to interpret correctly the meaning of these words or to distinguish the essential from the non-essential. It was, for example, this extremely thorough spy system that provided the Bavarian police with the material for the instructions published on May 17th, 1935, by the *Elsässischer Kurier* on " Safeguarding against the Jesuits," the full text of which was as follows:

Bavarian Political Police.
B. Nr. 18. 175-35. I i B.

MUNICH,
[*Strictly Confidential.*]   *April* 23rd, 1935.

To all Police Headquarters, State Police offices, District Office stations, Town Commissioners and Provincial Administrations. Concerning " Safeguarding against the Jesuits " and supervision of Catholic literature.

The Jesuits are instigating systematic and far-reaching activities in Bavaria to undermine the Third Reich and bring contempt even on the Führer himself. In various semi-scientific lectures the philosophic principles of National Socialism are submitted to an acrimonious criticism which is nothing more nor less than disguised incitement against the Reich. These lectures, moreover, are so ambiguously and cunningly composed that a judicial punishment of the lecturer is possible in only very few cases.

In order to check this subversive and rebellious activity of the Jesuits and to dishearten their propagandist efforts in Bavaria, increased attention must be paid to their public appearances; public meetings are to be prevented by all means; private meetings are to be watched, and the severest penalties must be imposed on offenders, statements injurious to the State being ruthlessly punished by " protective custody." Further, public appearances of the Jesuits are to be reported immediately and a negative report is to be made on the 30th of every month starting from May 30th, 1935.

Catholic literature must claim special attention. The bookstalls at pilgrimage shrines, in church porches, on railway stations, as well as all Catholic bookshops and publishers, are to be scrutinised continually and thoroughly, especial watch being kept on new publications of Catholic popular and pamphlet literature. This refers particularly to the book series:

" Catholic Pamphlets on Questions of the Day," published by Saarbrücker
    Drückerei und Verlags A.G., Saarbrücken.
" Clear Concepts," published by Dr. Heinrich Krone, Berlin-Wilhelms-
    haven.

"The Church in Our Time," published by J. P. Bachem, G.m.b.H., Cologne.
"For the Defence of the Faith," published by A. Huber, Munich.

Any publications injurious to the State are to be confiscated, and in doubtful cases three copies are to be sent in for examination.

A negative report is also to be sent in on the 30th of every month starting from May 30th, 1935.

Intensified activity in this sphere is enjoined as a strict duty. The instructions given are to be regarded as strictly confidential, not from lack of confidence, but from a wish to withhold from the adversary means for further propaganda. In the struggle against Political Catholicism the ordinary police authorities will be given the full support of the Bavarian Political Police.

To check these statements consult:

L.S. MUNICH, *April 23rd*, 1935.

Signed: ZELLER, *Police Secretary*.
J.B. signed: STEPP.

Further evidence of the hostility of the State is shown by the supervision of "Itinerant Preachers" which was enjoined by the police headquarters in Munich in May, 1936, in the following decree:

We have been informed that of late a striking number of regular priests, notably Jesuits, move from place to place as itinerant preachers. Special attention must be given to them, more particularly to the missioners. Observations are to be handed in at once with carefully checked particulars of the individual and depositions of witnesses for any sermon preached.

A few cases given in chronological order will serve to illustrate that as a result of these instructions the inevitable condemnations of many Catholic priests followed.

At Bonn the Catholic priest T. was fined 600 RM. on the grounds that in a sermon he spoke disparagingly of the Hitler Youth and the Racial Theory. At his trial the State attorney stressed the fact that, even as a clergyman, the defendant was not entitled to make such remarks, for the Concordat expressly states that a priest must conform to the laws of the State.[1] Again the Catholic parish priest of Koblenz-Neuendorf was sentenced to six months' imprisonment because, in a sermon on Christian charity, he had ridiculed—so they said—" the Winter Relief Work " and the National Socialist Welfare Work.[2] Similar arrests were made in the cases of a parish priest from Mayen, who received five months' imprisonment for insulting remarks on the Hitler Youth, and a curate M. of Mannheim, who was sentenced to four months' imprisonment because in church services and religious instruction, in his indignation at the damage done to show boxes outside the church and the alleged illtreatment of the forbidden Catholic *Jungschaar* (a Catholic Youth Organisation), he had spoken critically of the HJ (Hitler Youth) uniform.[3] Similarly in July, 1935, Professor Herm. Muckermann's series of sermons begun at Duisberg was prohibited by the authorities because members of the SA and HJ systematically disturbed law and order. These are only a few examples

---

[1] *Germania*, May 10th, 1935.   [2] *Germania*, May 12th, 1935.
[3] *Kölnische Volkszeitung*, May 18th, 1936.

from the long list of cases which have occurred in the years from 1933 to the present day.

Further evidence is furnished by the already quoted report of the Archdiocese of Freiburg, which states that the decree of February 28th, 1933, was used to veto the preaching of the Franciscan Father Elzear Wangler for a sermon delivered on October 16th, 1934, at Sigmaringen; the same authority was invoked for the veto on Father Stephan Schmutz of Beuron for a sermon given on November 4th, 1934. For a sermon on the patron saint of Bohlingen Fr. Adelhelm Jud was arrested in that town on November 12th, 1933, and Dr. Krebs, a university professor, was forbidden by the Gestapo to preach a sermon on Original Sin to men in Freiburg Cathedral; this sermon had been announced for November 29th. Needless to say all complaints to the Reich Ministry for Ecclesiastical Affairs in Berlin were unsuccessful, and, moreover, the police, who would not allow the placarding of invitations to sermons in the city (though this was later permitted), offered no such intervention to the placarding of notices concerning the public meetings of the German Christians and Old Catholics, though these were sometimes of a very polemical nature.

The ordinance of the Reich President of February 28th, 1933, the official Church report continues, laid the foundation for the so-called " protective custody " which was imposed for disapproved statements from the pulpit, and often for long terms of imprisonment. The number of those known to have suffered, some of them over seventy years old, was about fifty, but according to various reports received a far greater number of other Catholic priests of the Archdiocese has been called to account by branches of the police or the Gestapo for remarks made in either the pulpit or the school.

The incompatibility of the Church's injunctions on all conscientious Catholics to safeguard the Christian education of the young with the totalitarian principles of the State is amply illustrated by the report in the Berlin Catholic parish magazine of February 2nd, 1936, of the case against Canon Mgr. Moschner of Breslau.

The article is headed " A Dean of Breslau before the Special Court " and states that Canon Mgr. Moschner of Breslau, diocesan president of the Silesian Catholic Youth Associations, had to justify himself before the special court of Ratibor on counts against Para. 2 of the " Law against Malicious Attacks on State and Party," and § 130a of the Civil Code forbidding abuse of the pulpit. He was charged with uttering defamatory remarks against leading personalities of the State and the Party, and, as a clergyman at a religious meeting, of speaking of State affairs in a manner prejudicial to the peace. In reply the defendant declared that during a journey through the diocese he had held a meeting of the Catholic Youth in the Youth Hostel of Ratibor-Altendorf in order to encourage them and their parents and to discuss the attacks of such anti-Christian organisations as the Hauer movement. He had been very cautious in his statements, he said, because he knew that representatives of the Secret Police and others, as he had been informed, were present to spy on him. The charges against him had not been made by the police, but by persons summoned as witnesses for the prosecution, who declared at the trial that they had attended the meeting with the express purpose of noting any remarks hostile to the State. Notwithstanding his circumspection, they denounced his speech as antagonistic to the State Youth and as a veiled attack on the State and its institutions. In view of the evidence, the counsel waived the accusation concerning two of the remarks, but the rest he condemned as a violent and unjustifiable attack on the totalitarian principle of the State. The defendant had spoken with restraint, he admitted, but as the mouthpiece of the Cardinal of Breslau it was incumbent on him to realise his particularly great responsibility. In accordance with the recommendation of the prosecutor the defendant was fined 600 RM. for the offence against § 130a of the Civil Code. In its summing up the Court conceded to him the right to speak in religious assemblies about Christ and the Faith, but declared that the State would not tolerate any assertion that the Church, to the exclusion of its own rights, had sole authority over the education of youth, for such a claim would lead to civil discontent.

The dreadful plight of conscientious priests under the Third Reich, though sufficiently illustrated already, is further revealed in the cases of Mgr. Leffers, parish priest of Rostock, Fr. Rupert Mayer, S.J., and Canon Kraus of Eischstätt.

Mgr. Leffers was sentenced to one and a half year's imprisonment by the Schwerin special court held at Rostock. What led up to this sentence and the view taken of it even by people who have no sympathy with the Church is disclosed by the following commentary in the *Frankfurter Zeitung*:[1]

Three young University students, two of them girls, ardent supporters of Ludendorff's anti-Christian movement and similar activities, called on a Church dignitary in Rostock. In the course of a discussion on Rosenberg's " Myth " they " led him to think that they were seeking spiritual advice"; and in consequence he spoke openly to them. Afterwards the three young people drew up a report which contained damaging statements. The priest appeared before the special court, was faced with the sworn depositions of the three students, and was condemned to one and a half year's imprisonment. One of the three had already spoken with Mgr. Leffers' curate on the same subject, and had then given as the reason of his visit his desire to get a clearer understanding of the views of the Catholic clergy on National Socialism, as he himself was an upholder of Rosenberg's doctrine. His approach, however, to Mgr. Leffers cannot have been the same, for otherwise the DNB (German News Agency) report cited above would not have said that the priest acted on the assumption that he was asked for spiritual advice. The expressions, which were held by the court to be proved and which formed the grounds of its judgement, were not apparently criticisms of Rosenberg's book, but rather comments on the general political situation. The most convincing evidence of witnesses who testified that the defendant was a loyal citizen was unable to avert his condemnation. A University professor deposed that the student had, before that, distinguished himself by his great activity in Rostock.

From many points of view the whole incident has naturally caused consternation. The decision of the court cannot, of course, be checked without access to the official documents, and we must confine ourselves to what was authoritatively stated in that short report: the priest was deliberately given the false impression that these young Catholics were seeking his spiritual help; yet they had come to lay a trap for him. No matter what the priest may have said or thought and no matter what importance the students may attach to their political and ideological convictions . . . there is no justification for methods like these, which are barely distinguishable from those of the *agent provocateur*. These young people, who perhaps believe that they have done something meritorious, should be made to realise that their behaviour is worse than that of many of those informers whom highly-placed Party officials have, with commendable firmness, constantly repudiated in many public declarations.

The case of Fr. Rupert Mayer, S.J., is even more remarkable. Shortly after the authorities had forbidden him to preach altogether

[1] April 17th, 1935.

he was in June, 1937, strictly prohibited from preaching anywhere except in St. Michael's, Munich. With the approval of his superiors, however, Fr. Mayer continued his usual pulpit activities, and this led to his arrest on Saturday, June 5th. The news caused a great sensation, especially amongst the men, for the arrested pulpit orator has a high reputation both as a missioner and as a patriot.

On Sunday, June 13th, by order of the Vicar-General of Munich, a declaration was read from the pulpits urging all Catholics to refrain from street demonstrations and informing them that a protest and appeal for the release of Fr. Mayer had been sent to the highest authorities by both the Cardinal and the Vicar-General. It went on:

> Never can the Church accept the right of the State to impose even a partial veto on a priest who complies with the Reich Concordat. Such a veto would ultimately effect the complete paralysis of the Church's activities, among which preaching is of paramount importance; it would also be incompatible with the Church's freedom guaranteed by the Concordat and, above all, offend against Article 32. . . .

The declaration then concluded by ordering special prayers in all the parish churches of Munich.

The arrest of Fr. Mayer was the subject of a moving address given by his Grace Cardinal Faulhaber himself on July 4th, 1937, at St. Michael's. The sermon is reproduced in full,[1] as it is an illuminating commentary on the existing situation of Catholicism in the Third Reich. The conclusion of this outstanding case was that Fr. Mayer, although he affirmed at the assizes that he had only defended the Church against the slanders of the press, was sentenced to six months' imprisonment on July 22nd, 1937.

The last case is that of Canon Kraus of Eichstätt, an upright priest who as a major in the World War was several times seriously wounded. He solemnly protested in a sermon against the defamations of Catholic priests and religious which, with the consent of the State, the whole press was disseminating. His sermon was based on the following authentic and documented evidence. First, the *Stürmer* published a letter from a curate, Franz Steigerwald, who, according to the unanimous assertions of the German Vicars-General, did not exist. Secondly, he quoted the case of a secondary-school boy, Schülle, described by the whole press as a diocesan leader of the Catholic Youth, who was taken into custody on a charge of immorality, the Church being refused permission to publish the necessary corrections which placed the case in a quite different light. Thirdly, he referred to an interview between an editor and a so-called Catholic parish priest in the concentration camp of Dachau which was reported verbatim in a daily paper. Canon Kraus proved from an authentic communication of the Camp Director of Dachau that this case, in which the priest was said to be the connecting link between Moscow and the Vatican, was a sheer fabrication. The Canon's courageous sermon was answered by an order of expulsion

[1] In Appendix III.

from the diocese of Eichstätt. His bishop, however, declared from the pulpit that as his rightful superior he had given him strict orders not to leave. No further action against him has been reported.

3. *The Muzzling of the Catholic Press*

The Church, both as conscious of being the carrier of a divine message to men and as a living power intent on influencing both individuals and whole communities, may renounce anything else rather than a good press, and the press which German Catholicism had created, especially since the *Kulturkampf* of the eighteen-seventies, without any doubt deserved to be called good. For, besides an imposing number of Catholic dailies, which, thoroughly loyal to the Church, had secured for the Catholic cause a great measure of esteem and influence in public life, there were not only very many first-rate periodicals, but also a large number of distinguished publishing houses and libraries, which had allied themselves with the Church and upheld her principles.

All this now has gone, with very few exceptions, and what remains after five years of the new régime has been so altered and muzzled that it can no longer be considered a spiritual weapon in the hands of the Church of any use in the relentless warfare that National Socialism is waging against her.

Within a few weeks of the solemn ratification of the Concordat, in November, 1933, the Cardinal Archbishop of Cologne felt constrained to publish a declaration in which he spoke of attempts openly to question the right to exist of newspapers that complied in every detail with the requirements of Catholic Faith and morals, and he referred to the German bishops' declaration of the previous Whitsuntide, where it was asserted that the Church could by no means surrender that most modern instrument of ministering to the needs of souls, the Press, but must demand such a measure of freedom as would provide her with the means of continuing an activity hitherto so abundantly blessed.

That the fears of the Rhineland Metropolitan were not unfounded was soon to be proved. In December, 1933, there appeared the " Law concerning Editors " (*Schriftleitergesetz*), which delivered the whole press, with the exception of the official diocesan gazettes, into the hands of the State. Every editor of even the least important local religious magazine was obliged to become a member of the Literary Chamber of the Reich (*Reichsschriftumskammer*) and to follow for the future whatever directions it might give. In this there was given to the Government a most useful weapon, and one supported with the full force of law, for the ousting of the Catholic Press, and paragraph 14, which excluded from publication anything " likely to weaken the will for union of the German people and German culture " was, as will be seen, to render good service to those who framed it.

As was to be expected, the first attack of National Socialism was directed against the most important part of the Catholic Press, the dailies. Indeed, the very existence of a Catholic Daily Press is termed, after the promulgation of the Editors Law, a " disloyalty to the New State," as, for example, in the *Nationalzeitung*:[1]

It must be maintained with firmness, that according to the new Editors Law, which embodies the spirit of the National Socialist State, there are no longer Catholic or Evangelical editors, but only German editors. . . . National Socialism does not suffer this fundamental principle to be shaken or distorted.

Soon the President of the Reich Press Bureau (*Reichspressekammer*), Party-member Amann, deemed that the hour had come to give the screw another turn. On April 24th, 1935, he ordered that

newspapers, in what regards the arrangement of their contents, may not be adapted to suit the preferences of a group of persons, determined or determinable by their denomination, calling or common interests.

Henceforward, therefore, Catholic dailies which still dare to deal on a large scale with religious or ecclesiastical events betray themselves as " restricted by their denomination " and offend against the decree. The advancing of " denominational points of view " in newspaper reports is now severely punished. Detailed reports of a pilgrimage, for example, become an illicit proselytising campaign, and for an account of a " solemnity attuned to its denomination " at a convent chapel jubilee a newspaper, formerly Catholic, was severely reprimanded by the Reich Press Bureau.

It is easy to see that obedience to this regulation means a violation of the Catholic conscience. How is an editor, convinced of the truth of the Christian religion, to deal only with politics in his paper, when at the same time he has completely to disregard " denominational points of view," when his conscience tells him that religion moulds all the acts of men, when a thousand problems and questions of public life defined by the new State as " politics " refer immediately to the Faith and the Church? Nor does the National Socialist editor succeed in separating politics from religion. It is true indeed that he does nothing to help on the Christian creed, but instead he is for ever preaching what is precisely the opposite, the creed of National Socialism; yet the Catholic editor, in consequence of the Amann regulation, is forced to lend himself and his paper to the public propagation of things contrary to his conscience, witness the propaganda prescribed by the State for the " Immorality Trials " and the use made of them for the vilification of the Church. Should he, on the other hand, make any attempt, however feeble, to preserve freedom of conscience, there is always the menace of exclusion from the Reich Press Bureau, which entails the probable loss of his position and, maybe, much worse.

The immediate and most far-reaching effect, however, of the Amann regulation was its weakening of the Church, for from that time on the

[1] No. 92, 1934.

forming of public opinion on Christian principles was rendered impossible and Catholic influence was more and more eliminated from public life.

Indeed, it is not too much to say that that regulation was the death sentence of the Catholic Press, for it is evident that Catholic dailies could not compete with the other newspapers on the same political level, when these were being favoured and systematically pushed by all State and Party officials. Catholic papers could exist only because they stressed the religious point of view and, for this reason, commended themselves to Catholic subscribers. If Catholics still continue to support these newspapers after their complete co-ordination with the others, they do so solely from a sense of loyalty.

It should be observed, too, that the uniformity enforced by the Amann decree destroys the very essence of a daily press. For only then can the daily paper conduce to the good government of the State, demonstrate approval of public measures and contribute to consistency of thought and policy when it enjoys the confidence of its readers, and this is possible only when it is in touch with and represents spheres of the national life which are not bound up with politics. This the Catholic Press did. It gave a unity to the fertile Catholic life, used its religious power to the full and mobilised it as an asset to statesmanship. Bereft of the confidence of its readers and supported only by forced contributions, the Press loses its meaning.

Compared with these incisive regulations, the later pettinesses and annoyances were of no great importance. The Catholic Press was, for example, forbidden to take part in the Vatican Press Exhibition of 1936, or to print liturgical weekly calendars, announce monthly Communions, church meetings, assemblies of Catholic clubs and organisations or parish family festivals, etc. An illustration of how a harmless phrase can lead to the confiscation of a paper is furnished by the *Neue Münchener Tagblatt*, whose issue of April 13th/14th, 1935, was seized and destroyed by order of police headquarters in Munich because it contained the following:

> 1. Christ knew that man remains himself and is just as truly himself at the Crucifixion as at the "Hosanna," because both proceed from his own self-seeking. Palm Sunday, therefore, could not deceive Him. From such, however, as call themselves after Him, He expects indeed that they put off that old Adam of self-seeking, so that henceforth they may neither deceive themselves nor be deceived.
> 2. The blessed mysteries of this week reveal themselves to our eyes together with the mystery of iniquity. An Apostle betrays Christ: Israel calls down rejection on herself. All this should be a reminder to us and a warning of similar disloyalties and of the judgements of God in the days of the New Dispensation.

It can now no longer be said that there exists in Germany a Catholic Press. It is true that a number of the old names, once glorious, still remain, but the substance is gone: no more may they stand up for the honour of the Church and the maintenance of a vigorous Christianity —a terrible loss indeed.

72 INTERFERENCE WITH TEACHING OF THE CHURCH

That this co-ordination of the formerly Catholic papers should in the long run involve their entire disappearance will surprise no one. In this way in the territory of Baden alone the Church has been deprived of twenty-two dailies. In this way, too, the *Tremonia* in Dortmund came to an end, as did the *Münsterscher Anzeiger*, the *Echo der Gegenwart* in Aachen and, from January 1st, 1939, the *Germania* of old fame, which was soon followed by the *Märkische Volkszeitung* of Berlin. In their death they were preceded by the *Deutsches Volksblatt* in Stuttgart, the *Badischer Beobachter*, the *Limburger Kurier*, the *Trierischer Volksfreund*, etc.

In Austria likewise the Catholic dailies have been suppressed without exception or, what comes to the same thing, co-ordinated with National Socialism. The *Reichspost* and the *Linzer Volksblatt* at first were published under the old titles but with a changed spirit. In 1939 the *Reichspost* had definitely to suspend its publication. The *Salzburger Chronik*, since the Anschluss edited as the *Salzburger Zeitung*, disappeared as early as the summer of 1938.

A word may also be said of the many personal tragedies which lie hidden behind these prosaic facts. Many former editors were arrested, taken into concentration camps or turned out on to the street. Those who in an inferior position still may serve their paper under the new cause are perhaps even more to be pitied for their permanent struggles with their consciences. And of the numerous employees of the publishing houses, the typesetters, lithographers, newspaper boys, etc., how many have lost their livelihood only because formerly they had faithfully served the Catholic cause !

By the very fact that the Catholic dailies had been brought into line with the other newspapers, and so become useless as a weapon on the side of religion, the Catholic periodicals necessarily gained a greater importance in proportion as the fierce struggle for the Faith demanded ever more and more urgently a press that would take the part of the persecuted Church. From the very first, then, it was to be expected that, after the Catholic dailies, the numerous Catholic periodicals would be the next objective in the strategy of her opponents.

On February 17th, 1936, a regulation was issued by the Reich Press Bureau confining ecclesiastical publications to what was strictly religious:

> According to Article 4 of the decree of April 24th, 1935, newspapers, in what regards the arrangement of their contents, may not be adapted to suit the preferences of a group of persons, determined or determinable by their denomination, calling or common interests. It cannot be allowed that the kind of publication, which is excluded from the daily and weekly press, should find a substitute in the denominational periodicals, and therefore it can no longer be tolerated that these, though they omit all political news, should contain matter of general interest or of a didactic nature, whose selection is influenced by the fact that the subscribers are members of a certain denomination, whereas every article ought to have an exclusively religious content.

Hence for the diocesan press we order as follows: For diocesan papers edited by a diocese and sold only within that diocese, the following comes into force:

They must serve exclusively for the promulgation of Church announcements, of news referring to ecclesiastical events, of religious memorial articles on the history of the Church or diocese, of the treatment of dogmatic and moral questions, of reflections on and descriptions of the life of the Church or the Saints, of legends, and for the cultivation of Church music and Church art.

The acceptance of advertisements which refer to religious and ecclesiastica usages or which, permissible in other respects, have a special application to the readers as members of the Catholic denomination is allowed.

To Sunday papers and suchlike publications the following applies: They must serve exclusively for the development of a universally intelligible religious culture by treating religious and moral questions in such a way that each single part of the contents starts from a point of religion. . . .

The acceptance of advertisements is subject to the same regulations as apply to the diocesan publications. . . .

Signed: AMANN.

The gist and point of this diffuse decree (the style of which scarcely does credit to the Reich Press Bureau) is, then, that the whole of the contents, including too the sections of a more entertaining nature and even the advertisements, must be of a strictly religious character. Film criticisms, riddles, joke corners, novelettes, stories, etc., are therefore excluded, and any judgement of actual problems or of public events on Catholic principles, any discussion of neo-paganism is no longer possible. The " Sterilised Press " is now a reality.[1]

Close watch is kept to ensure that these regulations are strictly observed. A communication, for instance, of the same President of the Reich Press Bureau to the publishers of ecclesiastical publications contained the following:

In various periodicals of the Catholic ecclesiastical press there is an increase of advertisements in which, on the occasion of the conferring of Confirmation, articles for ordinary daily use are included. Under the decree of February 17th, 1936, only such advertisements may be accepted as, in their totality, apply to the reader in his quality as a Catholic, as Prayer books, rosaries, myrtle-wreaths, etc. . . .

Again, on December 6th, 1937, in a special circular of the Reich Press Bureau, a ridiculously fussy warning was issued to the Catholic Press, part of which reads as follows:

Of late I have repeatedly had occasion to state that in advertisements in Catholic church magazines an announcement admissible according to the decree of the President of the Reich Press Bureau is coupled with another not so admissible. In " situations wanted," for instance, the phrase occurs that the male or female applicant would " prefer " a situation with a religious institution, a parish priest, etc. Such wording of an advertisement admits the possibility that interested persons other than parish priests, convents, etc., may also communicate with the advertiser. Further I have had to state that girls who are fond of children are wanted even in households where there are no children at all. I demand that in future great care be taken that such advertisements be refused.

Signed: WILLI.

[1] *Cf.* also the remarks of Amann in the *Deutsche Presse*, organ of the Reich Union of the German Press, No. 21, of May 23rd, 1936, also the comments of Dr. Göbbels in the *Völkischer Beobachter*, Munich edition, of February 19th, 1936.

74 INTERFERENCE WITH TEACHING OF THE CHURCH

The narrow limits imposed on the Catholic periodicals by these regulations and by the insistence on the part of the State on their strict observance effectively prevented them from affording any substantial support to the Church. They were not allowed, for example, to say a word in defence of religious houses and priests at the time of the "Immorality Trials," and more than forty editors were dismissed (later, it is true, to be reinstated) because they had reproduced a statement of the Vicar-General of Breslau with reference to the Currency Laws. In July, 1935, the *Munich Church Magazine*[1] was seized and destroyed because it included an article on "The True Riches of the Monasteries," and because another article, "We Answer," contained the words: "A Catholic newspaper must consent to much." The *Berlin Church Magazine* of March 13th, 1937, refuted, calmly and incisively, an article which had appeared in the *Schulungsbriefe der NSDAP*[2] (Training Letters of the NSDAP) about the Church's conception of Womanhood, and for this it was severely reprimanded by the Ministry of Propaganda, as it was too, later, for an adverse criticism of the film "Youth," with its complete misrepresentation of priests and the priesthood.

From the very start, then, many problems and whole departments of life could receive no treatment in the Catholic Press. Prayers and discussions about the continued existence of the Catholic schools were from April, 1937, no longer allowed to appear: articles explaining the financial operations of the Church or treating of the question as to whether Christ was or was not of Aryan descent were not allowed—indeed, this latter has been finally settled by a theological *ex cathedra* decision of the Reich Department of Propaganda of Württemberg, that "today this question cannot be definitely answered." Any report about the Eucharistic Congress at Budapest of May, 1938, was forbidden. When the *Diocesan Gazette* of Freiburg of December 5th, 1936, dared to print a report on the events in Oldenburg, where attempts had been made to remove the crucifixes from the schoolrooms, the issue was seized and the paper subjected to the censorship of the Gestapo.

A glance at the *St. Konradsblatt*,[3] the Sunday paper of the Archdiocese of Freiburg, is very instructive. It is there reported:

> Switzerland. On Sunday, September 19th, the Swiss bishops caused a Pastoral Letter to be read in all the churches, in which Communism in all its different forms is stigmatised as the greatest enemy of the family and of any social, civil or national order.

That the Pastoral dealt with both the anti-Christian forces, Communism and State-deifying Nationalism, the diocesan paper dared not mention. Again, the same paper (No. 42) contained the following:

> The Holy Father has addressed an Encyclical about the Holy Rosary to all bishops of the Catholic world: "The dangers of the present time need not shake the confidence of the good Christian."

[1] No. 29, July 21st, 1935.
[2] NSDAP means National Socialist German Workers' Party.
[3] No. 41, 1937.

That is all that was mentioned on the Encyclical. What dangers of the present time were specified by it—Godless Communism and State-deifying Nationalism—at this the church magazine might not even hint, no more than it would have been allowed to reproduce the text of the Encyclical, despite the solemn guarantee of the Reich Concordat permitting it.

In October, 1935, a supplement to the *Diocesan Gazette* of Munich-Freising (No. 19), entitled " The Religious Situation in Germany," translated from the *Osservatore Romano*[1] was confiscated and for the future all translations from the *Osservatore* in diocesan gazettes were forbidden. In many places a house-to-house drive to increase the circulation of Catholic papers was prohibited.

The decree of October, 1937, ordaining that no organisation whatever should be obliged to subscribe to Catholic ecclesiastical periodicals, was later amended to the effect that periodicals should not be subscribed to by members of an organisation in common, nor should organisations undertake their distribution or the collection of subscriptions. This decree meant a serious loss to many Catholic magazines, because one of their chief supports was precisely the Catholic organisations.

There followed a new regulation according to which no reports on religious manifestations, etc., are permitted, not even from countries friendly to Germany, as Italy and Spain, and so the religious ceremonies, for example, that accompanied the victory celebrations of General Franco in Madrid had to be passed over in silence by the Catholic Press of Germany.

Among the Catholic periodicals the Church magazines, edited by the ecclesiastical authorities and addressing themselves to the faithful of a parish, town, or even a whole diocese, had become in the course of the last few years more and more conspicuous, and, in spite of frequent interferences, these papers have steadily grown to be a bulwark of the Church in the struggle for the Faith. A whole book, indeed, would have to be written if all the annoyances, restrictions, and molestations of this section of the Catholic Press were to be described, for there is certainly not a single Catholic Church paper in Germany which once, at least, has not been the victim of disciplinary measures on the part of the secular authorities. And yet it is interesting to observe that in spite of, or perhaps because of, this harassing the number of subscribers has continually been on the increase.

Of their sufferings a very deficient chronological list, yet drawn from absolutely trustworthy sources, is given in the following prohibitions:

On May 4th, 1934, the *Aibling Parish Magazine*.
At the end of July, 1934, the *Bonifatiusblatt*, No. 4.
In the year 1934 the *St. Konradsblatt*.
On January 20th, 1935, the *St. Konradsblatt*.
On March 8th, 1935, the *Essen Parish Magazine*, No. 10.

[1] No. 81, August 4th, 1935.

On March 21st, 1935, the *Essen Parish Magazine*, No. 12.
On March 22nd, 1935, the *Aachen Diocesan Newspaper*.
On April 7th, 1935, the *Berlin Diocesan Magazine*, No. 14.
On April 28th, 1935, the *St. Paulinusblatt* at Trier, No. 17.
On May 4th, 1935, the *St. Paulinusblatt* at Trier, No. 18.
On May 4th, 1935, the *Munich Catholic Newspaper*.
On May 10th, 1935, the *Kleine Katholische Kirchenzeitung*.
On May 28th, 1935, the *Leo*, No. 9.
On June 21st, 1935, the *Johannesbote Schneidemühl*, No. 26.
On June 24th, 1935, the *Dortmund Kirchlicher Anzeiger*, No. 24.
On July 14th, 1935, the *Munich Catholic Newspaper*, No. 28.
On July, 21st, 1935, Bishop Kaller announces that the *Catholic Church Magazine* of Ermland has been six times seized.
On August 30th, 1935, the *Würzburg Diocesan Magazine*.
On June 13th, 1936, the *Diocesan Gazette for Munich and Freising*, No. 16.
On June 21st, 1936, the *Berlin Diocesan Magazine*.
On August 2nd, 1936, the *Hildesheim Diocesan Magazine*, No. 31.
On December 5th, 1936, the *Freiburg Diocesan Gazette*, No. 40.
On March 1st, 1936, the *Kleine Katholische Kirchenzeitung* of Munich.
On March 20th, 1936, the *Cologne Catholic Newspaper*.
In spring, 1938, all the diocesan magazines in Austria.
On February 27th, 1938, the *Cologne Catholic Newspaper*, No. 9.
In September, 1938, the *Berlin Diocesan Magazine* forbidden for the future.
In the course of the year 1938:
The *Münsterisches Kirchenblatt*.
The *St. Liboriusblatt* of Paderborn.
The *St. Paulinusblatt*, Trier, etc.

To show how paltry the reasons frequently were for these prohibitions we give just one illustration. In the special First Communion number of the *Kleine Kirchenzeitung* of Munich[1] there was recounted an anecdote of how the Prussian General of Hussars, von Zitten, once returned a neat answer to old Fritz, when he was being laughed at by the German king for his Christian faith. This article had to be removed from the type-blocks to avoid confiscation.

In Austria there used to be a number of Catholic Press Unions with printing offices for the publication of Catholic literature. Now they have nearly all, with all their furnishings which were the property of the different dioceses, been taken over to serve the Party and in many cases to issue Party papers.

Besides the prohibition of some particular number or even the closing down of a paper as is outlined in the preceding list, there is another method frequently resorted to by National Socialism to ensure that nothing is written that can in any way be interpreted as a criticism of the régime. This method is the appointment of a censor to whom each issue must be submitted before publication and who, with or without sound reasons, can reject whatsoever he wishes, as is shown by the following declaration of the parish clergy of Münster in Westphalia read from the pulpits in December, 1936:

Of late we have repeatedly been asked why the *Münster Parish Magazine* no longer as formerly deals plainly and clearly with the struggle for the Faith and the religious errors of our times.

[1] March, 1937.

In order to leave no one in doubt as to the reasons for this, we wish it to be known that already for more than a year the *Münster Parish Magazine* has been censored by the police and that not infrequently, for quite inexplicable reasons, articles have been cancelled either wholly or in part. So, for example, from the issue for November 29th there was cut out a harmless saying of our great Westphalian countryman, Bishop William Emmanuel von Ketteler, though its meaning was crystal clear to any upright Christian. The saying in question, which describes what should be the attitude of any manly Catholic, is worded as follows:

Consistency

It is not possible to be a Christian in the family circle and a pagan in public life. That will not do. A man must be consistent or else he is not a man. Wherever you are or act, then you must act as a Christian man and try to exercise a steady influence according to Christ's doctrines and Christ's principles. Then you will be a true friend of your fellow-citizens and of your people, for if Christ's interests are taken care of, the welfare of the people is secured. WILLIAM EMMANUEL VON KETTELER.

Thus the parish magazine again and again is prevented from telling you what a parish priest would like to tell you. In the daily press, however, you are given accounts which do not always harmonise with reality, as a report about the much discussed events in Oldenburg has lately proved.

THE PARISH CLERGY OF MÜNSTER.

Some brief mention should be made, too, of the disciplinary measures taken against other Catholic periodicals than parish magazines strictly so called.

On March 7th, 1935, the *Junge Front* was forbidden by the State police of Düsseldorf because of inaccurate assertions in a local recruiting pamphlet, which had, incidentally, been printed without the knowledge of either the editor or the publisher, and on May 8th of the same year the *Christ-Königsbote* was prohibited until further notice for the alleged reason that, under the cloak of Catholic doctrine, the journal evoked antagonism against the National Socialist ideology, which for the security of the State was not to be tolerated. From December of the same year to the end of March of the following year the *Stimmen der Zeit*, a monthly conducted by the Jesuit Fathers, was forbidden in virtue of the law for the protection of the people and the State.

In January, 1936, the weekly *Michael* (the new title of the *Junge Front*), which had reached a circulation of more than 300,000, after repeated confiscations was definitely forbidden, and in spring of the same year the *Ketteler-Wacht* too, the former *Westdeutsche Arbeiter-Zeitung*, the official organ of the Catholic Workers' Associations with a circulation of 150,000, had to suspend publication.

In 1937 the *Weltmission*, an illustrated monthly of the Papal work for the propagation of the Faith (Francis Xavier Mission Union), was forbidden for the future on August 27th, by the Gestapo in Berlin. The reason given was that, " in consequence of the paltry and false way of representing conditions among foreign peoples and the glorifying of foreign races in comparison with Europeans, the prohibition of the above cited periodical has become necessary, as it constitutes a danger to the racial theory as the basis of the National Socialist State."

On August 28th of the same year the *Klerusblatt*, organ of the diocesan associations of Bavaria, was forbidden until further notice on the grounds that " the treatment meted out to the Church in Russia is represented in a way directly opposed to what until now has been published by the German Press about Russia and proved to be true. As the article is practically undiluted communistic propaganda, its publication would, at the very least, have an injurious effect upon the State." What, as a matter of fact, was not to the taste of the Gestapo was that the article in question described the revival of religious life in Russia and its triumph over the opposition of the State and the Party organisations.

Other periodicals that had to suspend publication in the course of 1937 were the educational journals, *Das neue Blatt für die kath. Lehrerschaft*, *Das kleine Schulkind* and *Das grosse Schulkind*, and also the *Altöttinger Liebfrauenbote*, *Die christliche Kunst*, and in 1938 *Die christliche Einkehr* because one of its articles, " We implore St. Michael,"[1] was considered liable to disturb public peace and order.

Also in 1938 the *Zweipfennigblatt*, the Catholic Parish Priests' journal, of Innsbruck[2] was forbidden because it printed the following quotation: " The slighting of religion in the schools is equal to taking the sun from the heavens and spring from the year.—The great pedagogue Willmann." The Viennese Sodality magazine *Fahne Mariens*, the *Kirche und Leben* of Düsseldorf and the Catholic young men's magazine *Die Wacht* were also suppressed in this year.

Early in the following year, 1939, the Catholic weekly for working women in town and country, *Ketteler-Licht*, was forbidden and in March also the *Heerbann Mariens*, a study-paper for lay-apostles, because in an article dealing with the early Church the police thought they saw a scornful allusion to the National Socialist Movement. This same year saw the suppression of the magazines *Familienglück* and *Myrthe* of the *Neulandbund* (May 15th), papers which had successfully arranged Catholic marriages for several years, but whose denominational object now was opposed to the idea of the community spirit of the people (*Volksgemeinschaft*); in May, of the magazine *Monika*, then in its seventy-first year, published by the Pedagogical Institute Casseaneum at Donauwörth, for Catholic mothers and housewives, whose circulation extended throughout all German-speaking countries; and in spring of the periodical *Die Seelsorge*, formerly the *Kirche im Angriff*.

A particularly heavy blow was the edict prohibiting all the Catholic Youth papers like *Die Jungwacht*, *Am Scheidewege*, *Der Kranz*, *Die Knospen*, *Frauenart und Frauenleben*, etc. (we have already mentioned the fate of *Die Wacht*), which before their suppression had had a very large circulation.

[1] No. 16, October 1st, 1938.   [1] No. 47, November 20th, 1938.

Catholic books, brochures and calendars, as was to be expected, met with no better fate than that of the Catholic periodicals, and, in particular, writings which took up the defence of the Church, which discussed the dangers of the day to the Faith and showed signs of becoming influential were immediately exposed to prohibition on the part of the State.

Among such publications, the place of honour was held by Dr. Algermissen's *Germanentum und Christentum*, one of the leading works written by Catholics about the German faith, which between November, 1934, and July, 1935, had six editions of 12,000 copies each. It was forbidden by the police, confiscated and destroyed. Similarly *Das Menschliche in der Kirche*, by Canon Simon, explaining to the faithful the human weaknesses in the Church and accounting for them from a Catholic point of view, was prohibited.

Many apologetical works, intended for mass-production, were confiscated. The *Studien zum Mythus*, published by the Diocesan Administration in Münster, were allowed to appear because, owing to the depth of their erudition, they would in any case appeal to only a very narrow circle of readers; but the popular refutations of the "Myth," as Dahl, *Zum Mythus des XX Jahrhunderts*; Anton Koch, *Der neue Mythus und der alte Glaube*; Generalvikariat Köln, *Zu Rosenbergs Mythus des XX Jahrhunderts*, were all confiscated.

In May, 1935, there were seized the *Kath. Volksschriften zu Tagesfragen*, Saarbrücken (Catholic Popular Pamphlets on Questions of the Day), *Klare Begriffe* and *Dem Glauben zur Wehr*, and in June of the same year Nos. 14 and 17 of the series *Dem Glauben zur Wehr* (Defence of the Faith Series), *Kirche und Kapitalismus* and *Die Freimaurer*, as well as the brochure of Worlitscheck, *Papsttum und Deutschtum*, were forbidden, seized and destroyed. In Munich during this month National Socialist students broke the shop-windows of the *Tyrolia* Bookshop, because it bore the inscription "The Catholic Book."

The suspicions of the Gestapo were not, however, allayed by the almost total destruction of the apologetical literature, but involved, too, that of a vast number of books of a purely religious character such as "Truths of the Catechism," edited by the Bishops' Conference at Fulda, explanations of the Catechism, sermons, conferences and brochures like those of Ludwig Biehl, Fassbinder, Heinrich Hesse, Stöbele, Jos. Teusch, and others.

In this way Paffrath's *Gottes Licht im Alten Testament*, a purely spiritual book, was seized, as also the leaflet *Mein Glaube und mein Schwur*, a kind of confession of faith, which was forbidden to be circulated in Baden, and a number of writings that gave an exposition of Catholic principles of education. Gensert's brochure, *Liebe deine Kirche*, was put on the list of injurious and undesirable books, and the remaining copies of Fr. Leo Schlegel's *Das Kleinod der christlichen Mädchen* and *Paradies auf Erden*, both of which extol the ideal of virginity, were confiscated by the Gestapo, as also was the pamphlet *Fürchtet euch nicht* (Herder, 1935), written by Fr. Pribilla, S.J.

Dr. Pius Fischer, in a brochure *Rückständiges Christentum, II. Priestertum - Ordensstand - Zölibat*, published by Huber of Munich, by quoting judgements of celebrated men, for the most part not ecclesiastics, had shown the ethical and social value of the orders and celibacy of the priests. It was seized by the Secret Police.

To sum up, it can truthfully be said that hundreds of Catholic brochures, especially those of an apologetic nature, fell victims to the State censorship.

Of calendars also a good number were forbidden. We only mention the *Franziskuskalender*, the *Marienkalender*, the *Christ. Elternkalender*. Of the latter, the 7,000 copies still extant in Munich at the school organisations and all the copies sent off to the Bavarian presbyteries, discovered with the help of the card-index system recording the recipients, totalling in all some 43,000, were confiscated. The printing costs alone amounted to more than 12,000 RM. There was seized also the *Dom Bosco-Kalender*—the whole of the 50,000 copies of which were at that time lying packed for dispatch post-paid. And lastly we mention the *Kath. Familienkalender*, edited by the *Verband Süddeutscher Kath. Arbeiter- und Arbeiterinnen-Vereine*.

It would seem, after what has been recounted above, that everything possible had already been done to destroy Catholic literature. But at the same time as the measures there described were being applied, an attack was being carried on against the Catholic publishing firms, which reduced their output still further. We have already mentioned that in 1937 twelve publishing businesses were declared " hostile to the State " and sequestrated without compensation for printing the Papal Encyclical *Mit brennender Sorge*. In some cases (*e.g.*, the firm of Valentin Höfling in Munich), the businesses are now being carried on under their old names by the State as National Socialist enterprises.

In Austria a fair number of Catholic publishing firms were closed or transformed by the authorities. *Tyrolia*, publishers in Innsbruck, centre of the great Press institute established by Mgr. Schöpfer, was liquidated in 1938: its printing office had already been taken over by the National Socialist *Deutscher Alpenverlag*.

Confiscation of whole firms, however, could hardly be carried out on the gigantic scale on which it was applied to their products and so the system of restrictions was resorted to, with which the firms had to comply. In 1939 decrees were issued giving bookshops and publishers the alternative of dealing with either purely Christian literature or profane, but they could not do both. In consequence an establishment that wishes to retain its Christian character must in future give up the sale of all secular literature, though it remains still somewhat doubtful as to where the line between religious and secular will be drawn, whether, that is to say, " Christian " will be allowed to include, besides strictly biblical, theological and edifying books, also such as may be called elevating and refined in a Christian spirit.

Non-Christian bookshops, on the other hand, are forbidden to recommend Christian literature in any form.

It is clear that this measure will spell *finis* for many firms, but in any case the number of Christian booksellers is deliberately being reduced to a minimum, and a further regulation, that establishments owned and run by companies must close and that only individually owned concerns may do business for the future, will quicken the coming of the end for many more.

Catholic libraries are also in a bad way. Rosenberg's books were missed from the Borromäus Libraries, so these " politically unreliable libraries " were closed for some days for examination and " purging." The *Borromäus Verein*[1] has, too, been greatly hit by the withdrawal of the booksellers' discount,[2] as the central office was largely dependent on the sale of books to the various libraries.

That thousands of school libraries are gradually being " purged " from all denominational influences needs not to be mentioned. In June, 1938, the Saxon Minister of Popular Education made known that the Department for the Distribution of Literature had submitted the elementary school libraries to an investigation. It was stated, he says, that the largest portion of the books were out of date and undesirable and so the libraries were obliged to remove all such books by July 1st, 1938. Further, there were to be withdrawn, besides Jewish writings, etc., all books which " in their purport are narrowly restricted by their denomination "—in other words, Catholic and Protestant books.

Finally, a few words should be added about the restrictions to which the Church in the use of occasional religious pamphlets is more and more subjected. As early as June 29th, 1934, the Baden Minister of the Interior forbade the circulation of religious pamphlets till further notice—*i.e.*, for ever. The placarding of posters of a religious character and the distribution of leaflets to invite to sermons or religious conferences, even if addressed personally to the various Catholics and distributed from house to house in closed envelopes, have been repeatedly prohibited. The people's mission at St. Rupert's in Munich could scarcely be prepared because the *Missionsbote* was confiscated by the police. Even private letters that contain spiritual advice and direction for souls cannot be dispatched with security, for they are liable to be ranked among the forbidden pamphlets.

---

[1] Association for the promotion of good books which maintains circulating libraries in practically every German parish.—*Translator's note*.

[2] *Cf.* the announcement of the *Börsenverein* in *Börsenblatt für den deutschen Buchhandel* of April 29th, 1939.

CHAPTER III

THE CHURCH IS EXCLUDED FROM THE WORK OF EDUCATION: I. THE DESTRUCTION OF THE CATHOLIC YOUTH ASSOCIATIONS

To educate youth is to train and form the next generation and means eventually the moulding of the future of the whole nation. The Church in Germany was, in this matter of education, in a very strong position. She had her schools: she had her associations for young people. Both were in a position which hardly another country could equal. When the Concordat came to be drawn up, one of the first and foremost concerns of the ecclesiastical authorities was to give to these schools and associations an unassailable legal position. In Articles 23 and 31 we find, therefore, that both these activities are definitely assigned to the Church.

That was the position in 1933. The position now as we write this in the summer of 1939 is that, practically speaking, Catholic schools and Youth Associations in Germany no longer exist. Both these means of formation have been taken over by the Nazi State and are being made to serve its purpose of de-Christianising the German people. And how did it come about?

In the preface attention has been called to the attitude adopted by Catholics in the spring and summer of 1933. All reserve was laid aside. They were confident that the heads of the new State would not meddle with the rights of the Church, while in actual fact the Nazi authorities were losing no time in preparing the way for the break-up of the Catholic educational system. The new leaders of the nation gave their foremost attention to the teaching profession, made its allegiance secure and hammered into it the new way of thinking. It is particularly from 1935 onwards that, one by one, the various strong points in the Church's position have been assailed. The Catholic Youth organisations are made suspect of being anti-national. They are represented as sabotaging the national effort. Their members are forced into the Hitler Youth by pressure being brought to bear on their parents, by terrorisation and by their being deliberately passed over when it comes to promotion, while at the same time the clergy and the members of religious orders are defamed and proclaimed unworthy to take part in the education of German youth. All the forces of propaganda are turned without scruple against the denominational schools. Articles throughout the entire press, public meetings, proclamations, propaganda speeches by public officials, and often enough open and covert threats are all used in a successful effort to break down the parents' resistance, so that in many places by means of the school election farce the National Socialist community school is established, while the remaining territories and provinces are " purged " of their denominational schools by simple decree.

There has been no want of official protests and courageous denunciations from the pulpit of the injustice of such methods: it was the only course of action open to the bishops. But it was all useless. In such an unequal fight the defeat of the Church was inevitable, and it is certainly not to her discredit that she was unable to compete in cruelty with the totalitarian State.

A few remarks must be made on the fundamental attitude of National Socialism to the question of education.

To the fact that the ruling party in the Third Reich intended to bring up German youth in a consciously anti-Christian spirit Baldur von Schirach, the Reich Youth Leader, bears witness with a remark made in the course of a Berlin speech as far back as November 5th, 1934: " Rosenberg's way is the way of German youth."

In May, 1935, a decree of Rust, the Minister of Education, provides, as he says, an entirely new foundation for the case of the young. The State considers its principal objective to be the furthering of the Hitler Youth and the ideological training of those outside it, which was to be done mainly through the medium of the so-called rallies of State Youth. In this discussion of fundamentals there is no word about the Church being a factor.[1]

More definite still was a statement made by the leading personality in the National Socialist Teachers' Union. In the course of a recruiting drive for the Hitler Youth from April 1st to 20th, 1935, District Leader Wächtler made an announcement to German teachers in which, among other things, he stated that the three great factors which had the right to contribute to the education of German youth were the family, the school and the Youth Organisation. In the same way, therefore, as Rosenberg and Baldur von Schirach had so often done, so District Leader Wächtler makes a deliberate exclusion of the Church as a factor in education. Later on these principles are often repeated, as, for example, in the speech of Rosenberg at Detmold, in which he affirmed that the education of youth was to be conducted by the State and the National Socialist organisation alone, and that this was a vital position which the Party could never abandon.[2]

1. *Catholic Youth Associations Guaranteed yet Doomed from the Start*

Nowhere—apart from the school question—did the fight rage so bitterly as around the Catholic Youth Associations. Naturally the victory rested in the long run with the State because of the stronger

[1] For the decree *cf. Köln. Volkszeitung* or *Germania* of May 10th, 1935.
[2] *Cf. Frankfurter Zeitung*, No. 32, January 18th, 1937.

84 DESTRUCTION OF CATHOLIC YOUTH ASSOCIATIONS

measures it was able to adopt, but that victory was merely an external one in the matter of outer organisation. Dissolution could not be avoided, but the young Catholics gave way only to force, while in their hearts they were able to preserve a strong sense of their own moral superiority and worth. Externally overpowered and disarmed, they kept alive spiritually a burning faith in their own undying ideals.

The reason of this obstinate fight for the Youth Associations and the strong indignation and sorrow which the Church expressed at their loss will become clear when the following two points are considered: first, the sort of country Germany would become when Catholicism was no longer able to exercise an influence on Catholic youth; and secondly, the knowledge that it was not a question of handing over the Youth Associations to some neutral and colourless system, but to one which was utterly anti-Christian.

The history of the struggle is a long one, and it is scarcely worth while now to follow it up in all its details: it will suffice to select the more important points. It will be seen that, while the direct destruction of the Catholic associations was prevented by the Concordat, nevertheless the full intention of bringing this about was in the minds of the leading personalities from the start, and we shall be able to watch the State and the Party bringing their whole strength to bear in favour of the Hitler Youth against the Catholic Youth groups. And yet in spite of it six years elapsed before the greater part of the Associations could be liquidated—proof enough of the mutual fidelity which bound the Church and the Catholic youth together.

On April 28th, 1933, the Chancellor, Adolf Hitler, wrote as follows to Cardinal Bertram:

> I can assure Your Eminence that there is no intention of proceeding against any such associations provided they do not indulge in party politics or foster any tendencies inimical to the present Government.

In the Concordat of July, 1933, Article 31 lays down:

> Those Catholic organisations and societies which pursue exclusively charitable, cultural or religious ends and, as such, are placed under the ecclesiastical authorities will be protected in their institutions and activities.
> Those Catholic organisations which to their religious, cultural and charitable pursuits add others, such as social or professional interests, though they may be brought into national organisations, are to enjoy the protection of Article 31, Section 1, provided they guarantee to develop their activities outside all political parties.
> It is reserved to the Central Government and the German episcopate in joint agreement to determine which organisations and associations come within the scope of this article.
> In so far as the Reich and its constituent States take charge of sport and other youth organisations, care will be taken that it shall be possible for the members of the same regularly to practise their religious duties on Sundays and feast days, and that they shall not be required to do anything not in harmony with their religious and moral convictions and obligations.

CATHOLIC YOUTH ASSOCIATIONS GUARANTEED

The Chancellor, Adolf Hitler, made on July 7th, 1933, the following statement concerning the Concordat:

The conclusion of the Concordat between the Holy See and the German Government appears to me to give sufficient guarantee that the Roman Catholic citizens of the Reich will from now on put themselves whole-heartedly at the service of the new National Socialist State:
I therefore decree:
1. The dissolution, carried out without directions from the Central Government, of such Catholic organisations as are recognised by the present treaty is to be cancelled immediately.
2. All measures taken against clerical and other leaders of these Catholic organisations are to be annulled. Any repetition of such measures will in future be unlawful and will be punished according to the normal legal procedure.
I am happily convinced that there has now finally come to an end a period in which it appeared that religious and political interests were unfortunately ranged against each other in an insuperable opposition.

Ministerialdirektor Dr. Buttmann, the representative of the German Government in the negotiations with the Holy See, wrote to Bishop Berning on July 31st, 1933:

I have published in the Press the principles which have finally been agreed to in Rome for the interpretation of Article 31.

Directions for Interpretation

In the application of Article 31 the Central Government adopts the following attitude:
The Catholic associations and organisations enumerated in Section 1 are to be allowed to conduct their own activities in their own way, in which matter the Government has no further title to interfere than that which it has in the general matter of the loyalty of citizens to the State.
Those Catholic organisations, however, which are enumerated in Section 2 may, but only if they so wish, be incorporated in the national associations, which incorporation does not deprive them of the right to wear a particular type of dress, to wear badges and to carry banners on public occasions, neither is it to interfere with the activities peculiar to those associations, their property, Catholic character and independence according to their constitutions. They are therefore to retain their present constitutions except where such constitutions contain aims which run counter to the nature of the new State. The heads of these associations are to be appointed as heretofore. Interference with the activities of the associations is to be avoided except in so far as a possible incorporation into national organisations may make the observance of such regulations necessary as the terms of incorporation themselves may impose.
The members of Catholic organisations are, on account of such membership, in no wise to be put at a legal disadvantage in school or State.
The Central Government presumes that the Catholic organisations, in the case of incorporation, will obtain the agreement of their ecclesiastical authorities.

A basis had therefore been obtained. However, results were not immediately forthcoming when it came to negotiations for the application of these directions, particularly in deciding which Catholic associations came under the various groups mentioned in the Concordat. The Catholic Youth Associations did their best, on the basis of their

86 DESTRUCTION OF CATHOLIC YOUTH ASSOCIATIONS

legally secured independence, to establish tolerable relations with the State Youth organisation. The newspaper reports of the latter months of 1933 leave one astounded to see the Catholic organisations going so far in order to demonstrate their goodwill and expressing so perseveringly their confidence in the Central Government in spite of already growing trickery and opposition. It became evident soon enough that no demonstrations of loyalty to the National Socialist State were going to save them.

Only a few weeks after the signing of the Concordat the public was surprised to learn that high authorities were resolved on the breaking up of the Catholic Youth Associations and the forcing of all young people into the Hitler Youth.

Lauterbacher, the Leader of the Western Regions (and later Chief of Staff to the Reich Youth Leader), declared at Coblenz in the January of 1934, a few months after the Concordat had been signed, that " the Hitler Youth will not compromise but will go its own way, which must necessarily lead to the destruction of all other youth associations." His speech lasted nearly two hours and he outlined the principles which were to guide the Hitler Youth in its work for the coming year. He said that after their first year of commencement a year devoted to interior formation of the National Socialist spirit was to follow: that the watchword for 1934 was to be the demand for the totalitarianisation of German youth: that character formation and physical toughening of German youth was the sole purpose of the Hitler Youth: that the totalitarian idea in the Hitler Youth required the dissolution of the denominational associations.[1]

In March, 1934, at a Hitler Youth demonstration in Cologne, the Regional Leader, Wallwey, stated:

> In the faces of all those who are endeavouring to drive a wedge into the unity of German youth we shout that the youth of Germany stands solidly together and is ready to employ the most energetic measures, should it be necessary, against these traitors. . . . Here in Cologne we have inflicted an overwhelming defeat on our enemies (the denominational associations), but we shall go on with greater determination still *until every single German youth stands in our ranks*, and to any who are watching for a further opportunity to carry on their underground agitation we have but one thing to say: " Be careful."[2]

On March 27th, 1934, the Reich Youth Leader, Baldur von Schirach, stated:

> The incorporation of the Protestant Youth associations will some time or other be followed, and necessarily followed, by that of the Catholic Youth. (Loud applause.) In a time when all are abandoning their private interests, Catholic youth has no longer any right to lead a separate existence.[3]

On November 5th, 1934, occurred in a Berlin speech of the same person the remark which we have already quoted: " The way of

---
[1] *Kölnische Volkszeitung*, January 14th, 1934.
[2] *Westdeutscher Beobachter*, March 12th, 1934.
[3] *Schlesische Volkszeitung*, March 29th, 1934.

CATHOLIC YOUTH ASSOCIATIONS DOOMED

Rosenberg is the way for the German youth." The *Leipziger Neueste Nachrichten* of April 9th, 1935, quotes a speech of von Schirach's in which it is said:

> It will be decided in the coming weeks whether the Catholics will possess enough sense to give up of their own accord this cliquish and disloyal system of theirs or whether it will be necessary to use force. . . .
> And, unless the devil himself is against us, we'll succeed in compelling the Catholics just as we've compelled the hundred and one other clubs and associations.

At the beginning of June, 1935, Baldur von Schirach made a speech which was transmitted by all German broadcasting stations and in which he said:

> The youth of the country is justified in asking why precisely the leaders of the Catholic Youth movement claim a right for it, which no other Youth movement any longer demands.

The *Reichsverwaltungsblatt*, the organ of the Ministry of the Interior, discusses, in its July number, 1935, fundamental points relating to the legislation for the State-organised youth: The Hitler Youth insists on its claim to totality. The only ones to remain outside the movement were the Catholics. Their formal existence could be said to be secured by the Concordat, not so, however, their material existence, so that when the time was ripe for the final step to totality to be taken by the Hitler Youth, the Concordat would be no obstacle. Though the Concordat guaranteed the formal existence of the Catholic Youth organisations, it gave no guarantee that Catholic youth would be exempted from a general and compulsory youth service, should such an arrangement come into existence. The Church ought now to cease distinguishing between " German " and " Catholic " and recognise that no purpose was served by keeping on the Catholic Youth Associations.

On August 27th, 1935, the Bavarian Minister of Education instructed the personnel of all secondary schools to give their fullest support to the Hitler Youth, since " it aimed at embracing the entire youth of the country."

In August, 1935, Baldur von Schirach repeated again that

> The Hitler Youth would take steps against any attempts to form denominational cliques and that their aim was one great community of Germans, in which no one would be asked about his religion or social position.[1]

On September 2nd, 1935, a leaflet was distributed on the streets in Munich. It was published on the authority of the Hitler Youth leaders and branded the members of Catholic Youth Associations as being enemies of the State.

On October 13th, 1935, at Limburg on the Lahn, Baldur von Schirach again repeated:

> There is no commandment of God telling the young people of Germany to join denominational associations and to fight against Adolf Hitler, and thus against the German people.

[1] In a Hitler Youth camp near Lenggries.

88   DESTRUCTION OF CATHOLIC YOUTH ASSOCIATIONS

On January 13th, 1936, Frick, the Minister of the Interior, likewise stated (at Saarbrücken) that the Hitler Youth must embrace German youth in its entirety and that therefore the Catholic associations would be destroyed.

> As leaders of the youth of Germany, you have an immense duty and responsibility. We must, however, in order to carry out this work, establish the fact that we of the Hitler Youth, and we alone, are to be responsible. We have to establish the absolute, totalitarian claim of the National Socialist State. . . . In future, to become a civil servant of that State it will be necessary to have passed through the school of the Hitler Youth and the State Youth.

On April 19th, 1936, Baldur von Schirach again in a broadcast address:

> Youth has, of its own accord, passed by the claim of certain clerical circles to educate youth outside that great community which bears the name of the Führer. The heart of youth is seen by God alone, and when the Leader whom he has given us is loved by them and they devote themselves to a true and courageous service of him and their country, then that must be called an interior mission which has been confided to them from eternity.[1]

At the end of April, 1936, in Heilsberg, Baldur von Schirach demanded that the denominational associations should make the sacrifice of their separate existence.[2]

It is strange how this steady contradiction of the Concordat continues. One is forced to presume that behind these similar utterances some planned method of procedure lies concealed.

On October 11th, 1936, at Düsseldorf, comes the final and most important statement from Baldur von Schirach:

> Things were once different when the Führer entrusted to us, his fellow-workers, the task of uniting the people, and to me the particular task of ridding the country of the multiplicity of organisations and associations and in their place to create the one Hitler Youth.

Now these are the words of the only really competent authority in this matter, and they make it quite clear that Adolf Hitler, when he signed the solemn Concordat with the Church guaranteeing to her the protection of her associations, gave simultaneously instructions to his colleague, Baldur von Schirach, to destroy those same associations.

It is therefore clear that the intention to destroy the associations was there. How was the intention carried out? Out of consideration for the Concordat there could be no question of an immediate and open prohibition of the Catholic Youth Associations, and so the main body of the attack is delivered in an indirect way. For example, life is made difficult for them, new recruits find things made unpleasant, parents are made nervous, the risks incurred by being members become unbearable, and so on.

Official decrees were not used until public opinion had been sufficiently prepared. As early, however, as July 30th, 1933, only eight

---
[1] *Völkischer Beobachter*, April 20th, 1936.
[2] *Märkische Volkszeitung*, No. 120, April 30th, 1936.

days, that is, after the signing of the Concordat, Baldur von Schirach had forbidden the simultaneous membership of both denominational Youth associations and the Hitler Youth. The reasons for this are as follows:

> The simultaneous membership of denominational organisations on the part of the Hitler Youth leads to continual nuisances, as the denominational associations do not limit themselves to their own proper sphere of Church activities. From now on, therefore, I forbid such simultaneous membership. . . . I make express reservation to myself of the right to change this regulation, should the denominational youth organisations confine themselves to their proper sphere of activity.
>
> Signed: BALDUR V. SCHIRACH.

These reasons are wide enough to allow of further development.

On July 23rd, 1935, therefore, two years later, a general police regulation brought about the limiting of Catholic Youth activity desired by the Hitler Youth:

> All activity which is not of a purely ecclesiastical or religious nature, in particular political and various sport activities, is forbidden to denominational Youth associations even if formed for the occasion.[1]

This may well be said to have sealed the fate of the Catholic Youth organisations. All public activity was denied to them. The means of training which they had possessed for years were taken away and without them no really serious training of young people could be undertaken. One thing only was left them to do: to give a last proof of their fidelity to their ideals and to die an honourable death.

Compared with the fateful decree of July 23rd, 1935, all the other official regulations have little importance. In May, 1936, for instance, it was forbidden to undertake any journeys abroad without first informing the Reich Youth Leader; in September, 1936, it was forbidden to wear the " Christus " badge in public; in October, 1936, the penalties for contravening the regulations of July 23rd, 1935, concerning sport activities and concerning the wearing of uniforms were considerably increased. A decree of December 1st, 1936, says: " The entire youth of Germany will, outside the home and the school, receive its training, physical, mental and moral, in the Hitler Youth, for national service in the spirit of National Socialism. The training of all German youth in the Hitler Youth is entrusted to the Reich Youth Leader of the German National Socialist Workers' Party. The Youth Leader of the German Reich ranks as a supreme departmental Chief of the Reich and is responsible immediately to the Führer and Reich Chancellor."

This decree appeared to doom once and for all the Catholic Youth organisations. It was, however, only a piece of intimidation, for the Reich Youth Leader hastened to announce that, in order to safeguard the volunteer principle, the decree would not be put into execution. But there was, in fact, scarcely any need for such a decree, since

Cf. Münchener Neuste Nachrichten, No. 203, July 27th, 1935.

a beginning had already been made with the compulsory dissolution of the Catholic Youth Associations in the various dioceses.

Actually there were not very many universal decrees against the Catholic Youth Associations. When, however, one comes to the various regulations, limitations, prohibitions and penalisations of merely local effect, which were levelled against the members of the Catholic Youth organisations, it becomes impossible to count them all. It must suffice to quote only a small fraction of those we have come across.

In June, 1934, the Catholic Youth Associations in the Province of Westphalia were forbidden to march in procession or to wear uniforms. A year later, in June, 1935, the Münster Youth was forbidden to make the pilgrimage to Telgte. In the Saar area demonstrations by Catholic Youth Associations were prevented by the police. In November, 1935, the Reich Congress of Catholic Young Men's Associations was stopped by the imposition of impossible conditions. From late 1935 on, proceedings against Catholic Youth and youth leaders were extremely numerous. One Catholic young man was, for instance, punished by a fine of 150 marks for marching his Youth Group in close formation over the Opel bridge at Mainz. On this occasion the *Mainzer Anzeiger*[1] remarked: " Denominational Youth Groups have no right to go parading. The streets are reserved for the Führer's Youth." Meetings in private houses, round games played at social evenings, the singing of folk-songs and marching tunes, the casual gathering together in the reading rooms of their club-houses, guitar playing, any gathering whatsoever even in a hall belonging directly to a church—a parochial hall, for example, in which on occasions a saloon might be opened, smoking indulged in or a dance held—such things were all considered as crimes and punished again and again with severe penalties. In a number of dioceses the police or the municipal authorities, without the slightest legal right, forced the clergy or the lay leaders to hand over the membership lists of their Associations.

In 1936, in the diocese of Passau, alone among all the other societies the Catholic Young Men's Association was not allowed to do theatricals. A little later it was announced in the district of Grafenau in the same diocese that, in accordance with instructions from higher quarters, all performances, meetings, gatherings, including those held privately among a small circle, would, irrespective of the place where they were to be held, not be allowed without permission having first been obtained.

Many Catholic Youth Associations were deprived of their meeting-houses or, when gathered together in them, subjected to so much interference and annoyance that they had continually to seek for new ones.

[1] November 13th, 1935.

2. Indirect Methods—Defamation

In this campaign of destruction the most dangerous weapons the Nazis disposed of were not those of normal official procedure, but the indirect forces of propaganda, terrorisation and, above all, economic pressure on parents and children. As early as the end of 1933 a leading authority in the Catholic Youth movement rightly recognised

" that our work was in danger of being destroyed indirectly " by these and suchlike methods. He enumerated them as follows:
1. The use of every means of propaganda by the new Youth organisations.
2. Work at school and the filling up of free time.
3. Preventing teachers and employees from co-operating with us.
4. Coercion practised in workshops and offices.
5. The difficulties consequent on having a double organisation, particularly in country districts.
6. The reduction of municipal subsidies and Government grants.
7. The economic strangling of unions and associations.
8. Difficulties in the use of Youth hostels and sports fields.[1]

That was in 1933. Events subsequently showed that the position was much worse.

The Hitler Youth asserted from the beginning that the existence of the Catholic Youth organisations impeded the work of national unification. In October, 1933, the *Fanfare*[2] referred jeeringly to the leaders of Catholic Youth as " operators behind the scenes who persist in refusing to fall into place in the great national front of the new German State." About the same time a sectional leader of the Hitler Youth " Bann " 69 (Upper Moselle) issued a proclamation: "German youth, join the Hitler Youth." In this we read the following:

There are still youths and girls whom an obstinate denominationalism prevents from reading the signs of the times. . . . Those who stand apart will, in future, be unable to bring proof that they think and act as Germans. They are particularists who are out to sabotage the work of our Government when it urges the youth to co-operate in the task of building up our country afresh.

On September 30th, 1933, a priest of the church of St. Stephen in Mainz who defended the Catholic Youth organisations was accused of belonging to those enemies of the Government who were more dangerous than the Communists. Then follows the assertion that

The totalitarian State must insist on the entire control of the coming generation . . . and it will have to keep a watch on those personages going round in clerical clothes whose attitude to the idea of a national community is criminal. . . .'[3]

On November 30th, 1933, the Hitler Youth headquarters published the following in the *Münsterische Zeitung*:

Is there no desire among you that your children should receive something of the new spirit which is creating a new Germany ? Do you want your children to be blamed later on with the fact that their parents did not make them bearers of this new Germany ?

[1] *Cf. Jungführer*, 1933, Nos. 3 4, p. 158.   [2] No. 5, October, 1933.
[3] *Cf. Mainzer Warte*, September 30th, 1933.

And then an instructive remark is added for the benefit of the children themselves:

> You know now what is to be done. You are to go immediately to the depot. There is no question of going first to your parents to ask them whether they will allow you to become members of the German Youth movement. It is obvious that they can have no objection, for they love you.

In *Fanfare*, February, 1934, the same accusation is repeated:

> Away with the denominational associations . . . it is impossible to allow the denominational youth to consider itself as a State within the State, protected by agreements, and to become a new party formation in opposition to the new and growing national idea. The Hitler Youth demands, in the interests of the nation, that all denominational associations be brought within its ranks. . . .

On June 21st, 1934, the feast of St. Aloysius, Mgr. Anheier, the well-known leader of the Catholic Youth of the diocese of Trier, published a leaflet in which he defended the Catholic Youth against the accusation that they were " enemies of the State, a danger to the people and even guilty of high treason." On March 28th, 1934, the Hitler Youth published in the *Ibbenbürener Volkszeitung* a propaganda article:

> It will have to be understood that in the new German State there is room for one Youth Association only, the Hitler Youth. Nationalist Socialist ideology differs so entirely from any previous one, that only when the youth of the country has been brought up in it will the people be able to call it their own.

On September 2nd, 1935, the leaflet was distributed in Munich of which mention has already been made. It came signed from the Supreme Command of the Hitler Youth and reviled the Catholic Youth Associations as enemies of the State.

In the summer of 1935 a vile calumny was spread abroad that the Catholic Youth Associations were saturated with Bolshevism and that they made common cause with the Communists. What gave rise to this ? The assertion was that leaflets had been found in Munich in which the Communist party proposed an alliance against Fascism to the Catholic Youth. The *Berliner Morgenpost* referred to this leaflet as peculiar, and so it was, but the most peculiar thing about it was that an offer to Catholic Youth emanating from the Communists should provide sufficient excuse for calling the former enemies of the State.

The easy readiness with which the Nazis took up the accusation is seen likewise in a publication of a colleague of Rosenberg's, a certain Georg Leibbrandt, entitled *Moskaus Aufmarsch in Europa* (Moscow's Advance in Europe). One chapter bears the heading, " Youth Internationals and the Catholic Youth Associations," and in it one may read that:

> The Moscow recipe for the defence of democracy and peace is the united front of the Communists and the Catholic mass organisations, Moscow's emissaries, of course, being the leaders, and the use of all disposable

means, even bloodshed, in the fight against the enemy, to which the school must educate the children in order to bring about the world revolution. These principles are of late again, and in all candour, being made known to the world by Moscow.

This is followed by six pages of quotations from Bolshevic newspapers and periodicals concerning the alleged " united front with Catholic Youth." An essay of R. Guillot, the general secretary of the Communist Youth International, receives particular mention and is quoted as saying:

In England and the United States co-operation with Church Youth Associations and certain other Catholic Youth Associations is already realised. In France, Czecho-Slovakia and other countries a beginning has still to be made. In Catholic Youth circles the united front idea is gaining ground.

Rosenberg's colleague went to a lot of trouble to collect such quotations from Communist sources in order to create the impression that the Catholic Youth Unions had actually accepted the Communist overtures, although in fact none of them had fallen into the trap. Having gathered together six pages of quotations from the Communist side concerning their aims of co-operation with Catholics, common decency should have required that the attitude of the ecclesiastical authorities clearly and emphatically refusing and forbidding Catholic Youth to co-operate in any way with the Communists should have been mentioned, for the utterances in question could not possibly have been unknown to the Nazi writer. He was obviously more concerned to calumniate Catholic Youth than to arrive at the truth.

On April 1st, 1935, there appeared in the *Kirchlicher Anzeiger* (No. 8) for the archdiocese of Cologne certain very instructive " Corrections."

On three different days (March 22nd, 28th and 29th) it was announced over the West German broadcasting station:

1. That an Essen troop of thirty boys with their leader had transferred themselves *en bloc* to the Hitler Youth.
2. That a troop in Essen-Karnap had gone over together to the Hitler Youth.
3. That in Essen-Bocholt a troop had attacked a Hitler Youth party and seriously injured the leader, who had to be taken to a hospital.

Our investigations show that none of these announcements is correct. Concerning the incident in Essen-Bocholt we find that a guest of the Catholic Youth was, while on a fenced-in piece of parish property, attacked and thrown to the ground by a party of Hitler Youth. On his way home he was again attacked, and this time his father came to his aid and, in doing so, injured the leader of the Hitler Youth. In a broadcast speech on Sunday morning the unfortunate incident was, without regard for the actual facts, imputed to the provocation of unscrupulous denominational circles.

In public speeches the members of the Catholic Associations were constantly distinguished from the " Germans " who compose the Hitler Youth, as people without a country and deracinated or else as being good-for-nothing. In November, 1935, for instance, in an address to the Hitler Youth in Saxony, Lauterbacher, Chief of Staff to the Reich Youth Leader, said that:

> The section of German youth still outside the Hitler Youth is for the most part second-rate and there are very few of them who could be of any use to us.

The kind of vilification the Catholic Youth had to put up with can be seen from the following announcement made by the Cologne clergy and read from the pulpits on February 4th, 1934:

> In obedience to the Holy Father and in accordance with the Concordat we Catholic priests endeavour in our work in the Youth Associations to draw youth to Christ.
>
> This is called in recent articles of the *Westdeutscher Beobachter* " black treason," and " misuse of youth for obscure purposes." They say it is base intrigue, alien provocation, misuse of priestly dignity and of pulpit prerogative, of ecclesiastical authority and of the confessional.
>
> Since no other way is open to us, from the pulpit we make, before God and the congregation here assembled, a solemn denunciation and an emphatic protest.
>
> The activities of the Catholic priesthood among your youth is clear and open to you all. May God our Lord and you, the faithful gathered here, bear witness to our consciences, so that to whatever height these calumnies may be heaped, they may still fail to reach even the soles of our shoes.
>
> Nothing shall lead us from our path and we shall continue to labour that German Catholic youth may remain the youth of Christ.
>
> THE PARISH CLERGY OF COLOGNE.
>
> COLOGNE, *February 4th*, 1934.

On March 31st, 1935, according to the *Munich Catholic Parish Magazine*,[1] no less a person than Baldur von Schirach, the Reich Youth Leader, made the following statement in Essen:

> It is their jobs they are concerned about, not religion. They say they devote themselves to religious education. The only God they have any devotion to is their bellies.

But this number of the *Munich Parish Magazine*, as well as No. 14 of the *Berlin Catholic Parish Magazine*, which had, in a most moderate way, refuted the assertion, were both confiscated by the police, in spite of the protests of several bishops, including those of Fulda and Münster.

Broadcasting, too, was used in order to heap insults on the leaders of Catholic Youth. On March 22nd, 28th and 29th, 1935, statements like the following were broadcast from the West German station.[2]

> Comrades ! What, I should like to know, has sport got to do with the denominations ? Has anybody ever seen a Protestant sport or a Catholic sport ? Does anybody know precisely what Catholic physical jerks or Protestant gymnastics are like ? It is nothing but the evasive talk of those who are for ever in opposition to Germany. What they are anxious about is not religion, but their jobs. They say they are in the service of religious education—the only service they know of is their belly.

Such specimens suffice.

---

[1] No. 15, April 14th, 1935.
[2] Quoted in the *Kirchlicher Anzeiger* of the archdiocese of Cologne (No. 8, April 1st, 1935).

3. Indirect Methods—Opposition in the Schools

The schools presented to the Nazis one of the most convenient instruments for depriving the Catholic Youth Associations of their members and for adding them to the State organisation, an instrument of which the enemies of the Church did not hesitate to make full use.

On August 26th, 1935, the President of the local government of the Düsseldorf district addressed a letter to Area School inspectors and the heads of secondary schools, from which a good insight can be gained into the extensive use that was being made of the schools. From a copy of the circular which lies before us we quote the following:

> I have been forced to conclude that the teaching staffs have not interested themselves to the necessary extent in recruiting for the Hitler Youth. I call attention to the decree of August 26th, 1933 (U II C 1562), and impose the following regulations:
>
> 1. Without exception all teachers are required to bring their whole personal influence to bear on all children above the age of ten, explaining the idea of, and encouraging them to join, the Hitler Youth. Henceforth, therefore, no teacher may in any way, directly or indirectly, encourage, work for, or give financial assistance to other youth associations.
>
> In accordance with the above-mentioned decree it is a teacher's duty to see that his, or her, own children are members of the Hitler Youth and serve thus as an example for the rest.
>
> It is furthermore an offence against the ministerial decree of February 27th, 1935 (RU II G No. 882-34 K II 1), for teachers not to prevent children under the age of ten from being taken into any other groups or associations, and thus being influenced against the State Youth.
>
> 2. In every school and classroom posters are to be exhibited which effectively and vividly illustrate the necessity for unity among German youth.
>
> 3. In every classroom numerical statistics, which must be kept up to date by monthly revision, must be posted up in graph form in a prominent place, showing the number of children in the Hitler Youth.
>
> 4. Precautions are to be taken that no children in the preparatory classes are organised into any groups or associations. Parents who do not conform to this are to be sent for and informed that their behaviour is an offence against school regulations and discipline.
>
> 5. In order to accomplish the complete organisation of youth, heads of schools shall, from time to time as shall appear necessary, call the parents together and impress upon them the necessity for unity among the youth of Germany.
>
> 6. Teachers who do not show the necessary enthusiasm for this unification of youth are to be reported to me by Area School inspectors, so that disciplinary measures may be taken against them for negligence.
>
> 7. The clergy are to be informed immediately by the heads of schools that when giving religious instruction they are subject to school regulations and, in accordance with the decree mentioned above, must desist from promoting organisations other than that of the State Youth. The clergy are to make a written acknowledgment of the receipt of these instructions, which is to be preserved by head-masters in the school archives. Members of the clergy who offend against their duty as teachers will be deprived by me of the permission to teach religion.
>
> 8. I shall hold the Area School inspectors, in particular, responsible for the carrying out of these regulations. Reports addressed to me are on each occasion to contain details of progress made.

Appendix for vocational and trade schools: The foregoing circular instruction No. 1, §§ 1 and 2, Nos. 2, 3, 7, No. 5 so far as applicable and No. 6 with the additional regulation that the reports are to be brought to me in the normal course, holds for vocational and trade schools.

By Order.

(*Signed*) PREMER.

This letter was implemented by a decree of September 1st, 1935, with the title " Mustering of the Entire Teaching Personnel to Complete the Enrolment in the Hitler Youth of Every Pupil over the Age of Ten." It was published in the *Official School Gazette* for the governmental district of Düsseldorf (No. 17) and contained in a slightly briefer form all the points insisted on in the circular.

As early, however, as the beginning of the year 1935 the Catholic clergy had been forbidden to commend Catholic associations and sodalities to their pupils at religious instruction, which created no little difficulty, since recommendation of Church associations formed a part of the regular plan of instruction.[1] A little later the screw was given another turn when teachers of religion were forbidden to direct or have anything to do with Catholic Youth Associations. On June 25th, 1936, for example, a decree of the Minister of Education for the Reich says: " It is decreed that clergy admitted as teachers of religion in schools must refrain from all activity in the organisations mentioned (denominational Youth Associations) and from all commendation of the same even outside the religious instruction classes."

On the other hand, teachers were strictly enjoined to devote themselves positively to the idea of the Hitler Youth:

> To support and recruit for the Hitler Youth is a part of the work and duty of all teachers at every school and, therefore, all activity on behalf of denominational Youth Associations both inside and outside the school is forbidden. The same applies also to the clergy allowed to teach religion in the schools during their religious lessons.[2]

The same instructions were sent to each teacher in every district of Germany. They were, therefore, even when they had the most serious conscientious objections, forced to use their whole influence for the Hitler Youth propaganda.

It was, however, not only Catholic teachers who were driven in this way, but pressure was often brought to bear also on the children. In October, 1935, for example, a teacher in a town in the Rhineland told her pupils:

> Girls, I am very fond of you all as if you were my own children, and I am going to give you a piece of motherly advice. Join up in the BDM (German Girls' League). When you leave school you'll be wanting to get a boy-friend, and if you've never been in the BDM you won't get one. And then when you get married, your husband will lose his job the second they find out you haven't been a member of the BDM.

---

[1] The education committee No. 1 of the Bonn rural area sent round a circular to teachers on September 9th, 1935, calling attention to the above decree.
[2] Bavarian Ministry of Education, August 27th, 1935.

INDIRECT METHODS—OPPOSITION IN THE SCHOOLS

Another teacher tempted the boys in his class with the following promise:

Every boy who joins up in the Hitler Youth gets a new inkpot.

A head-master (and with the title of doctor) dared actually to utter the following threats against members of a Catholic Youth group:

You set of stubborn and unteachable louts, you'll come to your end on the roadside yet.

As a result of pressure of this kind exerted by the teachers, in a large number of districts whole classes enrolled in the junior section of the Hitler Youth. In one case the best boy in the class was subjected to such mental torture by his teacher trying to force him into it that the child actually became ill and got fits of screaming. Teachers did not hesitate to insult and threaten: they called Catholic youngsters " Black spawn," told the children that they would be expelled from the school, and gave dictations like the following:[1]

Hitler Youth ! Every pupil in our school above the age of ten who does not join the Junior Section or the German Girls' League by to-morrow, October 19th, 1935, will have the following remark written in his report-book on November 1st, 1935: " In spite of all efforts this pupil was, on October 19th, 1935, still not a member of the Junior Section or the German Girls' League."

In many cases the school exerted still more pressure by threatening the parents. A circular, for example, of October 17th, 1935, from the secondary schools at Ludwigshafen on the Rhine to parents of pupils contained the following:

An attitude in or out of school which would be tantamount to impeding the progress of the national effort or of the State would lead to expulsion from the school. Such an expulsion would be an absolute hindrance to entrance into any other secondary school. A boy who persists in not joining the Hitler Youth is remaining of his own will outside the great community of the youth of this country, which is the preparation for the community of the whole nation.

One case occurred in which a school made use of the local police in order to warn the parents to enrol their children in the Hitler Youth. In Munich the managements of the elementary schools received the following communication of August, 1935, from Rudolf Hess, the Representative of the Führer, and it was taken round by the teachers when they visited the parents:

Those who, acting on hints and suggestions, refuse to grant their children's wish to join the Hitler Youth show a lack of responsibility and are to be considered as enemies of the National Socialist State and its Führer. The Führer and his assistants alone, and not some religious corporation, have to answer to God for earthly destinies. . . .

(*Signed*) RUDOLF HESS.

[1] In a Catholic elementary school of Westphalia on October 18th, 1935.

Another element in this pressure was the reduction of school fees. In the circular already mentioned of September 9th, 1935, of the Education Committee of the Bonn rural area No. 1 is the remark:

> Children who unreasonably and persistently refuse to join the Hitler Youth are as far as possible to be passed over in the matter of special preferences (scholarships, free places, etc.).

A similar notice in the *Bayerischer Regierungsanzeiger* of August 11th, 1938, was also from the Ministry of Education. The fourth section runs as follows:

> Reduced school fees (including those accorded to children of the same family) may, in all State and private schools, be granted only to those who belong to the State Youth.

These regulations were published and in many cases put into practice, in spite of the fact that, on August 16th, 1935, the Minister of Education in Prussia had ruled that reductions in school fees were not to be confined, on principle, to members of the Hitler Youth.

It was, too, lawful for the Hitler Youth, but not for the Catholic Youth, to admit members under the age of ten. In August, 1935, for example, Terboven, president of the government of the Rhine province, issued an order that the severest measures were to be taken against Catholic organisations which admitted children under the age of ten, stating that the norm for procedure was not the Concordat, but the instruction of the Minister, which forbade membership of children under the age of ten in any except National Socialist groups.

4. *Indirect Methods—Economic Pressure*

Perhaps the most brutal method employed by the Nazis against Catholic youth was to make the economic existence of parents and the chances of success in life of children dependent on whether these joined the Hitler Youth, a step which necessarily entailed their leaving the Catholic Associations. The whole vileness and rottenness of Nazi methods are seen in their true light only after an examination of the innumerable cases of intimidation of defenceless parents, who for conscientious reasons would not let their children join the Hitler Youth, while all the time and hundreds of times it was cynically proclaimed that enrolment in it was voluntary.

So numerous, indeed, are the cases where the employment of officials and workmen has been made dependent on the entry of their children into the Hitler Youth that it is no exaggeration to speak of a general catastrophe for Catholic employees. We give here only a few examples.

On July 21st, 1935, the mayor of Duisburg, Ellgering, announced:

> The definite attitude of our Minister, Dr. Frick, causes me to demand that all officials, employees and workmen who are subordinate to me surrender their membership of denominational and vocational associations and see that their children leave confessional Youth organisations. . . .

INDIRECT METHODS—ECONOMIC PRESSURE

On July 23rd, 1936, Baron von Holzschuher, President of the government of Lower Bavaria and the Oberpfalz, decreed:

It is not right for officials and servants of the State to let their children enter denominationally controlled Youth organisations as long as the ecclesiastical authorities do not succeed in bringing their politically-minded clergy to adopt a positive attitude towards the State and the Führer. . . .[1]

Similarly a regulation was published on July 26th, 1935, by the mayor of Würzburg and addressed to all the departments of the municipal administration:

Recent events and the ordinances of competent leaders in Party and State have decided me to make the following regulations: The heads of all departments are responsible for handing in by August 15th the names of those officials, employees and workmen in permanent employ whose children belong to denominational Youth groups. . . . Every official, employee or workman in permanent employ is to send a written statement that his children do not, or will no longer, belong to any association of either denomination.

The consequences of such regulations are not hard to seek. State officials and people who are in receipt of a pension or annuity from the State live in fear of losing their livelihood should they refuse to conform. Nor are their fears groundless, as the following examples show.

On February 4th, 1936, the *Kölnische Zeitung* (No. 64) contained a report of a General Congress of customs officials, in the course of which State Secretary Reinhardt stated that it was not sufficient for an official to be a member of the Party, but that it was essential for him to have his children brought up according to National Socialist ideas and to entrust them cheerfully to the arrangements made by the National Socialists for youth. Coming officials would be drawn exclusively from the ranks of the Hitler Youth.

In 1935 a Catholic employee who had already done six years in the service of a certain municipality and had a family of eight young children was dismissed by the authorities. His appeal for reinstatement was refused by the Labour Commission on the grounds that, though requested on several occasions, he had refused to enrol his children in the State youth and was, therefore, politically unreliable and averse to the State.

In 1936 another urban council dismissed a foreman who had been in their employ for nine years. The Labour Commission dismissed his appeal because the appellant himself admitted that he did not encourage his son to enter the Hitler Youth, but on the contrary allowed him to remain in the Catholic Young Men's Association, and further, because persons ill disposed towards the State could not be tolerated in public services, etc.

Or again, in the spring of 1935 a town council refused to continue payment of relief to a mother because she was unwilling to withdraw her son from a Catholic Youth group.

[1] *Cf. Augsburger Anzeiger*, No. 206.

Members of the various party organisations experienced the same pressure. In 1935, for instance, an announcement of the group of H. of the National Socialist Women's Union stated:

> In accordance with a regulation of district headquarters, children of members of the Women's Union may not belong to Catholic associations. The local group leader is accordingly to be informed within one week whether your daughter has given up any such membership, as otherwise you will forfeit your membership of the Union. Attention is called to the fact that nobody who has left the Union may be received into it again. Heil Hitler!

On May 25th, 1936, the following notice, originating from the Upper Bavarian headquarters of the Reich League of Civil Servants, was circulated in Munich:

> By May 27th, 1936, all members of the League must send in information concerning the number of children they have, whether these belong to the Hitler Youth or German Girls' League, and, further, whether they attend a Government or a denominational school.
>
> *(Signed)* ERNST WILL, *Hauptvertrauensmann.*

Finally we append a questionnaire which was sent round to officials in a town of Western Germany by the NSDAP and which they were required to fill up.

QUESTIONNAIRE

Address: Name...................... Party Unit.... Cell....
Residence................................

1. Have you any children?...... If so, of what age?........
   Are they members of the Hitler Youth?...... German Girls' League?...... Junior Hitler Youth?......
   Do they belong to some other youth association?...... If so, which?................
2. Do your women dependents belong to the National Socialist Women's Union?......
3. Do you take in the National Socialist newspaper?......
   If not, why not?......................
4. Do you possess a swastika flag?......
   If not, what kind of flag do you possess?...............
5. Are you, or were you, a member of a lodge of freemasons or similar body?......
   If yes, of what lodge, for how long and with what rank, giving name and address of lodge...
   Any concealment of such membership entails expulsion from the Party in accordance with § 4.
   Stamp of the National Socialist German Workers' Party.............
   Signature ....

Even parents in independent positions and their children were not immune. Threats are repeatedly made that young people who did not join the State Youth organisations in good time would have no chance of employment later, and these threats were, unfortunately, by no means empty ones.

In September, 1935, all the pupils of the elementary and secondary schools in Munich were given propaganda leaflets of the German

Girls' League to be passed on to their parents, to whom pressure was thus applied. The children were informed:

> The statement must be filled up and no excuses made. Those who do not enrol will not be able to obtain situations later. . . . Parents who refuse will be made to regret it, etc.

Of the facts to be found in the press of the Third Reich during the second half of 1935 a few examples only are here quoted.

On May 9th, 1935:

> According to a report in the *Angriff* the East Prussian master-craftsmen have agreed with the competent authorities to accept in future as apprentices only those who belong to the Hitler Youth.[1]

A similar resolution was passed by the master-craftsmen of Bavaria on September 8th, 1935,[2] of Amberg on October 4th, 1935,[3] of Upper Bavaria on October 3rd, 1935,[4] and of the Upper Palatinate and Regensburg on October 11th, 1935.[5]

Ministerial offices followed suit.

> The Reichsminister of Finance laid it down in an ordinance of October 25th, 1935, that in public offices and works preference is to be given, in admitting apprentices, to those who are members of the Hitler Youth, or, as the case may require, the SA and the SS, and have belonged to their organisations for at least a year. The German railways also announce that these regulations will be effective in admitting apprentices and workmen.[6]

The Prussian State administration made similar regulations.[7]

On July 2nd, 1935:

> Nobody will in future be allowed to enter the teaching profession who has not been a member of the Hitler Youth or the German Girls' League from the beginning.[8]

On October 23rd, 1935:

> The teaching profession is to recruit itself mainly from graduates who were already members of the Hitler Youth or the Girls' League during their school days.[9]

On July 31st, 1935:

> The administration of a mining company in Uebach-Palenberg has added its resolution to that of the industry of the Jülich district, in accordance with which no young persons will in future be employed unless they belong to the State Youth.[10]

Similarly on August 23rd, 1935:

> The works of the I.G. Dye Manufacturers at Leverkusen, Dormagen, Elberfeld and Krefeld-Uerdingen on the Lower Rhine have decided to employ only members of the Hitler Youth and the German Labour Front.[11]

---

[1] *Germania*, No. 129.
[2] *Völkischer Beobachter*, No. 251.
[3] *Amberger Volkszeitung*, No. 229.
[4] *Münchener Tageblatt*.
[5] *Neumarkter Tageblatt*, No. 242.
[6] *Das junge Deutschland*, vol. 30, No. 1, Berlin, 1936.
[7] *Preussisches Besoldungsblatt*, 1935, p. 256.
[8] Quoted from an address of Morgenthaler, Württemberg Prime Minister, on the subject of the ideological mission of a teacher. Cf. *Regierungsanzeiger für Württemberg*, No. 75.
[9] *Völkischer Beobachter*, No. 296.
[10] *Völkischer Beobachter*, No. 212.
[11] Second morning edition of the *Frankfurter Zeitung*, No. 429.

On September 17th, 1935: Notice for Post Office messengers, the future source of Post Office officials: Candidates from the Hitler Youth will be taken in preference to all others.[1]

On October 4th, 1935:

> General roll-call of the Werdenfels Youth. The headquarters of the Hitler Youth and Girls' League for the Werdenfels area (Wellheim, Schongau and Garmisch districts) have reached an agreement with the competent authorities of the German Labour Front—farmers', master-craftsmen's and shop-keepers' leaders—whereby only members of the Hitler Youth will be given situations in future, and such as are already in employment but do not yet belong to the Hitler Youth will be caused to enrol themselves without delay.[2]

On August 9th, 1935, the Opladen Town Council decided unanimously that:

> Contracts will in future be given only to those concerns of which every single employee and apprentice is a member of one or the other National Socialist organisation.[3]

A similar resolution was taken on October 5th, 1935, by the Area Council of Siegburg and the Town Councils of Bonn, Godesberg, Beuel, Rheinbach and Mackenheim.[4]

On August 13th, 1935: Herr Haidn, Chief Departmental Leader in the Reich Agricultural Corporation, has issued instructions that measures are to be taken among the farmers to ensure that their children keep clear of the denominational Youth Associations, in order to avoid the risk of being influenced against the State under the cloak of religious activity.[5]

In the publication *Die Meisterprüfung in Frage und Antwort*[6] (The Master-craftsman's Examination in Question and Answer), the following question may be read:

> What kind of youths or girls may the master-craftsman take? Answer: Now, only members of the Hitler Youth and Girls' League.

It will have been noticed that these announcements and regulations, applying to twenty-three places or professions, all appear within the short space of six months. It was a new stage of the campaign completed.

5. *Indirect Methods—Physical Terrorisation*

For years both the State and the Party have exerted all their influence and marshalled all their means of propaganda in support of the Hitler Youth. At the same time they have heaped insult after insult on all other Youth organisations, calling them "nationless," "politically unreliable," "State enemies" and the rest, and, stifling every protest and attempt at justification on their part, held them up to the scorn of all "true Germans." It will, then, come as a surprise to no one that the State Youth, taking its cue from its leaders, went so

---

[1] *Völkischer Beobachter*.
[2] *Völkischer Beobachter*, No. 277.
[3] *Völkischer Beobachter*, No. 221.
[4] *Völkischer Beobachter*, No. 278.
[5] *Völkischer Beobachter*, No. 225.
[6] Published by Lindel, 24, Rumfordstrasse, Munich.

INDIRECT METHODS—PHYSICAL TERRORISATION

far as physical violence. The attacks on Catholic Youth under official covering in the Press, the charges made in public speeches at meetings and in broadcast addresses, the outlawing of Catholic Youth in school and business necessarily stirred up the Hitler Youth to seek tangible expression for its contempt, and at the same time it knew that the authorities would, if not support, then at least silently condone its deeds.

In official reports certain characteristics about these bodily attacks appear with an almost unfailing regularity:

(1) They are spoken of as " spontaneous expressions of popular indignation." In reality the youths—often brought in from other places—are instigated to commit the excesses, while the poor people of the locality are disgusted witnesses and indignant, not at the actions of the Catholic youths, but at their helplessness. The spontaneity of the attacks is such that they only succeed when they have been prepared several days beforehand and outsiders in civilian clothes brought in from other places, etc.

(2) The attitude of the authorities has but the mere appearance of conforming to proper legal standards. In actual fact the police always arrive upon the scene too late, hardly ever arrest the miscreants and at best conduct a sham investigation.

(3) The net result is always the same: intimidation of Catholic youth and of the Catholic section of the population. Into the bargain, those who have been attacked and mishandled are penalised, mostly by the dissolution of their associations.

A few examples only are here quoted:

On February 4th, 1934, a protest of the clergy of Cologne was read out which complained of the ill-treatment and mobbing of Catholic youth in the following terms:

> With righteous indignation we have learnt that last Sunday the Catholic young men who had assembled for services in the various churches were provoked and ill-treated by other youths in a disgusting way before the very doors of the churches.
>
> With righteous indignation we experienced last Sunday that in several parts of Cologne, at St. Agnes', the Holy Apostles', St. Ursula's and in Zollstock, there was no respect even for the holiness of the House of God; that in a number of places there was no respect even for the holy name of Christ, for in prominent, even holy, places could be read: " Chi Rho " (XP) —*i.e.*, the initials of Christ's name—" be cursed."
>
> With righteous indignation we heard young Catholics and their priests abused in ribald songs.
>
> Reports differing from the above are incorrect. We learn that large numbers of our Protestant fellow-Christians and of the National Socialists themselves are disgusted.
>
> Catholic Youth, we thank you and your leaders for all the fidelity you have been showing towards us.
>
> Catholic parents ! Be mindful of the warning of the Holy Father and send your children to the Catholic associations: Go to Christ. . . .
>
> COLOGNE, *February 4th*, 1934. THE PARISH CLERGY OF COLOGNE.

From March 24th to April 7th, 1935, the Hitler Youth of the Ruhr and Lower Rhine region launched a spring campaign with the objective " to convince the remaining decently-minded German boys that they should join up in the Hitler Youth." The facts show that this offensive was directed almost entirely against the Catholic Youth Associations and that it led to many excesses.

But it was necessary to cover their brutal proceedings with some appearance of legality, and so the Hitler Youth spread reports that the Catholic Youth was responsible for a number of provocative incidents. On April 3rd, 1935, for instance, the *Rheinische Landeszeitung* wrote:

> The Catholic youth groups have allowed their fanaticism to carry them beyond all bounds. They are guilty of innumerable acts of wanton destruction and, in order to throw the suspicion on us, they have daubed deliberately distorted versions of our propaganda slogans over houses and whole streets. They are giving every kind of provocation. Pictures of the Führer have been torn down, swastika flags and Hitler Youth signs pulled down and destroyed. Such methods, however, bring their own retribution.

The suspicions cast in this article were vague and general and the leader of the Catholic Young Men's Associations asked the regional Hitler Youth headquarters to furnish proofs: names, witnesses, places. No answer was ever received.

On March 31st, 1935, the *National Zeitung*, of Essen, published an article under the heading " Those who oppose the Hitler Youth oppose the State." In it is stated:

> In Mülheim-Styrum members of Catholic Youth groups painted in prominent colours on a fence the words: " We've no more need of Hitler !" Similarly the Essen headquarters of the Hitler Youth were sent a leaflet containing the words: " We stand by our pastors, our parents and the Centre Party. The members of the Catholic Youth."

The Catholic Young Men's Association of Mülheim-Styrum accordingly wrote to the *National Zeitung* on April 2nd, 1935, a letter in which the following comments were made:

> It is to be very much regretted that your newspaper considers the Catholic Youth groups capable of this sort of hooliganism. At all events we should be very obliged to you if you would inform us where the statement was painted, for so far we have failed to find it. Even if, however, anything of it still be in evidence, there should be produced, too, witnesses who could prove that the Catholic Youth groups are responsible for it. Such steps as these are necessary to clear the matter up.

Again, no answer to this letter was ever received.

The kind of assaults and excesses to which the Hitler Youth lent themselves in the course of their offensive may be shown by the following selection, which, for brevity's sake, is given in précis style:

Between March 26th and April 1st, 1935, in Essen-Altendorf, Catholic youths were assaulted and seriously injured on many occasions, some beaten till unconscious; property also damaged and cases of arson. Speech of Reich Youth Leader, also wireless and press, misrepresent facts.

On March 30th, 1935, in Essen-West, a group of Hitler Youth, some drunk, armed with heavy truncheons and life-preservers, assault and

The Police Station at Essen during the Campaign of Violence carried on by the Hitler Youth against the Catholic Youth Associations.

"The police stands by the Hitler Youth."

THE VATICAN SOLVES THE RACIAL QUESTION.

INDIRECT METHODS—PHYSICAL TERRORISATION 105

inflict head and face wounds on a Catholic young man: medical treatment necessary.

On February 28th, 1935, in Limburg, about ten members of Hitler Youth assault two Catholic youths in most brutal fashion and inflict serious injuries. Vomiting, violent headaches, heart trouble indicate serious concussion of the brain. Condition grew worse. Taken to hospital: cerebral hæmorrhage. Middle of April: still in hospital. Medical opinion estimated four to six months for complete recovery. Police inspector in charge of investigation remarked: " We, too, used to have fights now and again when we were boys." The affair is deliberately minimised as if only a boyish quarrel. As result of the assault incapable of work for six months; attacks of dizziness render resumption of employment as electrical engineer impossible; and yet the public prosecutor for Limburg, in spite of all this, breaks off further investigation on account of " the trivial nature of the affair."

The attitude of the police during this offensive is particularly interesting, for a large poster was exhibited during it on the façade of the police headquarters in Essen, decorated with the coats-of-arms of both police and Hitler Youth and the words: " The police stand by the Hitler Youth."

This poster shows the true attitude of the police during the offensive. Of all the cases of assault, violence, battery, arson, insult, disturbance of the peace, damage to property, robbery and theft, not one is known where the culprits, though recognised, were brought to justice or, if unknown, have been identified through the efforts of the police.

In most cases the injured party took out a summons, but usually the proceedings were broken off " on account of the trivial nature of the case " or because the members of the Hitler Youth " were to be punished by disciplinary measures." In no instance among all the cases mentioned are the public prosecutors known to have filed a petition in the courts, though members of Catholic associations were arrested and taken into " protective custody " for the sole reason that they had defended themselves in the attacks.

At Easter, 1935, a pilgrimage of Catholic young men returned from Rome and was subjected to disgusting and malicious treatment at the German frontier. The German News Agency, however, did its best to represent the affair in as harmless a light as possible. It reported that " all that had taken place was a search for uniforms and other articles of equipment in order to ascertain whether any contravention of the regulations against wearing uniforms was taking place. One youth was held in custody by the police for two hours on account of rude behaviour, but afterwards released, so that he and his group were able to proceed on their journey according to plan."[1] A similar denial was issued by the German *Diplomatische Korrespondenz*. It was said that articles appearing in the *Osservatore Romano* and other foreign newspapers were obviously aiming at " establishing a causal connection between the pilgrimage to Rome and the alleged

[1] *Cf. Germania*, No. 125, May 5th, 1935.

appalling treatment of the young Catholics; in other words, they sought to create the impression that in Germany a manifestation of religious feeling brought with it a sequel like this." It was added that this was untrue, and official investigations showed the affair in question to have consisted merely of a search for uniforms and other articles of equipment.[1]

The " search for uniforms " was in reality as follows: Sixty out of sixty-one buses (one was missed " through error ") carrying 1,705 pilgrims were held up for as much as seven hours in pouring rain on the frontier at Constance, Singen, Waldshut, Erzingen, Oterbach and Munich between April 26th and 29th. They were thoroughly searched by Customs officials, who on the whole behaved well, and by SS-men and Secret Police, who were discourteous and insulting. Duty had to be paid on even such little things as the medal each pilgrim had received from the Holy Father. Everything that in the slightest resembled " equipment " or belonged to an " organisation "—including violins, tents, banners, etc., to the value of some sixty or seventy thousand marks—was confiscated, and what was not confiscated was thrown on the floor for the pilgrims to collect. And all this to the accompaniment of threats: " They ought to have their lives thrashed out of them and be sent to a concentration camp. Cutting their throats would be the best thing "; and insults: " So this lot are papists, the blokes who stabbed Germany in the back in 1918." When it was over, and all their tents, tarpaulins, even their knives and forks had been taken, they were allowed to continue their journey, with all their bedding sodden, nowhere to sleep and nothing with which to eat. Yet some of them had still three days and nights before they would reach home.

This " search for uniforms " was carried out, according to the Secret Police, because of " orders from superiors: ordinance of the Reichsminister of the Interior." It is true enough that in April, 1935, there was a regulation, based, be it noted, on Hindenburg's decree against the Communists, which forbade denominational Youth Organisations to adopt any uniformity of dress or to go about in close formation. At all events, such regulations were only local and by no means in force throughout the whole Reich, still less did they apply abroad, and it was precisely in the territory of Baden, where no such regulations against uniforms existed at the time, that this frontier incident took place. At that time, too, the obligation did not exist of procuring permission to arrange pilgrimages, even though they went outside the country.

These events were followed not quite two months later by an outrageous assault on Catholic Youth in Cologne by members of the SA and the Hitler Youth. On June 16th, 1935, a solemn service for Catholic Youth took place in the Cathedral. Eye-witnesses and those actually present at the service have declared themselves willing to assert under oath the veracity of the following statements:

While the service in the Cathedral was proceeding, increasing numbers of Hitler Youth began to gather in the space between the Cathedral and the

[1] *Cf. Germania*, May 11th, 1935.

central railway-station, some of whom, when interrogated later, stated that they had been expressly ordered to go there. Round the crowded Cathedral approach the illustrated Hitler Youth newspaper, the *Fanfare*, was ostentatiously offered for sale. Insulting slogans about the black criminals and phrases such as " Down with the parsons " were shouted by organised choruses, so that the service inside was disturbed and the crowd outside angered, and it started singing the Te Deum in German by way of reply. It would have been perfectly easy for the police to have dispersed the Hitler Youth, but they remained entirely passive. Many members of the congregation leaving the Cathedral after the service were assaulted by the Hitler Youth. Catholic youths who, on being assailed, shouted for the police were taken off in custody, while the Hitler Youth was allowed to go on with its hooliganism undisturbed as its numbers steadily increased. The congregation leaving the Cathedral were yelled at in chorus, and even those who had no part at all in the proceedings were interfered with. The Hitler Youth, and one SA-man with them, went on with their assaults while the police looked on, even while women and girls were struck. As the Hitler Youth made a rush on the banners, which were furled according to the regulations, these were taken back into the Cathedral. The Hitler Youth remained in front of the Cathedral until ten in the evening without being interfered with by the police.

The whole demonstration on the part of the Catholics was purely religious and took place within the walls of the church. The chief instigators among the Hitler Youth were regional leaders and suchlike, who were in many cases recognised and whose names were ascertained. The entire affair was witnessed by foreigners.

Three weeks later the following occurred in Rheingönnheim in the diocese of Speyer. The parish priest exhibited a poster inviting all young Catholics, whether members of associations or not, to a church service. On July 8th, 1935, members of the SA and SS, nearly all strangers to the district, gathered in a public square. They came, according to their instructions, in civilian clothes. Only the representative of the local leader and perhaps two others actually came from the district. A speech was made in which it was said that the parish priest was a disturber of the religious peace. They then marched to the church, and found the parish priest not at home. One of the churchwardens, a layman, was struck and injured. An attempt was made to break into the presbytery. Only the little parish hall could be got into, and here everything was wrecked. The church was then entered in order to hunt for the supposed hiding-place of the priest. The housekeeper in the meantime had phoned for the police and asked for a flying squad to be sent. It was answered that the request would be passed on. When a second request was made, the answer was: " We are not authorised to interfere." When all was nearly over, the flying squad arrived and remained at first inactive in front of the Mayor's offices, but afterwards arrested some Catholic young men who had dared to ring the church bells. The diocesan authorities of Speyer complained and demanded the punishment of those responsible. Not the slightest result was achieved.

There was a host of other incidents, too, as at Maising on July 14th, 1935, when some Catholic young men were assaulted in a youth hostel, and particularly in Berlin during July and August of the same year, where windows[1] were broken, insulting remarks daubed over walls and pavement,[2] attacks made on individuals or small groups,[3] and bands of Hitler Youth howled their notorious Currency ditty outside churches and parish halls,[4] while the police did nothing at all. At the end of January, 1936, members of the Hitler Youth broke into an old railway coach which had been converted into a Youth centre by the Catholic Young Men's Association of München-Sendling, stole some articles, upset all the Mass arrangements and desecrated a crucifix.[5]

It is, therefore, clear that there was no exaggeration when in May, 1936, in their Joint Pastoral Letter to Catholic Youth, the German bishops declared:

> Many of you have risked property, future, university career, employment, even loss of life and liberty; and you have made an offering of it to God, truly not merely for some association or pastime, but out of fidelity to your motto: " For the kingdom of Christ in the new Germany."

6. *The Result*: *the Dissolution of the Catholic Youth Associations*

The purpose at which all these activities which have just been described were aimed was, of course, attained. Wherever it appeared to the Nazis that public opinion had been sufficiently prepared, ruthless action was at once taken to dissolve the Catholic associations, and since 1939 the Associations of Catholic Youth in Germany have ceased to exist. Here and there an odd one may possibly be found, and one or two local groups, perhaps, may lead a precarious existence; but their doom is sealed, and the Nazis know quite well that, as long as any kind of connection between these remnants and any public appearances are prevented, they are incapable of exercising any influence worth mentioning.

The associations which, one after another, have been forbidden in the past few years can now be enumerated, but mention must first be made of a document of the year 1934 which probably is unique in modern history. It is the order of a Nazi Area Leader who declared on his own authority that the Concordat, which is a treaty between two sovereign States, was in his area null and void. It was published in *Mainfränkische Zeitung* and addressed to all Mayors, local and assistant leaders of the Schweinfurt administration area.

> 1. In accordance with the district order of April 25th, 1934, all Catholic Youth and Young Men's Associations are forthwith forbidden in the interests of public peace and order and for the protection of the State and its citizens.
> 2. The above order renders void the protection granted with reservations to the said associations under the terms of Article 31 of the Reich Concordat of July 20th, 1933, between the Holy See and the German Reich.
> 3. The prohibition extends to all registered and non-registered Catholic associations, and any bodies resembling such associations, which are

---

[1] St. Matthias' presbytery, August 17th.   Parish hall of same, August 23rd.
[2] St. Matthias, beginning of July and July 13th.
[3] August 16th, August 23rd.   [4] July 22nd-24th; August 11th.
[5] In this case, by way of an exception, the police acted promptly

DISSOLUTION

devoted to the care of youth. Associations which according to their constitutions concern themselves with the purely religious training of youth are likewise included.

4. It is the duty of political leaders to order the presidents of such associations to proceed to an immediate dissolution. This means that meetings of any kind whatsoever, whether in meeting-rooms or private houses, and any further relations between the former members, even of a social nature, including also the common subscription to and discussion of newspapers and periodicals of whatever kind, are forbidden. The movable property of the associations is to be transferred to the possession of the political leaders unless it can be proved that such property belongs to the Church or parish.

In the case of any disturbances during the execution of the order, especially of resistance on the part of the clergy or the leaders of the associations, area headquarters are to be informed without delay, which will, in conjunction with the political police, take the most energetic and immediate action should any opposition to the dissolution of the associations be made by their leaders or members or any third party.

(*Signed*) WEIDLING, *Area Leader.*
(*Signed*) ROHRBACHER, *Area Chargé d'Affaires*

SCHWEINFURT, *April 25th, 1934.*

1935. In April a decree of the Minister of Education in Württemberg forbade all children of school age to belong to the Associations of the Holy Childhood and the Guardian Angels, with the consequence that these two purely religious associations ceased to exist in that territory.

In May the police forbade the Catholic scouts and the *Neudeutschland* association of secondary school pupils in the town of Ulm.

On July 23rd came the prohibition and dissolution in the territory of Baden of the sport association for Catholic Youth known as *Deutsche Jugendkraft*. About the same time all Catholic Young Men's Associations in Württemberg were dissolved and their property confiscated.

In November the local section of St. George's scouts at Hausach in the territory of Baden was dissolved.

In December, the so-called " Youth House " in Düsseldorf, the headquarters of the Catholic Young Men's Association, was closed and sealed. The greater part of the personnel, the clerical and lay organisers, were arrested. The publications of the house, particularly *Michael*, with its circulation of 300,000, were forbidden until further notice. After some time *Michael* was allowed to resume publication and the " Youth House " permitted to resume its activities.

1936. The following were closed down: The training centres of the Catholic Young Men's Association, the national training centre of *Deutsche Jugendkraft* built in 1925 at Münster in Westphalia, and also the training centre for leaders which this last association possessed in Altenberg.

1937. The Catholic Young Men's Association in the dioceses of Münster, Breslau and Paderborn was dissolved and its property confiscated. In November of the same year the same Association was forbidden in the diocese of Trier. In the summer the *Neudeutschland*

League, together with its senior branch, was dissolved in the territory of Württemberg and its property confiscated. In October of the same year the same league was dissolved in Silesia; in December in the diocese of Limburg.

1938. The mortality among the associations assumed large proportions. On January 20th, the Catholic Young Men's Association with all its kindred organisations, the Catholic Young Women's Associations and the *Neudeutschland* League were dissolved in the diocese of Speyer and the eight Bavarian dioceses and their property confiscated. In the course of the year the same Association was dissolved in the archdiocese of Cologne and the diocese of Aachen. One of the publications of the " Youth House " in Düsseldorf mentioned above, *Die Wacht*, was suppressed. In addition, as early as March, 1938, a general prohibition of associations in Austria dissolved nearly all the Catholic Youth organisations.

1939. The Catholic Young Men's Associations and sodalities in the diocese of Osnabrück were dissolved. In February, the " Youth House " in Düsseldorf, the headquarters of the Young Men's Association, was finally closed. The training centre for leaders at Altenberg, the property of the Catholic Young Men's Association, was given over to the Rhineland Youth Hostels' Association. In the same month the Catholic Young Men's Associations of the archdiocese of Freiburg were suppressed and their property confiscated. In March the Austrian school children were forbidden to belong to any association whatsoever other then those of the National Socialists, which was a serious blow to the Holy Childhood Association. In the summer came the closing of the magnificently organised headquarters of the association of Young Women's Sodalities, the *Bundeshaus* (League House), in the Prinz-Georg-Strasse at Düsseldorf, and the consequent cessation of the high-class and widely read periodicals edited from it.

Survey of the Measures taken in the Territory of Baden up to the Beginning of 1938 *according to the Report published by Archdiocesan Authorities at Freiburg.*

Since the revolution of 1933 the difficulties of Church associations have increased steadily until by the end of 1937 the Youths' and Girls' organisations in Baden were completely paralysed.

In summer, 1934, the Catholic People's Association was suppressed by the police and its property confiscated, which affected some 450 societies with 30,000 members. The Guilds organised by the Church formed the secondary objective of the campaign of destruction. The fight against the Catholic Youth Associations was the most bitter. On July 23rd, 1935, contrary to the terms of Article 31 of the Reich Concordat an order extending to the whole Reich forbade the denominational Youth Associations to indulge in " any activity not of a purely ecclesiastical or religious character, particularly in the nature of politics, sport or drill, or in the organising of holiday camps." The wearing of uniforms and badges and the carrying of banners was likewise prohibited. The execution of this decree occasioned many interventions by the public authorities and the members of the State Youth, fines and even arrests. On July 23rd, 1935, the *Deutsche Jugendkraft* (the Catholic Athletic Association) was suppressed by the police in the territory of Baden, and on August 24th, 1935, it was suppressed throughout the Reich and its property confiscated. The suppression was preceded by a number of unpleasant incidents.

A decree dated July 29th, 1935, of the district headquarters of the Party—Baden district—forbade the children of officials to belong to denominational associations and instructed all party centres in the region to implement the order.

As a result of this pressure from all sides the Catholic Young Men's Association in the archdiocese, which formerly contained some 14,000 members in 338 societies, is greatly reduced in numbers.

The persecution of the Church Youth organisations has particularly affected *Neudeutschland* (Catholic Secondary-school Pupils' League), which numbered, in 1933, 52 groups with about 1,950 members. The president of the government in Sigmaringen dissolved the groups in Hohenzollern in 1937.

The girls' associations, however, have been able to continue their main activities, and the same can be said with even more truth of the Christian Mothers' Societies, which, in 1933, numbered 591 with 84,800 members.

The arrangement and pursuit of Church associations' activities were made very difficult by the prohibitions of 1935: the prohibition of activities of a purely secular nature, the obligation of obtaining approval for public meetings, the prohibition of organised hiking, the limitations of the theatre law and the cinema law.

7. *Post Mortem*

That these measures were intended to constitute part of a downright persecution of the Church was the firm conviction of the German bishops.

In November, 1937, the Bishop of Münster, Mgr. Count von Galen, in the course of a sermon protested against the dissolution of the Catholic Youth Association in the following courageous terms:

If we are misunderstood and abused by our own fellow-countrymen, even by representatives of the secular power, if we are forced to submit to treatment which we feel is bitterly unfair—that was the lot of Christ, and let us say with Him: " Father, forgive them, for they know not what they do."

I am fully convinced that many of them do **not** know what they do. They have no idea of the extent of their misunderstanding. They are blinded by prejudice, led into error by misrepresentation, and hence wrong the Church of Christ, the Holy Father, and the bishops, priests and the laity. They do not realise the extent to which they are injuring our people and our country when they refuse to the truth and teaching of Christ a way to the ears and hearts of the people, especially of the young.

On October 29th the Münster Diocesan Organisation of the Catholic Young Men's Association was dissolved. No intimation was first given of any illegalities. There was no possibility of defence or of going to court. According to the secret police order, not only is the Diocesan Organisation itself suppressed but also, it would appear, all affiliated parish societies for youths, even the sodalities of Our Lady, which can look back on many years of life, often even before the foundation of the Diocesan Organisation, and their property, including the dedicated church banners, has been confiscated. A decree of February 28th, 1933, of the late President Hindenburg, designed to meet Communist activities, is invoked in order to destroy Catholic associations. It is a perverse and wanton insult to German Catholics and their priests and bishops. It is a flagrant injustice to the leaders and members of our Youth Associations, who with untiring selflessness have successfully aimed at one thing only: to lead the youth of Germany to fidelity to Christ and to love of their Fatherland, to a sense of duty and common endeavour for the well-being of our fellow-countrymen. I have sent a telegram to the Führer and Reich Chancellor informing him of the dissolution of our Young Men's Societies and begging him to cancel the order of the Secret Police.

In the beginning of 1938 the same event caused the Bavarian bishops to publish the following Pastoral Letter:

DEARLY BELOVED,
The Catholic Young Men's Association and all its affiliated societies, the girls' sodalities of Our Lady, and the *Neudeutschland* league have been dissolved by an order of the Secret Police of January 20th, 1938, any further activity on their part forbidden and their property confiscated. . . .

The bishops then recall some of the acts of violence that had accompanied the suppression of the associations and protest against their being put on a level with Communist societies, when they had, in fact, been the backbone of the defence against Communism. They go on:

Our Catholic Young Men's and Young Women's Associations have been true to their principles and sought to labour for the well-being of the country, as numbers of you who took part in the May Day celebrations in 1933 will remember. Soon, however, the fight against the Church and her associations commenced. First simultaneous membership was prohibited. Then came the decree concerning the secularisation of public life; after that the restriction of the Catholic associations to the church and places immediately adjacent and the prohibition of any but purely religious activity. Then, because the associations still lived on, they were dissolved by the police. . . .
Article 31 of the Reich Concordat is a complete acknowledgment by Germany of the Catholic Church's juridical conception by which Church Associations as such are subordinate to ecclesiastical authority. By virtue, therefore, of our full spiritual authority and by virtue of the rights acknowledged in the Reich Concordat, we bishops declare: The Young Women's Sodalities of the Blessed Virgin Mary are neither dissolved nor forbidden within the area of our ecclesiastical jurisdiction. Ecclesiastically they continue in their full existence with all ecclesiastical rights, and with the favours and indulgences granted to them by our Holy Church which no power on earth can take away. . . .

The Pastoral ends with words of congratulation on the steadfastness of the faithful in so many trials and of encouragement, and exhorts all to stand firm and be constant in their reception of the Sacraments and their attendance at the services of the Church.

Two characteristics of this whole campaign against the Catholic Youth Associations stand out—its cunning and its ruthlessness.

It was, for example, cunning to have sought and signed the Reich Concordat in 1933 and, with that as a kind of alibi, to have set Catholic fears for their organisations and anxieties for their Youth at rest. Yet in 1936 it was let out that the Führer and Reich Chancellor had no sooner pledged himself to preserve the Catholic Youth Associations than he gave orders for their destruction.

It was cunning to have resorted so little to general direct prohibitions, but petty district regulations and local trickery could be so intensified as to lead to the same result, and indeed they were to be preferred for they made less of an impression. What in one diocese, province or district appeared as a severe persecution was either not found at all or only in a very modified form in the neighbouring one, and so general opinion could never crystallise. Meanwhile threats and warnings from the mouths of the highest officials kept parents nervous and confused the juridical issue, and yet, because the campaign was spread over so many years, left the hope that a solution acceptable to all might be reached, with the result that the innocent, who, as always, desired to avoid open conflict, were for ever dissuaded from marshalling all their forces of resistance.

It was cunning always to have found reasons, however trivial or trite, for the suppression and dissolution of the individual associations. If need be, the fact that three or four of its members had a game of football together or sang some song that was not a hymn sufficed to dissolve an association.

It was cunning, when a regulation had been imposed, to moderate it, or rescind it for a short time, only to renew it later in a more rigorous form. For example: In summer, 1933, Catholic Youth Associations were forbidden to wear uniforms in the Münster region of Westphalia; on September 1st, 1933, the order was rescinded, but in June, 1934, it was re-enacted in a more severe form together with a regulation against marching in formation in the streets. Or again, one year after the promulgation of the decisive decree of June 29th, 1935, a notice appeared in a number of newspapers that Göring, the Prime Minister for Prussia, had abolished it by a measure which was to take effect immediately. But the police continued to enforce the decree. Again, in November, 1935, the opinion was general that the end of the great Catholic Youth Organisation, the Catholic Young Men's Association, had come, because the " Youth House " in Düsseldorf had been occupied; but again this was only a temporary measure and a few weeks later the house was restored.

So, too, the meaning and scope of the decrees and prohibitions was deliberately left uncertain. When, for instance, it came to the interpretation of the expression " popular sport " (*Volkssport*) it was found to cover every kind of sport and athletic activity. Or again, denominational Youth Associations must confine themselves to what is " of a purely ecclesiastical or religious nature." But every pilgrimage is prohibited, every organised appearance in processions is prohibited, meetings for religious discussions are prohibited; in fact, any and every gathering outside the four walls of the church is prohibited.

The second characteristic of ruthlessness is to be found not so much in the fact that everything was destroyed, as in the way in which this destruction was carried out slowly and without any regard for the people's sense of justice and decency. On the one hand the young men of the Catholic Associations, one of the finest types of German youth, were expected to honour the State as a legal institution, while on the other the most solemn engagements were disregarded and they themselves treated as enemies and insulted. It was time and time again proclaimed by its official leaders that entry into the Hitler Youth was purely voluntary, and yet Catholic young men were persecuted and terrorised by the State-supported youth organisations till they joined, and Catholic parents, particularly civil servants, in hundreds of thousands were threatened with dismissal unless they made their children join, no regard being paid to the agonies of conscience that this step entailed in good Christian people.

The " Germans " of today are for ever prating of " German strength," " German heroism," " German ways," but little indeed of anything truly German can be found in those who carried out this slow murder of the Catholic Youth Associations. Such men don't know what it is to meet an adversary in fair and chivalrous battle; but one thing comes easily to them—the cowardly overwhelming of the defenceless.

CHAPTER IV

THE CHURCH IS EXCLUDED FROM THE WORK OF EDUCATION: II. THE DESTRUCTION OF THE CATHOLIC SECONDARY SCHOOLS

1. *The Aim from the Beginning*

WE have already indicated that in the attack on this position, which is probably the most significant and strategically important of all, we are dealing with a thoroughly well thought-out plan of campaign on the part of the Nazis.

From the very beginning, this campaign, as is proved by numerous utterances of official personages, had a definite aim clearly in view, which was the conversion of the Catholic schools into so-called "German Community Schools," entirely devoted to the interests of the National Socialist State. The school struggle in Munich in 1935 provided a sort of preliminary trial of strength in which the German community schools came off best; thereafter the Party concentrated all its resources on preparing public opinion for its large-scale offensive against the denominational schools.

In the actual onslaught on the Christian schools, we are able to distinguish, as it were, three different forms of offensive action which for the most part followed one another step by step, but which were also employed to a certain extent simultaneously—namely, (i) the destruction of the specifically Christian character of the denominational schools (removal of crucifixes from classrooms, etc.); (ii) elimination of teachers belonging to Religious Orders or Congregations; (iii) final conversion of denominational schools into NS (National Socialist) community schools.

We gain a specially clear insight into the whole spirit of National Socialism in this matter when we reflect that the Nazi State has shown that it is not even satisfied with the attainment of its aim of the introduction everywhere of the community school. It goes further by systematically working for the complete banishment of Christian religious instruction from the schools and the introduction of an outspokenly anti-Christian spirit, through suitable arrangement of the instruction given and the careful formation of a National Socialist teaching body.

Even before it took control of the State, the attitude of National Socialism to the school question was characteristic and significant. In all the meetings and discussions of the various regional congresses of the Party, it was never possible to elicit from any of the Nazi Reichstag deputies a clear statement in favour of the denominational schools; and this in spite of the fact that such a statement would undoubtedly have had considerable propaganda value for the Movement. So, for example, the *Kölnische Volkszeitung* wrote, in connection with the discussion on culture held on June 23rd and 24th, 1932:

> The Centre Party " asked the National Socialists a very precise question: Is ' Christian ' religious instruction to be understood as meaning denominational teaching—*i.e.*, Catholic, Protestant, etc.—or is this ' Christian ' instruction to be given on an undenominational basis which takes no cognisance of denominational distinctions ? In other words, does ' Christian ' school denote, or at least include, ' denominational ' school, or does it not ? Both questions, although they were asked on two occasions, remained *unanswered*. When the Centre Party's speaker drew express attention to this at the end of the discussion, the brusque retort was given: We have no intention of answering your question. You have already got to know far too much, without that."[1]

That was clear enough in all conscience !

The assumption of power by the Party followed, and with it, characteristically, a number of express and solemn assurances that the denominational schools would be maintained. Adolf Hitler pledged his word thereto for the first time in the Reichstag speech which he delivered on the occasion of voting the so-called " Authorisation Law"; and for the second time—in even more solemn fashion—when, three months later, he wrote his signature to the Concordat, in which Article 23 begins with the words: " The retention of Catholic denominational schools, and the establishment of new ones, are guaranteed."

Thereafter, in general, silence reigned over the school question until 1936, when with all publicity the " German Community School " was demanded, and public opinion assiduously influenced in this sense, though it is true that even before this there had been no lack of threatening signs. Dr. Rust, for example, the Minister of Education, in his speech at the dedication of a Teachers' College in Lauenberg (Pomerania), said:

> Our German schools have been teaching the individual for his own sake, and not for that of the nation. This is the decisive direction which the German school has to take today. . . . In the sphere of cultural education, the national State can brook no exceptions and indulge no special whims.

Meanwhile, in professional teaching circles, whenever the " coming school reforms " were discussed, the intention of capturing the school completely for the Nazi ideology and the Movement made itself clearly evident.[2]

In the year 1935, when the tendency became even more evident; Cardinal Faulhaber felt compelled to make a public protest against the propaganda for the community school.[3] One of the most tireless

---
[1] *Cf. Köln. Volksztg.*, No. 186, of July 6th, 1932.
[2] *Cf.* the basic principles of school reform propounded by Prof. Krieck in *Preuss. Lehrerztg*, November 3rd, 1934.
[3] *E.g.*, in his sermon on the anniversary of the Pope's Coronation, in St. Michael's Church, Munich.

protagonists in the campaign, Chief Urban School Inspector Bauer, gave answer to the effect that a too frequent or a too long-enduring intermixing of religious and temporal affairs could only lead to a profanation of holy things and applied to the denominational school question the words of the Führer: " Forget everything, your position, your profession, your ancestry, forget your religious persuasion and your education; one thing alone you must never forget: **Germany.**" On another occasion he declared that the application of the slogan " One People, One Reich, One Law " ought not to stop short of the school. Indeed, the slogan itself ought to have a fourth demand added to it: " One School. . . ." Nor is National Socialism in any way disconcerted if appeal is made to the rights of parents; the rights of the community stand higher than those of the parents.[1]

Little straws show which way the wind is blowing. The national-political camps and instructional courses, for example, for boys and girls from the secondary schools were always so arranged that children of the various denominations were mixed together. Or again, the fact that it contained a quotation from an episcopal utterance in favour of the denominational schools sufficed for the suppression in 1935 of the Catholic Parents' Calendar.

From 1936, attacks on the denominational schools from official quarters were multiplied. At the beginning of October, 1936, the German News Agency distributed an article in which it was maintained that the denominational school disturbed the community and destroyed the unity of the nation.

It is the task both of the State and the Party to ensure that the present unity of the nation is also made secure for the future by means of the uniform school. The denominational schools give us only conditional assurance on this point, or even no assurance at all.

The Bishop of Münster took this point up at once, in a declaration published in the *Münster Diocesan Gazette,* and asked some plain questions:

Is this contention true ? I address this question publicly to those under whose instructions the German News Agency is working. I address this question to those official quarters which have forced our local newspapers to print this article and disseminate this contention. Is it true, then, that the German State, whose Führer at a solemn moment announced to the whole world that the National Government regards the two denominations as most important factors for the preservation of our national heritage, . . . is it true that this same Germany today wishes to suppress and destroy the very foundation on which the maintenance of these factors depends—namely, the denominational schools ?

At the District Congress of Educators from Main-Franconia, held in Würzburg, Minister of State Adolf Wagner declared that the State would introduce the community school in spite of everything. Our generation's path through life must be National Socialist, and our

[1] *Der Reichsbote,* No. 16, April 21st, 1935.

children could consequently have but one ideal, and that was Adolf Hitler.[1] Moreover, Hitler himself, in his speech to youth on May 1st, 1937, declared:

> There is but one German people, and there can therefore be but one German youth. And there can be but one German Youth Movement, because there is but one way in which German youth can be educated and trained. The handful of people, who perhaps still cherish within themselves the thought that, beginning with youth, they will be able to divide the German nation again, will be disappointed. This Reich stands, and is building itself up anew, upon its youth. And this Reich will hand its youth over to no one, but will take its education and its formation upon itself.[2]

In Fulda, on November 24th, 1937, Minister Kerrl declared:

> We cannot recognise that the Church has a right to ensure that the individual should be educated in all respects in the way which she holds to be right; but we must leave it to the National Socialist State to educate the child in the way it regards as right.

In the same year (June, 1937) Reichsminister Rust declared that:

> The exercise of denominational influences in the education of the young is from now on, and for all time, impossible. From this it follows as a consequence that denominational distinctions between German schools should be brought to an end as soon as possible.

This comes from the lips of the very same Minister who, just two years previously at a district Party Congress in Guben, had stated: "We have conceded the denominational school in a Concordat. What we have promised, that we shall observe."[3] It is moreover revealing that the Minister of Education of the Bavarian Government, Adolf Wagner, expresses his thanks to all those " who have collaborated with me in the carrying out of the task with which I was entrusted (conversion of Catholic schools into NS community schools)."

With this evidence before us (and much more could be cited), we see that the Government of the German Reich has broken its word with conscious cynicism.

2. *Preparatory Steps*

The preparations for the great onslaught on the denominational schools were carried out at first in silence and secrecy. Early in 1935 an Educational Committee Law was passed, by which the participation of the clergy in Educational Committees, Boards of Management, School Councils, etc., which had hitherto been taken for granted as normal, was made dependent on the arbitrary decision of the State. Thus, in the Official Journal of the Reich Ministry of Education, Ministerial Director Bojunga lays down that:

> there is no question of the Church herself sending or appointing representatives, since the schools belong to the State. The State will decide for itself, on the advice of its School Inspection Department, whether any members of the clergy are to be appointed to Education Committees, and, if so, which members shall be so appointed.[4]

[1] *Münchener Tagblatt*, February 15th, 1937. [2] *Köln. Volksztg.*, May 3rd, 1937.
[3] *Germania*, No. 154, June 3rd, 1935. [4] June, 1935.

Meanwhile, in most districts and administrative areas, the most important posts on the Education Committees were " purged " of the old loyal Catholic members and handed over to creatures of the State.[1] In the whole of Catholic Münster there was appointed as school inspector for the Catholic schools of the town and its vicinity a Protestant elementary-school teacher without academic qualifications, who very soon distinguished himself by his animosity against the Catholic schools and by his tactlessness.

Early in 1935 a sort of trial attack on the Catholic schools was staged in Munich, with the result that at the school entry on February 13th only 65 per cent. of the children (as against 84 per cent. in the previous year) were entered for denominational schools, and, in consequence, twenty-five Catholic elementary schools were converted into community schools. Parents had great pressure applied to them. Schoolmistresses who had dared to inscribe their names for the denominational schools were howled down by the mob with cries of " Shame!" Meetings of Catholic parents had been forbidden on January 24th, 1935 (ten days after the Saar plebiscite). The *Münchener Tagblatt* commented pertinently on the results of this school entry:

> The result of this year's school entry is due to the extensive propaganda which has been conducted in favour of the community school. The advocates of the denominational schools had to confine themselves to warnings of an exclusively pastoral nature.

Even the municipal institutions (for example the orphanage, which was staffed by Catholic nuns) had to enter for the community schools all those children of school age who in the previous year had been attending denominational schools.

The trial attack was successful. It had now been confirmed that by means of terror, intimidation and propaganda the religious schools could be captured. (It was only in isolated cases that in 1935 Catholic schools were converted into community schools by the method of decree, as for instance in the dioceses of Hildesheim and Paderborn.) Now therefore the general onslaught on the denominational schools can be gradually set in motion. But before the enemy " goes over the top," he will seek to reduce the resistance of his opponents by putting down a heavy barrage of propaganda.

The entire Press, and especially the definitely Party organs, printed articles representing the denominational schools as intolerable from the standpoint of national unity. So, for example, the *SA-Mann*[2] wrote:

> The schools are financed by the State, the teachers are paid by the State. . . . The school is therefore the State's affair. . . . Here it is a question, not of denominational requirements, but of the requirements of the nation. . . . It is to the interest of the State that right from the very beginning the mind of youth should be seized by the community idea. It cannot therefore

---

[1] *Cf.* Urban Educational Committee in Munich.   [2] No. 40, October 3rd, 1936.

120 DESTRUCTION OF CATHOLIC SECONDARY SCHOOLS

approve a distinction between Catholics and non-Catholics in school matters. Quite apart from school organisation, the Church has its own institutions, by means of which she can prepare the individual for the next life.

In a paragraph in the *Schwarze Korps*,[1] under the headline " Crusade against the Community Idea," we read:

> It should be left to the Party and the State to judge what helps and what harms the German people and State, what strengthens or weakens them, and what is to be regarded as activity dictated by party politics. . . . By the conscious defamation of all the measures taken by the State, dubbing them " pagan," " anti-religious," " anti-Christian," etc., the Catholic Church carries on her century-old fight against the unity of the Reich.

People of influence, such as school inspectors, leading officials of the Party, teachers and others, were constantly reiterating, both in speech and in writing, the necessity of introducing the community school. So, for instance, a certain School Inspector Materna in the *Niederdeutscher Beobachter*:[2]

> The school, as a public State organisation for the children of all citizens, even of the most diverse religious convictions, will in future have to be accepted by all. . . . Millions of Germans keep right away from any denomination. . . . In view of these developments, which nothing at all can avail to bring to a halt, scholars and teachers cannot be expected to go on learning and teaching the Jewish national history which forms one part of denominational religious instruction. This sort of instruction has absolutely nothing to do with religion or a religious way of living, and belongs rather to the synagogue.

And a Regional Leader of the Hitler Youth stated in the *Völkischer Beobachter*[3] that, as a leader of Hitler Youth, he was in favour of the German community schools.

> The Hitler Youth is the community of the whole of youth, without distinction of religious denomination. It is in this very community that it finds its strongest and most impressive vital experience. This community experience is disturbed by educational separation in Catholic and Protestant denominational schools. Parents, therefore, who are zealous for the community of German youth will send their children to the German community schools.

In numerous public meetings, especially in those organised since February, 1936, by the " German Faith Movement," propaganda in favour of the community schools was carried on in all circles of the population.

After National Socialism had worked up public opinion sufficiently, it believed it possible without further ado to proceed to the attack on its real objective, namely the destruction of the Catholic schools and their conversion into a purely National Socialist educational instrument. Naturally, they did not attack this objective directly, nor attempt to carry the whole position at once—that is not the Nazi way. But step by step they went forward; isolated ordinances, little underhand tricks and bigger, restrictive decrees, etc., preceded the

[1] October 8th, 1936.   [2] September 6th, 1935.   [3] September 10th, 1935.

final and decisive measure, held in view all the time, the eradication of the Catholic school. As we have already pointed out, this attack was delivered in three steps: firstly the schools were robbed of their Christian character, then religious teachers and nuns were turned out, and finally the former Catholic elementary schools were converted into German community schools—in other words, into Nazi schools.

3. *Destruction of the Christian Character of the Denominational Schools*

In the Joint Pastoral from Fulda, read on September 20th, 1936, the bishops made a protest about this very point:

Opponents of the denominational school are trying in many cases to undermine the existing religious schools from within. Complaints are increasing about the un-Christian utterances of individual teachers, utterances through which the religious feelings of the children have been deeply wounded. Here and there religious pictures and crucifixes have been removed from the schools. Plans of study have been adopted and school books taken into use by which the denominational schools are largely deprived of their Christian character.

However, considerable difficulties still stood in the way of the complete de-Christianisation of the religious schools; above all, the Catholic teachers in many places would not lend themselves to such a campaign. But there was still something more that could be done without further ado by mere administrative decree—the external conversion of the schools, the removal of Christian symbols, principally of the crucifix.

The Cross in the Classroom

In 1936 there appeared a decree respecting the decoration of school classrooms, in which it was ordained that the picture of the Führer and Reich Chancellor should everywhere be accorded its rightful place.[1] Immediately, zealous provincial and local authorities set about removing the crucifix from the schools, or at least placing it in a subordinate position.

The reaction of the Catholic population to these measures was most striking. They quite rightly interpreted the gesture as a symbol of the de-Christianisation of the schools, and felt outraged to such an extent that their resistance manifested itself in public demonstrations —almost a unique instance in the Third Reich. In many localities, hundreds of men, sometimes whole villages, by their threatening attitude forced the authorities to restore the crucifixes to the schools. But these demonstrations did not have the practical effect they were designed to have; the authorities for the most part gave way for the moment, only to remove the crucifixes again at a more favourable opportunity. After all, how can organised groups of people, who scarcely even hear of the happenings in the next village, prevail against State authority armed to the teeth ? But the fact that there was so much open resistance, in spite of the fearful terror which reigned

[1] *Cf., e.g., Trier Diocesan Gazette*, No. 293 1936.

and the terrible risks which each and every demonstrator took upon himself, is the best proof of all that the most sacred feelings of the Catholic population were outraged to the very depths, and that they opposed the de-Christianisation of public life with deep horror and disgust; it shows, too, how little the Catholic population believed in the " positive Christianity " of a régime which was doing the same thing as the Reds were then doing in Spain.

Of all the excitement which followed, the occurrences in Oldenburg have become the best known. We give below the authentic report which the episcopal authorities caused to be published in the *Münster Diocesan Gazette*, Supplement 51:

On November 4th, 1936, the following Ordinance was issued by the Minister for Churches and Schools in the territory of Oldenburg:

MINISTRY OF INTERIOR AND MINISTRY OF CHURCHES AND SCHOOLS,
IV. 9607. OLDENBURG.
November 4th, 1936.

All public buildings of the State, communes or rural districts belong to the whole German nation, without consideration of the religious persuasions of individual citizens. This applies also to all elementary school buildings. It is therefore not permissible for public school buildings to be ecclesiastically consecrated or blessed. Special notice will be taken of future infringements under this head.

It has never been the custom to allow denominational symbols—*e.g.*, the crucifix or the picture of Martin Luther—to be affixed to public administrative buildings of the State. It is indeed necessary that this should be so, since the State comprises the whole people. This point of view must be normative for all public administrative buildings of the parishes, communes and rural districts. School buildings of the State, communes or rural district authorities are to be treated in the same way. Even elementary school buildings form no exception to this rule, for they belong to the community, and not to adherents of some particular faith or persuasion.

We consequently ordain that in future ecclesiastical and religious symbols of the sort mentioned above, or any of a similar character, are not to be affixed to any building belonging to the State, communes or rural district authorities. Such as are already so affixed are to be removed.

Reports on this matter are to be furnished by the fifteenth day of December of this present year.

Signed: PAULY.
Certified correct: WULFF,
Secretary to the Administration.

When Canon Vorwerk, of Vechta, the bishop's Official for the territory of Oldenburg, heard of this Ordinance of the Minister, in consultation with the Bishop of Münster he addressed to the faithful of his Officialate the following letter, which was read in all Catholic churches on Sunday, November 15th, 1936:

BELOVED CATHOLICS OF OLDENBURG,

By an Ordinance of the Oldenburg State Ministry of November 4th it has been decreed that all crosses are to be removed from Catholic schools by December 15th of this year. This news swept through the land like wildfire. Numerous utterances from all parts of the country and from all sections of the population bear witness to the deep distress and the tremendous shock which this Ordinance has caused everywhere. How indeed could it be otherwise? It is, and always must be, simply incomprehensible for an honourable Catholic that the Cross should be banished from the schools in which our children are to be trained in their faith and in the love of the Cross.

We are Christians, and that means that we believe that we have been redeemed by the Cross of Christ. It is for this reason that we see in the Cross the very heart and centre of our Faith. For us, any attack on the Cross is necessarily an attack on Christianity. The Reich Concordat and the School Law guarantee the maintenance of the denominational schools—*i.e.*, Catholic schools in which the doctrines and standpoint of the Catholic Faith are taught and recognised. We therefore make a most energetic protest against this Ordinance; for where there is a Catholic school, the Cross cannot and must not be banned. Where Christianity is, there stands the Cross also. With deep anxiety, therefore, we are forced to ask ourselves the question: Is there any room for Christianity where the Cross is no longer tolerated?

We heard with joy how the national movement in Spain has brought the Cross back into the schools from which it was removed years ago by a godless Government. They have done this, because in the Cross they see the battle-standard of the fight against Bolshevism. Shall the Cross, then, be banned from the school in Oldenburg?

It is a sacred duty in conscience for all Catholics to stand up for Christian education, for education in the Faith of the Cross, the sign of our Redemption. Consequently we can never give our approval to the banning of the Cross from the rooms in which our children are educated. We will do everything in order to avoid this. You must also help, and stand up for the retention of the Cross in the school. I hope before God that the unanimous desire of the people will meet with consideration. Let us pray for the blessing of the Almighty.

This letter is to be read on Sunday, November 15th.

Signed: VORWERK, *Episcopal Official.*

VECHTA, *November 14th, 1936.*

When the Ministerial Ordinance became known, it caused tremendous agitation among the deeply religious population. . . . From November 21st onwards deputations from almost every parish in the Oldenburg territory of the Münster diocese marched in procession to the Ministry in Oldenburg City. On Tuesday, November 24th, in the square in front of the Ministry, there were as many as seventy-five vehicles in which various deputations had arrived in order to lodge their protest and demand the cancellation of the Ordinance. These demands, however, continued to be met with a refusal. At Party meetings in certain localities speakers attempted to justify and defend the Ordinance, and an attempt on the part of the Minister himself to calm the excitement by announcing that the crucifix might be put up in the classroom each time that the religious instruction lesson was in progress was not successful.

A decision was finally come to, on November 25th, at a meeting in Cloppenburg which all Party comrades and members of the Nazi organisations of Münsterland were ordered to attend, and at which about 7,000 men assembled from near and far. The theme to be discussed was announced as: " What do the District Leaders of Münsterland think about it? . . ." The Reich Governor of Oldenburg was bound to admit that the assembly, and the population of Münsterland which they represented, regarded the Ordinance removing the Cross from the schools as a grave attack upon the Christian sentiments of the people, and that they intended to defend to the very last the Faith of their fathers and the honour of the Cross by which man has been redeemed.

In recognition of these sentiments of the people, the Reich Governor then declared: " A wise Government must even be able to reverse decisions that may have been wrongly made," and amid the renewed cheers of the meeting he continued: " The Ordinance of November 4th, 1936, is rescinded. The crosses shall remain in the schools." After this decision, it was impossible to hold the crowd in any longer; in happy excitement they streamed out of the hall, in order to carry the joyful news to all parts of Münsterland.

The Episcopal Official in Vechta ordered a Thanksgiving Service to be held in all churches of the Oldenburg territory on Sunday, November 29th, at which the following Pastoral of the Bishop of Münster was read:

MY BELOVED DIOCESANS,

On the First Sunday in Advent, by order of the episcopal Official, my representative in your territory, a Thanksgiving Service will be held in all the churches of our beloved homeland, and a joyful Te Deum will be sung. It had been ordered that the Cross should be removed from all public buildings, and even from the schools in which Catholic children were taught by Catholic teachers. When you heard that, and when we heard it, a thrill of horror went through our hearts. Had it then already come to this pitch? Was that to happen here, in our own home country, which was recently clamoured for in the *Durchbruch*, the paper which wages war for the so-called " German Faith Movement," when it wrote[1] " The Cross must go."? Was it to be here, in the Oldenburg territory of Münsterland, that the first fatal step was to be taken along the path of Rosenberg, which, according to the well-known saying of the Reich Youth Leader, is destined to become " the path of German youth "? Alfred Rosenberg, whose book, condemned by the Church though it is, is still forced upon those who attend Leadership Courses and Training Camps as indispensable for a right understanding of National Socialist ideals and outlook, expressly demands the substitution of other symbols for " the crosses representing the Crucifixion of Christ in the churches and village streets." Yes, Rosenberg makes his intentions quite clear: " A German Church will gradually replace representations of the Crucifixion in its churches by representations of the Spirit of Fire, of the Heroic in the highest sense."[2] So it is to come about " gradually "! We understand perfectly well. And is it now that it is to begin? " The Cross must go," first of all in the schools, so that the children " may bid farewell to the image of Christ."

My beloved Diocesans! Let us thank God that He has opened our eyes, and enabled us to recognise what an unholy development was taking place here in our midst and what immeasurable evils stood before us. You did recognise it, and because you did so you poured out your tears before the Almighty in fervent prayer; day after day in overflowing churches and in your family devotions before the Crucified you have besought God to avert this dreadful evil. But not only have you prayed, you have bestirred yourselves in the matter as well. From nearly every parish your representatives, brave German men, tried and tested both in war and peace, have

[1] No. 31.   [2] *Mythus*, p. 616.

journeyed to Oldenburg, and, casting aside the fear of men, have given witness for you and for your loyalty to Christ, the Crucified One. Thank God for this manly Christian courage, which is indeed at all times a Christian duty, but is more than ever necessary today. Thank God also that to the man whom the Führer has set in authority as Governor of Oldenburg He has given the vision and the courage to rescind that Ordinance of November 4th, 1936, whose execution we all regarded as an outrage in the face of God and a great evil for our people and our country. When at a gathering of more than 7,000 men at Cloppenburg on November 25th the Governor recognised that you all stood up as one man for the Cross, that our Münsterland will not be deprived of the Cross, that you wish your children and your children's children to grow up into German men and women in the shadow of the Cross, in reverence to the Cross and in love to the Crucified Redeemer, he publicly gave utterance to the principle: "A wise Government must even be able to reverse decisions that may have been wrongly made." And then he announced, loudly and solemnly: "The Ordinance of November 4th, 1936, is rescinded. The crosses shall remain in the schools."

"The crosses shall remain in the schools." Those are words which we hear with enthusiasm and with gratitude. The Cross shall remain in our village streets and pathways. The Cross shall remain in our rooms and in our churches. The Cross shall remain—and that is the most important of all—in our hearts. Nothing ought, nothing must, nothing shall separate us, our youth, our people or our homeland from the Cross. We will avoid all companionship with those who are the enemies of the Cross of Christ. We will read no books that shame the Cross of Christ, we will not suffer them in our homes, in our show-cases, in our shop windows. And if it should be our lot for the sake of the Cross to suffer shame and persecution with Christ Crucified, then we shall neither fear nor shrink. For then we shall think of Him Who, Himself dying on the Cross, yet won for us the victory of life eternal.

CLEMENS AUGUST, *Bishop of Münster.*

MÜNSTER, *November* 27th, 1936.

Not only in Oldenburg, but in many other parts of Germany, similar demonstrations took place, which showed how profoundly the Catholic population had been moved. For the diocese of Trier, an informative report was published by the Vicariate-General in the "Clergy Communications"[1]:

Great excitement was caused in all sections of the Catholic population by the local execution of the Ordinance on the Decoration of School Classrooms (K.A.A., 1936, No. 293), in the course of which crucifixes were removed from their place of honour, though in certain isolated cases, as in Kenn-on-the-Moselle, the picture of the Führer and Reich Chancellor was retained in its old place. The parents of Kenn-on-the-Moselle requested the Director of the school to restore the crucifix to its original position. As this request did not produce any result, a deputation of four men went to Trier, where they were refused access to the leading officials, and it was explained to them by some subordinate that what happened in the school was no affair of theirs—the Reich no longer recognised that parents had any rights in such matters. In Wenigerath near Bischofsdhron, representations to the Mayor having proved fruitless, the people themselves replaced the cross in its original position on January 6th. The result was that during the night of the 6th-7th of January, with the co-operation of the Trier Gestapo, the individuals implicated were woken up, taken to the school, and treated in an absolutely outrageous manner. Five of them were arrested.

Two arrests were made in Wolsfeld near Bitburg for the same reason.

[1] No. 2, 1937.

126 DESTRUCTION OF CATHOLIC SECONDARY SCHOOLS

They were charged with a breach of the peace. On an injunction being sought against these arrests, both men were released from arrest, and then taken into " protective custody." The Reich Commissar for the Saarland has informed us in this connection that his decree regarding the installation of the Führer's picture in classrooms did not imply any slighting of the crucifix, but left it open to subordinate school officials and teachers to give it a position in accordance with Christian sentiment and ancient usage. Complaints had been coming in from the authorities that here and there religious rubbish was still to be found in the schools. We ask you all, therefore, to co-operate in ensuring that in church, home and school the walls shall be decorated in a manner befitting the sublimity of things religious, and in accordance with the prescriptions of the Church.

There were also demonstrations in the Lower Rhineland. Thus in Bislich (Rees district) the population were successful in their stand for the retention of the Cross in the schools. Undeterred by drenching rain, more than 500 people demonstrated on the square in front of the school, and gave loud expression to their feelings: " We want to see the Cross in its place of honour in the school." The headmaster accordingly had the crucifix replaced in its former position. A resolution in favour of the retention of the Cross in the school was signed by 480 people.

Similar success was achieved by the Catholics of Palling near Traunstein. In April, 1937, the Mayor caused the crucifix to be removed from its usual place—over the dais—and the picture of the Führer to be hung there instead. The crucifix was hung on the wall at the back of the classroom, so that during prayers the children had to turn round. Some of the principal farmers of the district met together and went to see the Mayor at a time when they knew that he would be alone in his office, which was in the school buildings. They insisted that the cross should be restored to its former place. They said that they would not leave the building until the Mayor himself had replaced the cross. After a long discussion, he went himself into the classroom and restored the cross to its old place above the dais. The picture of the Führer was hung on the back wall of the classroom.

We have reports whose accuracy is vouched for of spontaneous manifestations of disapproval on the part of the Catholics in Castellaun-on-the-Moselle and Emmerich (Lower Rhine). In both places the police treated the Catholics with great brutality.

Similar communications with regard to the removal of the crucifix from the schools came in from several towns in the Baden territory. As the Bishop of Münster said in a Pastoral of December 21st, 1936:

> Quite recently in some parts of the diocese an order of the School authorities has been put into force, according to which the crucifix, the image of the Son of God, our Redeemer, is to be removed from the place of honour in the classroom, to be replaced by the picture of the Führer and Reich Chancellor . . . that children, easily influenced as they are, shall draw the conclusion that less honour is to be paid to Jesus Christ, our Saviour and our God, than to a mortal man. . . . If this be truly so, then the only interpretation that can be put on these measures is that they are an attempt to undermine the still remaining Catholic schools from within.

In Austria also since early 1938 the character of the Catholic schools has been systematically de-Christianised.

In spite of the hot resentment and resistance of the Catholic population, gradually the crosses were everywhere removed from the schools. The Bishop of Aachen, Mgr. Sträter, has given striking expression in a Pastoral to the distress of the Catholic population at these brutal acts of persecution:

> From all quarters tidings are brought to me of the profound emotion which the removal of the Cross has caused in the hearts of the Catholic population both in town and country. Among many Christian parents and children, among many religiously-minded teachers, hot tears have been shed and many a hand has trembled as it removed the Cross from its place of honour in accordance with the orders of authority.
>
> These are the crosses which hitherto have lent an air of consecration to our schoolrooms. These are the crosses upon which Christian parents have gazed in piety and joy, which a long line of your Christian forbears have venerated and loved. And now there arise anxious questionings: What will become of those crosses which were collected together and in some places taken off in large numbers in lorries? Truly, the Catholic population will never forget the occurrences of the beginning of this school year.

Undermining the Denominational Schools from Within.

The aim of depriving the denominational schools of their Christian character was pursued at the same time by other means, which were less conspicuous but for that very reason more effective. We give a short account of these additional measures below.

(1) In the year 1935 Minister of Education Dr. Rust issued the following order (appealing to instructions given by the Führer's Representative:

> (i) No child is to be compelled to take part in any school religious instruction which may be provided for in the curriculum, nor in any school religious services, school devotions or similar school arrangements. However, in order to avoid disturbances of school routine, the child's exemption from these activities must be registered by the appropriate school official.
>
> (ii) Teachers may not be compelled to give religious instruction, or to take charge of religious exercises or practices, or to take part in such, if they duly declare to the appropriate School Inspection Authority that they have conscientious objections to so doing.
>
> (iii) In cases where difficulties are put in the way of using the services of teachers who do not belong to any Christian persuasion, a report is to be furnished to this office.

(2) In many places the teachers were forbidden to co-operate in the school religious services.

(3) The President of the Regional Government of Cologne ordered that time allotted on school time-tables to religious instruction should not be used for the reception of the Sacraments. Directors of schools were to satisfy themselves personally that these instructions were duly observed. The reason for this prohibition was the fact that several classes went together to the church during the hour of religious

instruction for the purpose of making their confessions. The same instruction was issued for Austria at the end of 1938.

(4) On February 23rd, 1937, the Bavarian Ministry of Education sent the following communication to the authorities of the various secondary schools and senior schools:

> It has come to my knowledge that convent schools arrange " Days of Recollection " for their scholars. Functions and arrangements of this description are no business of the school. They are consequently to be discontinued in the future.

(5) Lay teachers in the Catholic elementary schools did not conduct themselves in a manner befitting Catholic teachers, or in accordance with the provisions of Article 24 of the Concordat. In particular, Bible instruction was given in certain cases in a manner which was incompatible with Catholic doctrine.[1] The Bishop of Münster raised objections on this score in his Pastoral of December 21st, 1936:

> In spite of our protests, in Catholic elementary schools of our diocese teachers are employed who have fallen away from the Faith or have left the Church, whose own children do not receive a Catholic education or have received an exemption from attendance at religious instruction. It is obvious that such teachers do not " accord with the special needs of Catholic schools," as is required by Article 24 of the Concordat. By the employment of such persons " the remaining Catholic schools are being undermined from within." They are certainly undermined from within " when teachers speak to the children slightingly of bishops and priests, or when teachers speak disparagingly of the Bible stories of the Old Testament and hold them up to contempt. They are undermined from within when teachers lay regrettable cases of offences against the Catholic moral law to the charge of the whole Church, or even to the charge of the priesthood or religious state as such. They are undermined when teachers or other Youth leaders, in their hatred against the Church and her priests, incite the children to disorderly conduct during the hour of religious instruction, to ask impudent questions, to create disturbances, and to ridicule the priest who is giving the instruction." These deplorable cases " must be publicly pilloried, so that parents may know what is happening and what is being tolerated in the Catholic schools that yet remain. . . . At the same time, these occurrences show parents just what they have to fear from the introduction of the German community schools. . . ."

(6) Children in Catholic schools were refused permission to take part in religious functions held outside the school, such as the devotion of the " Forty Hours," etc.[2]

(7) In many districts it was forbidden to make enquiries during the religious instructions in the schools regarding attendance at Divine Service.[3]

(8) The Bishop of Münster in the same Pastoral complained about the un-Christian books used in the schools:

> Parents are specially warned to exercise their vigilance in regard to the school books recently prescribed, particularly in the case of reading books and history textbooks. When we find that in such books our Christian heritage, Christian traditions, and Christian interpretation of world affairs

[1] *Cf.* Vicar-General of Trier in *Clergy Communications*, vol. 2, 1937.
[2] Trier *Clergy Communications, loc. cit.*   [3] *Ibid.*

and daily life receive little or no treatment or recognition, we at once realise how little authoritative circles are concerned to support and assist Christian parents in the Christian upbringing of their children by means of the school. In such books we find the spirit of the community school, which remains indifferent to the absolute values of Christianity. Such books can indeed be exploited for the purpose of undermining from within the schools that still remain to us.

(9) In many districts all pictures of the Saints and the portrait of the Pope were removed.

(10) Throughout the whole Rhineland, Catholic priests have been thrown out of the elementary schools, in which their work has been attended with such great blessings in the past.[1]

(11) The Bishop of Münster was forbidden to visit Catholic schools during his visitation tours, and so was deprived of the opportunity of exercising the supervision over religious instruction which was guaranteed in the Concordat.

(12) The Bavarian Ministry of Education announced:[2]

The organisation of religious services is the duty of the Church, not of the school. In future, therefore, no such services are to be arranged by the schools. Consequently, time spent in religious services is not to be given credit as part of the time allotted for instruction, nor may schools make any financial grant or allowance for them.

This order merely gives final legal sanction to a state of affairs that had already obtained for a long time in nearly the whole of Bavaria.

(13) In many places (*e.g.*, in Württemberg, in Austria, etc.) the use of church hymns in school singing lessons was forbidden in 1938. Hymns were said to belong rather to religious instruction, and for that reason their use in singing lessons was to be discontinued in the future. In singing lessons, besides folk-songs, the songs of the National Socialist Movement were to be used, and also soldier songs. The Feast Day of St. Leopold of Austria was no longer observed.

(14) In the year 1939, Herr Schwede-Koburg, District Leader and President of the Government of Pomerania, in a decree sent to the Presidents of Local Governments, drew attention to a number of former Ministerial decrees, in which it had been declared to be incompatible with fundamental freedom of conscience that scholars should be influenced by their teachers in favour of any particular Church or religious persuasion. It is particularly repugnant to fundamental freedom of conscience, says the decree, when Church functions of any kind, even denominational morning prayers, are held in the school. Consequently, so-called " school services " might no longer take place. Without prejudice to the Evangelical or Catholic religious instruction already laid down in the time-tables, it was not permissible to make arrangements for attendance at ecclesiastical functions, whether on the school premises or elsewhere. Even outside

---

[1] Bishop Bornewasser of Trier, in a sermon on New Year's Eve, December 31st, 1937.
[2] *Bavarian Government Gazette*, December 21st, 1938.

school-time, teachers were not to take the children to Church functions, or look after them while they were attending such functions. It was further not permissible for teachers or clergy to interrogate children at school with regard to their attendance at Church functions.

4. *The Dissolution of Convent Schools*

Since the middle of 1936 National Socialism has been aiming straight for its real goal, the destruction of the Catholic schools. In the first place the attack was concentrated on the many schools which were directed by members of Religious Orders and Congregations, which were, for the most part, secondary schools. Once they were disposed of, it would be easy to attack the last and most important rampart of the Christian religion, the denominational elementary schools.

In order rightly to estimate the importance of this step, it is enough to recall the flourishing state of these religious secondary schools in Germany. In the middle of 1936, when the onslaught began, there were in Germany 1,534 secondary boys' schools, of which 1,462 were public and 72 private. But of the 792 secondary girls' schools, only 508 were public and the remaining 284 were private. Catholic Religious Orders and Congregations had altogether 12 secondary schools for boys and 188 secondary schools for girls. In Prussia, the private secondary schools for girls had 26,522 scholars (63·9 per cent.), while the public secondary schools had only 14,968 scholars. For Bavaria, the corresponding figures were 10,332 (76·7 per cent.) and 3,128. In the whole Reich, 40,421 (64·2 per cent.) Catholic girls were studying at private Catholic secondary schools and 22,562 at the State secondary schools. The number of denominational boarding schools was correspondingly high.

The conversion of these Catholic private secondary schools was not carried out at one blow. As usual in its fight against the Church, the Nazi State was careful to accustom public opinion to these measures gradually by taking one step at a time and, for this reason, the final dissolution or conversion of these schools was preceded by a series of decrees which aimed at destroying the convent schools stage by stage. We give here a short summary of these official measures.

Hitherto there had existed in Bavaria sixteen training colleges for women teachers, all of which were conventual institutions with nuns as teachers and professors. On February 13th, 1935, there appeared a decree for the reorganisation of the training of teachers in Bavaria, in which the Bavarian Ministry of Education laid down that in future only four such conventual training colleges should exist, while the remainder were to take no new entries for the lowest class for the school year 1935-36, and their higher classes were to be dissolved at the end of the school year 1936-37. A specially serious feature of this decree was the stipulation that even the four training colleges still permitted to exist were only to be allowed to accept candidates for convent elementary school work—*i.e.*, only nuns could be trained in these institutions.

From the beginning of 1936 the State subsidies to men and women teachers belonging to the Religious Orders practically came to an end. Dr. Rust, the Reichsminister of Education, decreed on April 7th, 1936, that financial support could only be granted by the State in cases where the retention of the school was in the public interest. Naturally, a State which was endeavouring to secure the " elimination of denominational religion from public life " (Reichsminister Frick) had no interest in the continued existence of convent schools !

By a decree of the same Minister (Dr. Rust) of April 4th, 1936, it was ordered that for the future no new pupils should be enrolled in the so-called preparatory school classes. It was from these preparatory classes that the pupils of the secondary schools proper were for the most part derived, and such classes existed practically speaking only in Catholic convent schools.

In October, 1936, the President of the Government of the Rhine Province, Terboven, announced that it was the absolute duty of all State and municipal officials to send their children to the public schools where such existed. This announcement was clearly a blow aimed at the schools directed by the Religious Congregations. In the course of time, orders of a similar tenor were issued by authorities all over the country, and urged repeatedly by official quarters. In September, 1937, the Reichsminister of the Interior issued a universal prohibition to all officials against sending their children to private convent schools. Any exception to this ruling would require the approval of the superior of the official concerned. The point of view taken up by the Government is confirmed in *German Science, Education and Culture*,[1] the official journal of the Ministry of Education: " To send his children, without compelling reasons, to a private school is incompatible with the duty of an official of the National Socialist State."

Doubtless acting under instructions from higher quarters, the municipalities themselves have been erecting, since 1936-37, more and more middle and secondary schools, especially for girls, and so it is brought about that the convent schools gradually become " superfluous."

In those towns in which the only secondary schools for girls were convent schools, approval was given for girls to attend the public secondary schools for boys. (Formerly, in the days of political upheaval in Germany, it was the Marxists who called for co-education.)

A decree of the Bavarian Ministry of Education in February, 1937, prescribed that teachers even in private schools were to be examined as to their unexceptionable national sentiments towards the State.[2] Supervision of a national sentiment towards the State which would be free from any possible objection on the part of the Nazi State would indeed prove a useful method of sifting the personnel working in convent schools.

[1] *Deutsche Wissenschaft, Erziehung und Volksbildung*, No. 19, October 5th, 1937.
[2] Published in *N. Münchener Tagblatt*, March 1st, 1937.

It even happened at the beginning of 1938 that a Catholic mother was deprived of the custody of her own children by the Court of Chancery because she had enrolled them in a Catholic private school, and the official law journal *German Law* (*Deutsches Recht*) approved of this decision.

New taxation legislation, and especially the Reich Land Taxation Law of April 1st, 1938, added a tremendous load to the already heavy burden of taxation borne by the Catholic private schools. No relief or exemption could be obtained, since the maintenance of the denominational private schools " was not in the interests of the State."

Immediately after the Anschluss, members of the Party in Austria were forbidden to send their children to private schools any longer, and pressure was applied to produce the same result among State officials and employees, so that in Austria, too, National Socialism began its career with the systematic destruction of the Catholic schools.

In the summer of 1939 the Bavarian Ministry of Education forbade the clergy to exercise any function or activity in secondary schools, with the exception of religious instruction and instruction in the Hebrew language. Clergy were not even to act as substitute teachers in cases of necessity, even though they had passed their State examinations and possessed full qualifications for the teaching office.

Protests

In May, 1936, State Councillor Boepple of the Bavarian Ministry of Education, in a speech before 5,000 men and women teachers, declared that, of 1,600 teaching posts held by nuns, 600 would be handed over to lay teachers during the coming year. It was absolutely necessary to transfer all conventual teaching into lay hands, since " the State must be able to exercise a centralised control over all its educational affairs. . . . The National Socialist State wants a school, a youth, and a form of education in harmony with the National Socialist spirit. For this reason it can no longer entrust the care of State public elementary schools to Religious Orders. Even if in certain isolated cases convent teachers were willing to teach their pupils in the spirit of National Socialism, yet experience has shown that convent schools in general are not able to do justice, in the instruction they give, to the basic requirements of the new State or to the new educational aims it has adopted."

This utterance, deeply offensive as it was to all Catholics, was dealt with by Cardinal Faulhaber in a sermon:

I know that your souls are weighed down by a heavy burden, when you recall the violent measures by which parents were hustled into changing their children over from the Catholic schools to the community schools during the last school entry in Munich. There was no scruple against using economic pressure by threats against the means of livelihood of those who did not comply, often to such an extent that there was no longer any question of freedom of choice for the parents concerned. And now comes an official communication that 600 teachers in convent schools, and eventually all teachers in convent schools, are to be excluded from the public Bavarian school appointments. Women teachers who have passed their State examinations with the highest honours and distinctions are to lose their hard-won State recognition and the right to exercise the profession for which they have qualified themselves. The people begin to ask themselves: Are we Catholics then outlawed and proscribed? And are the wishes of the parents to count for nothing in this matter of education?

Shortly after, the Bavarian bishops issued a solemn collective protest against this proposed assault on the rights both of the parents and the Church. Here is an extract from their impressive Joint Pastoral:

We can scarcely believe that, in the name of the newly-won national unity, a law should be passed by which German women are singled out for such harsh treatment, and their rights trampled upon, because they wear the religious habit of nuns.

Attention is then drawn in detail to the services rendered to the nation by the Benedictine nuns, the " English Ladies " (Englische Fräulein), the Ursulines, the Servite nuns, the Cistercian nuns, the Clarissian nuns, the Dominican nuns, and not least by the Poor Sisters of the Schools. Emphasis is laid on the recognition accorded by the State to the work of all these Orders and Congregations. Reference is made to Bismarck's saying: " I have taken steps to acquire reliable information respecting the attitude of the Bavarian Government to the School Sisters working in that country. As a result of this information I have become convinced that the Bavarian Government itself would not approve of the removal of these Sisters." Reports and other documents are quoted, showing that the convent schools are among the best in the country.

The bishops then declare that the harsh measures which it is proposed to take against these Orders and Congregations are an act of ingratitude and of injustice, and are a misfortune to the whole community. " The right of the nuns to exercise their activities in the schools and in the education of children is guaranteed both in the Concordat with Bavaria and in the Reich Concordat. . . . According to Article 5 of the Bavarian Concordat, ' appointments of members of Orders and religious Congregations to teaching positions will be governed by no other conditions than those which apply to lay persons.' . . . How can the nun teachers be driven out of the schools without an open breach of the Concordat? What must the German people think and what must foreign observers think of German fidelity to treaties, by which the pledged word ought not be broken ?"

The Pastoral then goes on to deal with the burdens of which the Religious Orders have relieved the State. " Before the war the salary of a teaching nun amounted to no more than the slender wage of a domestic servant. There were teaching nuns who for a whole year of teaching activity received only 16 marks, and even today every teaching nun saves the State an average of 2,000 marks in comparison with the lay mistress who would otherwise have to be employed. It must be remembered, moreover, that no nun receives a pension, but the old and sick are cared for by the Order to which they belong. By the exclusion of teaching nuns from the schools the State's annual Budget will be increased by about four million marks." This sweeping aside of the teaching nuns is but another step on the way to the universal introduction of the community school, in which it is possible for the children of Catholic parents to be taught by teachers who reject Christianity.

The bishops finally emphasise: " Catholic parents wish to see peaceful relations as well between the Church and the State, as between the Church and the school, for the best interests of the nation and our youth. They consider that the war against our holy Faith, which has been set on foot by anti-Christian circles, and is being ever more fiercely waged, is a great misfortune, not only for the Church, but also for the State and the whole German nation."

The Bishop of Speyer had a notice put up in the church porches, asking for special prayers:

> For decades past teaching nuns have been working in the schools of our diocese to the great benefit and blessing of our youth. The announcement that all teaching nuns are to be driven out of the elementary schools fills me, and you also, with deep sorrow. The very thought that these beloved and revered nuns are to be banned from our schools is a source of bitter distress to all of us. Let us pray to God that the work of the nuns, which has been so richly blessed in the past, may yet not be lost to the school and the parish."

All protests, all representations, all references to the open violation of the pledged word and to the injustice exercised towards teachers, parents and children—all were in vain. Notice of dismissal was served on all teachers belonging to the Religious Orders. Actually it was not so much on them that this notice was served, as on the spirit of Christianity which they taught by word and example. A new spirit, with which the spirit of Christianity is utterly incompatible, the spirit of National Socialism, is from now on to be forced on the whole of German youth. That it was not the nuns as individuals, but the spirit of Christianity against which the attack was aimed, is shown by the fact that every objection to a teacher was withdrawn, if only she left her Order and changed her sentiments. At Amberg in Bavaria, a certain Sister Tiburtia left the Order to which she belonged (a very unusual occurrence, even in these times of terrible difficulty), in order to carry on as a teacher in a lay capacity. A public celebration was organised in her honour, at which the Area Leader, the Mayor, the Area School Inspector and various other officials were present. In a speech made in her honour it was said that Sister Tiburtia had shown by her action that her fidelity to the National Socialist ideology was true and genuine. Her defection from the Order was described as a " courageous step," and she was handed by way of a prize a book inscribed with a personal dedication from the town notables.

The Wholesale Dismissal of Teachers belonging to the Religious Orders

Blow after blow is rained down upon the conventual schools, and each of these blows is aimed at the Church herself. Let us give a short list of some of the results of this assault:

In 1937 the following were either closed or converted into State schools:

Secondary School and Boarding School of the English Ladies in Nympfenburg.

> Reasons alleged: There reigned in the Institute a spirit which was incompatible with the basic principles of the National Socialist State. The Institute had shown itself to be merely a training-ground for class

distinctions and social obscurantism. Difficulties were raised by the authorities of the Institute against the enrolment of pupils in the various organisations of the German Girls' League (BDM).[1]

The Educational Institute of the Salesians in Amberg.

Reasons alleged: A meeting of the Catholic children of the parish had taken place in this Institute.

The Mission School of the Benedictines in Schweiklberg.

Reasons alleged: The directors of the school refused to reappoint as a teacher a priest who had been dismissed from the Order.

A notice in the *Official Gazette of the Reich Ministry of Education* early in 1937 gave the following information regarding elementary school teachers belonging to Religious Orders:

In about 400 public elementary schools for girls the instruction of the pupils was confided to Catholic Religious Orders or Congregations of women. . . . The dispersal of such teachers is provided for in the bye-law of November 16th, 1936, to the School Provision Law. Of about 1,600 teaching posts occupied by members of Religious Orders at the beginning of this year (1937), 300 have already been made over to lay teachers. The remaining posts are to be vacated in the course of this year so that the entire elimination of teachers belonging to the Religious Orders is in prospect.

In his sermon on New Year's Day, 1938, Cardinal Faulhaber made known that " quite recently 750 teaching nuns have been dismissed in Bavaria alone." In the course of the same year (1938) no less than eighteen educational institutions for boys with 2,545 scholars disappeared in Bavaria—*i.e.*, all the middle and secondary schools (with the exception of the Mission Schools in St. Ottilien and Münster-Schwarzach), among them the Benedictine Gymnasium[2] of St. Stephen in Augsburg and the Benedictine Gymnasium in Metten. At the same time sixty-four convent schools were closed down, with 12,957 pupils, and the boarding schools attached to many of these institutions suffered a like fate. (In many cases the dissolution of the school was effected in stages; at first new enrolments for the top and bottom classes were forbidden, and then later the remaining classes were dispersed.)

By a decree of the Ministry of the Interior in Vienna dated July 19th, 1938, by a single stroke of the pen all the Catholic private schools in Austria were deprived of public recognition and rights. The final closing of these schools, or their conversion into State institutions, followed for the most part immediately.

In Vienna itself all Catholic Institutions, Students' Homes, Boarding Schools and private Training Colleges for Teachers were closed by a decree of the City Educational Council on August 3rd, 1938. Among these schools were world-renowned institutions such as the " Schotten-Gymnasium " directed by the Benedictines in Vienna. (This college,

---

[1] Thus the *Bayerlscher Staatsanzeiger*, April 7th, 1937.
[2] A " gymnasium " corresponds, more or less, to our secondary school.

136 DESTRUCTION OF CATHOLIC SECONDARY SCHOOLS

whose foundation goes back to the thirteenth century, was at one time directed by Scots Benedictine monks, hence the name it still bore when it was suppressed.)

Things went in much the same way in the remaining parts of Austria. Thus, in September, 1938, the *Schweizerische Kirchenzeitung* enumerated the following Catholic educational establishments, schools, colleges, etc., that had fallen victim to the Nazi hatred for the Church.

The Borromeo Seminary for Boys in Salzburg was confiscated for use as offices by the Forestry Department. The Paulinum Seminary for Boys in Schwaz (Northern Tyrol) was taken into State service as a lay institution. The Teachers' Training College belonging to the School Brothers in Tisis was appropriated by the State and placed under lay direction; the School Brothers were swept entirely on one side and excluded from their own college. St. Joseph's Home belonging to the Ingenbohl Sisters of Feldkirch, which comprised a commercial school and a continuation school of domestic economy for girls, was taken over by the State and laicised. The House of St. Francis Xavier, belonging to the Missionary Fathers of the Precious Blood, was handed over to the Hitler Youth. The girls' Lyceum " Marienberg " of the Dominican nuns in Bregenz was converted into a training institute for business women, taken over by the State and put under lay direction. A State Youth Hostel and a business academy for boys was installed in the school buildings and boarders' quarters of the Cistercians at Mehrerau. The Students' Hostels, Homes, " Pensionats," etc., associated with so many Catholic private schools, naturally suffered the same fate as the schools themselves.

In the summer of 1939, Dr. Rust, the Reichsminister of Education, made a new and more vigorous onslaught on the denominational boarding schools. He stated that the task of the secondary schools, as indeed of German schools in general, was the education of the individual National Socialist in collaboration with the parents and the Hitler Youth Organisations. " If children leave the parental home, and are sent to boarding schools, then these latter establishments must have the same aim in view." Chief Councillor in the Ministry of Education, Dr. Heckel, gave a commentary on this new regulation of the Minister in the Ministry's official Gazette, and said that the political educational aim and function of the boarding schools was such as to forbid any form of training which was in opposition to National Socialism, whether directly or indirectly. This applied also to the exclusively denominational boarding schools. National Socialism only took cognisance of the individual as a German, not as a Catholic or Protestant.[1]

We reproduce here a letter sent by the Regional Educational Council of Salzburg to the authorities of the Borromaeum private Gymnasium at St. Rupert near Bischofshofen, which shows how thorough the Nazis were in their work of destroying the Catholic schools:

Quoted in *Junge Kirche*, No. 6, 1939.

[*Urgent.*]
REGIONAL EDUCATIONAL AUTHORITY OF SALZBURG
Number: 7339/38 L.Sch.R.
SALZBURG.
October 21st, 1938.

Subject: Closing of the Denominational Schools and Boarding Schools.
To the Directors of the Borromaeum Private Gymnasium, St. Rupert, near Bischofshofen

In consideration of the various events which have occurred in recent times, and bearing in mind the necessity of educating the whole of youth in the National Socialist spirit, the Minister for Internal and Cultural Affairs, in his decree Zl IV-2a-38211-a of October 17th, 1938, has ordered the closing, with immediate effect, of all denominational private schools (whether publicly recognised or not) belonging to the elementary school scheme, secondary schools (senior schools), training colleges for men or women teachers, commercial and industrial schools, including schools of domestic economy and professional schools for women.

The aforesaid decree applies also to all denominational boarding schools, under whatever name or title they may be conducted.

The Regional Educational Authority is therefore under the necessity of dissolving the Private Gymnasium of St. Rupert as a denominational institution. In order, however, that the pupils may not be prejudiced or disturbed in their studies, the Regional Educational Authority has made a request to the Ministry that the Private Gymnasium of St. Rupert should be converted into a State gymnasium.

Pending the granting of this request, instruction in the gymnasium should proceed as usual. Moreover, the Regional Educational Authority will endeavour to take over the teaching staff of the Private Gymnasium for the public State Gymnasium into which it is to be converted.

The renting of the buildings will be carried out in a manner similar to that hitherto adopted by the Borromaeum Private Gymnasium. The Regional Educational Authority requests that the terms of the lease be communicated to it.

Chairman of the Regional Educational Authority,
SPRINGENSCHMID.

Zl.400, *October 22nd,* 1938.

Towards the end of 1938 and in the early part of 1939 most of the Catholic private schools that still remained were closed, both in Austria and in the Old Reich. Among these were institutions of international reputation such as the Stella Matutina College at Feldkirch, the rooms of which were used to house a Reich School of Customs and Excise; the College of St. Blasien, the German division of the Austrian Stella Matutina; the College of St. Aloysius in Godesberg, one of the most modern in Germany; the Seminary of the Augustinian Fathers in Münnerstadt; and others.

Sentence of death was pronounced on the last remnant of Catholic private schools in a decree of the Minister of Education, Dr. Rust, in the summer of 1939. Among other Catholic educational institutions on the condemned list were: the Episcopal College for clerical students at Gaesdonk (Diocese of Münster); the boarding college of the Sacred Heart nuns near Bonn; the boarding college of the Holy Cross Sisters in Aspel near Rees-Rhein; and also the boarding college of the Sisters of Our Blessed Lady in Mülhausen near Kempen. By April 1st, 1940, at latest, all Catholic private schools, even Mission Schools, had to be finally closed down.

These relentless measures involved thousands of members of Religious Orders and priests, with long years of good and meritorious service behind them, in the direst misfortunes. Many religious houses, especially convents of nuns, were completely ruined economically. Hundreds of nuns, in order to keep alive at all, were forced to give up community life in their Orders and throw themselves on the charity of their relatives. Others tried to earn a bare subsistence by home crafts; others, again, had no alternative but to seek industrial employment. Thus, for instance, in the summer of 1938, forty-one former nuns were at work in a textile factory in Baden. A certain number of these dispossessed members of the Religious Orders succeeded in obtaining visas to leave Germany, and went off to seek some new field of activity overseas. Only in quite exceptional cases have nuns put off their religious habit—these of course at once received State appointments.

In their Pastoral of August 19th, 1938, the bishops of Austria bewail the destitution and distress to which these dispossessed Religious of both sexes have been reduced. They point out that by driving the Religious from the schools—

a large number of Religious Sisters and Brothers and priests were deprived of the bread they had honourably earned, while many old teachers belonging to these Orders and Congregations, who had retired and are no longer fit for work, but shared the livelihood earned by their younger colleagues, have been condemned to spend their declining years in anxiety and want. . . .
We, and the whole of the Catholic faithful with us, deeply deplore the fact that the right of education has been withdrawn from these religious schools, and that thereby the teaching personnel belonging to the Orders and Congregations has in many cases been reduced to destitution, while many Catholic parents have been restricted in the exercise of their free choice of a school to which to send their children.
We regard it as our duty, beloved faithful, to urge you with the greatest insistence to help these nuns who have been so harshly treated, at least in supplying their immediate and urgent necessities. These Religious Sisters who have been banned from their schools will have to turn to some other kind of work to gain a scanty living. Here is where the Catholic spirit of sacrifice and Christian charity must step in; and we must take every possible opportunity of standing by them in genuine German national solidarity. Of all the houses upon which these harsh official measures have fallen, none must be allowed to want because of any failure of Christian charity among the Catholic population. During the decades of crisis and want through which our country passed, hundreds stood daily at the doors of these convents and religious houses, and were fed there with bread and soup. If at the present time in these houses benevolent and philanthropic activity has given place to anxiety for the very means of livelihood, they must certainly not be allowed to suffer through any lack of sympathy in the hearts of the Catholic people.

Even if the economic and professional ruin of thousands of innocent citizens caused no concern to the Nazi State, so long as they were merely Catholics or only just nuns and religious, yet one would have thought that the enormous additions to the State's financial burdens might have given the authorities pause. But this factor does not seem to have worried them in the least. The millions of additional expenditure caused by the closing of the Catholic private schools were without more ado passed on to the German tax-payer by the State and the municipalities. The following interesting facts emerge from a report on schools and education in the city of Nürnberg that appeared in the middle of May in the South German edition of the *Völkischer Beobachter*:

By reason of the dissolution of schools under denominational management, the city was forced to undertake an increased development of the existing facilities for the education of girls. In recent years, consequently, the subsidies required for senior, secondary and professional schools for girls have been rising steadily; for the financial year 1937 they amounted to 732,538 RM., in the 1938 Budget with their Supplementary Estimates they reached 825,928, while in the new Budget they have risen to 940,603.

Thus the war against the teaching nuns cost the city of Nürnberg alone more than 20,000 RM. a year! We give a few more statistics below:

I. MEMBERS OF RELIGIOUS CONGREGATIONS OF WOMEN DISPERSED

In accordance with the Ministerial Decree of December 29th, 1937, teachers who were members of Religious Congregations were excluded from all convent educational institutions for girls, and from secondary schools for girls, including senior schools and boarding establishments connected with them. That gives a total of—

64 institutions with	.. 12,957 pupils.

These institutions conducted:

10 secondary schools of 9 classes each, with	..	766 ,,
63 secondary schools of 6 classes each, with	..	8,087 ,,
53 secondary schools of 3 classes each, with	..	4,104 ,,
58 boarding-schools, with	..	2,818 ,,

II. MEMBERS OF RELIGIOUS CONGREGATIONS OF MEN DISPERSED

In accordance with the same Decree, teachers who were members of Religious Orders or Congregations were excluded from all establishments for the higher education of boys, including seminaries reserved for the education of aspirants to the priesthood or the Religious Orders (with the exception of the two establishments conducted by the Missionary Benedictines of St. Ottilien). This gives a total of—

18 institutions with	.. 2,545 pupils.

These institutions conducted:

3 secondary schools of 9 classes each, with	..	1,229 ,,
9 secondary schools of 6 classes each, with	..	981 ,,
6 grammar schools of 1-5 classes each, with	..	335 ,,
18 boarding schools, with	..	1,975 ,,

DESTRUCTION OF CATHOLIC SECONDARY SCHOOLS

The Judgement of the Church

In a Pastoral of September 4th, 1938, the Bavarian bishops placed on record the injustice of these measures and the grave damage that had resulted therefrom:

BELOVED DIOCESANS,

Among the bitter sufferings and persecutions with which our Church is visited in our German Fatherland today, not the least of our sorrows is the removal of the Catholic Religious Orders and Congregations from the sphere of education. With sinister speed the dispersal of Religious teachers and of schools directed by Religious is proceeding month after month, and has already been carried through to such an extent that we see to our horror that the final destruction of all such schools is not far off. We know that large sections of our people are not informed on this matter, or insufficiently informed. We bishops feel that our consciences and our duty to our flocks oblige us once again to raise our voices in protest, and in the name of justice and religious peace to issue a solemn warning, even at this eleventh hour, against developments whose only aim is the total exclusion of the Church and of Christianity from the education of our German youth.

And first of all we have to give you a report of the distressing occurrences of the last few months. In 126 parishes in Bavarian Government territory teachers belonging to the various Religious Houses in those parishes have been excluded from teaching in the elementary schools. By this new decree 367 teaching nuns have been thrown out of work and prevented from exercising their profession. For decades, in many places for nearly a century, the Religious Orders in the parishes have worked devotedly for the benefit of youth. Enjoying the confidence of the parents and the affection of the children, these nuns have spread abroad the blessings of a Christian education and character formation that has been passed on from generation to generation as a precious heritage in the family.

If we ask why it is that these convent teachers have met with such a hard fate, there is probably no one who can bring any personal reproach against them, or cast doubt either on their loyal devotion to their calling or on their professional abilities. Only one thing is held against them—namely, that they wear a religious habit, and by their sacred vows have consecrated and devoted themselves in a special manner to God and the service of youth. For this reason and for this reason alone have these nuns been declared unfit for the instruction and education of German youth. It is for this reason alone that they have been excluded from the teaching profession for which, just like their lay colleagues in that profession, they had prepared themselves by passing the State examinations with honour. Surely these events must necessarily deeply wound our religious sentiments and outrage our sense of justice!

Since January 1st, 1937, in a short year and a half, more than twelve hundred nuns have been dismissed in this manner from the public elementary school service. To these must be added month by month the ever-growing number of Sisters who have been expelled from the nursery schools, infants' schools and kindergartens, for the good odour of Christian education is to be banned even from these sanctuaries of innocence and hope. There must further be added all those nuns who are now no longer allowed to carry on their needlework classes and their schools of domestic economy, by which our young women were prepared for their future work as housewives and mothers, and provided with all sorts of knowledge useful to them in their future careers. How is it possible to justify this sort of thing in the name of a new-found unity of the nation and the people?

An attempt has been made to justify the expulsion of the nuns from the elementary schools on the plea that these schools were the property of the

State and of the civil parishes, that the duty of education was incumbent on the State and the civil parishes, and that consequently the dismissal of the teaching nuns involved no violation of the rights of the Religious Orders. But at Easter this 'year the Bavarian Ministry of Education, at one blow, ordered and effected the closing or progressive dissolution of eighty-four schools managed by Religious, sixty-four of them being secondary schools for girls and twenty being secondary schools for boys, and all these institutions were beyond any doubt the actual property of the Orders and Congregations concerned. Already for a long time past the way had been prepared for this destructive blow by a series of measures which added burden after burden to the load of these religious schools, and inflicted one injury after another upon them, though their loyalty to their work remained unshaken and their spirit of service continued unabated. Thus last year, by State decree, it was forbidden to send the children of State officials and of employees in the public services to schools managed by Religious. The dissolution which is now ordered means the complete destruction of conventual secondary school education in Bavaria. By way of a reason for this decree of destruction the Orders and Congregations are simply told that there is now no further need for their schools to exist. But since the necessary school places for their 16,000 former pupils were lacking almost everywhere, the civil authorities of the parish areas have been ordered to proceed with a rapid building of new schools, and a special law has been brought into operation, by means of which they may, where necessary, take possession of the conventual school buildings and classrooms by compulsory appropriation. Again we ask whether such an attack on the rights of others is in any way compatible with the basic moral principles of justice and equity.

Nor does unemployment among lay school teachers afford a plausible pretext in these days, since there is such a shortage of lay teachers, both in the elementary and in the secondary schools, that fears are entertained as to their efficient continuance, and there is danger that educational progress will be retarded. Notwithstanding all this, however, hundreds and hundreds of professionally qualified religious teachers of long experience are disqualified by these decrees. But the State and municipal budgets will have to provide for an additional annual expenditure of many millions of marks. Thus, however we look at it, the elimination of the religious teachers and of their schools is a calamity to the nation, an act of injustice, and an act of ingratitude.

A public declaration was recently made to the effect that neither the personal integrity nor the professional efficiency of the expelled religious teachers, nor the past achievements of the schools which they directed, provided any ground for reproach. But, it is said, they must be eliminated from the educational field of today, since by reason of their religious vows they are unable to fulfil the ideological requirements of the National Socialist State in the education of youth.

In answer to that, we bishops have the following declaration to make: The Church and the Religious Orders in their educational work for youth have always and everywhere observed our Lord's injunction: " Render unto Cæsar the things that are Cæsar's and to God the things that are God's." True to this rule of conduct they have always conscientiously fulfilled the claims which the State justly makes in regard to the education of German youth, in the interests of the common good and of the special tasks which confront the nation today. In teaching and training our Christian youth to be loyal to the Faith that is in them, the schools of the Religious have laid special emphasis on building up that sense of patriotism, citizenship and social duty which the spirit of Catholic Faith and morals enshrines. Youth that is trained to be loyal and true to the Faith will certainly fulfil its natural duties towards the nation and the State, especially in the hour of sacrifice. Thus it is that these conventual schools, from the beginning of German history, have proved themselves as the seed-ground and nursery of Christian and German education and character formation in our Fatherland. Is it not an intolerable contradiction that such schools as these should today be destroyed and rooted out from our homeland, just as has so recently been done in Bolshevist countries, . . . and that at a time when the German nation conceives it as its historic task to combat anti-Christian Bolshevism, and appeals to the rest of the Christian world to aid it as comrades in the fight ? How long will the State continue to reject the co-operation of the Church and of her Religious Orders in carrying out the German national task of today, the fight against Communism ?

In the Concordat the German Reich guaranteed that peaceful co-operation with the Church should be permanently maintained and consolidated, especially in the sphere of activity common to both parties, the education of German youth, and made a threefold promise to that effect, a promise binding in loyalty and good faith. For the State promised:

(i) That the Orders of the Catholic Church should be entitled to establish and conduct private schools as hitherto, subject to the general laws governing education.

(ii) That these schools of the Religious Orders should be able to give the same qualifications as the State schools, in so far as they fulfil the curricular requirements which hold for the latter.

(iii) That the State authorisation of members of the Religious Orders to engage in teaching, and their appointment as teachers in elementary, senior and secondary schools, should be governed by such conditions as are obligatory on all, and not by special and exceptional legislation applicable to them alone.

Having drawn your attention to these solemn undertakings in the very words of Article 25 of the Concordat, we ask you, Beloved Diocesans, whether the attacks on our Religious Orders which we have reported to you—the mass dismissal of more than 1,200 nuns from our elementary schools, the dissolution of all secondary schools belonging to the Religious Orders, whether for boys or for girls, and the exclusion of members of Religious Orders from all educational establishments of whatever kind—are compatible with the unequivocal undertakings given in the Concordat. We ask whether they are compatible with German fidelity to solemn obligations and treaties, with the common good of the German people, or with the rights of the Church and of parents to the Christian education of youth.

Conscious of our duty, and of our responsibility before God, before the world and before history, we once again demand justice for our Religious Orders, and peace and freedom for their work in the service of Christian education. And we exhort you, Beloved Diocesans, to pray earnestly for these intentions, and to unite your prayers to the prayer which each Sunday rises to Heaven from the priest at the altar in the name of the whole parish: *We beseech Thee, O Lord, to take our Fatherland into Thy continual protection. Enlighten those who govern it with the illumination of Thine own wisdom. May they know what is for the good of our people, and in Thy power achieve that which is right. Amen.*

THE BISHOPS OF THE DIOCESES OF BAVARIA.

CHAPTER V

THE CHURCH IS EXCLUDED FROM THE WORK OF EDUCATION: III. THE DESTRUCTION OF THE CATHOLIC ELEMENTARY SCHOOLS

1. *Destruction by "Parents' Vote."*

THE actual conversion of the denominational schools into German community schools was carried out in two ways: either by means of the so-called " Parents' Vote "—and this was the method most resorted to at first—or by means of official ordinances, the method adopted later.

Munich, 1936.

At the time of the school entry of 1936 a relentless propaganda for the community schools was set on foot in Munich. In eighty public meetings, in wireless broadcasts, in systematically conducted house-to-house canvassing, pressure—in some cases even economic threats—was brought to bear on parents to make them vote for the community schools. Cardinal Faulhaber found himself obliged to issue a special warning to parents from the pulpit: " Catholic parents ! It is a clear duty of conscience to remain unshaken, even when you are threatened with the loss of your means of livelihood. It is your duty to enter your children for the Catholic schools. No law-abiding State in the world can rob its citizens of those rights which it has guaranteed itself." In spite of this warning the results were crushing. Out of 55,220 children, 35,954 were entered for the community schools —*i.e.*, 65·11 per cent. (as against only 34·55 per cent. in the previous year). For the denominational schools 19,288 children were entered —*i.e.*, 34·89 per cent. (as against 65·45 per cent. in the previous year).

That the " election " was, as a matter of fact, a mere farce, is shown by a pulpit pronouncement issued by the Munich Diocesan Administration on August 30th, 1936:

> In the last few days the newspapers have printed statements made by the Munich Director of Education at a meeting of the City Council, according to which it has been decided, in spite of the protests of the diocesan authorities, to convert forty-four denominational schools in Munich into community schools, or, as they were formerly called, undenominational schools. It is maintained that this mass abolition of Catholic schools has been carried out in response to the desires of a majority of the Munich parents, and as a result of the registrations made at the recent school entry. But complete silence is maintained as to the means by which these school-entry results were secured, and nothing is said about the matters complained of by the diocesan authorities.

We wish, therefore, to make the following points perfectly clear: The results of the recent school entry were secured by means that were entirely unjust and illegal. The afflicted parents of Munich know this only too well by bitter experience, and it is proved up to the hilt in the episcopal protest, which contains a comprehensive list of incontestable facts. Indescribable terrorism, that contravened every principle of law and justice, made it simply impossible for thousands of parents to exercise their right of entering their children for the Catholic schools. The entire educational organisation of the city was ordered by the Munich Director of Education to obstruct enrolment for the denominational schools. The whole of the teaching body was officially called upon by the authorities to work for the recruitment of the community schools. All the resources of propaganda at the service of the Party, the daily Press, thousands of handbills, hundreds of public meetings, even the Air Raid Precautions organisation and the official radio broadcasts were employed for the purpose of branding the denominational schools as harmful to the nation, and the supporters of these schools as enemies of the State. Workmen, employees and officials were threatened with economic disadvantages and even with the loss of their means of livelihood, in order to induce them to withdraw their children from the Catholic schools and send them to the community schools. Parents in a state of poverty had their allowance from the " Winter Relief Work " cut down or withdrawn. A special canvassing and checking service was officially organised by the Party, by means of which house-to-house visits were carried out and pressure brought to bear on mothers and fathers of families to an extent which they were not able to withstand. In contrast to all this, not one word could be said or published in favour of the denominational schools outside the walls of a church, without being at once violently silenced as a disturbance of public order. The police even confiscated a parochial letter circularised by the parish organisations to Catholic parents.

All these lamentable facts have been brought to the notice of the responsible State authorities, in the letter of protest from the diocesan authorities. In the light of these facts, that letter puts a plain question: Where in all the world is an election result, secured by such illegal methods, by such a stifling of the power of free choice, by such violence offered to freedom of conscience and to the rights of parents—where is such an election recognised as legally valid and as a free expression of the parents' wishes ? Wherever right and justice and freedom in matters of conscience are still respected, such an " election " must be regarded as void and of no effect.

Württemberg, 1936.

The school elections in Württemberg on April 21st, 1936, were carried out in exactly the same way as in Munich. Once again the results were what the Nazis desired: of 28,000 schoolchildren, about 26,000 were entered for the community schools—*i.e.*, about 93 per cent.[1] The remaining 7 per cent. created no difficulty, of course, so that in March, 1937, President Mergenthaler of Württemberg was able to announce that the denominational schools in Württemberg had " disappeared into little fragments." Even these last few fragments will soon become a thing of the past, for according to a statement of the Ministry of Education, the last denominational elementary schools in Stuttgart were closed at the beginning of February, 1937, while the last seventeen denominational schools left in the whole of Württemberg were closed on June 4th, 1937.

[1] *Völkischer Beobachter*, April 26th, 1936.

Nürnberg, 1936.

In much the same way, the victory of the community schools was ensured from the very first by an expensive propaganda organisation, by the bludgeoning down of any Catholic counteraction, and by economic threats brought to bear on officials, employees, etc. Out of 4,871 new entries for the school year 1936-7, 3,999, or 82·1 per cent., were for the community schools.

Munich, 1937—The Master-Stroke.

Nazi circles were not content with the results achieved in Munich in 1936. Early in 1937 they therefore staged a school campaign which really is a classical example of the way in which the Nazi State attains its ends by the use of force as an instrument of policy, while at the same time preserving an external façade of freedom. It will prove instructive if we sketch out the main features of the organisation of this campaign.

The following agencies took part in this great drive for the community schools:

(i) *The Party.*—(a) The so-called " Block Wardens " (supervising officials and other trusted agents of the Nazi Party—the NSDAP —designated for a particular block of buildings or group of streets) obtained from the teachers lists of such children as were still attending the denominational schools. They then visited the parents of these children in their homes, and worked on them with veiled threats ("I shall be keeping a close eye on you, you know . . .," " I strongly advise you . . .," etc.).

(b) In " Children's Hours " organised by the schools, the new entrants for the community schools were presented with gifts in the presence of their parents.

(ii) *School Authorities and Teachers.*—(a) The school authorities held several "Parents' Evenings," during which the parents' opinion was worked up in favour of the community schools.

(b) Through the post and through the children the teachers sent appeals for the community schools to the parents, enclosing a printed entry form, already filled in and only requiring to be signed "on the dotted line." At the same time, the teachers sought to influence the parents by hints given through the children—suggestions that it was a long way to the nearest denominational school; reminders that religious instruction was also given in the community schools, etc.

(c) During visits to parents in their homes, teachers represented that it was very doubtful whether the denominational schools could continue to survive. To parents living in the centre of the city they said: "Perhaps you'll have to send your children to some denominational school right away on the outskirts"; parents living on the outskirts were told: " Perhaps your little ones will have to go to some denominational school right in the middle of the city "—in both cases trying to exploit the unwillingness of parents to see their children going long distances to school. They also suggested that the education given in the denominational schools would not be so good, since the diminishing enrolment would involve the combination of several classes. Their talk was interlarded with such expressions as: "Of course, we don't want to put any pressure on you," etc., but at the same time the whole tenor of their message was: "Woe to those who set themselves against the will of National Socialism."

(iii) *The State.*—(*a*) Immediately before the school elections, Minister of State Adolf Wagner instituted an "Enrolment Week for the German Schools," and entrusted the arrangements for this to the community schools' chief protagonists, the so-called "German School Union," an organisation composed principally of neo-pagans.

(*b*) Minister of State Adolf Wagner himself delivered the inaugural speech of the "Enrolment Week for the German Schools," at a public meeting of January 23rd, 1937. Here is an extract:

> Looking at it as a whole, the Party and the State have become one; and this is true also of the separate organs of the State—thus the Party and the administration are one, the Party and the police are one. And now there is laid on me the new task of bringing about this unity of identity between the Party and the school. There is no task more important for the Party and the State than the education of youth in the spirit of the National Socialist ideology, which is the ruling ideology in Party and in State today. If some traces of an outmoded conception of education still survive anywhere in any of our German elementary schools, secondary schools or universities, what I have just said should serve to eliminate them finally. . . .
>
> The teacher should also be interiorly free. Church supervision has, indeed, been done away with in the schools, but there are still a good many clerical gentlemen up and down the country who have not yet reconciled themselves to this. They will, however, have to do so, for today the teacher enjoys the protection of the National Socialist Reich. In this Third Reich we shall at length bury those last remnants of institutions which may have had their justification, value and meaning during the Middle Ages or at the end of the last century, but which are today obsolete and unsuited to the times. The cleric may continue his work in the Church, but to the teacher belongs the school. In the school it is the teacher's task to make our youth German. This alone shows how unsuited to the times we live in is the system of the so-called denominational schools.
>
> I address an appeal to the Churches to exercise their discernment, and not to attempt to stem this development which is in any case most certainly coming. The community school guarantees religious instruction exactly as the denominational school does. It passes on to the children the same spirit, the same matter, the same knowledge, the same abilities. What more do the Churches want? Why should they hold fast to an institution which belongs to an epoch that is past? Why do they expose themselves to the loss of prestige which will certainly come, as more and more of those who are qualified to teach desert the denominational schools for the community schools? Here is a problem by its attitude to which the Church may demonstrate its willingness to co-operate with the new movements of progress. We believe in a life that strides vitally onwards, and for that reason we affirm that the denominational school, as the last remnant of denominational dictatorship in the educational field, is doomed to disappear.

(*c*) Minister of State Wagner issued an appeal for enrolment in the community schools, which was broadcast in the daily Press, by means of placards, by handbills given out in the streets and even by notices affixed to the church doors.

(d) The same Minister took up the cudgels against the pulpit manifesto of the parish clergy, and had a counter-statement or *démenti* published in the stop-press columns of all newspapers. It read as follows:

> The Information Bureau of the Bavarian Government released on January 25th the following statement of the Minister of Education, Adolf Wagner:
> " On Sunday the 24th of January, in connection with the question of school enrolment, an authoritative declaration was read in the churches of Munich which contained misrepresentations and untrue statements. I therefore deem it necessary to give a correct account of the facts.
> " The Bavarian Educational Authority has always laid stress on the fact that the character of our community schools must be in harmony with the theistic sentiments of the German people, and has taken proceedings whenever deviations from this norm have come to its notice. Such isolated misconceptions and deviations are, of course, in no case to be laid to the charge of the community schools as such, since similar occurrences have also taken place and been censured in the denominational schools. The Bavarian Government has never tolerated the removal of the crucifix from schoolrooms, nor did it forbid at Regensburg the sign of the Cross and the joining of hands during prayers. It is entirely untrue that responsible quarters have held up the fundamental principles of Christianity to ridicule before the Munich teachers.
> " The manifesto read on Sunday in the churches was obviously designed to influence those concerned in favour of the denominational schools with a view to the forthcoming school entry. Since I observe that in this case false statements are being exploited, as the chief supervising school authority in Bavaria I am bound to take action. In the most express manner possible I draw the attention of parents to the following:
>
> " (i) The community school is, in the present state of the law, a school in which, according to the regulations, religious instruction is guaranteed exactly as it is in the denominational schools.
> " (ii) The present state of the law allows parents to decide freely to which form of school they shall send their children.
> " (iii) Separation of children in the schools according to their religious persuasion is not desirable. It no longer fits in with the Third Reich in which we ought to realise, and must realise, that—whether we are Catholics or Protestants—we are Germans. In the same way, we no longer make distinctions of class or condition, between high and low, rich or poor."

Let us now examine this *démenti*. It is maintained that in the community school the same provision has been made for religious **instruction** as in the denominational schools. That was never disputed in the pulpit manifesto, rather it was said that it was not true that in the community school religious **education** was equally safeguarded. Further, the pulpit manifesto described the case of a community school in Regensburg where the sign of the Cross and the joining of hands at prayers had been forbidden. The Minister of State corrects this by saying: "The Bavarian Educational Authority has never forbidden this." Quite so. The veto in this case came not from the Government but from the Party!

(e) Other State officials and organs joined in the enrolment drive. Thus the President of the Reich Postal Service in the Munich district did his part by sending to every post office official a handbill in favour of the community schools. Similar help was given by the German State Railways and many other public services.

(iv) *The City Authorities.*—(a) The City provided 16,000 RM. for the purchase of gifts to be presented to the children at the "Children's Hours."

(b) City School Inspector Bauer gave a radio broadcast " triologue " with two representatives of the parents as a recruiting appeal for the community schools (January 28th and 29th).

(c) Inspector Bauer on January 28th addressed a meeting of the Catholic parents of the children attending the convent school at Anger advocating the conversion of this training college and practice school directed by the Poor Sisters of the Schools. The speaker appealed to the wish of the Führer to safeguard national unity.

(d) Necessitous minors were sent to the community schools by the Mayor through the respective guardians. In this dignitary's letter, which we reproduce below, especial significance attaches to the phrase: " I accordingly take your agreement for granted."

The Mayor of Munich,
    City Youth Department.
(*Necessitous Minors.*)

MUNICH.
January 21*st*, 1937.

Subject: Enrolment in Elementary Schools.

In accordance with your request, the City Youth Department has arranged for your child (ward) to be placed, for care and maintenance, in the charge of foster-parents at the public expense, for the purposes of guardianship and education. In pursuance of the educational aims laid down by National Socialism, the City Youth Department will employ all such means as are calculated to ensure that the child shall be trained to be one who feels, thinks and acts, morally and socially, as a German, and who is aware of his solidarity with, and of his duty towards, the national community of the German people. The guardianship of the City Youth Department is based upon the feeling of German nationality and is designed to kindle devoted love for Fatherland and Führer, together with a National Socialist cast of mind which is ready for deeds. Exclusiveness and splitting-off of particular sections of the population, social grades, parties and religious communities run counter to this idea of one great national community.

For these reasons the City Youth Department will, at the forthcoming school enrolment, cause your child (ward) to be entered for his elementary education in the German community school, unless indeed he already belongs to it.

According to the National Socialist conception of the law, in contrast to former notions, parents no longer enjoy complete dominion in their own right or independently of the will of the State in this matter of education, but are rather trustees for the people. I accordingly take your agreement with the action of the City Youth Department for granted.

Should you, however, German citizen or German citizeness, have other opinions on this matter, which we do not anticipate, you should communicate at once with the undersigned department of the City Youth Department.

(v) *The Police.*—(a) The police prohibited the distribution of the "Parish Letter" issued by the parish priests of the City at the time of the school entry.

(b) From Wednesday, January 27th, onwards, the police kept a day and night watch on the offices of the Diocesan Administration and on all Catholic presbyteries to ensure that no printed matter in favour of the denominational schools came in or went out. Part of the "Parish Letter" was confiscated.

All that the Church was able to do by way of Counteraction.—
(i) Visits paid to the parents in their homes by the clergy. This was done as far as possible.

(ii) Pulpit pronouncements. Three of these pronouncements are available. The first is in the form of a statement to parents signed by Cardinal Faulhaber:

> It would be a grave burden on our conscience were we to remain silent at this decisive time. And so we address ourselves to you, Catholic parents, pleading with you and warning you to remember your responsibilities and to enrol your children for the denominational schools.
> For it is not true, as is said, that religious education is secured in the community school just as well as in the denominational school. Already in a community school in Regensburg, Catholic children have been forbidden to make the sign of the Cross and to join their hands when praying; already in some places the crucifix has been removed from the schools; already, at a meeting of the Munich teachers which all were obliged to attend, authoritative personages have held up the fundamental truths of Christianity to ridicule.

The second pronouncement is a declaration written by Cardinal Faulhaber and issued by him at the conclusion of the school enrolment. It was couched in almost the same words as a protest issued by the Diocesan Administration and ends:

> When, in spite of this, forty-four denominational schools in Munich have been suppressed, appeal to these " election " results being made by way of justification, then justice and equity and the freedom of conscience of parents have been trampled under foot. Equity and freedom of conscience are the greatest treasures of a people. He who despises these treasures brings harm to his people.

The third pronouncement is the concluding declaration of the Catholic parish clergy which was read from all pulpits on the last Sunday in January:

> . . . We had hoped against hope that the election this year would perhaps be a free decision of conscience on the part of Catholic parents. But our hopes have been bitterly disappointed. . . .

It then referred to the injustice of the measures adopted by the public authorities and to the suppression of every public attempt to express Catholic views and continued:

> In view of all this, we maintain that the conditions necessary for a free expression of their desires on the part of the parents are no longer existent. Catholic parents cannot indeed relinquish a right that is guaranteed to them both by the law and by the Concordat, but we must nevertheless declare that it has been made impossible for them under the pressure which has been brought to bear on them to exercise this right with the true freedom proper to citizens. Only one path still remains open to us.

We shall address a petition of right to the highest competent authority in the Reich against this election which, under the circumstances we have instanced, would better be described as a sham election. Might does not give birth to a new right, and thus the right we have to our denominational schools can never disappear. . . .

This time the opponents of the denominational schools could be content with the results of their " free " school elections. Out of 7,654 children enrolled, 7,322 (95·6 per cent.) went to the community schools, and only 332 (4·4 per cent.) to the denominational schools.

The Saar Territory and Trier, 1937.—This example was followed in March in the District of Saarpfalz. We have the same familiar picture; or, if there is any change, we see at most a greater confidence as to the results, and therefore somewhat less strenuous efforts on the part of the Nazi opponents of the denominational schools. All was over within three days. One morning District Leader Bürckel ordered the local group leaders and cell leaders to carry the election through before evening; he even forced Catholic parents to make house-to-house visits with lists of parents to recruit for the community schools. Various other circumstances attached to this election which did violence to the conscience of the parents. Again the results were what might have been expected—97 per cent. for the community schools.

We quote two documents emanating from the Church authorities in which the methods employed in this election are pilloried. The first is a joint declaration issued by the two Bishops of Trier and Speyer on March 23rd, 1937, of which the following are the more important extracts:

On Saturday, March 20th, 1937, the authorities suddenly imposed an election, for or against the community school, on a section of the parents and guardians of the District of Saarpfalz.

According to newspaper reports, the great majority of those concerned pronounced for the community school. An ecclesiastical investigation as to how the number of those who voted for the community school was arrived at has so far yielded surprising results. When the investigation has been concluded, the results of it will be communicated to the competent authorities.

We know that many Catholics, in spite of the pressure brought to bear on them, have acted in accordance with their Catholic convictions. In doing so they had not the least intention, by taking up a hostile attitude to the community school, of giving expression to any hostility towards Christians of other persuasions. They live in peace with them, as we all do. They know the judgement passed on the community school by our Holy Father and by their bishops; it is evident to anyone with even a passing acquaintance with the educational developments of recent years that these schools are not and never will be truly Christian, and this indeed is already confirmed by certain school books which have been taken into use. They know, moreover, that the Catholic school with its genuinely Catholic teachers is not only the best from a religious point of view, but also from the standpoint of the State and of the nation.

We know also to our sorrow that a number of Catholics, against their better knowledge, have been disloyal to their conscientious convictions by casting their votes in favour of the community school. We do not judge them—we leave that to Almighty God.

We know that the hearts of Catholics who are loyally devoted to their

Church are today filled with sorrow, especially the hearts of those who, in the face of the indescribable pressure brought to bear on their consciences, finally gave their vote for the community school. Our Holy Church mourns with them. For the sake of parents, children and nation the Church has fought energetically for the denominational school. She was able to do so with all the greater insistence since the Reich Government, in the Concordat with the Holy See which, on its ratification, became part of our law, has pledged itself to the maintenance of Catholic schools and the erection of new Catholic schools. As recently as 1935, at the District Party Congress in Guben, the Reichsminister of Education declared: "We have guaranteed the denominational schools in a Concordat. What we have promised we shall observe."

As a sign of the mourning of the Catholic Church and of the loyal Catholic faithful, in the whole district of Saarpfalz the bells of the Catholic churches will remain silent on Easter Sunday. At the usual times for Holy Mass, Low Mass will be said without singing or organ music.

This Pastoral Message is to be read at Divine Service on Good Friday and on Easter Sunday.

LUDWIG, *Bishop of Speyer.*
FRANZ RUDOLF, *Bishop of Trier.*

Speyer and Trier, *March 23rd,* 1937.

The second document is an extract from the *Clergy Communications*[1] published by the Vicariate-General of Trier:

Although the existence of the denominational schools is protected by paragraph 33 of the Elementary School Law and by Article 23 of the Reich Concordat, many efforts are being made to destroy the denominational principle in elementary education. Thus, for instance, the joint Catholic school of Kappel and Kludenbach has been suppressed, and the Catholic children of Kludenbach are thus obliged to attend the Protestant school of that locality. Similar attempts are being made in certain other places in our diocese—*e.g.,* in Gornhausen, Neunkirchen-bei-Schönberg, and Talling. In many places the parish council has decided to introduce the community school—*e.g.,* in Rhaunen, Wallmenroth and Klosterchumd. In the district of Baumholder they have begun to collect signatures by way of preparing for the introduction of the community school. In certain elementary schools a Catholic teacher has been substituted for a Protestant teacher, and a Protestant for a Catholic; and in Sien, for instance, Catholic and Protestant teachers were pooled for a whole series of different school subjects. The excitement caused by these events led to a school strike in Heinzenbach-Unzenberg, but the parents and guardians concerned were fined 10 RM. for each child who did not attend school and the father of a big family, who could not pay these fines, was punished with a sentence of three days in prison.

Overcoming the Will of the Parents by Violence

We offer a few more examples of the way in which the parents' wishes were violently over-ridden:

(i) **Rush Tactics and Falsification of Election Results.**—In a communication to his clergy of December 21st, 1936, Count von Galen, the Bishop of Münster, said:

In the Archdiocese of Cologne, by means of house-to-house canvassing, the population was actually invited to put their signatures to lists drawn up in favour of the community schools. Since this agitation was started suddenly, giving no time for thinking the matter over and forestalling any possibility of giving advice and explanation regarding the consequences of

[1] No. 2, 1937

the steps proposed, a certain amount of success was achieved. It is therefore urgently necessary to warn the faithful everywhere . . . to maintain the greatest vigilance against an agitation which may break out suddenly.

The Bishop of Speyer, Mgr. Ludwig Sebastian, in a Pastoral of April 11th, 1937, gives some almost incredible instances of surprise attacks and falsification in these so-called " elections ":

They appeal to the " overwhelming results of the election on March 20th " to prove the necessity of the community schools. I know that I shall have the agreement of all of you when I assert in all candour the community school has not come into being by legal methods or by methods which are in accordance with the principles of justice. . . . It has been spoken of as being seen " in the brilliant clearness of the actual fact of the election." But we maintain that this election was not sponsored by a German sense of honour. . . . Everything which makes an election a free election was absent in the great majority of cases. . . .

In many parishes, in which it was known that an overwhelming majority for the denominational schools existed, no election at all was held and yet 100 per cent. success for the community school was announced! Let me give an example: In one parish the parish councillors were invited to a meeting by the Mayor. It was suggested to them that, in view of the overwhelming results of the elections in the rest of the district, it would be well for them to pass a motion in favour of the community school for their own parish. Without further consideration the Parish Council gave its agreement. At once a telegram went off to the Government stating that the locality had declared itself 100 per cent. in favour of the Christian (*i.e.*, NS) community schools.

In another place an election was held on March 20th. At first, out of 100 parents and guardians, only six voted for the community school. From the Parish Council offices further recruits were worked up until the number rose to twelve. The newspapers on Monday morning reported that 100 per cent. had declared in favour of the community school.

Here is another case which shows how many votes were won by sheer rush tactics. A workman writes: " On Saturday evening I came home from my work without any inkling of what was impending. I was at once brought out of my house and taken along to the Parish Council offices. On arrival there I at once declared, ' I want the Roman Catholic school,' and wished to leave forthwith. The local ' Cell Leader ' held me back and wrote a note to my firm declaring that in consequence of my declaration I was dismissed from my job. A police constable told me that if I did not sign I could never again obtain any public work. It was urged: ' The community school will come in any case; you're only making trouble for yourself.' I signed in a state of excitement and confusion. I never wanted, nor do I now want, anything else but the Catholic school. I did not sign of my own free will. I declare that my signature was extorted by force and is void in law."

In other districts in which the first election resulted in 100 per cent. votes in favour of the denominational school the election was not allowed to count, and a second and even a third election was held in which wholesale pressure was applied, both by individual persuasion and by other means.

Here is an example: In a certain place the first election took place on Saturday, March 20th; 94 per cent. of the votes were recorded against the community school. This election was entirely free. Although this election was completely valid and the parents had voted freely according to their own convictions, the results were not published and, contrary to all expectations, a second election was ordered for the 23rd of the month. Printed forms were brought into the homes of the parents with the words: " I hereby declare that I wish to send my children to the Christian community school, in which denominational religious instruction is guaranteed." These forms were to be signed by the parents and given in at the Mayor's office from 10 o'clock onwards. Most parents crossed out the printed words and wrote across the form: " I do not recognise any school other than the Roman Catholic school." Large numbers of Catholic men and women gathered at the Parish Council offices during the afternoon. The results of this election were almost the same as in the case of the first election. The Election Commission was not even satisfied with this second valid election, and staged a third election for Wednesday the 24th. Printed forms with the same wording were once again distributed, and the parents asked to attend at the office. A great number of Catholic parents appeared, and declared that they would vote according to their consciences. Meanwhile a telephone message was sent to a man by a business firm, telling him to send in his resignation as their local manager, since he was a spokesman for the Catholic schools. He was told: " If you support the community school, you can retain your position as manager." The man concerned replied: " I should be a dirty blackguard if I were to buy the manager's position at the price of my convictions."

On October 25th, 1937, in Neukirchen-bei-Sulzbach (Oberpfalz), the parents were summoned to a meeting, the purpose of which was not announced, though it was proclaimed: " Those who do not attend this meeting will be taken as agreeing with the resolutions passed at it." Out of 65 Catholic parents qualified to vote, 20 stayed away. After an address on the subject of the community schools and the denominational schools, 11 people left the meeting in protest because no discussion was permitted. Of those who still remained, 16 voted for the community school and 9 against it. The next day the " election results " were published: that 47 votes had been given for the community school and 9 against it. The 47 alleged favourable votes were reckoned up in this way: 20 non-attendants, 11 withdrawn in protest (these were absent during the actual voting, and the suffrages of absent or abstaining voters were taken as affirmative) and only 16 actual favourable votes, making a total of 47 ! An " election " was held under similar circumstances on October 23rd, 1937, in Königstein (Oberpfalz). Once again absentees and those who withdrew in protest were counted as voting for the community school. Result: 92·7 per cent. for the community school !

We have the following authentic report from Frankfurt-am-Main:

On May 24th, 1938, the parents of school children were summoned to a meeting by the members of the Frankfurt School Union for the purpose of deciding the question of the German community schools. Numerous Catholic parents and guardians presented themselves at the time announced, but on their arrival they found to their astonishment that the large assembly hall was nearly full of Party functionaries, SA-men, SS-men and Hitler Youth, so that only a few Catholic parents were able to find places. The Nazis had all appeared in uniform. The meeting lasted scarcely fifteen minutes. The Nazi chairman of the meeting gave a propaganda speech of about ten minutes in favour of the Nazi community schools, and was repeatedly interrupted by thunders of applause from the Party ranks. At the end of his " election speech," in which more was said about national unity than about the community school, the chairman called upon all those who were against the community school, and consequently against national unity, to leave the hall. Four of the parents protested against this measure. The chairman then declared, with the unanimous agreement of the Nazis, that the Catholic parents had voted 100 per cent., with only four exceptions, in favour of the community school.

The Bishop of Limburg, Dr. Hilfrich, took up this matter in a letter of protest to the Reichsminister of Education dated June 11th, 1938:

> Catholic parents have been roused to the greatest indignation by this " interrogation " which has been held, and by the specious and inaccurate declaration of the parents' decision, on all of which information has been submitted to the President of the District Government in the report of my Ordinariate. Since it was made quite impossible for these parents to make known their wishes, in the name of the Catholic parents and guardians I enter an emphatic protest against this method of " consulting " parents in order to introduce changes in the conditions of education laid down by the law and, on my own account, I appeal to the Reich Concordat which guarantees the maintenance of denominational schools and even the erection of new denominational schools.

(ii) **Direct Deception is also Employed.**—In Upper Bavaria the parents' elections on the question of the community schools were, in a large proportion of cases, carried out in the following manner:

> Without any previous warning the parents in the various localities were summoned to the Mayor's office. There they were asked: Do you wish the school to remain Christian as hitherto ? Do you wish the crucifix to be retained in the school as hitherto ? Do you wish religious instruction to be given in the school as hitherto ? If you want this, then sign this form on the dotted line. The parents, thinking that the State had given in over the school question, and that the denominational schools would be retained, were most ready to sign the form. In the evening it was announced: By a completely free election of the parents, Upper Bavaria has declared itself 97 per cent. in favour of the community schools of Adolf Hitler.

In the Pastoral of the Bishop of Speyer of April 11th, 1937, which we have already quoted, the following example was also given:

> Some of those engaged in recruiting for the community schools deceived unsuspecting womenfolk and induced them to give their signatures by saying, for example: " Nothing is going to be altered in the school"; " You are being asked to add your signature in favour of the retention of the religious instruction in the school"; " We are collecting signatures so that what the parish priest wants may be secured"; " In any case, it is impossible for you to do anything about it—everyone has already declared in favour of the community school." Another instance: In one place the election was held on Saturday between 12 midday and 2 o'clock, at a time therefore when most of the men would be away working in the factory or in the woods. Without any previous warning, those whose task it was to secure the agreement of the voters simply appeared in the various parents' homes, where in most cases only the wives were at home. These were not very conversant with the matter, but for the most part believed the information given to them by the canvassers, who said: " That is the right form. The parents are being left in full control. It's quite all right, I'm a Catholic myself," etc. When these good people realised what it was that they had signed there was general mourning and tears, and many passed sleepless nights. When the womenfolk saw how they had been deceived, and wanted to withdraw their signatures, they were roughly refused.

(iii) **The Use of Threats and Other Forms of Pressure.**—In Regensburg the pressure brought to bear upon the Catholic parents was so

THREATS AND OTHER FORMS OF PRESSURE

strong that there can be no question of a free expression of their wishes. The Bishop of Regensburg accordingly instructed the Catholic parents of his diocese to send letters to the parish priests of their parishes, withdrawing their vote for the community school, on the ground that it was extorted by force.

The violent over-riding of the wishes of parents was pilloried in the following words by Cardinal Schulte, Archbishop of Cologne, at the beginning of January, 1937:

> You are being ruthlessly oppressed; advantage is being taken of your economic dependence to stage mass meetings in favour of the community schools and to give them the appearance of being voluntary. They seek to deceive you with false notions, your patriotism and your solidarity with the nation is called in question, threats are applied in order to intimidate you, in order at last to gain your signature for the community school, and even to oblige you actively to engage in recruiting for this school.

The description given by the Bishop of Trier, Mgr. Bornewasser, of the way in which terror was brought to bear on the consciences of the voters is specially shocking.[1] The Bishop of Speyer, too, in the Pastoral of April 11th, 1937, parts of which we have quoted already, makes a similar denunciation:

> Fear played a great part in the enrolment for the community schools. Can it be denied that hints of economic disadvantage were given, or that threats were made that public assistance or work or position might be lost? In most cases in which Catholics gave their signatures against their convictions, fear was at least a contributory factor. As a matter of fact, those parents and guardians who voted for the denominational schools were excluded from any participation in the Winter Relief.
> In one parish, those who would not at once sign in favour of the community school were told: " The school question is a question of bread and butter." One woman replied: " For me it is not a question of bread and butter, but a question of conscience. I am responsible for the education of my children." In one parish, in the course of the election day, about thirty men and women came to the parish priest, some of them in a state of confusion, some weeping, some full of discouragement and despair, to bewail their spiritual distress.

In Berlin, Bishop Preysing found himself forced to have a statement read from the pulpits on January 30th, 1938, in which it was said:

> Various school authorities in Berlin have made attempts to bring Catholic parents to change their minds about sending their children to Catholic schools. The parents have made a protest to the competent Catholic authorities, in consequence of which the bishop put the formal question to the City President of Berlin as to whether the appropriate provisions of the Concordat (Article 23) were still valid. An affirmative reply was given. Catholic parents are accordingly once again warned not to allow themselves to be dissuaded from sending their children to Catholic schools.

Disciplinary measures taken against Catholic fathers in dependent positions caused many parents to waver. Thus in 1936 in Munich, for instance, a postal worker was dismissed from his position and left without resources, because he had entered his three children for the denominational schools. Any number of similar examples can be quoted.

[1] This Pastoral is given in full on pp. 160-162. *Cf.* especially p. 161.

156 DESTRUCTION OF CATHOLIC ELEMENTARY SCHOOLS

(iv) **The Use of Sheer Force.**—The case of the village of Weldirgfelden (Kreis Künzelsau) illustrates this. Since the parents refused to send their children to the community school, the Catholic school was closed out of hand and the children distributed among various villages in the neighbourhood. Most of them had to go to school on foot every day to Hermuthausen, a Protestant village, so that throughout the whole week they were unable to go to church. All complaints from the parents were in vain.

From many other places reports are also constantly coming in that recalcitrant parents have been subjected to disciplinary measures—*e.g.*, fathers have been deprived of the special allowances made for large families; teachers who refused to lend themselves to community school propaganda have been punished by being transferred or retired, etc.

Results of Elections that were Really Free

Irrefutable evidence of the fact that the State elections were nothing more than an elaborately staged farce is provided by the results of the enquiry which in some dioceses the bishops caused to be made by the clergy and in the churches. These elections, which were not influenced by any sort of threats or promises, gave the following results in favour of the denominational schools:

	Per Cent.
In Essen by means of written statements (by reason of absence from home, etc., many could not reply)	79·29
In twelve other parish districts of Essen	92·2
In the Deanery of Neuss by means of written statements (7 per cent. declared that they wished to hold aloof from the matter)	89·1
In the Deanery of Grevenbroich	95·8
In four parishes of Düsseldorf	82·0
In one parish in Cologne	88·0
In Berghausen	68·0
In Zons	79·0
In Kirchherten	90·0
In Immekeppel	91·0
In Lengsdorf	99·0

The following figures were obtained in the Diocese of Münster: Out of roughly a million Catholics of the diocese, 824,122 adult Catholics attended the morning services in the churches. They were asked to indicate their desire to retain the Catholic schools by raising their hands, and 813,471 adults raised their hands, thus giving free expression to their desires. This figure is equivalent to about 98·7 per cent. A similar election was carried out in Oldenburg, and here the figures were still better, amounting to 99·18 per cent. (These facts are taken from a letter from the Bishop of Münster " to the Führer and Reich Chancellor, Adolf Hitler," dated March 8th, 1939.)

In a Pastoral read from the pulpits in April, 1939, the Bishop of Münster said:

In spite of the free and open manifestation of the will of the people, by which they declared almost unanimously for the retention of the Catholic schools—a fact which has been brought to the knowledge of the officials and the highest authorities in the Government—at the beginning of the new school year Catholic denominational schools have been closed in many places in this diocese.

After it had been made known that those concerned had the right to enter their objections within four weeks, tens of thousands of letters of protest were sent to the educational authorities, but, without any attention being paid to them, the Catholic schools were closed and converted into community schools.

Bishop Damian of Fulda issued a Pastoral, in which he makes the following remarks regarding the attitude taken up by the faithful in his diocese to the school question:

Out of about 64,000 parents and guardians in the diocese of Fulda, in spite of the premature suspension of registration which became necessary in many places, 50,800 registered their votes on the question of the Catholic denominational schools. Out of these 50,800, no less than 50,467 have declared to the bishop that they desire the Catholic denominational schools to be maintained. Out of about 64,000 parents and guardians, therefore, 80 per cent. have registered their opinions with regard to the denominational school question, and of these 99·6 per cent. have declared themselves in favour of the retention of the Catholic schools.

At the beginning of March, in many parishes of Upper Silesia, the faithful were requested to signify their desire for the retention of the Catholic schools by rising from their places. Eye-witnesses tell us that practically everyone gave this sign.

From the Nazi *Schwarze Korps* we learn that in the district of Dachau a certain Baroness von Gumppenberg gave the following reasons for voting at the election in favour of the denominational schools:

I cast my vote against the community school:
(i) because I am a Roman Catholic, and therefore do not wish my children to be brought up in the spirit of neo-paganism, since from this spirit and outlook it is but a short step to complete cultural Bolshevism;
(ii) on account of my national and thoroughly German attitude, for I cannot and will not contribute by such a step to the fulfilment of a demand which the Communists have been making for years.

Those who are acquainted with the tone of the *Schwarze Korps* will not be surprised to read in it the wildest abuse of this upright Catholic woman and mother: the Baroness " reveals herself as a docile parrot of those experts in deceit, the clergy," etc.

2. *The Shorter Way—Dissolution by Decree*, 1938 *and* 1939

The school ballots just mentioned had already become exceptional, for in general from the year 1938 the simpler method of official enactment was followed. So in the district of Oldenburg, for example, as the periodical *Nationalsozialistisches Bildungswesen*[1] reports, first the smaller denominational schools were gradually abolished by the authorities and then the schools in the larger areas and towns were joined together into National Socialist community schools.

[1] No. 10, 1938.

158 DESTRUCTION OF CATHOLIC ELEMENTARY SCHOOLS

It is interesting to observe these measures in detail. We are enabled to do this by a Pastoral of the Bishop of Münster of July 31st, 1938, from which we give the following extract:

The National Socialist Government of Oldenburg published on June 11th, 1936, a new school law for the district of Oldenburg in which the denominational character of the elementary schools was once again legally recognised. This new law expressly determines: " The schools are to be organised according to religious persuasions." Nevertheless the same Minister, Pauly, who put his signature to this law, at Easter, 1938, suppressed numerous denominational schools without further ado. This measure, which was carried out contrary to established law, aroused " the greatest excitement " among the faithful of both denominations. In many districts it came to strong demonstrations of protest on the part of parents, which were suppressed by force of arms. Thus, for example, after such a demonstration of protest in Goldenstedt a number of men of repute in that district were arrested, not indeed to be brought before the court, but to be put in a concentration camp, where twelve of them still remain today. The National Socialist Minister, Pauly, issued a communication to parents and guardians, at the conclusion of which he threatened that those parents who kept their children away from the community schools would be imprisoned by the Secret Police without judicial proceedings and legal sentence.

The bishop then enumerates a list of further arrests, expulsions and punishments of Catholic priests and laymen. Even the official representative of the bishop in Vechta, Mgr. Vorwerk, was expelled by the Gestapo.[1]

Since February 15th, 1938, there are no longer any Catholic schools in Würzburg. By a regulation of the Government of Mainfranken all Catholic and Protestant elementary schools were immediately transformed into community schools.

On June 9th the German News Agency announced: 500 Berlin elementary schools have been converted into community schools.

The Bavarian Minister of Education announced with pride in the *Völkischer Beobachter*:[2]

The denominational schools throughout the whole of Bavaria have now been transformed into community schools. At this turning-point in the history of our public elementary school system I thank all who have co-operated with me in the fulfilment of the task which I set.

Signed: ADOLF WAGNER.

In Austria the shortest work possible was made of the Catholic schools. The regional Educational Councils with a stroke of the pen ordered the closing of all private schools and the transformation of elementary schools into community schools.

On January 1st, 1939, the general situation was as follows: There were no Catholic elementary schools at all in Bavaria, Württemberg, Baden, Saxony, Thuringia, Oldenburg, Saarpfalz (the former Saar district), large parts of Prussia and the whole of Austria. By this date, then, altogether more than 10,000 Catholic elementary schools in the Third Reich had been suppressed or converted into National Socialist community schools.

[1] *Cf.* p. 43. [2] South German edition, October 27th, 1938.

DISSOLUTION BY DECREE, 1938 AND 1939

Then in the spring of 1939 reports follow in rapid succession that with the beginning of the new school year denominational schools would be transformed into community schools by force of law. This transformation is being arranged, for example, in Gelsenkirchen, Bottrop, Recklinghausen, Frankfurt-am-Main, Düsseldorf, Cologne, Berlin and throughout the whole diocese of Münster. In April the *Kölnische Volkszeitung* reported that from April 18th on, in the Rhineland, the " German elementary school " had taken the place of the denominational school as the school of the community, and this formerly Catholic newspaper adds the laconic note: " The classrooms which are emptied by the introduction of the ' German elementary school ' in the district of Cologne are being put to other uses; arrangements have been made to use them as homes for Hitler Youth, kindergartens, etc." These losses can be rightly estimated only when it is realised that in the Rhine Province in 1937, according to the " Statistical Year Book for the German Reich," there were 3,317 Catholic elementary schools attended by 651,518 pupils. These reports were further supplemented in the months following, so that finally in the summer of 1939 it is true to say there are, practically speaking, no more denominational schools in Germany.

Even the Kindergartens

Because National Socialism wants the whole man, body and soul, for itself, it will not allow the Church even to take care of the children in the kindergartens. The Württemberg Chief State Councillor, Drück, gave expression to this principle in his address to parents in November, 1936:

> According to our racial principles we demand that in questions of education German national interests be pre-eminent and everything else be subordinate to them. There must be no doubt on this point either—namely, that even in kindergartens the denominational principle must disappear, and so, for the future, the municipalities and the National Socialist Welfare Organisation will be responsible also for these. If the children go through the kindergarten, the German community school and the Hitler Youth and hold together there, then they will hold together also when they have grown up.

In the course of recent years the kindergartens have been more and more taken out of the hands of Catholic nuns. Thus, to name but a few cases, in 1937 the Catholic kindergartens in Trier, Ravensburg and Heilbronn were closed; in 1938 nearly all those in Austria; in 1939 the remainder throughout the Reich.

As early as 1936 the Bishop of Trier made the following telling remarks in a Pastoral Letter written on the occasion of a charity week:

> There is a movement also against the kindergartens under the control of the Church, which are said to impede the growth of the spirit of national unity. With talk of this kind attempts are made to persuade parents not to send their children any longer to the nuns and their kindergartens. It really is remarkable: how can children of the age of two to six upset the national community by their harmless games and innocent joys ? What is

one to say, when certain official bodies no longer send children to our Children's Convalescent Homes, because they loyally hold fast to their general religious character; while other organisations, which till now have used our homes, even made the inconceivable demand that we should lock the doors of the chapel, take the education and care of the children from the hand of the self-sacrificing nuns, forbid access to all clergy and remove all religious pictures and objects of devotion which remind children of their religious creed?

At the conclusion of his Pastoral, Bishop Bornewasser emphasises that the Church would never consent to such demands, and consequently exhorts the faithful to be more than ever loyal towards the hard-pressed institutions of the Church that are engaged in charitable and educational activities.

3. *A Final Judgement*

Several bishops exposed from the pulpit the illegalities of these measures and their far-reaching consequences for the German people. We shall, however, content ourselves with quoting the stirring Pastoral of Mgr. Bornewasser, Bishop of Trier, which was circulated by courier in December, 1937, and consequently was not available for reading everywhere. We reproduce this powerful document of the *Kulturkampf* in its entirety:

BELOVED FAITHFUL OF THIS DIOCESE,

My reason for addressing you again today is my desire to stand guard over the right, the truth, and the freedom of conscience of the members of my flock. You all know that on November 2nd the community school was suddenly introduced in Trier, Wittlich, Bernkastel-Cues, Ehrang, Konz, Karthaus and other places. Last Sunday I appealed to you to make use of the right of protest which you enjoy according to the law. Many thousands have done this, unconstrained, uninfluenced, by a free decision and in the open light of day, in spite of much espionage. All these thousands of people wished publicly to protest the fact that the denominational schools were destroyed overnight and the Catholic children forced into the community schools, in contravention of the provisions of the law for the maintenance of elementary schools and of the Reich Concordat. I know that quite as many thousands of people support the denominational schools in their hearts, but refrain from registering the fact openly, since, under present circumstances, they fear for their livelihood.

The protest lists have been, and are being, guarded from all possible attack or misuse. One single page of signatures was confiscated at the door of the church of St. Matthias in Trier. That same evening four of the Trier clergy, after attending a conference, were taken to the State Secret Police and subjected to a thorough personal search, without result, however. If then during this week our opponents have been bandying about such remarks as, " We have the lists in our possession," or " The lists are now in Berlin, and are being sent to us," they were telling deliberate falsehoods calculated to deceive and intimidate.

I have been shocked and deeply distressed by what I have heard in the course of the week about these counter-measures which have been taken against the Catholic protest. I am unable to rid myself of the conviction that they are likely to spread among the people an oppressive feeling of legal insecurity.

This week I have seen that in this diocese of Trier, whose soil was in the past so often reddened by the blood of the martyrs, living martyrs are still to be found today—men and women who are suffering a terrible interior martyrdom for the sake of their Faith and their loyalty to the Church.

It has been said by someone: " We do not intend to make any martyrs." But they are making martyrs, many martyrs whose interior sufferings afflict both body and soul. As at all times in the Church's history, it is on them that our hopes of better times rest.

It has been said: Officials who have made their voice heard against the introduction of the community schools would be dismissed; pensioners would lose their grants; the children of those who had entered their names in the lists would never succeed in finding employment; shop-keepers would be boycotted; threats of dismissal were made by factory managers, etc. Here and there officials were required to state under their service oath whether they or any of their family had signed. Block wardens went from house to house, trying in many cases to intimidate even women, and force them to withdraw their objections. They even spoke of sabotage of Government measures, of national unreliability, of sentiments of enmity towards the State, of disciplinary action on the part both of the State and of the Party. In this connection the Mayor of Trier—not, it is true, until eight days after the community schools had been introduced—issued a statement on November 10th expressly recognising the right of appeal provided for in the law of July 28th, 1906, and announcing that this right could be exercised within four weeks at the City Education Department.

My appeal of last Sunday and your signatures to the protest were entirely unobjectionable from the point of view of the State law. So far as the registration of protests at the City Education Department is concerned, the experiences of recent weeks lead one to doubt if many will take this step. During the canvassing of the past few weeks, all sorts of reasons have been alleged by way of enticing harassed individuals to withdraw their signatures to the protest: it was desired to spare the Protestant children the long journey to school; traffic dangers made it necessary to make the journey to school as short as possible; many Protestant parents had already sent their children to near-by Catholic schools; in Trier the new schools would save the city about 18,000 marks a year; schools of this sort had already existed in other German towns for 100 years and more. But of course no mention was made of the fact that, although these schools were really " Christian undenominational schools," in which both Catholic and Protestant children were taught together, yet they had never been approved by the Church.

I must leave my hearers to judge for themselves how much these alleged reasons are worth. It is not difficult.

But as a German bishop I have grave words to say on another topic— namely, on the validity of the Reich Concordat. This Concordat is a solemn treaty, which gives certain rights to both parties, but which is also binding on each in the same way.

State authorities are painfully careful in ensuring that the Concordat is faithfully observed by the bishops. They have a right to do this, but this right carries with it a sacred duty to ensure that they themselves observe the provisions of this treaty between two Sovereign Powers. In this solemn treaty we read a sentence of fundamental importance: " The maintenance of the Catholic denominational schools and the erection of new Catholic denominational schools are guaranteed." This sentence of Article 23 is clear and unambiguous, if words have any meaning at all. And the decision of the Supreme Court of Appeal in Württemberg, to which reference has so frequently been made in the course of this fight against the denominational schools, rightly declared in so many words: " Article 23 of the Reich Concordat, in the light of Article 146 of the Weimar Constitution, refers to public schools, and indeed elementary schools, and lays down that the maintenance of the Catholic denominational schools and the erection of new Catholic denominational schools are guaranteed."

We all know the real reasons for which the community school has been introduced in contradiction to the law as it stands, and with complete disregard of the rights of parents. It is because they wish to destroy the educational influence of the Church completely. This is why the private schools have been harassed, cut down and limited, and finally destroyed; this is why our clergy have been excluded from giving religious instruction; this is why they have dissolved our Catholic Guilds, Associations and even religious Youth Societies; this is why steps are taken against the religious instruction given to the children in the churches; this is why the denominational schools have been closed.

Beloved Faithful ! I suffer with you under the unspeakable oppression of conscience and the bitter distress which has so unjustly been brought upon you. In order to protect you from threats and insults and economic damage —and only for this reason—we have suspended our efforts on behalf of the denominational schools guaranteed to us by law, and have not sent on the protest lists. The whole of the parish clergy was of one mind in its determination to make visits from house to house, no matter what unpleasant consequences might ensue for them. It was only on my instructions that they refrained from doing this.

In view of the distressing events of this week, I shall naturally send another letter to the Minister and to the President of the District Government, in which the most energetic protest will be made against the violence done to conscience and to our legal rights. My demand for the denominational schools, guaranteed to us by the law of the land and by the Concordat, will not be silenced. It is unnecessary for me to say that our demand for Catholic schools for our Catholic brethren does not involve the very least reproach to our Protestant fellow-citizens. I do not think that any Protestant Christian who knows me and my ways will have any doubt on that point.

We still remain loyal and true to our nation and our Fatherland, as we have been in the past, and carry out our duties as citizens in the most conscientious manner possible. But I demand *freedom of conscience* for you, and *justice*. That is your bishop's duty as a Catholic and a German. May the blessing of God be with you all.

Your bishop,
✠Franz Rudolf.

CHAPTER VI

THE CHURCH IS EXCLUDED FROM THE WORK OF EDUCATION: IV. RELIGIOUS INSTRUCTION

1. *The Abolition of Religious Instruction*

IN its agitation against Catholic schools Nazi propaganda has worked for years with the catchword: " In the German community schools everything remains as before; not a finger is laid on the Christian religion; it is just as secure in the community school as in the denominational school "; above all, the continuance of religious instruction was emphasised. In dozens of gatherings, in the whole National Socialist press, on the radio, in the speeches of official personages including several Ministers, this promise was formally given. " Religious instruction in the schools will never be interfered with," said, for example, Dr. Kerrl, the Reichsminister for Ecclesiastical Affairs, at Fulda on November 24th, 1937, and Reichskommissar District Leader Bürckel, in his speech of August, 1938, to Germans living abroad, gave the assurance that, though the State was primarily responsible for the education of youth, the Church could give this youth its religious formation.

This promise, too, of National Socialism turned out to be mere propaganda phraseology. If one looks back on the actual development of the schools question, one cannot but conclude that the responsible men of the Party had from the outset determined that, when once the denominational schools with Christianity as the ruling principle of education had been got rid of, the next item on the programme would be the abolition of all religious instruction. The bishops had expressed this fear years before—*e.g.*, the Bishop of Berlin said in a Pastoral read from the pulpits on October 10th, 1937:

> Under the shibboleth of secularising public life, measures are continually being planned to choke the voice of the Church in public. . . . The campaign against the Church is being conducted stage by stage, but the end is held steadily in view. In the sphere of education also there have been several such stages. At first the cry was: " Away with the denominational school; the unity of the people demands it !" Then: " The priests must get out of the schools." What will be the next step ? Will religious instruction be completely abolished and an anti-Christian ideology forced on the children ?

The fears expressed in the Pastoral were well grounded. Since the summer of 1939 the whole assault of the Nazi press and of Nazi associations has been concentrated on this last prop of Christianity, religious instruction, which was then still preserved, at any rate, in a number of schools. Nor is there any doubt that this assault, too, will end in an easy victory over the Church.

On June 14th, 1939, the Munich City School Inspector, Bauer, gave a lecture on " Ideology and Education " in which he publicly announced his new school programme: Removal of Christian religious instruction from the curriculum of the community schools and the introduction of the National Socialist ideology. He said:

> The Catholic Church maintains that National Socialism is not strong enough to overthrow Bolshevism. The Bavarian bishops also asserted this in their Pastoral Letters of 1937. But we tell the Church that it is Hitler, and he alone, who saved Germany, and we will tolerate no mystifications on this point. He would not have won the victory if his ideology had not been the strongest and the best.
> Religious instruction must disappear from the schools. We make our demand: Instruction in the German faith by German teachers in German schools ! The man who is tied to the dogmas of the Churches need look for nothing from us in the future.[1]

The displacement of religious instruction begins in practice—as always happens in such cases—with a host of restrictions.

According to Article 21 of the Concordat, religious instruction was compulsory in the vocational schools. Yet, as early as 1933, the year in which the Concordat was made, the report was being spread that the fulfilment of this solemn promise was not as yet to be expected.[2]

In his Pastoral Letter of December 21st, 1936, the Bishop of Münster asserts that, despite the renewed assurance of the Reichsminister for Ecclesiastical Affairs,

> religious instruction has been abolished in many places—for example, in the agricultural schools. In many towns officially appointed teachers of religion have been retired before attaining the age limit on the pretext that, for reasons of economy, the position of an officially appointed teacher for this regular subject must be dispensed with. In many places it has been laid down that religious instruction in vocational schools is no longer to be given during the ordinary school hours, but during free time, before and after compulsory classes. The Minister for Science, Education and Popular Culture replied on January 16th, 1936, to our complaints on this matter " that the subordinate authorities have received instructions from me to allow as little change as possible in the giving of religious instruction in the vocational schools." Despite this, it is being more and more displaced as a compulsory subject in such schools, and according to reports which lie before us there are not a few vocational school teachers and directors who constantly and expressly indicate to the pupils that attendance at religious instruction is not of obligation. It is obvious that inexperienced young men, who cannot yet appreciate its value for their present and future lives, regard this indication as an encouragement and enticement to absent themselves from it, especially as attendance means the sacrifice of some of their free time and, perhaps, getting up earlier in the morning.
> This experience, therefore, with the vocational school (which, of course, is already a " community school ") gives us an example of the value attached to religious instruction by the defenders of the community schools, and, at the same time, shows how easily it can, even though it remain recognised as a " regular subject,'" be rendered almost useless in practice.

[1] *Cf.* also the criticism of this speech in the *Osservatore Romano*, July 8th, 1939.
[2] *Cf. Kölnische Volkszeitung*, No. 292, October 26th, 1933.

VOCATIONAL SCHOOLS

Barely a year later, in November, 1937, the Bishop of Münster complains that religious instruction has been taken from the clergy and handed over to lay teachers.

Without any attempt to secure the agreement of the bishop, as is laid down in the Concordat with the Reich, the clerical religious teachers of the vocational schools have been turned out, and, without any reference to the bishop, the giving of religious instruction has been entrusted to lay teachers. . . . I publicly charge those who are responsible for this of setting aside a solemnly enacted law and of violating a treaty concluded by the Government of the German Reich.

I repeat publicly today what I wrote to the President of the District Government: Those persons who have been summoned and commissioned by secular authorities to give religious instruction in Catholic vocational schools, now that the clergy has been expelled from them, have not received the necessary ecclesiastical sanction and therefore have not the right to teach that subject. Pupils of both sexes, who voluntarily attend the religious instruction of such teachers, have no guarantee that what they receive is in the spirit of the Catholic Church. . . . If teachers, who have interiorly lost the Faith, were to venture still to give what is supposed to be Catholic religious instruction, then woe to the poor children who fall into the hands of such impostors. Better no religious instruction at all in the school than one which offers poison in place of true nourishment.

By a decree of April 17th, 1939, religious instruction was limited to half an hour a week in those vocational schools in which it was still given and, soon afterwards, there followed another decree by which it was finally altogether abolished in all vocational and continuation schools, despite the express guarantee of Article 21 of the Reich Concordat.

The same kind of tactics was followed in other types of school, too. In 1937, for example, the State, without any justification, interfered in the internal arrangement of religious instruction by prohibiting several religious textbooks approved by the Church—for example, *Glaube und Leben*, by Dr. Martin, the *Merkbüchlein für den kath. Religionsunterricht an den bayerischen Fortbildungsschulen*, as well as the textbook of Cohnen and Andres, *Die Lehre von der Kirche*. Or again, when in 1935 a number of school periods had to be cut out owing to the institution of the State Youth Day,[1] it was the teaching of religion that suffered the most serious curtailment.[2] In South Germany, already from the school year 1935-36 onwards, the number of periods for religious instruction had been decreased from four to three and shorter periods of forty-five minutes introduced. Cardinal Archbishop Schulte of Cologne complains in his Pastoral Letter of the beginning of May, 1937, that at Easter of that year religious instruction in the three upper classes of the boys' secondary schools was limited by a stroke of the pen to one period in the week, but, despite his protest, this same limitation was extended at the beginning of the school year 1938 to the fifth class. In the spring of 1938, by decree of Dr. Rust, the Reichsminister of Education, the

---
[1] A weekly holiday, devoted to athletics and ideological instruction.—[*Translator's Note.*]
[2] *Cf.*, for example, the ordinance of the Area School Inspector in Arnsberg of June 1st, 1935.

number of religious periods was fixed in general at two a week, while one a week was considered sufficient for the sixth school year. On April 17th, 1939, Bavaria likewise fixed two periods a week. (It should be noted, incidentally, that throughout the Reich five periods a week were allotted to physical exercises.)

But, besides these curtailments in the number of religious periods, there are further restrictions as to their allocation. For instance, religious instruction in Bavarian schools, by decree of the Bavarian Ministry of Education of March 17th, 1939, is squeezed in at inconvenient hours. In summer, 1939, the Ministry of Education in Vienna similarly decreed that in all schools in which religious instruction is given it must take place either after the conclusion of the morning's teaching or in the afternoon, and the Ministry of Education of Baden passed a similar decree for the Baden schools.

The restrictions we have just outlined naturally have the effect on the youthful mind of making it underestimate the importance of religion. The same intention underlies, too, a number of other innovations. So, for example, the marks for religion on a pupil's report no longer count for the assessment of his general proficiency. Also, in official school documents, especially in report sheets, the term " religion " has given way to " denominational instruction," and since the school year 1939-40 religious periods are no longer an integral part of the school time-tables drawn up by directors of schools. Schools, it is true, provide classrooms for the purpose of religious instruction, but, for the rest, the Church itself has to see to its organisation,[1] and in many districts (*e.g.*, in Saxony, in the Arnsberg district, in Bochum, etc.), from as early as 1935, schoolrooms are no longer provided for such religious teaching as is not strictly a school subject—*e.g.*, instruction for Confession and Communion.

The Exclusion of the Clergy

In 1936 the claim was put forward that, to give religious instruction in the schools, even the clergy should have the express permission of the President of the local Government, which, as a matter of fact, was often refused, as in Münster, Hildesheim and elsewhere, on the flimsiest of pretexts—*e.g.*, " your conduct shows that you are not willing to put yourself unreservedly at the service of the State," or " because there is no need of it," etc.

The Bishop of Trier declared in a Pastoral of December 21st, 1936:

The State now makes the demand, based on a law of February 18th, 1876, passed during the *Kulturkampf*, that the clergy, in order to give religious instruction in the schools, must apply for permission. But, when they do apply, months often elapse before it is granted; in many cases it is refused and in others it is taken away, because, as is alleged, they are not considered fit persons to educate German youth. Recently it has been decided that certain priests are to be deprived of this permission or shall not receive it, because they rightly refuse to make the declaration that they will no longer engage in pastoral work with the purely religious Youth Associations.

[1] Ordinance of the Viennese Ministry of the Interior of April 18th, 1939.

The allegations of the Pastoral were borne out by the facts. In many districts—*e.g.*, Württemberg—the Government attempted to hand over the teaching of religion to the laity in order to exclude the clergy, and in a number of dioceses (Ermland, Freiburg, Trier, Hildesheim, etc.) permission to teach was refused to the clergy, because they happened to be directing a Catholic Youth Group.

On October 10th, 1937, there was read from the pulpits a Pastoral of Mgr. Graf von Preysing, Bishop of Berlin, in which he stated:

> It is with deep sorrow that I have to announce to you that from now on your priests, with but few exceptions, may no longer give religious instruction in the schools. By this step the expulsion of the Church from the schools has been completed. . . . No reason for this step has been given to me as bishop. . . .

In November, 1937, the Bishop of Münster, in a sermon, addressed the following words to Catholic parents:

> A few weeks ago I informed you in a short Pastoral that, according to an ordinance of the Reichsminister of Education, all the official religious instruction in the elementary schools was to be given exclusively by secular teachers: that, consequently, all clerics are excluded from giving such instruction in those schools. No reasons for this have been communicated to us and our request for such reasons has as yet been given no reply. It is evident that the carrying out of these measures expresses a lack of confidence in the Church and her priests, the injustice of which cannot but fill us with poignant grief. We recognise in this measure the endeavour to alienate the hearts of children from the servants and followers of the children's Divine Friend.

In Trier in 1937 complaints were again made, this time by the Vicar-General,[1] that the reply of the Government to the requests of the clergy for permission to give religious instruction was frequently delayed for months. Such tactics brought results, for towards the end of 1937 there were, according to trustworthy reports, already 250 clerics in the diocese of Rottenburg alone who had been deprived of official permission to teach religion. So on March 10th, 1938, the Bavarian Government passed a law which laid down among other things:

> In order to give official religious instruction in elementary schools, the clergy need the permission of the President of the District Government. This permission is to be refused if the cleric is non-Aryan or politically suspect or unsuitable as a teacher.

After the Anschluss the same plan was followed in Austria, where a large number of teachers of religion and catechists were forbidden on various pretexts to give religious instruction.

Besides the obstructions to the teaching of religion, there were others to impede episcopal supervision. An example of this we have already mentioned, when Mgr. Graf von Galen, forbidden to visit the Catholic elementary schools in his diocese of Münster, was prevented from fulfilling his duties of supervision as bishop. In some parts of Austria this ecclesiastical right was officially abolished in 1938 and

---

[1] *Clergy Communications*, vol. 2, 1937.

with it the obligation on the part of lay teachers, entrusted with the giving of religious instruction, of being canonically approved.[1] In the spring of 1939 a new Schools Law did away with the ecclesiastical supervision of religious instruction throughout the whole of Austria.

Difficulties for Teachers and Pupils

Instruction in Bible History offered the first and easiest field for this form of attack, and more than one teacher, under the influence of the Party agitation against the Jews, has in fact refused to teach it. Here the Nazi Teachers' Union has been very active, and its authorities have made it difficult for teachers not to conform to Party ideas. In this regard we may quote a questionnaire sent round in the winter of 1938 by the Area Leader of the Nazi Teachers' Union of Fürstenfeldbruck, near Munich, which has come to our hands and which reads as follows:

NSLB Fürstenfeldbruck, near Munich.

To all teachers of the Fürstenfeldbruck area.

You are requested to answer the following questions:
1. Do you still give instruction in the Bible?
2. If so, what is your reason?
3. Can you bring instruction in the Old Testament into harmony with your views on race?
4. Do you wish you could stop giving instruction in the Bible?
5. Do you still have to play the organ?
6. If so, are there any special reasons for this?
7. Do you wish you could give this up?
8. Do you belong to the Party?

Gruber,
Area Leader of the NS Teachers' Union.

N.B.—The answering of questions 2 and 3 is voluntary.

In November, 1938, the Nazi Teachers' Union instituted a drive to abolish Bible-teaching especially in German Upper Silesia, and pressure was put upon teachers in Gleiwitz, Oppeln, Beuthen, Hindenburg, etc., to get them to sign the following document:

In consequence of the dirty Jewish assassination in Paris, I cannot bring myself any longer to extol in my teaching the national figures of a people which thrives exclusively on hatred of Germany. I declare myself, therefore, unable to impart religious instruction. . . .

Every effort, too, was made to influence the children, and for this end it had been repeatedly and most solemnly emphasised by ministerial decrees that no pupil might be compelled to attend the official religious instruction given in the schools, but that from the age of fourteen any pupil might, on his own initiative and simply by making the necessary declaration, give it up entirely, just as at the same age he might announce his complete withdrawal from his Church.

---
[1] By decree of the Vienna City Schools Board and the Schools Board of the Lower Danube District; *cf.* the *Vienna Diocesan Journal*, December 17th, 1938.

The inducement which lies at the back of the repeated publication and emphasising of this regulation has had, as a matter of fact, remarkably little success. We know that since 1919—over a period, that is, of twenty years—despite the very active propaganda previously carried on by the Marxists, not even 2 per cent. of the elementary school pupils over the whole of the German Reich (Old Reich) withdrew from religious instruction, and this although in recent years they could take this step at the age of fourteen on their own account and without any written declaration from their parents.[1]

It was otherwise in Austria. There the Marxist apostasy propaganda had enjoyed great success for a time, but it was checked by the Christian school policy which Dollfuss and Schuschnigg deliberately pursued. In the spring of 1938, however, the Ministry for Internal and Cultural Affairs, " in order to come into line with regulations already in existence in the Old Reich," passed two decrees of far-reaching cultural and political importance, in which it was laid down that pupils need not attend religious instructions, services, devotions and similar religious functions contained in the school programme if a formal declaration had been made of their withdrawal from them. Up to the age of fourteen this declaration had to be made by the parents; after that age, pupils were perfectly free to decide this most important question for themselves and school teachers could not be compelled to co-operate in such religious functions in the schools. By the second decree " the right of free choice of Religious Confession for everyone " was to be restored, for which nothing more than a declaration of change of religion, made to the District Commissioners, was necessary.

The aim of both these decrees is avowedly the destruction of the Christian educational policy introduced by Dollfuss in 1933 and the restoration of the conditions which obtained in Austria before that date, though, to be sure, no hint is anywhere given that those former conditions were for all practical purposes no better than Bolshevism pure and simple. For the truth is, of course, that the decree on religious instruction, superseded by these measures, was intended to replace the notorious " Glöckel Decree " of the Red School dictator of Vienna, and that the difficulties put in the way of an easy change of religion were aimed at setting a check to the communistic anti-God propaganda rife in Vienna and the rest of Austria.

With reference to this ministerial decree the Cardinal Archbishop of Vienna, Mgr. Theodore Innitzer, made a forceful appeal to Catholic parents, in which, among other things, he says:

> The decision as to whether your children attend the religious instruction and other school religious exercises rests with you till they reach the age of fourteen. Take this your duty deeply to heart and see to it that no child of yours absents himself from the instruction in the Catholic religion which is given in the schools. It is a question of an individual and sacred duty exclusively yours, the entire responsibility for which rests upon you

[1] *Cf.*, *e.g.*, *Bayerischer Regierungsanzeiger*, No. 67, 1938.

personally, a responsibility of which no one can relieve you. Almighty God, who has entrusted your children to you as a precious possession, will one day demand an account of you.

The open way in which parents and children were invited by those in official positions to make this declaration of withdrawal from religious instruction is illustrated by the " important explanation to parents " issued by the District Schools Board of Salzburg in October, 1938, immediately after the violently hostile speech of the Reichskommissar Bürckel:

After allusions to Bürckel's foiling of the " Church's attempts at camouflage," the document unequivocally appeals to the people to keep their children away from religious instruction. The parochial clergy and missioners, arguing as though the Church had a monopoly of religion, had in recent weeks warned parents of their duty, but National Socialism had proved " that it is capable of giving youth a moral and religious education without the assistance of the Church." The declaration of withdrawal from religious instruction, so the parents are told, is by no means the same thing as a complete absence of religion, for " whoever believes in the Führer and his work, believes consequently in the people as a creation of God: therein lies a deeper faith than in the vile attempt of the Christian *Ständestaat* to foster disunion in the German people by mediæval methods."[1]

This systematic opposition to religious instruction on the part of National Socialism and its frightful consequences are described in the following terms by the official report of the Freiburg Diocesan Administration, to which we have referred several times already:

The Baden Concordat of October 12th, 1932, in the final protocol to Article 11, lays down: " In its application of Reich and State legislation, the Free State of Baden will continue to uphold the existing rights of the Catholic Church with regard to religious instruction in the Baden schools." According to the then existing law, religious instruction was one of the subjects obligatory in every school. The imparting, direction and supervision of it belonged to the Church, as well as the drawing up of the curriculum and the choice of textbooks. Such elementary school teachers as had been certified as competent religious teachers by the ecclesiastical authorities were placed by the State at the disposal of the Church for six periods a week, and so in the appointment of teachers careful consideration was to be given to the religious denomination to which the children belonged. In the elementary schools there were for the children three periods of religious instruction a week, in the secondary schools two, and in the continuation and trade schools one. " Nevertheless, since 1933 the Church has had to suffer, even in this Archdiocese of Freiburg, the most grievous encroachments on the part of the State in the matter of religious instruction. The Baden law of January 29th, 1934, concerning the elementary and secondary schools ignored a whole mass of assurances given in the Baden Concordat, a procedure against which the Archiepiscopal " Ordinariate " immediately protested in the most solemn manner. Nevertheless, the Baden Government has continued, since 1935, to withdraw from an ever-increasing number of Catholic clergy authorisation to give religious instruction, especially from such as have been the object of an investigation by the State Secret Police. All protests, however, against the illegality of this procedure have availed nothing, and at the present time thirty-two members of the clergy of Baden are still banned from the schools.

The attempts of the clergy, thus shut out from the schools, to repair the

[1] *Ostschweiz*, October 19th, 1938.

defect by instructing the children in other buildings than schools, especially in churches, were combated in every way by the Baden Ministry of Education as an evasion of the State's prohibition, and it was for this reason chiefly that the parish priests of Schapbach and Waldhausen, Frs. Seifried and Herberisch, were finally removed by force from their posts. In Hohenzollern, too, by decree of the President of the Government of October, 1937, permission to give systematic religious instruction in the schools was withdrawn from eight parish priests and, by a decree of the Reichsminister of Education of November 18th, 1937, examinations in religion by ecclesiastical boards are suspended until further notice.

The first encroachment on the Church's prerogative to select its own religious textbooks was the prohibition, " to be notified to all teachers of religion," issued by the Baden Educational Authorities, of the use of the " Truths of the Catechism " drawn up by the Fulda Conference of Bishops, and the confiscation of the booklets in question, which were taken from the children by the teachers sometimes in a manner far from edifying.

Then by a communication of July 24th, 1937, the Baden Minister of Education forbade the further use of the Bible History, which had been introduced at Easter, 1936, into the schools of the Archdiocese and had long been in use elsewhere—the words of Christ in the incident of the Samaritan woman at Jacob's well, " Salvation is from the Jews," were considered particularly offensive—and this prohibition was extended to the secondary schools in February, 1938. Finally, on November 29th, 1937, the Baden Minister of Education even insisted that the ecclesiastical authorities should no longer allow the Old Testament to be treated of at all during religious instruction.

Numerous complaints have come to the ears of the ecclesiastical authorities of odious attacks made by elementary school teachers on Catholic doctrines and institutions. Not less than thirty-seven teachers resigned in the course of the year 1937 from giving religious instruction in Baden, while others either disregarded the Old Testament in their classes or threatened that, if the Church insisted on its being treated, they would resign from giving religious instruction altogether.

A strong agitation to induce as many as possible to make the official declaration of withdrawal from religious instruction set in from the year 1937, especially among trade school pupils, an agitation which was for the most part inaugurated or directly supported by the school managements themselves, or by teachers or guilds. The official notification of the Ministry of Education, according to which the weekly period of religious instruction in trade schools was to be decreased from an hour to half an hour, which in some cases is relegated, too, to the end of the school day, signifies a further important step towards the complete abolition of religious instruction from these schools.

In Baden, as elsewhere, religious instruction was cut down to one period a week in the sixth, seventh and eighth classes of the secondary schools and since Easter, 1937, the devoting of part of the singing lesson to the teaching of hymns has been stopped. Not infrequently in these schools, too, odious attacks are made on the Catholic convictions of the pupils by the teachers and, in some cases even, anti-Catholic literature has been distributed. Official religious teachers have not been appointed to secondary schools in Baden since 1935, while, from another aspect, by the transformation of Classical schools (*Gymnasium*) into Upper schools (*Oberschule*), not only in Baden but also in Tauberbischofsheim and Sigmaringen, and by the abolition of the teaching of Hebrew, considerable difficulties have been put in the way of vocations to the priesthood. . . .

In the course of this campaign there has been issued, too, a whole series of official regulations with the object of limiting more and more the content of the religious teaching, and for this the Old Testament provided a welcome handle. As early as 1936 the *Westdeutscher Beobachter*[1] published communications from teachers demanding the abolition of the Old Testament from the syllabus " in order that the children might be spared conflicts of soul." Similarly the *Kölnische Volkszeitung*[2] announced that the President of the District Government of Münster, in view of the recent limitation of the number of weekly periods allowed for religious instruction, had decided that a corresponding reduction was necessary in the subject-matter of those classes and that this was to be effected by the exclusion of Old Testament teaching. The Government of Anhalt, too, emphasised anew in January, 1939, that the Old Testament, including the Psalms and Prophets, as well as St. Paul, were not to be treated of in religious instruction.

The Bavarian bishops, therefore, complain in their Pastoral Letter of December 13th, 1936: There are teachers " who bring an unchristian spirit into their teaching and even give instruction in the Bible in such a way that the children must become confused in their faith."

In a sermon preached in the *Dom* of Münster, the Bishop of Münster, Mgr. Graf von Galen, betrayed the same anxiety:

> We cannot but fear that not all the teachers who are now being appointed to give religious instruction in the elementary schools in place of the clergy are competent and willing to give it in complete agreement with the doctrines and principles of the Church. Wherefore I exhort anew the fathers and mothers of our Catholic school children to be ever deeply conscious of the heavy responsibility they bear for the Christian instruction and education of our children. They should make sure that the whole of the Catechism and the whole Bible History of the Old and the New Testaments are taught in the spirit of the Church and according to the prescribed schemes of studies in their entirety and without arbitrary omissions.

The regulation, promulgated as early as 1936, forbidding teachers of religion to make enquiries during religious lessons about attendance at religious services, was a serious encroachment on the rights of the Church to use such occasions for pastoral purposes. Similarly the Württemberg Ministry of Religion, which had already in 1935 forbidden teachers of religion to recommend in class religious magazines or other publications, delivered another blow at the Church by a regulation of 1938, which laid down that only such hymns could be practised during periods allotted to religious instruction as were common to the religious services of both the Christian denominations.

Complete suppression of religious instruction is, of course, the final aim of the movement, and it is rapidly and systematically being attained, in some cases by indirect methods, as when, as often happened, the post of religious instructor in secondary schools becoming vacant, for example, by death, no further appointment is made; or directly, as in the case of a number of the Berlin community schools where in autumn, 1937, religious instruction was suddenly and completely done away with and parents were informed by a circular letter that if

[1] October 25th, 1936.   [2] January 8th, 1936.

SUPPRESSION OF RELIGIOUS INSTRUCTION

they really wanted their children to have it they could get it for them outside of school; or as in the case of the trade and commercial senior schools of Austria, where religious instruction, though regulated by the Austrian Concordat of 1934, was abolished in 1938 by a stroke of the pen.

In the elementary schools also it is being more and more suppressed in practice, nor are the authorities at a loss for pretexts. When, for example, the Diocesan Administration of Munich declared on April 27th, 1939, that, owing to the shortening of the religious periods, religious instruction in the upper classes would have to be given solely by the clergy, the city school authorities seized the opportunity to appeal to all the teaching body to resign from all religious teaching—that is, in the lower classes, too—as a protest against " this insult to the teaching profession," and many of them responded to the appeal. This is a clear case of the exploitation of a deliberate and malicious misinterpretation of the Diocesan Administration's decree, since it was well known that the teaching of religion in the upper classes demands a training which lay teachers but rarely possess, and that, as a matter of fact, lay teachers are officially approved by the Church only for Bible History and the simpler catechetical instruction of the first and second school years.

At any rate, as a result of these and other methods there is now, in every diocese, a large number of schools in which religious instruction is no longer given, and this number is increasing year by year as the " old " teachers are gradually dying off.

It can cause us no surprise, therefore, that nearly all the bishops of Germany have arranged for the religious instruction of the children to take place no longer in school buildings, but in some hall or other belonging to the parish, and that they exhort parents urgently and repeatedly to send their children to these private religious classes.[1]

2. *Nazi Exploitation of the Schools*

What does the National Socialist State intend with regard to the community schools it has striven for with such clearness and tenacity of purpose ? Those in authority have often declared their intention—to permeate youth through and through with the Nazi ideology. This ideology is to be not merely a subject of instruction, but the very principle of instruction. We should be quite wrong were we to conceive of the new community school as of a school in which religion was a merely neutral factor in the manner of the old undenominational schools. An article from the *Frankfurter Zeitung*,[2] for example, would correct that impression:

It must not be forgotten that between the undenominational school and the community school there exists an essential difference, inasmuch as the

---

[1] *Cf.* especially the Joint Pastoral Letter of the German bishops on " Care for the Children's Spiritual Life," which was read out in all churches in May, 1938, and in which it is said: " Unfortunately the religious instruction given in the schools today is no longer sufficient. . . ."
[2] May 26th, 1938.

former derives from the mutual tolerance of Christian creeds, while the latter, in accordance with the National Socialist ideology, is based on the superiority of the idea of national unity to the denominational divergencies of teachers and pupils.

A characterisation even more pertinent and clear was given in his newspaper, *Weltanschauung und Schule*, as far back as 1935 by Professor Bäumler, Chief Sectional Director in Rosenberg's department, under whose charge is the whole ideological education of Party members. He declared that the community school was no mere undenominational school, because it was no more a mere State school. It was rather an ideological school, a school of the National Socialist creed. In 1939 at one of the jubilee celebrations of the National Socialist Teachers' Union the following was stressed among its guiding principles: " National Socialism has not dissolved the denominational schools in order to secularise them: it has turned them into schools professing the creed of National Socialism."

National Socialism, then, is itself convinced that the ideology which it is to teach in its new schools is incompatible with Christianity. For, did it consider possible a union of Christianity with itself, it would not have laboured with such zeal and determination to convert the hitherto Christian school into the German community school. The opposition of this school to Christianity will be laid bare to the public—of this there can be no doubt—as soon as the long-heralded definitive school law is published. Even as it is, the notes which mark the attitude of the community school to Christianity are clear enough.

So, for example, we can read in the declaration of the Bishops' Conference of 1937 at Fulda:

We see in the projected community schools not only no support of the Christian faith but, on the contrary, as is demonstrated by unambiguous pronouncements, an effective means to crush the Catholic faith and Christianity in the growing youth and so endanger the welfare of the whole German people. Consequently it is misleading and false to maintain that with the community schools things are as they were formerly.[1]

Besides the community school, National Socialism has made for itself an ideal type of school in the so-called " Adolf Hitler Schools," in which the recruits for the leadership of Party and State are formed from their sixth to their eighteenth year. It is a hard-and-fast rule that in these schools no sort of religious instruction may be given and that the pupils have no opportunity to fulfil their religious duties, but in place of Christian religious instruction there is given an ideological instruction, for which Rosenberg's ideas form the basis. The atmosphere of these schools is, therefore, explicitly hostile to Christianity.

Teachers, too, are trained in a spirit hostile to Christianity and are constantly being influenced by the authorities in the same sense. For instance, all Catholic teachers have to leave their own Catholic Associations and, on occasion, this is enforced by the definite threat of loss

[1] *Cf.* also the Pastoral of Cardinal Schulte of May 3rd, 1937.

of membership of the National Socialist Teachers' Union and consequent loss of economic existence.

In the training colleges for teachers, whose classes naturally contain people of different creeds, the students are trained wholly in accordance with Rosenberg's ideas, so that, while they are still immature, they are won over to oppose the Church with superficial notions and distorted ideas, and even with hatred and contempt.

Then, too, the officially conducted training courses, school camps, etc., are imbued with this same spirit and what the Catholic considers holiest is there most bitterly attacked. We know, for example, from Catholic women teachers that they weep at night over the things that they have to listen to during the day.

With what an anti-Christian spirit the National Socialist Teachers' Union—a professional organisation, membership of which is compulsory for all, Catholics as well—is full, we shall show later. For the moment suffice it to say that Catholic teachers have to take assiduous precautions to avoid arousing even a suspicion that they are in any degree under the influence of their parish priest—even taking part, for example, in retreats (that is, in strictly religious functions) has been forbidden to the teachers by the authorities.

As far back as 1937 it was said that school prayers were falling into disuse. An order, for example, of the Area Leader of the National Socialist Teachers' Union forbade the children of the Hans Schemm School at Regensburg-Schottenheim to join their hands or make the sign of the Cross at prayers—this is a case of a German community school of 500 Catholic and 35 Protestant children. Again, scarcely was the Catholic elementary school of Neumarkt (Oberpfalz) converted into a German community school (October 14th, 1937) than a circular was sent round the classes by the school inspector (October 30th, 1937) forbidding to all the classes, even the purely Catholic ones, the sign of the Cross and the Our Father.

Since the change of the denominational schools as a whole into the " mixed " community schools Christian prayers have been practically everywhere abolished. The Educational Authorities of the Upper Danube district, for example, based their prohibition of school prayers on the grounds that the saying of the conventional prayers of the different creeds caused an " injurious straining in the classrooms of that true national community spirit." In their stead have been introduced to a greater and greater extent forms of prayers and formulas connected with Nazi festivals which foster " a sense of religion, which is superior to that of the denominations." So, in many districts, the six to ten year-old school children say the following " prayer ":

> Mighty hand of mercy rule
> Thou the labours of our school,
> O'er our Führer wide extending,
> Him from ev'ry ill defending.
> Bless our land and people aye:
> Be thou our God eternally.

For the school children between ten and fourteen an appropriate text from the " Book of Rites and Solemnities " of the Hitler Youth has to be chosen.

Characteristic is what a head-master propounded at a parents' meeting at Bad Gastein in the autumn of 1938: that even if religious instruction were made optional, the children would, for all that, by no means be brought up without religion; religion was above all creeds; the present-day German youth was the most devout in the whole world; " it was bent on accomplishing the very best for the Führer, sent of God, and the people, produced of God." It was interesting, he continued, to know that during the Czech crisis the prayer of many an Austrian school ran: " People will cleave to people and blood to blood, despite rampart and frontier; German for ever !"—in such a vow there lay deeper religion than in the inattentive grinding out of an Our Father.

The new school books are, of course, designed to further the spread of National Socialist ideas. The rôle assigned to them is to present to the immature mind a series of ideas and pictures quietly, almost imperceptibly, but in such a way as to create a corresponding bias in their favour, and in this way to keep the Christian faith far removed from the child's mind or even to suffocate its young growth, if it has already begun to strike root there. So, for instance, in the uniform reader which in 1936 appeared for children in the fifth and sixth years at school there is offered a long extract from Schenzinger's *Hitlerjunge Quex*:

A youngster who has lost his mother is taking part in a " service." " ' Mother is dead,' he was thinking all the time he was standing there with his hands joined; ' Mother is gone; gone for ever. Where has she gone to ? But surely she must be somewhere.' That something that has once existed should absolutely cease to be—no, he could not believe that. He struggled fiercely, like someone drowning. He was repeating with the rest the words of the invocation which the troop leader had first recited, when suddenly it came upon him: ' Mother is within me. Something of her is here yet; I can feel it !' He was happy again: his burden was lighter and, as the throng dispersed, he joined in once again with the laughter of the others " (p. 369).

That is the belief in immortality which the children of Christian parents learn from their school books in the schools of the Third Reich !

In the summer of 1939 a new history book was introduced into the secondary schools, *Führer and Völker* (Leaders and Peoples), by Minister of State Dr. Paul Schmitthenner, professor of the University of Heidelberg. In it Church and Papacy are painted in the blackest colours as the mortal enemies of the German people, and the principles of the Catholic faith are characterised as being in direct opposition to those of the true Germanic tradition. So, for instance, it says on pp. 16-17:

The Cluniac Movement.—It was a foreign Roman spirit which originated in the romanesque Cluny, a spirit of penance and priestly domination.

The unnatural law of celibacy, with its contempt of marriage, flatly contradicted the original Germanic outlook. So very un-German was it, that it made a sharp distinction between things of the spirit and things of the earth. The most dangerous thing about it, however, was the law against simony and lay investiture, and, had the king been deprived of these powers, it would have been the end of his authority. But the main aim of the Cluniacs was to work, not merely for the emancipation of the Church, but also for its mastery over all the kingdoms of this world.

On the " Crusades and their dreadful consequences for the German people " it says:

The sum total of those who fell in the Crusades has been reckoned at many millions, mostly pilgrims and fighting men of northern stock. Not for People and Fatherland, but for a delusion, a foreign project that had nothing to do with the People, did uncounted Germans go to their death.

Luther is extolled as the " great leader " of the German people, as the one who " unmasked the Roman lie and fraud and with the might of a hero of old joined battle with the sworn arch enemy in Rome," and manfully led the fight against " the calculated robbery of the Papal budget."

The Jesuits are represented as the " most formidable Romish fighting force." The Constitutions which St. Ignatius gave to his Order are " diametrically opposed to what is most fundamental in the German creed." Every rusty weapon is hauled out of the Liberal arsenal to induce the rising German race to shudder at this " crafty and unscrupulous army which, now more than ever before, menaces freedom."

These are only some examples: all the new National Socialist primers and textbooks know only the glorification of the " Leader " and the German Aryan race, while they pour scorn upon the Church, her servants and her institutions.

A variety of other means is used in the schools to discredit Christianity. In the secondary schools, subjects for exercises are set which have to be treated in a National Socialist—which is the same thing as anti-Christian—sense. For instance, one such subject for a composition was: " Why is the Catholic Church harmful to the Nation ?" Another type of example is furnished by the elementary school of München-Feldmoching, where in the spring of 1939 a " Healthy People " exhibition was presented to which the sixth class of boys made the following contribution:

To illustrate the title " Spiritual Poison " a kind of tableau was shown which consisted of six figures. In the foreground stood two Jews with the Talmud under their arms; behind them were two Communists with a dead man lying at their feet and, close by, were two other figures clearly recognisable as Catholic Religious. Of these, one represented a monk, dressed in cassock and clerical hat, holding in one hand a staff and in the other a scroll with the inscription: " All men are equal ! Love your enemies !" and the other, apparently a nun, was kneeling at a prie-dieu which carried on a placard the inscription: " Mortification, renunciation of the world " and in one hand she held a scourge. Above the whole group a star had been fastened bearing the subject title of the tableau, " Spiritual Poison," and in front lay a page from the *Völkischer Beobachter*[1] with pictures of Cardinal Mundelein, Mr. Eden, several Jews, etc., on the upper border of which someone had written by hand the remark: " For such as do not understand the tableau."

Such things are, indeed, not at all hard to understand.

National Socialist Ideological Instruction substituted for Christian Religious Instruction

As early as 1937 the German Faith movement had organised a kind of pagan religious teaching and had set up a so-called faith instruction in the schools. We read, for example, in the January number, 1937, of *Der Vorstoss*[2] (*The Advance*), the organ of the German Faith movement in Bavaria: " In Munich we are able to carry out the faith instruction in every single school. It is a national duty for parents to send their children to instruction in the faith."

The authorities of the community school in Kirchheim, too, as can be seen from *Das Schwarze Korps*,[3] decided to institute special study periods for instruction in National Socialist ideology. As justification for this measure it was alleged that these courses of instruction were to fill a gap, since Christian religious instruction was receiving ever less and less encouragement, and, in any case, there was the danger that the school children were growing up without any ideological bearings. *Das Schwarze Korps* went on to remark:

> That is a problem which will have to be solved for the whole German school system. . . . One cannot expect from a child's mind that in one lesson it should rise to an understanding of the race theory and of the individuality of the nation's life, if in the next lesson it will be taught that all men, Germans, Hottentots and Jews, are images of God. Experience also teaches that dogma-believing Christian zealots handle the children's souls in their religious, Bible and Confirmation classes all the more obstinately and brutally if they know that their pupils are at the same time receiving instruction in the national ideology. Here there can be only an either . . . or.

In a number of schools in Württemberg a beginning was already made in 1938 with these classes in National Socialist ideology as a substitute for religious instruction. As an indication of the general lines of this teaching, a plan of the subject-matter was put together with an introduction signed by Dr. Erich Keller, and to this the Ministry of Education, Department for the Elementary Schools, has given official support in that it has directed that this outline may be put into the hands of such teachers only as can be guaranteed reliable in their ideological outlook, and, even then, they may have it only where it is necessary and by way of a loan. It is forbidden to make a copy of the scheme or to let it fall into other hands. The instruction is to be consciously arranged in an anti-Christian sense.

[1] No. 43 February 12th 1939 p. 3.   [2] P. 4.   [3] June 1st, 1939, p. 19.

SUBSTITUTION OF IDEOLOGICAL INSTRUCTION 179

The content of this scheme embraces the whole of primary education from the first year at school onwards. It provides for a division of the matter into two parts: (1) Perception of God in nature and (2) Experience of the community of blood; initiation into the world of German standards. In order to deepen the effect, first importance is to be given to influencing the child on the emotional side, and so, whatever points have been gone through in class, have then to be pressed home in the lesson devoted to singing and folklore.

This ideological instruction proceeds from a conception of God which has been radically falsified and robbed of its true content. The presence of God in nature is to be discerned in the regularity and order of the change between day and night, of the seasons, of the years. To the young children in their first year at school this experience is explained and illustrated by means of fairy tales like Sleeping Beauty, Lady Holle, Little Red Riding Hood, Willie Winkie, the Goose Girl, etc. It is put before the middle classes by means of myths of the gods and sagas of the heroes, the *Götterdämmerung*, legends of *Gudrun* and the *Nibelungen*. History, too, if carefully chosen to suit their purpose, can serve as illustration: northern beliefs in very early historical times (a subject about which nobody knows anything definite); the destruction of the Ostro-Goths; Witukind and the Saxons; the massacre at Cannstadt; the Crusades as misdirected idealism of Nordic knighthood. Easter becomes the Feast of Life; Whitsun, the Feast of Joy; Christmas, the Feast of Light.

The sixth year at school brings something more: the migration of the nations; Kaiser and Pope; Luther as a German champion against Rome; Germans sent to the stake as heretics and witches by the Church; the heroic deeds of Andrew Hofer, Schlageter, Norkus; the Führer's birthday—all have to be treated of. Even in the lower classes attention has to be paid to questions of the day that affect national life, but in the senior classes, from the seventh year on, the analysis of these questions is accorded the most important place, and it is here that the anti-Christian tendency manifests itself more and more clearly.

As an outline of the subjects which the seventh-year scholars have to handle, the following are suggested: **Relations with other Powers**: Attitude to Christianity, the Jewish World Outlook, Jewry and Jewish Morality, Jesus and Jewry, Jews in Modern Life, the Origin of Christianity and of the Church, the Origin of the Bible (for which George Schneider's *Völkische Reformation* is given as a source book), Political Catholicism, the Mastery of Souls, the Inquisition, the Waldenses, the Huguenots, Freemasonry and Marxism, Bolshevism and the Godless Movement, and the position of the Church with regard to all these questions. The eighth-year classes have the following subjects to work upon: **The Movement Hostile to the German Spirit**: Jesuits, the Centre Party, the World War, Erzberger, Catholic Action and its Camouflage in the Third Reich, Protestant Pilgrims to Rome, Champions of the German Spirit (Rosenberg, Ludendorff), Point 24 of the Party Programme. The new dogmatic system[1] in this ideological instruction includes the following points: Divine Revelation in Nature, in Blood, Race, People and Fate; Restricted and Free Religion; Original Sin and Veneration for Ancestors.

In the secondary schools the highly contradictory attitude of Christianity to the questions of life has to be stressed before everything else. Such themes as these are characteristic: The Denial of Life and Joy of Existence; the Kingdom of God and World Dominion; Sinfulness and the Need of Redemption. Christianity is expressly characterised as an alien religion and, following Rosenberg, certain adulterating elements are designated as a mingling of Jewish, Greek and Roman ingredients, as, for example, the Papacy.

In the advanced course of the secondary schools the object is to work out a German faith which is to be achieved through the following antitheses: Scholasticism—Mysticism; the Church's system and belief—the Reformation and the impetus to research; Rationalism (Idealism, Materialism, Marxism) in opposition to the beliefs of National Socialism; the mythical conception of the Church, of Individualism, and of Personality in Humanism and the Reformation as opposed to that of the People in National Socialism. The net result is to be that German faith takes its rise not from any foreign authority but from the blood.

In this way a substitute for Christianity will be evolved. Divine authority is of no value whatever: it will be absolutely swept away through the denial of revelation. In practice the aforementioned teaching develops into a full-blown denial of God. God is still spoken of, of course, and spoken of a good deal, but He is denied as a spiritual and supernatural being, deprived of His eternity and put on a par with Nature and Blood. The history of mankind and of the Occident is falsified in the spirit of Rosenberg and Ludendorff. And so naturally the reading matter given as sources and material derives almost exclusively from the Ludendorff Press or from the pens of Rosenberg's associates.

There was also a course of study mapped out for German primary schools in Saxony during 1939, and delivered to the school teachers in the Dresden district. From the very interesting introduction to this scheme let us quote the following sentences:

The consideration of the German people and of the laws of life given by Nature imperatively demands a complete reshaping of religious education in the school. Bible criticism and historical research, national psychology and folklore, critical dialectics, study of adolescence and, in addition, the knowledge of religious emotion and experience have shown that for every people there is an experience of religion peculiar to it whose expression does not agree with the beliefs and practices prescribed by the Churches. Contemporary forms of religion have been very markedly influenced by non-German and Oriental elements.

It is what men do that reveals the vigour of a religion. The really redeeming act, one which gives a meaning and form to life, is possible only if a man penetrates to the intimate connection between his own little bit of life and

[1] The expression " dogmatic " does not come from us, but is used in the conspectus itself.

SUBSTITUTION OF IDEOLOGICAL INSTRUCTION 181

the life of the whole. The purer the outlook on life is, the clearer is the experience of the vital values in our consciousness. These values are intimately bound up with the race: respect for the body, life, property and tradition; the will towards right and truthfulness; readiness for sacrifice, racial pride and real social convictions, and, as a consequence of these, courage, loyalty, a sense of national unity, bravery, a sense of duty, desire of achieving great things, organising capacity and inventiveness—all these invest our racial history with its characteristic traits.

The marked sense of honour of the German, however, is the expression of national religion, because this sense of honour is the consequence of a special power of assessing things at their true value. The aim of our education is to increase the emotional capacity of the individual to appreciate these values, in order that he may strive to acquire them as characteristics of an independent and self-determining personality. Genuine religiousness finds its expression in all walks of life. Hence all means of education have something of a religious character. That is what this scheme seeks to show, and the teacher who does his utmost to bring all his class-work to bear in one direction does the very best service he can do.

In what has been said so far, no mention has been made of what is far and away the most pernicious element in the National Socialist management of the schools for their own ends, and that is the gradual falsification of Christian religious instruction. The name " religious instruction " is indeed retained, but the substance is so altered that whatever in it is not in harmony with " Germanic feeling " is eliminated and at the same time the content is increasingly interpreted to suit their race ideology.

As examples of this hybrid mixture of Christian and National Socialist ideas—where, needless to say, the Christian component is sadly maltreated—we offer two documents. The first is a series of directions issued by the Anhalt Ministry of Education (1935) and runs as follows:

Anhalt Government,
    Department of Education.

To all School Authorities

Many questions touching the treatment of the Old Testament in the schools necessitate the issue of temporary instructions, pending the appearance of the syllabus to be issued by the Reich Ministry of Education.

Within the framework of the syllabus of religious instruction the scholars are to be directed to the two main sources of German faith—namely, the Germanic experience of the divine and the Christian doctrine of salvation: these two subjects are to be brought home to the minds of the children by vivid and glowing descriptions of models of German piety. There is no need of any Old Testament stories about the Patriarchs or Kings; but the effect of the personality of Jesus on the life of great Germans is to be described in inspiring stories.

The religious attitude as represented in the Old Testament will be given its right valuation in the eighth year at school when the search of the peoples after God and their outlook on things eternal are presented and correlated. In addition to the religious testimonies given by German men and women and by representative German spiritual lyrics, some few Psalms may also be introduced here.

The typical characters of Jewish religion will be set forth in the senior schools in the ninth year by directing the scholars' attention during history classes to the march of Nordic Man and the fate of ancient cultures.

In this connection the mission and activities of the Prophets are to be propounded, but only for purposes of comparison. The primary concern is, and must remain, the whole body of beliefs of the German people.

Signed (for the Ministry): SCHULZE.[1]
State Government of Anhalt,
Department of Popular Education.

The second example is also in the form of directions, issued this time by the Ministry of Education of Thuringia in 1937, and containing a general syllabus for religious instruction in the following main proposals:

1. Both syllabus and teaching must lay particular stress on the manly and fighting character of Christianity.
2. Both syllabus and teaching must aim at attaining a lively interaction between Christ and the German National Socialist mind, which is to lead to the maximum of endeavour for the fulfilment of duty to country, nation and Führer.
3. The religious instruction lessons are often to be transformed into special celebrations of a solemn and impressive character, so that the whole soul may be penetrated by the divine revelation manifested in Christ, the German People and the German soil. In these celebrations use should be made of vigorous and lofty sayings from Scripture, of the most sublime German hymns and of works of German religious art.
4. All teachers should have committed to memory a good stock of specially chosen sayings and poems.
5. Religious instruction must be regularly made to correspond with the German year. Popular and local holidays, Church feasts and Party celebrations as they occur are to be made the subjects for the religious classes in all divisions of the school.

The Minister has directed that for the future any treatment of Old Testament Bible History, Jewish religious instruction and other Old Testament matters is to be wholly discontinued in middle and senior schools. Jesus Christ must be portrayed as an anti-Semite, and subjects prescribed as school compositions for those in the fifth year at elementary schools are: "Jesus' fight against Jewish selfishness for a kingdom of love, honour, purity and strength"; and for the sixth year: "Jesus' fight against Jewry and clericalism in the person of the Pharisees and the priests."

We read of a similar attempt at falsifying religious instruction in the *Schwäbischer Mercur*:[2]

With reference to the well-known decree of the Minister of Education of April 28th, 1937, on religious instruction in which, among other things, it was said: "The education of German youth must, without any deviation whatsoever, be carried out in a National Socialist spirit. This principle must be applied to each and every subject taught in the schools, and so, since Religion is part of the school syllabus, it must necessarily apply also to the giving of religious instruction, in which, therefore, nothing that does not harmonise with the moral sense of the German race may find a place."
The *Official Gazette* of November 2nd, 1937, writes as follows: "An attempt has recently been made to show that this decree goes against the promise that was given concerning the teaching of religion in the German elementary schools, because, as is asserted, on the introduction of German community

---

[1] *Neue Freie Presse*, Vienna, January 27th, 1937. [2] No. 257, November 3rd, 1937.

schools it was provided that such teaching would be given according to the principles of the Lutheran and Catholic Churches, from which the above-mentioned decree is a departure.

"But it is obvious that the Minister of Education cannot allow anything which infringes on National Socialism. And to treat of matters which run counter to the moral sense of the German race entails such an infringement. No promise in this regard can, therefore, be given by a National Socialist Minister."

The fear that religious instruction would be used by neo-pagan National Socialist teachers as so many opportunities for inculcating their own views is expressed in a Pastoral Letter of the Bishop of Berlin of October 10th, 1937. The writings and words of those responsible for the cultural life of the nation, writes the bishop, make it abundantly clear how Sacred Scripture is spoken of and the Catholic Church reviled:

> Men and women teachers, trained in such a spirit, will work like poison on the minds of the children. Such teachers, whether they be men or women, as no longer take their stand on the firm foundation of the Catholic Faith, should of their own accord withdraw from giving Catholic instruction, for any other course would be dishonourable hypocrisy before God and man, and a deliberate perversion of the religious instruction they pretend to give.

The Bishop of Münster in a sermon in November, 1937, gave expression to his deep sorrow and anxiety at the thought that unbelieving teachers would misuse religious instruction in order to destroy the Christian religion:

> If teachers, who have interiorly lost the Faith, were to venture still to give what is supposed to be Catholic religious instruction, then woe to the poor children who fall into the hands of such impostors. Better no religious instruction in the school than one which offers poison in place of true nourishment. Whoever denies the immortality of the individual human soul and tries to satisfy man's hope of eternity and his longing for life everlasting by prating of an "eternal Germany" and of an eternal consciousness consisting only in the awareness of the past and the future of the People, such a one teaches no true religion, but destroys all religion; he offers the children a religious substitute which cannot instil any lasting sense of personal obligation, but can only destroy and corrupt it. It is indeed only too true that when teachers are required to be instrumental in giving to the children entrusted to their charge a substitute religion which avails itself of the old religious terms only to disguise its enmity against Christianity and its principles that contradict Christian truth, then indeed, as Pius XI says, " the more necessary is a vigilant distrust and distrustful vigilance stimulated by bitter experience." Christian parents, when teachers dare to forbid your children to relate to you at home what they have been taught in school, or to repeat the remarks that have been made with regard to religious truths, then know and be sure that something is happening in the school which they would keep secret from you, something which will alienate from you the hearts of your own children. This being so, you are justified, nay obliged, to protest to these Educational Authorities that employ such teachers, and through petitions and complaints and all lawful means to prevail upon them to remove people who are destroying both the children's trust in their parents and proper family life, to remove them from a position which they can worthily fill only by co-operating in all honour and loyalty with the parents of their pupils.

Allusion is also made to this insidious perversion in the German community schools of Christian religious teaching in a Pastoral Letter of the spring of 1938, in which the Bishop of Mainz deplores the difficulties placed in the way of religious instruction and its final abolition:

> Our sorrow (at the closing of the Catholic private schools) would be easier to bear, did we but know that the children could go into other trustworthy schools, but, instead, we see them faced with an education that causes us deep concern. For years we have followed with the greatest sorrow the progress towards complete abolition of religious instruction in the non-private schools of our diocese. The number of the religious instruction periods has been continuously curtailed, the clergy have been more and more excluded from teaching, and now only in exceptional circumstances are they allowed to give religious instruction in the schools. Then the bishop clearly stated what we have been able to prove from other sources: " Lay teachers often use this instruction in a way that is diametrically opposed to the precepts of the Church. Large portions of the Old Testament, although they are part of the Word of God, are completely ignored. Religion is no longer taught according to the traditions of God's divinely appointed Church, but according to a race theory which places no importance whatsoever on the eternal salvation of man's soul."

In an earlier part of this chapter mention was made of the compulsion exercised on teachers to induce them to refuse to give religious instruction. Lately, however, incredible though it sounds, they have been openly asked to continue in this teaching, but in a National Socialist spirit. One highly placed Party member, for instance, urged teachers to become " believers in God " (*i.e.*, neo-pagan) and then to carry on religious instruction in this neo-pagan sense.[1]

The undisguised way in which such advice is given, as, for instance, by the Bavarian State Minister, Robert Wagner, can only be described as cynical. We give here, as an example, the pertinent passages from an address he delivered to teachers on February 13th, 1937:

> One thing I do beg of you. Up till now there have been here and there— well, let us call them National Socialist teachers, who have refused to give religious instruction. Well now, I want everyone to know what I am now going to say to you. Comrades, I would much rather see **you** as teachers in the schools than many a clergyman, and so I ask you earnestly to remain there and to teach religion. What is it that makes you want to get out of it ? Why ? What is your aim ? How then dare you reproach me for not doing a thing properly, for not doing my duty ? I would like to see the man who would say that to my face with impunity. And yet another point. We National Socialists never retreat. Where we once are, there we stay. We never again go away. Not even the Church will get us out. We are there to stay. It is absolutely unthinkable that we should budge an inch. So I beg of you, remain in the schools, and you yourselves give the religious instruction.

And so Christian doctrine is to be used to destroy Christianity. The name " religious instruction " is abused in order to screen National Socialist teaching.

---

[1] *Cf.* Streicher's speech to the teachers of Franconia quoted in *Reichszeitung der deutschen Erzieher, NS Lehrerzeitung*, Heft IV, April, 1937, p. 117.

At this point we reproduce an article from the *Völkischer Beobachter*[1] which corroborates only too well the exposition of the Nazi point of view described above:

Sectarian Education or National Religious Education?

It is incumbent on the State to ensure that popular education in schools —the " State element " in the structure of education—corresponds to the vital needs of the German race, and harmonises rather than clashes with other normal channels of influence—the home, the Hitler Youth, etc.

To this end it is essential that the State, in its educational capacity, should completely eliminate every alien influence and take full charge of all education provided in schools. It alone is authorised to deal with such education. By virtue of this exclusive educational right the State must control every aspect of school life. It cannot allow—indeed, it has no right to allow—other organisations (and religious denominations come under this heading) which do not guarantee complete conformity with National Socialism and complete harmony with the life of our race to educate youth for ends other than those demanded by the interests of the people. Those who take their orders from centres outside the nation (*e.g.*, Rome) may never hope to be entrusted with the education of German youth by any conscientious Government. . . .

The same principles in their entirety hold good for teachers, in so far as they are official representatives of the State. . . . Those who do not see the root and the aim of all education in the race may no longer function as teachers in German schools, and no teacher, whatsoever his subject, may be regarded as an exception to this rule. Every school must be a self-contained centre of education. . . . It must be impossible for a teacher in the course of one type of instruction to repudiate what is elsewhere proclaimed a fundamental principle of moral conduct. Our concept of the racial structure of the German people either holds good in every possible sphere or it holds good in none at all. Moreover, we cannot admit that children in their most receptive years should be presented on the one hand with the conception that membership of the German nation, irrespective of social status and religious denomination, is the fundamental principle of national life, and on the other hand be presented with another fundamental principle in the shape of membership of a denomination which ignores all racial and national distinctions. Similarly, it is out of the question to indicate to German children that service rendered to the people is the moral basis of conduct and, at the same time in other portions of the curriculum, to base the acceptance or rejection of some line of action on the hope of an expected reward or on the fear of a subsequent punishment. Does anybody really believe that youth can be brought up to be religious by means of such a dichotomy ? . . . German Youth must be protected from any such treatment. It would be better to exclude denominational instruction altogether, rather than risk the destruction of all sense of religion amongst German youth, as the result of denominational squabbles.

From all this the fact plainly emerges that National Socialism not only seeks to drive the Church out of the schools, but that it wishes also to eliminate the Christian religion from religious instruction. And the basis of this policy is not Secularism, but religion itself ! Former types of religious instruction are not rejected because the teaching given in other subjects is anti-religious, so that such a rejection is demanded by the need for pedagogical uniformity. Denominational religious instruction has to disappear precisely because certain

[1] Vienna edition, March 29th, 1939.

other subjects—Biology, History, German Literature, Geography, Gymnastics—are the chosen mediums of an exclusive, totalitarian religion.

" Religion," says the writer further on, " being as it is one of the most fundamental and important cultural factors in the life of a people, is like all other activities of life based on the people's specific racial characteristics. The logical conclusion drawn from National Socialist educational principles demands, therefore, that all teachers, even those giving denominational instruction, who do not accept these principles, and so ignore the vital necessities of the German nation, should be barred from having any part in the education of German youth. This has nothing whatever to do with hostility against religion, let alone with atheism. . . . It is therefore a National Socialist and consequently a religious act for the State to ordain that denominational religious instruction is to be given only by such lay and clerical teachers as can be expected not to abuse the school for denominational controversy and strife. . . . It must lead to hypocrisy if young boys and girls are compelled to observe denominational practices which are for them of no religious significance."

May God spare the German people the catastrophe of a young generation brought up on such principles.

CHAPTER VII

THE OBSTRUCTION OF THE CHURCH'S PASTORAL
WORK: I. THE DESTRUCTION OF CATHOLIC
ORGANISATIONS FOR ADULTS

To those who have read thus far it will scarcely be a matter of surprise that in the National Socialist campaign against the Church not even her pastoral work was exempt from attack; part of it, indeed—and not the least important—was destroyed by the suppression, already described, of the Catholic education of the young. But actually National Socialism goes far beyond that; bit by bit it is destroying the entire pastoral economy of the Church with its unions and associations, both lay and ecclesiastical. In what follows we shall show, in the first place, how those important instruments of pastoral activity, the ecclesiastical organisations for adults, are being broken up; secondly, how that sphere of the Church's activity which bears on the public life of the nation is restricted and rendered impossible; and finally, how step by step systematic warfare is being waged against religion itself—against the administration and reception of the sacraments, against attendance at religious services, and even against the mere fact of Church membership.

1. *The Occupational Organisations*

In her various associations and societies for adults the Catholic Church of Germany had created a very important instrument for the exercise of her pastoral work among various classes of the people. These organisations—some of them based on the natural divisions of age and sex, and others on differences of occupation—did immense service, not only in establishing and deepening faith by means of their religious training, but also in impregnating with the Christian spirit the whole sphere of business and family life. The methods by which they were destroyed were exactly the same as those employed against the Catholic Youth Associations. The authorities gave them the assurance that they could continue in existence and even promised them the protection of the State; but at the same time these very authorities began to restrict their activity in every possible way, to exert pressure on their members, and finally, on a variety of pretexts, to dissolve one organisation after another.

Yet as early as April 28th, 1933, in a communication to Cardinal Bertram, the President of the Fulda Conference of Bishops, Adolf Hitler had given the assurance that so long as the Catholic associations " do not indulge in party politics or further any tendencies inimical to the present Government, there is no intention of proceeding against them."[1] On May 18th, 1933, the Vicar Capitular of Münster, too, basing his assertion on " trustworthy information," had declared that the threat to the independence of the Catholic associations—*i.e.*, the danger of being absorbed by the NSDAP—was a question of " misunderstandings or encroachments by local authorities, which have not the support of the Central Government." It really seemed that the safety of the Catholic organisations was secured. In the June of 1933, and so before the conclusion of the Concordat, the Catholic Workers' Association and the Catholic Journeymen's Association were temporarily enrolled in the German Labour Front. On this occasion Dr. Ley, the Leader of the German Labour Front, declared:

> Now that both Catholic and Evangelical Workers' and Journeymen's Associations are enrolled in this German Labour Front, such action as might seem to have been directed against them is to be discontinued. . . . Some statements of mine have been erroneously taken to mean that I regard the Workers' and Journeymen's Associations as hostile to the State. That is not true: I only pointed out that if the denominational unions resisted their organic incorporation into the new State, they would then be regarded as its enemies."[2]

With the signing of the Reich Concordat on July 20th, 1933, the National Socialist State itself seemed to have guaranteed the further continuance of the denominational associations, for in Article 31, sect. 2, it is expressly stated:

> Those Catholic organisations which, to their religious, cultural and charitable pursuits add others, such as social or professional interests, even though they may be brought into national associations, are to enjoy the protection of Article 31, sect. 1, provided they guarantee to develop their activities outside all political parties.

Furthermore, on July 18th, 1933, representatives of the Government of the Reich and of the German bishops came to the following agreement on this Article about an eventual incorporation in national organisations:

> The incorporation of these associations is not to deprive them of their own corporate life and property. . . . Interference with the activities of the associations is to be avoided. . . . The Reich Government presumes that the Catholic organisations, in the case of incorporation, will obtain the agreement of their ecclesiastical authorities.

The First Prohibitions

On April 28th, 1934, within a year of the events just mentioned, the Leader of the German Labour Front, Dr. Ley, issued the following regulation:

> There is occasion to point out that members of other vocational and class organisations, especially denominational Workers' and Journeymen's Associations, cannot be members of the German Labour Front. In cases of such double membership—both of the German Labour Front and of

[1] Quoted in the *Münster Diocesan Gazette*, January 2nd, 1935, p. 4.
[2] *Cf.*, for example, *Münsterscher Anzeiger*, June 30th, 1933.

one of the above-mentioned Associations—membership of the German Labour Front must be cancelled forthwith.

This regulation caused great uneasiness and anxiety to countless Catholic workmen and journeymen, since, trusting in the assurances given by the State, at least 90 per cent. of the men and women who belonged to the Catholic Workers' Associations had, as individuals, become members of the German Labour Front. Cardinal Bertram of Breslau and Bishop Baris of Berlin lodged vigorous protests, but without any result. Any hope, however, that might have remained was shattered by another speech of Dr. Ley's almost a year later (April 25th, 1935), in which he asserted that the denominational organisations had pledged their word eighty times, but in reality had thrown all honour overboard. (Thus organisations which had made sacrifices second to none in the World War—55,000 members of the Journeymen's Association took part in it and 17,000 of them were killed in action—were publicly accused of breaking their word.) Journeyman apprentices, declared Dr. Ley at a farewell demonstration for itinerant apprentices held in front of Berlin Castle, were in future to be true to what their name originally implied. (As though the Catholic associations had not sent thousands of apprentices on the road and kept countless craftsmen from becoming submerged in the proletariate.) " Therefore," he continued, " we want to demolish the last remains of the denominational Journeymen's Associations. For we cannot tolerate disunion and discord in this field." The prohibition, therefore, which he had decreed against double membership remained in force.[1]

A few weeks later there appeared in the newspaper of the German Labour Front, the *Angriff*,[2] a proclamation by Schürmann, the District Leader of the German Labour Front, which was also brought to general notice by the radio:

> I take occasion to refer again, and in most emphatic terms, to the ruling of the National Director, Dr. Robert Ley, according to which a double membership of the German Labour Front and of the denominational Workers' Union is not valid.
>
> I have recently been informed that a certain interested party is spreading the rumour that the prohibition of double membership has been repealed. I take the opportunity, therefore, to assert publicly that the ruling of Dr. Ley is still in force. Double membership entails exclusion from the German Labour Front.
>
> Hereby any doubts occasioned by the spreading of unwarranted rumours should be removed. The local Leaders of the German Labour Front are personally responsible to me for the carrying out of this regulation without unreasonable severity. In accordance with the desire and will of the Führer the German Labour Front is the sole representative of all who work with brain and muscle. To it alone belongs the ideological and socio-political education of the workers and the arrangement of leisure-time amusements.
>
> As National Socialists we recognise no Evangelical locksmiths or Catholic joiners, but only German workers, whose welfare we serve regardless of

---

[1] Quoted in a Pastoral Letter issued by Cardinal Faulhaber and Bishop Hauck of Bamberg on June 1st, 1935.
[2] May 23rd, 1935.

their religious denomination. The denominational Workers' Associations have no longer any right to exist in Germany now that the German Labour Front, in virtue of the ordinance of the Führer of October 24th, 1934, has been commissioned to watch over the interests of all German workers.

Signed: SCHÜRMANN,
District Leader of the German Labour Front.[1]

It was in vain that the bishops appealed to an agreement of July 18th, 1934, between the Government of the Reich and the Episcopate, in which it was stated: " The members of the Catholic organisations are not, on account of such membership, to be put at any legal disadvantage in school or State."

A month later Dr. Frick, the Reichsminister of the Interior, expressed similar opinions concerning the Catholic Civil Servants' Unions. Without giving a vestige of proof he asserted in a conference quoted in the *Völkischer Beobachter* of June 9th, 1935, that the Catholic organisations were still under the influence of the political Centre Party. Again, on the South Westphalia District Party Day in Münster in Westphalia (July 7th, 1935), Dr. Frick declared in a public speech:

I must add that the Catholic professional associations, like the Journeymen's Associations and the denominational Youth Organisations, no longer suit our present age, and that they often busy themselves in spheres which the National Socialist State must claim solely for itself for the fulfilment of its tasks.

On July 22nd, 1935, the National Socialist *Parteikorrespondenz* published a repetition of Dr. Ley's ruling of the previous July and added:

" We have occasion to point out that members of the denominational Workers' and Journeymen's Associations cannot be members of the German Labour Front. Where there is a case of double membership—*i.e.*, membership of the German Labour Front and of one of the above-mentioned unions—the membership of the German Labour Front is to be cancelled forthwith." The motive alleged for this recent strengthening of the Ley decree is that the efficient organisation of the national work within the operatives' community cannot be secured if that community remains divided on account of the existence of denominational Workers' and Journeymen's Associations, which have become a rallying point for former trade union secretaries.

At the same time, in the Labour Front's *Informationsdienst*, the District Director of the German Labour Front in Düsseldorf, Bangert, attacked the denominational workers and recalled the ruling " according to which any double membership of the German Labour Front and denominational Workers' Associations is inadmissible. All works' managers and local administrators are urged to compel those who are still members of a denominational workers' union to decide whether they adhere to the Führer, Adolf Hitler, or cling to the subversive spirit of the Centre Party, which entails exclusion from the ranks of the German Labour Front."

As early as 1934 a decree had been passed in many towns of Germany prohibiting the Catholic associations from holding meetings—a prohibition which remained in force during the following years. In some places leaders of associations were threatened with arrest merely

[1] *Cf. Germania*, No. 144, May 24th, 1935.

because they sought approval for meetings to be held outside the church; in others each individual meeting held outside the church required the permission of the police, which was often refused, even when the purpose of the meeting was purely religious.

The appearance in public of Catholic organisations has been prohibited since 1935 in practically every part of Germany.[1] On February 27th, 1936, the Bavarian Ministry of the Interior laid it down that permission for religious associations to hold meetings outside the church could not be given. In the summer of 1935 Catholic organisations were forbidden (*e.g.*, in the diocese of Passau) to take part in civilian dress in purely ecclesiastical celebrations such as the Corpus Christi procession, or to carry a banner; and members of the Men's Sodalities had even to take off their Sodality medals before the procession began.

The *Berlin Catholic Parish Magazine* for July 2nd, 1935, gives a whole list of cases in which Civil Servants have been urged by their superiors to give up their membership in the denominational organisations, and such cases have grown more numerous since the summer of 1935. An illustration of the methods employed is afforded by a characteristic declaration of the President of the District Government of Münster. In reply to the enquiries of a certain subordinate Mayor he bade him have no compunction about urging Civil Servants to leave denominational organisations; the refusal of such a request out of a spirit of opposition did not as yet, it is true, constitute a disciplinary offence, but certainly justified authorities in not showing special favour to such a Civil Servant in granting leave of absence, affording extra help in critical times, and facilitating promotion; moreover a report of this kind could be entered in the person's dossier.

Invitations, which left no doubt of their meaning, to resign from such organisations often took the form of questionnaires in which the authorities made enquiries about membership of any kind of Catholic organisation, even strictly religious ones. Even the fact that children belonged to the Parish Youth had to be acknowledged, as though the Parish Youth, to which every Catholic youth belonged by baptism, constituted an association ! It was also expressly asked whether the Civil Servant had belonged to or still belonged to a Sodality of Our Lady. The following announcement, for example, was published in the *Neues Münchener Tageblatt* of September 11th, 1935:

> By October 1st, 1935, every Civil Servant must declare on his Service Oath what associations he has belonged to since the war or still belongs to, no matter whether they are denominational or not. The declaration will be included in the personal records, though for the present (!) no conclusions will be drawn from these declarations.

As in the case of the propaganda for the community schools, so here too the authorities did not shrink from using economic pressure to make Civil Servants more amenable. This being so, we can easily understand the full significance of a resolution of the Mayor of the

---

[1] *Cf.*, *e.g.*, *Germania*, No. 129, May 9th, 1935.

town of Laufen, published in the *Rupertigau-Boten*.[1] It states that none of those who were in business in the town of Laufen, nor the members of their families, could belong to a denominational organisation. In the future the town of Laufen would place its undertakings and contracts in the hands of such business people and craftsmen only as belonged to a National Socialist organisation, and not with those who were either themselves members of a denominational organisation or had relatives and employees belonging to one. In this same year, too, the periodical *Freiheit und Brot*[2] contained the following:

> The headquarters of the Munich-Upper Bavaria District insists with all emphasis that it should be obvious to every member of the Party that the accommodation which they have available under the Children's Country Holiday Scheme should be placed at the disposal of the National Socialist Welfare Service only—the bureau established for that purpose by the National Socialist German Workers' Party. This communication has been made because during the present year a variety of organisations and associations have operated this scheme.

Compulsory Resignation

The Nazi authorities did not content themselves with invitations, requests and threats. Taking their stand on the decrees cited above, which forbade the double membership of National Socialist organisations and Catholic unions, they compelled numerous Catholics—sometimes by delivering ultimatums with a time-limit—to resign from the Catholic organisations, guaranteed though these were in the Concordat and " protected by the State." On July 11th, 1935, for example, the Mayor of Dortmund sent round a circular referring to the declarations of Dr. Frick, the Reichsminister of the Interior. In this he says, among other things:

> I must demand that those Civil Servants, employees and workers who are under my authority immediately give up their membership of the denominational organisations which correspond to these employments, and that they see to it that their children resign from the denominational Youth organisations. . . . I do not intend by this regulation to exercise any moral compulsion on the Civil Servant, etc., under my authority (!). But I must assert the principle that the State can demand of those whom it has chosen as collaborators that they give to the State what belongs to the State. I am of the opinion that those who believe that they cannot conform to this ruling will have to give up the idea of collaborating further in the building up of this State. I shall shortly institute an inquiry to see whether this regulation has been observed.

To assure Civil Servants that he has no desire to exert moral pressure and in the same breath to threaten them with economic ruin, can only be described as cynical!

According to the demand which the Area Leader of Freisung made on July 11th, 1935, even the wives of the Party members were to resign from their various denominational societies, and by the 30th of the same month every Party member of the district had to report that his wife had been enrolled in the National Socialist Women's Union.

[1] No. 200, August 31st, 1935.   [2] Munich, August 29th, 1935.

In municipal offices, railway and tramway companies, etc. (as, for instance, in Ellwengen, Ahlen, Munich and elsewhere), many people were forced to leave their denominational societies and, in a number of places, their resignation was exacted under a declaration on oath. As can be proved from a whole series of cases, refusal to comply resulted in summary exclusion from the German Labour Front. This is what happened to a number of Munich tramway employees, for instance, just because they were members of a Sodality of Our Lady. In many places, too, town councillors were requested to get their wives to resign from the Union of Christian Mothers.

On August 19th, 1935, the local headquarters of the German National Socialist Workers' Party in Dinkelsbühl issued to members of the German Labour Front and of the Party an ultimatum which gave them till August 24th to declare their resignation from the Catholic Journeymen's Association. Anyone belonging to a denominational association was an enemy of the State ! The alternative, of course, was expulsion from the Labour Front. That may not sound very terrible, but we should remember that anyone expelled from one of these compulsory organisations cannot, as a rule, obtain any other post and has to face financial ruin.

In a circular issued in August, 1935, by the town of Waltrop, we read:

Do you want to remain a member of the German Labour Front, or do you want to uphold the false prophets of an outworn system, and allow yourself to be exploited for political ends (that is, do you want to belong to a denominational organisation) ? If, then, you want to remain a member of a Church occupational group, we require you to surrender your membership card of the German Labour Front by August 15th either to your sectional warden or at our offices. Failing this you must hand in to us the declaration that you are a member of the German Labour Front only:

" I hereby declare on oath that I have read the above document and have made my declaration in all truth."

....
(*Personal Signature*.)

Waltrop, *August*, 1935.

Labour Front Group Supervision in a certain locality in Lower Franconia required members of Catholic organisations to declare:

It has been brought to my notice that double membership of the German Labour Front and of denominational associations is unlawful. Hereby I declare on oath that I belong to no denominational association or union (Catholic Apprentices', Journeymen's and Workers' Associations). I bind myself not to take part in any functions of the above organisations, since it is not fitting that members of the German Labour Front should do so. I sign this declaration on oath freely, recognising that the only organisation for all German workers is the German Labour Front, to which I also belong.

In this connection there is the ruling of the Führer's Representative, Rudolf Hess, of May 15th, 1936, which should be quoted. It runs:

In the interests of the homogeneous adjustment of the German Undergraduates' Union I hereby forbid Party members and members of Party organisations still studying in German universities and technical schools to belong to any other existing Undergraduates' Union or Association.[1]

[1] *Cf. Münchener Neueste Nachrichten*, May 16th, 1936.

194 OBSTRUCTION OF CHURCH'S PASTORAL WORK

What in the first years of the Nazi persecution of the Church was left to the initiative of individual authorities was made general for the whole of the Reich in 1938 by a decree of Reichsminister of the Interior, Dr. Frick, on October 4th. By this decree the membership of practically all denominational associations was forbidden finally and without exception to all Civil Servants, teachers, and employees of the Third Reich. Among the forbidden organisations are mentioned the Catholic Workers' and Journeymen's Associations, the Catholic Graduates' Union, the Union of Catholic German Women Social Officials, the Reich Union of Catholic Women Shop Assistants and Officials. Then in the summer of 1938 a report appeared in the Press that the soldiers of the former Austrian Army had to resign immediately from the denominational soldiers' associations which had been established in recent years in Austria.

Compulsory Surrender of Membership Lists

In order to bring effective pressure to bear on individual Catholics, especially Civil Servants, employees and workmen, the authorities tried to get hold of the lists of the members of the Catholic associations and unions. In very many cases, especially during 1935 and 1936, the local chairmen of the associations were summarily requested to surrender their lists of members to the Mayor or to the Party officials or, as was most frequently the case, to the police. Although the bishops made a protest, referred to the ecclesiastical character of these associations, and required parish priests to refuse to comply with the demand, often enough the surrender of the lists was enforced by threats.

The answer of the President of the District Government to the complaints of the Vicar-General of Hildesheim of August 29th, 1936, shows what a bad conscience the authorities themselves had over this affair. The answer reads:

> With reference to the discussion over the telephone today between my Secretary and the Vicar-General, Dr. Offenstein, I inform you that the issuing of the order to the police authorities of this district concerning the surrender of the membership lists of all Catholic organisations was due to a mistake of a subordinate official (!). I regret that this has happened and I beg you to accept my apologies. I have immediately cancelled the order.
>
> For the President,
BACKMEISTER.

Nevertheless the Government of Upper Bavaria declared that the authorities were acting within their powers in demanding the surrender of these lists, since the fundamental laws of the Constitution of the Reich were annulled by the decree of February 28th, 1933. Once again, therefore, the Emergency Decree, which was directed against the machinations of the Communists, was made to serve the purpose of aiding the attack on the Catholic Church.

Only a few cases of the ill-treatment which members of Catholic associations have had to suffer in recent years can be enumerated here.

A meeting of the Catholic Workers' Association in Wolfratshausen was held on August 15th, 1935, with the approval of the authorities. No sooner was it ended than seven people with parts of the SS and SA uniform showing beneath their civilian clothes appeared in the assembly room; they jeered at the association members present, threw a glass of beer in the face of the chairman, destroyed a picture on the wall by hurling an ash tray at it, and tore the badges of office from the breasts of some of the officials. One of the priests, on his way home from the meeting, was knocked about and beaten with rubber truncheons in the open street by five men wearing parts of the SS and SA uniforms.

Shortly before this, on August 5th of the same year, a meeting of the Catholic Journeymen's Association had taken place in the same town with official approval. Several Catholic journeymen had already been threatened by some SS-men on account of this meeting, and on the way home three of them were overtaken by a car in which three SS-men and a civilian were seated. The journeymen were taken off in the car and beaten, one of them being maltreated in an exceptionally brutal fashion. They had to make a three-hour journey back by foot.

But it was not the perpetrators of this outrage who were punished but the Catholic Associations, inasmuch as the administrator of the Rural Area Council of Wolfratshausen decided on September 2nd, 1935, that Catholic organisations could only hold meetings when they had the written approval of the authorities.

On March 31st, 1935, the house of the Catholic Workers' Association in Rhede in Westphalia was raided by SA-men from the camp in Bocholt. Catholic members of the Association were maltreated and the platform and all the furniture of the room were wrecked. When the police flying squad arrived, the SA-men had already marched off in formation. Yet, although the raid had taken place in broad daylight, the Public Prosecutor's office decided on June 18th of the same year that legal proceedings could not be taken, as the perpetrators were unknown.

The Dissolution of Catholic Associations

It will always remain a glorious page in the history of the Catholic Church in Germany that National Socialism, even by the methods of ruthless restriction and attrition which we have described, did not attain its end—the destruction of the Catholic Associations and Unions. Despite external obstruction and libellous reports, and despite the enormous pressure which was exerted on their members for years on end, these organisations showed very little sign of dying the natural death that comes of a decrease in membership. So there was nothing for it but to abolish them by direct prohibition, and this, accordingly, was what was done. They did not indeed prohibit them all at once, but one by one, and on a variety of pretexts, for the determination to destroy them all, which was present from the very beginning, was not to be disclosed too soon.

In September, 1935, by order of the Gestapo the Catholic Workers' Association in the district of Münster was dissolved then and there, and its assets confiscated, the only justification forthcoming being the allegation that the Association had engaged in activities which were hostile to the State. The Brochure published by the Diocesan Administration of Cologne in 1936, " The Church and the Catholic Workers' Associations—an Episcopal Defence," was prohibited and confiscated by the orders of the Ministry for Ecclesiastical Affairs. Then in 1938 the Catholic Workers' Home in Würzburg was confiscated, the justification again being that it had furthered movements against the interests of the People and the State, and this was followed in 1939 by the dissolution of all the Workers' Associations still existing.

As regards the Journeymen's Associations, in 1935 all local groups in the district of Lüdinghausen were dissolved, without any notification being given to the Diocesan Administration of Münster. In November, 1937, the *Kolpinghaus* in Osnabrück was closed and the Journeymen's Association in the whole municipal borough of Osnabrück dissolved, with the usual excuse that the *Kolpinghaus* had become a rallying point for elements hostile to the State. In 1938 the Catholic Journeymen's Institution in Würzburg was taken over without indemnity by the Bavarian government, once more on the grounds that the Würzburg establishment had promoted movements against the People and the State. Then at the end of 1938 the large *Kolpinghaus* in Berlin was also confiscated by the Gestapo and its flourishing Berlin Association dissolved.

A long-expected blow was at last delivered, immediately before the Bishops' Conference at Fulda in 1937, in the compulsory dissolution of the Catholic Women Teachers' Union. This Union, unlike the corresponding one for men, had refused to dissolve itself, and the admirable example of this refusal was approved by all Catholics and not least by the bishops. Though from the beginning, when it had first come under the protection of the Concordat, many attempts had been made to induce it to break up, its members met such efforts by the unanimous resolution to yield only to force. A notice in the *Clergy Communications*, published by the Office of the Vicar-General of Trier,[1] shows how much the members of this Union had to suffer:

> Although the highest authorities have declared that membership of the Union of Catholic Women Teachers is not to prejudice the professional careers of these teachers, not only have many women been excluded from the National Socialist Teachers' Union,[2] but also many have been suddenly removed to other places under particularly aggravating circumstances.

[1] 1937, Heft 2.
[2] Especially after the decree of Wächtler, the Reich Leader of the NS Teachers' Union, on September 29th, 1936.

Then at the end of July, 1937, the local offices of the Union were searched by the Gestapo, who confiscated the membership lists as well as the cash balances. The reason given for this dissolution was "faulty finance."

Since the seizure of power by National Socialism the Catholic Undergraduates' Unions were made the victims of petty persecution on an ever-widening scale, and in order to avoid compulsory dissolution by the State they had to give up their denominational character. Some of the Unions—the undergraduate section—considered it right to dissolve, while the groups known as Old Alumni Unions continued in existence. When, however, the National Socialist Undergraduates' Union, despite full official support and all the terrorising it could employ, failed to carry its point at the Universities, the last and most radical measures were resorted to in 1936. Reichsminister Rudolf Hess laid down in May of that year that no member of the German National Socialist Workers' Party or of any of its organisations could be a member of a non-political Undergraduates' Union; all Party members, therefore, could draw their own conclusions. This practically sealed the fate of the Catholic Unions.

The Catholic Graduates' Union, which was founded in 1913 and in its 180 odd local groups numbered about 13,000 members, was dissolved without further ado in January, 1939, in virtue of the decree for the Protection of the People and the State, passed by the President of the Reich on February 28th, 1933, against the intrigues of the Communists.

Towards the end of 1939 the Secret Police prohibited and dissolved the Central Association of the Sodality of Our Lady for girls as well as the central association of the Unions for Catholic Women and Mothers, though the reason given for this step (" continued activity hostile to the State and the People ") is without any justification. The assets of both these associations as well as their common central office buildings were confiscated and their publishing house closed.

What a serious blow this dealt at the Catholic life in Germany can be gauged from the statistics published in the *Osservatore Romano* of May 4th, 1935. They deal with the work done by these Associations in that year—*i.e.*, at a time when both could work with comparative freedom. There were then 22 diocesan associations, with about 800,000 members, attached to the Central Association of the Sodality of Our Lady for Girls. The periodicals of the association enjoyed a remarkably wide circulation. *Der Kranz* (a periodical for girls over eighteen) had a circulation of 170,000, *Knospen* (the corresponding periodical for girls between fourteen and seventeen) of 68,000, while the circulation of *Die Quelle* (a periodical for country girls) was 11,000. *Frauenart und Frauenleben*, a periodical for clerical directors, which enjoyed a high reputation even outside Germany, had a circulation of 3,500, and finally the figures for *Jugendführerin* and *Vorstandsblätter* are 13,000 and 9,700 respectively. The Union of Women and Mothers' Associations, which likewise had its central office in Düsseldorf, had no less than 980,000 members, and the Union periodical *Frau und Mutter* had a circulation of 780,000.

Thus, by the closing of the Central Offices, which were furnished in a tasteful and practical style and had departments for periodicals, a library, archives for pictures and photos, editorial offices for the various publications, conference rooms, etc.—all at the service of an eminently cultural work of a thoroughly religious nature, a centre of religious influence for close on two million Catholic women and girls was done away with and periodicals with a total circulation of over a million were suppressed.

Of the remaining Catholic organisations which have been dissolved in the course of recent years we may mention: the Catholic Civil Servants' Union; the Albertus Magnus Union for the support of Catholic students;[1] the Women's Association for assisting priestly vocations; a large number of Sodalities of Our Lady; the diocesan Unions of Catholic Clerical Teachers; the Union of Catholic Clerical Teachers of Bavaria; the Christian Union of German Railwaymen; the German Catholics' Peace Association; the Reich Union of Catholic Ex-Servicemen with its subordinate organisations; the Archconfraternity of St. Sebastian, which comprised very numerous Catholic Rifle Clubs in the Rhineland and Westphalia, etc.

In Austria, hardly three months after the Anschluss, by far the majority of the Catholic Unions and Organisations were compulsorily dissolved. According to a report of the Diocesan Gazette of Linz[2] such has beent he fate in Austria of (1) the Catholic People's Union, (2) the Organisation for Catholic Women (with the exception of the Railway-Stations' Mission, the Society for Care of the Destitute, and the *Elizabethtisch*), (3) the Union for Clerical Teachers in Secondary Schools, (4) the National League and its Junior Section, (5) St. George's Scouts, (6) Austrian Athletic Union, (7) German Christian Gymnasts' Society, (8) *Neuland*, (9) National Union of Catholic Girl Associations, (10) Union of Catholic Undergraduates, (11) Union of Catholic Workers, (12) *Katholischer Landesarbeitsbund* with its associated organisations.

There survive for the time being only charitable organisations, those concerned with church music, and—as bodies engaged in purely religious activities—Confraternities and Sodalities.

The Catholic Journeymen's Associations were dissolved without exception and their assets were confiscated. The small saving banks were for the most part taken over by the State. Even the assets of purely religious bodies, such as pious Confraternities or ecclesiastical Associations, were confiscated, although in almost every case the sums concerned were parochial property. In this connection there is a most instructive report which was published in the spring of 1939 by Hoffman, the *Stillhaltekommissar* or Commissioner for winding up the entire system of Unions and Organisations. He gives a survey of the " New Organisation of the Unions," that is, of the complete

---

[1] Lay students—not seminarians.   [2] No. 5, 1938.

destruction effected since the Anschluss of all free activities in Austria. 115,000 associations had been " investigated " and 110,000 of them dissolved, the remaining 5,000 being brought into line with—that is, incorporated into—other associations.

The report admits that the co-ordination—*i.e.*, the destruction—of the organisations in Austria is much more radical than in Germany, but " The Commissioner for liquidating the Associations has created conditions in Austria which promise in great part to serve as a model for the length and breadth of the Reich."

Apart from the fact that the Catholic Journeymen's Associations were obviously superfluous, it was found necessary to dissolve all denominational organisations without exception. The mistake which was made after the assumption of authority in the *Altreich* was not repeated in Austria. For here in Austria countless organisations and associations have been dissolved which—as we have already said—still survive in the *Altreich* in a similar form. Thus the procedure adopted in Austria can serve as a model for the whole Reich—*i.e.*, no organisation is allowed to exist which is not completely subjected to the sovereign authority of the German National Socialist Workers' Party. There no longer exists here any political and sectarian life or activity enjoying corporate independence.

The declaration of the report that the liquidation of the 110,000 associations involved the dismissal of 25,000 employees gives an approximate idea of the extent of this movement of co-ordination and dissolution. Immediately after the Anschluss the assets of all associations were blocked and finally confiscated, a process which brought 2,000,000,000 marks to the State.

National Socialism is perfectly clear about the great pastoral importance of the Catholic Associations, and therefore it takes the most careful precautions to ensure that in the future no Catholic organisation can develop in spheres that are strictly ecclesiastical. In December, 1937, the Gestapo issued an order of Herr Kerrl, the Minister for Ecclesiastical Affairs, to the various departments, in which it was stated:

It is my firm conviction that the Church must confine itself to the purely religious sphere. Apart from the actual church building and its sacristy, we can only regard as necessary an adjoining room for weddings, baptisms, etc., and a hall for Bible-classes, Passiontide devotions, etc. This holds good likewise for the houses of parish priests and vergers: only auxiliary rooms of the sort described are to be considered necessary. Building enterprises which overstep these limits are a violent intrusion of the Church into the secular domain, and this cannot be tolerated.

I request that precautions be taken by appropriate measures to ensure that in the future (*a*) no Church taxes be applied, and (*b*) no State or public subsidies be granted, for the construction of ecclesiastical buildings which are to serve other than religious purposes.

I urge that attention be paid to the above decree, and I require to be informed if any attempt should be made to construct, let us say, assembly rooms in the churches.

Signed: BRUNNER.

2. *The Wrecking of Catholic Charities*

From earliest Christian times the Church's works of charity have been intimately bound up with her religious life. Catholic Germany possessed, especially in her *Karitasverband*, a model organisation which right up to most recent times has, despite all obstruction, achieved wonders. In what follows a few details are quoted from the official ecclesiastical report on the services of the *Karitasverband* in the year 1935.

As a result of the State regulation of organised charity in Germany, the activities of Catholic charity for some years past have consisted chiefly in the work done within the walls of her charitable institutions. In 1935 the Religious Orders in their hospitals performed the following services: 1,600,000 in-patients were cared for, the number of day cases treated exceeded 60,000,000, and the number of night cases 1,400,000. Services to out-patients numbered 4,300,000.

Moreover, in 1935 the *Karitasverband* provided over 400 crèches for small children, and more than 5,000 establishments whose chief work was the nursing of out-patients. In these establishments more than 11,000 Catholic Sisters gave their services without any remuneration. The number of sick attended to in the establishments themselves was about 1,500,000. Besides this, 3,500,000 attendances during the day and 675,000 night nursings were carried out in the homes of sick persons; and there were other minor services which amounted to the number of 10,400,000.

Besides this truly heroic and thoroughly Christian service rendered to the German people, special mention must be made of the unobtrusive services rendered by Catholic Sisters to families and to women in child-bed. In 1935 about 600 of these Sisters took care of 24,000 families and 5,600 women; 80,000 whole days of attendance, 17,200 half-days and 200,600 hours were given, besides 8,500 night-watches and 126,000 other minor services.

German Catholicism may look with pride on these records of its charity, for they demonstrate the spirit of sacrifice living in the Church and her Orders and Congregations. Their work is all the more praiseworthy as they do not advertise it and in most cases give their help without remuneration to the poorest of the poor.

The National Socialist Press, of course, took no notice of these remarkable achievements. On the contrary the Prussian Staatskommissar for the Regulation of the Public Welfare Service laid down rules as early as 1934 which were clearly aimed at cutting down private—and above all, Catholic—charity in favour of the State's Winter Relief Work.

The number of collections for charity was considerably curtailed; collections could only be made from April 1st to October 31st, and all street and house collections required the special approval of the Staatskommissar.[1]

So as to leave the field clear for the collections organised by the State and the Party, the *Karitasverband* was allowed to organise a general collection for only one week in the year and that with special permission. Its " independent and responsible " participation in the Winter Relief Work of the German People in the winter of 1935-6

---

[1] *Cf. Münstersche Anzeiger*, February 21st, 1934.

amounted to this, that it had to make a public renunciation of its claims to its own organisations and to exhort the people to contribute generously to the general Winter Relief.

The general *Karitas* collection which took place with official approval throughout Germany on May 18th, 1935, was accompanied by the wildest disturbances on the part of bands of men in uniform; countless collectors—men and women—were maltreated, often under the eyes of the police, and the Munich authorities took these artificially provoked disturbances as a pretext for prohibiting the collection throughout Bavaria.

Collections which had been traditional for many years and which had come to be very important for the Catholic *Karitasverband*—as, for instance, the long-established autumn collection of provisions —were summarily prohibited in 1935.

The year 1936 brought further restrictions. While in former years the large Christian charitable organisations and the interdenominational associations were allowed to organise public collections on different Sundays and weekdays, the Government informed the *Karitasverband*, the Interior Mission of the Evangelical Church, the Red Cross, and the People's Society for the Care of War Cemeteries that all four organisations were to be content with a single collection on one Sunday, on the grounds that such collections were to be limited as much as possible in the future. Thereupon the President of the *Karitasverband*, Mgr. Kreuz, addressed a proclamation to all the Catholics of Germany, in which he placed the collection of the *Karitasverband* under the protection of St. Martin, the great Saint of Charity. Immediately, however, there came a prohibition forbidding the distribution of the St. Martin's badge.

In June, 1936, there followed the formation of a " Reich Union for Public and Private Welfare Work " which was put in the charge of Hilgenfeldt, Head of the Central Department of Public Welfare in the German National Socialist Workers' Party.

" Starting from the principle," says the Press announcement, " that National Socialism recognises only one united National Socialist Welfare activity, it has the duty of dealing with all the tasks which jointly concern public and voluntary Welfare Work, and thus of securing a Welfare Work organised according to uniform National Socialist principles."

In 1937 the time allowed for street collections for the Catholic *Karitasverband* was reduced from six days to two. The generosity of the people, however, was so great, that in those two days almost as much was collected as in the usual six.

Despite the great generosity and loyalty shown to Catholic charitable enterprises, the official prohibitions of collections caused them, nevertheless, serious injury, though they did not succeed by any means in throttling them altogether, and that is why, especially since 1936, National Socialism has launched an attack on the good name of these undertakings. Archbishop Gröber replied to these libellous attacks in a Pastoral Letter which appeared on Charity Sunday, 1936:

> Steps are being taken to do away with the clinics of the Sisters under the pretext that the activity of the *Karitasverband*, as a denominational association, is impairing national unity. Such a procedure is contrary not only to the principles of the law and to elementary gratitude, but also to the general economic situation. Let them tell us what offence these Sisters have committed against the German people, and in what their opposition to national unity consists. It is nothing but an empty catchword to assert that a Christian love that is not based on the idea of blood challenges the whole concept of German life, and that, therefore, it must be replaced by a love that is Nordic, racial and natural. The Catholic *Karitasverband* has ever been reviled as a manifestation of a priestly craving for power, which, under a parade of unselfishness, is in reality out to domineer and exploit. The person who does not understand such heroic courage, and even judges it to be a senseless waste of human energy on what is of inferior value and degenerate, certainly cannot be accused of sentimentality, but at the same time he is utterly ignorant of what national unity really means. For the spirit of a deeper national unity does not confine itself to what is healthy and strong but includes also among its tasks the relief of life's needs and miseries, if it does not wish to degrade mankind to the savagery and brutality of the beast. . . . Christian charity does no harm whatsoever to the State health institutions, but supports them by the very strength of its Christian purpose—a motive much deeper and far more enduring than any borrowed from Nature and racial unity alone. For Christian charity has its roots in God Himself, and is, therefore, far more effective in keeping man's unruly selfishness under control than the thought of race and a common Fatherland, though we have no wish in any spirit of bad will to deny these their natural values.

It was due to the initiative of the Catholic *Karitasverband* that thousands upon thousands of German children living beyond the German frontiers could spend their holidays every year with Catholic families throughout Germany, and yet as a reward for these good offices, in June, 1936, the State excluded the *Karitasverband* from the " Children's Country Holiday " organisation.

Another very important sphere of activity was taken from the Catholic *Karitasverband* on August 1st, 1936—namely, the Employment Agency. The Reichsminister of the Interior forbade this activity as " inexpedient " and vouchsafed no reply to the solemn protest of the Fulda conference of bishops against this injustice.

The increasing difficulties placed in the path of the Catholic *Karitasverband* are recounted—very discreetly, of course, and mostly by implication—in a report on the work performed by that organisation in 1936 in the diocese of Berlin. In this report we read:

> The way of the *Karitasverband* in 1936 was particularly thorny. The struggle for the preservation of Christianity in public life left its mark also on the *Karitasverband* to the detriment of many people in need of help, for there is nothing of equal value to replace what is being taken from them, as the *Karitas* does not look to the needs of the body only, but also to those of the soul.
>
> One of the spheres of activity included in the present yearly report had to be given up in the course of the year. We refer to the Employment Agency, for whose services there has been great demand for many years and whose

THE CROSSED ADDER forces its way into all places of rottenness and decay in the homes of all peoples and races, multiplies with extreme rapidity and becomes the terror of the inhabitants. Nations, unable to defend themselves against its poison, are doomed to ruin.

[*Durchbruch*, Dec. 2nd, 1937.

Fort trot
Faulhaber
dem Judenfreund!
Dem Handlanger
Moskaus!

FAULHABER AND MOSCOW.

"Away with Faulhaber, the friend of the Jews, who gives the hand of friendship to Moscow."

work has been richly blessed. Last year's report mentioned that the *Karitas* Employment Agency in Berlin has secured 3,822 posts for workers. In virtue of the law of November 5th, 1935, concerning Employment Agencies, Teachers' Agencies and agencies for giving advice on careers, in future free Employment Agencies working for the public utility may cater only for such persons as are not capable of full-time work. All the same, by August 1st, 1936, when the law came into force, it was possible to secure 2,668 posts.

The Children's Holiday Department of the *Karitasverband* experienced further obstruction. The reduction of 75 per cent. granted to Children's Holiday Organisations by the German railways in arrangement with the Public Welfare Bureau was no longer allowed for the larger part of the children sent by us—namely, for all those sent to country families or to such homes as were not recognised by the Public Welfare Bureau as reception centres. Nevertheless we succeeded in sending the usual number of children for holidays and in counterbalancing the loss of the railway fare reduction by increased sacrifices on the part of the parents and of the *Karitasverband* itself.

In 1937 Party members were forbidden to belong to the *Karitasverband* and from that year onwards systematic endeavours were made to remove Catholic Religious from charitable institutions and to replace them by the " Brown Sisters," an organisation founded by the Nazis specifically for this purpose. This process of substitution goes forward very slowly, but that is certainly not because National Socialism appreciates or welcomes the services of the Catholic Religious in this sphere, but it is due solely to the fact that it is finding it impossible to replace the self-sacrificing Sisters and Brothers fast enough.

The declaration of Dr. Gröber, Archbishop of Freiburg, on Charity Sunday, July 3rd, 1938, brings home to us the difficult position of the Catholic *Karitasverband* in the Third Reich, a position which, humanly speaking, is hopeless. He says:

The fulfilment of the duty of charity is more important than ever today. Or is it that the people of my archdiocese do not perhaps realise that, as there are fewer opportunities than in former times to make public collections, we have to use these opportunities with a greater spirit of sacrifice ? Yes, unfortunately we realise only too well that, owing to the pressure exerted from various quarters, a state of distress is slowly but steadily developing for the *Karitasverband* and charitable institutions, and this can be remedied only by exceptional generosity on our part. If, against our will and to our sorrow, certain spheres of public welfare work are forbidden to the Church, then our manifest inability to make any effective resistance is no fault of ours.

For Christian charity with its joy in sacrifice there is no comparable substitute. Times of distress have proved this often enough. But to the great joy of the Archbishop, " thanks to the clear recognition of the present danger, Catholic unity and resolution is revealing itself more and more in a multitude of ways." This must assert itself, too, in the matter of charity.

In the report, frequently referred to above, published by the Freiburg Diocesan Administration at the beginning of 1938 on the tribulations of the Church in Baden, we find the following details concerning the destruction of Catholic charitable activity:

The charitable work of the Church has been deliberately driven out of public life since 1933 by every possible device. The *Karitasverband* today is almost completely excluded from co-operating in public welfare work which the Welfare Authorities have entrusted exclusively to the National Socialist Public Welfare Department, the Winter Relief Work, and the National Socialist Women's Union, and since November, 1935, the Catholic Girls' Protection Society has not been allowed to act as an employment agency.

In the matter of Social Services, as a result of the principle that the care of those who are healthy in body and mind belongs to the State and its Welfare Institutions, ecclesiastical charity has been driven more and more in the last five years to looking after such as do not enjoy this physical and mental health, and these same principles are being applied also to the social services for prisoners, for drunkards' families, for people with hereditary diseases, etc.

In what regards Welfare Work for Mothers and Children (care for their health and during convalescence), the Church has almost completely lost the goodwill and support of official departments, the reduction in railway fares, medical attendance on mothers and children, and is thrown back entirely on its own resources to find families and homes to afford hospitality to the children in the country. The carrying out of all these tasks is a serious financial strain and suffers severely from the rivalry of the National Socialist Public Welfare Department and other official organisations.

As for Child Welfare itself, the Church is no longer allowed to co-operate in the legal management of Infants' Homes and Day Nurseries. The erection of new kindergartens and other Children's Homes has been rendered extraordinarily difficult by the withholding of official approval, and for the future they cannot be erected unless a real need for them is recognised. On the other hand, in the institutions that already exist, the Sisters of Religious Orders are being increasingly replaced, through the action of the municipal authorities, by unemployed members of the National Socialist Public Welfare Organisation.

Especially in recent years, the different Orders and Congregations of nuns have suffered many severe losses in kindergartens, needlework schools, medical surgeries for out-patients and Social Service Institutions. So, for example, the Sisters in the *Mensa Academica* at Heidelberg, Karlsruhe and Freiburg and those in other public catering institutions had to make way for a secular personnel, and about twenty kindergartens have been handed over to the " Brown Sisters."

Since the whole system of ecclesiastical institutions has now lost the status of a public utility service it has been burdened with new taxes retrospective to the year 1934, and all the large Mother-houses and other large institutions throughout the diocese are now being assessed for taxes.

The enrolment of new members for the *Karitasverband* and for the local charitable unions is made exceedingly difficult, and unfavourable reports are spread among the people that the charitable work of the Church is breaking down and that its services are less efficient.

The so-called Collecting Law which limits and obstructs to an extraordinary degree Church collections for ecclesiastical and charitable purposes would need a treatment for itself alone.[1]

The closing of countless Catholic charitable institutions and their transference to non-Catholic management has been going on constantly, especially since 1937. In this way the Catholic *Karitasverband* lost at least the following institutions in 1937 itself: 2 hospitals, 6 sanatoria, 2 clinics, 2 convalescent homes, 2 crèches, 8 kindergartens, 3 students' hostels, 6 orphanages, 6 reformatories, 2 apprentices' hostels, and 3 schools for domestic economy. In the course of the same year Catholic nuns were turned out of 18 hospitals, 76 kindergartens and 4 homes for the aged.

[1] *Cf.* p. 52.

The same tendency is showing itself in Austria since the Anschluss Catholic charitable activity is rigidly controlled by the secular authorities and is subjected to a great variety of obstructions. The State Commissioners charged with its supervision make themselves extremely unpleasant and put all possible difficulties in the way of the Religious in hospitals, orphanages, welfare homes, etc.

In the Sudetenland, the charitable organisations were to a large extent handed over without further ado to the National Socialist Public Welfare Organisation. Elsewhere the Government or the Party is trying to penetrate, step by step, into their management in such a way as to deprive them completely of their independence and their Catholic character.

The plight, therefore, of Catholic charitable enterprises in the Third Reich seems, humanly speaking, hopeless. But it will continue to live on even if it is no longer in control of the associations and institutes which have been so brilliantly built up in the past, complete in every detail of organisation and training. It will be carried on by those who, despite all the additional State taxes, have given it such decisive support up to now—by the faithful, that is, whose names will remain ever unknown, and on whom more and more the fate of Christianity in the Third Reich depends.

CHAPTER VIII

THE OBSTRUCTION OF THE CHURCH'S PASTORAL WORK : II. SUNDRY APOSTOLIC WORKS

1. *The Secularisation of Public Life*

THE secularising of public life, which was proclaimed, for instance, by Dr. Frick, the Reichsminister of the Interior, on July 7th, 1935, has remained throughout recent years one of the most important aims of National Socialism. Not that National Socialism will remain satisfied even with the removal of everything Christian from public life alone; as a radical totalitarian system it intrudes into every private activity—there is no real private life on National Socialist principles —into the conversation at the family table, into the most personal thoughts of the individual members of the nation. All the same, the purging of Christian elements from public life was the first objective in the campaign against the Church and was to be pursued remorselessly.

The first moves in this campaign were the abolition of ecclesiastical feast days, the prohibition of any religious demonstrations out of church, the restriction and obstruction of pilgrimages and processions, the suppression of Catholic morning radio services, etc. These measures must appear in a very remarkable light when one reflects that the Nazi régime is constantly using such phrases as the Unity of the People, Blood and Soil, the upholding of old traditions, the care for the national heritage, and the like. For what is more closely bound up with this national heritage than precisely the Christian feasts and festivals, the pilgrimages and processions in which for centuries the real life of the people has flowered in verse and song, in colourful festal garb, in pageants and in rhythmic dances? Once again we come up against that untruthfulness inherent in the system which we have already had to point out so often. In the course of German history no system of government has deliberately destroyed so many of the popular traditions as this one which professes to be their guardian and upholder.

Feast days which are rooted in a tradition which goes back through centuries are abolished by a stroke of the pen. Thus, for example, since 1935 the feast of All Saints is no longer a public holiday in Upper Silesia. Businesses remain open, public works are carried on, the miners must go down the mines, although the Catholic population on the eve of All Souls celebrates the memory of the dead and goes in procession to the cemeteries. In Catholic Bavaria the Epiphany has been a public holiday from ancient times. In 1937 there appeared, a few days before the feast, a proclamation of all the Bavarian Cabinet Ministers in which it was laid down: " The ecclesiastical Feast of the Epiphany (January 6th) is not accorded State recognition." In the same year the Reich Ministry of the Interior in agreement with the Reich Ministry of Propaganda confined the State " protection " of the days on which the Church especially recalled the memory of the dead (All Souls and the following Sunday, *Toten Sonntag*) to the hours between 6 a.m. and 7 p.m. Up to then these festival days had been " protected " from midnight to midnight—*i.e.*, during this time dances, films and plays of a light character, public processions, sporting events and the like were prohibited. Since 1937 all these restrictions have been abolished for the eve of the feast, and on the feast itself they do not hold after 7 p.m. In February, 1938, the President of the Government of the Rhine Province passed a decree which withdrew all State " protection " from the Catholic Feast Days of the Epiphany, SS. Peter and Paul and the Immaculate Conception, and gave instructions that all schools should open and all the usual lessons be given on these days as on every other. In the remaining provinces similar decrees seem to have been passed in the meantime.

In the spring of 1938 there followed a decree of Dr. Frick to all Presidents of Provincial Governments, laying down that, on all ecclesiastical festivals not recognised by the State, work in all municipal offices was to continue as on other weekdays. The reason given was that the National Socialist State was not interested in the maintenance of denominational distinctions, but was rather intent on the restoration of the National Socialist spirit of unity.[1] In consequence the authorities of various dioceses took the occasion to point out in their official gazettes that the law of the Church affecting Holidays of Obligation was not abrogated by these civil measures, and that consequently all the faithful had the duty of attending Mass and of abstaining from servile work.

For Austria, Reichskommissar Bürckel decreed in the summer of 1938 that the Feast of SS. Peter and Paul, hitherto a feast day of high rank in Austria, was to be treated as an ordinary workday, and that work was to go on as usual in all factories, etc. The reason he gave was that this matter of feast days, too, must be brought into line with conditions in the old Reich " in the interests of national economy as well as of all the workers."

The feasts of the patrons of the different Federal States comprised in the former Austria were also abolished by official decree. In October of the same year there followed an ordinance of the Reichsminister of the Interior, which enacted that no flags were to be flown on public buildings to celebrate ecclesiastical events or on festivals no longer recognised by the State.

Der SA-Mann in February of 1938 gave a fuller explanation of the

[1] *Cf. Frankfurter Zeitung*, May 8th, 1938.

attitude of National Socialism to Church festivals when it observed that an overwhelming majority of the German people has not the slightest interest in seeing all sorts of days, as, for example, December 8th, printed in red on the calendar as the Feast of the Immaculate Conception. . . . The majority are not in the least concerned as to when the Feast of St. Peter's Chair is, or on what Sunday after the Epiphany, after Easter, after Pentecost they can have a day out in the country. They are just as indifferent to the date of the Feast of the Guardian Angels, the Blessed Trinity, Christ the King or Low Sunday. Much more important is it for the calendar to inform them of the date of One Dish Sundays, and to give a list of the National Socialist Memorial Feasts, etc.

At the end of 1934 Hermann Göring, the Prussian Ministerpräsident, issued a decree (presumably occasioned by the Konrad von Parzham Celebration held by the Berlin Catholics in the Sportpalast), which prohibited the Church's public celebrations, in order to protect them from " profanation." The decree reads as follows:

BERLIN.
December 7th, 1934.
The Prussian Ministerpräsident,
    Chief of the State Secret Police.
    II 1 B 1 2492-34.

Express Letter Ordinance

In recent times it has become increasingly evident that denominational functions are being held for reasons of propaganda in secular enclosures devoted to sport or pleasure. It is, however, the business of the State to prevent purely religious functions, as, for instance, the honouring of a Saint, from being brought before the public in a way which is more like a profanation of religion than a religious celebration. Mass organisations of this kind and the accompanying propaganda that is carried on under the cloak of religious celebrations not only disturb the security of the people, but also give the enemies of the State a welcome shelter for camouflaged activity. They are consequently injurious to the unity and safety of the National Socialist State. Therefore, in virtue of § 1 of the Ordinance of February 28th, 1933, in conjunction with § 14 of the P.V.G., all public celebrations and demonstrations of an ecclesiastico-denominational character are prohibited, and this order is to take effect immediately. Celebrations in churches, long-established processions and pilgrimages, Christmas celebrations of a private character and Nativity Plays are excepted.

Some four months later the National Socialist District Headquarters of Mainfranken insisted in a circular of April 2nd, 1935, that no political leader, Mayor, municipal Councillor, etc., could take part in his official capacity in processions or ecclesiastical festivals. There was no prohibition against their participating as private individuals, but at the same time they were warned against this, since the Church was carrying on a constant campaign against National Socialism.

When in May, 1935, the Catholic men of Essen wished, as in former years, to honour the Mother of God on the Adolf Hitler Platz in front of the ancient and celebrated picture from the Münster Church,

Maria in der Not, the function was not allowed by the police. In the same year in Cologne the celebration that was to be held in the large Meeting Hall on Low Sunday for all the First Communicants of the town was forbidden by the Gestapo. The Württemberg Minister of the Interior went much further, for on June 21st, 1935, he summarily forbade all public ecclesiastical functions and justified his action by referring to Göring's decree, according to which such celebrations provided a " shelter for the enemies of the State." On July 24th, 1935, an ordinance of the Reichsminister of the Interior was issued which laid down that all public functions of an ecclesiastico-denominational character required the express permission of the Gestapo. In Gleiwitz, therefore, and numerous other municipalities of Upper Silesia where parochial celebrations were to be held as usual on the feast of Corpus Christi, 1936, late in the afternoon of the preceding day an agent of the Gestapo handed to the parish authorities an order prohibiting the celebrations with the excuse that it was not suitable at the moment " to celebrate uproarious feasts." A similar reason was given by the President of the District Government of Oppeln, who replied to a protest made by telephone that parochial celebrations did not suit " the dignity of the Feast of Corpus Christi." In the same month a communication of the Gestapo was read out from the pulpits of all Berlin churches forbidding the celebration of Catholic parish festivities which had hitherto been customary. These festivities, which have not the slightest political significance, are the last traces of the parish fairs which used to be celebrated with great splendour.

We may remark, incidentally, that in numerous cases application to hold Church processions on the occasion of First Masses, Parish Jubilees and the like were rejected by the police. In one case in 1937 the reason given was that, in view of the general attitude of the ecclesiastical authorities towards the National Socialist State, it did not appear to be feasible to give State protection to functions of this kind. Reference was also made to the " immorality " trials against priests and Religious which, it was claimed, had stirred up sentiments of hostility against the Church.

We must also mention the fact that in October, 1938, Dr. Frick forbade all officials throughout the Reich to take part in denominational functions in their official capacity.

A further means for ousting the Church from public life is the prohibiting of the display of ecclesiastical banners on festive occasions. On October 4th, 1935, the Reichsminister of the Interior issued instructions that the law concerning the displaying of flags which had been decreed at the Reich Party Congress should be enforced. In that law it was laid down that whenever the State orders the displaying of flags on public buildings, churches also must display the Swastika. Although this ordinance constituted a manifest encroachment on that purely ecclesiastical terrain which had been protected by the Reich Concordat, it was carried out practically everywhere.

Later, however, the State authorities made further claims. Hitherto it had been permitted to fly the Church's colours along with the national flag, but now these had to disappear.

In May, 1936, for instance, the Bavarian State Ministry issued the following decree which the Diocesan Administrations were to bring to the notice of the clergy:

The following are the days on which flags must be flown: New Year, the Reich Foundation Day (January 18th), the Day of the National Resurgence (January 30th), the Heroes' Memorial Day (fifth Sunday after Easter), the Birthday of the Führer and Reich Chancellor (April 20th), the National Feast Day of the German People (May 1st), and Harvest Thanksgiving Day.

Besides these days there are other special occasions on which the compulsory flying of flags can be ordered and these will be made known by the Press and Radio. Churches may fly the national flag only and may not fly, as was customary, the Papal colours alongside it. The time for flying begins at 7 a.m. and ends when darkness sets in. On days on which the flying of the national flag is ordered, churches and church buildings may fly the national flag only, even if the day also happens to have a special ecclesiastical significance or festal character. If the churches want a display of flags for some other reason they can display the Church colours. The Churches themselves have the right to appoint such days, but if on these occasions they fly the national flag together with the Church flag, the former must always occupy the position of honour.

In Austria, however, since the spring of 1938, the fact is that by an order of the local authorities the Church colours could no longer be displayed even on ecclesiastical feast days, and at the beginning of February, 1939, the Reichskommissar, Bürckel, ordered that the regulations of the *Altreich* in this respect were to be universally observed in Austria. It goes without saying that private individuals, even on such festal occasions as Corpus Christi processions, may display only the Swastika.[1] People were repeatedly punished for hanging out yellow and white colours or for decorating the fronts of their houses, altars, etc., with yellow and white flowers or garlands.

Under various pretexts the holding of purely religious pilgrimages, too, has been obstructed and made impossible in recent years. We have already mentioned[2] what happened to the 1,705 Catholic young men at the Swiss-German frontier on their return from a pilgrimage to Rome at Easter, 1935. We now proceed to enumerate a number of similar cases. In August, 1935, the pilgrimage to Wemding (Bavaria) for the Fatima Day was forbidden. In the same month sentence of imprisonment was passed and fines were imposed on a curate and several Catholic nuns from Neunkirchen on the Saar because they led a pilgrimage at which religious hymns were sung. In accordance with an old tradition there were annual pilgrimages from Anrath and Körrenzig in the Lower Rhine District to the shrine of Our Lady in 't-Zand near Roermond, but in August, 1936, when the processions came to the frontier, they were stopped by officials of the Gestapo and forbidden to cross, and there were many others also, private pilgrims, who were forced to turn back.

[1] *Cf. Münchener Tagblatt*, June 18th, 1936.   [2] P. 105.

The imposing demonstrations of faith which have taken place for years at St. Annaberg in Upper Silesia, especially the traditional pilgrimages for men in which hundreds of thousands take part, have been systematically hampered in recent years. With this end in view, a " Thing Place " (*i.e.*, a meeting centre) of the Hitler Youth was erected there in 1936, while three years later orders were given for the closing of the Catholic Pilgrims' Hostel, a fine building fitted out on modern lines, nor was any explanation offered to justify these orders. In the same year, 1939, every possible device was employed to prevent Catholic men from taking part—the special trains that had been ordered were not provided, railway reductions for travelling parties were withdrawn, all sorts of Party assemblies were fixed for the same Sunday, and finally a vexatious control for cars, motor bicycles and bicycles was ordered.

Five hundred members of the Young Ladies' Sodality of Saarbrücken had arranged to make a pilgrimage on September 5th, 1937, to Marienthal near Bingen in a special train, when, two days before the day fixed for departure, all those who were to take part had the railway fares (RM. 4.80) which they had already paid returned to them and were notified that, as the provision of special trains had been refused, the pilgrimage would not take place. Again, the Dutch Catholic daily paper, *De Gelderlander*, reports that the Catholic Workers' Union in Stokkum (Holland) appealed to its members to make a pilgrimage to Kevelaer by bicycle at the end of September, 1937. Arriving at the Dutch-German frontier, the pilgrims showed the customary common passport for the whole party and were informed that such passports were not recognised for Kevelaer, but that there was nothing in the way of their visiting other places across the frontier. Under these circumstances the pilgrims decided to go no further. It is, no doubt, still fresh in everyone's memory how in 1938 the German Catholics were forbidden at the last hour to take part in the Eucharistic Congress in Budapest, for which the magnificent number of 40,000 pilgrims had already given in their names. The flimsiness of the reason given for this measure—namely, the scarcity of currency—was shown up by the fact that at the same time thousands of " Strength through Joy " travellers were spending their holidays at the expense of the Reich on the Dalmatian coast and in other foreign resorts.

The Polish population of German Upper Silesia was also forbidden by the authorities in the spring of 1939 to make the popular pilgrimage to Our Lady of Czenstochau.[1]

Here is what the official report of the Diocesan Administration of Freiburg has to say on the obstruction of pilgrimages:

> The Chief of the Secret State Police had already treated of the subject of ecclesiastical pilgrimages in a decree of December 7th, 1934. The Reichsminister of the Interior on August 17th, 1937, recalled this decree (according to which only " long-established " pilgrimages were permitted), and explained it in the following way: " The term ' long established ' is not to be taken

Cf. La Croix, May 25th, 1939.

exclusively in this sense that a determined number of definite pilgrimages are allowed, but it implies that everything about these pilgrimages is also of long standing—that the occasion, the arrangement, the make-up and the purpose, for instance, are still the same. If a pilgrimage differs in any one of these respects from former pilgrimages, then it is not a pilgrimage of long standing." The Minister adds that the same prescriptions apply to functions arranged in honour of Our Lord and Our Lady and other celebrations of similar character in so far as they are merely substitutes for pilgrimages.

Catholic demonstrations of faith on a large scale are made impossible by these official instructions, especially as, recently, the use of loud speakers at Church festivals has also been forbidden, and a severe blow has been dealt at Church pilgrimages. Today, especially, there is a wide demand for these, as is clear from the pilgrimage to the Aachen shrines, which in July, 1937, were visited by nearly a million people. In 1937 a pilgrimage of the men of the Sacred Heart Parish, Freiburg, to the nearby cemetery was not permitted, though everything had already been prepared down to the last detail. It has further been established that Party authorities in Constance required all subordinate officials to report the names of those Civil Servants who, in the summer of 1937, took part in the traditional men's pilgrimage to Birnau at which Archbishop Gröber spoke.

The Hindering and Prohibition of Processions

The story of the way in which the Church's processions have been hampered and prohibited forms a specially painful chapter in the history of the Nazi persecution of the Church. In many districts—e.g., in the diocese of Passau—even as early as 1935, Catholic organisations were forbidden at the last moment by the police to take part in Corpus Christi processions. Often the prohibition was not made known until the various associations were actually drawn up in line. It has sometimes happened that members of the Young Ladies' Sodality have had to take off their medals and roll up their banners at the request of the police. In Munich several groups of the Hitler Youth had to go on duty at the time that had been fixed for the Corpus Christi procession, and on July 18th, 1936, the following classical proclamation was put up on the notice board of the Hitler Youth in one of the city schools: " The real Hitler Boy will stand firm against all difficulties which certain parties are creating. He will not remain at home like a ' rabbit ' and a mother's darling. Walking in the procession would show more grit than that." On this same feast in 1935 there were members of the Hitler Youth in front of Cologne Cathedral just at the hour for Mass. With conspicuous zeal they were offering for sale copies of Streicher's smutty paper *Der Stürmer* and from time to time they shouted in unison " Germany, awake !" Between them and the churchgoers, who were provoked to indignation, a quarrel ensued. This developed into a fight which was only stopped by the intervention of a detachment of police. The crowd of many thousands assembled before the Cathedral, which included, moreover, a party of American tourists, must have realised once again what National Socialism understands by religious freedom and the protection of ancient traditions.

In numerous districts of Bavaria, autumn processions in thanksgiving for the harvest were a centuries-old custom, but in 1935 they were prohibited by the Secret Police, on the score that demonstrations outside the church had to be discontinued. This prohibition, which in many cases was communicated at the last moment when all preparations had been made, caused great astonishment and bitter feelings.

In June, 1936, the following regulations for the celebration of the Feast of Corpus Christi were made first for Lower Bavaria and the Oberpfalz, and, a few days later, for the whole Reich:

1. There is to be no display of flags on public buildings.
2. The decoration of private buildings with ecclesiastical banners and colours will be viewed as a deliberate repudiation of the National Revival. The display of the yellow and white colours of the Roman Pontifical State (!) in the form of flags of any kind, wreaths, garlands, etc., is a deliberate disturbance of the public peace and order and will be punished by the police.
3. Civil Servants are not to participate officially; therefore there are to be no groups of Civil Servants in the procession. Participation in a private capacity is allowed.
4. Denominational Associations may take part in the processions and may carry purely ecclesiastical banners. All display of a purely associational character is forbidden. There must be no marching in ranks to and from the procession, and no association banners, pennants or uniform dress.

At the same time the episcopal Vicariate-General of Münster in Westphalia made known the following regulations of the Government of the German Reich:

BERLIN, N.W.40.
May 29th, 1936.

Concerning the display of flags, decorations on public buildings and participation of Civil Servants in Corpus Christi processions. In May, 1936, the following ministerial Ordinance was issued: " According to my decree of June 8th, 1935, concerning the regulation of the display of flags on public buildings, orders may only be given for such display on public buildings on the occasion of local festivals if the special importance of the case justifies official participation. In agreement with the Minister for Ecclesiastical Affairs for the Reich and Prussia, I do not consider that this condition is fulfilled on the Feast of Corpus Christi. Therefore the display of flags on public buildings on this day is out of the question. I also consider that the decorating of public buildings for the Corpus Christi procession to be neither necessary nor appropriate.

There is no objection to Civil Servants taking part, as private individuals, in the religious service and the accompanying procession on the Feast of Corpus Christi. The Minister for Ecclesiastical Affairs for the Reich and Prussia has requested the President of the German Conference of Bishops to take steps to ensure that in the preparation and carrying out of the religious service and of the procession there should be no separate grouping of Civil Servants in the church or at the procession."

For the Minister,
Signed: PFUNDTNER, *Secretary of State.*

The Diocesan Administration of Münster adds the dry comment:

The foregoing decree is hereby brought to your notice, and we may point out in explanation thereof that it is not a local authority but the Government of the Reich which is responsible for the fact that, even in places where it has been the immemorial custom to decorate the whole processional route, now, on the occasion of the Corpus Christi procession, no decoration whatever is permitted on official and public buildings, including Catholic schools.

It was in 1936 that the Reich Ministry for War forbade for the first time the participation of officers and soldiers in formation in Corpus Christi processions or in the lining of the road by troops, and this only three years after Vice-Chancellor von Papen and the Elz von Rübenach, Reichsminister of Transport, had taken part in the Corpus Christi procession at St. Hedwig's in Berlin, together with numerous officers and soldiers.

There were also individual cases of processions being disturbed. In Limbach (Saar), for example, a Catholic procession was assailed by SA-men in uniform; banners and religious symbols were torn from the hands of children, and only with great difficulty could the clergy prevent further disturbances.

A typical example of the petty trickery which was resorted to in order to hinder long-established and popular processions is the case of the world-famous spring procession at Echternach. The procession, which moves from the Prussian part of Echternach over the Sauer bridge to the Luxemburg part of the town and ends up in the Basilica there with great solemnity, was visited in former years by thousands of German pilgrims from the Saar and the bordering Eifel district. In 1937 the great crowds of German pilgrims were missing, because, as the *Luxemburger Wort* proved from the reports of eye-witnesses, the German frontier officials behaved in an absolutely petty way. Passports had to be shown at two different points and, so, numerous pilgrims from the Saar who had come in motor buses with a common passport could not get through. The pilgrims from Prümm, who had been met as usual by the Echternach clergy, also had difficulties. They were received at the Echternach-Brücker customs office by a large detachment of customs officials. At the turnpike there was a careful scrutiny of passports, and anyone who had no passport— none was necessary the preceding year—had to go back, with the result that many of the pilgrims had to return, after a journey of $37\frac{1}{2}$ miles, without ever setting eyes on the grave of St. Willibrord. The *Luxemburger Wort* made the further complaint that the open-air sermon of the bishop was interrupted in an insulting manner by excited Prussian officials shouting from the frontier barriers.

In the same year the Corpus Christi procession was forbidden at the last moment in Berchtesgaden on the ground that it would disturb the local traffic; while in Freiburg in Breisgau, in addition to the prohibition of a band, there was also an order forbidding the procession to pass along the Kaiserstrasse, which had been the usual route for centuries. Certain of the organisers who expressed their dissatisfaction at this spiteful measure were placed under arrest. The procession of the Precious Blood, as it is called, which proceeds from the Lower Rhine districts of Kevelaer and Goch to the small town of Boxmeer in Brabant, and which is an event as old as human memory, was also prohibited by the Gestapo.

We have already quoted frequently from the official report of the Diocesan Administration of Freiburg: On the prohibition and obstruction of pilgrimages and especially of Corpus Christi processions. The facts given in this report are very illuminating. We read there:

> The new civil ordinances concerning processions and pilgrimages have created fresh difficulties in the life of the Church. The ordinance of the Reichsminister of the Interior of November 5th, 1936, declares with reference to § 33 of the Street Traffic Regulations: " It has been proved that in various districts of the Reich religious demonstrations, pilgrimages on foot, processions, especially Corpus Christi processions, and funeral processions are in part the cause of serious traffic obstruction, so that the removal of these demonstrations and processions from main thoroughfares will have to be contemplated, even in cases where such routes have hitherto been traditional." The instruction for the execution of this ordinance given in the Baden *Administrational Gazette* of November 6th, 1936, declares that all processions along public streets need official permission, and tells the competent authorities that they must enquire strictly into each application. The general principle to be applied is that such functions are not to take place on arterial roads and important thoroughfares, but that where a diversion of the processional route is not feasible the obstruction of traffic is to be reduced to a minimum, and the streets must immediately afterwards be tidied up at the expense of the organiser of the function.
>
> The application of this regulation in Baden in 1937 to the traditional processions for the Blessing of the Fields, the Patronal Feast and Corpus Christi led to considerable difficulties in many places. The Freiburg Corpus Christi procession, for instance, which is famed throughout Germany and beyond for its splendour, had to follow a partially modified route. We may add, incidentally, that soldiers, Civil Servants' Groups, the Fire Brigade and to a large extent Old Soldiers' Associations were forbidden to take official part in the 1937 procession.
>
> The fact that official bands (those belonging to the Post Office Workers, Fire Brigade and Ambulance Corps) were forbidden to take part in the Corpus Christi procession was no less offensive. In Freiburg one of these bands was called away during the procession itself, but to make up for this the Air Force, making a considerable noise, was permitted to fly very low over the procession for a long time. A painful impression was also made by the fact that a fee had to be paid for permission to hold this procession which dates back for centuries.
>
> The introduction of new processions to celebrate special events is practically impossible in this state of things; and now the customary torchlight processions at the conclusion of missions to the people are officially forbidden. The two new Reich Ordinances concerning the regulation of street traffic the decree of November 13th, 1937, and the Circular of the Baden Ministry of the Interior of December 27th, 1937, did nothing to lessen the difficulties.
>
> Moreover, as time went on, complaints began to multiply that Civil Servants and teachers were taken to task by Party officials for their participation in religious services and in the life of the Church, and that Civil Servants who took part in processions and pilgrimages, even in the Corpus Christi procession, were in many places photographed and had to expect a setback in their careers. Indeed, one Party official did not hesitate to describe the participation of Civil Servants in a Corpus Christi procession as a demonstration against the present Government.

In 1938, in spite of all the trickery, it was possible to hold Corpus Christi processions in practically all Catholic districts of the Third

Reich, and the number of the faithful who took part in them was greater than ever. The anti-Christian outbreaks were few in number and these passed off without incident.

The Catholic population of Munich in particular gave a splendid testimony of its loyalty to the Faith. Despite the fact that the municipal authorities had made it clear to the Civil Servants and employees that they would look unfavourably upon any participation in the procession, more than 12,000 of the faithful took part in it. In many cases Catholic Civil Servants were transferred to provincial districts with loss of rank because they made no secret of their religious convictions and declared their intention of taking part in an ecclesiastical celebration which was protected by the Reich Concordat. It is this sort of economic coercion that explains why the vast majority of those who followed the Archbishop, Cardinal Faulhaber, in procession through the streets of Munich were women, while the police, armed with cameras, were hunting round for Civil Servants and State employees. The army was not represented and the Papal colours were nowhere to be seen.

A further step towards secularisation was taken in this same year 1938 when the Feast of Corpus Christi was no longer recognised as a civil holiday. Throughout the whole of Catholic Upper Silesia, for example, work went on in all Government and municipal offices, there was no whole holiday, and in this effort to eliminate the feast the mines and foundries had also to do their bit. In some mines it was given out that work not done on Corpus Christi could not be made up at another time, a thing which under other circumstances would have been allowed. However, Catholic tradesmen showed their Catholic spirit by keeping their shops shut on the feast.

In Austria, within a few months of the Anschluss, principles similar to those of the *Altreich* were applied by the authorities, and so Civil Servants were no longer permitted to take part in the procession officially, nor were schools allowed to take part in groups.

In 1939 Corpus Christi processions were forbidden in many districts as a result of the agitation which had been conducted against them for years by the Nazi Press, which represented them as " demonstrations of political Catholicism " and the like. In this year, too, the long-established Easter Procession in Vienna was also forbidden because " the streets were too narrow," and the Corpus Christi Procession at Graz met with the same fate.

The procession in Aachen was, on the important roads, confined to the pavement and was subjected to a variety of restrictive regulations. The strewing of flowers, for example, was no longer permitted, for it was suddenly discovered (after all these years) that this procedure might lead to accidents. This year the procession was only allowed to use a few small streets in the vicinity of the Cathedral, and, though in former years Benediction was given on the Market Place in front of the famous Town Hall and in front of the Eliesenbrunnen in the Holzgraben, this year only one altar could be erected —behind the Town Hall. A propos of Aachen in particular, the detail is worth mentioning that a large Nazi meeting was arranged precisely for the feast of Corpus Christi.

The hampering of Church processions by petty restrictions like these is reported from all districts of the Third Reich, for the ordinances concerning processions and pilgrimages laid down on November 5th, 1936, by Kerrl, the Reichsminister of Ecclesiastical Affairs, afforded the National Socialist local authorities a legal handle for their interference with Church life. . . .[1]

In 1939, a few weeks before the Feast of Corpus Christi, a compulsory meeting of all male and female Post Office workers took place in Frankfurt-am-Main in the hall of the Zoological Gardens. The Party speaker declared: The time for Corpus Christi processions is shortly coming round again. It has been clear for years that Corpus Christi processions are not religious functions at all, but demonstrations of political Catholicism, and so, as regards the participation of Civil Servants, let each one of them realise this: " The person who expects to get his bread and butter in the future from the Catholic Church can go to the procession; but anyone who expects to get it from the State is hereby given serious warning."

As was to be expected, many Civil Servants and State and municipal employees were deterred from joining in the procession by threats and pressure of the type described above, but in spite of that, and in spite of all the other difficulties that were put in their way, the unanimous verdict of the reports is that in 1939 an exceptionally large number of people took part in the Corpus Christi processions. In Munich, for example, 16,000 of the faithful, including a striking number of young people, 600 University students of both sexes and many older men followed the Blessed Sacrament; and in Frankfurt-am-Main the number of men who took part was greater than ever before.

We have received a very interesting account of the great torchlight procession, organised every year by the Men's Sodality of Our Lady, on Trinity Sunday in Munich. The account is from one who took part in it in the year 1937.

This year, too, despite all veiled warnings and threats, thousands of men carried their coloured lighted candles through the streets, but the most striking thing was the very large number of young men who took part. Everyone looked extremely grave, for the revered President of the Munich Men's Sodality, Fr. Rupert Mayer, was not allowed to give his traditional sermon, as the prohibition to preach was still in force against him. As in other years, however, Fr. Mayer went with his Sodalists to the Cathedral, where, at the conclusion of the imposing ceremony, he addressed a short word of thanks to the men who were so loyal to him. They were deeply moved when they heard the voice of their spiritual leader to whom the erection and flourishing condition of their Sodality was due. Thousands of the faithful stood by in reverent silence in the streets of the city during the torchlight procession.

In German Upper Silesia, too, all means were tried to create the impression, on account of the small number of people that took part in the Corpus Christi processions, that the thoroughly Catholic popula-

---

[1] *Der Deutsche in Polen*, June 18th, 1939. The nature of these ordinances and the instructions issued as a guide to their application have been described already (p. 215) and so need no further comment here.

tion of these parts was turning away from the Church more and more. Official restrictions on the arrangements for the processions had proved ineffective in the past, and so on this occasion the managements of the big industrial concerns were utilised in order to give more emphasis to the boycotting movement. A few days before the feast managerial announcements appeared on the notice boards of pits and foundries summoning the workers to work on Corpus Christi on account of the necessity of extra production, a move quite in the style of the godless propaganda in the Soviet Union. The overseers were not a little astonished that their words produced no effect save on a minute fraction of the workers, and that the only result of this manœuvre was to make the number of Catholic men who took part in the procession greater than in former years.

In conclusion it may be pointed out that the campaign against processions did not confine itself to the processions themselves. Even films representing the public celebration of religious festivals were repeatedly confiscated and prohibited, as, for instance, an instructional film on Lourdes in 1936 and, in 1939, a film of the Eucharistic Congress in Budapest.

The Abolition of Church Broadcasts on the Public Radio

As early as 1936 several German radio stations, including Hamburg, taking their cue from the " secularisation of public life " policy enjoined by the State, decided to cut out the broadcasting of religious and liturgical functions from their programmes. In December, 1936, the Evangelical Bishop Tügel gave utterance to the feelings of Christians on this matter in the following apposite remarks in the *Hamburger Kirchenzeitung*:

In cutting out the Church more and more the Radio is doing away with something that is essential. Let them restore to us the Radio Religious Service and fulfil what is the clear wish of many of our fellow-countrymen, and, no doubt, the secret wish of the majority of the North German people. Let them not appeal to the so-called " secularisation " of public life. The suppression of a thing which belongs to every German as much as his nationality, and which concerns what is ultimate and most profound in human life, would also inflict an injury on this same national character and, at the same time, not benefit the people, but expose them to peril. History affords abundant proof that the neglect of a people's soul brings bitter consequences.

While the heathen German Faith Movement was allowed to use the radio for propaganda purposes (on November 28th, 1937, for example, a neo-pagan morning service of the Silesian section of this organisation was broadcast by the Breslau Radio Station and its two dependent stations, Gleiwitz and Görlitz), the broadcasting of Christian religious services and celebrations was curtailed more and more. The following answer was given in April, 1939, to a petition sent to the Berlin Radio Station: " In answer to your communication we inform you that the difficulties of covering our essential programme prevent us from broadcasting any more denominational morning services in the future."

Just so—but the Nazi organisations, of course, and especially the Hitler Youth, continue to broadcast their pagan morning services.

We may fittingly conclude this section with a piece of information that is highly revealing. In the autumn of 1939 the Catholic Press in the Third Reich was forbidden to give the title *Volk* to those who took part in ecclesiastical functions, for the term *Volk* means for National Socialism not the members of a separate denomination, but the general community comprising all the various religious denominations.

The determination of National Socialism to oust the Church from public life is also shown by the brutal interference of the police in public manifestations of religion. But we shall deal with these incidents separately when we come to describe how German Catholics are being deprived of their legal rights.

2. *Interference in the Purely Pastoral Work of the Church*

The more important part of the Church's work for souls lies not in the directing of associations, or in pilgrimages and processions, useful though they are, but in the regular and everyday labours of the priest, his Mass, his conferring of the Sacraments, his visits to the sick and dying and the rest, and the importance of his work grows in proportion as the more indirect means of sustaining the faithful are curtailed and destroyed. But it is not to be expected that a Government which takes such pains to do away with the less essential would not do its best to maim and destroy what is vital and necessary for the religious life of its Catholic subjects. In what follows we present, from the vast number of instances available, a few representative cases of this interference, in order to give some idea of the way in which National Socialism obstructs the priest in his pastoral work and prevents the faithful from taking advantage of it.

We can begin with an example that illustrates the close watch kept on all the Church's pastoral activities. These official instructions were sent to an official of the German National Socialist Workers' Party, who was to see that careful watch was kept on the following:

I. 1. Sermons of the local pastors: the nomination of confidential persons to listen to sermons. Attention here to be paid to the combating of the Race Theory and the history of German origins; to any sympathy expressed for the Jews; to opposition to the sterilisation campaign.

2. Religious and pastoral courses held in the parish: particulars to be ascertained.

3. The Retreat Movement: Retreat Houses and those who take part to be under observation.

4. Missions to the people to be reported on: the Order the missioners belong to; the names of their Superiors.

5. Collections for foreign missions: The Association of the Child Jesus; the Louis Missionary Association.

6. Pilgrims to Rome from the individual parishes to be ascertained: report on pilgrimages to Rome made by the individual associations.

7. The erection of Catholic schools, new churches, new religious houses and Orders.

II. 1. The attitude of the Catholic clergy towards the new State to be reported on.
2. The attitude of the clergy to the new German greeting.
3. The combating of measures taken by the State.
4. The spreading of atrocity reports.
5. Clerical offences against morality.
6. Behaviour of clergy on the frontier to be observed.

III. 1. Catholic Associations to be ascertained.
2. Close watch on specially named Catholic Associations: the Catholic Women's Union; the Catholic League of Charity, associations for men, the Young Men's Association.

The knowledge that every word and action was watched was, in itself, a sufficiently grave handicap to efficient pastoral work, but besides that it suffered severely from the fact that priests were expelled from certain Government districts without any consideration for the religious needs of the faithful, and episcopal petitions for new appointments to their posts were answered very slowly. Again, a small point but a symptom of the times, the small chapel in the main railway station of Munich, where every Sunday Mass had been said at a very early hour specially for people setting off on excursions, had to be removed.

Another form of interference was the confiscation and prohibition, without any justification in law, of letters, handbills, placards and the like, which were nothing but invitations to purely pastoral functions. So, for example, in 1935 at a place near Munich a girl was put under arrest by the Mayor and brought before the police, because she had distributed round the houses printed invitations to girls to make their Easter Confession. Again, a placard with the title " Catholic parents, you are warmly invited to the parents' hour," printed in May, 1935, by the Huber Printing Establishment, was confiscated, withdrawn and forbidden. So, even today, in many districts notification of religious Youth weeks by means of placards and handbills is not allowed. It is obvious that by restrictions of this kind the preparation for popular missions and things like religious weeks, in particular, is very seriously hindered and in large parishes rendered practically impossible. But that is not all, for there is, too, a long list of district authorities to be notified weeks before the projected mission—a purely pastoral work —and these demand to be told exactly the times of the sermons, whether schools or associations will take part, the names and addresses of the clergy co-operating, etc.

According, however, to an announcement of the German News Agency, the imposition of all these restrictions did not prevent Dr. Kerrl, the Reichsminister for Ecclesiastical Affairs, from declaring to an editor at Hanover on December 11th, 1937: " Never has any parish priest been hindered in the exercise of his office. Not a single religious service, not a single Mass has been disturbed." Even the second part of his statement is untrue, for in actual fact disturbances and interferences of this kind have happened often enough. For example, to mention only a few cases in the diocese of Hildesheim—to which Hanover belongs—in Münder on the Deister, in Winsen on the Lahe and in Hessen in Braunschweig, the celebration of Mass itself was disturbed. In the middle of the Mass, which for lack of a church was being celebrated in a room (and even this was forbidden for a long time in Münder), a police sergeant at the command of the Gestapo entered the room and cried aloud: " Heil Hitler ! The service is forbidden." Again, in Wesermünde a special religious service had been arranged for the Labour Service camps, but the Gestapo would allow it only once a month.[1]

At other religious services disturbances were frequent. On March 31st, 1935, for instance, at a place near Trier, large numbers of uniformed members of the Hitler Youth—not, be it said, from the place itself—interrupted the sermon with laughter and *sotto voce* remarks and sang the line of the hymn " Christ, Thou Lord of the new age " in the blasphemous form " Hitler, thou lord of the new age." Or, again, the authorities in charge of the *Hochland* camp at Lenggries went so far as to allow the boys to march past the open-air altar during Mass singing the notorious " Currency ditty " and other songs of the same sort.

That was a device frequently resorted to, and Party groups often deliberately disturbed religious services by marching past churches in step, singing songs usually, of course, of an unpleasant character. So, for example, on August 11th, 1935, a column of Hitler Youth, singing abusive songs, marched past the Church of St. Matthias in Berlin during the 9 a.m. and the 12 a.m. services.

In September, 1939, there came into force in parts of the Third Reich a decree which prohibited all extraordinary pastoral functions. This, a quiet step towards the systematic restriction of pastoral work, was a severe blow particularly to parish life, since, among other things, it put a stop to popular missions and retreats—among the most valuable means of renewing the spiritual life of a parish.

The Church's work for souls in the parts of Poland occupied by Germany, especially in the district Gnesen-Posen, has, since the outbreak of war, been brutally obstructed. We take the following details from a thoroughly trustworthy source (the report is of January, 1940):

> Many churches in the parts of Poland occupied by Germany were closed out of hand, but this measure was not carried out everywhere in the same way.
> In the Archdiocese of Gnesen, the Cathedral, which had been recently restored and refurnished, was closed by the police on the pretext that it was in a dangerous state of disrepair, and now behind its locked doors concerts take place which are recorded on gramophone discs. The Church of the Holy Trinity, the chief parish church, was profaned. Churches which still have priests—and half of the parishes of the Archdiocese of Gnesen have no priests—may be opened only on Sundays, and then only between 9 and

---

[1] A favourite form of interference was for the authorities to arrange parades, route marches, etc., for the various NS organisations for the hour of Mass. *Cf.*, *e.g.*, p. 374.

11 a.m., except in Bromberg, where there is a somewhat greater freedom. The result is that at 9 a.m., as soon as the churches are opened, a crowd of people streams in to get their children baptised, to go to Confession, Communion, etc., and so great is the throng that the priest scarcely has time to finish the Mass at the stipulated time, 11 o'clock. In Bromberg the magnificent, recently completed church of the Lazarist Fathers was taken from them and withdrawn from religious services.

The following details concern the Archdiocese of Posen: The Cathedral of the city of Posen, which is at the same time the parish church for 14,000 souls, was closed by the police under the pretext that the fabric was in a dangerous state, and the keys are retained by the Gestapo. The most beautiful church of Posen, the collegiate church of St. Mary Magdalen, which is also a parish church for 23,000 souls, was similarly closed, and the Jesuit church there met with the same fate. In those churches of the archdiocese that may still be used, religious service may be held only on Sundays between the hours of 9 and 11 a.m. Individual priests began to celebrate Mass also on weekdays at a very early hour and behind locked doors, but that, too, was forbidden, though here and there in the course of the week the celebration of a Requiem Mass is allowed.

The restrictions that Germany, because it had gained the mastery, could impose on the Church's pastoral work in Catholic Poland make sad reading, but sadder still are the accounts of its treatment of those who are completely in its hands, its prisoners. It is an undeniable fact that it has been well-nigh impossible, often even expressly forbidden, for prisoners in concentration camps and elsewhere to receive the sacraments, and under any and every pretext priests are refused access to those in custody. In Austria, for example, in 1939 a priest who wished to hear the confession of a prisoner met with the greatest difficulties: the prison superintendent refused to go out of ear-shot and was unwilling to allow even the pronouncing of the words of absolution on the ground that they were in a foreign language.

But saddest of all is the lot of patients in hospitals since the seizure of power by National Socialism. Real pastoral work in hospitals in Austria, for example, has practically been made impossible. Before a priest can be summoned a long list of formalities has first to be gone through, while the hospital personnel, instead of supporting this pastoral work, places further obstacles in the way. In consequence the sick, people who are seriously ill or already on their death beds, are deprived of priestly assistance. According to the *Vienna Diocesan Magazine* of September 30th, 1938, the Ministry of Education of Vienna passed a decree on July 22nd of the same year, according to which the reception of the Last Sacraments was only allowed if the patient in question applied for them in writing and they had then to be administered in a separate room. This decree, issued on August 1st, 1938, by the Regional Authorities of Upper Austria, reads as follows:

To all Public and Private Institutions for the Sick in Upper Austria.

In order to avoid both inconvenience and the risk of impairing medical treatment in institutions for the sick, it is ordained that for the future the ministration of priests at sick beds is only to be allowed in the case of those patients who have expressly desired it.

Wherefore hospital authorities are instructed to draw up, with due regard for the local circumstances of the various institutions, regulations concerning priestly ministrations, to the effect that every day the nursing staff is to receive the wishes of the patient in this matter, and they are to be forwarded in writing to the various rectories either directly or through the management at a *fixed hour*.

Only in special cases—a sudden turn for the worse in the condition of patients, the urgent necessity of a serious operation or the reception of people in a dying condition—may requests be forwarded at any other time, and then only if the house surgeon or the doctor in charge thinks fit. These requests must contain the name of the patient, number of room or bed and the spiritual ministration that is desired.

In this matter it is forbidden for any member of the staff whatsoever to influence patients in any way.

The carrying out of priestly ministrations must always conform to the directions laid down by the medical authorities of the institute concerned. So, for example, for medical and psychological reasons the Sacrament of Extreme Unction must never be conferred in a room in which there are other people seriously ill.

These regulations were commended to the authorities in question by a decree of the Ministry for Interior and Educational Affairs (Zl. 53,632 of July 22nd, 1938) with a request that its contents be brought to the notice of hospital managements, departments and chaplains.

Interference with the Laity

It is well known that the Catholics of Germany lay great stress on retreats and days of recollection as means for deepening and enriching their spiritual life. These religious exercises are simply a school of Christian piety designed to encourage men to strive after sanctity and, as such, far removed from any political or merely profane purpose. Nevertheless they do not meet with the approval of the leaders of the Third Reich, who have devised various ways of making attendance at them difficult. For Retreat Houses outside Germany, Currency laws[1] and passport regulations were invoked, and, thanks to these latter, in 1937 the well-known Retreat House of the German Redemptorists in Vaals on the German-Dutch frontier had to close.

In order to keep a check on people making retreats, and above all in order to bring pressure to bear on Civil Servants and employees, there appeared in July, 1937, a decree of Himmler, the Reich Commissioner of the German Police, which enacted that those who went to Retreat Houses, convents or houses of religious orders to take part in retreats must be reported to the local police authorities within twenty-four hours of their arrival. The Church, quite justifiably, regarded this oppressive measure as a device to deter men from making retreats, and the president of the Fulda Conference of Bishops, Cardinal Bertram, appealed to the Chief of the German police to repeal the decree, but in vain. Such is the spirit of the new régime, and we know

---

[1] In 1935 the Aachen Customs Investigation office tried hard to discover cases of registered marks being given and accepted as payment in Retreat Houses beyond the borders.

cases of men who had to endure the most brutal bullying from their National Socialist fellow-workmen for having taken part in a day of recollection in their parish.

Nevertheless National Socialism still tries to persuade the world outside Germany (and not without success) that in the Third Reich there is no such thing as a religious persecution and its authorities have frequently asserted with indignation that no one is hindered in the exercise of his religion. Yet the cases in which attempts have been made to hold back Catholics from attendance at religious services, for example, are so numerous and recur with such regularity that no one can doubt that they are symptomatic of a general policy. It is the National Socialist organisations which exert the greatest pressure in this direction, but we shall refer to this further on when we come to treat of the action of the Party against the Church. Here we present a short collection of the official measures taken by the State.

For example, Wagner, District Leader and Reich Governor of Baden, made the following announcement at a service roll-call at the district headquarters in Karlsruhe on May 26th, 1937:

> It can no longer be tolerated that Civil Servants should listen in silence and without protesting in a legitimate and respectful manner to invective against National Socialism at meetings and services which do not deserve to be called religious. In future I shall take disciplinary action with a view to dismissal against Civil Servants who offend in this way against loyalty and faith. Those who refuse to take notice of this warning must abide by the consequences. The same applies to members of the Party.

Once again we see reflected in this decree the complete dishonesty of the National Socialist system. Its leaders have not the courage openly to forbid the attendance of all Civil Servants and Party members at religious services: therefore they demand from them a protest " in a legitimate manner." What exactly is such a protest ? And who is to decide which religious service no longer deserves the title of " religious "? What exactly comprises invective against National Socialism ? Obviously in order to superintend the fulfilment of this prescription an army of spies has to be sent to the religious services. Yet it has its effect. Many Civil Servants and Party members will now no longer dare to visit a church, for they would not like to expose themselves to the necessity of " protesting in a legitimate manner " at a religious service. By these indirect methods National Socialism once more attains its end—it stops people from practising their religion.

Here are more examples. As early as 1935 in villages and small towns of Sauerland (Province of Westphalia) officials were called to account and threatened because they went to church too often and were religiously " too active " altogether. In a town of South Germany a tramway worker was summoned before the management and given a warning because he had ventured to attend the religious service on Easter Sunday afternoon and took in the *Munich Parish Magazine.*

Of Austria it is true to say that after the Anschluss Catholic youth was systematically hindered by party organisations and State authorities from taking part in Church life. It has, in fact, happened often enough—and recently the cases are being multiplied—that Catholics have been punished or warned because of their attendance at religious services.

In view of these facts (many more of which we shall enumerate later)[1] our verdict on the reiterated assurance from official quarters that nothing is put in the way of attendance at religious services[2] must be that it is the usual Nazi dishonest juggling with words and a cowardly attempt to disguise their action. It was nothing but outrageous cynicism when Adolf Wagner (Minister of State and District Leader) declared on May 2nd, 1937, at an Area Congress in Reichenhall (Upper Bavaria): " It is not our fault that the churches are getting emptier and emptier, while the people stream in their thousands to National Socialist demonstrations." The director of the Nazi training centre at Vogelsang in the Eifel made the matter more explicit when he gave this explanation: " Junkers (the people who were taking the course) may attend religious services in civilian dress "; but he added immediately with a sneer: " The majority of our people have no civilian dress with them."

It is due to National Socialism, not that the churches on the whole are becoming emptier, for that is a lie recognised by everybody who goes to church in Germany, but that many sections of the Catholic population, especially men, youths and children, are hindered from attending religious services on Sundays, even for months on end. For it is National Socialism which arranges parades, route marches, rifle practices and celebrations on Sundays and Holidays of Obligation in such a way that for many the fulfilment of their religious duties is rendered impossible. It is only necessary to glance at the Monday editions of the newspapers to see at what an early hour on Sundays the SA had to begin route marches, camp duties, etc., how early the Hitler Youth set off for ski-ing. It is National Socialism that by its ban on uniformed attendance at church[3] prevents in practice thousands of Catholics in the organisations from attending religious services. It is National Socialism which makes attendance at religious services absolutely impossible for months on end for those in the Labour Camps. If then the churches are becoming emptier, it is because National Socialism has left nothing undone to bring this about.[4]

Allied to the measures adopted to keep people away from church is the endeavour to separate the people from the priest. According to the declarations of both the Catholic clergy and the laity this has been attempted time and time again right up to this year 1940. It is entirely typical of the aims and methods of National Socialism that even

[1] P. 342.
[2] *Cf.*, for example, the decree of the Bavarian Ministry of Education of June 2nd, 1933.
[3] *Cf.* p. 335.   [4] *Cf.* p. 374.

soldiers at the front are given secret orders before they go on leave that they are to avoid contact with priests, since these latter are enemies of the State. But, it must be frankly confessed, such endeavours are to a large extent rendered ineffective by the army chaplains, whose work is much appreciated and supported by the military authorities and exercises a wide influence.

3. *Official Measures to Promote Apostasy*

All the decrees, regulations and measures which we have described in the preceding pages are, after all, only preliminary skirmishes, designed to lead up to the real aim of National Socialism: formal apostasy from the Church.

Here it is much more difficult than elsewhere to distinguish between propaganda directed by the State and that directed by the Party. For high officials in the Party are for the most part also important State officials, and so their action is, in reality, an example of State pressure brought to bear upon the subject.[1]

The account of this apostasy campaign forms one of the most unpleasant chapters of the whole persecution of the Church, for here above all National Socialism is most careful never to fight with open visor. The higher officials are careful to avoid anything like decrees or public utterances which might provide a legal basis for the charge that they are responsible for it. But if the frontal attack is avoided, the indirect approach is all the more ruthless, systematic and thorough; and if the higher circles do not show their hand, subordinate departments and ordinary Party members are all the more active in the cause.

In what follows we shall indicate, together with the relevant facts, three means by which the apostasy movement is officially set in motion: (1) apostasy is facilitated, (2) attempts are made to change popular opinion in its favour, and (3) abandonment of the Church is suggested by questionnaires, and urged by economic pressure and the example of high officials of the State and the Party. The official propaganda of ideas in National Socialist literature, in Party organisations, etc., will be described in one of the following sections.[2]

In what regards the young, National Socialism found an extremely useful legal ruling ready to hand. By it parents of children under the age of twelve can, without asking their consent, declare that they are no longer members of the Church. For children between the ages of twelve and fourteen the child's consent is necessary, but anyone over fourteen can, without stating any reasons for it, by a simple declaration made before a civil magistrate withdraw from his Church. The German regulations did not hold in the former Austria, where the law strove to protect children against the apostasy movement rife during the period of Austrian Bolshevism. In the new

[1] The propaganda of the NS organisation is very briefly treated on p. 336.
[2] Part III, Chap. I.

Austria the German regulation has been applied since the spring of 1939, so that now, when parents change their religion, children must necessarily do the same.

In order, however, to induce apostasy on anything like a wide scale the stigma attaching to it in the minds of all decent men had to be removed. One step towards this was the prohibition of announcing from the pulpit the names of those who had renounced their religion,[1] and allied to this is the fact that no criticism of religious apostasy is allowed in the press, no matter how light the criticism may be. For example, the Munich *Messenger of St. Gabriel* ventured in 1937 to touch on this question. It received a warning, on the grounds that the expressions " lapse," " disloyalty to Christ," etc., were an insult to those who had severed their connection with the Church.

The favourite method, however, of National Socialism is to mask unbelief with the honourable designation of " belief in God." National Socialist circles realise, of course, that words like " unbeliever," " free-thinker," " pagan " have an unpleasant ring for the German people, among whom Christian instincts have taken such a deep root that even those liberal circles which retained so little of the substance of the Faith looked on themselves still as " Christians " and repudiated completely anything like radical unbelief or such descriptions as " godless " or " pagan." Whatever the tendency of this purely destructive freedom of thought—materialistic, pantheistic or what not —National Socialism proceeded to call all those who professed it by the completely misleading name of " believers in God." To merit this description it was enough to believe in the " god " of Race and Blood. Yet, to call things by their proper names and refer to these neo-pagans quite simply as " pagans " was to incur, quite often, the penalties of the criminal courts for slander.

In February, 1937, the Reichsminister of the Interior ordained that in official lists and documents there were to be three religious categories: (i) members of religious denominations (*e.g.*, Catholics, Protestants and Old Catholics); (ii) believers in God; (iii) unbelievers. In various dioceses, therefore, the ecclesiastical authorities explained to the faithful that

the new official designation " believing in God " does not indicate those of our fellow-countrymen who believe in God because they belong to the Church, but rather those who deny and reject Christianity and belong to no definite Church.

The consequence is that sound Catholics who are unaware of this declare themselves to the authorities as " believing in God " and are considered officially to have left the Church. For this reason Catholics are strictly forbidden to inscribe themselves or have themselves inscribed under that designation in official lists or documents.

For in the State registers those who " believe in God " are those who deny the Triune God, Jesus Christ the Redeemer and true Christianity. It

[1] *Cf.* p. 15.

would therefore be a denial of the Faith, an external lapse from the Faith, were a Catholic to declare himself to the State as a " believer in God." In official transactions Catholics must designate themselves simply as Catholics.

So this is the pass to which things have come that, in the Third Reich, anyone who believes in the true God of Christianity may not describe himself as a " believer in God,"; it is the unbelievers, the modern pagans, who are the " believers in God "! Here then, too, National Socialism remains true to its own standards of truth and honour, for if it calls the destruction of the most primitive rights of man liberation, and the persecution of the Church the protection and salvation of religion, why should it not call paganism belief in God ?

With these measures to protect and camouflage renegades went others to produce them. Among these, the first place can be assigned to the endless questionnaires that the German, especially the Civil Servant and the State or municipal employee, has to fill in. While it is true that these do not contain any direct prohibition against belonging to a Church, the numberless questions to which the State demands an answer certainly suggest one. It asks whether a man is a Catholic, what are his real beliefs and what he used to believe; how thoroughly he practises his religion; whether he belongs to any Catholic organisation and since when; whether he belonged to one in the past, etc. It never tires of asking him about all this and, when it has got its information from the man himself, it wants it then from his wife and his children, and perhaps even from his parents and grandparents, if not in questionnaires, at any rate in countless verbal interrogations. Right from his school days—even from his kindergarten—up to his Training Courses, Labour Camps, Service parades and so on, the Catholic has to keep on putting up his hand, remaining behind, stepping out of the ranks: in other words the Christian, from the very fact that he is a Christian, is for ever being forced to make himself conspicuous in the eyes of his comrades and his superiors.

Eventually even the simplest man comes to understand the meaning of this endless questioning: he gradually perceives what it is that is wanted of him and comprehends the barely half-concealed threat.

To take but one example. How thoroughly distasteful must have been the searchings of heart of those forty odd Bavarian junior barristers who were required to fill in the following questionnaire at the Munich Court in 1937:

Profession (married women with no profession give profession of husband).........................
Place of residence.................... Age (completed)......
Religious denomination (yes or no ?)............... Sex......
1. Do you believe that there is a God ?
2. If so, do you believe in the teaching of the Church to which you belong, or have you got a different idea of God and his relations to men ?

3. Do you believe in the divinity of Christ ? Do you believe that Christ was born of a virgin ? Do you believe that Christ rose again after the crucifixion ? Or do you believe that Christ was only a man ?

4. Do you believe that the Bible is the word of God—*i.e.*, that its content was given by God to those who wrote it and that God's will is to be found in it ?

5. Do you believe in an after-life of the soul after death ?

6. Do you believe in a divine justice—*i.e.*, that after death man is rewarded for a morally good life and punished for an evil one ?

7. Do you pray to God, and do you believe that God hears prayer ? Do you believe that God allows Himself to be influenced in His actions by prayer ?

8. Do you believe that the Christian religion is indispensable as a moral foundation and authority for human morality and education ? Or do you believe that a belief in God which is not bound up with Christian teaching is also sufficient for this ? Or do you believe that another moral foundation can have the same authority as faith in God? And if so, which?

9. Do you believe that Christian teaching is of an eternal and universal value ? If not, do you believe that of some other teaching ? If so, of which ? Or do you believe that religious and moral teaching differs according to historical periods and races and should be accommodated to them and change with them ?

10. Do you believe that the soul is something in man that has a separate existence—*i.e.*, that man is composed of two parts, body and soul ? Do you believe that matter and spirit in the world are things that have an independent existence, but work in co-operation ? Or do you believe that the soul is merely a reflection of the body—*i.e.*, that all spiritual experiences can ultimately be reduced entirely to bodily experiences ? Do you believe, therefore, that matter is the sole basic constituent of the world and of men ? Or do you believe, on the contrary, that everything material is a reflection of spirit—*i.e.*, that bodies and their energies are only reflections of spiritual experiences ? Do you believe, therefore, that spirit is the sole basic constituent of the world and of men ?

11. Have you before this busied yourself with religious and philosophical questions of this nature ? Or do these questions find no particular place in your reflections ? How often in the past year, as far as you can reckon, have you attended religious services—*e.g.*, Mass ?

12. Do you wish to make any special remarks ?

(In the original document space is left for answers to all the questions.)

To a junior barrister, who enquired whether this questionnaire was an official document, the answer, so characteristic of National Socialism, was given: " Not as yet." A variation of this method is for employers and managers to put to workmen questions like this: " Do you hold with a foreign power (the Pope) still having a say in Germany ? " What can a man answer to that ? The result, of course, is that time and time again in recent years people from State and Party organisations, especially SA- and SS-men, come to the parish authorities lamenting that they can no longer resist the extremely strong, though indirect, pressure brought on them to make them apostatise.

Another means is economic pressure, so strong and so generally applied, that Cardinal Faulhaber could say publicly:[1]

A form of propaganda has been introduced which employs every means, even economic pressure, to de-Christianise the public life of our people and to force as many as possible to apostatise from the Church. This propaganda

[1] In a sermon on the Holy Souls delivered in Munich Cathedral on November 8th, 1936.

is applied to Civil Servants and to officials in the movement and to such professions as are economically dependent. But the number of those who have left the Churches is—at any rate among the Catholic population—not so great as fanatical exaggeration makes out.

To give a concrete case from the year 1936. An unemployed artist was engaged to do some work, but only on the condition that he became a member of his union and produced the necessary attestation of his racial purity. His union leader told him that he could begin on the work straightaway if he would break with the Catholic Church. Or, again, to induce people to escape the growing burden of taxation by apostasy, in many places (in Duisburg, for example, in 1937) three-quarters of a year's civil taxes were collected from many people at the same time as the Church tax.[1]

The example of high officials in State and Party is a powerful recommendation of apostasy, for the overwhelming majority of the élite of the Party (who also hold high offices in the State) has never left any doubt as to their attitude to the Church, even though most of them at one time belonged, at least nominally, to one of the two Christian denominations. The year 1936, and especially the spring of 1937, saw a striking number of apostasies among these officials. To name but a few who had apostatised by March, 1937: von Ribbentrop, then Ambassador in London; Reich Leader Borhmann of Munich; Reich Governors Mutschmann of Saxony; Röver of Oldenburg and Robert Wagner of Baden: District Leaders Grohé of Cologne, Florian of Düsseldorf and Wächtler (Leader of the National Socialist Teachers' Union); Deputy District Leader Holtz of Nürnberg; Chief of Staff Lutze gave notice that his children had left the Church. In the course of 1937 further Party officials followed suit (among others District Leader Joseph Wagner, President of the Government of Silesia) and at the same time Catholic records reveal a remarkable number of apostasies on the part of Civil Servants.

On the whole the number of apostasies is exaggerated by the National Socialists, but the fact remains that, with its purposeful propaganda and its unscrupulous employment of every possible means of pressure, it has succeeded in thousands of cases. In the year 1935, for example, 2,913 and in 1936, 3,805 apostasies from the Church were recorded at the Berlin District Courts.

The Results of the Apostasy Movement

In the Archdiocese of Cologne, as can be seen from the official statistics, the total number of apostasies from the Church in the first half of 1938 was 8,495, and for the same period of 1937 the number was 10,059. The large cities of Düsseldorf, Essen and Wuppertal are mainly responsible for this decrease, while the city of Cologne itself remains above the average for the diocese. This less favourable

Cf. p. 51, note.

development in Cologne is to be explained by the economic pressure exercised by National Socialism on Civil Servants and employees. The statistics for March, 1938, are particularly instructive, for in that month, as a consequence of a special propaganda drive, the number of apostasies shows a 100 per cent. increase over some other months.

In the summer of 1939 the Bavarian Statistical Bureau published the figures of religious apostasies in Bavaria for 1938:

The total number of persons who left the Churches is 17,892, compared with 26,570 in the year 1937. Of these, 11,199 were men and 6,693 women. Catholic losses were 5,754 men (9,024 in 1937) and 3,236 women (4,271 in 1937). Evangelical losses were 5,369 men and 3,321 women. The remainder is divided among the Jews and the members of other officially recognised religious communities.

The statistics are an impressive proof that the falling away from the Churches is in no way proportionate to the propaganda directed to this end and the pressure exercised in its suppprt. Compared with the figures for 1937, the total number of defections has apparently decreased and is proportionately much higher among Evangelicals than among Catholics. The apostasies from all religious denominations number for the city of Munich only 4,406, for Nürnberg 2,309, for Würzburg 280.

Archbishop Gröber, in the authoritative report we have already frequently cited, writes as follows concerning the apostasies in the Archdiocese of Freiburg up to the beginning of 1938:

The hostile attitude towards the Catholic Church, combined with an ever-increasing, and in large measure undisguised, agitation for religious apostasy must necessarily reveal itself in the numbers of renegades from the Catholic Church and in the decrease in the number of conversions. The apostasies in the Archdiocese of Freiburg, according to official figures, reached their peak in 1931 and 1932 with 2,527 and 2,750, owing to the unrestrained, free-thinking anti-Church movement especially in social democratic and communistic circles. In the two following years they sank to 2,108 and 1,646, but in 1935 they rose again to 1,966 and in 1936 shot up to the highest recorded figure of 2,798. The decrease in the number of conversions should be traced to the same source. Ecclesiastical statistics give 763 conversions and 214 reconciliations for 1932, but these numbers sank in 1933 to 693 and 376, in 1934 to 592 and 261, in 1935 to 588 and 227, and in 1936 to 459 and 145. Of special interest are the ecclesiastical statistics for 1937, completed at present only for the first nine months, according to which there were from January to March, 1937, in all 633 apostasies, of which 15 were of teachers, 28 of Party officials and 44 of Civil Servants; from April to June (immorality trials !) the number grew to 841—28 of teachers, 42 of Party officials, 115 of Civil Servants; in the third quarter, July to September, 606 apostasies were registered, in which 10 were of teachers, 26 of Party officials and 69 of Civil Servants; in the fourth quarter 1,294 apostasies were recorded, of which 30 were of teachers, 53 of Party officials and 150 of Civil Servants. The agitation against Christianity and the Church, conducted in organisations, schools and assemblies, in the public press and by private individuals, and accompanied with the exercise of official influence, was therefore not wholly without effect.

In Austria there was from the summer of 1938 considerable apostasy propaganda, quite different in character from that of the Marxist régime. Catholics were urged to apostatise from the Church for the most varied reasons. They would, for example, be informed of the economic disadvantages which their remaining in the Church entailed or be terrified with descriptions of enormous Church taxes in the future. There is no need to say more than that already in 1938 apostasy formulas were in print and were being distributed to the people and that many had hardly the courage to refuse the signature demanded.

To give some statistics. Catholic circles in Austria estimate the number of apostasies from the Church in Vienna in the six weeks from the annexation till April 24th at 46,000. On an average about 6,000 people a week apostatise from the Catholic Church, and of these by far the greater part goes over to the Evangelical Church, though some 5,300 have joined the Old Catholics and 460 have chosen to belong to no denomination.

Of the Provinces, Styria and Carinthia register most apostasies. From the middle of March to the middle of April there were 18,600 apostasies from the Catholic Church in Styria, 11,000 in Carinthia, 9,200 in Upper Austria, 9,000 in Lower Austria, 7,100 in Salzburg, 5,800 in Burgenland and 5,400 in Tyrol and Vorarlberg.

The specially large number of apostates in Vienna is to be traced to the National Socialist anti-Church propaganda exercised among the police, the teachers and the employees of the State and the municipalities. Of the police, for instance, it is said that more than 2,000 in Vienna alone have yielded to the pressure exercised on them from above.

In April, 1939, statistics were published of the losses suffered by the Catholic Church in Salzburg in 1938. Of the 78,244 Catholics in the city of Salzburg, 3,987, or 5 per cent., fell away, though the total for the whole diocese was only 5,424, or $\frac{1}{2}$ per cent. On the other hand, the number of those who have returned to the Church was very small—in the whole archdiocese only 67, of whom 43 were inhabitants of the city of Salzburg. The following detail is of interest: According to the reports of the Salzburg Registration Office, from October 14th—*i.e.*, the day after Bürckel's Vienna speech—to October 25th in Salzburg alone 1,219 persons left the Churches. Of these, 630 were men and 589 women, 1,154 were Catholics, 60 Protestants and 5 Old Catholics. This large number of women is especially noteworthy, as this marks a fundamental difference between the National Socialist apostasy movement and that of the Marxists in post-war Austria, for in the latter it was mainly men who left the Church, women being influenced much less.

The number of the apostasies in the capital of Styria and the second largest city of Austria, Graz, which since the beginning of the National Socialist régime has called itself the " city of the National Rising," is relatively large, for in the year 1938 about 16,000 out of a total population of 153,000 left the Catholic Church. The anti-Church agitation there is appreciably more severe than in Vienna.

On the whole, however, it must be recognised that in Austria, too, the National Socialist propaganda has by no means effected the large number of apostasies which it had hoped.

Christianity today is full of conflicting tendencies, and as we concentrate on one or the other our views are equally conflicting, darkly pessimistic or full of rosy optimism. About the figure of Christ there is a constant coming and going. The steady falling away from the Church speaks to us in accents of woe: men on whom we thought we could count forsake the company of Christ. Yet others there are who are coming over to Him, men of whom, but yesterday, we could not have believed it possible. No one dare foretell today what the morrow will be. It is true we mourn each soul that turns its back on Christ—for each is our brother signed with the Blood of Christ—but we can still say, broadly, that one who *today* cleaves to Christ is worth ten who have stood by Him through mere force of habit and have forsaken Him at the first alarm. There are many, too (we need only refer to the statistics), who spend but a short time in the chill darkness of separation from Christ and, let the door open ever so slightly, are straightway back within their Father's house.

CHAPTER IX

THE REFUSAL OF LEGAL PROTECTION FOR THE CATHOLIC CHURCH

ONE of the highest goods of human society is *law* and, therefore, from the remotest times there has been agreement among civilised nations that one of the most important duties of the State is to uphold the law. Even those who have but a slight acquaintance with the mentality of the German people know how deeply rooted in them is this idea of *law*. The sense of order and discipline for which that people is famous arises from, and is supported by, respect for the law, and history shows that lawlessness, insurrection and revolution had always to be covered with a cloak of legality in order to secure acceptance.

National Socialism has therefore, very wisely, retained this idea of law, though it is true that it is only the outer husk which is preserved, emptied of all its content. Probably at no time in the history of the German people has there been so much talk of law, so much emphasis placed on the law, so much appeal to law on all sides, or so many institutions set up for the enforcement of the law, as is the case under National Socialism. And yet the Nazi system, with its glorification of force, its worship of success, its proclamation of its own infallibility, its absolute claim to the precedence of the Party over the whole State, and its outlawry of all other agencies, such as the Church, the family and the individual, which claim to have legal rights, cannot escape the reproach that it has opened wide the door to all sorts of illegality, and even destroyed the very idea of law itself.

Since it is not our task here to give a complete discussion of the National Socialist system in its entirety, we must refrain from undertaking any closer examination of this matter in general. We will content ourselves with exposing some of the actual illegalities of which National Socialism has been guilty in its relations with the Catholic Church.

Proceedings which are Incompatible with the Claim to be a Constitutional State founded on Law

We must first of all make some brief reference to the procedure (in itself illegal) by means of which the attack on the Church's legal rights was made possible and carried out within a pseudo-legal framework.

Of primary importance here is the practical abolition of the independence of the judicature in the Third Reich. In order to make this point clear, we quote *verbatim* from an article published under the National Socialist régime on the essential changes which have taken place in the idea of the functions of a *judge*. It was written by Professor Eduard Kern of the University of Tübingen and appeared in the leading German professional law journal *Gerichtssaal*.[1] According to Professor Kern, this is what has happened to the judge and his relation to the State as a whole in Germany today:

By comparison with the law as it existed before the year 1933, the guarantees of judicial independence have been diminished:
(i) The objective conditions and reasons for the dismissal or transfer of judges have been widened. The interchange of judges for service reasons and the relegation of judges to a state of retirement for reasons of political unreliability are now permissible throughout the Reich.
(ii) Relegation to the retired state according to paragraph 71 of the Officials Law and declaration of nullity of appointment is now permitted without judicial sentence.
(iii) In formal disciplinary service proceedings, besides sentences of admonition, sentences of reprimand and fines can be inflicted. No appeal against such service disciplinary measure is allowed to a service tribunal, nor is such an appeal allowable against other measures of the service administrative authorities, such as admonitions and censures.
(iv) Legal claims of judges in financial matters may no longer be pressed through legal channels, but only through administrative channels.
(v) A particularly important modification has taken place in the legal position of the judges of the Reich Supreme Court. Although hitherto members of the bench of judges of the Reich Supreme Court could not be subjected to service disciplinary proceedings, they now become subject to the same conditions as other judges in general. The only exception is that in cases of formal service disciplinary proceedings against judges of the Supreme Court the decision in first instance and in final instance lies with the special service disciplinary senate of the Supreme Court.
After enumerating the above facts, Professor Kern comes to the general conclusion that in the Third Reich judges have exactly the same legal position as any other official of the régime; according to Hitler's "Officials Law," the judge can be removed from his office by a simple decision of the Führer in agreement with the Ministry of the Interior on the motion of a departmental Minister, if " his words or behaviour make it appear that the National Socialist State can no longer rely on him unreservedly."

Now what does this mean in practice? It simply means that it depends on the good pleasure of the Nazi regional or district leader of the place in which a court of justice is situated just how far and in what manner a judge can exercise his office. It is true that a legal judgement, once it has been delivered by a judge, still remains immune from the intervention of the Führer and Reich Chancellor. But this is now a matter of mere formality. If the judge's decision in a particular case is not such as to please the Party authorities, the "Officials Law" provides them with all sorts of handles for procuring his dismissal; the case is then sent up to a higher court, which will have been rendered more compliant with the dismissal of the judge of lower instance before its eyes, and so the judgement can easily be revised in accordance with Party interests.

[1] Stuttgart, vol. cx.

Confirmation of the fact that the judges in the Third Reich are no longer free and independent may be found in the reasons given for allowing an appeal by the court of second instance in the following case: A number of youths were charged with wandering in bands and violating the Presidential Ordinance of February 28th, 1933, for the suppression of communistic activity endangering the State. The Petty Sessions judge in Hagen acquitted the youths, on the ground that " hiking " in bands and participating in sporting activities under the ægis of a Catholic Youth Organisation did not involve communistic activity, or activity endangering the State, or any act of violence, and that the regulations of the State Police based on the anti-communistic Ordinance of the Reich President went far beyond the provisions of that Ordinance and were consequently void in law.

An appeal was entered against this decision by the prosecution, and the case came before the High Court in Berlin. Since it could not very well be said that Catholic organisations were communistic, this court elaborated for itself a new concept of " mediate danger " for the State. Such indirect danger to the State would exist if " tendencies were manifested in public which could be characterised as an expression of discontent with the new order of things, and could thus be said to prepare the ground for a fresh outbreak of communistic endeavour."

It will perhaps be instructive to read the following tortuous and involved " explanations " of the court's decision:

National Socialist ideology seeks to attain the true union and community of our people by bridging over all the manifold oppositions which may exist, as, for instance, between social classes, religious persuasions, etc. The division of religious persuasions within the German nation must, according to the political developments of the times, be regarded as contradictory to these unifying endeavours whenever the adherents of these religious persuasions give concrete visible expression to their views otherwise than in the course of strictly ecclesiastical activity, thus manifesting the fact that they are separate and different from others. This sort of emphasis placed on internal division contains within itself the seeds of dissolution for the German people. And any such inchoate dissolution is calculated to assist the endeavours of the Communists and to support the aims which they have in view. The regulations of the State Police Bureau are, therefore, based on the fact that the various activities which it prohibits are, under present political conditions, equivalent to an expression of opinion which is disturbing to the public peace, and could, therefore, re-awaken the hopes of others in communistic circles and at least indirectly favour their communistic activities, notwithstanding the fact that the agencies affected by the police regulations are themselves opposed to atheistic Communism, etc.

Another factor which serves to bend the law to the service of the party is the exceptional and privileged position accorded to the State Secret Police, the Gestapo. As is well known, the Gestapo is completely independent and cannot be cited before a court; in its activity it is not subject to any higher authority, and there is no legal remedy or recourse against its decrees. We are thus faced with this unique state of affairs, that executive organs of the State enjoy complete exemption from the provisions of the law, while at the same time their arbitrary acts receive the fullest legal protection. We must, therefore, not be surprised if we find that in the course of the struggle against the Catholics the Gestapo is guilty of brutal acts of violence which are checked by nobody and carefully kept from the public notice.

Yet another agency operating outside the sphere of law is the concentration camp. What happens to those who are sent there and how long they remain is, according to the principles of the Third Reich, immune from judicial investigation.

Of the other factors which could be mentioned, the exceptional position enjoyed by the Party should be indicated. It is true enough that this has its own courts to which its members are subject, but against the Party as such no legal action can be taken. It is a major Nazi principle that " the Party is in command over the State." Actions of the Party, or of Party formations, of the Government's executive organs such as the police or judiciary, cannot be discussed in court. The consequences, naturally enough, are devastating. It is quite sufficient to call to mind the incredibly arbitrary acts and interferences on the part of the SA, SS, the Hitler Youth and other Party formations in order to understand what it means when the police do not dare to interfere or to give their protection to others against the arbitrary actions of Party members acting as such, particularly when it is a question of an active persecution of the Church.

The lack of impartiality on the part of the police is well illustrated by the photograph facing p. 105, showing the police headquarters in Essen with a large notice across the main front: " The Police stand by the Hitler Youth." The notice was to be seen precisely during those weeks when the Hitler Youth, by means of incitement, terrorisation and threats, were carrying out their grand offensive against the denominational associations.

Finally, attention is called to a legal principle of National Socialism. Competent lawyers took every opportunity of emphasising that the norm for the whole judicial system of the Third Reich was the people's sense of justice. What, one may well wonder, has the German people's sense of justice to say to the following cases taken from the judicial proceedings of the past few years ?

In 1935 a police detective sent his wife to Confession to a Catholic parish priest. In the confessional she was to ask the tricky question, whether she ought to let her son take part in the Land Year. The unsuspecting priest said that the parents would, of course, have to make sure that the boy's religion would not be endangered and that it would be possible for him to go to Mass. Thereupon the detective made a formal accusation against the priest, who was at once arrested and detained in prison for months by the Secret Police, after which he was condemned to a five-hundred-mark fine instead of imprisonment for having misused the confessional for political purposes, thereby shaking confidence in the Land Year organisation. It is left to the reader to judge on whom " the German people's sense of justice " would lay the guilt of misusing the confessional.[1]

The investigations and examinations carried out by the police, particularly the Secret Police, form an ugly blot in German legal practice. There are dozens, probably hundreds, of cases in which they have been guilty of " framing " witnesses and extorting confessions by threats and promises. Examples will be found further on in the pages on the " immorality " trials.

What sort of justice is it when persons, priests as well as laymen, are detained for months and even years in prison without being brought in a proper way to trial ? What legal justification is there for taking off priests and laymen to concentration camps without judgement, or even any attempt at a judicial investigation. There is certainly no written law to support it and to bring forward the German people's sense of justice to legalise it would be a serious insult to the German people. A declaration ordered by the Bishop of Münster to be read from all pulpits on the last Sunday of July, 1938, confirms what has been said:

> I have already mentioned that twelve greatly respected men from the neighbourhood of Goldenstedt have been arrested and, without hearing or judgement, held in protective custody since the beginning of May.
> Similarly at the beginning of May the two curates of the parish of Goldenstedt were expelled from the territory of Oldenburg by the Secret Police, so that an old and infirm parish priest is now left alone to care for his flock of two thousand souls. The two curates had not been heard or judged. They were not confronted with proofs of punishable offences. They had no chance of defending themselves. Again without judgement in court and having had no occasion to defend themselves, the sixty-eight-year-old parish priest of Löningen and his sixty-three-year-old curate were driven from their parish and expelled from the territory of Oldenburg by the Secret Police on June 28th. They had to leave immediately and abandon their duties, as they were threatened with arrest if they did not leave the same day.
> The vicar of Visbek was expelled from Oldenburg and on July 6th taken to the boundary by two policemen. Again no judgement in court was passed, nor was there chance of defence against possible accusations. Neither to me nor to my representative for Oldenburg in Vechta was any communication made concerning complaints against these priests or concerning the punishment of expulsion which was inflicted.[2]

Another form of illegal action was the sticking of posters (which as often as not were of a character offensive to Catholics) on the walls of private houses and, by choice, on churches and presbyteries. Quite apart from the words of the posters, the question may be asked: Has a German citizen no right to remove bills from his house when they have been put there without his consent, seeing that it is an offence punishable in German law to make free with the property of another, to disfigure it, etc. ? It is certain, however, that in the Third Reich nobody has been brought to justice for fixing posters on other people's property. Punishment was, indeed, meted out—and that not infre-

[1] For the similar case of Mgr. Leffers, cf. p. 67.
[2] For the similar case of Mgr. Vorwerk cf. p. 43, and for that of Canon Kraus, p. 68.

quently—but only to those who removed the posters from their own houses.

This kind of activity was particularly rife at the beginning of August, 1935. For example, a certain poster was stuck up on the Cathedral of Passau, on the parish presbytery and on private dwellings, and a number of people were punished for removing it. In the same year there were similar cases in Würzburg, where picture posters insulting the Catholic priesthood were stuck round the Cathedral. Complaint was made, with the result that the same poster appeared at the entrance to the Bishop's chapel and on the dwelling of a well-known priest. Again in October, 1935, placards were fixed on the presbytery in Traunstein without the consent of the owners (the placards showed an SA-man and a member of the German Girls' League in light athletic costume). The police, when approached, refused to take any action, which was understandable, seeing that the posters were put up by the Party, and the police in the Third Reich may not enforce the law against them.

In March, 1936, it was the election posters that were stuck by preference on Catholic presbyteries. On this occasion the following incident occurred in a town of Bavaria. The parish priest's sister, thinking it to be within the rights of a house-owner, removed the posters which had been stuck on the presbytery, while the sacristan removed those which had been stuck on the church. Thereupon a police inspector appeared and took them both into protective custody. This is the sort of thing that happened in the March of 1936 in the National Socialist " law-and-order State."

Nor again was the procedure of the SA in Unterspiessheim in the Gerolzhofen area on August 18th, 1935, when they took over the Catholic Youth Association's house, particularly characterised by law and order. Six lorries full of SA-men followed by a number of other cars made their appearance in the village, with their occupants shouting insults in chorus against the Catholics. From among the villagers themselves only the teacher and the Mayor took part. The SA-men, numbering some two hundred, marched to the Youth Association's house, which had already been forced on the previous day by two SA members, occupied it, made speeches, and hoisted the Swastika flag. The Christus sign was smashed with a hammer and the episcopal coat of arms was torn down. Then it was declared that, as the priest had refused a peaceful solution of the matter, they had resorted to this violent method, and that the house was now the property of the SA.

The Protests of the Ecclesiastical Authorities remain Unanswered

The *Munich Diocesan Gazette*[1] gives a long list of complaints and protests which the ecclesiastical authorities of the diocese made in the course of only two months to the various territorial and national

[1] No. 19, October 10th, 1935, pp. 232-235.

departments and which in most instances remained unanswered. Here we give only a synopsis.

(1) At the Bavarian Ministry of the Interior:

> (*a*) Protests against distribution of " currency ditty " to SA at Munich[1] and Freising.[2]
> (*b*) Enquiry[3] whether the prohibition against uniforms, badges and sports holds in Bavaria. Reply: " Present practice may be followed till further notice."

(2) At the Reich Ministry for Ecclesiastical Affairs: Protests against violence at Wolfratshausen;[4] against utterances of National Socialist officials;[5] against seizure of *Munich Parish Magazine* for quoting a Pastoral;[6] against action taken against distributors of the same Pastoral;[7] against expulsion of Catholics from German Labour Front for being members of a Sodality;[8] against demand for membership lists of Catholic Youth Association of Rosenheim;[9] against resolutions to accept only members of Hitler Youth and BDM as apprentices.[10]

(3) At the Reich Ministry of Justice: Enquiry about illegal sticking of posters on private houses and ecclesiastical buildings.[11]

(4) At *Hochland* headquarters of Hitler Youth: Protests against insufficient announcement of hour of Mass and interference with those wishing to attend it;[12] against distribution of hymn of German Faith Movement.[13]

(5) Various: Protests to Bavarian Ministry of Education against articles in *HJ-Zeitung*;[14] against a Nazi marriage ceremonial at Altötting (to Führer and elsewhere);[15] against interference with Catholic associations;[16] against misuse of schools.[17]

In 1936 an emergency Pastoral, issued by the Bishops' Conference of the Cologne and Paderborn Provinces, which later was ordered by Cardinal Bertram to be read in the East German ecclesiastical province, bears further witness to the sad state of affairs. It was signed by thirteen German Bishops and states explicitly that all the protests made to the Government authorities by the Bishops had been useless and that, therefore, the time had come to appeal to the public. In the same way Dr. Bornewasser, Bishop of Trier, had complained already (July, 1935) that the representations made by him concerning incidents that had occurred during his Confirmation circuit in Kreuznach remained unanswered. In 1935 and 1936 various bishops had complained to the proper authorities of the non-observance of provisions of the Concordat. The Bishops' Conference at Fulda in August,

---

[1] On August 7th.
[2] On August 23rd.
[3] On August 8th.
[4] On September 3rd; *cf.* p. 195.
[5] On September 3rd, 23rd, October 5th.
[6] On September 7th.
[7] On September 7th and 9th.
[8] On September 7th, October 3rd.
[9] On September 11th, October 4th.
[10] On September 23rd, October 3rd and 4th.
[11] On August 14th, 26th and 30th.
[12] On August 5th.
[13] On August 8th, when it was replied that distribution, if any, was unofficial; on August 20th and October 8th against continued distribution.
[14] On August 13th.
[15] On August 8th, 9th and 17th.
[16] On August 8th, 16th, 17th.
[17] On September 23rd and October 8th.

1935, had made representations to the Führer and Reich Chancellor, Hitler, yet a whole year elapsed and still no answer had been received, while in the meantime the matter complained of had by no means improved. Immediately prior to the Reichstag elections in the spring of 1936 a German Cardinal addressed an official protest to the competent authorities complaining of the silence with which all representations, even in the highest places, were received. The Austrian episcopacy, too, addressed numerous protests to the Government without the slightest success.

Desecration of Sacred Places and Religious Symbols

The enmity, however, against the Catholic Church which raged undisturbed in the Third Reich did not confine itself to attacks on presbyteries and Youth houses and to the plastering of bills on the walls of churches and private houses, but led to atrocities and desecrations which are, perhaps, unique of their kind. Certainly in no other country would they have been possible—except Bolshevik Russia. From 1935 onwards things which the Catholic holds sacred—chapels, crucifixes, pictures of Our Lady and of the saints—were desecrated and destroyed.

These atrocities reveal a great deal: the utter inability to obtain legal redress of more than thirty million Catholics, who were forced to put up with the most outrageous insults from small groups of neo-pagans and fanatical Nazis; the powerlessness, or worse, the active sympathy with wrongdoers of those whose duty it was to enforce the law, but who did nothing at all; and the coarseness and brutality and appalling hatred of religion generated by the vulgar anti-Christian propaganda disseminated under the direction of Alfred Rosenberg among the German people in thousands of meetings, writings, speeches, training camps, etc.

Here we cannot give details of all these blasphemies and desecrations; of the wrecking of dozens of wayside crucifixes, and the robbing of churches.[1] We content ourselves with one particularly revolting example and one diocesan list.

In Wuppertal-Barmen, in summer, 1935, Hitler Youth pulled down a mission cross which stood outside the church and put it up during the night in the sports stadium. It was seen that the boys with the cross as target held shooting practices with rifles and pistols. Part of this practice took place after dark, and the boys illuminated the cross-beam of the crucifix to improve the target. When the metal plate with the inscription I.N.R.I. fell down, the boys started to set the crucifix on fire. The metal plate was then taken during the night and, with shouts of ". The Jewish king has fallen," and " Down with the Jews and the Christians," nailed on to the premises of a Jewish firm. The Catholic clergy made formal protest concerning this desecration

---

[1] These acts of desecration and wanton destruction were so numerous and throw such light on the sad state of irreligion of the youth of Germany that they cannot be altogether omitted. They will be found, therefore, in Appendix IV.

242 REFUSAL OF LEGAL PROTECTION FOR CHURCH

In the Archdiocese of Paderborn, in April, 1937, the Archbishop, Dr. Kaspar Klein, gave a sermon in which he enumerated a number of outrages on crucifixes and desecrations of shrines which had been reported to the Vicariate-General since the middle of 1935:

1. In June, 1935, a cross near Grevenbrück in the Olpe district was desecrated and shattered. The miscreants were found out and condemned to two months' imprisonment.

2. In the summer of 1935 a statue of St. Joseph was removed from a shrine at Westernkoten near Lippstadt and broken.

3. A statue of St. John Nepomucene was found broken and shattered in Erwitte near Lippstadton the same night. The miscreants could in neither case be discovered.

4. On the nights of March 25th and 27th, 1936, the figure was torn down from a crucifix in front of the Maria Hilf Chapel near Geseke and hung on a tree.

5. During the same period a second crucifix was desecrated in the vicinity of Geseke. The culprits remained unknown.

6. A wayside cross near Neheim was found knocked down and broken during Lent, 1936. Investigations were broken off because the President of the Government decided that no indications had been discovered that the cross had been wilfully knocked down and damaged.

7. On the night before Easter Sunday, 1936, the figure was pulled off a wayside cross near Willebadessen (Paderborn) and one arm of it broken. No one was found out.

8. At the beginning of May, 1936, a shrine was broken into and a statue of St. Joseph broken just before a special procession day at Körbecke in the Soest area. The culprits were not found out.

9. On the night of July 5th, 1936, the figure was knocked off a crucifix near Balve, Arnsberg district. No one was discovered.

10. On June 29th, 1936, a cross made of box-tree evergreen hanging over a shrine in Hellefeld in the Arnsberg area was torn down with insulting remarks. There were clear witnesses as to who did it, but it was said that investigations had no result.

11. On July 31st, 1936, a window of the kindergarten in Oeventrop, Arnsberg district, was broken and the crucifix taken.

12. On the night after Christmas Day, 1936, the figure of a crucifix which had just been repaired was torn down and broken in Wewelsburg. The perpetrators were detected as being two members of the Labour Service camp at Wewelsburg. The President of the Government stated on January 14th, 1937, that the two men had been handed over to justice. Nothing further is known.

13. On the night of March 17th, 1937, the elementary school in Holzwickede, the Hans-Schemm school, was broken into and the cross taken away from one of the classrooms. The figure was thrown on to the street and broken, while the desecrated cross was thrown into the river Emscher.

14. The most terrible, so far, of all the crucifix desecrations occurred in Balve, Arnsberg district, during Holy Week in 1937.

Concluding this terrible enumeration the Archbishop of Paderborn said:

These numerous and terrible sacrileges stir both you and us to the depths. There can be no doubt that they are a consequence of the anti-Christian influence and incitement that is making itself everywhere evident both in word and writing, and in reply we unite as one man in the glorious salute of our Church: " Hail, O Cross of Christ, in Thee alone we place our hope."

There was no cessation of these atrocities in the following years. A particularly unpleasant case occurred on Easter Sunday, 1939, in

Badisch-Laufenburg, where in the guest-room of an inn there was a cross hanging on the wall. A leader of the Labour Service took offence at it, removed it from the wall and, using insulting language and amidst the jeers and yells of his men, marched with it down to the Rhine and threw it into the river. The outraged population had to stand and look on.

In May, 1939, it was broadcast from the Vatican station that the sacrilegious outrages in the Archdiocese of Freiburg had reached such terrible proportions that the diocesan authorities had deemed it necessary to instruct all parish priests to keep the churches closed during certain hours of the day.

In the diocese of Danzig, too, the Nazi incitement of youth bore due fruit. In the autumn of 1937 a shocking outrage occurred in the church of St. Nicholas. Unknown persons forced a way into the church and destroyed all the banners and flags of the Catholic Youth Associations, tearing them and slashing them with knives, or, when it was a question of a valuable piece of material, stealing it. The flags belonged to the parish. As early as 1936 a number of such outrages had been perpetrated within the area of the Danzig Free State and the Bishop at the time, Mgr. O'Rourke, used the most severe terms of condemnation in a Pastoral.

For the honour of the German people it must be said that the indignation over all these outrages was genuine and deeply felt and in almost all the parishes concerned the services of reparation were attended by immense numbers of people. Concerning those responsible there is but one opinion among the people of Germany: they are those who, with the toleration and connivance of the Nazi authorities, preach the campaign of hatred against Christianity. Above all it is the leader in the fight against the Catholic Church, Alfred Rosenberg, and these shameful deeds are the visible results of his slogan: " The Cross must vanish from Germany."

Catholics are Outlawed

There are, unfortunately, only too many cases which go to prove that the idea that in the Third Reich the police are there to protect the citizen is entirely misleading. The reader may judge from the following:

On May 18th, 1935, a street and house-to-house collection throughout the whole country was started by the Catholic *Karitasverband* for which the express approval of the Ministry of the Interior had been obtained. Groups of students marched through the streets of Munich shortly after the commencement of the collection, carrying placards of the latest newspaper reports concerning a currency smuggling action then in progress against a nun and shouting in measured chorus: " Not a farthing for the currency smugglers ! Germans, don't send your money to Rome ! Give it all to the National Socialist Public

Welfare." Many of the students followed the collectors step by step in order to stop passers-by from contributing by constant reference to the currency case and by the threat: " Those who give money will be photographed; they are supporting high treason." A number of men and women who had volunteered to collect were insulted and interfered with, but when they asked for police protection the police could only say that they couldn't do anything against the demonstrators without orders. In the early afternoon Wagner, Bavarian State Minister, stopped the collection in Munich and forbade the wearing of the collectors' badge. A few hours later the collection was stopped, too, in other Bavarian towns—*e.g.*, Freising, Pasing, Rosenheim.[1]

In Duisburg Hermann Muckermann was to hold a series of conferences from July 8th to 10th, 1935. Members of the SA and the Hitler Youth, both in uniform and plain clothes, made such a commotion in front of the church and presbytery that by July 9th the Gestapo had sufficient pretext for prohibiting the last two conferences. Thus again it was not those who disturbed the peace, but the people whom they threatened, the Catholics, who were made to suffer. Those police who wanted to restore order were laughed at and told: " We'll ust see who's in charge on the streets." That from the Führer's Youth to the officials employed by the State for the protection of law and order !

In a village in South Germany a priest spoke somewhat sharply to a Hitler Youth boy for being rude and impertinent. A few weeks later a car drew up outside his house and the occupants, who said they were political police, ordered the priest to go along with them. They took him to a near-by forest and subjected him to such inhuman treatment that when he dragged himself to a doctor there was found not a single white spot left on his body, which was covered with one big bruise. The investigations of the political police furnished, naturally, no result.

In 1936 some eighty members of the SA, some of them in uniform, appeared in front of a Catholic presbytery and shouted: " Hand over the traitor and we'll beat him dead." They then saw the parish priest in the garden of the house, knocked him down, kicked him, and then drove him out of the village to the accompaniment of the yells of a crowd of onlookers. He was kicked down the road towards the next village, several times being knocked into the ditch. Finally, a motor-car came along and took him into the prison of the nearest large town. The leader of the attack threatened the relatives of the priest with reprisals if they said a word about the affair. The next morning the parish priest was released by an official of the area authorities, but not before he had undertaken not to return immediately to his parish. His clothes were still dirty when he left the prison, his head swollen and his eye badly bruised. Nearly all the adult members of the parish signed a declaration stating that they were very saddened by

---

[1] For the incidents at Wolfratshausen *cf.* p. 195.

the events and considered them abominable and at the same time requested the bishop to send back the priest to them. Not very long after, on Maundy Thursday, 1936, the Area Leader appeared in the village and held a public meeting at which the chairman was the very man who had led the attack against the parish priest. The Area Leader announced that the parish priest had not used his vote at the election and was a traitor to his country and that he would see to it that he did not return, no matter how many signatures were collected. He had already had one man arrested for calling the proceedings disgraceful barbarity and now he threatened the neighbouring parish priest with something similar if he didn't behave himself.

The events which took place at the time of the Reichstag election of 1938 in Fellbach are typical. The *Schaffhausener Zeitung* gives the following report:

A messenger came to the parish priest's house on the day of the election and told him that he would have to go to the election as a duty. Accordingly Father Sturm, the parish priest, went shortly after three to record his vote. In the election room there were no booths so that the voting should be secret, but it was open to anyone to see how others used their vote.

About nine o'clock on the evening of the same day a group of SS- and SA-men with some civilians, altogether about fifteen or twenty people, gathered outside the presbytery. The parish priest himself was not there, but his curate was, together with some relations. The windows were broken, shutters thrown into the rooms and an entrance forced. All the rooms were turned upside down and everything knocked about in the search for the parish priest. The curate stood in the way, but was pushed aside with the remark, " He's not the one. He voted all right," though later he was struck and wounded, as happened, too, to the sister of the parish priest. It was not long before the parish priest appeared, and he was surrounded before he got through the garden of the house. " Which way did you vote, eh ?" He did not answer. They took hold of him and threw him into the street. Then for an hour and a half he had to run the gauntlet through the streets of Fellbach. From all sides he received kicks and blows so that he collapsed. They spat on him and kept an electric torch shining on his face and shouted in chorus: " There's the traitor to his country, Father Sturm."

About eleven o'clock he was brought into the police station at the town hall in a pitiable condition. The Mayor, Adelheim, asked him the question on the spot: " What have you been doing ?" " Nothing." " But you must have done something." " Nothing that I know of." Then the Mayor asked: " How did you vote ?" The priest said that the election, as was well known, was a secret one. Thereupon he received the answer that a parish priest should know what Christianity was, but in this case apparently he didn't. Then followed a lecture on the Christian duties of a parish priest, which the priest, after a while, interrupted with the remark that the Mayor could spare himself his pains, that as parish priest he knew what his duties were. Political instruction about the Führer he also energetically and with dignity declined to receive. He was kept at the station until a little before twelve o'clock for his own security and then brought back to his house by the police.

It is of interest to note that on the Tuesday the town-hall authorities exerted themselves to the utmost to force the parish priest to put his house, which had been completely devastated, into proper condition again.

In a room used for public business by the canteen manager at the repair works of the German railways at Freimann near Munich the following " verse " was written up in 1936 on the wall in large black letters:

> When will man's heavy bonds be cut ?
> When will earth's gloom be banished ?
> When, strangled with the last priest's gut,
> The last of the Jews has vanished.

There is no need nowadays to do more than walk through the streets of German towns and villages in order to witness how the clergy are more and more insulted and shouted after with expressions such as: " Black scoundrels !" " Currency profiteers !" and so on.

Whenever it was a question of Catholics being interfered with and assaulted the police remained passively in the background, but acted with all the more vigour when the Catholics undertook some activity themselves such as a demonstration in honour of a Bishop, or when a Pastoral Letter was read or some religious celebration held. Then the police would be sure to be there in time, if not, indeed, before time, carefully taking all necessary precautions. In such cases there is no difficulty in dealing with large crowds by means of baton charges and fire-hoses, and they are generous with their arrests, careful and skilful in their investigations, so that their general efficiency leaves nothing to be desired. The reader will find in the following passages a small selection of such disgraceful affairs.

On Trinity Sunday, 1936, the day on which Catholics make a profession of Faith, a vast crowd gathered on the spacious Cathedral square in Münster in Westphalia in honour of their courageous bishop, Clemens August von Galen. The police, supported by the SS and the SA, tried to disperse this great demonstration of faith, and the truncheon was not spared. When the bishop spoke from the window of his residence and urged the people to remain true to the Faith of their fathers the Gestapo turned fire-hoses on to the crowd, but they cheered their heroic bishop enthusiastically, sang hymns and, in spite of all the attempts to break it up, the stirring demonstration continued to the end.[1]

The entirely Catholic villages in the deanery of Gangelt were decorated and beflagged on the occasion of the Confirmation visit of the Coadjutor Bishop of Aachen. The competent police authorities ordered all the flags to be taken down, but, as the Catholic population did not obey, the Gestapo proceeded to remove the flags themselves and to confiscate them. In Hastenrade even the minute yellow and white flags were taken from the triumphal arch in front of the church and presbytery, while the Bishop, Dr. Sträter, protested in vain against this savagery from the windows of the presbytery. In other places the police removed the decorations completely and forbade the solemn reception of the Bishop. The population of the deanery in Gangelt gave expression to its disgust by a big demonstration in honour of the Bishop.[2]

On Monday, July 8th, 1936, the Great Procession of Thanksgiving

[1] *Der Deutsche in Polen*, June 21st, 1936. [2] *Ibid.*, October 4th, 1936.

took place in Münster. This procession is an ancient institution full of old traditions, which has taken place in the July of every year for more than 550 years in commemoration of the saving of the town from fire and pestilence. In the Cathedral after it was over the Bishop of the diocese, Count von Galen, mounted the pulpit and gave the following address to the great crowd which packed the ancient Cathedral to the doors. This is the account of one of the congregation:

My dear Catholics of Münster, we have just come to the end of the great procession by which the city of Münster pays its homage to Our Lord and Saviour, King of the whole world, Sovereign over all peoples, the German people included. As we came back across the Cathedral square I noticed that a large part of it had been roped off by the police and was under guard.
The police have never done this before and neither I myself, nor any of the Cathedral canons, nor the procession committee was informed of it. The way across to the bishop's house is also roped off, which would indicate that the police intend to prevent you from accompanying your bishop back, as you have done on former occasions. I wished to inform you of the closing off of these areas, as it has come as a surprise, and many of you, without doubt, have not noticed it. I beg you to yield to force and to give up the intention of accompanying me home. I have no desire to see a repetition of the incident which occurred on the evening of Trinity Sunday when faithful Catholics who were mere onlookers paying their respects to their bishop were struck and arrested. . . .
But one thing must be said. If anybody thinks that physical force, ropes and police measures are going to separate me from you, or you from me . . . (Prolonged cheering.) I thank you for the approval your cheers show. If, therefore, anybody thinks that physical force is going to separate us, he is making a serious mistake. The bonds between you and me have been fashioned by God, by fidelity to Our Lord and Saviour whom we have publicly confessed this day, by the fidelity of which the ring I received at my consecration and have ever since worn is the symbol. The bonds between us can be destroyed or broken by no one as long as we continue together through life in the following of Christ.
May God bless Münster, where once again, with the exception of those buildings where it was forbidden, all the houses along the procession route were decorated. How foreign to us is the spirit of those who issued such a prohibition. It shows what little idea they have of the dignity of our Faith and our own staunchness. God will reward your fidelity. . . . Not on Palm Sunday alone and cheering with the whole world, but on Good Friday, too, must we follow him, though it be to prison and death. . . .

The address was punctuated by prolonged applause, which grew to thunder when the Bishop left the Cathedral and came on to the square in front, the whole western side of which had been roped off and was guarded by a strong police cordon right up to the doors of the Cathedral. That did not, however, damp the ardour of the faithful.[1]

In February, 1937, the teacher of the village school at Castellaun on the Moselle removed the crucifix from the schoolroom. This caused considerable agitation among the population and a large crowd gathered and marched to the school demanding that the teacher put it back, but, before it was possible for any discussion to begin, the teacher's wife had phoned for the flying squad. The police, in an

[1] *Der Deutsche in Polen*, July 26th, 1936.

attempt to find out who it was who had advised the demonstration, collected all the men of the village and drove them into a yard to examine them. They all refused to mention any name and the police, thrusting their pistols against the men's chests, threatened to count ten and shoot if they did not name the person. Nobody, however, betrayed him and the police then rounded them up and took them off to Trier, where they were brought up for a breach of the peace.

In Emmerich on the Lower Rhine the anniversary of the national Socialist revolution was celebrated in this way. The head teacher of the Legmehr Catholic elementary school, Keminski, had the crucifixes in all the classrooms replaced by pictures of Hitler and explained to the top class that Christianity was foreign to the Germanic nature because it was a product of Judaism.

The Catholic parents got to hear about this and decided to arrange a protest for Monday, February 1st. The decision was passed in secrecy from one to another, and on Monday morning more than 500 parents gathered in front of the school with the demand that a deputation from their number should interview the head teacher. In the meantime members of the SA from neighbouring places had collected in the school yard, while Hitler Youth gathered in the school, but Keminski would not appear. The SA threatened the officials who were among the crowd and told them to leave, but the crowd in reply demanded the replacement of the crosses and sang hymns. Thereupon the Hitler Youth appeared in the yard under the leadership of the head teacher, tried to shout them down with Nazi songs and, when they did not succeed in this, commenced beating drums for all they were worth. Flying squads of the Gestapo finally appeared and were greeted by the crowd with *Deutschland über Alles*, whereupon Zell, the Gestapo chief, shouted to the parents that they were singing this out of sarcasm and ordered the street to be cleared, a proceeding carried out only with difficulty, as a number of the demonstrators resisted and one policeman was badly bitten in the hand. Several persons were then and there arrested and later more than a hundred of the demonstrators were examined by the police and further arrests were made. A deputation of five of the parents then went to the President of the District Government at Düsseldorf, but the crosses were not restored. The only result of the parents' protests was further restrictions: clerics were forbidden to give religious instruction at this school after February 8th. Not a single word of all this, however, leaked out in the German press and some officials who had taken part in the demonstration were immediately dismissed.

The successful defence of the Cross by the Oldenburg Catholics has already been reported.[1] In March, 1937, they were able to record yet another success as a result of their fidelity to their Faith and their bravery. The Encyclical of the Holy Father on the " Situation of the Church in Germany " was read during the afternoon service on Palm Sunday in the village of Essen, Oldenburg. After it had been read

[1] *Cf.* p. 122

the priest called attention to the distribution of the text after the service. Young girls, members of the congregation, were engaged in this, when suddenly two policemen appeared and confiscated the Encyclicals in the church porch, on ecclesiastical ground. The clergy protested, whereupon the police official, Pietrowski, ordered the girls to go to the curate's house, where the Commissioner declared the seven girls under arrest by orders of the Gestapo, despite the assertion of Fr. Niermann, the curate, that as he was responsible, if anyone was to be arrested, it should be he. To this the Commissioner replied that he had definite orders not to arrest any of the clergy.

Meanwhile the crowd had again assembled in front of the curate's house where the girls, whose conduct was exemplary, were being detained and examined. One of the policemen went to get a car to take them away, but everybody refused to give him one, so that one had to be sent for by telephone from Quakenbrück, five miles away. The crowd became increasingly hostile and refused to let the driver approach the curate's house. As it was not possible to provide for the further transport of the girls, the Mayor and the police arranged to let them go, but the crowd refused to take the Mayor's word when he announced this, saying that they had been tricked like this before and the shouts for the release of the girls were renewed once more. About seven in the evening the girls appeared in the doorway and were greeted with wild enthusiasm. The girls went off in a group to the church and all the bells suddenly began to ring. The crowd pressed after the police as they retired and demanded the return of the confiscated copies of the Encyclical. The situation became serious and the police drew their revolvers and threatened to arrest them. The crowd dispersed slowly, but the high state of tension in Essen remained.[1]

In November, 1938, the three hundredth anniversary of the erection of the *Mariensäule*, the Pillar of Our Lady, in front of the Munich town hall was the occasion of a triduum of services in St. Peter's church nearby, the oldest parish church in Munich. The congregation streaming out of St. Peter's gathered round the Pillar, richly decorated with flowers and lit up by fairy lamps, and sang hymns in honour of Our Lady. But it was not long before some of the heroes of the new age disturbed the singing, broke through the crowds, put out the lamps and destroyed the decorations. By Sunday, November 13th, however, the decorations had been renewed, the lamps were burning again and St. Peter's was so packed that many hundreds were unable to enter. The closing service of the triduum was to have been given by the Archbishop, Cardinal von Faulhaber, but he did not appear in order to avoid possible demonstrations. After the service the crowds flocked again spontaneously over to the Pillar, those who could not find room round the column filling the wide pavement. The hymn *Maria zu lieben* . . . was sung, and when a second was begun, suddenly shouts of " Stop that singing !" were heard. The noise increased,

---

[1] An account of the imprisonment of twelve Catholics of Goldenstedt who protested against the new NS community school is given on p. 158.

but the crowd was not disturbed, though determined Party members tried to disperse the people and shouted:

" Munich is the centre of the movement."
" That's out of place nowadays."
" This is blocking the traffic."
" Where's the flying squad ?"

They had not long to wait for it, but in the meantime the faithful had dispersed of their own accord to avoid incidents.

The foreign press published the report of Mgr. von Ronay, a Hungarian, clerical director of the Austrian Catholic Scouts Association, and it gives an insight into the savagery that accompanied the arrests of priests in Austria after the Anschluss. From the report, based on Mgr. von Ronay's own experiences, we give only the following excerpt:

It was really heartrending to see the single file of prominent men of the old régime trotting round the yard of a prison in an Austrian town. Priests, a regional Government chief, a leader of the Fatherland Front, officials of long service and officers with royalist views, whether they had weak hearts or whether they were strong, whether young or old, fat or thin, it mattered not; they were forced to run round and round by the hour. It stands to reason that many an elderly man, corpulent perhaps and asthmatic, broke down under it, and then the SS-man on duty would kick him into getting up and continuing.

The treatment of Colonel C—— is an example of the coarse brutality of these brown beasts. Every day he was asked: " Who are you ?" To which he was forced to reply: " I am a mangy hound." " And why are you a mangy hound ?" " Because I persecuted the National Socialists." He was then struck in the face until mouth and nose started bleeding.

A fifty-year-old priest who suffered from a weak heart collapsed in the prison yard. He raised his hands begging: " For the sake of Christ: I cannot go any further." " Get up, you bloody parson-swine, and keep on running," was the answer.

Am I to give still further instances ? What's the use ? It all occurred in the days after the change-over. One's heart ached at the sight of all the sorrow and misery when the wives of those arrested came to me and begged me to intervene. How many fathers of families were dismissed from their posts and deprived of their pensions for the sole reason that under Schuschnigg they did their duty, obeyed their superiors and intervened when the Nazis started throwing bombs. These are the unemployed and the breadless in Austria now, while the new lords blare forth that unemployment has vanished. And then, what of the Führer's promise: " We shall draw a line under what is past and persecute nobody just because he did, and does, think differently from us ?" Fine phrases, but empty, empty.

MGR. AUREL V. RONAY.

The whole brutality of Nazi " law and order " was exposed when in the winter of 1939-40 the Catholic Poles were evacuated from the area which had been set aside for the Germans. The source of the following facts, based entirely on the evidence of eye-witnesses, is above suspicion:

From the Archdiocese of Gnesen a considerable number of priests, a number steadily increasing, was transported into Germany and there is no further news of them.

In the November of last year 300 families in Gnesen were taken and imprisoned in the warehouse of a leather factory. They had been taken abruptly from their homes, many even from the streets as they returned from church. Seven priests were imprisoned with them and later a further 150 families were added to them. After a time they were all taken off in goods trains to the *General Gouvernement*. Numbers of priests were deported from the Archdiocese of Posen, also to Germany or to the *General Gouvernement*.

The number of Catholic lay-folk, representing all grades of society, but particularly the educated classes, who have been deported with their families and sent to the *General Gouvernement* runs into tens of thousands. All their movable and immovable property has been taken from them, without compensation, without mercy. Conditions in the town of Posen are particularly inhuman. No less a paper than the *Ostdeutscher Beobachter*[1] published the decree framed to prevent anybody from hiding himself and avoiding expulsion. Jews and Poles were forbidden under severe penalty to be outside their dwellings between seven-thirty in the evening and six in the morning, and during this interval the Gestapo would unexpectedly enter first one house and then another and take off the inhabitants in the middle of the night. Each time, some five hundred would be led away and not a few would have to spend the night without sleep or, at least, without being able to take off their clothes, as those who were being taken away were only allowed a few minutes to prepare. The various groups would then have to wait on the streets under an armed guard of the Gestapo until the bus which was going round collecting them arrived, with the result that old and sick people, women and children, would be kept standing about for as long as four hours in a temperature of thirty degrees of frost Fahrenheit. The people would be taken first to a barracks, where they would have to remain with only rotting straw to lie on and without even the most primitive toilet arrangements. The food is unutterably bad, there is a great deal of sickness and numbers die. No food may be sent in from outside. From among these prisoners the men who are strong and healthy are sent to Germany and that is the last heard of them. A considerable portion of the girls are sent off under compulsion in the direction of Berlin. Those who remain, old and sick people mostly, and women and children, are removed after a few days—sometimes a few weeks—and despatched in goods trains to the *General Gouvernement*. The waggons have to remain completely shut throughout the journey, and their occupants are so exposed to the cold and suffer so much from hunger that on every journey several die. Nearly all are ill when the destination is reached.

Attacks on Catholic Bishops

One of the most distressing features of this fight against the Church are the attacks, developing often enough into assaults, on bishops of the Catholic Church. If the reader has any idea of the reverence, the respect, the religious awe which the Catholic people of the German dioceses show to the consecrated successors of the Apostles, if he has ever seen both young and old devoutly kneel to receive his blessing, then he can form some idea of the frightful destruction wrought by Naziism in the hearts of the youth of Germany when he hears how the children of that same people—too often the fanatical sons of sincere Catholic parents—abuse the bishop in chorus, demand his death, crowd round to spit on him, upset his car and so on. Then will the words addressed by a Vicar-General to the Government be understood in their full meaning: " That seed to which the German bishops

[1] December 10th, 1939.

have been calling attention for years we can now with the greatest sorrow watch growing and ripening." In these circumstances it is more easy to understand why the Catholics seize every occasion of paying homage and showing their loyalty to the bishops. The Nazi authorities have on the whole been too nervous to arrest a Catholic bishop, though the reasons they had for arresting priests and laymen held a hundred times more often and with far more force precisely in the case of the bishops. But the Nazis know the loyalty of Catholics to their bishops. In order, therefore, to lessen the esteem in which the bishops are held and the influence which they exercise over Catholic Germans, this anti-Christian system is forced to seek out other ways and means. Its organised—often uniformed—bands, for instance, pretend to represent a people roused to spontaneous indignation, frequently and unfortunately to the detriment of the bishop's health and danger of his life. The reader will find in the following a chronological list of the cases given in authentic reports:

At the beginning of 1935 the murder of Cardinal von Faulhaber was demanded in public meetings in Munich with such cries as, " Hang him; put him up against the wall," without the police taking any action. For example: on February 15th, 1935, at a meeting of the German School Union in which the City School Inspector, Bauer, spoke; at a meeting on June 13th, 1935, in which the speaker was a certain Dr. Engel of the Ludendorff movement; in particular at a meeting of the German Faith Movement on May 17th, 1935, with Backofen, Director for Bavaria, as speaker. After this last meeting three Catholic young men, whose behaviour had been absolutely correct, were knocked unconscious by members of the SS.

On May 12th, 1935, the Archbishop of Paderborn, Mgr. Kaspar Klein, paid a visit to Hamm. On his arrival he was mobbed in the wildest fashion by the Hitler Youth, and the currency ditty and insults shouted in chorus greeted him. The Hitler Youth attempted to prevent the bishop from getting into his car, but, failing in that, as it moved off they jumped on to the running board, spat inside, tried to overturn it and attacked with their " dirks of honour " some Catholics who tried to protect their bishop. They then marched off to the St. Agnes-Kirchplatz and furiously shouted insults in chorus against the Church and the priests, so that the address of welcome to the Archbishop had to be abandoned. The flying squad arrived, but only when everything was over. After the bishop had entered the church the bawling and shouting went on for a long time outside on the church square and the church door was repeatedly hammered on. The whole disgraceful scene had been carefully prepared and songs and chorus-shouting practised beforehand. Hitler Youth leaders from Dortmund and Hamm took part in it.

Bishop Bornewasser of Trier had rendered great services to the German cause during the plebiscite activities in the Saar Territory. In June, 1937, despite his seventy-two years, he was the object of deliberately organised, ferocious protestations in several parts of the

Hunsrück area and it was with great difficulty that a strong force of police prevented bodily harm being done to him. Two years previously, on May 26th, 1934, he had been subjected by the Hitler Youth to outrageous insults and interferences at the end of a Confirmation service in Kreuznach.

On July 20th, 1935, the Bishop of Münster was due to administer Confirmation in the Sacred Heart parish in Hamm, where it was the custom on these occasions for the Bishop to be met and conducted to the church by four mounted men. This was forbidden by the police. The parish priest then applied for at least the permission for the Bishop to give an address in the church square, as a large number of the faithful was expected and the church would be filled by the six hundred odd Confirmation candidates. The permission was not granted.

On July 20th the people living in the Münsterstrasse had decorated their houses with flags and garlands for the passage of the Bishop. At six in the morning the police arrived and ordered the removal of the decorations. Later on, however, the people put the decorations back, and the more they were interfered with the more enthusiastic they became. When the Bishop arrived he was met at the town boundary by a large flying-squad car and four smaller cars full of police and accompanied by them to the church. They remained in the church square all day and went with the Bishop to the schools. Nobody was allowed to remain standing except in the church square, and even there the police tried to make the people move on or go into the already overcrowded church. Secret Police were present in the church during the administering of Confirmation and the sermon. The Bishop on leaving the church was greeted with an immense ovation, and it was in vain that the police tried to suppress it. When the Bishop arrived at the steps up into the presbytery he turned to say a few words of thanks, but was stopped by a police secretary who jumped up and called out aloud: " Your Excellency is not allowed to speak."

The insult to which the Archbishop of Freiburg was subjected in September, 1935, may be gathered from the following protest issued by the Vicar-General of the archdiocese:

ARCHBISHOP'S HOUSE,
FREIBURG IM BREISGAU,
September 26th, 1935.
No. 14091.

Inscriptions on the Walls of Ecclesiastical Buildings in Freiburg.

On Saturday night, September 21st, 1935, unknown persons inscribed the following expressions on buildings in Freiburg:

1. On the wall of the presbytery of the Maria Hilf Church: " Hang the black traitors." The writing is 60 feet long and 3 feet high.

2. On the garden wall of the theological students' hostel: " Down with the black wire-pullers," with the head of a priest drawn on the left, and on the right what, to judge from the head apparel, is likewise meant to be a priest. The letters cover a space of 45 by 3 feet.

3. On the yard wall of the Studer prebendary house, opposite the chancel of the minster, the words : " Away from Rome," measuring 24 by 3 feet.

4. On the two pillars flanking the entrance to the archiepiscopal residence: " Away from Rome."

This is a grievous insult to the Archbishop and the Catholic clergy. It is an incitement to abandon the Faith and to acts of violence against priests. We have therefore made formal complaint to the competent authorities in Karlsruhe and Berlin. Such occurrences will, we hope, only help to increase the devotion of Catholics to their Church and to strengthen her divinely appointed superiors.

This protest is to be read at Holy Mass on Sunday, September 29th.

Signed: RÖSCH (*Vicar-General*).

During May and June, 1936, in Munich: In a meeting of the German Faith Movement on the eve of Corpus Christi the Corpus Christi procession was referred to as " Faulhaber's route march." In other public meetings, for instance in the beer-halls of the Löwenbräu and the Bürgerbräu, shouts were continually heard of " Down with Faulhaber," " Hang him," " Shoot him," " Send him to Dachau " (a notorious concentration camp), and no measures were taken to suppress them. About the same time a certain Dr. Schott gave lectures in Munich and exhibited in the course of them a portrait of the " Grand Penitentiary " with the question: " Does anybody notice a similarity to a certain person ? Imagine the beard not there. . . ." There was a pause until somebody called out: " Faulhaber." " The name wasn't mentioned by me," declared the speaker, while those present at the meeting shouted in a frenzy: " Hang him," " Shoot him," and so on.

Witnesses described the abuse with which Cardinal von Faulhaber was met outside the Holy Cross Church in Giesing, Munich, on October 25th, 1936. About a dozen men and youths surrounded the Cardinal's car and with whistling, swearing and vulgar expressions tried to drown the cheers of the faithful. After the Cardinal had entered the car, one of the louts endeavoured to break the window next to him with his fist.

The lawless excesses and personal attacks on the Bishop of Rottenburg, Mgr. Sproll, received only brief notice in the foreign press. They were, however, described in an official ecclesiastical announcement which was read in several German dioceses on the last Sunday of July, 1938. The most important passages are reproduced here:

Following instructions from the Holy See, Dr. John B. Sproll, Bishop of Rottenburg, returned to his diocese on Friday, July 15th. He informed the Reich Governor of his return. On July 16th he sang the traditional Solemn Requiem for his predecessors in the Cathedral and on the evening of the same day the Bishop's house was the scene of the wildest excesses, which extended also to the offices of the Diocesan Administration. In the afternoon information had already been secretly brought in. Towards a quarter to eight in the evening about 100 young people, few of them from Rottenburg itself, gathered in the *Hindenburgplatz* in front of the stone steps. First for an entire hour they shouted out various slogans in chorus, many of which were also exhibited on placards: " Bishop Sproll, traitor to his country," " Down with the traitor," " We want a German bishop," " Who's got his trousers full ? Bishop Sproll." The more they shouted the more excited they became. Repeated attacks were made on the doors of the

Bishop's residence, and eventually about nine o'clock an entrance was forced into it through the chancellery. The crowd then scattered over all parts of the first and second floors, where the Blessed Sacrament was reserved. A group of them came shouting and yelling and entered the chapel, but when they saw the Bishop kneeling in front of the altar, they hesitated and then withdrew, making contemptuous remarks. The domestic chapel was then shut. Shortly afterwards a second party arrived in front of the chapel and forced the door in such a way as to lift it from its hinges and throw it inwards. This party likewise withdrew when they saw the Bishop in prayer. Finally, the editor of the *Flammenzeichen* of Stuttgart with five others appeared. He approached the kneeling Bishop and accosted him with the advice to leave. The Bishop replied: " I shall not discuss the matter with you, least of all here in the chapel. I shall not leave the chapel, and will die rather than do so."

While this scene was going on in the chapel, the rest of the intruders ransacked the offices and private portions of the Bishop's abode. Boxes were opened, bedding thrown about and doors damaged. Somebody took a white Mass vestment from a cupboard, dragged it about through several rooms and left it on a table. After this had gone on for more than an hour, the mob left the palace when ordered to do so by its leaders. One heard, for instance: " Get out now, the police will arrest him." Outside somebody shouted: " The Bishop says he won't go. We'll come again and go on coming till he leaves Rottenburg." The *Horst Wessel* song and *Deutschland über Alles* were then sung and the demonstrators marched off. About ten o'clock an official of the Stuttgart Gestapo rang up the Vicar-General and asked for an appointment. When this had been granted, he expressed the wish to speak with the Bishop himself and said: " I have been ordered to advise you most earnestly that, under the circumstances, you should not remain any longer in Rottenburg. The demonstrations will be repeated." The Bishop replied: " I have strict orders from the Holy See to return to my diocese. I am Bishop of Rottenburg and I shall remain in Rottenburg." The Gestapo officer repeated his advice, but the Bishop would not go back on what he had decided and added still more emphatically: " I shall remain, even if I lose my life in doing so." After the interview the official inspected the damage done by the demonstrators and then departed shortly before midnight.

On July 18th another demonstration occurred. This time the demonstrators numbered between 1,500 and 2,000 and again the majority had come in from other places. The demonstration gave the impression of being well ordered. It began punctually at nine o'clock and finished after ten. In chorus the Bishop was denounced as being a traitor to the country, a black gypsy, a whore's boy and suchlike, and the demand was made that he should leave the town. One of the demonstrators made a speech and said: National Socialism is not persecuting the Faith or the Church, but is merely trying to prevent their being used for political purposes. The people were being given the freedom they so earnestly desired, before National Socialism had released them from the compulsion exercised by the Church. Germany was a land of law and order, the speaker emphasised, and then urged the crowd to keep discipline. Songs were then sung and the threat made: " We shall keep on coming till the Bishop goes." It was repeatedly shouted: " We're not going without the Bishop. He's got to be hanged." No entrance was forced into the residence, but windows were broken with very large stones. In the Bishop's study alone were four large stones which had broken the windows and covered the room with splinters of glass. On this occasion likewise the police did not intervene.

A third demonstration occurred on the evening of July 23rd. The District Administrator of Rottenburg and the Gestapo of Stuttgart knew of it beforehand, and later the Public Prosecutor in Tübingen, informed by telephone, was asked for police protection for the person and dwelling of the Bishop, but, in spite of all this, no counter-measures were taken. Those taking part in the demonstration, who had been brought from as much as thirty miles away in cars and buses, formed up at various points for a procession through the town. Four columns, in all some three thousand men, converged on to the Bishop's house, to the tune of the marching-song, " Put the Parsons up against the Wall." It was past nine o'clock when the demonstration began with the letting off of fireworks, so-called cannons, and then there followed a deafening roar of shouting, whistling, howling and the usual threats and abuse. It was obviously the intention to secure the person of the Bishop, who had taken what precautions he could by fastening all the doors and windows so that they should be able to withstand any ordinary attempts to enter. Soon, however, several window shutters were broken and door panels were rammed and burst in and some sixty or seventy men got in through the openings. The intruders got into the offices and study, threw papers and documents out of the window, and the situation became serious when the smell of burning was noticed, but one of the inmates of the house found the bed in a guest-room on fire, and succeeded in throwing the burning parts out of the window. The demonstrators forced their way into the chapel also. Here they found the Archbishop of Freiburg, who had arrived in Rottenburg, with the Bishop, the Vicar-General and some of the Cathedral canons, all in prayer before the Blessed Sacrament exposed. The Archbishop was subjected to some annoyance and the chapel door was taken off its hinges and carried out into the corridor. One of the canons, who had put himself in front of the Blessed Sacrament in order to defend it, was told by one of the demonstrators that the blacks would have to get out of Germany, to which remark another added: " Yes, with a free ticket to Moscow." For something like a quarter of an hour about twenty of these people remained in the chapel, some of them smoking cigars and cigarettes and with their hats on their heads. They departed only when the police came and drove them gradually out of the house. At a word of command the formations which were outside likewise moved off.[1]

From a protest of the Diocesan Administration of Freiburg concerning the coarse utterances of the Area Leader Dr. Fritsch against Archbishop Gröber and Bishop Sproll, the Swiss paper *Schaffhauser Zeitung*[2] printed the following extract:

Area Leader Dr. Fritsch, according to reliable information, made the following statements before a thousand political leaders of the Freiburg district in the Festhalle at Freiburg on August 28th, 1938:

Dr. Fritsch put the question whether a Catholic could be a National Socialist. To such a one, he said, he would propose two questions:

1. What was his attitude towards the Old Testament, which was a product of Jewish mentality; in fact, the only one.

2. Whether he agreed with the racial doctrine. In which case the words " Go ye into the whole world " became a dead letter.

The " old gentleman " in Rome had recognised that all right. With Kaffirs and such rabble we could not share the same ideology. It was a tremendous victory for the National Socialist way of thinking when the racial idea was adopted in Italy. It was thanks only to the National Socialist sense of discipline that the ideological war in Freiburg was being conducted in such a gentlemanly fashion. For the same reason the Archbishop should be thankful that he was still able to reside in his house and had not already received the proper answer to his goings-on. This " ragamuffin " was spreading lying statements in the foreign press, and that was high treason. Raising his voice, the speaker continued: " Here and with all publicity I call him a knave, a liar and a traitor to his country. I hope he brings an

[1] Concerning the third demonstration on July 23rd, 1938, *Der Deutsche in Polen* printed (August 14th, 1938) a copy of the authentic information sent by the diocesan authorities to the Reichsminister for Ecclesiastical Affairs.
[2] September 13th, 1938.

action against me, so that we can at last get a chance to say in open court what we've got against him."

Dr. Fritsch continued: We would have done that long ago on our own initiative, but we want to avoid making bishop-martyrs. He then turned his attention to press statements of Thursday and Friday in the *Freiburger Zeitung* and *Alemanne* that Bishop Sproll had been residing at Freiburg for the last few days. He said that Freiburg was no asylum for traitors. " If the gentleman does not clear out within the next few days, then we shall see to it that he gets the same treatment here as in Rottenburg. We shall not be short of the necessary men. And when it comes to that, the second gent will go with him. And why hasn't it been done already ? Not because we hadn't got the courage—no courage is required to chase wops out anyhow—but because we didn't want to dirty our fingers on such swine."

The speaker then proceeded to deal with the coming Party Congress, the yearly pilgrimage of the Party members and the " unique religious experience " of gazing on the Führer. He encouraged the leaders not to tire or let themselves be disheartened by failure in minor conflicts. One thing at least the Pope had discerned with accuracy when he said that there could never be a compromise between the Swastika and the Christian Cross of the Roman Catholic Church.

Fight without compromise, without concern for success or failure. The youth will carry on the fight. If one could write on one's grave-stone the saying of Hutten's, *Ich hab's gewagt* (I have dared to do it), one would certainly have held one's own better than those who always ran to the Church.

There is no need to draw attention to the very poor service indeed which such utterances render to the true national unity of the German people. They have caused profound sorrow and bitterness in the widest circles. There is, for instance, a letter to Bishop Sproll[1] which reveals the inner feelings of disgust of even SA-members who had been ordered to attend and take part in the Rottenburg excesses:

YOUR EXCELLENCY,
There is something for which I ask your pardon. I was one of those present last Saturday—not, indeed, of my own free will, but there by order. I have always been proud of my country, but last Saturday I was, for the first time, ashamed to call myself a German. And a number of the comrades of my section think the same as I do. We were ashamed of ourselves for having—without our knowledge—allowed ourselves to be used for such a scandalous affair. When those who share my opinions were quite alone after the return from Rottenburg, we gave free vent to our indignation. What we thought was: now we see why the Bishop abstained from voting. By staging this demonstration the Party has given us an involuntary proof that you acted rightly on April 10th. The fact alone that the SA had to attend in civilian dress indicated that the Party itself had the feeling that what was happening was not the proper thing for the " dress of honour " of the SA. Anybody with a spark of decency remaining in him ought to be ashamed of the things that happened last Saturday evening in Rottenburg. I come from .... I am an SA-man and, apart from that, I am also ...... so you will understand that under the circumstances I do not sign my name, for I cannot tell who might get hold of my letter. But I had to write to you to ease my conscience, and perhaps these lines will compensate you in some small way for the outrage committed on you. You have proved by the courage you have shown that you are a German bishop to the core.
Yours sincerely,
N. N.

[1] Printed in *Ostschweiz* October 13th, 1938. It was received by the bishop a few days after the incidents to which it refers.

258 REFUSAL OF LEGAL PROTECTION FOR CHURCH

At the end of November, 1938, reports circulated in the foreign press concerning a demonstration of National Socialists against Cardinal Faulhaber, in which windows of the archiepiscopal residence had been broken. *Der Deutsche in Polen* of November 27th, 1938, published a report of an eye-witness which shows that the affair was by no means so trivial.

" The demonstrations," says the report, " were of a very serious nature. It was also no mere chance that they followed on a speech of Wagner, the District Leader and Bavarian Minister of State, who can be looked upon as instigator of the disgraceful behaviour. Wagner made a speech in the Krone Circus which was relayed to loud-speakers in twenty other halls in Munich and its environs, in the course of which he said: ' It would not surprise me if this sort of thing happened to Cardinal Faulhaber ' (viz., acts of destruction which had taken place the previous day in the Munich business quarter). These were his actual words and they show plainly enough that a licence, as it were, had been granted for what happened in consequence the following day.

" During the day there were rumours that there were going to be demonstrations against Cardinal Faulhaber that evening. They found their way into the archiepiscopal residence and police headquarters were informed so that the necessary steps could be taken. Copies of this communication to the police were sent to the Reich Governor, Ritter von Epp, and to the Bavarian Government. Herr Wagner did not omit to read out at the meeting the communication from the archiepiscopal authorities and to add some odious comments of his own. The concern expressed in the communication was completely justified, as can be seen from the report of eye-witnesses present at the incidents in front of the archiepiscopal palace:

"Shortly after ten o'clock, immediately after the meeting in the Krone Circus, uniformed detachments in motor-cars and on motor-cycles, about seventy in number, arrived in front of the residence of Cardinal Faulhaber. As if at a word of command a hail of stones was directed against the windows, while the men shouted such insulting expressions as: ' Take the hound into protective custody,' ' Take the rotten traitor to Dachau.' And in imitation of Catholic gatherings: ' We want to see our Bishop,' ' Dear Bishop, be so good as to come and show yourself at the window.' In the meantime material for throwing at the windows was gathered from a bank opposite, where building alterations were in progress, and next morning the domestic chapel was scattered with it, some of the bricks thrown having penetrated as far as the walls opposite the windows. With crowbars and baulks of wood the window frames and shutters were shattered, but the ' brown heroes ' could not get in on account of the iron bars. So orders were given to bring an iron cart from the builders' place and an attempt was made to ram the heavy oak doors, but it failed on account of the beam fastening them from the inside. Then the demonstrators started shouting again: ' Come out, you swine,' ' The blighter ought to be hanged,' and other remarks too bad to be printed here. A woman who said, ' It's no use, he's not inside,' was knocked down and remained bleeding on the ground. This Nazi élite kept up their ferocious demonstration for nearly an hour till the flying squad arrived[1] and forced them off into the side street, but, as usual when ' the German people gives expression to its indignation,' no arrests were made."

The peak of the attacks of the Nazi hordes against the Catholic Bishops was reached with the excesses of Saturday, October 8th, 1938,

---

[1] *Translator's Note.*—The Cardinal's residence in Munich is only a few hundred yards away from the headquarters of the flying squad.

in the residence of Cardinal Innitzer in Vienna. The following was published in the *Osservatore Romano* of October 15th, 1938:

On Friday, October 7th, a service for Catholic youth took place in St. Stephen's Cathedral. The Cardinal Archbishop also gave a sermon in which he encouraged the young in their faith and religious activities, and when he left the Cathedral some six thousand of them gave expression to their loyalty and sang the hymn to the Sacred Heart. The Hitler Youth and the SA had gathered there, too, and started counter-shouts and whistling: " Down with Innitzer. Our faith is Germany." The young Catholics were numerically the stronger, but they made no answer and dispersed quite quietly. In spite of that, bands of SA-men gathered together in front of the Bishop's residence and staged noisy demonstrations with the shout that the Cardinal should be taken to Dachau. They next tried to break in the door of the residence, but the police intervened to protect it and it was not until towards eleven o'clock in the evening that the demonstrators, with rowdy threats, left the place.

The next day, Saturday, October 8th, at eight-fifteen in the evening, the demonstrations started again from all sides, including the Rotenturmstrasse, so that the residence was entirely surrounded. Stones came from all directions, and all the windows were broken. Again and again the police were asked for assistance, as the demonstrators were endeavouring to break in, and several police stations promised to give aid. In spite of this, however, the heavy door was broken a quarter of an hour later and a disorderly crowd poured in, destroying everything they came across in the antechambers and on the staircase. The inmates of the residence hurried towards the chapel to the Cardinal's protection. It was feared that the Blessed Sacrament would be the object of a sacrilege and a priest consumed the Sacred Hosts—and indeed it was high time, for the intruders had reached the episcopal chapel, struck a secretary of the Cardinal unconscious, destroyed the statue of a saint and, pursuing their vandalism, stormed the study of the Cardinal, where they broke open a writing table and smashed a crucifix. The purple pectoral cross and ring of the Cardinal were stolen, and everywhere the furniture was smashed, pictures slashed and objects of art demolished. The Archbishop's Master of Ceremonies was hit on the head with a candelabra, and one of the priests was dragged to the window and only just saved from being thrown out. As he pluckily defended the chapel the mob shouted: " Well, was it better under Schuschnigg?" and other insults.

At length the rumour spread among them that the police were on their way and that they had better disperse. The withdrawal then began, but not before they had demanded from the inmates of the residence a signed statement never to say a word about what had happened. Not one of the intruders, who left singing *Deutschland über Alles,* was in any way interfered with on going out, and one solitary arrest was made. (This was the correspondent of *The Times.*) One of the broken clocks had stopped at five minutes past nine—the police had taken no less than forty minutes to reach the inner region of the town.

The crowd had insulted the Cardinal in a most violent and vulgar way. His life had, indeed, been saved, but in another house of the Cathedral *Curia* very brutal things had occurred. The house was first thoroughly damaged and then a curate, Fr. Kravarnik, was taken and thrown out of a window. He was seriously injured, and it is said that both his legs were broken so that his life is in danger.

Outside on the square the Cardinal's purple mantle, some articles of personal use, furniture, carpets, etc., were burnt. The outrages were not reported in any of the Vienna newspapers.

It would be difficult to imagine anything more cynical than the speech made by Bürckel, the Reichskommissar, some eight days later on the *Heldenplatz* in Vienna to " explain " these outrages. The staffs of the various works were compelled to attend the meeting. On large banners were to be read inscriptions such as:

" The parsons to the gallows ! "
" Down with the clergy ! "
" To Dachau with Innitzer ! "
" To hell with the Jesuits ! "
" To build up Germany, we shall use
 No help from Rome nor from the Jews."
" The members of our firm have left the Church *en bloc*."

Reichskommissar Bürckel stated that the reports published abroad concerning the events of the previous Friday and Saturday were twisted and distorted, and that the actual facts were as follows: A number of political clergy had endeavoured to work the people up to a *putsch* against the Government which had not succeeded, and on the following evening a group of young men had marched to the archiepiscopal residence, where a few excesses had taken place. From the Government's point of view there had been disturbances of public order—a prohibited political demonstration on the one side and a few excesses on the other.

The speaker then accused Cardinal Innitzer of having tried to come to terms after the Anschluss because at the time the political power of the Church was at a low ebb. In reality, however, the entire Austrian clergy was only waiting for a political opportunity, and a few days ago a conference of these clerical politicians had decided on calling the people to a demonstration for the Faith, which was nothing else but a political demonstration. Innitzer had openly exposed his political aims.

In conclusion Bürckel declared that discussions and negotiations with the clergy had now finished for good and he then announced a series of measures.

In view of the fact that the majority of those who had taken part in the demonstrations had been Jews and Czechs, he, Bürckel, had decided:

1. That all Jews of Czech citizenship and Czechs without an entirely clean record would be given the shortest notice to quit Vienna.

2. That the intention entertained till recently of permitting the Church, in spite of everything, to retain one or other *petit séminaire* would now be abandoned, since the recent exhibition on the part of the political clergy gave no guarantee that the boys in them would be brought up decently.

3. That the amnesty which, on account of the great victory in the Sudeten districts, had been planned for denominational politicians would now have to be postponed.

4. That the various sections of the clergy who had petitioned for the release of Schuschnigg should see Innitzer about it (*i.e.*, that there was now no question of release—*Translator's note*).

Relations between Party and Church are henceforth to be governed by the following:

Religious matters are the private affair of the individual. Anybody profaning a crucifix or suchlike object makes himself thereby an enemy of National Socialism. If anybody wants to go to church, let him go. If he doesn't, let it be a matter for his own conscience. But any church, as the house of God, in which the Führer or the National Socialist cause is condemned is not the place for a National Socialist.

On November 8th, 1938, the Bishop of Münster, Mgr. von Galen, went to several parishes in the deanery of Sterkrade to administer the Sacrament of Confirmation. On his arrival a short service was held in the parish church and afterwards the Bishop walked slowly to the Dean's house, blessing the crowd as he went. He had gone a few yards in this fashion, when suddenly a police inspector rushed up to him and informed him haughtily that he couldn't proceed in this style blessing the people, but would have to take to his car, and about twenty policemen appeared at the same time to back their chief in case of need. The Bishop was indignant and replied: " Nowhere in the whole diocese has anyone yet denied my right to go about accompanied by my priests. Your conduct is doing more harm to the cause you stand for than you imagine, and I demand to go home in this fashion." " And I forbid you to," the police inspector shouted back at him. " You have got to take the car."

In the meantime the crowd, aware now of what was going on, began to throng round the Bishop and the policemen and finally to assume such a hostile attitude towards the police that the latter thought it better to let the Bishop proceed in his own way. However, the police inspector obviously wanted to preserve some of his authority, so he forbade the Mass servers to remain in the procession. The people crowding the square hurrahed the Bishop so that the lusty cheering could be heard a long way away and, much moved, the Bishop continued on his way blessing the people until he reached the Dean's house. The cheering continued, and when the Bishop entered the house the crowd started chanting in chorus: " We want to see our Bishop." After some time he appeared at a window and addressed the crowd in a strong voice: " I shall give you my blessing and after that you must all disperse quietly to your homes." Everybody knelt down, received the Bishop's blessing in dead silence and then went quietly away.

In May, 1939, abusive demonstrations against Cardinal von Faulhaber were renewed in several places in Bavaria. An authentic report says:

1. In Gars, whither the Cardinal went to give Confirmation on May 8th, and at Wang, where he was to consecrate a church on May 9th, 1939, there were to be encountered at several places along the way large painted inscriptions: " We don't want him, the traitor Faulhaber." The parish priest of Gars made a very strong protest about it.

2. On Tuesday, May 23rd, and on Wednesday, May 24th, Confirmation was due to be administered in Mühldorf on the Inn, where the Mayor was a former Protestant pastor who, for three days, had been Bishop of the German Christians.

During the night before the first day of the Confirmations the really simple decorations at the entrance to the parish church and to the presbytery were torn down. During the night before the second Confirmation day posters were fixed up at seven or eight points round the town displaying: " Away with Faulhaber, the friend of the Jews and the agent of Moscow."[1] The entrance to the presbytery garden was smeared with paint and above the door were written the words, " Priest swine," flanked by two Swastikas. A board full of mortar was fixed up against the door in such a way as to fall on the head of the first person coming out, and this happened to the parish priest Fr. Altinger.

When in June, 1939, Cardinal Innitzer journeyed through the northern parts of Lower Austria for visitation and Confirmation purposes he was subjected to such outrages and mobbings that he decided to break off his journey. When he was administering the sacrament of Confirmation in Nieder-Russbach, the godless Brown Shirts kept up an inferno of noise outside the church all during the service, and in Ziersdorf the windows of the presbytery where the Cardinal was staying were broken, as well as the windows of his car.

In Königsbrunn these disgraceful scenes reached a climax. The Cardinal preached on peace. Crowds of Nazis outside shouted: " Take him off to Dachau. He is talking of peace and means war. Away with the political priests." In order to avoid further incidents the Cardinal covered his dress with the parish priest's cape and left the church. He was recognised, however, by a teacher, who gave the signal for attack, and was bombarded with rotten eggs and potatoes and struck at with umbrellas, while shouts were raised: " Cardinal, your hands are dripping with the blood of Holzweber and Planetta " (the executed murderers of Dolfuss).

The great number of these incidents gives some indication of the results that the unrestrained National Socialist agitation produces in certain sections—not, indeed, the best—of the population of Germany. It has happened, though not often, in German history that in a conflict between Church and State—the *Kulturkampf* of the 1870s, for instance—Catholic bishops were punished, imprisoned and expelled. But in the whole course of German history never till now have Catholic bishops been attacked by the street rabble and threatened with death. The merit of having brought about this state of affairs belongs to Church-hating National Socialism.

[1] *Cf.* illustration opposite.

CHAPTER X

ATTACKS ON THE HONOUR OF THE CHURCH

NATIONAL Socialism regards honour as one of the most valuable of national possessions and the ruling party does its utmost to implant a deep-rooted esteem for honour in the mind of the people. For all that, the fact is that it is precisely in the Third Reich that the honour of the Church may be trampled underfoot with impunity. If anything, that is very much of an under-statement. For, where the defamation of the Catholic Church is concerned, the Nazis are not merely passive spectators: they are the very ones whose deliberate aim it is to wipe out the Church's good name.

The Nazis know quite well what they are about. If honour is a thing of outstanding value for the individual, something that enables its possessor to live a decently human life as a member of a community, it is doubly so for an institution like the Church, which has a religious and moral character. A Church deprived of its honour or a Church whose official representatives are held up to the public as dishonourable, hypocrites, secret criminals and the like is bound to lose, sooner or later, all moral credit and with it all influence over its members and over outsiders.

And that is precisely what the Nazis are out to achieve. They have no use for a Church that is alive and influential. Hence, the defamation of the Church is part of the plan of campaign and the destruction of her good name is a strategic objective. To achieve this purpose every means in their power is brought into play with a singleness of aim that is utterly ruthless and a cunning that is utterly without scruple. We have met it before.

Hence we observe that it is the official organs of the State and of the Party that launch the chief attack on the honour of the Church. All the means for influencing public opinion that an all-powerful State has at its disposal are set in motion to bring the Church, her leading personalities and her ordinances into contempt.

While the conflict as a whole in all its length and breadth will be dealt with in the second part, our chief concern at present is to bring together defamatory measures that bear a more official character, for which in consequence the State and its officials are strictly responsible. We shall enumerate in the form of a brief statement of fact a series of malicious attacks which are brought home to the public in a large variety of ways—on posters, in songs, in films and on the stage, in public speeches, in demonstrations and in the Press. In most cases comment would be superfluous.

ATTACKS ON THE HONOUR OF THE CHURCH

The Church is defamed—

1. *By Posters*

In the summer of 1935 there was a poster, " German People ! Attention !" which was highly offensive to the Church and to every Catholic. This was stuck up on many presbyteries, private houses and even on churches—on the *Dom* at Passau, for instance. If the proprietor ventured to remove the placard from his own property he was punished.

In August, 1935, likewise, SA-men affixed to the *Dom* in Würzburg a poster bearing abuse and insulting caricatures of the Catholic clergy. In the same August posters were stuck up in the public squares of Bad Tölz. They bore the following legend:

" Rome for the Parsons,
Palestine for the Jews,
But Germany for the Germans."

The following poster, meant to be an answer to the Fulda Pastoral of August, 1935, was affixed to the fire station at Frauenberg (Bavaria) on September 1st of that year:

A Preliminary Explanation of Today's Pastoral.

1. The authors of this composition have repeatedly violated the Concordat they are so fond of quoting, and *by this very Pastoral* they have done so once again.
2. No one asks people to leave the Church—a flat lie of the Bishops.
3. Religious gatherings outside the Church have never been forbidden. Look at today's procession. So—lie No. 2.
4. The Press publishes articles as formerly. Lie No. 3.
5. The assertion about pagan propaganda is a dirty lie.
6. It is precisely the National Socialists who uphold the sacredness of Marriage; look at the Free Love and the Abortion clause of the Parties linked with political Catholicism.
7. The attacks on the tribunals set up against currency wanglers can be proved from documentary evidence.
8. Attacks on the Hitler Youth. Members of the Hitler Youth are always enabled to practise their religious duties.

The whole Pastoral is a piece of calumnious agitation and shows very little Christian charity.

Heil Hitler !

In July, 1937, there appeared on the poster of the *Stürmer* in Forstenried (Bavaria) a caricature of Cardinal Faulhaber; in August there was a caricature of Cardinal Pacelli, at that time Secretary of State. The latter is turning round and saying to a Communist who is bearing his red train: "Thank you for your help; I'll give you my blessing for it afterwards."

In the shop window of the Ludendorff Book Company in Munich there is an almost continuous display of posters containing the dirtiest gibes against the Church and against priests. Take, for instance, the bill that recommends the book " The Pope enjoys Himself " (by W. Löhde, RM. 2.85). At the bottom we read:

Pius II (1458-64) led a dissolute life and wrote erotic poems. When he was Pope and grown old he wrote: "I can no longer serve the pleasure of any woman nor can any minister to mine. Wine is my food, my joy and my diversion; it is the source of all my happiness. Truth to tell, Venus flees from me more than I from her."

On the large poster itself there is a picture of a smiling Pope in full pontificals surrounded by various heads that peep out from behind his vestments.

2. *In Songs*

The following abusive ditty was regularly practised and sung by numerous groups of the Hitler Youth and other formations in the year 1935; it was, for instance, given out at the *Hochland* camp of the Hitler Youth at Lenggries—*and* to Catholic members.

> Autumn's storm blows o'er the stubble
> And rages o'er fallow and mead;
> A new thousand years begins for the world,
> Oh, *Deutschland* creative, take heed.
>
> The Pope sits in Rome on his silk-covered throne
> And settled on us are his parsons.
> And what, pray, has any man-jack of us all
> To do with the Pope and his parsons?
>
> Our sires were as heretics burnt at the stake
> To crown the Church mil'tant with glory;
> The deserts of Asia and Palestine's soil
> With life-blood of Germans was gory.
>
> With blood of the Saxon the Aller ran red,
> And slain were the brave men of Steding;
> And monks took the peasants' poor chattels abroad,
> In exchange their indulgences shedding.
>
> The years passed away, but the parson stayed on
> The German to rob of his might;
> And, Romish or Lutheran maketh no odds,
> Spread always the old Jewish light.
>
> The years of the Cross are in truth past recall,
> And sunlight begins for us now;
> So we shall be free with the help of the Lord
> With honour our land to endow.
>
> No go-between need we to bring us to Heaven—
> The sun and the stars light our way.
> And, even to Heaven, Blood, Sunshine and Sword
> Are with us, allies in the fray.

Das Schwarze Korps published in its edition of June 12th, 1935, a currency ditty. Here are a few stanzas:

> While Brother Medardus strode over the land
> His feats to perform brave and big,
> On an endless conveyor were prayers rattled off
> In the Abbey of Thing-a-ma-jig.
>
> They fasted (in spirit), did penance and prayed;
> "Will he pull the thing off?" then they hollered:
> "O Lord, do Thou watch o'er these marks" (umpteen thou.),
> And meantime Medardus was collared.

266 ATTACKS ON THE HONOUR OF THE CHURCH

> The Prior in a tantrum went scarlet and cursed
> Old Medardus: " Now we'll be pinched. Yes,
> Th' eleventh commandment went out of your head:
> ' Thou shalt not be found out ' 's what it says.
>
> Foreign Exchange ? Well, Brother, you know
> What the laws of the Index enact.''
> " O Father, O holy Simplicity," quoth
> Medardus, " I'll swear to the fact."

Since 1935 they have been singing the following song in the Hitler Youth and other formations:

> The old Jewish mess is swept up at last,
> But the gang of Black Racketeers still holds on fast.
> Oh, German *Volk*, is this to be ?
> Shall these Black Swine still spit at thee ?
> If not, then beat 'em up, till high
> The sparks fly up into the sky.
> Hall', Hallo. . . .
>
> German men and women all,
> Enough of this Faulhaber tack;
> German men and women all,
> Pulverise this riff-raff black.
> And if, just like stuck pigs, they squeal,
> Stick in 'em something they will feel !
> Hall', Hallo. . . .
>
> Every faith we honour, although it be not ours,
> But no one's going to rob us of what we dearly prize.
> The German *Volk*, the *deutscher Gott*,
> Tower high above the parson's rot;
> And rogues who wallow in this sludge
> We'll batter till they cannot budge.
> Hall', Hallo. . . .
>
> To honest German brothers we'll give a friendly paw;
> For agitating clerics—a sock right on the jaw !
> 'Twill soon be light, 'tis break of day,
> And Judas soon will have his pay,
> Strung up on the gallows rude—
> 'Tis what he's asked for—ravens' food !
> Until he swings upon the tree,
> We shall not from such rogues be free.
> Hall', Hallo. . . .

The following song was sung by the Hitler Youth in a Württemberg village on the children's Confirmation day in the summer of 1935:

> The " blacks " are all seducers,
> They fight not for their home;
> As ever they are liars,
> They fight for wealth and Rome.
>
> 'Tis clerics make " Reaction "
> And good-for-nothings—so
> Let's beat up all the traitors
> Nor any mercy show.

The following *Divisenschieber-Lied* (Currency Ditty) has had a tremendous vogue since 1935. It has been rehearsed and sung in

IN SONGS

public in every part of Germany by various National Socialist formations, especially by the Hitler Youth.

> When first they went a-smuggling
> To Holland, three they were,
> A Father and two brothers,
> All currency smugglers,
> A nun was also there.
>
> But when they journeyed further,
> Ah ! Now they were but three,
> The priest in quod, the dodger,
> They'd necked him well, the codger;
> The joke was his to see.
>
> The nun she whispered softly,
> " It's your turn now, me fears."
> And his head shaven bald,
> When at judgement day he's called,
> Will shine—an arse with ears.
>
> And when they gained the frontier,
> Ah ! here the brother's hoard
> Was snaffled by a copper,
> And now the pious brother
> Has lodging free, with board.
>
> The nun and t'other brother
> Went on, and she and he
> Made prayer in accents greedy:
> " Grant, Lord, Thy clergy needy
> Their foreign currency."
>
> The last one then was collared
> And locked up safe in clink.
> " Thy neighbour shalt thou cherish,"
> And not for treason perish—
> So from money-smuggling shrink.
>
> The Pope at Heaven's portals
> Salutes him with a kiss:
> " Come in, you money-clearer,
> To me there's no one dearer;
> We'll have a drink on this."
>
> The thing got to the papers:
> There was a fine to-do.
> The Bishop's Mass was solemn,
> His great gob . . .

Here is a similar effort which was printed and distributed to the people during the SA propaganda tour in Freising on August 18th, 1935:

> "Adieu," the maiden murmurs:
> Clangs fast the convent door.
> The Pope gives her the order
> To smuggle o'er the border
> The coin he needs so sore.
>
> And as they went a-smuggling
> The company was three.
> A priest and two lay brothers
> Composed this gang of smugglers—
> The nun was with the three.

And as they journeyed onward
Survived now only two:
The priest caught by the collar
Was left in jail to holler.
The joke was wearing through.

" Ah ! like a backside bordered
With ears," she whispers sweet,
" Your pate shines cleanly shaven.
Ah, comrade, be not craven
The heavenly judge to meet."

The following song above all was sung in the Hitler Youth Groups:

Song of Religious Life

Oh, the cloistered life is jolly !
Nowadays, instead of prayer,
Smuggling money is the business;
Forth on this sly sport they fare.

Swift they say a Paternoster,
Priest and monk and pious nun.
Swifter then with zealous purpose
Smuggling currency they run.

Laden with the goodly specie
Slinks the nun from place to place.
No one would suspect the creature
From her modest pious face.

To the monk she slips the packet
Puts the swag into his hand.
Out he sallies bold and merry,
From his German Fatherland.

One fine day the whole thing ended;
One fine day the racket crashed.
And the news of this rare scandal
Far and near to all was flashed.

Priest and nun and holy friar—
What a horror, they're in clink !
From the labours of their smuggling
To a well-earned rest they sink.

To the priest the nun soft whispers,
" Glorious was the task and grand,
Backing up our Holy Father,
Smuggling money through the land."

3. *In Public Exhibitions*

Here are two specimens:

The *Grüne Woche* in Berlin, 1935:

In the *Berlin Catholic Parish Magazine*, No. 5, of February 3rd, 1935, there is a highly informative critical notice of this Exhibition. Therein we read:

Among the expressions of high feeling and indignation that have been written about the anti-Christian spirit that is displayed in the *Grüne Woche*, there occurs the following from a foreign visitor: " While passing through Berlin, I paid a visit on Sunday, January 27th, to the *Grüne Woche* on the Kaiserdamm. In the section ' From Odal Right to the Reich Heredityfarm Law '[1] (in the sub-section entitled ' Infiltrations of Roman Law destroy German Law ') there are inscriptions that are quite out of place and are an insult to the Catholic Church. I mention only the worst, which runs: ' It is not necessary for priests to marry while peasants have wives.' I spent a long time in this place listening to the guide and to the troops of people he was piloting round. Time and again the worst possible construction was put on the sentence just quoted." We protest most strongly against this insulting attack on the honour of our priests; for the rest, we leave it to our readers to judge of its indelicacy and its thoroughly bad taste.

At the same time, in the entrance hall of the Exhibition, in the section that bears the description " German Odal Right," we were surprised (and angry) to read the following categorical assertion:

" The introduction of the *Seelgerät*, which was part and parcel of the Christianising process, reduced the German yeoman to the level of a tenant farmer. The Christian Church claimed the right of *Seelgerät*. According to this—in defiance of the primitive German law of inheritance—the owner of a farm, with the idea of delivering his soul from Purgatory, could bequeath part of his farm to the Church. In most cases the *Seelgerät* was drawn up in a form according to which the dying peasant bequeathed his farm in its entirety to the Church and his heir received it back as a fief encumbered with rent. It was thus that a great part of the German peasantry lost its independence."

On the whole, Christianity and the Church come off very badly in this Exhibition. We feel that we ought to mention that the explanations of the young guides in the " Odal Right " department met with lively protests from the visitors. What filled us with concern was the manner in which a young guide, scarcely more than a boy, explained to the assembled company the need for large families and the evil results of birth control. This was in the section devoted to " The Blessing of Children and Public Health." He dealt with his subject in the language of the stud-farm. The views of these young men on Christian teaching and on Christian charity as it affects sufferers from hereditary disease are so crude that there is no point in discussing more in detail these profundities that they have got off so well.

The German farmer will preserve happy recollections of this Exhibition. But he will have made one unpleasant discovery—namely, that there is one continuous line of development linking up the German Farmers' Almanac with the " German Odal Right " part of the show. But that line he will not follow, since he knows that it leads him away from his most sacred and most precious possession, the Christian Faith.

The German Book Exhibition in Budapest, 1937:

About this the German correspondent of the *Wiener Reichspost* wrote in that paper on November 19th, 1937:

For many years past a German Book Exhibition has been held in Budapest every autumn. This year's Exhibition opened a few days ago and remains open for a fortnight.

---

[1] *Odal Right.*—" The homestead of the original settler . . . with the share of arable and appurtenant common rights bore among the northern nations the name of Odal or Edhel " (Stubbs' "Const. Hist." § 34). Odal Right comprises the ancient Germanic, pre-feudal laws and customs of property inheritance. The outstanding features of the system were the preservation of absolute ownership and the various provisions designed to keep the estates intact among the kindred. The *Erbhofgesetz* or hereditary-farm law of the Third Reich looks back towards this primitive Germanic property law and is part of the National Socialist agricultural policy based on the " Blood and Soil " principle. One of the cardinal aims of that policy is to bind the farmer closer to the soil and so to prevent the migration to the cities. " Amongst other things the *Erbhofgesetz* decrees that no mortgages of any kind may be registered on hereditary farms, so as not to expose the owner of the hereditary farm to the danger of being ' blackmailed ' for the payment of mortgage interest " (Dr. J. O. Reichenheim, *Tablet*, June 8th, 1940).

The Hungarian Press is devoting to it very detailed reports. No attempt is made to conceal the view that, in this year's Exhibition, the motif of political propaganda is very much overstressed. Here the Hungarian Press is openly protesting against the boosting of the writings of Rosenberg. Of course, the picture that adorns every room is that of Reich Chancellor Hitler. For all that, it is difficult to rid oneself of the impression that in this year's Exhibition it is Rosenberg who takes the chief place. In order of precedence he ranks next to Hitler, but in reality he is the centre of the Exhibition. The other intellectuals and writers of National Socialism are left a long way behind. " Rosenberg and in particular his ' Protestant Pilgrim to Rome,' " declares Buchhändler Knapp, the steward of the Exhibition, " is the big draw of the day."

4. *In Dramatic Performances*

We take the following sentences from the *Kölnische Volkszeitung's*[1] detailed review of *Uta v. Naumberg*, a play by Felix Dhünen:

Is this, then, meant to be an attempt at German tragedy ? It would seem that the essential tragedy lies in this, that the lovely noblewoman, through the prejudices of her day and through the Christian law already proclaimed on Sinai—this point is strongly stressed—loses her right to love whom and how she pleases. Her villainous enemy is the Church—embodied in the person of a fanatical witch-hunter. It follows that the hero of the piece is Graf Dietmar Thoren. He contrives to extort the promise of secrecy from the monk and thus to cast him into torments more terrible than those of the funeral pyre. The " heroic " quality depicted by Felix Dhünen in this young man displays itself in this, that Dietmar by an act of self-renunciation, as it were, burns himself on the very pyre that he had prepared for his enemy.

A good deal could be said about all this. We merely point out that if the intention is to portray the conflict of German and Christian man as that conflict declared itself more than a thousand years ago, there must be more respect for accuracy. Felix Dhünen has understood neither the character of the founders of Naumberg Cathedral nor the tenth and eleventh centuries. He carries his tenth-century prejudices into the era that witnessed the building of the Naumberg *Dom*. While defending the Liberal view of marriage, he idealises it with romantic conceptions that belong to the Courts of Love. Then he confounds Cluny with La Trappe—story-book " Jesuits " from the " Gothick " thrillers of the Enlightenment with monks who lived about the year 1000—the witch superstitions of the late Middle Ages (drifting further and further away from the basic ideas of the Church) with the Demonology (foisted by him on the Church) of that early Germanic period that was still half heathen.

From 1935 onwards *Die Liebesbeicht* (The Confession of Love), a piece of uncouth invective against the Church, was performed again and again—by touring companies of the Strength through Joy Organisation, for instance. The show bill gives it out that the play deals with the " spiritual effects of celibacy."

Touring companies of the Strength through Joy Organisation also played *Die Kreuzlschreiber*, in which Papal Infallibility is derided.

Here, too, must be mentioned " The King Rides," a play by Frau Anders, which, since October, 1936, has been performed repeatedly in the Prince Regent Theatre (now the People's Theatre) in Munich. The figure of the Bishop of Mainz in the play is the last word in out-and-out vulgarity and wickedness.

[1] No. 375, December 7th, 1934.

The *Berlin Catholic Parish Magazine* points out on January 19th, 1936, that in the "Little Theatre" *unter den Linden* plays like *Die Kreuzlschreiber*, "The Parish Priest of Kirchfeld" "Magdalena," "The Medal" were performed by the so-called Thoma Company "all of them products of that period that had set itself against everything ecclesiastical and every absolute moral code, a period we believed had long since passed away." The same number protests above all against the Thoma Company's performance of the play "The Last Peasant" by Anderl Kern. The following gives some idea of the contents of this abusive play:

The parish priest of a place has an illegitimate child by his housekeeper. The latter is the sister of a farmer who had lost his son and heir in the war. The farmer, who is aware that the parish priest is the father of his sister's child, would have liked to have adopted the boy as his heir, but the youth's parents want to force him to become a priest that he may atone for their sins and pray for them.

The young seminarist comes home in the holidays and explains to them that he has no inclination for the priesthood, that he wants to be a farmer, and that he is in love with his uncle's maidservant: he tells the parish priest that he has already notified the bishop that he is leaving the seminary. The parish priest threatens him with excommunication, etc., but all to no purpose. At this, his mother goes out of her mind and, regarding the young maidservant as the chief obstacle, she tries, rosary in hand and a prayer on her lips, to stab her. Here the old farmer steps in. He taxes the parish priest with his sin. The latter, contrite now, explains how he fell into temptation and yielded. It was only under compulsion and from his unnatural relationship to his child that he had become so harsh and tyrannical. The farmer declares that the young man shall be his heir and that he shall marry the maidservant. . . .

Minor characters: a sanctimonious, hypocritical seminarist and a gossip to represent the Young Women's Sodality. All the members of the company take holy water, make the Sign of the Cross and use the Catholic greeting. The parish priest himself exhibits every evil trait: he is intolerant, domineering, a legacy hunter, etc.

And it was this play that was acted amid thunderous applause before hundreds of the Hitler Youth and the German Girls' League, ranging in age from the eleven-year-olds to the "Leaders."

The *Berlin Catholic Parish Magazine* is fully justified when it says:

"The play is an attack on the priesthood and, through it, on the Church, such an attack as we have not met with for many a long year. As its artistic merits are well below the usual Berlin standards, it would, perhaps, have been better to have taken no notice of it. But as this play, through associations of dialect and local colour, is bound to be regarded by the Berliner (who is little conversant with things Catholic) as a revelation of the background of popular Catholicism, we are forced to disown it in the most emphatic manner." The magazine concludes with a quotation from *Germania*,[1] which, under the headline "A Caricature of a Priest," attacks the play:

[1] January 15th, 1936.

" We could indeed go on for some time describing all the little touches that the author includes to complete his caricature of the priest. But the account of its contents given above is proof enough that we have in this first-night performance the *dust-bin sweepings of nineteenth century Liberalism*: in a word, a painfully effective dramatic rendering of Corvin's ' Mirror of Priestcraft.' "

The *Schwarze Korps*[1] makes fun of a passage in the Catholic Youth paper *Die Wacht*, which pillories the anti-Catholic and malicious tone of several plays. The passage runs:

It is almost impossible to go to any modern play without having one's religious' convictions so affronted that one would have been afterwards ashamed at not having publicly protested. It is not merely that peculiar zeal is shown in presenting historical themes which portray the political machinations of the Church's leaders, who were princes as well as bishops, in any case. Quite apart from that, the facts themselves are travestied and set aside in defiance of all truth and justice, and staged with a vulgarity that makes one shudder. Here we have not only an insult against the Church and an offence against history, but all authority is undermined. . . .

The *Schwarze Korps* treats this complaint from the Catholic side as something funny, and replies with references to the offences and misdemeanours of the Church in past and present.

In the Vienna paper *Das kleine Frauenblatt* a Youth Leader gives some information about a play that was staged by members of the Junior Section of the Hitler Youth, whose ages ranged from ten to fourteen:

We put on a play. Here are the characters: a podgy prelate, Herr Schuschnigg with an umbrella, Prince Starhemberg and a Jewish bank director. Dramatic ending—all run away. An unexampled success: roars of laughter.

In May, 1939, the first performance of a new comedy by Curt Götz took place in the Munich *Schauspielhaus*. The comedy is entitled: " The Liar and the Nun." There appear in it a spiteful pompous abbess and half a dozen nuns. We are told in the Munich edition of the *Völkischer Beobachter* that the enjoyment of the audience was prolonged and unrestrained.

5. *Films*

In the latter half of the year 1938 there was shown throughout the Third Reich a film that enjoyed great popularity in the National Socialist press and aroused a burst of enthusiasm. The film is entitled " Youth," and its story derives from a play by Max Halbe that goes back to about 1890. The chief characters in this film are two priests: one of them, the parish priest, Fr. Hoppe, is a kindly man, a philanthropist, a man of experience who welcomes life, while the other, the curate von Schigorski, is a morose and fanatical zealot, a puritan whose ideas and behaviour, as is noted, are in no way typically Catholic. The parish priest's niece is the heroine of the film, and after the curate has driven her to death there is a violent discussion between the

[1] May 6th, 1937.

two priests over her bier. The old parish priest blames the " dogmas " of the Church and " priestly fanaticism " for the girl's death. He declares that the Church is an " Institution " that holds man back from God and is fruitful in such calamities.

The Vicariate-General of the Archdiocese in Paderborn felt obliged to issue an official declaration in which the film is described as a " concoction," " such a disgusting travesty of Catholic belief and of the priestly character that the Catholic public cannot allow it to go unchallenged."

In addition, the *Berlin Catholic Parish Magazine* discussed the film in detail in several articles[1] and repudiated it in no uncertain manner. It points out in particular that the portrayal of the film curate is completely out of character; that he stands for principles that have been condemned by the Church as heretical, and behaves in a manner that would have led any bishop to proceed against him. The film presents a completely distorted view of the Catholic priest and of the Catholic ministry.

Under the pressure of effective public opinion in various parts of the Catholic Sauerland (South Westphalia) the film had to be taken off the programme. The official Party organ of the SS, *Das Schwarze Korps* of November 17th, is very angry over " this unheard-of terrorising by the Church " and writes under the headline " How about a Waldbreitbach Film ?":

> If at this stage the German bishops have the audacity to attack by means such as these a film that is perfectly innocuous and markedly friendly towards the Church—so much so that it not only passed the State censorship without a hitch, but is a production of the highest distinction—some idea may be formed of what will happen if we try to show a film of the present time under National Socialism: a film, for instance, that deals with the war of extermination waged by the Roman Church against the German people in Austria. Unless here and now we give a rap over the knuckles to these gentlemen who interfere in matters that do not concern them, we shall have them dictating some day to us what films may be shown in German cinemas.

6. *In Speeches*

In the speeches of the leading representatives of the State and the Party, the Church and her good name are the constant object of gibes and insults. Here we can give only a small selection from the abundant material. It is, however, worthy of note that the Führer is, in this respect, very restrained in order to create the impression among the people that he does not share the anti-clerical sentiments (and measures) of his colleagues.

The Führer and Reich Chancellor Adolf Hitler.
Anyone who interferes with the mission (of the Führer) is an enemy of the German race, no matter whether he attempts this as a Bolshevik or a Democrat, a revolutionary Terrorist or a reactionary Visionary. In an emergency like this it is not the man who loafs round the country with Bible texts and spends the livelong day partly in doing nothing and partly in

---
[1] No. 25, June 19th, 1938; No. 28, July 10th, 1938.

criticising the actions of others, who acts in the name of God, but the man who impresses on his soul the highest form that unites a man with his God: the form of work.¹

Reichsminister Dr. Göbbels.

Those who collaborate with the National Socialist Welfare Service are in truth the apostles and missionaries of National Socialism. They have exhibited the Christianity of deeds and true charity, what time the Churches, by theological hair-splitting which has no interest for anyone, have striven to break the bonds of confidence between Führer and people.²

We are doing the Churches no injury. The Church has no longer any clear connection with the nation. A nation that has passed through four years of war and fifteen years of Marxism has no comprehension of theological hair-splitting. It envisages a Christianity of deeds and it finds this embodied far more in the Winter Relief Work than in the theoretical systematisation of so-called articles of belief. (The true attitude of the people may be gauged from the huge religious demonstrations, the spontaneous ovations offered to the bishops, the mounting revenue of the *Caritas* Collections, etc. Given the German nation its freedom, you will see on which side it will stand.) . . . We regard ourselves as the political pastors of our people and are convinced that it is our task to diminish and assuage the cares with which the soul of our people is afflicted. This festal centre is meant to be a political Church by which men will be brought up as true National Socialists for years and years to come.³

We have become a soldierly nation and if, for example, the pastors say that they are the ones who have the ear of the Lord, well, anyone can say that; for the Lord cannot be monopolised. He gives His blessing to those who are in the right. The true political pastors of the German nation are the National Socialists, while the Church squabbles about the administration of the Eucharist under one kind or both. The National Socialist régime provides no titbits for the belly, but it does furnish delicacies for the soul. . . .⁴

What these good Cardinals say in the churches themselves is entirely their own business. But the political arena and the streets belong to us.⁵

Reichminister Dr. Frick.

It would be a good thing if the spirit of the Centre Party had entirely departed. But it still haunts our life far too much—yes, and right here in Münster. What am I to say when people think it still possible in our new Germany for a high ecclesiastic to present the Government with the demand that the Reich Leader of the ideological training of the Party be prohibited from speaking in Münster ? . . . There are at present all sorts of organisations, ostensibly non-political in character, which attempt by roundabout and backstairs methods or by the misuse of religion to exercise political influence in Germany. . . . We have still in German public life organisations which try to perpetuate the denominational division of the people. We National Socialists demand that the whole of public life be purged of its denominationalism. Today, is there any point in having Catholic public service organisations ? What we want is just German public officials. Or is there any point in still having a Catholic daily press ? We want a daily press that is neither Catholic nor Protestant, but simply German.⁶

Reichsminister Dr. Kerrl.

We hear often enough from the Churches that faith can remove mountains, but we do not see anything like this being done." Beyond

¹ Speech in the Reichstag, February 20th, 1938. *Cf. Völkischer Beobachter*, No. 52, February 21st, 1938, p. 2.
² In an address to the National Socialist Welfare Service and Winter Help Organisation in September, 1937.
³ At the dedication of the Nordmark-Feierstätte in Bad Segeberg, October, 1937.
⁴ In the Berlin Sportpalast in November, 1937.
⁵ October, 1938, in the Hanseatic Hall at Hamburg.   ⁶ In Münster, July 7th, 1935.

question there has been far too much toleration extended to religion, but, in spite of this, clergymen of both denominations have gone on stirring up trouble for the State. In proof, there are the 7,000 prosecutions that have been reported since January, 1933, against representatives of the Churches. . . . Furthermore, Christ did not teach men that they must fight against the National Socialist race doctrine: rather did He wage a relentless war against the Jews, who on that account slew Him on the Cross. . . . The German nation will not allow itself to be held up in its march towards the future by confessional circles dabbling in politics.[1]

The Evangelical theologian Dr. Dibelius sent a letter to Kerrl, Reichsminister for Ecclesiastical Affairs, in the spring of 1937. Here is some of what he wrote:

Herr Minister, your speech of February 13th to the Presidents of the Church Committees is meant to be a clarification of the new decree for the Evangelical Church. The Führer's decision has set it completely aside. According to the report before me, you said on that occasion: " The Catholic Bishop Count Galen and the Evangelical General Superintendent Zöllner want to tell me that Christianity is in essence the acknowledgment of Jesus Christ as the Son of God. That is ridiculous and a point of minor importance. To allow the figure of Jesus to work upon one and to live a Christianity of deeds, that is everything. . . ."

If Jesus was a man like ourselves, no more and no less, then anyone may criticise His doctrine and the sacraments of the Church have no longer any value. Then no more has the Church the right to oppose the Gospel to the " Myth " of Alfred Rosenberg. What must be the feelings of German Christians when the Minister for Ecclesiastical Affairs sums up all that as " ridiculous "?[2]

Reichsminister Frank.

On no account must the National Socialist ideological structure be imperceptibly falsified by denominational ideas.[3]

Reichminister Rust.

The idea of " race " gives us an insight into the very relative importance of the denominations.[4]

Minister of State Adolf Wagner.

In the days that lie immediately ahead of us the fight will not be against either Communists or Marxists, but against *Catholicism*. Everyone will find himself faced with a serious question: German or Catholic ? This struggle will not be easy. Catholics have been schooled in their ideas for centuries; they have any number of institutions in which to subject their people to jesuitical teaching. By comparison, the schooling in the hands of National Socialism is very inferior. In the contest that is about to begin the utmost caution must be shown. We must see to it that in this encounter the other side takes the initiative.[5]

With a few trusty followers, of whom Alfred Rosenberg was one, Adolf Hitler took up the fight against the ever-increasing Red tide. And when the black International took the place of the dead Bolsheviks, there was no change on the battle-front of the young National Socialist movement. *For the enemy was still here:* he had merely changed his colours. . . .[6]

We are very glad that it is precisely Rosenberg who has been given charge of the National Socialist ideology in the Party. The principles of National

---
[1] On November 23rd, 1937, in Fulda.
[2] *Reichspost*, March 12th, 1937.
[3] In Hamburg. *Cf. Westdeutscher Beobachter*, October 13th, 1937.
[4] In Berlin, November 27th, 1937.
[5] At an Education Day of the SA Leaders in Erding, July 13th, 1935.
[6] In a speech. *Cf. Münchener Neueste Nachrichten*, No. 165, June 18th, 1936.

Socialism are the principles of the Reich. There is nothing to be altered there and it is foolish to attack these principles. Everyone has to respect them, including the bishops.[1]

It is not our fault that in the two thousand years of Christianity's existence the great God preached by Christ has become a thousand little gods. On the contrary, we shall not suffer the thought of God to be torn out of the heart of this magnificent people. We want to erect a bulwark against this attempt. As National Socialists we have no need to be told how to believe in God. We *are* the believers in God. . . . The constant and everlasting watchword of our movement is: the fight against every force that would destroy our right to live, that comes among us to take our people out of their path: an unending fight against the Jews, and in this fight it makes no difference to us whether the eternal Jew runs about in the red rags of the Bolshevik or in the black clothes of the Ultramontane.[2]

Unless this pastoral business, etc., stops, we shall stop collecting the Church revenue for the parsons. . . . Teachers are more suitable than parsons for the work of religious instruction. The parsons should be given a rap over the knuckles. . . .[3]

There can be no peace in Germany until such time as these political priests are utterly wiped out. Our fight is not against the church-goers, but against the priests who under the cloak of their priestly office are perpetually agitating against the National Socialist State. We see today how a Faulhaber has pushed into the place of Held and Wohlmuth (former leaders of the Old Catholic Party of Bavaria). . . .

We began our fight with political Catholicism in March, 1933. The time has now come to continue this fight. Away with political priests ! Down with political Catholicism ![4]

Secretary of State Waldmann.

In the spring of 1933 we began our work in the State, added stone to stone and brought things into line. There was only one exception—the Churches. Up to the present these have formed an enclave within the community and it has got to be removed.[5]

Reich Leader Alfred Rosenberg.

It is a fact of the first importance that with the National Socialist revolution the Middle Ages came to an end once and for all. The fall of the Centre Party was not merely the fall of a political party; it was the fall, too, of the fifteenth and thirteenth century conception of the State. We do not hold today that the nation is a means to sectarian domination as an end, but just the opposite: the value of a religious denomination is just its capacity for advancing and strengthening the noblest values of a nation, and nothing else.[6]

A senile belief is unwilling to give way to the outlook of a new phase of development. . . . The laws of the evolution of the Blood were not discovered by the Councils of the Church, but by the keen-eyed and reverent researches of good Europeans whom these very Churches threatened with death. In the same way, as the race theory is not the discovery of the preachers, they are not competent to pass judgement on it. . . .

Today people cannot be intimidated as effectively as in times past by the idea of eternal punishment in the next life, and in the course of the present century wrathful fulminations against scientific discoveries, grounded as they are in obstinate error, have altogether lost their power on men.

By a lengthy struggle we have managed to acquire this gem of inner wisdom,

---

[1] In the NS Culture Association. *Cf. Osservatore Romano*, July 10th, 1936.
[2] At the Area Meeting of the Munich NSDAP, October, 1936.
[3] From a speech at the District Meeting of the NS Teachers' Union in Würzburg, 1937.
[4] In March, 1938, in Munich at a NS mass demonstration.
[5] In the summer of 1936 at an Area Meeting of the NSDAP in Bad Mergentheim.
[6] In Erfurt, June, 1935. *Cf. Köln. Volkztg.*, No. 153, June 3rd, 1935.

which we should like to express to you today in this way: If there is a Heaven, a Heaven it may be of which we can form no clear idea in our present state, then the man who fights with honour and makes sacrifices for his race and its highest values will more surely get there than the man who with prayers in his mouth betrays alike his people and his country. . . .[1]

We have every reason for thinking that without the German, Christianity would have remained an affair of the Middle Ages. . . .

The common outlook that dominated German life for hundreds of years has passed away, as the result of new scientific discoveries, as a result of the establishment of Church leadership, as a result of the awakening of a consciousness of German rights.[2]

I am absolutely clear in my own mind, and I think I can speak for the Führer as well, that both the Catholic Church and the Evangelical Confessional Church, as they exist at present, must vanish from the life of our people.

I am perfectly well aware that the situation in Austria is essentially different: if we take steps there, we shall find terrible corruption. The exact time of our intervention, however, has to be left to the Government.[3]

This same Alfred Rosenberg spoke on March 31st, 1939, in Troppau. The main points of his speech were: Marxism, the Jews and the Church. Here is part of what he said on the subject of the Church:

From 1933 onwards the German Reich has taken pains to keep religious teaching and political power, generally speaking, apart.

We feel bound to confess that we had not much faith in this attempt, but for the name of the State we had to make the effort. We were answered by ever-increasing encroachments on a sphere that belongs, so we hold, to the fundamental principles of our Reich. The so-called persecution of the Jews was hailed as unchristian in bishops' Pastorals and in the Sunday sermons of the clergy. The racial legislation of the Reich was set down as pagan and it is still described as pagan today.

In any case, these things are in no way to be regarded as religious matters at all, as matter upon which the Pope and the bishops are entitled to pass judgement. The Church, moreover, thinks that the State and our ideology are two different things.

We must state at once that we do not make this distinction, and shall never make it. According to the bishops it is quite right and proper to acknowledge a State that is an honest and industrious tax collector for the Church, that affords protection for the bishops' palaces and provides an efficient postal service for the transmission of their pastorals; but the moment the State tries to be something more than a night-watchman or an efficient policeman, then these people have no time for it. The moment the State is no longer a pale image of itself, but stands for a clearly-defined ideological outlook, then people feel suddenly restricted in their deepest religious convictions. Be that as it may, we still have got to say: We National Socialists have created this State; we are going to hold on to this State; and we shall never let go of this State.

They would not give way one step before those gentlemen with their protests and complaints about persecution. When had these same gentlemen ever practised toleration? The speaker believed

---

[1] At the Discussion on Civilisation of the Nürnberg Party Congress, 1936.
[2] At the Torgauer Area Meeting of the NSDAP in October, 1937. *Cf. Köln. Volkztg.*, No. 287, of October 18th, 1937.
[3] In an unpublished speech at the German Culture Discussion, Nürnberg Party Congress, 1938.

that 99 per cent. of the German people were at one with him in thinking that there never had been a more merciless and bloodthirsty period of German history than the days of the tortures of the Inquisition.

The latest example of the development of these ideas is the Church State of Austria. What was going on there was nothing less than an attempt, against every healthy German instinct, to enact over again the bloody Counter-Reformation. . . . But we have not dealt with these clergymen as they have treated us. We have let loose on them no massacre of St. Bartholomew, as they have deserved, but we have promised them religious toleration and we have fulfilled our promise. . . . For today they are free to speak without reserve in every church. They have the right to receive everyone who still believes that he can find religious consolation with them. Further, if they want to protest, they have their Pastorals. But we must make it clear that we must award to all other religious bodies a like measure of toleration.

However, it was not the largest majority of the religious bodies that the speaker had in mind. The Catholic Church could no longer be regarded as an official State Church. The Catholic Church was freer in Germany than in the many other States which she would like to play off against us. . . .

For the rest, I think that once again an effort is made to distort the historical situation. For today it is not we who occupy the dock, but there stand before the judgement-seat of the German people all those Prelates who raise such an outcry. Well, we put up with all that, but there is one thing that is beyond us, that we cannot do: we cannot expect our youth to sit at the feet of those who have acted as traitors to the German people. . . .

Rosenberg concludes with the words:

We have a vision of a Reich, in which every town and village shall have its community house, where on Sundays the young people of town and country will meet and from whose belfries there will ring forth the peals that will call all Germans together. We know that in this Reich that we have in mind the whole German nation will wend its way to Nürnberg, where German youth will vie in sport with German youth as in the days of yore, where in this Congress Hall all will be gathered together as in a German Cathedral there to debate the questions of German destiny and to gather new strength for the future. And we know that there will be above all the graves of our martyrs to which on fixed days the nation will make its pilgrimage. Of that martyrdom the Eternal Watch in Munich will be the emblem and over all there will fly the flags of victories mightier than ever before, as symbols of a new life and a new order. If we devote ourselves to the service of our country, to affirm the destiny of this era, then we have the right to feel that we are the standard-bearers of the greatest epoch in Germany's history.

From this speech it follows that the object in view is an untiring effort to wipe out the Church.

Dr. Wagner, German Doctors' Leader.

Our ideal man is no longer, as in the past, the man who is ready to submit himself humbly to his fate, who slides round on his knees, supplicates for grace and tries, perhaps, even in this world to get a mortgage on heaven; but our ideal is the German man, strong, efficient, powerful, the man who is ready to master his fate.[1]

[1] From a speech at the first National Conference of the German National Health Movement August 8th, 1937.

THE TWO REDS.

Card. Pacelli: " Thanks very much, my friend, and now I'll give you my blessing."

[*Brennessel*, Aug. 3rd, 1937.

CATHOLIC RELIGIOUS HOUSES.

"The good God sees it, but Dr. Schacht doesn't."

Herr Schmidt, Head of the Central Training Department of the NSDAP.

On October 23rd, 1937, Herr Schmidt of Berlin, Head of the Central Training Department of the German National Socialist Workers' Party, made a speech here (in Münster i.W.) to the teachers and educational workers of the district, Westfalen-Nord. In this speech all supernatural religion, including Christianity, was not merely denied, but also scoffed at and ridiculed. He expressly denied the " eternal life " of each individual human soul. He declared that Heaven and Hell were a fairy-tale and asked the teachers to make a special point of ridding the children of this belief in Heaven and Hell. I have been informed that a section of the teachers present applauded the speaker—even at those passages that contained a denial of the truths of the Faith. . . .[1]

District Leader Julius Streicher

Of all those who libel the Church, the lowest and the most vulgar is without question District Leader Julius Streicher, the editor of the *Stürmer*, whose attacks are characterised by their vague insinuations and the low level to which they sink. The only purpose we have in view in the following is to show to what depths of vulgarity and filth high Party officials can descend with impunity in their public speeches.

There is a chaplain in the neighbourhood of Nürnberg who at the moment is under trial. He would say Mass in the morning and in the afternoon go to the station and hire male prostitutes of sixteen and lie with them in the evening. Next morning he would say Mass again, elevate the Host (Streicher imitated this), and the faithful would genuflect before it (Streicher mimicked this, too).

If you only knew the sort of letter we could publish—a letter written by a highly-placed bishop—then you would see that these people are men, too.

In the bedroom of a priest whose brother is a bishop we found things so abnormal that the average man would have no inkling of their use. We brought away from a convent of nuns, which, by the way, is still entrusted with the task of bringing up young girls, a whole heap of pornographic literature.

If only you knew the sums we were offered to suppress the Currency trials !

I was always a bit of a bad lad. When I had to go to the war, my sister said: " You'll have to learn to pray now, all right." I didn't. In a barrage, when people were falling right and left, there was a country lad who began to recite the rosary out loud. I said to him: " God in Heaven ! Away with you and your rosary." So long as he stuck to God the Father, I didn't mind. But when he began, " Holy Mary, pray for us " (Streicher imitated this), then I said to him: " God in Heaven ! We don't want any women. This woman doesn't hear you."

Christ mixed a good deal with women. I believe that He stayed with one who was an adulteress—so I have heard.

Whenever we are seen with a decent woman we are taken to task by red and black newspapers (I mean the press of that lot in vestments), since they think that we are the same dirty sows as they are. . . . Monks and nuns have got a walk like eunuchs.

I'll now give you an example. Someone might go home today after this meeting and then later say to the Rabbi: " Julius Streicher said such abominable things that I want to become a Jew." Then the Rabbi says: " In that case you'll have to be circumcised." Then they go into a room. Then he comes out with his finger in a bandage (roars of applause). After-

---

[1] The Bishop of Münster, Mgr. Graf v. Galen, in a sermon preached in the *Dom* at Münster, November, 1937.

wards he goes to his colleagues and says: " Don't you see any difference in me ? " They say: " You look really awful." (Streicher then said something about trousers.) Then the man we are talking about says: " I'm a Jew." To which the others reply: " You're a bloody fool. It's race and not circumcision that makes a man a Jew." (That gives some idea of the level of his speech.)

The speaker harped incessantly upon his main comparison between Christ and the movement. He always referred to the disciples as the SA and SS of Our Lord. After he had done this several times, he begged pardon and said:

It is only on one or two exceptional points that Christ and Hitler stand comparison, for Hitler is far too big a man to be compared with one so petty.[1]

The Ministers of both Confessions baptise the descendants of Christ's murderers. They baptise the descendants of the Jews of whom Christ said that their father was the devil. If ever I should have any children, I should think twice about allowing one of them to be baptised, for I'd say to myself: That's fine company for my poor child to mix in.

An Evangelical SA-man comes to the priest with a Catholic girl and asks to be married. The parish priest has scruples about mixed marriages. What does the young chap say to the parish priest? Do you want me to tell you? Am I to tell you really what he says? He says: "Lick my . . ." Then the young man says to his girl: "Come on, let's go for a walk and sing the grand song, *Wer uns getraut* " . . . (Who marries us . . .).

When I die Almighty God will ask me: " What's your name ? " " Julius Streicher." "Oho, so you're old Streicher, are you? Well, what do you want here ? " " I'd like to come into Heaven." " Well, and what's your religion ? " Then I shall say to Him: " It hasn't actually got a name. I was baptised a Catholic, but we mustn't mix up a man's denomination with his religion." Then the Lord will say: " H'm, this is rather a cheeky way of going on ! " And He will send me to Hell. Then perhaps old Grohé (the Cologne District Leader) comes to die. Let us suppose that he is a Protestant (I don't know whether he is or not) and that he's due for Heaven. He looks in and sees Herr Kaas, Dr. Wohlmuth, the Bishop of Meissen, sitting there for the greater glory of God. At that Grohé says: " Then I'm going down to Streicher in Hell. Down there, at any rate, business is more on the level."

The Pope, who was born in Italy of an Italian mother, is more attached to Italy and to his own people than to the outside world. But we have bishops and cardinals who are more attached to the rest of the world than to their own people !"[2]

Along with the deliverance of the German people there goes the deliverance by Adolf Hitler of other afflicted peoples who cannot as yet help themselves. . . .

When bishops become suddenly friendly I always say, " Don't let yourselves be taken in by decent Jews: don't let yourselves be taken in by these so-called bishops," I always say: " You can bet he's a bit of a Jesuit."

The Ten Commandments given to the Jews on Mount Sinai were afterwards handed on to us. There is no need to tell a decent man not to steal, not to commit adultery. With a naughty child you may keep dinning in " Thou shalt not steal," but the child will certainly become wicked, because that is how it is made. For instance: Some fool of a Protestant allows himself to be married as a Catholic for the sake of his wife, who has always been an ardent church-goer, and is a virago without an equal. . . . First a

---

[1] In a speech at the end of the discussion on schools by the German Academy of Education held in Munich from July 19th to 26th, 1935. The speech was on July 26th; we give it as taken down by one present.

[2] At a great demonstration of the NSDAP in the Rheinland Hall at Cologne, December 4th, 1935.

Protestant, then a Catholic, perhaps next he'll let himself be circumcised . . ., but he can let himself be baptised, he can let himself be circumcised, he's still a shit-bag all the time. It's all no help to him, even being baptised, for with this scar, I can't do a thing. (Thunderous applause.)

Then the Protestants come along and say: " We want to run missions in Africa"; then the Catholics come and say: " We are the people for that." And the niggers say: " Lick my arse ! "

He (the speaker) said to a priest who refused him absolution because he would not reveal his occupation (at the time he was an assistant teacher in the vicinity of Kempten): " Herr Stadtkaplan, if *you* won't absolve me, than I shall be forgiven all right. So long ! I'm not coming into the ' box ' again and I'm having nothing to do with people who have drifted so far from their position as God's representatives. . . ." Referring to the rumour that he had left the Church, he said: " I hereby let all the people know; I just hadn't time to carry out all the necessary formalities ! . . ."[1]

Streicher made a wild onslaught on the Church, bishops and priests in speeches which he delivered in several towns in Baden in October, 1936. His talk was all of " parsons." About the miracle of the Red Sea: " Do you really believe in this fraud ?" In expounding race pollution he used the comparison of two dogs coupling. In front of young girls of the BDM and members of the Hitler Youth he said things like this: " There are girls who have been slept with and girls who haven't." He insinuated that priests use the sacrament of Confession for immoral purposes and he embroidered this theme with a complete lack of shame. Oral Confession was rendered contemptible. The Blessed Sacrament was reviled. As a matter of course, the speech was full of " parsons "; several dogmas were made ridiculous.[2]

In the speeches which he delivered in many towns of Baden in October, 1936, Julius Streicher inveighed specially against Archbishop Gröber. He got on to the same thing on other occasions—in a speech, for instance, that he made to the whole Teaching Body of Nürnberg on January 25th, 1937. Against the Archbishop, Streicher uttered the calumny that he had written a love-letter to a twenty-year-old Jewess: he also had a love-letter of the Archbishop's read out loud together with a number of police-documents bearing on the same affair.[3]

It is much better to play football than to attend divine service. It is much better for the children's health for them to scramble through the woods than for them to go to church. That must be made quite clear to all those who today are still hanging back and wavering. And, addressing the women, Streicher's worthy henchman declared: " You're doing much better working round the house and getting a good meal ready for your husbands than running off to church; that's no good at all."[4]

Deputy District Leader Holz.

You arse-hole ! you who run round with your hymn book and prayer book ! Ours is a Christianity of deeds ! Look at our Winter Relief Work.

[1] From a speech on October 23rd, 1936, in the Herkules-Saalbau in Nürnberg
[2] In his speech to the NS Women's Union at Nürnberg on January 17th, 1937.
[3] *Cf.* also the *Fränkische Tagesztg.* of January 27th, 1937.
[4] From a speech made by the Adjutant of Gauleiter Streicher at a Party meeting in which a sprinkling of children took part.

But these are shit-bags. You ought not to give money for missions in Africa to get clothes for Kaffirs. It's hot enough there, as it is. Let them run round as God made them. We have enough of our own poor. . . .[1]

Various Other Party Members.

The doctrine that the Son of God chose to come into this world by an immaculate conception implies fundamentally that all human conception must be regarded as something impure. How can we fulfil the fourth commandment and honour father and mother, if we are to hold that we owe our existence to the lusts of the flesh and to Original Sin, and that the whole human species is corrupt in the germ and begotten of seed that is sinful?[2]

The subject of our speech is: "The Men behind the Scenes in Modern Life!" It is with a great shock that millions have read in the papers during the last few days how German women in the habit of nuns have committed high-treason against their country. These women are going to prison for five years. . . . These women have never done all this on their own: they have acted on secret orders. But just as these men behind the scenes gave their orders in secret, so now they lie low and let these women serve their five years' imprisonment. That is the revolting part of the whole thing. . . . They have vowed themselves to a different outlook on life, an outlook that on a basis of distorted history has brought nothing but blood and tears into the world for the last 1,800 years.[3]

Party-member Rittweger said inter alia:

Today in the German Reich there are only two categories—National Socialists and swine.[4]

Dr. Schwarz, Darmstadt:

Christians can never feel that they are true followers of the Führer. They always feel that they are in a morass of sin, which can bring forth nothing but marsh-flowers. National Socialism stands on a moral plane far above the ethics of Jesus. We do not want to sink back into Christianity, but to soar far above it. It is no longer the case that the individual must suppress the risings of his sexual nature; rather, he should embark on sex experience as a duty to society.[5]

Dr. Schott spoke on "Popular Fairy Tales." He expounded "Little Red Riding Hood." He interpreted it as the encounter of the German Ur-mother with the ambush of an alien Christianity. "The Hunter was also on the spot. He kept his watch. Now we have ripped open the belly of the Black Wolf. However, that was but a beginning—very much as the doctor taps to see how deep the pus lies. But we shall go on with our work and not rest until the Wolf's hood and bed-jacket are completely torn off."[6]

Roder of the Ministry of Education:

I was delighted—I say it again, delighted—to wipe twenty monkish training colleges off the face of the earth with one stroke of the pen. I say, nevertheless, that was but a beginning. . . .[7]

---

[1] From a speech delivered in Herzbruch on October 27th, 1936.
[2] Ministerial Councillor Dr. Stähle, Stuttgart, on November 16th, 1935; in the City Hall at Münster in Westphalia; quoted in the *Bavarian Medical Journal*, No. 14, of April 4th, 1936.
[3] State Councillor Professor Börger on May 29th, 1935, at a demonstration of the German Workers' Front held on the cycle-track of the Köln-Müngersdorf Stadium. *Cf. Köln. Volkszeitung*, May 31st, 1935.
[4] Reich Education Conference of the German Academy of Education, July 19th to 26th, 1935, at the University of Munich.
[5] *Ibid.*   [6] *Ibid.*   [7] *Ibid.*

We did not build the Third Reich for dried-up high-school professors nor yet for the prayer-mumblers of both sexes. . . .

God and Christianity are in no danger, but only those who have introduced all this hocus-pocus into the Church services, those who have extinguished the candles and covered the altars with black. They have reduced a couple of old hags to tears, but that will not happen a second time. Christ and Luther are Crown witnesses for us. The Confessional Front has betrayed Luther.

Franciscan Brothers are swinish priests. Protestant Deans and training-college professors have done similar things.[1]

There is nothing heroic about allowing oneself to be shot down shaking at the knees and sighing out prayers—the sort of thing that has been happening in Spain. All the tears of the Holy Father and all the prayers of the nuns didn't help there one bit. For National Socialism the purpose of human life can be put in a sentence: We are here on earth to maintain the species.[2]

The second, Politico-philosophical Front—he would not call it the " Inner Front," since the fight was carried on from outside the country as well—could be expressed in three international ideas: Judaism, Moscow and Rome. Fights in which people struggled for their national existence could be waged in a spirit of chivalry. But the clash between conflicting ideologies had to be regarded differently, since they were mutually exclusive. The national States stood in the way of those international currents. The enemy within the gates was one of the means used by our opponents.[3]

At a meeting held on the Shooting Range at Eichstätt on December 15th, 1937, there were two speakers on the subject of " The Church and the Community Schools."

There has never been heard in Eichstätt anything against religion so incredibly low as the effort of the two speakers from outside. Time does not allow of anything like a verbatim report of all these foul attacks. I can only make particular mention of one or two.

It was insinuated that the army chaplains of the Great War avoided the front line and kept well back in the rear. The administration of the Sacraments in a military hospital was sneered at and ridiculed in a most revolting manner.

The Vatican Council which defined the infallibility of the Pope in matters of faith and morals—a purely religious topic—was dragged into the discussion. And, of course, the moral theology of St. Alphonsus Liguori, of which the speaker quite certainly had never read a line—that, too, had to be dragged in. His knowledge of it chiefly came out of the notorious " Mirror of Priestcraft."

The mystery of Christmas, the Virgin Birth of Christ, and the Sacrament of the Altar were vilified and held up to ridicule with a foul-minded suggestiveness that will not bear repetition.

He boasted that he was never going to enter a church again, spoke blasphemously of the joys of Heaven and—just like the Marxists of happy memory—renounced his own prospects of Heaven. He preferred Hell to Heaven, since in Hell there were a number of good fellows, while in Heaven there were only hypocrites. He took occasion here to revile the memory of the two million who died in the World War without the ministrations of a priest.

He described the Gospel as not worthy of credence, called priests cowards and hypocrites, and spoke of bishops with the utmost disdain.

---

[1] Albert Roth at the solemn opening of the Economic Production Campaign in the Festival Hall at Hüfingen.
[2] Chief City School Inspector Bauer at a training course for teachers, Munich, December 13th, 1936.
[3] Ministerialdirigent Dr. Best, Deputy Chief of the Public Safety Service, at an evening class in Cologne for the members of the German Police Force. *Cf. Köln. Volkztg.* of November 27th, 1937.

When men holding high positions in the Party do not know the proper way to speak of a bishop, it is no wonder that all the rowdyism in front of the bishop's residence does not cease, it is no wonder that a mob of half-witted hooligans (as happened this morning at a quarter to five) prowls up and down before the bishop's residence growling: " Come out, you old rogue ! Down with you, you old rascal!"

Here is a thing that I have emphasised on several occasions and I do so once again: All these attacks and insults, all this suspicion and contempt which is such an affront to the most sacred feelings of Catholics, all this, I say, occurred at a meeting that was political.[1]

Everything that has happened in the Christian Corporative State from Dolfuss to Schuschnigg must be set down to the account of the Church. The bishops are the enemies of the German people. Even the bishop's palace is not the property of the Church, but belongs to us National Socialists. And as in Salzburg there is a shortage of room, the State will take over the room he happens to have.

Everything is meaningless unless we set our much more forceful political beliefs against the political Church.

In Adolf Hitler's Reich God is not monopolised by the Church. For us Germans there are many other paths along which God can be found. It is for that reason, too, that we have prohibited the Church from imparting religious instruction. The Church does not teach religion. The Church teaches a sectarian creed. The religion of Germans is summed up in the sentence: " Everything for Adolf Hitler."

In no other way can I bring the Lord God before my mind than as the One who protects and guides our Führer. In no other way can I serve Him better than by working for the Führer.[2]

7. *In Public Demonstrations*

On the evening of June 16th, 1935, a motor-car crowded with Hitler Youth, some standing even on the running boards, drove up before the residence of the Bishop of Rottenburg, and all shouted: " Black Gypsy, play us a tune."

On August 4th, 1935, about 150 SA-men drove in four or five railway motor lorries to Altötting. They came out of the München-Freimann Railway repair shops; on the lorries was written in large letters: " Political Catholicism is public enemy No. 1. Our faith is Germany. . . ." In Altötting a so-called German marriage service took place on the Kapellenplatz in front of the shrine to the great indignation of the Catholics. A sentence in the matrimonial address ran: " We are not concerned whether we go to the angels in Heaven or to the devil in Hell."

On Sunday, August 11th, 1935, the SA of Munich organised a demonstration drive similar to that of Altötting on the preceding Sunday. About thirty lorry loads of SA-men shouting in unison drove through the various streets of Munich. Phrases like " The Youth belongs to us and not to the parsons " were chalked on the lorries, and on one of them there was a caricature of a fat religious, and under it the words:

> Were I a little angel slick,
> I'd slip across the border quick.

---

[1] Fr. Kraus, parish priest of the *Dom* in Eichstätt, in his sermon on December 19th, 1937. For this sermon he received an order of expulsion.
[2] State Councillor Springenschmidt in the Opera House, Salzburg, October 18th, 1938.

The SA-men shouted in unison, " Stick the parsons and the Jews against the wall," and other similar expressions.

On August 13th and 16th, 1935, the SA drove through the streets of Freiburg-im-Breisgau. On the lorries were sixteen " guys " representing priests and nuns with large streamers bearing inscriptions such as

> O holy " Mark " (*Devisia*), pray for us.
> Beware of the Jews and parsons.

And the SA-men yelled in unison:

> Jews, parsons and reaction are the enemies of the nation.
> Thou shalt love thy neighbour and not wangle currency.

The SA-men made a terrific din before all Catholic institutions, especially the presbytery in the Herrenstrasse and the archiepiscopal residence, and shouted:

> The parsons must go to the gallows.
> Down with the parsons.

On the doors of the residences of the Archbishop and of his coadjutor and of all parochial buildings they stuck the placard about the " Black-Hand Gang " which had been officially released the day before. On the first lorry there was a " guy " representing a Catholic nun, on the second another representing a Catholic priest, and on the third a gallows had been erected. On the evening of the same day there took place in the Church of St. Conrad a religious service in honour of Our Lady of Fatima, whose picture is there held in special veneration. Every seat in the church was filled. During Benediction members of the Hitler Youth created an organised uproar.

Archbishop Gröber was absent from Freiburg when these excesses took place, but on the following day he went up into the pulpit after Mass and stigmatised such proceedings as a disgrace not only to Freiburg and the Party, but to the whole of Germany and to civilisation. Archbishop Gröber had never spoken with so much vigour and emotion before. He said that he had always sought to live at peace with the Third Reich, and had always been moderate; yet now the time for silence was past.

In August, 1935, members of the *Hochland* camp of the Hitler Youth organised a public procession through Lenggries, singing a chorus which ran, " What's to be done with the priests ? Hang them, hang them !" In the same month the Black Guards and the Storm Troopers organised a demonstration in Kolbermoor, Bad Aibling and Burckmühl near Bad Tölz, using cars on which appeared phrases such as:

> " Rome for the Priests,
> Palestine for the Jews,
> GERMANY FOR THE GERMANS."

286 ATTACKS ON THE HONOUR OF THE CHURCH

In September, 1935, on the eve of the installation of the new Bishop, Dr. Stohr, Storm Troopers marched through the streets of Mainz shouting anti-clerical songs with the notorious refrain:

> Black rats and moles, . . .
> We shall smite them, we shall rout them out of Germany.

The Storm Troopers were active during the night, and next morning those streets through which the episcopal procession would pass displayed the notorious red poster, "*Deutsches Volk horch' auf!*" ("German people, listen!").

On July 12th, 1936, the Storm Troopers organised a procession in Prien. One of its cars was inscribed, "You should love your neighbour, not play swindler's tricks with the currency"; the other had a picture of a Jew and a Bolshevik with a priest between them, and over the picture was written, "Enemies of the State." These Storm Troopers had come from Munich.

In 1938 Hamburg was the scene of a horrible example of blasphemy, exhibited at a National Socialist rally. The *Osservatore Romano*[1] gave an account of it, and illustrated the account with a photograph painful to Catholics and disgusting to all decent people. The scene shown in the picture is visible through dense masses of curious onlookers who stand under houses decorated as if for a procession. In the centre is something resembling an altar, flanked by figures bearing candles or torches and wearing garments resembling those worn by members of a choir. If the Swastika was not shown on their breasts and elsewhere in the picture, one might think that it represented a Corpus Christi procession. Over the sham altar rose an object resembling a monstrance, in which, in place of the Host, appeared a Swastika against a white background. Under this picture the *Osservatore Romano* wrote, "Doctrinal parodies; a parody of the Blessed Sacrament of the Altar displayed in Hamburg." The picture is characteristic, and the "anti-God" spirit which lies behind it is worthy of Moscow. It is actually a typical expression of the Nazi outlook, the outlook of a "substitute religion" which opposes a union of blood and race to the conception of a spiritual union in Christ.

On October 17th, 1938, at 6.30 p.m., a crowd of some forty people gathered in the Kapitelplatz in Salzburg, in front of Archbishop Waitz's residence, to make a demonstration against him. They marched in formation to the Stadtbrücke, then returned, more than a thousand strong. There they chanted demands for the Archbishop's resignation on the grounds that his extreme connection with political Catholicism had rendered him unbearable. After this demonstration a representative of the District Leader, standing in front of the residence, requested them to depart, and after 8 p.m. the crowd dispersed, prudently refraining from any show of violence.

On June 15th, 1939, the predominantly Catholic city of Paderborn

---
[1] July 24th, 1938.

was the scene of a grossly insulting demonstration against its Archbishop, Dr. Kaspar Klein. A fortnight later the Archbishop addressed the following protest to the District Leader of Münster, Dr. Alfred Meyer:

PADERBORN,
June 30th, 1939.

A regrettable incident obliges me to have recourse to you. On Thursday, June 15th, there took place a procession of the Old Guard of the Führer in the morning, and in the afternoon a so-called historical pageant, which is the occasion of my protest, paraded through the streets.

A few days before the 15th it had been rumoured in the city that the procession would have an anti-Catholic character, and on that account many Catholics refrained from being present. The pageant which actually took place can only be described as a reversion to the worst excesses of the anticlericalism of bygone days. On a moving stage inscribed with the tag, " On with the movement away from God," was displayed a Rabbi on terms of intimate companionship with an individual robed as a Catholic priest, who sprinkled water over the crowd with a lavatory brush in contempt of the Catholic use of holy water. The inscription on the stage was interpreted by onlookers to signify that the German clergy, or at least the clergy of my diocese, had joined forces with Jews and Communists in the " Away from God " movement before 1933. That is sheer falsification of historical facts, the gravest slander that has as yet been cast against the clergy.

On another cart was written: " Jesuits and Hirelings of the Priests lead Wichart to Judgement." On the cart stood three actors, dressed as Jesuits, who made ludicrous Signs of the Cross over the spectators, in mimicry of the blessings given by bishops and priests. In order to make the mockery complete, a few spectators knelt down in front of the Academy and the Fransciscan monastery, and made the Sign of the Cross. This derision was all the more pointed because the inscription gave the impression that Jesuits had acted as catchpoles in bringing Wichart to trial.

The phrase " priests' hirelings " could only have one meaning under present circumstances. According to Richter's " History of the City of Paderborn," Wichart was punished for " sedition, gross slander and other activities directed against the prince and the State "—that is, he was condemned to death for high treason by the regular courts of the city, and then, according to the cruel customs of the times, his living body was quartered. I feel certain that those who organised this pageant used the word *Pfaffenknechte* in order to suggest that the soldiers of those days, who were merely carrying out the commands of their lawful superior, were inferior, despicable creatures.

Another scene represented Pope Leo III seeking help from Charles the Great at the Paderborn Parliament. The gestures of the Pope and of his companion, who wore a monk's greasy habit, were calculated to give an impression of Jewish bargaining and unworthy cringing. The whole aim seems to have been to provide amusement at the expense of the Pope.

Finally, complaints have been made to me with regard to certain portions of the entertainment which ended the pageant, portions of a dubious character, which cannot but have had a demoralising effect on young people. In particular attention was drawn to the representation of life amongst young people as it was before 1933, and to Hans Sachs' farce, *Das heisse Eisen*. I am at a loss to understand how anybody could produce that piece, which treats adultery as a mere trifle, amongst young people and before an almost wholly Catholic population which regards adultery as a serious sin.

I feel sure, Herr Gauleiter, that you will agree with me in condemning such provocative and insulting exhibitions of bad taste. They have aroused great indignation amongst Catholics in Paderborn and in the surrounding district, and seem to come, at least in part, within the scope of § 166 of the penal code. I have felt obliged to institute legal proceedings against those persons whose mockery of holy water and of the Sign of the Cross have given such deep public offence.

Public displays of pageantry such as took place on June 15th ought, in my view, to aim at the laudable object of upholding German national prestige and the unity of the German people. If they are employed in this frivolous fashion, they can only have the contrary effect. They sow seeds of bitter hostility and raise fresh barriers between the different sections of the community. They open up wounds long healed and inflict fresh injuries which cannot be quickly cured. For us Catholics, no injury is harder to bear than public mockery of things that we hold sacred.

DR. KLEIN, *Archbishop of Paderborn*.[1]

8. *The Press*

From the contents of all periodicals in the German Reich, and especially of those which are repeatedly recommended by the State and the Party, one can deduce with absolute certainty that the struggle against the Church is conducted systematically in official quarters. With a very few exceptions, all periodicals display an anti-clerical spirit in the form of endless malicious attacks on the Church itself, on bishops, priests, dogmas and standpoints peculiar to Christianity. At the same time the literary value of such attacks is negligible. Writers whose command of the German language is so slight that they could never write even a story competently achieve sales running into tens of thousands with their " yellow press " propaganda. It has become impossible, moreover, to put forward any defence of the Church through the medium of the press, or even to reply to gross calumnies.

Of the many pamphlets which circulate freely we give below a few specimen titles; the title is normally sufficient indication of the anti-Christian nature of the contents: " *Heil Deutschland!* Jesuitry a Danger to the German State," " Out with the Jesuits," " Auricular Confession," " The Sins of Rome," " Vatican and Kremlin," " A Roman Gossip out of School," " The Road of Sorrow for German Women," " The Reich Rises against Rome," " Heaven, Hell, and Currency Exchange," " The Clerical Underworld," " The Catholic Church Endangers the State," " The Perversion of the Soul in Convents," " Materialism in Christianity," " Jesuit Morality a Danger to State and Morality," " Rome against the Reich," " Adulteration of Racial Purity," " Treason for Heavenly Rewards," " The Status of Women in Christianity," "A Priest's Cry: Away from Rome and Christ," " Christian Cruelty to German Women," " Immorality Trials throughout Sixteen Centuries," " Escape from the Convent," " Two years behind Convent Walls," " Pope Joan," " Jesuitical Tricks," " Jesuits as Legacy Hunters," " Jesuits as Murderers," " Jesuit Education."

In addition the following are worth recording:

Bernhard Wiedenhöft: " Women under the Cross: The Status of Women in Christianity." (*Durchbruch-Verlag, Friedrich Böhler*, Stuttgart.)

H. Igler: " The Roman Church and Bolshevism." (*Adolf Klein Verlag*, Leipzig, 1937.)

[1] The text of this letter was published in Italian in the *Osservatore Romano* for August 14th, 1939.

THE PRESS

Erich Thomassin: " I was a Catholic: A Letter to a Friend." (*Durchbruch-Verlag, Friedrich Böhler*, Stuttgart.)

Burghard Assmus: " Convent Life: Revelations of Immorality in Monasteries." (*A. Bock Verlag*, Berlin.) 51st to 53rd thousand.

Martin Lintl: " Escape from a Monastery: Confessions and Revelations of M. L., a Carmelite Prior." (*Deutscher Verlag für Politik und Wirtschaft*, Berlin, 1939.)

Hellmuth Neumann: " How Rome Works." (Supplement to *Der Vorstoss*.) Published by *Verlag Deutscher Druck*, Munich.

Hellmuth Neumann: " The Prince Bishop Kohn to his Beloved Brother, Prince Bishop Faulhaber." (*Deutscher Hort Verlag*, Dessau.)

Hans Obermeister: No. 3 of the *Arischen Wehr*, 1936: " False Teaching of the Church." (1) The Put-up Job of Peter; (2) The False Doctrines of Protestantism Today. (*Verlag Ernst Pistor*, Berlin.)

In October, 1937, Cardinal Faulhaber felt obliged to refute an outworn slander which had been circulated in the Hitler Youth periodical, *Wille und Macht*. His letter to the editor is reproduced below:

MUNICH,
October, 8th, 1937.

With reference to your issue of October 2nd, 1937, in which a certain untruth was served up once more, I wish to make the following declaration on oath : On the night of November 8th to 9th, 1923, I did not receive any visit from the then General Commissary, Herr Kahr, neither at 3 a.m. nor at any other hour before or after; nor did I have any relations with Kahr, either over the telephone or through the medium of any third party, or in any other way whatsoever, so as to attempt to influence the decisions of the Government at that time. I am at a loss to understand how this ancient lie, already six times stigmatised as false before the courts or by public declaration, can be repeated once more today. I am obliged to infer that this repetition is intended to arouse political passions to fever pitch at the present moment. I demand a rectification of this slander, whether it has been made by reprinting an old poster or has been imprinted in the plastic minds of young people who are in no position to investigate the actual, legally-established facts of the case.

Signed: CARDINAL FAULHABER,
Archbishop of Munich.

On Sunday, October 16th, 1937, the Archbishop of Freiburg, Dr. Gröber, assisted at the closing celebrations of a Catholic " Youth Week " in Tauberbischofsheim. As isolated cases of foot-and-mouth disease had been reported in the district the Archbishop took the precaution of asking the local authorities whether the meeting ought to take place, and full official permission was granted. On the day following this brilliant profession of Faith the local Nazi leader in Tauberbischofsheim, Dr. Schmidt, published the following " Open Letter ":

To the Archbishop of Freiburg,

Moved by a deep sense of responsibility, the National Socialist Party forbade all meetings or gatherings in the district threatened by foot-and-mouth disease. It took all possible steps to prevent the disease from spreading. Nevertheless you, my Lord Archbishop, thought good to allow your well-known obstinacy to override all prohibitions, and held your assembly in

Tauberbischofsheim on Sunday ! You have thus lost all respect in the eyes of the people, for you have shown plainly that you consider the good of the community less than the satisfaction of your personal ambition. You would have done better to have stayed in your episcopal palace at Freiburg. Your opinions have stirred up a wave of hatred against you.

In a letter which was sent to all parishes of the archdiocese and which was in some cases read from the pulpits, the Archbishop pointed out the unrestricted nature of the permission granted to him, and added that on October 16th the Nazi Party had held a mass meeting in Freiburg for Alfred Rosenberg, in spite of the fact that foot-and-mouth disease had affected places in the immediate neighbourhood of the city.

A leader of the Secret Police, Herr Heydrich, published an article in the *Völk. Beobachter*[1] dealing with the campaign against enemies of the State, in which he compared the bishops to traitors and Communists. The four capital enemies of the Third Reich were Jews, Communists, Freemasons and politically-minded clergy. The struggle against neo-paganism he described as high treason and supreme hypocrisy. Episcopal pressure on elections he called " camouflaged high treason." " Surely this skilful undermining of unity in the political will of the German people is far more dangerous than the treasonable activities of Communism, precisely because it cannot be immediately detected by everybody."

In a report issued by the German News Agency, and widely employed by newspapers on or about January 25th, 1936, the parish priest of St. Josephs, Essen-Steele-Horst, was bitterly attacked on the grounds of a funeral sermon in the course of which he referred to the dead man's marriage as not having been solemnised by the Church. (He was a miner who had met with an accident.) The *Berlin Catholic Parish Magazine*[2] compared this account with the true state of affairs and with the exact phrase employed by the preacher, proving plainly that the accusation implied in the News Agency's report was sheer slander.

A somewhat similar case occurred in 1935, when the parish priest of a central German town was slandered in connection with his refusal to allow Catholic burial. The dead person had not practised his religion for fifteen years. On hearing, however, that the deceased's family were angry, the priest decided at the last moment to grant leave for the burial, and greatly pleased the family by informing them of his decision. The same evening he was removed from his presbytery by some two or three hundred members of the Party, and was led through the streets with a placard attached to him. He was then taken into custody and recommended, " for the sake of quiet amongst the people," to go away for some time. The material of this incident was carefully worked up by Nazi papers—*e.g.*, *Der Führer*, the Party's organ in Baden.

Canon Kraus of Eichstätt exposed in the pulpit a whole series of tendentious calumnies, concentrating in particular on the case of the *Augsburger Nationalzeitung*,[3] whose editor, Dr. Seewald, had published

---

[1] April, 1936. [2] February 23rd, 1936. [3] December 5th, 1936.

an article entitled, " As seen in Dachau." In it he described an interview with a prisoner, under the headline " I am a Priest," and reported the following conversation between himself and the prisoner:

" Why are you here ?"—" For unnatural vice."
" Good Heavens ! What is your occupation ?"—" I am a Catholic priest."
" Incredible ! Where did you study ?"—" With the Jesuits in Innsbruck."
" Did you work anywhere else ?"—" Yes, in Rome. I acted as an agent between the Vatican and Moscow."
I was struck dumb. The commandant of the camp who was standing near us nodded and said : " Yes, that is the case. He is speaking the truth."

Commenting on this in his sermon Canon Kraus observed:

The sound good sense of Catholics has reacted to all this, as letters addressed to me show, with incredulity. " Absolutely impossible." " Sheer romance." The *Klerusblatt*,[1] indeed, has stated: " In connection with this newspaper report, which has also been utilised at public meetings, we have word from Dachau that no Catholic priest is at present in the camp." This brief assertion, which was read from many pulpits, has been described by Dr. Seewald as " systematic propaganda from the pulpit."[2] However, this " pulpit propaganda " induced Dr. Seewald to visit the camp at Dachau once more to investigate the prisoner's record. Later he wrote: " My investigations show that this prisoner studied theology abroad, but was unable to complete his studies on account of grave moral defects. He describes himself, both to the other prisoners and to the authorities, as a man who has completed his course, although in reality he is but a student. These are the facts, and they cannot be controverted." What is one to say ? It is best for us to remain calm, even though this irresponsible news report makes our blood boil. As for Dr. Seewald, we reply: " Against these ' facts ' many objections can be raised. There in Dachau you have a prisoner who makes himself out to be a priest; he says he was a student in Innsbruck with the Jesuits, and acted as an agent between Rome and Moscow. The commandant is standing near, a man who has access to the prisoner's record; he does not say: ' The fellow is talking nonsense, is making idiotic exaggerations.' No, he merely nods and says: ' Yes, that is the case; he is speaking the truth.' As a result Catholic authorities make investigations and learn from Dachau itself that no Catholic priest was in the camp. Only then did Dr. Seewald act as he should have acted in the first instance. And yet even Dr. Seewald's second report cannot be accepted. It is full of patent contradictions. Now we hear no reference to a Catholic priest, or to a student in Innsbruck, or to a liaison agent between Rome and Moscow. And, from beginning to end, the name of the prisoner is carefully concealed. This is truly remarkable. Why so much modesty ? Is it possible that it is concealed in order to prevent Catholic priests from corroborating this second statement of facts ? Dr. Seewald has asserted, and repeated his assertion at a local meeting, that the Catholic parish priest at Dachau made no inquiries of the camp authorities either personally or in writing. Yet I have here a report from Fr. Pflanzelt, the parish priest of Dachau, in which he states that Standartenführer Baronovski of Dachau has twice informed him that no Catholic priest is present in the camp. This report was sent to his Ordinary in Munich by Fr. Pflanzelt on December 14th, 1936."

The preacher ended his remarks on Dachau and Dr. Seewald with the following telling sentences:

You may judge for yourselves whether I had not some excuse for righteous indignation when I stated that you may consistently regard newspapers as lying if they publish scandal-mongering stories about the Church and about

---

[1] No. 51.   [2] *Augsburger Nationalzeitung*, January 27th, 1937

priests. And if I make such a statement, if I throw light on the truth and set accusations in their true perspective, am I to be accused of " abuse of the pulpit "? Does that make me a " political priest "? Is the rejection of calumny and the correction of lies to be styled " indulgence in politics "? Surely all honourable German citizens, who value straight dealing and truthfulness in public life, must welcome the action of a priest who observes and defends the eighth commandment.[1]

It was not enough to employ official refusals and confiscation in order to make replies and refutations of this deplorable press campaign impossible. The Catholic press has not even been allowed to report the existence of such a campaign. For example, the *Munich Catholic Parish Magazine*[2] published the following sentence: " In this connection we should like to point out that during the last few weeks a host of attacks has been made upon our beloved pastors "; and for this observation the number was confiscated.

The attitude which the Hitler Youth was permitted to indulge with regard to the bishops may be gathered from a libellous article in the *HJ*,[3] in which Archbishop Gröber was wildly attacked for his pamphlet, " Youth for Christ." One may compare two other articles in the *HJ*,[4]—" Wolves in Sheep's Clothing " and " A Great Fuss about a Searchlight " (the latter article displaying lamentable ignorance of the doctrine of the Immaculate Conception). On similar lines was the mockery directed against a Pastoral Letter of the German Bishops in *Durchbruch*,[5] and against a similar Letter issued from Breslau for Matriculation candidates in *Die Bewegung*, the official organ of the Nazi Students' Union.[6] The *Schwarze Korps* repeatedly published coarse attacks on Cardinals and Bishops—*e.g.*, " Who is Lying, Herr Cardinal ?",[7] " The End justifies the Means."[8]

It would be almost impossible to record the vast quantity of propaganda against the Catholic Church and its official representatives which was published in periodicals such as *Durchbruch*, *Nordland*, *Blitz*, *Der Romfreie Katholik*, *Positives Christentum*, etc. Hitler Youth periodicals contained attacks on the Church, the Papacy and the bishops in almost every number. Perhaps the lowest and most disgusting examples of irresponsible hatred directed against the Church were to be found in *Die Brennessel*,[9] a weekly paper directed by the Party. Every issue sought to throw mud at Christianity by means of articles and cartoons. We reproduce a few specimens of its vulgarity, the first a piece of doggerel taken from No. 31, August 3rd, 1937:[10]

THE ASCETICS

By Gerhard Schumann

The murky sons of darkness
Burrow dimly on through time:
They grudge us joy and gladness
In the creatures of our clime.

[1] *Riechspost*, April 13th, 1937.
[2] No. 10, March 8th, 1936.
[3] No. 35, 1935.
[4] February 15th, 1936.
[5] February 20th, 1936.
[6] March 11th, 1936.
[7] February 20th, 1936.
[8] February 13th, 1936. *Cf.* also July 1st, 1937.
[9] *Parteiverlag Franz Eher*, Berlin.
[10] P. 362.

THE PRESS

> To decency oblivious,
> In all they sin divine,
> These he-goats, sly, lascivious,
> These wallowing, filthy swine.
>
> Is the world, then, but the measure
> Of our fall to Hell ? Oh ! what,
> To God, to us, the pleasure,
> If the devil took the lot.

In No. 30, July 27th, 1937, p. 352, the following " Sayings for Wearers of Cowls " appeared:

> God is everywhere, except at Rome, where He has His deputy.
> The most stupid people are found where monasteries are most numerous.
> Where the lion fails the fox succeeds; where the fox fails comes the Devil; where the Devil fails the Jesuit wins through.
> They must eat much blessed meat in convents, said the daughter who came home pregnant from the convent !
> In many a monastery you will find two pairs of slippers under the bed.
> In the shade of the cloister all things corrupt—only women become fruitful.
> The nearer the monastery, the poorer the peasants.
> The Devil himself would not dare attempt what a monk will try.
> A well-filled pair of corsets makes a fine dish, say the priests. Thirteen nuns, fourteen children.

Similar " Sayings " appeared in No. 31, August 3rd, 1937, p. 372—*e.g.*:

> When the Pope needs money he peoples Heaven.
> Priests do not marry Poverty so long as the peasants have wives.
> If God could not swim He would long ago have been drowned in the wine swilled by priests.

9. *Cartoons and Caricatures*

We have reproduced some specimens from the vast number of cartoons dealing with the Church, the clergy and ecclesiastical institutions which have been published both in the official German press and in private publications. The following caricatures of cardinals and Bishops in the *Schwarze Korps* are also worthy of note: issues of July 8th, 1937; January 23rd, 1937; May 27th, 1937; June 3rd, 1937. *Cf.* the *Stürmer*, No. 31, 1937.

A little reflection on the attacks directed against the honour of the clergy and of ecclesiastical institutions, which we have recorded above, obliges one to agree with the Bavarian Hierarchy in its protest recorded in the Christmas Pastoral, 1936:

> The Concordat with the Reich grants official protection to the clergy against slander.
> What has become of this protection in view of the continuous campaign of gross calumny which is waged against the priesthood in speeches, books, periodicals and pictures ? What kind of official protection is granted to the good name of priests in view of cartoons which are publicly posted up everywhere, even in the tiniest villages, so that every child can read them ? Has the priesthood ever been held up to ridicule so much as it is today in

papers whose circulation runs into hundreds of thousands and in speeches given everywhere in Germany, given even by public officials ? We have even learnt of the case of a teacher who displayed a vulgar, anti-clerical cartoon in the schoolroom, and refused to remove it when asked to do so by the priest who was giving religious instruction. . . .

The Concordat ensures protection for priests and for the good name of their calling; nevertheless the bishops in this country are being subjected to unparalleled attacks. . . .

CHAPTER XI

THE CURRENCY TRIALS AND THE " IMMORALITY " TRIALS

1. *The " Currency Trials " (Devisenprozesse)*

WE do not propose to discuss here the purely legal aspect of this matter. In some cases it was clear that the defendants were aware of having acted contrary to the Currency Laws, and the offence was openly condemned by the ecclesiastical authorities. Our aim is to show, by means of the following facts, that National Socialism welcomed the *Devisenprozesse* as a weapon of primary importance in its attack on the Church.

Using every available means of propaganda at its disposal, National Socialism exploited these trials in order to slander the Church. Throughout the summer of 1935 the Nazi press and radio broadcast information about members of religious Orders who had infringed the currency regulations. More especially in the press of the Party were sensational accounts of these cases put forward, usually under large headings—for example, " Pious Tricksters go to Prison," " Brazen Blasphemy,"[1] " Millions skilfully Smuggled from Convents,"[2] " Martyrs and Clerical Currency Tricksters."[3] In this last case caricatures of Sisters of Mercy dressed in their habits were printed on the first page.[4] This same number of the *Schwarze Korps* contained the following passage:

We have no particular interest in the private lives of individual monks, nuns and secular priests who have been arrested at the Customs barriers, but when priests and religious whose dubious love affairs are all too well known are suddenly decked out with halos and martyrs' crowns and presented as innocent victims of the National Socialist State, we feel ourselves obliged to reply to such manœuvres with all possible emphasis. It is our duty to point out to faithful German Catholics the gulf which exists between the moral teaching of the Church and its fulfilment by a large section of the priesthood. Nothing will prevent the National Socialist State from following the path which morality and law point out for it. It can only regret that its progress is being hindered by certain people who preach morality and law, but have no respect for either in their own case.

Members of religious Orders were held to be devoid of all national sentiment and accused of considering nothing but their own financial gain; and in spite of the fact that ecclesiastical superiors had explicitly

---

[1] *Angriff*, May 18th, 1935. [2] *Ibid*, May 17th, 1935.
[3] *Das Schwarze Korps*, May 22nd, 1935. [4] *Cf. Angriff*, May 20th, 1935.

condemned this particular offence, the Church as a whole was held responsible. Speeches dealing with charges against the accused were given the greatest publicity, while speeches for the defence either passed unreported or were allowed only a few lines. Frequently, too, when much had been made of a condemnation, nothing was allowed to be published about the subsequent appeal and acquittal.

In many similar financial cases of embezzlement, etc., in which ordinary citizens and, more especially, members of the National Socialist Party were involved, the Nazi press reported nothing or practically nothing. This policy of slander on the part of the press was in no way checked, but rather encouraged, by responsible officials. Moreover, at official Party meetings, in camps, etc., the malicious Currency ditty was regularly sung.

The legal conduct of these cases proved the existence of a malicious attitude towards religious Orders and the Church, though it must be admitted that the courts were careful to commit no legal blunders. At the same time the following facts should be recorded:

(A) State attorneys went to the length of putting Catholic nuns on the same footing as Galician Jews and traitors to the community, and to insinuate that they were trying to put aside an illegal hoard; and, moreover, that through the agency of Dr. Hofius, the financial adviser of almost all the Orders concerned in the trials, Jewish capital had been employed in order to finance the designs of the Catholic Church in Germany.

(B) Although the Currency trials were held before special courts designed to give speedy verdicts, a large number of the accused, invalids amongst them, were detained in prison for a month or longer.

(C) In the conduct of these cases it was noticeable that even the physical welfare of the accused received little attention. In the case of a Canon Heisig, from Lauban, the doctor stated that the accused was suffering from a complete nervous collapse and was not responsible for his words or actions. In spite of this fact, and in spite of his solicitor's request for an acquittal, he received a sentence of three and a half years' imprisonment, no extenuating circumstances being taken into account.

(D) Defending solicitors repeatedly complained of the inadequate time allowed for them to prepare their cases and to discuss the complicated details with the accused. A good example is the case of the Redemptorist, Fr. Aigner. The solicitor stated:[1]

A short period of three hours, in which some thirty points had to be discussed, was insufficient for a clear understanding of the case. I beg you not to take up the accused's words too sharply. He has been in prison for four months, and cannot rely with absolute accuracy on his memory alone, just as a chief cashier of a bank would be unable to give an exact record of the transactions of the last two or three years without his statement of accounts.

[1] August 5th, 1935.

(E) Bound as they were to give true, unbiassed judgements, these courts were further bound to pay attention to the following psychological and ethical considerations as, at the least, extenuating circumstances.

In all these " crimes " the initial inpulse came from Dr. Hofius, who, as a professional, was able to influence members of religious Orders, and who always guaranteed the legitimacy of the proposed transactions.

In the case of the accused Sisters of Mercy, a factor of importance was their ignorance of the world and a certain simplicity in money matters. Since they dealt exclusively with charitable administration and not with ordinary business affairs, their knowledge of commercial dealings and of scientific book-keeping, etc., was incomplete. It is certain, moreover, that these Religious did not realise the extent to which their transactions were liable to disturb German currency, and they had little practical understanding of what was signified by the Currency Laws.

One might add that the very complicated nature of the Currency regulations should have been taken into account. A lawyer named Reichling, of Münster, who acted as defending counsel in the trial of the Hiltrup Fathers, stated on July 22nd, 1935:

> I have known experienced lawyers, who have fought their way through many Currency trials, remark in the course of private conversations that not only their colleagues, but even judges and State attorneys, had fallen into theoretical errors in matters of Currency Law.

It is true, also, to say that whenever Religious profited by legally incorrect transactions, their profit was completely devoted to charitable objects—*i.e.*, to the welfare of the German people. Justice demanded that every aspect of each case should have been taken into consideration, and that motives should have been carefully weighed. There could be no question of avarice or of selfish desire to enrich themselves amongst these accused Religious. Both before and after their Currency transactions they lived in poverty. In one case (against a missionary of the Sacred Heart, of Hiltrup) the financial dealings with which he was charged were intended to benefit German nationals in the South Seas, and both the accused and the Superior of his Order—whom the State attorney labelled a " swindler "—should have been regarded as pioneers of national German interests.

It is a fact that these psychological and ethical considerations which we have indicated were *never* taken into consideration, and never served as a motive for leniency. In practically every case the courts inflicted the severe punishments demanded by the official accusers and ignored all representations for the defence.

2. The So-called " Immorality " Trials

The " Immorality " trials represent a particularly malicious aspect of the attack upon the honour of the Church. It has been suggested that a Church whose " elect " have been convicted of such gross crimes has irreparably damaged her own good name, and cannot complain of slander from the world outside. To this one may reply that, although the courts brought regrettable misdemeanours to light, two general assertions must be emphatically contested or denied—viz.:

1. That the public learnt the whole truth;
2. That the rulers of the Third Reich employed these cases as a means of improving moral standards and conduct.

A. *Documentary evidence shows that the public did not learn the whole truth.*

1. An objective account of the real facts was made impossible by tendentious reports.

As soon as the first of the " Immorality " trials had begun in Coblenz in 1935 a veritable barrage of reports appeared in the Nazi press on the subject of supposed immoralities committed by Catholic priests and members of the religious Orders. The majority of these reports either had no foundation in fact or consisted of incredible exaggerations and generalisations of individual offences. None of these false statements was ever recalled, and no national journal ever dared to publish any correction or modification. The Church was obliged to look on helplessly while the reputation of her representatives was dragged in the mud.

Some examples follow:

(A) The *Alemanne* [1] (a Baden paper belonging to the Party) published an article under the heading, " Purity and Modesty ? Catholic Student of Theology exposed as Sexual Criminal."

The Facts of the Case.—This " theological student " was in reality a student in one of the lower classes of the secondary school at Sassbach. After a short probationary stay there he was dismissed for unsatisfactory conduct and work by the authorities.

(B) By an order issued on December 28th, 1936, the Bavarian Ministry of Education declared the Marist Brothers, the Brothers of Christian Schools and the Augustinian Hermits to be unfitted for the control of educational institutions and withdrew all licences for that work. The official grounds given referred to the existence of grave immorality in their institutions, and this fact was repeatedly mentioned in the press. The Ministry's decree, together with details of individual accusations, was sent out to all officials of the Party who had control of the different local groups, and they were instructed to broadcast information about the matter to the best of their abilities.

[1] July 15th, 1935.

To illustrate the true state of affairs we may take the case of the Marist Brothers as typical of the rest:

1. In a boarding establishment for schoolboys at Traunstein a Brother Ludwig was found guilty of misconduct and received sentence of two years' imprisonment. As soon as the school authorities learnt of the matter the Brother was sent away from the house and dismissed from the Order.

2. Several cases concerned the secondary school and hostel at Mindelheim. In each case we give first the terms of the accusation, then a brief comment on the facts.

(a) A former Spiritual Father, Dr. Schwarzer, was sentenced to two years' imprisonment in 1927 for sexual misconduct with schoolboys. Schwarzer was not a member of the Order, and was only connected with it as an occasional helper who had been highly recommended. The offences were committed outside the college buildings, and Schwarzer was instantly dismissed by the management on the very day that his offences became known—viz., ten years previously, on April 14th, 1927.

(b) A house-servant named Hamm, employed in the same college, was condemned to prison for immoral practices with a grown-up person. Hamm was not a member of the Order, nor even a servant in the house, but a hired assistant working in the grounds. He had no contact with the life of the school or with the pupils, and the offence was committed with a person unconnected with the college.

(c) Lutz, another house-servant, was imprisoned in 1936 for high treason. He had no connection with the Order, and the management of the college still remains uninformed as to the real nature of the charge against him. Police officials maintained that he was in communication with his brother, a person accused of communistic activities.

3. At the *Karls-Realschule* and boarding-house in Bad Reichenhall, a Brother Remigius was accused of misconduct with a schoolboy and sentenced to imprisonment. In actual fact the school authorities discovered the offence in 1936, and dismissed him from the Order on the same day.

To sum up: in Traunstein a single case occurred, which resulted in the immediate dismissal of the culprit by his Superiors. Three cases in Mindelheim were in no way connected with members of the Order. For these offences and that of Brother Remigius the Marist Brothers were deprived of their control over *eight* institutions.

Similarly, in the case of the other Orders named above, the actual offences committed were negligible in comparison with the outcry raised in the press. One may reasonably ask: Is it possible for any school, however well conducted, to guarantee absolutely that no unsuitable person is included amongst those under its supervision? Can one reasonably demand more than instant dismissal in such cases? Is it, moreover, correct according to German legal conceptions to seize upon such isolated misdemeanours in order to conduct systematic official propaganda, or to punish whole religious Congregations with what is almost complete destruction?

(c) In January, 1937, the whole German press printed a report from the German News Agency concerning a Catholic theological student who had been condemned by a jury court in Offenburg for incest and other sexual crimes. He was described as a student whose educational expenses were being paid by the Church, and as " Leader of all Catholic Youth Associations in Baden." Following up this report the Nazi and neo-pagan papers surpassed themselves with base attacks upon the Catholic Church. Thus the *Schwarze Korps*[1] printed the headline, " From Incest to Ordination," and lower down, in thick type:

> As in the case of all crimes committed by members of Roman Orders, so now in the case of the beastly crime of incest the Roman Church has sheltered the sins of one of its members. This underhand behaviour seems to us worse than the offence itself !

Early in January the diocesan authorities of Freiburg-im-Breisgau issued the following declaration, to be read from all pulpits:

> The daily papers have recently published accounts of a trial held in camera of a young man who had committed serious sexual offences with members of his own family. This nineteen-year-old youth was not a Youth leader of all Catholic Youth Associations in Baden, as has been repeatedly stated, and his connection with such organisations was limited to work lasting roughly six months, some two years ago, with the diocesan leaders of the Catholic Youth League. Since April last he has attended the Upper Fifth class of a private secondary school in Baden.
> We wish to state with the greatest possible emphasis that the deeply offensive insinuation of continued official, ecclesiastical patronage being given to this young man's education contains no grain of truth. The ecclesiastical authorities knew nothing of the unhappy youth's crimes until his imprisonment was announced.

As a result of this announcement the Propaganda Ministry obliged the whole German press, even ecclesiastical journals,[2] to print a " refutation " of the official ecclesiastical declaration, under the title, " The Schülle Case Again," and specimen copies had to be sent to press censors before publication. (In connection with this incident it is worth noting that no means was left to the bishops for announcing their opinions beyond the pulpits of their dioceses.)

The real facts of the case were well presented by Canon Kraus in a sermon delivered[3] in the Cathedral of Eichstätt. He said, in effect:

> Schülle was not a student of theology, but a student at a secondary school. Had a boy at that school, who intended later to become an officer in the army, committed the same crimes and been described in the papers as a standard-bearer, every officers' mess would have protested, and the papers would have been obliged to withdraw the statement. It has further been stated that Schülle could have continued his studies under ecclesiastical patronage even after such offences had been discovered. Father Dettinger has sworn under oath that he never said anything of the kind, least of all on the solitary occasion when he had a talk with Schülle. His statement on that occasion expressed the opposite of what has been asserted. It is said, too, that the Archbishop himself promoted Schülle to be a diocesan Youth leader. The fact is that

---

[1] February 4th, 1937. [2] *E.g.*, *Der Katholik*, February 7th, 1937.
[3] January 31st, 1937.

the Archbishop had never even heard of Schülle until he was sent to prison. Finally, it is said that the Archbishop has visited Schülle in prison. The fact is that the Archbishop paid a visit to a priest imprisoned at Kislau, and happened to speak to Schülle for a few minutes at the same time.

(D) The German press dealt in the same unprecedented fashion with the " Criminal Assault and Murder at Manage," in Belgium. Thus, for example, the *Schwarze Korps*[1] published an article on the subject under the title " It Stinks to Heaven," along with a repulsive cartoon. As might be expected, the Belgian monastery in which the crime took place was made fully responsible for it, and it was assumed as self-evident that the murderer must have been a Brother of the Order. The article, therefore, consisted of wild attacks on the morality of monastic houses. For example:

> How much, how very much must go on behind the walls of monasteries amongst Catholic communities of Brothers ! How much, for which no atonement is ever made in the public courts ! One wonders how much clerical circles have managed to hush up ! The tension which these cases display between " ideal and reality," between " God and all that fights against Him " cannot be explained away merely by the " human side of the Church." It is the outward expression and the natural effect of a system which has exalted the unnatural to the level of a general principle, of an organisation which has freed itself from public control. That is proof enough that such things occur repeatedly amongst the clergy !

A large number of extra copies of this *Schwarze Korps* article were printed and pushed through letter-boxes in Munich and other cities, and in one case were even placed in the pamphlet-box of a church. Even papers formerly Catholic[2] were forced to print the report of the German News Agency in full.

The facts of the case:

1. The institution in Manage was not a monastic school, but an industrial school run by the *Frères de la Charité*.

2. The murderer was not a brother, but a house-servant who had only recently been employed there.

3. While the German press was raging, the young man was being medically examined for suspected mental aberrations.

4. Although more than ten thousand of these Brothers of Mercy work in Belgium, nothing prejudicial to their moral reputation was known.

5. The Belgian Foreign Office requested the German Radio authorities to correct their previous announcements, since the murderer was not a Brother but a house-servant. The correction was indeed made, but as inconspicuously as possible—between 6 a.m. and 7 a.m.—and only one newspaper mentioned the matter in a couple of lines at the end of its editorial section.

(E) During the summer of 1937 another disgusting crime was worked to death by the German Press in its efforts to slander the Church. The case was one of criminal assault and murder committed by a seventeen-year-old boy against a child of thirteen. At first the murderer was described as a lay-brother; and later, when this false-

[1] April 15th, 1937. [2] *E.g., Kölnische Volkszeitung,* April 4th, 1937.

hood could no longer be maintained, he became a pupil in a monastery school. He remained such, in spite of the fact that the press could not avoid circulating a report that he had been expelled from a monastic school on account of misdemeanours which were attributable to ill-health, and had been sent to a municipal hospital. The press reports found nothing blameworthy in the fact that the boy was able to leave the hospital secretly, but reproached the school authorities bitterly for their carelessness in allowing the murderer's victim to be secretly removed. " The extraordinary circumstances of this murder are only explicable in the light of the conditions peculiar to denominational boarding-schools, conditions which reflect a mentality utterly unsuitable for dealing with children." Some reports went so far as to make Archbishop Gröber indirectly responsible for the murder: " It is worth noting that, only a few days before, Archbishop Gröber made a highly controversial speech at Villingen, in the course of which he referred to the martyrdom suffered by the Catholic priesthood. . . ." All the unsavoury details of the murder were fully described, no respect whatever being shown for the feelings of the readers. Celibacy and chastity were bitterly attacked, and every effort made to stimulate dormant prejudices. The supposed indignation of parents and of the teaching profession was also described in detail, and the reports closed with the following observation gratuitously attributed to Catholic parents: " Catholic parents who have been approached are unanimous in stating, ' Never again shall we entrust our children to such schools, for their unhealthy atmosphere is a veritable breeding-ground for such criminal abnormalities.' "

The real facts of the case were explained as follows by Father Ackermann of Rodalben in a sermon delivered on the occasion of the victim's burial:

I have rarely felt so depressed as I feel today, standing beside the grave of this budding flower so ruthlessly plucked by the hand of a murderer. It was a flower developing and opening out under the tender care of the Teaching Brothers of Maria-Tann. I wish to stress this fact, since the poor afflicted parents were completely satisfied with the physical, moral and spiritual development of their child at that school. The boy was devoted to the school, and all those placed over him were delighted with his zeal and good-will. All was going well until the powers of evil crossed his path. In every flock there exists some black sheep ! Every experienced teacher will tell you that children exist whose mental or moral balance is disturbed by some kink, and in the case of this unhappy murderer such a kink seems to have been at the root of the trouble. A mental rather than a moral kink, most probably, for I am in a position to affirm that the immoral practices of which so much has been made consisted in the fact that the murderer kissed his victim's feet. Such conduct is much more likely to arise from some mental disturbance than from moral corruption. On May 26th this madness showed itself, and only then did the school authorities become aware of the murderer's former eccentricities. The Brother Superior did his duty immediately by sending the offender to the hospital at Villingen, about an hour's walk from Maria-Tann. The boy's father was at once informed, and told that the school could no longer keep his son amongst its pupils. All the father's efforts to make the Superior change his mind had no effect. Indeed, had the father but obeyed the Superior's urgent request to remove his son from the hospital to his own home, this shocking misfortune would never have taken place. There is no question whatsoever of attaching any blame to the school, a fact admitted by the committee appointed to investigate. . . . The murderer was certainly not in full possession of his reason at the time of his crime. . . .

(F) On May 25th, 1937, the *Völk. Beobachter* published the following account:

AN ILL-CHOSEN CHRISTIAN WORKER

Three Years' Imprisonment for the Founder of a Catholic Youth League: Sentence given in Munich on May 24th

A forty-four-year-old Munich man, Karl Krieger, appeared before the Munich court to answer a charge of criminal assault upon a minor. Krieger was the founder of a Catholic Youth League, *Jugendlust*, the result, he confessed, of his personal interest in Christian social work. Once already, in 1930, Krieger was involved in a case of unnatural vice, but escaped punishment with the aid of medical evidence. The court sentenced the accused to imprisonment for three years.

Some facts about Krieger:

1. This " Christian worker," founder of a " Catholic Youth League," was not a priest.

2. His " League " was not a Catholic Youth organisation, though Krieger may well have disguised it with some such name.

3. Neither Krieger nor his League was known to ecclesiastical authorities.

(G) The following case may conveniently be included at this point. On May 29th, 1937, the *Völk. Beobachter* published an account under the heading, " Over the Frontier with False Passports," and on the following day the *Münchener Neueste Nachrichten* published the same account under the headline, " Jesuit Father Forges Documents." In each case the article dealt with the persecution on May 28th of the Alexian Brothers in Bonn. One of the accused, Ernst Walter, deposed that he had received forged papers—baptismal certificate, certificate of good conduct, etc.—from Friedrich Schmidt, a Munich Jesuit, which were intended to aid his flight from justice. On the strength of this statement the case for the State presumed the existence of a regular bureau for the forgery of passports and papers.

Some facts of the case:

1. The accused was called Walter Raupp, not Ernst Walter.

2. Neither in Germany nor Austria was there any Jesuit Father bearing the name Friedrich Schmidt.

3. No address in Munich answered to the description *Am Dom Nr. 5*," the supposed residence of the supposed Father.

4. In Munich there is not even a street named *Am Dom*. The court refused to give credence to the accused's statements on account of this falsehood, but the newspapers did not follow suit.

(H) The Vienna *Reichspost* published the following statement on June 14th, 1937:

Certain North German papers published an account of dreadful immoralities practised in a monastery at Biberach. A little later it was clearly established that no monastery exists at Biberach, and that nobody living there knew anything detrimental to the character of any members of religious Orders. In the neighbourhood of Biberach three or four priests reside and manage a Retreat House, and they stand very high in the esteem of their neighbours.

(I) Another case of malicious slander directed against the Catholic priesthood was connected with an episcopal declaration, read from all pulpits in the diocese of Munich, towards the end of June, 1937. The declaration ran:

A Munich paper with a wide circulation has published articles in which a priest attached to the parish of St. Margaret's, Munich, is accused of misusing the confessional in order to screen persons liable to court proceedings on account of immoral practices. Here we wish to state that the priest in question is an old Father who, held in the highest respect by all who know him, can look back on fifty years of highly fruitful activity in the care of souls. In the course of his long and exemplary priestly life no shadow of what is alleged in this dreadful accusation has ever arisen to darken his work amongst varied classes of society. It would appear that the accusers have not even taken the trouble to get into touch with the parish concerned, but have relied on the unverifiable and almost incredible statements of children in order to attack not only a widely-respected priest, but the holy Sacrament of Penance itself. For all the faithful the confessional is a holy spot, a place where the most complete trust can be placed in priests whose lips are permanently sealed. The faithful know well the true value of these attacks with which we have dealt.

(J) The *Stuttgarter NS.-Kurier*[1] published a report of proceedings at the criminal court of Ellwangen under the following large headline: " Lay-Brother at the Monastery of Neresheim Convicted of Twenty Offences against Public Morality."

Dealing with the case, the Benedictines of Neresheim issued a circular for the use of parish priests, in which they asserted categorically that of these twenty offences attributed to Schlipf, only one had been committed while he was a Benedictine Brother, the rest as a layman. It was for the one committed within the monastery that he had been instantly dismissed by his superiors.

(K) Towards the end of 1937 appeared a pamphlet entitled " The Truth about the Immorality Trials," by Herr Schwäbe, editor-in-chief of the *Westdeutscher Beobachter*. In the course of this work certain statements were quoted, said to have been made by a Catholic priest, Fr. Otto Schwab of Bamberg. Yet in the whole Archdiocese of Bamberg no priest of that name was known, and no other German Bishop had a Fr. Otto Schwab in his territory.

2. Wild exaggerations and generalisations made in connection with these trials.

National Socialism was not content with mere false or tendentious reports such as those we have cited above. Ministers of State and other responsible personages in the Third Reich entered the lists, backed up by the vast circulation of the Nazi press, and, unchecked

[1] No. 607, December 30th, 1937.

by any considerations of truth or decency, raged against monasteries, the priesthood and the Church in speeches which the wireless made accessible to the most remote villages. Herr Frick, for example, was not ashamed to speak as follows at Coblenz in 1936:

> In this connection I must add a few words in reference to the deplorable trials which are taking place at present in this city of Coblenz, and say something of the scandalous deeds which have taken place in certain monasteries. The German public has been deeply shocked by the depths of depravity which it has been obliged to contemplate. Religious houses, which ought to be centres of contemplation and pious prayer and praise, have shown themselves to be mere breeding-grounds of vice.

The Propaganda Minister, Dr. Göbbels, excelled all others in the propagation of incredible charges against the Church. In a speech relayed by all German wireless stations on May 28th, 1937, his assertions were so sweeping and the style adopted was so vulgar and savoured so much of market-place oratory that one can only assume that hatred of the Church carried the able Propaganda Minister away, and made him incapable of realising the disastrous effect of his attacks. This speech, which aroused indignation in all foreign countries, contained the following choice remarks:

> A vast number of Catholic clerics have been tried for sexual crimes. . . . It is not a matter of regrettable individual lapses, but of a general corruption of morals such as the history of civilisation has scarcely ever known. . . . No other class of society has ever come to shelter such depravity. . . . In our civilised world no other class of society has contrived to practise immorality and indulge in filth on a scale resembling that achieved by the German clergy in all its ranks. . . . We cannot possibly impose legal sanctions on unnatural vice and at the same time allow thousands upon thousands of priests and brothers of religious Orders to escape scot-free. . . . A very large number of these priests and Religious work in the confessional. . . . There is no doubt that even the thousands of cases which have come to light represent but a small fraction of the total moral corruption.

We shall deal below with other sections of this speech. For the moment we wish to stress the fact that Herr Göbbels spoke of thousands upon thousands of crimes committed by Catholic priests.

Herr Kerrl, Minister for Ecclesiastical Affairs, spoke at Hagen in Westphalia on November 30th, 1937, and gave the following figures for the " Immorality " trials. Persons condemned: Priests, 45; Brothers and nuns, 176; employees, etc., 21; total, 242. Cases still in progress concerned 93 priests, 744 Brothers and nuns, and 118 employees, a total of 955. Cases withdrawn or convictions not obtained concerned 29 priests, 127 Brothers, 31 employees, a total of 187. Shortly after, on November 24th, 1937, the same Minister spoke at Fulda of some 7,000 convictions of Catholic clergy since 1933.

This type of statistical reckoning was dealt with neatly by the Lucerne paper *Vaterland* on December 14th, 1937. We give a summary of the article as follows:

> The Minister so juggled with his figures, quietly including cases of libel " abuse of the pulpit," offences against the Flag Law (*i.e.*, enjoining the flying of the Swastika on stated occasions), and so on, that he over-reached

himself in his efforts to show that the *Sittlichkeitsprozesse* represented a perpetual practice of vice on the part of the priesthood as a whole. It is obvious, for example, that " abuse of the pulpit " must occur more frequently amongst priests than amongst other members of the community ! Similarly, the figures given of 7,000 cases involving 16,000 members of religious Orders for men was only arrived at by adding into the sexual offences many other infringements of the law on the part of nuns and secular priests. Anything to give an imposing total ! One can only conclude that such figures are a striking testimony to the good repute rather than the depravity of the German clergy; for such juggling with figures is surely a sign of a deplorably weak case !

Similar statistical exaggerations were indulged in by District Leader Streicher in speeches which he made during the summer and autumn of 1936 in Baden. Thus he declared that against the clergy of Baden alone 100 trials for sexual offences were in progress. At the same time Archbishop Gröber of Freiburg testified that the total was at most five or six, and pointed out that convictions in these cases were by no means a foregone conclusion.

The Real Figures.

It was clear that the ecclesiastical authorities could not remain passive while these accusations were being made, and in June the bishops published the following declaration through the only channel left open to them—the pulpit:

We have asked all German bishops to send in exact statistics of priests and members of Congregations who have become involved in " immorality " trials. Of the Congregations, representing some 100,000 men and women, exact figures are not yet forthcoming. With reference to priests, however, we can state that of the 21,461 secular priests in Germany, 49 have been involved in these trials. Of these, 21 have been convicted, 28 still await sentence. Of 4,174 priests belonging to religious Orders, 9 have been charged, 1 convicted; the rest are still on trial. Out of a total, therefore, of 25,634 priests, 58 cases have arisen, accounting for about 1 priest in every 500.[1]

We add some official figures for individual dioceses. In Münster, with over 1,000 secular priests, only 6 priests were involved in accusations of sexual misconduct from 1933 to 1937. Of these, 2 were acquitted, 1 case was dropped, and another was still undecided in May, 1937. In 2 cases sentence of imprisonment was passed. Of 270 priests, members of religious Orders in the diocese, 1 was accused and condemned to imprisonment. Of some 500 Brothers in various congregations, 13 were accused, 4 were condemned, 5 acquitted, 3 cases were dropped and 2 were still undecided in 1937. Of the 1,200 nuns working in the diocese, not one was condemned on a charge of immoral practices.

In Bavaria the figures for the various dioceses were as follows:

In 1936, priests from the eight dioceses of Bavaria appeared in the courts on a variety of charges to the number of 164. Fifty-five of these cases were State prosecutions (offences against the pulpit regulations, the law about public meetings, the Flag Law, etc.), and of these 19 were suspended, 23 ended with acquittal, 3 with a pardon, 5 with fines and 4 with imprisonment.

[1] *Osservatore Romano*, June 9th, 1937.

This means that during 1936, only 13 representatives of the Bavarian priesthood met with legal punishments. One should consider, too, that some of these cases were very trivial—*e.g.*, the result of not hanging out a flag on a church on some special occasion.[1]

For the large Archdiocese of Freiburg, Archbishop Gröber declared that the number of priests and Religious charged with immoral practices did not exceed four or five. In the diocese of Meissen only two such cases occurred since 1933 against secular priests. One of them was sentenced to one and a half year's imprisonment, the other, after seven months' detention, was acquitted. Finally, in the diocese of Würzburg, with its 1,041 priests, only one was sentenced in these trials between 1933 and 1937.

These examples may be taken as typical of other German dioceses. In reply, therefore, to the Nazi charge one may legitimately ask: Can any other large section of society boast of so small a percentage of unworthy elements in its midst ? Indeed, one cannot escape the fact that the German public was deliberately and systematically deceived in the accounts given of the " Immorality trials."

3. The suppression of vital circumstances.

Correct statistics were not the only factor connected with these trials about which the public was misinformed. A whole group of other circumstances, which would have thrown light on those cases of clerical misconduct which did occur, were systematically glossed over. Thus, for example, the speeches for the defence were not published. A casual glance at German newspapers issued between 1935 and 1937 gives an impression of continuous reports devoted to " Immorality trials." The case for the State is fully written up, the speeches often quoted verbatim, but any search for a report of the defence is fruitless. At best the papers allowed it a few words.

Similarly, in very many cases in which the accused was described as a " Brother ", the fact that he had long been dismissed from his Order was suppressed. Nor did the reports state that religious Orders had very often dealt with the case themselves. The phrase " member of an Order " was frequently used to include lay-people—*e.g.*, servants or employees in house or grounds—and, apart from their obvious lack of connection with the Order as such, it is impossible to regard the Order as responsible for their moral defects.

The press reports suppressed the relatively numerous acquittals in the *Sittlichkeitsprozesse*, or at most referred to them as inconspicuously as possible, after the fullest conceivable description of the charges, and made a special feature of the large numbers of clergy " arrested," without ever making it clear that these figures included mere witnesses. For example, early in 1937 huge headlines announced " 276 Religious before the Courts for Criminal Assault, etc.," and the report which followed spoke of 106 Brothers as arrested. In actual fact this " 106 " included many witnesses against whom no charge was made, the real

[1] *Reichspost*, June 1st, 1937.

number of accused being 50 or less. Moreover, even this latter figure included persons who had once been—often many years previously—novices or postulants in some religious Order, or had been connected with it as servants, etc.

On June 14th, 1937, the Vienna *Reichspost* dealt with a typical example of this unscrupulous use of press reports:

> Twenty-three Alexian Brothers were charged, of whom 14 were condemned, 6 acquitted, and 3 did not appear. Of the 14 convicted, 11 had severed connection with the Order, in some cases many years previously. In the case of one of the acquitted, the accusation stated that he had allowed boys to get drunk with altar wine as a preliminary to assaulting them, and this savoury detail was fully exploited. As for his acquittal, no mention was made of it, etc.

These illustrations will suffice to establish our contention that the public was systematically deceived.

B. *The aim of the Sittlichkeitsprozesse was to undermine the good name of the Church.*

In using the " Immorality " trials in the Russian fashion as a kind of exhibition, a continuous serial picture, the Nazi authorities had no intention of purifying the Church or national morality. To them they were simply just another means of destroying the Church, a weapon in the fight. The moral indignation expressed by these leaders and by the press of the Party was sheer hypocrisy, and its only aim was to arouse in the public, and especially in the minds of Catholics, a certain horror and disgust at the very sight of priests and Religious, and thus to alienate them from the Church.

Certain aspects only become intelligible in the light of this assumption. For example, the leading part played by the Propaganda Minister; the systematic and widespread wooing of public opinion; the unprecedented methods adopted by the police and the courts; and the attempt made to burden the bishops with the ultimate responsibility. One can summarise all this as a conscious and deliberate exploitation of the cases to defame the Church.

1. **The part played by the Ministry of Propaganda.**

For this we have a witness above all suspicion—viz., the Minister of Propaganda, Herr Göbbels, in person. In his wireless speech delivered on May 28th, 1937, he twice expressly emphasised the fact that he felt called upon to deal with the trials in his professional capacity. Yet it is obvious that the Ministry of Propaganda has no direct connection with the courts of law. Göbbels himself stated that the *Sittlichkeitsprozesse* would be officially dealt with by his Ministry. The result of this promise was a complete absence of any attempt to discover the real state of affairs or to atone for any error; on the contrary, the cases became a mere quarry for the anti-Christian propaganda of the Party. The German public could scarcely be surprised, for the sudden appearance of the trials, presented one after another like successive blows of a hammer after the promulgation of Papal Encyclical *Mit brennender Sorge*, had given sufficient warning.

It would seem that the " Immorality " trials had been held back or reserved for use at a psychological moment, and an interesting confirmation of this deduction may be found in a periodical, *Die Deutsche Justiz.*:[1]

> The Führer has given orders that for political reasons no more public trials should be held for the time being (from August, 1936),in criminal cases concerning currency, immorality and malicious attacks on the State.

Much the same idea was discernible in a speech delivered at Lörrach by a high official, Herr Wagner, Reich Governor of Baden, in autumn, 1935:

> The Catholic Church need not imagine that we are going to create martyrs. We shall not give the Church that satisfaction—she shall have, not martyrs, but criminals. I assure you that as soon as the list of currency charges has been dealt with we shall proceed with a fresh collection.

2. Systematic formation of public opinion.

We are able to print at this point an authentic document which both bears out what we have indicated above and demonstrates clearly that the whole machinery for the dissemination of news was officially and deliberately directed from above. This document, an official circular, appeared in the course of March, 1937, and was addressed to those in charge of Law Court news and reports:

> The Press Department of the Ministry of Justice draws attention to regulations affecting the reporting of criminal proceedings against priests and Religious, and of all cases affecting the relations of Church and State. The following directions have been issued by the Minister of Propaganda:
>
> " It has been decreed by the Minister of Justice that the postponed charges against priests and Religious referring to cases of immoral conduct will shortly be carried through. The reports of these cases will now be controlled by regulations which I shall order. Through collaboration with the Minister of Justice, the gravest cases will be set apart for full reports . . . and significant specimens of the remaining cases will be dealt with primarily by local news agencies. . . . Only the very worst cases will be handled by the whole national press; the rest will be briefly reported by the German News Agency, which will give the nature of the offence and details of the punishments allotted. These latter reports may also be used by the press as a whole."

These general regulations were then worked out more fully. For example:

> Since the Minister of Justice . . . will be fully informed of all charges made against Catholic priests he will be in a position to select the gravest cases which best meet the requirements of the national news service, and these will be proposed to the Ministry of Propaganda for " general release."

We have first-hand authority for stating that certain newspapers which hesitated to report the first *Sittlichkeitsprozesse* in Coblenz received written admonitions from the Reich Press Bureau. When the first group of charges against Brothers were made, the *Koblenzer*

[1] No. 1, January, 1937, p. 9.

Volkszeitung (formerly a Catholic paper) pointed out the undeniable fact that many members of the Franciscan Brothers' Congregation of Waldbreitbach had joined that Order during the period of unemployment and economic distress, driven often by sheer famine. The implication was that the necessary spiritual requirements for monastic life and monastic work had been wholly absent. The paper then received a sharp reprimand from the District Office of the Ministry of Propaganda, and was obliged to print the following " correction ":

> In our comments upon the legal charges presented in the courts last Wednesday we suggested that unsuitable elements had introduced themselves into this Congregation of Brothers to escape unemployment and economic distress, and that it was these elements that had later shown criminal tendencies. We may have given the impression that whatever corruption arose had its origin in these persons. In actual fact the reverse was the case. Many of the accused entered the Order as early as 1900, and later became seducers and corrupters of youth.

Several editors in Western Germany who did not wish to commit themselves to an unrestricted use of these news reports found themselves threatened, on account of their " passive resistance," with removal from the list of officially recognised editors.

The Vienna *Reichspost* correctly summarised the state of affairs as follows on May 15th, 1937:

> The bullying of Catholic Action has now reached a high-water mark which can scarcely be exceeded; and at the same time a systematic poisoning of public opinion, a deliberate incitement of the people and especially of the young has become a positive epidemic, the violence of which can scarcely be conceived in foreign countries. The malice which underlies this campaign manifests itself in the fact that not only wireless and press are fully mobilised to broadcast the existence of cases against the clergy, but the very style of the accounts is manipulated in a diabolical way so as to generalise individual cases. In one paper, for example, which has a circulation of almost half a million, parents were solemnly warned against entrusting their children to institutions in which " thousands " of sexual criminals were " let loose " on the children. Church magazines . . . may not correct these falsehoods . . . priests who use the pulpit for that purpose are either sent away or forbidden to preach. . . .

A good example of the reckless use of generalisation was given above from the *Schwarze Korps*.[1] Similarly, in its leading article for June 18th, 1936, the same paper said that some excuse might have been found had the monks charged with sexual crimes been really mere individual cases of mental aberration, etc.

> On the contrary, almost a whole Order has shown itself answerable for unnatural vice perpetrated at the expense of minors; not in a house here and there, but in twenty of its houses, involving 500 of its members, of whom 267 have already been legally convicted. . . .

During the period of these trials, almost every issue of the *Schwarze Korps* contained gross attacks on Christian morality, and other papers controlled by the Party, as well as those belonging to the " German Faith Movement," vied with it in its efforts. The show-cases of the

[1] P. 301.

SYSTEMATIC FORMATION OF PUBLIC OPINION

Stürmer, displayed in the streets of German cities, were lowered so that even children might feast their eyes on the accounts of the trials. In view of the character of the *Stürmer* and of the various filthy cartoons which were published, one might summarise the situation by saying that politics had changed to pornography.

This policy of wild exaggeration was indulged in by political leaders in speeches, and from time to time by the wireless. In February, 1936, for example, the German wireless made much of the imprisonment of Father Franz Johannis of Rosenberg, who "had violated school-girls on at least fifty occasions," and whose crimes, "committed in the schoolroom, were witnessed by the boys in the school." On closer investigation it appears that this charge had not even been dealt with by the courts, a circumstance which did not check the wireless accounts. The wireless report added that the local political leader in Rosenberg was responsible for Father Johannis's arrest, and expressed itself as not surprised, as the Father had been a well-known worker for the Centre Party in former years.

Even "pilgrimages" were organised to the courts in which cases against the clergy were being held. On July 9th, 1937, for example, the *Völk. Beobachter* announced that a trial in Coblenz was attended by 150 leading citizens (often Mayors) from Upper Bavaria. Another heading, of July 10th, 1937, ran: "114 Citizens Present at a Case against a Monastery"; and there followed the names of some of these, with quotations of their opinions.

It is obvious that this type of activity achieved the very opposite of what it professed to desire. The public, and particularly children, were not "protected" by such measures, but inoculated with poison. It is, indeed, no exaggeration to say that the unscrupulousness of the Nazi press far excelled that of the Communists.

The declarations which German bishops made by way of protest had absolutely no effect. We shall quote a few passages from these documents.

Konrad von Preysing, Bishop of Berlin, issued a Pastoral Letter in June, 1936, in which he said:

> Any careful reader of daily and weekly papers, who studies their contents and line of attack, will discover that they are filled with scandals . . . and tendentiously interpret trivialities drawn from every possible source and every period of history. The whole aim is to be sensational, to present the opponent as ridiculous and his activities as despicable. Pictures and caricatures seek to make past events live again. We must rely on truth, righteousness and honour as our weapons in an emphatic counter-attack on these devices.

The issue of the *Berlin Catholic Parish Magazine* in which the Bishop's address was printed was confiscated by the police.

Shortly afterwards Archbishop Gröber of Freiburg made a firm stand against the "Monastery Trials" in an announcement read from the pulpits of his diocese.

> Whatever is good is passed over, while all that is evil is shouted and broadcast throughout the country. In the end even the most susceptible hearers

become bored and need an ever greater display and exaggeration at the expense of the truth. . . . Whenever a priest or Religious fails in his duty the fact is elaborated with full deliberation, and whatever defence may be offered receives either practically no publicity at all or some contemptuous notice.

The Bishop of Münster, Mgr. von Galen, wrote to the same effect.

3. Unprecedented methods adopted by the police and the courts.

We wish to assert and then to prove that the object which the police had in mind when carrying out investigations into supposed immoral conduct amongst the clergy was not the discovery of the truth but the discovery of material damaging to the Church.

In the course of 1937 the Secret Police carried out investigations in almost all monasteries in order to record the names of candidates, novices and formed members who had left the Order concerned, either of their own free will or because they had been dismissed. Such persons were closely questioned as to the reasons for their departure or dismissal, and particular pains were taken to discover any instances of sexual misconduct which might have taken place in such houses. Cases were recorded which had occurred many years previously. A similar procedure was adopted in monastery schools and boarding-houses which were conducted by the clergy, and in a number of hospitals. In the case of the Brothers of Mercy in Pilchowitz, Neustadt and Breslau, who were accused of immoral practices, patients who had been under the care of the Brothers as much as four years before were visited by the Secret Police and asked whether they had noticed any cases of unnatural vice during their stay at the hospital. Not only ordinary citizens, but " convinced National Socialists " as well, were visited and asked to make depositions on these lines. This round-up of patients was made possible by the existence of official hospital records. We are unfortunately not in a position to record the extent to which this census gave satisfaction to its instigators, and thus check the constant reliance which was officially placed on such depositions. It is certain, however, that even old adherents of the Party were disgusted with the methods adopted in order to entrap the Brothers of Mercy; and it is a fact that the net result of the investigation was the release of the arrested Brothers in Pilchowitz, since it had shown the charges to be untenable. The precise result of the investigations made in Neustadt is not yet known, and so far only a few of the Neustadt Brothers have been released. In Breslau, too, the Secret Police found its efforts useless.

A word should be said, too, about the manner in which such personal investigations were conducted. The officials interrogated lay-Brothers, school-children and other minors with disgusting questions, drawing their attention to matters of which they had previously had no knowledge. In institutions such as orphanages the Gestapo asked hundreds of children questions of this type, and often relied on the merest suspicion to which these unreliable sources might give rise in order to arrest a member of the clergy. In Bavaria, moreover, in 1937 the police and other officials were ordered by the Gestapo to record the names of any priests who had had children or had paid maintenance allowances, etc., and careful attention was to be paid even to the merest suspicion of such a case. A Commissioner of Police informed a priest explicitly that he had been ordered to address enquiries of this kind to all priests in his district.

In the course of such verbal interrogations the officials of the Gestapo often employed promises and threats in order to extract compromising statements, especially when the person questioned was a minor. Many of the victims were interrogated, not by the ordinary officials, but by special detachments of the Gestapo. It is known, too, that the first set of cases, the Coblenz trials, were held before a special court delegated for the purpose from Berlin. In these so-called special courts of justice the personnel frequently lacked the necessary training, and it was a common thing to rely on the evidence of children without calling upon the expert evidence of doctors.

The following examples of methods of interrogation are worth recording, since they were given under oath. Children were bribed with sweets to speak against members of the clergy. . . . Others were threatened with the concentration camp, and when they held to their own accounts were made to sign a form which was said to consist of a committal to the concentration camp. . . . Pressure was brought to bear on one witness by throwing him against a wall and beating him, threatening him with a revolver, etc. More than once such witnesses visited priests and told them that they had had to act despite themselves, and in the end had simply signed whatever paper was put before them. It often happened, too, that the accused and even witnesses were questioned night after night until they broke down under the strain.

4. **The utter absence of impartiality in this attack on the honour of the Church.**

The wave of indignation which the immoral conduct of some priests and Religious aroused was stilled and practically non-existent whenever similar incidents occurred within the ranks of the Party. Then there was no question of " public interest " to be served by the exposure of crime. On the contrary, such incidents were systematically hushed up.

In his famous sermon (for which he was exiled from Eichstätt by the Gestapo) delivered on January 31st, 1937, Canon Kraus brought to light two official testimonies for his assertion that National Socialism had a double standard ready for dealing with all cases of immorality which should arise. The Canon said:

> The Papal Secretary of State, Cardinal Pacelli, on May 30th, 1936, wrote as follows, with reference to the Coblenz trials: " The Holy See has it on the best authority that in many cases of such sexual offences taking place within the Party or other State organisations, when a punishment was inflicted,

every possible means was taken to prevent the public from realising the connection of the offender with that organisation. It has even happened that Catholics whose conscience has impelled them to act as witnesses in such cases have been themselves punished, while the actual offenders escaped."

Cardinal Pacelli wrote in similar terms to the German Government on June 13th, 1936:

> The Holy See wishes once again to assert that in cases of moral misconduct by persons connected with the Party—arising sometimes from abuse of an official position of responsibility—the authorities have made no effort to enlist the customary channels of public exposure, or even to take any steps in the matter. Hence that absence of impartiality which we have suggested is no mere insinuation, but a charge based on solid fact.

The *Schwarze Korps*[1] wrote as follows about moral lapses within Party organisations:

> Our Party courts would not, unlike the Church, stoop to concealment of such base crimes. In any such case the offender would be ignominiously expelled from the Party, and would then have to answer for his misdeeds before the public courts.

Herr Göbbels expressed himself even more vigorously in a speech delivered on May 28th, 1937:

> The Party has set a clear example. In 1934 more than sixty members who had indulged in this vice were shot, and the Party gave the greatest possible national publicity to its procedure.

By way of comment on these assertions the following points should be noted:

(A) On June 30th, 1934, the Reich Press Bureau of the National Socialist Party announced tersely that Röhm, chief of staff of the SA, and some of his comrades, had been executed on account of a conspiracy against Hitler. No mention whatever was made of sexual misconduct as a reason for such measures, even though its existence was widely known both within the Party and outside it. On the contrary, Adolf Hitler stated that he had " for years shielded Röhm from violent attacks."

(B) On June 30th, 1934, Hitler, as Supreme Leader of the Storm Troopers, issued orders, of which the seventh section ran as follows:

> I expect all leaders of the Storm Troopers to assist in maintaining and consolidating its reputation as a clean and wholesome institution. I should like conditions to be such that every mother can give her son to Party organisations and to the Hitler Youth without fearing in the least any danger of moral corruption. I desire, therefore, that all Storm Troop leaders should take great care to punish all offences against § 175 of the Code with immediate exclusion from the Storm Troopers and from the Party. I intend only real men, not unnatural animals, to wield the leadership of the Storm Troopers.

We shall seek in vain for any trials arising from this command. From the ranks of the Storm Troopers or the Hitler Youth not one has come to our notice. It is certain that none received a publicity faintly approaching that given to the " Monastery Trials."

June 18th, 1936.

(C) On July 14th, 1934, Hitler spoke once again in the Reichstag of a " conspiracy amongst leaders of the Storm Troopers contrary to the normal views of a healthy people," and of " elements united by similar tastes and tendencies." The question arises: When were charges made against the guilty parties, and where are detailed press accounts to be found ?

(D) It was well known throughout Germany that Hermann Esser, the Bavarian Minister of State, an early supporter of the Party and head of the Bavarian Chancellery since 1933, led an openly scandalous life in Munich. He was actually driven out of a public-house by the owner, riding-whip in hand, for violating the publican's daughter, a young girl. Yet there was no news of this man's expulsion from the Party, or of that appearance before the public courts of which the *Schwarze Korps* spoke. Herr Esser was, indeed, eventually removed, simply because Munich became too hot for him; but a new post was specially created for him—viz., director of a Tourist Traffic Bureau. Nor was the case of Herr Esser the only example of such an " exemplary " attitude on the part of the Party. There was, for example, the gross and open scandal of Heinz Rutha, an architect, the right-hand man of Konrad Henlein (then local " Führer " of the Sudeten Germans), who had for years lived a notoriously immoral life while working in the offices of the Nazi Sudeten German Party in Prague, and had involved more than fifteen other Party members. Not a word of all this ever appeared in the German national press.

(E) One might ask, too, for some traces of moral indignation aroused in the Nazi press by the notorious immorality which was rife in some Hitler Youth camps. There was no mention of those ill-supervised relations between the Hitler Youth and the German Girls' League, which aroused so much horror in innumerable families throughout Germany; nor of the appalling number of cases of sexual misconduct between leaders of Party organisations and the children under their care. It was useless for newspapers to mention such cases if they at the same time suppressed the connection between the accused and his position in some section of the Party. We give a few typical examples of such procedure.

On January 24th, 1937, the *Völk. Beobachter* reported that a person accused of criminal assault had received sentence of three years' imprisonment. The name of this twenty-two-year-old criminal was not given, and the fact was suppressed that he was a Hitler Youth leader whose misconduct had corrupted six children.

In December, 1936, investigations were made on a considerable scale concerning offences amongst members of the Hitler Youth against § 175 of the Criminal Code. The press reported absolutely nothing of this.

On January 30th and 31st, 1937, the *Bayerische Ostmark* reported that a young man, twenty-four years old, had committed offences against minors and had been sent to prison for ten months. The paper did not add that he was a Hitler Youth leader, or that his offences had been committed within a Hitler Youth camp. Similarly, the *Bayerischer Anzeiger*[1] reported that two youths had been tried before the Juvenile Court for offences against children under fourteen years of age, and had received sentences of imprisonment for two years and six months respectively. The fact that one was a Patrol Leader and the other a Junior Leader in the Hitler Youth was not printed, nor was the public informed that the offences were committed during night marches, sing-songs held at night, etc.

On January 27th and 28th, 1937, two Leaders of the Hitler Youth in Regensburg were found guilty of serious sexual offences; and within two months two more serious cases had to be dealt with. The press made no mention of them. In March, 1937, three Hitler Youth leaders were arrested in Straubing for homosexual offences, yet the press remained silent about the matter. On May 8th, 1937, the *Bayerischer Anzeiger* reported that two cases of immorality had received light sentences of imprisonment, but did not report that one of them was a Troop Leader of the Storm Troopers.

On May 25th, 1937, the Vienna *Reichspost* published a compendious account, from its own correspondent in Munich, of cases tried for offences against § 175 of the Code. All mention of these cases had been forbidden to the German press.

The Mayor of Grenzach and Herr Vogt, the Political Leader of Pforzheim, and a close friend of Herr Wagner, the Reich Governor, were condemned for homosexual offences. The following received sentences of several years' imprisonment for assaults on children: the schoolmaster of Hottingen (near Säckingen), a trusted agent of the Nazi Teachers' Union and a friend of Uttentaler, the Mayor of Säckingen; and the schoolmaster at Birndorf (near Waldshut). At Tiengen, near Waldshut, a (Nazi) Brown Sister was found guilty of producing abortion, a case which, in the newspapers, was said to concern an *Ordensschwester* (viz., a member of a Congregation—*i.e.*, a nun !). " In Mannheim more than sixty youths appeared before the judge, accused of homosexual practices—a case which the judge described as the most filthy he had ever encountered. All were members of the Hitler Youth. At Alzey, near Worms, over seventy members of the Party were arrested for immoral practices. At St. Peter, near Freiburg, the local Hitler Youth leader was arrested, and at Offenburg the leader of the corresponding organisation for girls was charged with homicide and abortion. She was released through the influence of the Party, and any criticism was stifled by the threat of punishment."

On August 1st, 1937, the *Völk. Beobachter* reported sentences of imprisonment ranging from eight months to three and a half years, for four youths charged with immoral conduct, but did not report that the case concerned leaders of the Hitler Youth.

A final example: On November 26th, 1937, the *Bayerische Ostmark* reported that a certain Richard St. had been sentenced to two months'

---
[1] No. 30, 1937.

imprisonment for assault, but refrained from stating that he was a local director of the German Labour Front and had been detected in offences against working women.

Such examples lead us to conclude that the Nazi Party was anything but " exemplary " in this matter. A double standard was always employed. Moral indignation, moral purification, the protection of the young—these were loudly urged, but urged only when the offenders happened to be connected with the Church.

It can be proved, moreover, that the Party made a permanent arrangement by which sexual crimes within its ranks could be " legally " shielded behind a wall of silence. On December 1st, 1936, a law was formulated with regard to the interrogation of leaders of the Party and of its various organisations. It was decreed that all Party members in key positions would require special permission in order to give evidence or expert opinions on matters covered by their duty of discreet official silence. In the detailed explanation of this law it was stated that such permission would be refused whenever the welfare of the State demanded it, and it was made clear that, since the State and the Party are closely united, the welfare of the Party must be put on the same footing as that of the State. Commenting on this, Michael Germanicus was justified in writing as follows in his " Open Letter " to Dr. Göbbels (after the latter's speech on May 28th, 1937): " Do you know what this means, Herr Minister ? It means lavish corruption for the benefit of the Party under the cloak of legal terminology."

(F) How is one to explain the fact that the alarmingly rapid growth of juvenile crime in Germany during the last few years has aroused absolutely no " moral indignation " in the Nazi press ? And this is the case, even though the phenomenon clearly coincides with the development of National Socialism.

In this connection an article written by the well-known Swiss Deputy, Dr. Wick, in the Lucerne *Vaterland*,[1] is very much to the point. We quote a few passages:

The education given in the Hitler Youth, with its water-tight organisation and its stress on its independence of school, home and Church, has led to grave moral delinquency. As early as January, 1938, Günther Kaufmann, editor of Baldur von Schirach's *Wille und Macht*, complained as follows: " Our ideological conquest of the conceptions of sin and penance, the destruction of the teaching authority once wielded by priests, and the renewal of a healthy joy in living, have acted for some as signals inviting them to lay aside so-called ' outworn morality. . . .' "

Statistics throw an alarming light on the growing corruption of German youth. According to the official " Statistical Year Book of the German State " the number of juveniles convicted of immoral practices in 1932, the year preceding Hitler's rise to power, was 619; in 1933, 612; in 1934, 779; in 1935, 1,058; in 1936, 1,465; in 1937, 2,374. Further figures under this heading are not to hand. Figures for " criminal assault on children " were 1,065 in 1937 as against 478 in 1934; for " unnatural vice," 973 in 1937 against 121 in 1934. The figures for homicide and abortion amongst girls rose from 57 in 1935 to 158 in 1937, and the figures for the first half of 1938

[1] May, 1939.

were already 109. For manslaughter the following figures were given: 18 (1934), 42 (1935), 65 (1936), 70 (1937), 45 for the first six months of 1938. For damage to property the number of condemnations amongst children had risen by 250 per cent. from 1934 to 1937. For theft 6,947 children were condemned in 1934, 12,475 in 1937.

One must not omit to consider the fact that the " honour of the Party " causes many things to be passed over and hushed up nowadays, while much that would formerly have been called moral degeneration now passes as racial *Weltanschauung*. Parents complain with such rapidly increasing bitterness of the moral degeneration of their children that we may rightly entertain doubts about the moral outlook for a " noble " Aryan race in Germany.

The matter of this section should have made it clear that the Party is less concerned with purifying public life and protecting children than with damaging the good name and weakening the very existence of the Church.

5. Attempts to make the bishops bear all responsibility.

We have shown that from the very beginning National Socialism sought to exploit all cases of immorality which were tried in the courts as a weapon against the Church. With this end in view an effort was made to attach blame to the bishops as chief overseers of the Church. Both the press of the Party and several Ministers of State charged them with deliberately concealing cases of immorality amongst priests and members of religious Orders. Dr. Frick, for example, stated at a public meeting in Coblenz in June, 1936:

> This evil cannot be dealt with by concealing it under a cloak of silence or of Christian charity—and in this connection I am unfortunately obliged to point out that ecclesiastical authorities have knowingly laid themselves open to blame by neglecting their office of supervision, and have countenanced a conspiracy of silence. There is no other way of explaining the extent to which this evil has developed. The National Socialist press was only doing its duty in publicly exposing such a state of affairs, and the State, which has charge of the welfare of the nation, will be no respecter of persons in fulfilling its duty of uprooting all such evils which strike at the foundations of a people's strength. It will not make any distinction between ordinary folk and those inmates of monasteries who may, indeed, change their names when following their heavenly vocation, but whose earthly proceedings are subject to the law.

On May 28th, 1937, Dr. Göbbels made a speech at the Deutschlandshalle, Berlin, in which he stated that both Church and Hierarchy had tried to prevent the State from punishing perverts and crushing immorality, and he accused the Hierarchy of trying to conceal cases which might be dealt with in the future.

This accusation was not justified. The bishops punished such cases as came to their notice according to ecclesiastical custom. It is possible, indeed, that these ecclesiastical judges, being pastors as well as judges, listened more patiently and optimistically to promises of amendment on the part of guilty persons than secular judges would have done, and relied on such assurances. The assertion that sin was concealed by the bishops is a gratuitous calumny. The bishops did not protest against the institution of legal proceedings in such cases, but against the unprecedented publicity given to them in the press. A few quotations from episcopal Pastorals may serve to establish these points.

On June 2nd, 1936, the Bishop of Münster issued a document in which he stated:

> We feel the deepest sorrow at the thought of those lapses which have actually occurred and have been proceeded against in the public courts. By means of such things deep offence has been given to God, our fellow-men have been scandalised, and our holy Church has been disgraced. We are all the more distressed when we consider that the perpetrators of such deeds should have had certain words of Holy Writ more at heart than the rest of men—" You shall be holy, for I am holy " (1 Peter, i. 16). . . .
> Acting on the orders of the Holy See, the Bishop of Trier has already been engaged for several months on a visitation of all houses which have been concerned. He is being assisted in this work by prominent and well-informed priests. Why should I mention this to you ? Because I wish you to realise that the ecclesiastical courts are seeking, as soon as any misdemeanours come to their notice, to rectify matters by every means in their power. And you should note that their powers do not include open force.

On August 20th, 1936, the German Episcopate issued a Joint Pastoral Letter with regard to the cases which had arisen in Waldbreitbach. It opened as follows:

> For some time nothing has caused us so much distress as these crimes. Our condemnation of them is no less severe than that of the secular court, which we do not reproach with any disregard for law and right judgement. We regret these crimes, not because they have aroused great indignation and given rise to bitter attacks and calumnies, but above all because they have gravely offended God.

On May 9th, 1937, the Bavarian bishops issued a Joint Letter in which they wrote as follows:

> 1. We must protest in the name of truth against the reiterated accusation that German bishops have neglected to condemn the moral failings of priests and members of religious Orders. Indeed, in connection with the Brothers of Waldbreitbach, in September, 1936, we stated from all pulpits that we condemned these crimes no less severely than the secular courts. Today we wish to repeat that condemnation with all possible emphasis. We lament the errors and offences of which priests and Religious—people bound to strive after a special degree of perfection—have been guilty, for by these things God has been outraged, men have been corrupted, the Church, the Bride of Christ, has been insulted, the priesthood and religious life degraded, and the Faith and loyalty to the Church of many very sorely tried.
> We repeat that judgement of our Saviour, who, in spite of His mercy and generosity towards erring men, cried out, " Woe to that man by whom the scandal cometh"; and who, at the solemn hour of the Last Supper, spoke those dreadful words about Judas, the traitor within the circle of His closest followers, " It were better for him, if that man had not been born."
> 2. In those cases into which conclusive investigations have been made the Church has already inflicted ecclesiastical punishments, and will proceed in the same way in the future. The Bishop of Trier has declared before the court that he has concluded arrangements with Rome for the expulsion of more than thirty Brothers in religious Orders. The Congregation of Franciscan Brothers at Waldbreitbach has been dissolved by the Holy See itself, and in its place the " Congregation of Priests and Brothers of the

Holy Cross " has been instituted, in which the chief offices will, in future, be administered solely by priests.

The Vicar-General of Cologne has stated before the court at Bonn that proceedings have already been instituted with a view to dissolving the community of Alexian Brothers at Cologne.

It is not, however, customary for ecclesiastical courts to publish full details of investigations and judgements in such delicate matters, as is, indeed, the case with other types of disciplinary proceedings instituted by other authorities.

In a sermon preached on Trinity Sunday, 1937, Cardinal Faulhaber said:

We shall never shelter anything that is evil. . . . You may feel assured that ecclesiastical authorities will investigate all such evil abominations in holy places, and will proceed against them with the fullest severity.

In a declaration made by Count Preysing, Bishop of Berlin, and read in all Catholic Churches in Berlin on May 9th, 1937, it was asserted that the bishops had condemned such offences no less forcibly than the secular courts. "Even if whole branches of the mighty organisation of religious life within the Church were to become infected, they would be ruthlessly cut off from the body of the Church." In a Pastoral Letter which was read in all churches of the diocese the bishop stated:

Faith teaches us that sin is worse than its consequences. I wish explicitly to renew my former condemnation of such things as publicly as possible, with reference to all cases which have been clearly proved. The Church does not in any way take a stand against the sentences passed by the State; she has, in fact, proceeded already with ecclesiastical sanctions against those in whose cases conclusive investigations have been made. She does take a stand, however, and takes it most decisively, against the procedure by which cases already judged and others awaiting judgement are being systematically and deliberately exploited, with all the help that propaganda can supply, against the Church, the Church's teaching, and the Church's labours.

In carrying out the administration of the Church the German Episcopate has inflicted punishments in a number of cases of immoral conduct and other offences. The means which the Church has at her disposal for applying punishments and disciplinary measures are, however, limited, and must be adapted to her nature, and it is clear that in their application human error and human limitations will play their part as they do in the case of all superior authorities. Government authorities and responsible superiors in the Party cannot but be aware of the difficulties which arise within their wide experience in passing weighty judgements upon offences which demand some definite treatment of the offender. It is an open secret that the National Socialist movement, priding itself on severity and indifference to persons as something fundamental in its activities, has nevertheless, under certain circumstances in which the personal element was prominent, shown itself by no means wholly indifferent or impartial.

The reproach which was frequently made against the bishops, that they did not dissociate themselves sufficiently plainly from moral delinquents, can only be described as cynical; for it is plain that the bishops were not allowed to make their position plain to the public. Thus, for example, the *Bayerische Katholische Kirchenzeitung* for June 21st, 1936, was confiscated precisely because it published an episcopal statement about the trials in Coblenz. By way of justification the police explained that the publication of such episcopal letters was forbidden.

6. Conclusions drawn by the promoters of the moral "Kulturkampf" from every aspect of the attack.

From speeches made by Nazi leaders and from representative publications of the Party one can clearly discern not only the line of thought which was being fostered, but also some of the means which the Party desired to bring into action against the Catholic Church. We shall summarise briefly some conclusions which were drawn officially as a result of the " Immorality trials."

The Catholic Church is corrupt through and through, and must disappear.

Such was the gist of a leading article in the *Völk. Beobachter* for May 30th, 1937:

> In the solid mass of so-called " regrettable individual lapses," in the over-tolerant attitude of clerical superiors, and in the lying propaganda of this international body under the guidance of Roman or Vatican laws, we perceive symptoms of a disease leading to the complete internal decay of an institution which, up to now, has not achieved its aims among us and never shall.

The *Durchbruch* wrote more explicitly:[1]

> All who today bear the name of Christian share responsibility for all those ecclesiastical sins of past days whose expiation the Lord of righteousness is now completing. The Church richly deserves to be swept away in the revolution heralding a new era.

The very foundations of Catholic morality must be attacked.

This necessity was expounded by Dr. Ley in June, 1936 (at Coblenz):

> Their negative attitude to life led these men to enter the Franciscan Order; by contrast, our positive attitude to life, summed up in our ideological and philosophical position, leads the way to organisations of happy youth. Two worlds are represented here, struggling for a hold on our hearts.

An official paper, *Die HJ*,[2] reproduced the words of a State Attorney, Herr Hattingen, against Fr. Leovigil, a Franciscan:

> We must not blame the agents of these deeds so much as the system. It is a system which has brought untold misery on mankind, a system corresponding to the Middle Ages rather than to modern times. Perhaps Saints can manage to live according to the rules of these Orders; certainly ordinary, natural men will only attain a sham sanctity !

It is noteworthy that the sect of " Old Catholics " distributed on a large scale pamphlets describing " Immorality in Monasteries," and strove with the help of such pornographic literature to attack the " unnatural obligatory celibacy of the Roman Church " and to advocate the marriage of all clergy.

The Catholic Church must be prevented from having anything further to do with the education of youth.

[1] No. 15, 1937.   [2] June 27th, 1936.

In November, 1937, District Leader Julius Streicher spoke at a political meeting in the Rheinland Hall, Cologne, and was reported as saying that the feeling in favour of religious life, always particularly strong in the Rhineland, would be overcome. There had been many "Immorality" trials, and, if there was a temporary lull, more serious cases would soon be dealt with. If the representatives of the Church proved unable to protect youth, the representatives of the Party must take over that charge, as High Priests of the nation.[1] A little earlier, on May 13th, this same District Leader had spoken as follows in Munich: "Those who take young people out of the world and shut them up behind monastery walls commit a crime."[2]

In an article entitled "It Stinks to Heaven" the *Schwarze Korps* wrote:

After the experiences of the last few years we no longer have any faith in your morality. We feel anxious about those young people who are entrusted to your care, about the people whom you watch over, about the economic resources which you control. You are guarding and educating the youth of the race, and therefore the race and the State have the right and the duty of keeping a careful watch in order that this education may follow the lines of public morality. . . . Youth is too precious to us to allow a mere passive silence. . . ."

Similarly the Swiss *Baseler Nachrichten*,[3] reported Herr Rust, Reichsminister of Education, as saying at a Congress of the Teachers' Union that the continued influence of the denominations upon education must, for the future, be impossible in Germany. As a natural result of this the division of German schools according to denominational prejudices must be brought to an end as soon as possible.

Complete State control over all Church property must be introduced. On April 15th, 1937, the *Schwarze Korps* stated:

Our policy is not dictated by hatred of religion or of the Church. No reasons of that kind urge us to demand State control of clerical possessions. We consider ourselves better Christians in that we demand State supervision in order to prevent immorality in those places where it . . . has continuously flourished in its most unsavoury forms. Where clerical organisations fail the State must step in.

We cannot end this chapter better than by reproducing an "Open Letter," written under the pseudonym Michael Germanicus, and secretly distributed and reprinted on an immense scale in Germany during the summer of 1937. It was a striking answer to a speech made by Dr. Göbbels on May 28th, 1937, and it reflects perfectly the attitude of honourable German people everywhere.

AN OPEN LETTER TO DR. JOSEPH GÖBBELS, MINISTER FOR ENLIGHTENMENT AND PROPAGANDA

That old and tried friend of the Germans, the Samaritan of starving Germany, Cardinal Mundelein, spoke to 500 of his priests on the occasion of the "Immorality" trials about German justice, and in the Cardinal's declaration you found the opportunity you had sought for to comment, in your speech of May 28th in the Deutschlandshalle, on the trials which the

[1] *Kölnische Volkszeitung*, November 14th, 1937.
[2] *8-Uhr-Blatt*, Nürnberg, May 13th, 1937.   [3] May 31st, 1937.

German courts are staging in imitation of the Russians. It is true that you had not once the courage to explain to your uncritical public what precisely Cardinal Mundelein had said. Why this fear? Nobody will ask you for evidence, and you will find none to contradict you. You have the power! The possession of this power did not, indeed, help your régime in its weak protest against the Holy See; but if your declarations are true, Mr. Minister (and we shall make an exception in believing you), then Cardinal Mundelein must have said that in Germany justice and law are only used as tools for personal and selfish ends. This charge you meant to answer in your speech; but your very words made it clear that the Cardinal was not far wrong in his accusations against Brown Shirt rule.

All civilised countries try their criminals as soon as they are detected and arrested. In Germany, as in Russia, it is done otherwise, so that criminals are either left alone for a time or kept under arrest. Real or alleged offences are kept in cold storage, to be brought forward on suitable occasions as best serves the interests of the Party. So far as priests and Religious were concerned, the suitable occasion was the Pope's Encyclical *Mit brennender Sorge*.[1] Do you really wish to have the world believe that the production of cases long awaiting attention occurred just after the publication of the Papal Encyclical purely by accident? No, Mr. Göbbels! No doubt Hitler's assertion that mankind—*i.e.*, the German people—is stupid through and through[2] is true enough; yet, in spite of his " Give me but four years," the German people is not yet so utterly stupefied that it cannot observe the way in which legal action is made to subserve official propaganda in Germany. We may count ourselves lucky indeed that at least the conduct of such cases is still left to the care of the judges!

It was, perhaps, a little tactless of you to let out the fact that the " official materials " of these trials were " departmentally and officially " prepared by the Ministry of Propaganda. Surely it is an unparalleled scandal that the boundaries separating the Ministry of Justice from the Ministry of Propaganda in the Reich should thus be blurred and confused. It would seem that the German Ministry of Justice is obliged to work for a department foreign to its nature. And yet you dare to state that it is pure libel to assert that in Germany justice and law are used for personal—*i.e.*, for Party—ends. You have, indeed, stretched our credulity still further in the course of your speech. You threatened that " if any doubt is thrown on the truth of the immorality trials in the future, within Germany or without, you would oblige high ecclesiastical officials to testify before the courts under oath." Mr. Göbbels, did you not realise the extent to which you irremediably compromised German justice by that remark? For you yourself stated that in Germany the Ministry of Propaganda is able to set legal machinery in motion through a compliant judicial organisation!

You also mentioned, Mr. Minister, if I may refer to another of your remarks, " official materials." What materials do you mean? Possibly the accusations which, as everybody in Germany knows, were served up by the Party and its hirelings for treatment in the courts. May we perhaps remind you of the words of the judges of the Leipzig court in the course of the abortive trial for high treason in 1933: " The materials supplied by Party sources are either worthless or are forgeries." Or did you, perhaps, mean the materials supplied by declarations made at certain sittings by children and semi-imbeciles? Mr. Göbbels, what precisely is the meaning of these " materials " in **your** hands? Is it **your** job to direct the judges as to what possesses value and what lacks value, and as to the nature of the required verdict?

Possibly you meant " materials " of the irrefutable kind supplied by that " sadistic sex murder," of which you spoke, at the Belgian monastery of Manage? Not even the foreign Communist press, though its outlook is much the same, dared to exploit that deed of a weak-minded Belgian Religious. Moreover, Mr. Göbbels, when you were obliged to withdraw your charge,

---

[1] March 21st, 1937. [2] Popular edition of *Mein Kampf*, p. 412.

you did so in a most peculiar way, and managed to serve up the same old dish once more.

On the one hand you asserted that "*countless* priests and Religious have offended against the law in Germany," that "*countless* priests and Religious harm their penitents in the confessional by their pathological mentality." And, on the other hand, in the same speech you speak of "*thousands* of respectable priests who, as innumerable letters go to prove, note with the deepest sorrow the decay and corruption of the Church." Mr. Göbbels, apart from the fact that we are well able to count the number of priests and Religious, is the first or the second of your two statements wild exaggeration ? We can answer for you; both are such ! *Countless* priests have not offended; nor have *thousands* of priests sent in such letters. If you are fibbing, your fibs fall at least within the domain of mathematical calculation, within the calculation of probabilities. And still worse followed in your speech. You dared to say that the *countless* priests who have sinned, and the " thousands upon thousands of cases which have come to the notice of the law," represent but a fraction of the real extent of this moral wilderness, but a fraction of the total figures.

Mr. Göbbels, one hardly knows whether to be more amazed at the colossal clumsiness into which wild exaggeration has led you or at the utter shamelessness with which you formulate such libellous generalisations in the face of a complete lack of evidence. What, then, is to be said of your *thousands* of respectable priests ? Mr. Minister, we hereby demand that you should produce your documentary evidence ! Put it before the court of the world in facsimile ! You are not short of money to do it, in view of all the pennies handed in by wireless listeners who daily enjoy your lucubrations !

You stated, too, as the second main item of your speech, that the bishops have shielded offenders amongst priests and Religious. You know full well, Mr. Minister, that it is untrue. The bishops have taken all the means in their power (and it should be remembered that they are hampered to some extent by a certain sacramental obligation). That they have allowed a certain " right to grace " to operate[1] corresponds to the tradition of the Church. The indignation displayed by your obsequious State attorneys was somewhat superfluous. You have proposed the German National Socialist Workers' Party as an example of the treatment which offenders should receive from their own brethren, saying that " the Party has set a healthy example, and in 1934 shot sixty members who had offended. The Party then openly informed the public of the incident."

Mr. Göbbels, few statements in your speech have amazed thinking Germans so much as this indiscreet reminder of June 30th, 1934. First of all, you are very much in error if you imagine that even today, after three years, such summary " justice " as was administered on June 30th, 1934, and still is administered today, will make any impression on the world. By such things the régime but shows its weakness. Even today it dare not allow the accused to speak for themselves. Not by means of summary executions is justice served; rather they cover up corruption in the Party. May we, further, refresh your memory a little ? On July 7th, 1934, a fortnight after the Party purge, Herr Hitler stated in the Reichstag that seventy, not sixty, members of the Party were concerned. Three victims committed suicide. And others (*e.g.*, Beck, Edgar Jung, Dr. Gerlich, Dr. Klausner, Dr. von Kahr, Willy Schmidt, etc.), who were murdered by Göring when that gentleman extended " the scope of his labours," are not included ! You cannot be so naïve as to believe, or to think that anybody else believed, Hitler's fantastic story in the Reichstag. You assert on the strength of your own reputation that Röhm and his companions were not executed for *high treason*. Yet you have not proved that they were executed for homosexual practices. As a matter of fact, the well-known homosexuality of Röhm and the others only became a crime when they ceased to be *politically* acceptable, and when the public had forcibly to be filled with horror at their crimes. Listen to Hitler

---

[1] *Cf.* Code of Canon Law, c. 2214, § 2, " cum misericordia udicium. . . ."

himself on Röhm. . . . " For years I shielded this man by virtue of my unshakeable comradeship. . . ." At the beginning of 1934 Hitler wrote to Röhm as a personal friend. The facts, then, are as follows: Hitler, and with him the whole Party, indulgently protected for many years the bestialities of Röhm and of a whole crowd of notorious SS and SA leaders. Further, it concealed many other little trifles (*e.g.*, murderous attacks on Edmund Heines and other opponents of the Party—Potempa, etc.). Indeed, we hereby assert that the Party indulges in wholesale concealment of every scandal within its ranks, so long as the concealment involves no special difficulties. From December 1st, 1933, onwards, Mr. Göbbels, you have set up a judicial machine within the Party itself, and as cases from every part of Germany show, its sole purpose is to withdraw Party offenders from the normal channels of justice, so that all may be officially hushed up. You have fabricated a get-away so that, whenever things became a little too hot, the so-called interest of the State could be invoked in order to deal quietly with whatever might be compromising for the Party. Do you really think observant people did not notice how, acting on the respectful recommendation of Dr. Gürtner, the Reich Government passed a law on December 1st, 1936, bearing upon the examination of leaders of the German National Socialist Workers' Party and its various offshoots ? That law laid down that such leaders holding responsible positions require express permission in order to act as witnesses with regard to any circumstances which might be regarded as coming under their obligation of official reserve and secrecy. The annotations to this law state that the permission must be refused if the " welfare of the State " is at stake, and that the unity existing between the Party and the State implies that the welfare of the Party and that of the State are of precisely equal importance. Do you know, Mr. Minister, what that means ? It means lavish corruption for the benefit of the Party under the cloak of legal terminology !

No, indeed ! It would bode ill for the welfare of the Party were the people to get a glimpse of the bottomless pit of your Party, were it to know of the colossal extortions practised by Party members through the connivance of officials in Düsseldorf and elsewhere, of the swindles perpetrated in Lübeck and by the *Winterhilfwerk,* or of the sexual excesses in hostels and Hitler Youth camps. It would not do for the people to learn something of the gross immorality of your camps, something of the statistics concerning girls of fourteen or sixteen years of age who are ruined physically and morally in Hitler Youth camps, etc., returning to their homes as " young mothers." Nor must they hear of the luxurious homes and cars and sports enjoyed by the leaders of a so-called " Workers' Party." No, all that would not serve the " welfare of the Party." How you must thank God that you are in a position to hush it all up !

Mr. Göbbels, you would have served your Party better had you better observed the " sphere of silence " which you lauded in your speech. Do not concern yourself about the Church ! The Catholic Church knows how to discard undesirable elements, and will reform where reform is necessary. Keep your eyes on your own Party, for, by your own admission, that is where the seeds of corruption lie; and German justice stands forth in the service of that legal corruption !

That is the conclusion which clearly emerges from your speech, the conclusion which has angered all true German men and women and all friends of Germany throughout the world. Cardinal Mundelein may well feel satisfied with you, Mr. Göbbels, for your speech has proved up to the hilt that his charge was true !

MICHAEL GERMANICUS.

PART THREE

THE NATIONAL SOCIALIST PARTY AND THE CHURCH

IN the second part of this work we have shown that in the Third Reich the Government by means of its official measures is actively persecuting the Church, and already several times we have had to point out that the real driving force is not the Government officials, but the Party.

The Party's influence can hardly be overestimated, for, as is frankly admitted by many of those most highly placed, it is the Party's function " to govern the State." Without the Party's consent the State can do nothing. The hierarchy of the Party officials which co-exists with the State officials considers it its duty to supervise and direct the State: indeed, most of the really important posts in Party and State organisation have long since been united and, at every social level, the influence of the Party penetrates far deeper than that of the State. There are, besides the organisations for the training of leaders such as the SS, SA, and the *Ordensburgen* (with the " Adolf Hitler Schools " as the foundation) designed to form leaders, compulsory organisations for the mass of the people, to one or other of which, according to his occupation, everyone must belong, and for the young the Hitler Youth for boys and the German Girls' League.

The aim and purpose of all these organisations is to serve as instruments for ideological training. The means they employ are the publication of the organisations' papers (which all the members must take in), training camps, special courses, endless night classes, parades, etc., so that from the age of ten onwards a German's life is one long round of organised activity: Junior Section of the Hitler Youth, Land Year, Hitler Youth, Labour Service and military service, followed by the different professional organisations such as the Labour Front, the Reich Agricultural Corporation, Civil Servants' Union, National Socialist Teachers' Union, National Socialist Undergraduates' Union, etc. In addition the German citizen can be a member of the Party, which, of course, means compulsory attendance at further training courses. It is, then, absolutely impossible for anyone living in Germany to escape the activity of the Party or remain uninfluenced by its systematic ideological training.

It is the Party and the Party alone that penetrates, educates and directs the people. The restraining influence that might be exercised by other institutions such as the family or the Church is not only very weak on account of the amount of time that has to be given to Party activities, but it is not wanted—at least it is never allowed to challenge the National Socialist ideology.

This unremitting, abiding and systematic influence of the National Socialist Party is, however, avowedly anti-Christian, and it is the purpose of this section of the book to show this, first, by exposing the means used in the attack on the Church, and, secondly, by a more detailed analysis of the underlying ideology. Among the means, we treat first of those officially instituted by the Party—*e.g.*, Party offices, élite formations, compulsory organisations and other institutions for the training and care of the people—and then of those more private weapons which are tolerated or even supported by the Party (books, periodicals, magazines, meetings, etc.). As to the ideology underlying all this, we shall consider it first in its direct, and secondly in its indirect conflict with the Church. From all these details one fact will emerge that is of paramount importance and has terrible implications—the fact, namely, that the German nation is being brought up entirely and systematically in an anti-Christian spirit.

CHAPTER I

THE PARTY ORGANISATIONS AND THEIR PUBLICATIONS

It has been stated again and again by official leaders of the Party that the German National Socialist Workers' Party as such is entirely indifferent as to whether its members belong to a religious denomination or not. Thus, to quote just one instance, District Leader Florian of Düsseldorf declared in a circular of December 14th, 1936:

> I wish to state that wrong ideas are systematically spread and fostered among the population by our notorious political enemies, the assertion, for example, that the Party recommends and indeed urges its members to leave one of the big denominations or the innumerable sects in my district.
> That is not true. The Party desires no such thing. . . . If anyone has become convinced that he can no longer bind himself to one of the denominations, or if he has come to the conclusion that he can no longer remain dependent on one of them and its dogmas, let him as a free man do what his conscience bids. But if any Party leader should bring pressure to bear, he acts wrongly, and against my instructions. I allow everyone freedom in matters of religion. The only thing I as a National Socialist am asking for, is that with all the devotion of his German heart he may believe in the Creator of all things, God, and that in this belief he may serve his country.
> Heil Hitler !
> Signed: Florian.

In what follows we shall see what such declarations are worth. We shall have to state the fact that the Party organisations, its press and training institutions attack not only Christian dogma and Christian morals, but also members of the Church and its institutions, with every kind of abuse and ridicule; further, that it is precisely the Party that is most anxious to foster in every possible way the German Faith Movement and similar neo-pagan groups and movements, while at the same time the life of the Church is being strangled; finally, that National Socialism is educating the nation, especially the young, in an anti-Christian spirit and urging men to leave the Churches. Let us turn to facts.

1. *Party Papers and Periodicals of a More General Character*

Later on we shall treat of the special periodicals belonging to the different organisations, and so we confine ourselves here to publications common to the whole Movement. We can, however, give only a few extracts from each, sufficient to indicate its general tendencies.

The *Völkischer Beobachter*, official organ of the German National Socialist Workers' Party. Article: " Russian Longings in the Vatican."[1] Cartoon[2] of three bishops in full pontificals, who, standing in front of the German frontier, pick up mud from the street and throw it across the border. Heading: " Sport in Politics," and underneath we read the calumny: " Mud-throwing, the favourite sport of the Austrian Bishops."

In the supplement, " Popular Usages, Art, Science, Short Stories,"[3] we find the following verses:

Obscurantists

You fashion eternities
Out of nothing.
Who does not believe you—is thrown for ever into Hell;
Who follows you—has an eternal Heaven
As reward.

Thus you allot punishment and reward,
And God, whom you fashion in exactly the same way,
Stretches forth His protective hand
Above your Doings and Undoings.

You know exactly how greatly you are blaspheming
By giving and refusing already now
Places in the other world—
The best ones are, of course, reserved for you yourselves.

If all eternities have been created
Only for your poor corpses,
That they may burn or rise again,
If even God has been instituted for this,
Then we are " poor pagans,"
For such an eternity is nothing to us.

The article,[4] " Fighting the Enemies of the State," written by a Chief of the Secret Police, Heydrich, accuses the ecclesiastical authorities of using religion as a cloak for establishing the world hegemony of the Church.

A more serious publication is the *Nationalsozialistische Monatshefte*, the chief political and cultural monthly organ of the German National Socialist Workers' Party, editor Alfred Rosenberg. An article,[5] " Ernst Haeckel, a Pioneer of Biological National Thinking," fully approves of Haeckel's outlook on life, which is diametrically opposed to Christianity.

" Speaking of Ernst Haeckel's importance for the biological mentality of the present day and our modern way of viewing organic relations within a community, it must be allowed that his attitude towards man, man's nature and man's origin are of fundamental importance. An answer to the ' question of all questions ' of man's nature and origin is given in the doctrine of evolution itself." The article goes on to speak of the " insecurity of the Church's dogmatic system"; of the ideological struggle for biological

[1] January 12th, 1936.
[2] No. 353, December 19th, 1938.
[3] February, 1936.
[4] No. 120, April 29th, 1936.
[5] No. 69, December, 1935; *cf.* also No. 72, March, 1936.

thinking which " is going on in the entire German youth with one end in view—viz., the intellectual emancipation from all elements of clericalism which are alien to our race and our life and have no share in the aspirations of our nation."

The *Osservatore Romano* of February 8th, 1938, gave the following collection of insulting references to the Catholic Church and its adherents, all taken from the *Nationalsozialistische Monatshefte*: " Blood poisoning, Bastardisation into one single race muddle, Race death, Race swamp, Race contamination, Race tuberculosis, Race chaos, Soul murder, Lower order of mankind, Priest politicians, Patent Christianity, Obscurantists, Agitator curate, Business Catholicism, Sorcerer of Rome, Cæsaropapistic danger, Soul slavery, Medicineman's philosophy, Orientalised Christianity."

An article entitled[1] " The Roman Church turning away from Europe " stated that among the great international spiritual powers, which are bitterly opposed to a predominantly nordic and white family of nations, is also the Church of Rome. . . . The Myth of the twentieth century is written for Europe. . . . The Roman Church is preparing the rally against the Germanic world.

A less academic type of publication is represented by *Der Schulungsbrief* (Training Letter), the central monthly of the German National Socialist Workers' Party and the German Labour Front (chief training department of the Party and of the Labour Front; editor, Dr. Ley, Reich Director of the Labour Front; circulation, $3\frac{1}{2}$ millions).

According to an instruction by Dr. Ley of January 21st, 1937 (quoted in *Der Schulungsbrief*, No. 3, of March 1937), these training letters are

" the only official ideological training bulletins of the Party and the German Labour Front. For all political leaders and for Labour Front officials, subscription to these training letters is an evident duty. Without exception all those who have joined the Party since 1933, and especially those who have been received during last year and this, should subscribe to the training letters." Generally speaking all those should subscribe " who are interested in a profounder knowledge of the National Socialist ideology or who are in any way entrusted with the care of others."

In summer, 1938, the Commander-in-Chief of the army ordered that the training letters should be introduced into the army as a valuable means for education on National Socialist lines. The paper is meant in the first place to serve the leaders of companies, batteries or squadrons as a basis for instruction. After having been used for that purpose, the copies are displayed in reading and recreation rooms, etc.

In a special edition for the National Labour Day (second year, May, 1935) we find under the heading " The German Book " a review of Rosenberg's latest book, *An die Dunkelmänner unserer Zeit* (To the Obscurantists of our Time). The Introduction says that, for the majority of Germans, who see " in the Roman mentality and in the destructive penetration of jesuitical ideas among our people one of

[1] No. 104, November, 1938.

the chief causes of our national decay," Rosenberg's " Myth " was like a redemption. By a mere minority working under clerical leadership the work has been continuously attacked—an attack aimed ostensibly at Rosenberg himself, but in reality an attempt to undermine the very foundations of the National Socialist ideology. The review goes on to say:

> A long, hidden and bitter struggle has at last been brought to light by the solemn condemnation of the " Myth " by the Catholic Church in 1933, and this struggle has been continued ever since with great obstinacy in almost every sphere of our daily life. In this the clergy together with some wire-pullers of the late " Centre Party " have used, to broadcast their ideas, a pamphlet entitled " Studies on the ' Myth of the Twentieth Century,' " which contains an introduction by the Bishop of Münster. In it anonymous " experts " with typically jesuitical ingenuity employ all sorts of tricks and even open fallacies in their efforts to disprove scientifically the contention of the " Myth."
> The " Studies," however, did not prove a tower of strength in the struggle against the National Socialist ideology, but rather a house of cards which is now falling apart in all directions, since Alfred Rosenberg has answered his, and therefore also our, enemies. The title of this book is " To the Obscurantists of our Time," an excellent sequel to the " Myth," written not only with some asperity as the occasion demands, but also with all that serene clarity of vision and objective sincerity that has always characterised this distinguished philosopher. But, more than that, this new work of Rosenberg's is a pledge of religious freedom, which in the Third Reich shall never be lost through the intolerance of a small minority allied with Rome; and at the same time it is a warning to all who may still be under the delusion that they can impose on the entire German nation a foreign way of thinking and feeling. May Rosenberg's book, therefore, find its way into the hands of all those who, as true Germans, are seeking individually to form their own minds.

Another article entitled " The Historical Turning-point of the Middle Ages," in the October number of 1936, attempts to prove that Christianity has destroyed the national values of the Germans. " The missionaries were agitators protected by the authorities " (p. 389). We also find the usual accusations against the Church's indulgences. " How should he (Luther) have known that . . . the Hierarchy is the typical creation of the Mediterranean mind ?" (p. 397).

The November number of 1936 again propagates Rosenberg's ideas. We often find quotations from the " Myth " (*e.g.*, p. 419) or from Houston Stewart Chamberlain (p. 420). A long line of heretics is hailed as representing heroes and martyrs of Germanic ideals. " All the noblest men were persecuted with poison and gold " (p. 422; *cf.* also the attacks on the Church on pp. 417, 423, 427 *ff.*, etc.).

The February number of 1937 collects in an article, " The Idea and Worth of Woman in the Middle Ages," everything said by ascetical and religious writers that can be interpreted as lowering the ideal of " Woman." The Church is alleged to have been the cause of much immorality by its depreciation of " Woman."

In the March number, 1937, an article entitled " Fight against Three Foreign Ideologies " tries to show how the Jew Paul " with his Jewish intellect destroyed that German ideology which was based on the common link of blood. . . . With the help of this spiritual Internationalism founded on equality of souls, political clericalism has constructed one of the greatest terrorisms that the world has ever witnessed."

The April number, 1937, contained an article entitled " Free World Outlook," arguing that three intellectual movements, working on the ground prepared by the Reformation, liberated the German mind from those ties that the mediæval domination of the un-Germanic doctrine of the Church of Rome had imposed on it—humanism, free natural science and enlightenment. All three movements had to concentrate their main attack on Scholasticism, through which the Church of Rome's doctrinal system had reached the climax of its power over German national education.

In the May number, 1938, an article, " Labour and Race," explains how the Church " despises and curses labour," a scorn based on Jewish theology which had been taken over by the Christian Fathers, etc. This attitude " contributed considerably to the spread of Jewish contempt of labour and thus to a weakening of moral fitness for work among European nations."

A daily paper, the *Westdeutscher Beobachter* (*West German Observer*), official organ of the German National Socialist Workers' Party, writes on January 27th, 1936, with reference to the Pastoral issued after the Bishops' Conference at Fulda:

The warning against " certain " training courses and youth meetings, against " certain " books and periodicals is couched in that cryptic language which, quite clearly, is intended to mean something different from what it says. It cannot be gainsaid that this Pastoral deserves the reproach that it increases the already existing uncertainty about the clergy's attitude towards important events of the day: nay, one is even compelled to suspect that this is, in reality, a large-scale attack on National Socialist literature. Perhaps the training courses of the Party and of the State are among those " certain " things against which this Pastoral " gives a most emphatic warning "? The notorious anonymity of such Pastorals will certainly not destroy the widespread conviction among the people that certain clerical circles preserve only an external attitude of loyalty, and in a State which does all in its power to protect and preserve the Christian Faith the use of the word *Kulturkampf* is most objectionable.

With reference to a discourse by Rosenberg at the Party Rally at Nürnberg, 1937, the *Westdeutscher Beobachter* wrote on September 9th, 1937:

Now the two opposing camps are clearly marked. On the other side we find the bloody dictatorship of Moscow, of the tyrants, and there, too, muddle-headed Church leaders of all shades, while on our side works Creative Personality with power from above.

In the *Schwäbische Rundschau* of September 7th, 1936, District Director Drewitz writes about the Church's insistence on " denominational schools" and their inability to stem the Bolshevist assault by denominational education:

> Even in these days, when the whole nation is thanking National Socialism for the overthrow of Bolshevism, ecclesiastical circles are a source of worry to the simple faithful citizen. . . . Only the denominational school, so they say, is in a position to realise the important, decisive task of bringing religion and life into a powerful union. But perhaps we are justified in still having some little doubt about the truth of this assertion when we think of Spain, where the entire education of the people was entrusted to the Church, for there a nation which for centuries has been brought up entirely in a Catholic and therefore Christian spirit is murdering, burning, destroying all cultural values of the past. Is this, then, to be taken as a proof of incapacity to educate the people, or of negligence on the part of those who were responsible for that education, or—as we believe—evidence that religious ideologies cannot influence political life? One thing at least is evident—in Spain this religious ideology has failed.

2. The Department of Racial Policy of the German National Socialist Workers' Party

This department is one of the most important factors in the ideological struggle against the Church. Its director, Dr. Gross, delivered in the middle of June, 1938, an instructional lecture in Mülheim to the leaders, both boys and girls, of the Hitler Youth of the Ruhr and Lower Rhine district, about which the *Essener Nationalzeitung* reports:

> He proceeded from the fact that in the Germanic-Nordic race we find the best, the highest virtues of nobility and courage living on, imperishable, but that it was always those elements of the nation which from the racial point of view were of the highest value which had continually offered the greatest sacrifice of their blood. So it was at the time of the feuds among the German tribes, so in the Middle Ages when the best sons of the German nobility and knighthood joined the Crusades for foreign aims and left their bones somewhere in the arid deserts of Asia Minor, while the second sons lived generally as monks and abbots in celibacy: so it was at the time of the knightly feuds, of the Thirty Years' War and of all internal German wars and, finally, also in the Great War. The best and the most valuable blood was always shed first. . . . The nation must become ever stronger, better, more worthy within itself: the best racial blood must prevail; then Germany's future will be safe.

The Department of Racial Policy distributes through its chief district leaders, by canvassing from door to door and not through ordinary booksellers, literature which without any doubt aims at substituting the racial ideology for Christian ideas.

The bulletin of this department of the German National Socialist Workers' Party, *Bevölkerungspolitische Blätter*, in the April number of 1937 attacked the celibacy of the Catholic clergy which is to be considered extremely harmful to the vital forces of the nation. In view of this biological danger to the nation, all doubts founded on tradition are to be disregarded. Celibacy is not a question that concerns the Church, but the whole nation, for in Germany there are 19,000 priests, 13,000 monks and 74,000 nuns who remain childless.

The paper reaches the offensive conclusion that the Catholic portion of the German nation is less highly gifted than the Protestant. This, to say the least, is a very incautious statement to make in the Third Reich, where leading personalities were originally Catholic. By this enforced non-propagation of talent for generation after generation the Catholic section of the nation has suffered much. On the supposition that among Catholic Germans there are about 260,000 persons who should be classified as " highly talented," about 20,000 of these would be members of the clergy, so the conclusion must be drawn that about 8 per cent. of all " highly talented " Catholics are not in a position to multiply themselves. From this it would follow that celibacy, prolonged through many generations, would finally have the result that among the Catholic population high talents would completely disappear.

Openly anti-Christian ideas are also disseminated by the periodical *Neues Volk* (*New People*), published by the same department. In some cities, as, *e.g.*, Braunschweig, every newly married couple receives as a wedding present a free subscription to this paper.

3. The " *Schutzstaffel* " (*Protective Guard*): " *SS* "

On September 20th, 1935, the Reich Leader of the SS, Himmler, issued the following proclamation:

What the Representative of the Führer proclaimed on October 13th, 1933 (*Verordnungsblatt der NSDAP*, second year, No. lviii, October 31st, 1933), is and always has been the guiding principle of the SS—viz., " No National Socialist shall ever be at a disadvantage because he does not belong to any definite creed or denomination, or even to any denomination at all. Religion is a personal question for each individual to settle for himself at the bar of his own conscience. There must be no compulsion in matters of conscience. This proclamation is the foundation of our National Socialist formulation of the ancient German right of freedom of conscience. Just as in the SS it is not allowed to influence, still less to compel anyone in the direction of any denomination, so I shall never allow any member of the SS to ridicule or blaspheme any conviction or opinion which is sacred to other German citizens. Under this prohibition I include also the singing of songs which insult religious objects or mock at ecclesiastical customs and institutions. Just as we are still indignant that certain unauthorised persons quite unnecessarily cut down the trees which to our ancestors were holy, not as gods but as God's works, in the same way I should find it detestable if even one member of the SS should ever fall back into the barbarity of those unauthorised persons and touch, even though with only one finger, what is sacred to any single denomination, be it picture, statue, building or anything of the sort. I shall expel from the SS any of its members who err in this respect, for they are unfit for the fellowship and the order of the SS."

With these words one may compare the following deeds:

The SS in their barracks are forbidden (1) to leave barracks without uniform and (2) to enter a church with uniform. In this way it is made impossible for all SS-men to attend any religious service during the three years of their barrack training and, it is to be noted, the barracks at Munich alone usually house some 2,000 men.

In the SS duels are compulsory. An order of November 9th, 1935, states that each SS-man has the right and the duty to defend his honour by arms.

No doubt, officially, the SS has nothing to do with the German Faith Movement. Nevertheless members of the SS actively canvas for the neo-pagan movements. We quote from the *Reichswart* of April 14th, 1935:

> *District of Württemberg :* . . . Ellwangen, the Swabian Nazareth, a stronghold of Catholicism, was . . . specially taken care of and many have joined our ranks there. This is most of all due to the activity of the local leader, SS-Commander Eyselc. . . . In Stuttgart, Tübingen and Reutlingen, training night-classes are being held based on the books of Hauer and Reventlow. These works, which wonderfully supplement each other, are guides to the most profound questions of religious life. They give us strength to fight Christianity not only in easy controversy on superficial questions, but, knowing the superiority of our German faith, to attack what is most fundamental in the enemies' creed.

Though we are assured that the SS has never issued orders to enforce apostasy,[1] it is nevertheless true that members of the SS have been compelled, under threat of expulsion from the Party, to abandon the Church, as many testify who in their trouble of conscience have consulted their parish priests. The extent to which pressure is exercised upon members of the SS appears from the following authentic document from which we have, of course, to omit all personal details:

SS Reserve.
Ref.: Leaving the Church.
May 3rd, 1936.

To. . . . .

You must by 11 a.m. Tuesday report by telephone whether and when the troop leader and such subaltern leaders as are in charge of groups have left the Church; or, alternatively, when they can be counted on to leave. Otherwise state their denominations. The report is to be made on the specified date to the SS Rotten-Stabsführer. . . .

Signed: . . . .
The Leader of the SS Reserve.

In the light of such documents the following facts will come as no surprise: In the summer of 1936 Heinrich Himmler, Reich Leader of the SS and Chief of the German Police, ostentatiously left the Church, and his example was followed by SS-men in considerable numbers, led by the members of the Bodyguard of Adolf Hitler. So in Munich alone during the last months of 1936 there left the Church:

October, 1936: 9 SS-leaders in high positions.

November, 1936: 18 " Obersturmführer."
       6 SS-men.

December, 1936: 31 SS-leaders.
       10 SS-men. (Was it pure chance that on one day in this month in one Munich Registration Office 38 SS-men registered their apostasy ?)

---

[1] *Cf. Mitteilungsblatt der NS-Pastoren Mecklenburgs*, January 11th, 1937.

January, 1937: 13 Group leaders (Scharführer).
12 Aspirants (SS Anwärter).
4 Storm leaders (Sturmführer).
3 Storm men (Sturmmänner).
9 other SS-members or their relatives.

At Dachau 214 members of the SS left the Church, 48 of them between August 1st and December 31st, 1936, the rest between January 1st and March 31st, 1937, as also did 250 SS-men from the guards of the Sachsenburg concentration camp at the beginning of 1937. It is much the same with the SS Leaders' School, Wewelsburg, and the *SS-Verfügungstruppe* (troops for special disposition) at Arolsen (Waldeck). Who would say that such mass defection is merely fortuitous?

A disgusting display was staged on Corpus Christi, 1937, in the SS barracks of Munich-Freimann, where in the barrack yard a burlesque procession was held with a canvas attached to four poles to imitate the canopy used to protect the Blessed Sacrament. Some SS-men draped themselves in linen rags, etc., to represent vestments, others walked in the procession saying their " rosary " and other " prayers," while the great bulk of the SS-men watched the " show " from the barrack windows.

That the *official* celebrations of the SS are a very poor substitute for religion one instance will show. At the King Henry Festival on July 2nd, 1938, at Quedlinburg, Reich Leader Himmler placed a wreath of oak leaves in the Wygpert Crypt at the foot of Castle Hill and, according to the *Nationalzeitung* of July 3rd, 1938, he then ascended the hill between two rows of pylons decorated with Victory runes of the SS.

From sacrificial bowls huge flames blazed up to the night sky. . . . Under the plain crypt, near a grating under which the stone coffins of the king and the queen are visible, stood SS-men, guns in their hands, their helmeted heads inclined in an attitude of mourning, and in the breathless silence was heard the voice of the Reich Leader of the SS as he recalled in simple words the memory of the king and deposited large wreaths on the royal tombs. While the participants were standing at the vault, the names were announced of those towns which Henry I had founded and which now in his honour gave wreaths of German oak.

On this, the *Schwarze Korps* gave the following very instructive explanation in terms of the race myth:

This deep night, so instinct with life, gave rise to thoughts and impressions in the minds of all who were hastening with prayer and thanksgiving to this hall, where the king's bodily relics are to us symbols of his earthly sojourn and where wreaths of green oak are placed in his honour. When, outside the hall, sharp volleys greeted the new day, we felt the boundless eternity of a life dedicated to the service of the nation. In His great men we believe we are near to God Himself. In them we ever seek, meet and find His law, that in working for the nation, as the most beautiful revelation of His greatness, we are also nearest to His inmost and genuine Essence.

The weekly organ of the SS, the *Schwarze Korps*, is thoroughly anti-Christian. Although Herr Himmler in the circular which we quoted forbids his men " to ridicule or blaspheme the opinions and convictions of other German citizens," he knows perfectly well, nevertheless, that in the whole National Socialist literature there is no paper which ridicules and blasphemes the convictions of other German citizens as spitefully as this *Bulletin of the National Headquarters of the SS*, for which Herr Himmler himself is responsible.

A few instances will prove this. In the issue of May 1st, 1935, an article on " Infidels " states:

> The clerical gentlemen are surprised that the number of those who remain outside the churches is steadily increasing. This they can no longer deny. Ignoring, however, the necessary self-criticism involved in the search for the real cause of this development, they have chosen an easier way out. They say that the responsibility for the fact that large sections of the German nation are turning away from the Church today rests with those forces which are propagating the " Myth " of the blood—a dangerous statement, because it bears witness to the truth of their opponents' ideas. Moreover, the " apostates " are called neo-pagans or infidels.
>
> Are they really infidels—*i.e.*, men who do not believe in the existence of a creative power, a higher order or whatever one wishes to call it ? Generally speaking it will be difficult to answer this, as in almost every case one will have to conclude from individual cases. A very instructive illustration was offered in this respect last Friday by the gigantic meeting of the German Faith Movement in the Berlin *Sportpalast*, where it made its first public appearance in that setting. Many may have come only for the sake of curiosity, others with a genuine interest. It was evident, however, that the majority of these many thousands were no longer mere seekers, but had a clearly defined idea of God in their hearts. Proof of this is in the extraordinary enthusiasm of the applause which greeted not only the director of the German Faith Movement, Professor Hauer, but also his representative Count Reventlow. . . . Nor were these people who had come in such great numbers to this historic place the " dregs of society." Only very occasionally did one notice an individual here and there who seemed remarkable: the type of the eternal bird of passage or a lass in country dress; the great mass of the visitors, however, showed in their external appearance certain clear signs of an inner unanimity which was the more impressive in that it was not the expression of opposition to some rival movement, but of the vivid and joyful approval of their own idea.

The German Faith Movement demands observance of that regulation[1] of the Leader's Representative in which he, Rudolf Hess, assured to every German freedom of religious opinion. In this Professor Hauer is in complete agreement with the views of National Socialism.

> We have always advocated that in matters of faith there must be no coercion, but that, as the great Prussian king used to say, everyone should work out his own salvation according to his own fashion. This principle of spiritual freedom we shall hold also in future in opposition to all denominational totalitarian claims.

On June 26th, 1935, an article appeared in the *Schwarze Korps* on " Spicy Stories from the Confessional." Another article on " Race, Faith, Creed "[2] contained the following remarks:

> We should not be worthy exponents of our great philosophy of life if we remained on the defensive. No, we are attacking because Right is on our side. It is not we who have begun this struggle, but our adversaries.

[1] October 13th, 1933. [2] July 17th, 1935.

THE CONFESSIONAL GOWN.

God does not like to see us as He made us, but the confessor must see the interior. So this gown, with zip-fastener from top to bottom and indulgenced medal tag, is "correct" for confessional wear.

CLERICAL MODES FOR SUMMER.

The need is now felt for a costume which allows greater freedom of movement. We therefore recommend our "Mantle of Christian Charity," a garment cut so generously that it may be thrown over everything in the twinkling of an eye. This garment has, of course, full episcopal approval.

CATHOLIC FASHIONS.

[*Das Schwarze Korps*, July 1st, 1937.

FOUND OUT AT LAST.

[*Der Heidelberger Student*, May 4th, 1935.

It is not we who are overstepping frontiers and interfering with the affairs of other people, it is rather that foreign powers have trespassed into our territory.

Our adversaries are no strangers to us. We know them from our own struggle for power and from the century-old struggles of our people. They are those who in the name of Love have destroyed entire nations; who speak of God and mean themselves; who speak of the needs of the Church and mean the possession of a benefice; who chatter about their leader and mean the great gentlemen in Rome or at Doorn; who say " Creed " and " Faith " and mean by this opposition to the new Germany. Though they are utterly insignificant as regards numbers and intellectual capacity, all the same we cannot always afford to be carrying the dead-weight of our reactionaries, grumblers and quarrelsome parsons ! Our fathers may have given their lives for German freedom in the course of the centuries, our mothers may have been burned at the stake by mad criminals; we in our Brown Shirts are the avengers of our ancestors and the builders of the new Reich. . . . One can understand why they refuse to accept our racial point of view and why they attack our racial laws. We can also understand why the " Holy " Father rejects sterilisation. But we cannot understand why Roman priests in German Church magazines have often ranked mental defectives, negroes and Jews above healthy Germans. . . .

We are essentially men who take their stand on *this* earth, and refuse to be moved. For we are not of the number of those who say:" Our kingdom is not of this world." We leave it to them to establish the other world, but they will have to realise one day that only a people which has been preserved here on earth by healthy and constructive forces can be led into Heaven.

We stand by our field-grey comrades of the Great War who gave their lives for their people; we stand by our dead Brown Shirt comrades; we stand by all who are fighting for the German cause; and this profession of our principles rises infinitely above those sham professions of faith which nowadays certain quarters opposed to us find it so easy to produce. . . .

Similar material appeared in an article, " The Miracle Happened," on August 21st, 1935 (p. 13):

There is something strange about political Catholicism. As often as Christianity is in conflict with its earthly surroundings, public opinion is diverted from the shortcomings of the system by mystical portents. When the Pope declared the dogma of the Immaculate Conception, as recently as the middle of last century, there was considerable controversy in scholastic circles. The Virginal Conception (!) had not been proclaimed at the same time as Christ's Birth; rather it was an achievement of introspective philosophers whose horizon was limited by the cloister walls. Entire orders emphatically opposed this revelation and there were heated controversies which gravely injured the Church's prestige and divided the multitude of the faithful into two camps. Rome therefore resolved to put an end to all the learned discussions by simply declaring the " Immaculate Conception " a dogma, and after that a miraculous well began to flow at Lourdes and the Friars, shrugging their shoulders, had to resign themselves to the inevitable.

As further illustrations we quote some of the headings from the issue of December 5th, 1935: " Clerical Campaign against National Unity " (which refers to a booklet by Fr. Kassiepe on mixed marriages); " Parasites of the Post-War Era " (referring to Catholic religious Orders); " Darkest Backstairs Morality " (directed against the moral doctrine of the Catholic Church in matters of the State and taxation). A detailed description is given of the ride of a " clerical railwayman," ridiculing ecclesiastical personalities. A poem, " St. Leonard's Chapel," follows on " Christianity's Failure and the Victory of German Nature Worship." " What a Lady wrote 220 Years Ago " derides the virginity of nuns. " How Sister Lioba smuggled out Millions " is another attack. On the same page appeared pictures under the heading, " O You, My Austria,"[1] depicting a high ecclesiastic blessing a gallows, and underneath: " The end justifies the blackest means." A series of pictures follows with the object of representing priests, nuns, and bishops as enemies of the people. Another picture is of a Catholic priest blessing an Italian tank (with an interpretation which has been since proved to be a grave error). Then " Water-flushed Salvation of Souls " ridicules a pious pamphlet found in the w.c. of an express train. All this is to be found in one *single* copy of the official SS paper.

In the *Schwarze Korps*, No. 5, 1936, appeared the following:

Yes, we are prepared for the 1936 athletic season ! A *Leibstandarte Christi*—i.e., Christ's Bodyguard—has been founded and in the Kolping Unions[2] relay racers are in training, so that malicious rumours may be spread in record time over the Marathon course.

Already the competitions for the title of " Well-greased with all Unctions " may be regarded as decided. They are reserved for the " Black." The heats will be highly interesting, as they are a " Charitable Association Limited," in favour of some Friars who so far have always succeeded in preserving the appearance of amateurs.

In the team events we expect the Kolping Union to contest every award tooth and nail with the various Journeymen's Unions. Between these the champion titles will be contested in a gymnastic display, soul gymnastics and spiritual jerks. Awaiting the winners are valuable prizes, among them three absolutely plenary indulgences.

There are divergent opinions about the result of the obstacle race for skiers. The course is particularly difficult and no little courage and resolution are required to avoid touching any of the little posts which bear the numbers of the different paragraphs of the new German Penal Currency Code, which have led to severe falls and reduced several of the competitors to five years on the sick-bed with loss of civil rights. In the women's competitions, at the steep slope Sister Currentia, the hot favourite, took a fall and tore a muscle badly, on account of the breaking of her ski-sticks. Out of the broken cane came some bank notes, so that the public prosecutor disqualified her, in spite of strong protests from the sports committee.

The issue of the *Schwarze Korps* for April 8th, 1937, makes use of Communist pictures from Spain in order to ridicule the Church. By printing spiteful cartoons the paper intends to prove how widespread were the abuses of the Church in Spain. The complacency, however, with which all this dirt and all the other anti-clerical articles of the same issue are spread before the eyes of the 500,000 readers shows sufficiently the real attitude of this inspired organ of Adolf Hitler's bodyguard.

An entire page is filled with faces of priests with the comment beneath: " God created man after His own image." The devil and the priests are represented shaking hands and saying: " We are good friends, we need each other." A bishop is depicted with a

---

[1] Well-known song.—*Translator's note*.   [2] Catholic Journeymen.—*Translator's note*.

pig's head, sitting with several monks at a solemn banquet, while a poor family is hungry at an empty table. Finally, there is shown a gigantic statue of the Sacred Heart, covered with embrasures from which machine-guns and big guns are firing.

On the same page is a reproduction of the illustrated cover of a book by the apostate priest Juan Garcia Morales, *El Cristo Rojo* ("The Red Christ"). "As Holy Orders cannot be annulled, this priest has still to be considered a Catholic," concludes the *Schwarze Korps*, suggesting once again the calumny that Catholics are friends of the Bolsheviks.

Another copy of the *Schwarze Korps* for October 27th, 1938, contains in large type a leading article of several columns criticising " that section of the clergy that mixes in politics." In this are attacked the Fulda Pastoral of the German Bishops, the " climax of episcopal insincerity," and also Archbishop Gröber, Bishop Bornewasser, Count von Preysing, Bishop of Berlin, and the Evangelical Confessional Church. The " political clergy " are accused of " having faithfully supported the enemy in the German nation's decisive hour." A service of intercession for the preservation of peace arranged by the temporary heads of the Confessional Church for September 30th, 1938, particularly aroused the anger of the SS paper, which called them " political demonstrations of treason and sabotage in face of the united readiness of the nation in an anxious and fateful hour," and then demanded: " Stop it ! The nation's safety imposes upon us the duty of destroying such criminals of the State !"

In the leading article of the issue of March 30th, 1939, we read:

In his titanic work the Führer presses for the construction, stone by stone, of the sanctuary of our Reich; let us, the faithful and enthusiastic, lend him our support. At the same time we must keep an eye on the vermin that is unable to reach even the soles of the Führer's boots. Occasionally we notice movements of these dust-bound creatures who are vegetating in their own dirt. We notice the existence of a caste of priests moved with the lowest instincts and filled only with hatred and envy. . . .

The *Schwarze Korps* of May 11th, 1939, regrets that Rev. N. N. Gutsfeld has left the National League for the Care of German War Cemeteries. This clergyman justified his action in the following words:

My reason is the article in No. 3 of the *Kriegsgräber Fürsorge* of March 12th, 1939, in which Major A. D. Lemke writes: " Whether they remained out there or whether they have come home—they are united by that invisible bond of the same faith—they all believe in Germany as in a God." I find it impossible to approve of such principles. For me God's first commandment holds good: " Thou shalt have no strange gods before Me."

On this the *Schwarze Korps* remarks:

One can hardly be mistaken in terming this strange attitude the result of religious " hybris." What must be the value of a Christian doctrine that has such a disastrous effect on the common sense of a grown man ?

The same issue defends those who are leaving the Church in these words:

> Whosoever leaves the Church nowadays does so nearly always for very well-founded reasons. He sees that the preachers of Christian doctrine are in opposition to our State. He hears their sermons and instructions which, between the lines and under biblical allegories, discredit National Socialism and try to disturb national unity. He is aware of the international relations that exist between ecclesiastical fanatics and the manufacturers of atrocity stories in foreign countries. He has to witness the Churches denying the greatness of our time. He sees the miserable behaviour of morally corrupt priests and of political pastors engulfed in petty quarrels, with no other end than the preservation of their benefices and the securing of Church taxes.
>
> And then, filled with horror, such a man turns away from an institution which, entirely ignoring its real object, achieves not the care but the corruption of souls for its own selfish purposes.

The leading article of the same issue, " Model Praying," says among other things of the peace message of President Wilson: " It was just like the vow of chastity in that priestly league of men which, since its existence, has been striving only for power and the realisation of its desire to domineer. It was given with the consciousness that the spell of its words would be so strong that, fascinated by this miracle, nobody would remind the speaker of the fulfilment of his words."

4. The " Sturmabteilung " (Storm Troopers): SA

At the regular meetings of many of the local groups of the SA (as, for example, in Munich during the summer of 1935) it is part of the official programme to practise songs which mock at the Church and her institutions. So, for instance, in Mecklenburg[1] there were publicly sung at an SA singing competition songs designed to arouse feelings against certain ecclesiastical dignitaries, and a similar thing happened in the case of the SA regiment of Recklinghausen in January, 1936; and in all this Catholic members are often obliged to take an active part under threat of expulsion. Indeed, in one place in the Rhon district, towards the end of August, 1935, some Catholic members of the SA were punished by an SA officer for the " crime " of attending Church. That this last instance is indicative of a general attitude is demonstrated by the following regulations issued at Nürnberg in November, 1936:

> 1. I hereby forbid from henceforth the wearing of SA uniform on such occasions as weddings, baptisms, etc.
>
> 2. I forbid groups, flag deputations and individual leaders and men of the SA to take part in funerals, as long as representatives of the Church are present. In future provisions will have to be made in the case of deceased members of the SA that the funeral ceremonies are arranged at such a time that the official functions of an ecclesiastical representative are performed either before or after the participation and the mourning service of the SA. The SA rejects in future any connection with denominational organisations.

The attitude of the Chief of Staff of the SA, Lutze, is characterised by the following letter:

---

[1] *Cf. Niederdeutscher Beobachter*, 12th year, No. 9.

BERLIN, W. 8,
September 30*th*, 1936.
Voszstr. 1.

The Supreme SA-Leader R-R.
Bureau of the Chief of Staff.
Ref.: 9370-36-I-1.
Concerning Baptism of Infants.
Ref.: *Ibid.*, letter of September 16th, 1936.

To the Catholic Parish Priest of St. Bernard's, Berlin-Dahlem, Königin Luisestrasse 33

YOUR REVERENCE,

Your letter of 16th inst. has been referred to the Chief of Staff, who gives the following reply:

It is true that a son (whose name is Adolf Hermann) has been born to the Chief of Staff. The infant is not baptised and the Chief of Staff has no intention of having his child baptised by any one of the two principal religious denominations in Germany. The Chief of Staff is led to this attitude by the following consideration:

With deep anxiety he has long been watching the lines along which the two principal denominations are moving. Truth is among the highest ideals of mankind, as the Christian religion again and again maintains in its writings and doctrine. As a truthful man it is with deep sorrow that the Chief of Staff has noticed the many attacks full of lies and hatred made by both denominations against the State of today. It is inconsistent for a Christian religion to demand of its followers " not to give false witness against their neighbours," and, on the other hand, for the official representatives of this religion to give from the pulpit " false witness against the State." This must be unintelligible to any truthful and sincere character. The religious officials paid by the present State are indebted to that State for saving the meeting-places in which they preach their religion from being burnt as a dreadful illumination of Germany's night skies, and themselves from being brutally massacred by a Red mob, as has happened and is still happening in hundreds of cases in Spain, where anti-Christian Bolshevism rules.

If " Thou shalt love thy enemies " is still the Christian message, it is illogical for religious preachers to fight the modern State even on the supposition that they are its " enemies," for even as " enemies " of the modern State they would still have to love it, and one cannot insult what one loves !

They preach, " Thou shalt live chaste and modest in words and in work," and yet the official preachers of this doctrine have to be put behind iron bars for considerable periods for the most beastly obscenities. Is, then, the " chaste and modest living " asked only of the followers, and are the criminal sexual excesses of the preachers quite in order ? For it has been proved that these obscenities were known to and tolerated by higher quarters until at last the State tore away the protective veil and branded the overmastering instincts of sexual perversion among the servants of Jesus. It is nowhere written in Holy Scripture that to the preachers of Christianity sexual excesses are allowed; yet the lives of the Christian preachers should be regulated by Holy Scripture.

In 2,000 years not only has the Christian religion not succeeded in making men as good as the commandments and the Bible urge them to be, but, over and above, it has not even succeeded in making its preachers good men.

A few out of hundreds of inconsistencies are mentioned here. But young people, aware of all these contradictions, become involved in considerable spiritual conflict which must have most disastrous consequences on their whole lives. As one holding to his belief in God and as the devoted father of a family, the Chief of Staff finds it impossible to take this responsibility. He has to exclude any possibility which could expose his children to the danger of becoming immoral through contact with sexual hedonists in clerical robes. Over and above this, he has to protect them from the contamination of false doctrines. They are being brought up pure and to believe in God without being tied to any denomination.

The fact that the letter from the Catholic Rectory did not conclude with " Heil Hitler " is considered by us as mere forgetfulness.

Heil Hitler !

The First Adjutant of the Chief of Staff.

Signed: REIMAN, *Brigade Leader*.

An occasional remark in the official weekly published by the National Headquarters of the SA, *Der SA-Mann*, shows that the SA expects its Catholic members to leave either the Church or the SA. In No. 30 of July 27th, 1935, for example, is written:

> In those districts which are predominantly denominational many an SA-man will have to face the question whether above his faith in Germany he places a spiritual-secular power which has not even its seat in Germany. If so, he should have the decency to honour the SA with his presence no longer.

This is plain enough.

A Catholic SA-man who had asked for his honourable dismissal from the SA because he was unable to reconcile the ideas published in the *Stürmer* and in Rosenberg's " Myth " with his conscience, was punished with perpetual exclusion from the SA, the reason given being that

> there is only one National Socialist ideology . . . whether in the Führer's speeches, or in the *Stürmer*, or in the " Myth " . . . all are expressions of the one great idea for which X has no more enthusiasm. By this X reveals an attitude of mind hostile to the Movement and the State.

At the public demonstrations against the Church which we described above[1] the SA generally took the lead. To the incidents already mentioned let us add the following: In 1934 and 1935 SA-men at Borken-i-W. tore down the decorations in the streets during the night before the " Great Procession "; and in summer, 1935, they raided the headquarters of the working men's union at Ehede near Borken-i-W. and inflicted numerous injuries on Catholic men. Again at Borken-i-W. on June 25th, 1935, a fire broke out in the Catholic church, and SA-men from the camp of the " Austrian Legion " were seen in the vicinity. Before the court gave its verdict it was announced by press, wireless and posters that a certain Mensink, a pious church-goer and member of the Catholic Guild of St. Cecilia, was the culprit ! The suspicion was founded on the fact that his hat had been found in a confessional. Mensink admitted his guilt, but retracted it two days later, and on July 9th, 1935, he was able to prove his alibi.

At Schleissheim the SA arranged some sort of propaganda tour on August 18th, 1935, which the SA-men themselves conducted in a manner which was most offensive to Catholics.

The tone of this organisation's official organ, *Der SA-Mann*, may

[1] P. 284.

be judged from the following quotation—the first from the correspondence columns of its issue for July 20th, 1935, under the heading:

Religious Activity in the SA

It is and always has been a fundamental principle that religion is a private affair. In the SA there is no religious activity !

A SA-man at Oppeln, Oberschlesien, is in doubt whether he can be a good SA-man if he is a believing Catholic. Certainly he can, and we do hope he really is. Untrue and false is the opinion that the nation's unity has been disturbed by those who left Christianity. As a Catholic he ought to know the intolerance of this struggle better than anybody else. Each of us had to struggle hard until he found the correct attitude. For the rest we have been long enough active members of the SA to know that here " religion is not insulted," but the men object, and quite rightly, to the highly treasonable and criminal intrigues of certain representatives of this religion. If we neglected this we should be no fighters, and so lose the right to wear the Brown Shirt. We let everyone work out his own salvation as he pleases; we keep, however, a watchful eye on the increasing activity of those who still refuse to admit that the Centre Party in Germany is a thing of the past, and that the days when one could mix religion and politics with impunity are gone for ever. . . .

There is no objection to a discussion of the ideas of the " Myth of the Twentieth Century " if it is done in the proper way. . . .

In the *SA-Mann*, No. 30, of July 27th, 1935, we read the following:

Every Roman Church magazine is nowadays attacking National Socialist institutions partly by open, partly by hidden means, always, however, by malicious criticism. . . . There is very little in the Third Reich that meets with the approval of Catholicism. Paragraph 24 of the National Socialist Party's programme, which mentions positive Christianity, is at the moment a particularly favoured object of attack. The only thing these gentlemen forget is that they themselves are very far from positive Christianity. The German National Socialist Workers' Party has created the institution of Winter Relief and the Public Welfare Service; there is no better proof of positive Christianity. It is worth while for every director of a SA training camp to contrast the accomplishments of the above-mentioned National Socialist institutions with the accomplishments of the Churches of both denominations. The surprised SA-men will have to note the fact that the comparison is very unfavourable to the Churches. . . .

The *Hochland-SA*, a supplement to the *SA-Mann* of March 6th, 1937, gives a description of " The Bearer of an Indestructible Faith," a choral play that was performed in the Krone Circus, Berlin. Among the verses quoted were the following:

> They are dead who weakly perished,
> Who, whining, cringed before a life to come;
> Who, craven, hope for priestly pardon cherished
> And ended, blind before the gleam of life's last sun.
> To us they're dead.

The *SA-Mann* of April 3rd, 1937, is all worked up over the parish priest of Miesbach (Archdiocese of Munich) in that he " slandered " the dead memory of Frau Hümmer, the head of the local National Socialist Women's Union, by stating in his funeral oration that she died a Catholic. We give the words of the writer:

And so a parish priest turns a grave into a political platform and misuses it for his own unscrupulous ends. . . . The good Father Confessors take all possible care not to chatter about the things that the robber assassin and other criminals tell them under the seal of Confession; but here is a parish priest who did not think it beneath the dignity of his office to take the random utterances of a dying woman and, with malice prepense, to shout them from the house-tops.

The title of the whole article runs: " Clerical counter-measures against the Nazis and those of like mind. The inexhaustible impudence of our politician clerics. How long are we going to show indulgence to all this sheer effrontery ?"

In the *SA-Mann* of April 3rd, 1937, we learn that the cleavage between " the organic life conditions of the nation and the dust-covered oriental dogmas of the Church " is becoming more and more marked.

The *SA-Mann* of May 18th, 1937, takes the field against the use of Christian names.

The *SA-Mann* of July 24th, 1937, attacks the Catholic conception of marriage and the fertility of purely Catholic marriages.

The *SA-Mann* of February 26th, 1938, publishes in this and the following numbers a series of articles on Catholic action under the general heading of " The Black International." Catholic action is described by this paper as a purely political instrument which only came upon the scene when the power politics of the Papacy and the Church fell into a decline. " The layman is roped in for the sole purpose of maintaining the power of the Church." The main purpose of the articles is to call in question and deride the purely spiritual aims of the Church: " Under cover of a divine commission a large-scale campaign is organised which has nothing to do with inner spiritual values, but is concerned simply and solely with the advancement of the external power and domination of clerical dignitaries. . . . The sphere of Catholic action is extended further and further, and its policy in Germany is to carry on the aims and programme of the Catholic Centre Party by working away steadily below the surface. . . ."

Catholic veneration of the Saints is set down as a " degradation of the Führer-idea," and it is regarded as prejudicial to that idea that Catholic action should strive to have new Saints—men like Kolping, the Father of the working man—" thrown on the market." Throughout, the lives of Catholic Saints are presented deliberately and consciously as typical of everything that the German attitude towards life rejects. Catholic feast days are simply " counter-propaganda against national festivals." Thus May 1st is devoted to the " Queen of May " and celebrated with all due pomp. On the Summer Solstice Day the feast of the martyrdom of St. John the Baptist is celebrated. In any case, it is intolerable that Catholic action should dare to foist St. Christopher upon Catholic drivers as their Patron Saint. " Of all those who have his image hanging up in their cars, how many know that he is also the Patron Saint of the French line of fortifications along our frontiers ?"

The *SA-Mann*[1] on the page headed " The Political Soldier " has a

[1] No. 34, 1938.

section on the National Socialist theory of art. Here again its enmity to the Church comes out. A couple of examples: The words under the picture of the thirteenth-century church of St. Patroclus in Soest run:

> This Church, in all its proud and sturdy self-reliance, gives practical expression to the truth that it is in peasant life that the community has its roots. Such a building has less to do with the sects or even with Christianity itself than with the strivings of the Germans of the period to lay hold of all that was best in the spiritual and artistic sphere while keeping their feet firmly planted on mother earth.

Beneath a picture of the Freiburg Minster we find:

> It was not *by means* of dogma but *in conflict* with dogma, in conflict with a rigidly literal spirit of belief, that the German soul created this perfect edifice that has wellnigh lost its vital contact with the soil beneath and simply soars aloft to the heavens above. The yearning for a greater spiritual expansion, frustrated in the spiritual sphere, found an outlet in stone. The structure . . . soars aloft into the wide air of the spirit, up and away from the gloom and narrowness of the times.

We shall now give some quotations from three *hand-bills* which have printed at the bottom: " Issued by the SA of the German National Socialist Workers' Party, Starnberg." It will be noticed how the fight against Bolshevism is made to serve as a justification for the fight against so-called political Catholicism, which is taken as the equivalent of Catholicism itself.

On the *first hand-bill* we have:

> To every German! The man who fights against National Socialism fights for the Bolshevik World Revolution and is a traitor to the German nation. Who is it that is out to destroy all religion? The Bolshevik! And not the National Socialist!
> Germans! Yes, we do attack political Catholicism because:
> 1. It smuggles abroad the pennies of the poor widow and thus defrauds our fellow-countrymen.
> 2. It regards our people merely as something to be exploited for the increase of its own world power.
> 3. Political Ultramontanism is allied with the Jews and other enemies of our people and is a traitor disguised in clerical attire.
> All for each and each for all! Our Führer, Heil!
> Germany for ever!

The *second hand-bill* begins with the following sentences:

> To every German! Something for you! Can you still allow your child to be brought up as a bigot behind the walls of religious houses? Look at the happy Hitler Youth, at the SA as they sing their way along, self-reliant, courageous German men, the future hope of our Fatherland, fine and free.

And the *third hand-bill*:

> To every German! join in by deed and word! Be proud to live in the mighty days of struggle! Destroy the traitors who come to you in their black garb or in their fine frock coats. They want to smash your courage and your hope, so that once again they can lord it over you.

5. *The Training in the " Ordensburgen " (National Training Centres) and in the Adolf Hitler Schools*

Since 1937 National Socialism has planned and carried through a closed system of training for its führer caste. What are called the *Adolf Hitler Schools* form the base of the whole educational pyramid. In these, youths from twelve to eighteen years of age who have been selected as the führer of the future are trained and educated. They are admitted after they have done six years in the Elementary School, but only after a selection made in the first instance by the Hitler Youth and then subjected to further sifting by the Local Leader, the Area Leader and District Leader of the German National Socialist Workers' Party in turn. The principles of selection are good health, racial " soundness," and the extent to which the parents have been active in the Party. The Adolf Hitler Schools are units of the Hitler Youth, which in addition is represented on their boards: each school forms a " Bann " (troop). The self-governing principle of the Hitler Youth is retained; the head of the school belongs to the Hitler Youth. Breaches of discipline are visited on the whole school. The Party bears the costs of the training. Throughout these six years all the lads are, from the material point of view, on an equal footing: they all get the same pocket money and private allowances from parents are not tolerated. The selection for the next level of the pyramid is not effected by means of yearly tests or a final examination, but by means of " constant observation." (Dr. Ley has not defined in greater detail the principles of selection.) From eighteen to twenty-five years of age, those who have passed out successfully from the Adolf Hitler Schools are freed for their duties to the State. They have their labour service and military service to fulfil, and after that, as active members of some branch or other of the Party, they have to serve their time in Technical High School, University or in industry; and of course they have to perform their marriage duty by the State. During this time their names are kept on the books of the German National Socialist Workers' Party Personnel Department.

Twenty-five is the entrance age for the *Ordensburgen*, but, before admittance, there is still another weeding-out, as a result of which not more than a quarter of the total number may remain. The training in the *Ordensburgen* covers four years, which are spent successively in the four castles of Crosinsee in Pomerania, Vogelsang in the Eifel, Sonthofen in Allgau, and the historic castle of Marienburg. In the training scheme for the *Burgjunker* (as the inmates of these castles are called) Crosinsee caters for " elementary scientific instruction," swimming sports, gliding and athletics; speaking of Vogelsang, Dr. Ley was able to say that " the largest sports stadium " was being built there, " one that would surpass similar structures anywhere else in the world." At Sonthofen (which was dedicated by Adolf Hitler on November 23rd, 1937), the Junkers spend a year and a half, and here " besides the work of ideological formation, winter sports are the chief interest." This stage of the training is rounded off by the half-year spent in the East at that *Ordensburg* near Marienburg that stands on " the historic soil of German colonisation."

During the four years in these castles there takes place the last sifting out for the apex of the pyramid, the *Hohe Schule*. In each of the castles a nucleus of 140 men is chosen, each of whom has already occupied during his training a position of leadership in the lower branches of the Party. Finally, the flower of this cadre is chosen to receive " the final polish " at the *Hohe Schule* established on the Chiemsee in Upper Bavaria. In this, " the highest training institute of the German National Socialist Workers' Party," it is Alfred Rosenberg who in the last resort supervises the process of ideological formation. It is here that the following establishments are to be placed: (1) The " National Socialist Academy." (2) The " Institute of Research," with its Central Library. (3) A centre at which every year for four weeks the teachers in the Adolf Hitler Schools and the *Ordensburgen* " will be thoroughly overhauled in matters ideological." (All the quotations are from the *Völkischer Beobachter*, November 24th, 1937.) (4) A model Adolf Hitler School.

This system is meant to set its stamp on the new National Socialist man that it turns out. He has to be at once a " soldier and a preacher," and so the German National Socialist Workers' Party conceives it to be its most solemn duty to create a sort of " Order " whose chief task it is to propagate the new religion, for, more and more, that is what National Socialism shows itself to be. The danger that arises from this quarter is much greater than any arising from direct attacks on the Church and Christianity and from external persecution. This " intensive *Kulturkampf* " is the one which is truly dangerous.

We have treated above[1] of the spirit that prevails in the Adolf Hitler Schools. Here we may add another piece of evidence. According to the *Reichspost* of November 11th, 1937, this is what was written by one Kaufmann, head of the Hitler Youth Press Department, in No. 18 of the Hitler Youth Press Service:

> In the *Adolf Hitler Schools*, of course, no *sectarian instruction* in the tenets of the numerous Churches and religious denominations can be imparted. . . . Hence, religious instruction is concerned with the religious teaching of mankind in general, so that the young men may come to know something of the aspirations and strength of will of all whose mighty spirits have wrestled for the soul of man at all times and among all peoples. . . . The *Reichsjugendführer* has expressly enjoined that the religious convictions of others must be respected. But he has also pointed out that to serve under the flag of Youth is to serve Germany, and to serve Germany is to serve the great and almighty Being who is over our people. When the Reich Youth Leader dedicated new flags for the Hitler Youth in Wüstrow, he saw in them symbols, not only of the National Socialist Movement, but also of the power on earth of the Eternal God.

There you have it quite clearly stated that the religious instruction of the future is to be freed not only from all denominational ties, but also from every connection with Christianity.

[1] P. 174.

At the beginning of May, 1938, the new arrivals from the Adolf Hitler Schools were given a solemn reception at the *Ordensburg* of Sonthofen. The new " year " consisted of 340 young lads, twenty of them from Austria. In the course of his address, Reich Leader Dr. Ley said:

> There is one thing, boys, you have got to bear always in mind: From this moment you belong to Adolf Hitler ! The principles that have determined the selection of you lads are quite few in number. The primary consideration has been the test of blood, your Race. Today the Race-postulate is for us something that is self-evident, a sacred article of belief. Twenty years ago this was by no means the case. You have been chosen, and in that choice your racial purity was a central factor. In this matter we admit no manner of compromise. Again, we have put you to the test to see whether you are at the moment thoroughly fit to endure physically the demands we have to make on you. Finally, the way your parents have behaved as members of the national community has had its due weight in determining our choice.

After what has been said, the tone and outlook of the Junker brought up in the *Ordensburgen* can now scarcely be a matter of doubt. Naturally, not very much gets out about this strictly secluded élite. The little that does leak out is clear enough. As may be seen from the report of an interview with Dr. Ley given by the *Frankfurter Zeitung* for July 19th, 1936 (see also the *Westdeutscher Beobachter* of the same date), the *Ordensburgen* aim at the formation of the whole man along National Socialist lines.

To characterise the type of man they are out to produce, Dr. Ley uses an expression which has a distinctly religious flavour: " Preacher and Soldier." As we know from certain unimpeachable sources, it is pointed out quite candidly to the Junkers that there is no room for the future Führer in the Christian Churches, and that those who make difficulties about putting their apostasy into effect are jeopardising their future prospects. It is, therefore, no wonder that the Junkers for the most part take this warning to heart. The District Court of Gmünd in Eifel, for instance, which embraces within its jurisdiction the *Ordensburg* of Vogelsang, had at one period to register a distressing number of apostasy declarations. (In all, 118 teachers, pupils and employees left the two Christian Communions between May and December, 1936.)

We proceed to quote part of what was said at a talk given to the permanent staff and some of those following a course in one of the *Ordensburgen*. (For reasons which can easily be conceived, we cannot give more detailed circumstances.)

> Whereas at the Party Congress at Nürnberg considerations of foreign policy had to be kept in view, we can here speak quite frankly the language of the Party. The Party has two great enemies in Germany. Communism is one, Catholicism is the other. And by Catholicism is to be understood the adherents of the Church of Rome. In every branch of the Party this enemy has to be recognised. Its Press—*i.e.*, the Catholic Press—has been reduced to a remnant. And we are going to finish this off, too. Catholicism still survives chiefly in its organisations and its societies. . . . We must be through with this job in three years' time. By that time all this church-

going, which already has noticeably declined, will have ceased altogether. We have attained our object in the schools. The bishops have not offered any resistance worth speaking of . . . National Socialism has got to renew the face of Germany. . . .

6. *Other Arrangements for the Training of the Party Élite*

The *Völkischer Beobachter*[1] has a report of a lecture course in Rissen b/Hamburg for the *District Commissioners for Party Literature*. In this course a number of anti-Christian ideas were aired, especially in favour of the Race theory.

In a course delivered in 1936 in the Training Centre of the Munich-Upper Bavaria District for the *Mayors* of Upper Bavaria it was possible for the following sentence to be written up on the board time and time again without evoking any protest: " Better with Rosenberg in Hell than with Faulhaber in Heaven." Occasionally this aphorism served as a sort of grace before meals.

During November, 1936, in Stettin, there was an instructional Congress of the *German Women's Work* (Pomerania District). Those who were present (the Leader of the National Socialist Women's League for the area, the Leader of the Instruction for Mothers branch and the chief women organisers) were told in the course of an address: " Women with scruples of conscience who are for ever running off to church must be got rid of."

At the beginning of January, 1939, a Congress was held at the National Instructional Centre at Erwitte b/Lippstadt in Westphalia at which Dr. Ley and Rosenberg were the chief speakers. It was there that the heads and teachers of forty-seven *District Instructional Centres of the German National Socialist Workers' Party* as well as other outstanding personalities in the " work of ideological instruction " were given their " lead in matters practical and theoretical " for the year 1939. In the course of 1939, so it was revealed at Erwitte, more than 60,000 *Party officials*, mostly local leaders and heads of smaller rural groups, were to be given special training along the intimate and confidential lines laid down by Rosenberg and Ley. What is more, we are told by the National Socialist papers that religious and philosophical problems had a special rôle to play in these training courses. This work of training undertaken so systematically by the German National Socialist Workers' Party, the enormous number of men that it covers, and the fact that every one of these holds a position of influence all go to show the tremendous danger of the National Socialist propaganda against Christianity. No one can doubt for a moment what is meant by the statement that religious and philosophical problems " play a special rôle " in these training courses, particularly as they are followed by an enormous exodus from the Church. Here, for example, are some of the figures for the apostasies that took place in 1936: At the National Instruction Centre at Erwitte there were 43 apostasies. On October 20th and 21st, 1936, between 70 and 80

---
[1] No. 189, May 18th, 1936.

Catholics and Protestants left the Church in a body, and between August and Christmas practically all the followers of a certain course, 250 strong.

At the *Ordensburg* of Sonthofen in Bavaria in the spring of 1939 there was a Congress for all the *Area Leaders and District Heads of Departments*. Dr. Rosenfelder, of Alfred Rosenberg's special department, who acquired an unenviable reputation for his venomous newspaper articles against Pius XI, held forth for two hours. His theme was " The Attitude of the Roman Church and of World Protestantism towards the National Socialist Polity and the World Effects of that Attitude." From documents in his possession, wrote the *Völkischer Beobachter*, the speaker disclosed what lay behind many of the hitherto unintelligible moves of the clerical politicians.

District Leader Bürckel was another of the speakers at this Congress. The closing speech was delivered by Alfred Rosenberg in person. He exhorted his hearers to carry through the ideological fight of our times with the same stubborn and uncompromising severity that was evinced in the struggle for political power. Today Germany was no longer a State of religious sects, but the first truly German national State. It was not enough to have overcome Democracy and Marxism in the German nation; there were other ". ideological survivals" which had to submit to the National Socialist age. The " Führer's official commissioner for all spiritual and ideological formation " left no room for doubt that by " other ideological survivals " it was Christianity that he had in mind.

The organisations we have outlined above are all open, questions of age apart, to all Germans. They, and particularly the SS, are the special organisations for the ardent supporters of the régime. Besides those, however, there are other organisations arranged according to occupation or profession, and we shall devote the next chapter to a treatment of these.

CHAPTER II

OCCUPATIONAL ORGANISATIONS AND THEIR PUBLICATIONS

NATIONAL Socialism means to reach every member of the nation and to imbue him with its own ideology. To effect this, every occupation and profession has its organisation (something like our Trades Unions) and its publication, and everyone who follows an occupation must be a member of the corresponding organisation and take in its paper. Below we give a short account of the most important of these.

1. *The German Labour Front (DAF)*

In a previous section we have already explained how the German Labour Front, by forbidding its members to belong to other bodies as well, forced the Catholic Workmen's Guilds and other Catholic associations to disband.

On May 25th, 1937, S———, a member of the German Labour Front and a lecturer of the District Training Centre, gave a talk on " Business Staffs and the Labour Front " to the staff of a medium-sized factory (about forty people). One of those present reports the following passage from his address:

What ! Keep the ten commandments, just because once upon a time they were made by *a Jew* ! Well, I ask you ! If you keep company with a woman—that is called a sin; but the other fellow can take up with his cook, such a chic and fashionable cook (don't you know?), and that is no sin at all !

The Economic Group " Hotels and Boarding Houses " held a meeting in January, 1939, on the question of putting up pictures in guest-rooms. The Headquarters of the Area Propaganda Department for Berchtesgaden-Laufen issued the following circular:

On the occasion of his speech in the Kurhaus at Bad Reichenhall the Area Leader revealed that most of the guest-rooms in that area were without a picture of the Führer or of any of Germany's leading men. On the other hand, he had to say that in various rooms pictures of the Saints and the like had been hung up. These facts did not accord with the fame that our region had the honour of enjoying, as our Führer's *homeland by adoption*.

We make our own the Headquarters' point of view, and we ask our members to see to it that the rooms at the disposal of visitors are adorned with suitable pictures. This country of Berchtesgaden, as the Führer's adopted home, is doubly obliged to put up his picture in the reception-rooms.

It should be noted that apart from the *Angriff* (the Labour Front's daily paper) there is a large number of papers brought out by the particular occupational groups that are included in the German Labour Front. On April 6th, 1938, the total output of the press of the German Labour Front was estimated at 18,350,000 copies.

The *Angriff* is constantly printing malicious attacks on Christianity and the Church. Here are some examples:

In its number for October 4th, 1937, the *Angriff* attacks the " Protestants who make eyes at Rome." In its number for December 12th and 13th, 1936, it publishes an article entitled " We are in the Know," which treats the doctrines and dignitaries of the Church as objects of ridicule.

The *Angriff* of January 16th, 1938 (No. 14) publishes, under the heading " The World's First Emigrant," a cynical account of the Fall in Paradise which makes fun of the biblical narrative and of belief in Heaven, Original Sin, etc.

A leading article of its issue of October 27th, 1938, headed " Punch Pius XI " abuses the Pope for his address to the archæologists.[1]

Under the heading " The Pope Personally " the *Angriff* of November 17th, 1938, sneers at the Head of the Catholic Church.

> There are occasions when the highest authority has to declare itself and there are others on which it is better for it to refrain.
>
> Pius XI—so the *Osservatore Romano* now reveals officially—has expressed himself in very personal letters to King Victor Emmanuel and to Mussolini against the promulgation of the anti-Jewish marriage law that has been recently issued. Because his most exalted wishes were not taken into account, the law is particularly disgraceful. And so the Pope has intervened personally for the retention of race pollution. The Chief Rabbi of the Egyptians can really be quite easy in his mind; and, of course, a warm shower will descend on the Vatican coffers.
>
> But why at this juncture does Pius XI have his intervention on behalf of race pollution reported as a personal failure? The very announcement of this is a further political move: the pious Italians and the open-handed Jews are meant to learn what very malicious and inconsiderate men the King of Italy and the Duce are, to be *so* tiresome and vexing for an old man. . . .
>
> We do not know which is the more shocking, the unfortunate setback for the Pope or the clumsy bad taste of Vatican newspaper politics. In any case, for the future we are going to speak of the Pope as the Jew-Pope. For that, you can blame Pacelli.

Some quotations may likewise be given from the organs of the various occupational groups.

The *German Metal Worker*, No. 19, gives its account of the gathering of the German Faith Movement at the *Sportpalast* under the general heading of " Home Politics." Apart from the mere detail that here a purely religious movement is reported under the heading of politics, that meeting of the German Faith Movement was described with a warmth and appreciation that was quite striking! The issue, too, of December 15th, 1934, prints a picture that cannot but prove offensive to religious feelings. In it God is caricatured as a " Jewish " God. Kneeling before Him are various figures representing members of the Austrian *Heimwehr* and a Jew.

[1] *Cf.* p. 425.

In the news-sheet[1] of the Chemical Works Industrial Group, one Paul Hoffman inveighs against the *Dunkelmänner*, and when he describes them the following are the expressions that come from his pen: " a pitiful crew, cowards, jesuitical quibblers, footpads in ambush, poisoners of wells, mischief makers," etc.

The paper[2] of the Non-Fermented Fruit Products Industry and Fresh Fruit Interests deals spitefully with " the heroic fall of the Stedinger peasants in their fights against the bloodhounds of Rome."

In the *Schwippbogen*,[3] the professional journal of the *Deutsche Bank und Diskontgesellschaft*—a cell of the Reich Business Association—we are informed that the members of the editorial staff as " old National Socialists " stood their ground under the Weimar régime not only against Jews, Marxists and Freemasons, but against Jesuits as well. The paper takes over without the slightest reservation Ludendorff's view that the Jesuits share the guilt of the murder in Serajevo of Franz Joseph, the successor to the Austrian throne. Jesuits in the entourage of the Archduke had led the Archduke to Serajevo,

that he might be murdered there by his Freemason assassins.
The Jesuit had let the Freemasons get ahead. He had not stopped the Archduke from going to Serajevo (!), although there were circles in Rome that were watching Serajevo with close attention. With suspicious eagerness, he focussed attention on the guilt of the Freemasons.

2. The Reich Agricultural Corporation

At the end of 1934 there appeared a *German Farmers' Almanac* for the year 1935, published by the Reich Agricultural Corporation. In the *Official Gazette of the Diocese of Trier*[4] the Bishop of Trier wrote about this Almanac as follows:

I am surprised and deeply shocked that the Reich Agricultural Corporation, to which every German farmer, man and woman, must belong, should have offered this Almanac to the Christian German farmer. It has no business to be in the house of any Catholic farmer.

And why ? Because it is a deep insult to every Christian and Catholic feeling. The Saints' Days, the mention of every Christian Feast Day, even Christmas, Easter and Pentecost, have disappeared. January 6th (The Three Kings) is " The Three Äsir Day." February 22nd (the Feast of St. Peter's Chair) is the " Feast of Thor's Chair." Ash Wednesday is " Ash Woden's Day." On Maundy Thursday, the feast of the institution of the Blessed Sacrament, there takes place the " consecration of night-light oil " (!). Easter, the Resurrection of Our Lord, is the Feast of " Ostara " (a German Spring goddess). Ascension Day is " Rescue of Thor's Hammer." SS. Peter and Paul is the " Half-year Feast of Tiu " (god of War). The feast of St. James (July 25th) is " Thor and Sif." Christmas Eve is " The Birthday of Baldur, god of Light, and the Visit of the Infant Yule." Good Friday, when we commemorate Our Saviour's death on the Cross, is the Remembrance Day " of the 4,500 Saxons massacred by Charlemagne as well as of the 9,000,000 others—fighters for the right, heroes of the faith, heretics and witches—who were murdered, tortured to death and burnt at the stake."

[1] Hanover, No. 20, May 25th, 1935.
[3] July 1st, 1935.
[2] 5th Annual, No. 3.
[4] February 1st, 1935.

This is not the place for me to labour the point that all this is disastrous for national unity. To desecrate Good Friday by associating it, to the detriment of the Church, with Charlemagne's struggle for political power, to drag in all that stuff about the " 9,000,000 " murdered heretics—long since exploded by the research of scholars as the product of hatred of the Church—all this, I say, is to destroy that community of spirit of which we stand in such bitter need.

The Catholic farmer, conscious of his own Catholicism, will most decidedly not stand for this slight that has been put upon his Faith and upon his Church. The farming population of the Trier countryside—100 per cent. Catholic in both numbers and conviction—will echo wholeheartedly the blunt and straightforward statement that a Westphalian farmer sent to the Berlin *Germania*: " We reject in conscience this Almanac and the mentality that it exhibits. We want to remain what our fathers were before us, Germans *and* Christians; not merely the one and not merely the other, but both—and both completely and together. It seems to me that it is rather the business of the Reich Agricultural Corporation to support our efforts in this direction instead of working against us."

Trier, *January 29th, 1935.*   FRANZ RUDOLF, *Bishop of Trier*.

On February 26th, 1935, Walter Darré, Farmers' Leader in the Reich, made public the following explanation:

To those among the public who have taken exception to the Farmers' Almanac for 1935, which bears the name of the Reich Agricultural Corporation as publishers, we must in the first place make it quite clear that the Almanac was issued from a private press and not from the press of the Agricultural Corporation. As the Almanac had appeared under my name during the days of struggle and as (for general reasons) the 1934 Almanac had to be set aside, the printers were allowed to print the name of the Agricultural Corporation as publishers in order to preserve propagandist uniformity. A further explanation offers itself in the fact that the Almanac had to be dispatched in time for Christmas, which was not very far off, and only a very hasty revision could have been undertaken. As it did not cross anybody's mind that the Almanac was not just as usual, it was not, in fact, revised. Legally, the blame for the contents of the Almanac devolves upon the reviser and not upon the Agricultural Corporation. As the reviser does not belong to the Corporation, this body is not in the position to bring him to book. The associates of the Reich Agricultural Corporation are hereby instructed to pass on to the printers all complaints about the Almanac.

But the fact of the matter is that Reichsbauernführer Darré was not merely named as the producer of the Almanac, but, in his capacity as a Reichsminister and Farmers' Leader for the Reich, he prefaced it with a lengthy message, all complete with a facsimile of his signature. In this message it was explicitly stated that the Almanac of 1935 carried on the work of its forerunners. As a further testimonial, it was declared that it manifested a well-informed appreciation of the history of the German peasantry (*cf.* the description of the Stedinger peasants slaughtered " by the bloodhounds of Rome "!) and hence helped to restore the good name of our German forebears.

If one takes a glance at the further development of the Reich Agricultural Corporation, one cannot help doubting the *bona fides* of this explanation of the Farmers' Leader. After his public disavowal of the 1935 edition of the Almanac it might have been expected that its anti-Christian and indeed frankly pagan tone—intruded, to be sure,

THE REICH AGRICULTURAL CORPORATION

by " private " interests !—would have been dropped. The fact is that since then this tone has been more sharply, if more discreetly, emphasised. The first *Grüne Woche* (Agricultural Show) in Berlin, by exalting everything pagan, prepared the ground for the de-Christianisation of the German farmer. In this Agricultural Show and in others held at Whitsuntide, 1935, the customs of ancient Germanic heathendom were very much to the fore. There were, too, representations of the Stedingers' fight with the Archbishop of Bremen and of the Widukind legends. The connection between the customs of the countryside and the Church is being slowly undermined. Local leaders among the farmers receive frequent and pressing invitations to neo-pagan Congresses. Pagan ideas are coming to prevail more and more in such periodicals as the *Odal Zeitschrift*, the leading publication devoted to agricultural policy. The blood and soil idea serves to lead the farmer away from traditional Christian usages towards a new indigenous faith, to what practically amounts to full-blown Nature worship. It is furthermore significant that by far the greater number of the leading personalities in the Agricultural Corporation belong preponderantly to the SS, a body that is sharply anti-Christian. In the Corporation it is the anti-Christian influence that is gaining ground, especially in the non-Catholic provinces, in the Protestant north and east. Every supernatural tie is abandoned in favour of a vague sentiment. By degrees belief in a transcendent God is being slowly superseded by a fanatical belief and confidence in Hitler. " Hitler," said a Farmers' Leader, " is our Saviour; it is to him that we must pray."

In a number of conferences organised by the Reich Agricultural Corporation wild attacks were made on the Old Testament. In 1936 the Farmers' Association of the Rhineland Province compelled Catholic apprentices to leave their Catholic organisations and to join the Hitler Youth. The programme of the Farmers' District Meeting in Passau on Sunday, March 15th 1936, was so arranged that it was impossible for the young Catholic farmers to go to Mass.

In a circular[1] of the Farmers' Leader for the Province of Westphalia there was the gibe: " As the place one expects to get in Heaven depends in all circumstances upon one's cash payments to the Church, the farmer regards almsgiving to the Church as a good investment."

3. *The National Socialist Civil Servants' League*

As early as 1935 attempts were made to make it compulsory for Catholic Civil Servants to buy Rosenberg's publication *An die Dunkelmänner unserer Zeit* (To the Obscurantists of our Time). A reference to this move is to be found in a passage of the *Frankfurter Zeitung*[2] which runs:

> According to *Germania*, the Vicar-General of Cologne announces that when the authorities laid on Catholic officials the obligation to obtain the

---

[1] August 8th, 1936.   [2] June 4th, 1935; Nos. 281, 282 of the Reich edition.

work "An die Dunkelmänner unserer Zeit" and to sell as many copies as possible to their acquaintances, this was the result of an error and that accordingly the regulation has already been rescinded.

But over the question of the Civil Servants' oath a firmer line was taken. It was repeatedly and officially stated that this oath must be taken without any reservations whatsoever, and as a result Catholic officials got into difficulties with their conscience. The *Frankfurter Zeitung* of August 1st, 1935, for instance, published the following report from Darmstadt:

> The central department of the Hessian Government has communicated to all subordinate authorities and public bodies the following ordinance of the Reichsminister of Education for their instruction and direction:
> "I have occasion to call attention to the fact that, according to the law, it is part of an official's duties to take the oath prescribed for Civil Servants by the act of August 20th, 1934. Anyone refusing to take the oath must in consequence leave the service in one of the normal ways (retirement or penal dismissal). The taking of the oath with reservations is reckoned as a simple refusal to take it at all: an oath of loyalty does not of its essence permit reservations to be made. Any official, therefore, who in spite of this is ready to take the oath only under reservation should, as an honest man, draw the correct conclusion and surrender his office of his own accord. If he does not do so, then he must expect the same consequences as one who refuses to take the oath altogether.
> "It is requested that all staffs be informed of this in due course."

In view of this the German Bishops decided that it was necessary to draw attention to the Catholic attitude towards this matter of civil oaths.[1]

There are innumerable cases where Catholic officials were forced very much against the dictates of their conscience to withdraw their children from Catholic organisations and enrol them in the Hitler Youth. The loyalty they had sworn to the Führer was exploited on such occasions, and they were told that from the ideological point of view the Hitler Youth provided the only genuine training ground for young Germany. Often these demands were made in the form of threats of dismissal, exclusion from the German Labour Front and so on, and the same threats were used to force the officials and their dependents to sever all connection with Catholic organisations entirely.

This anti-Christian attitude finds clear expression in the *Handbuch für den Beamten* (Civil Servants' Handbook):

> We shall strive, as long as we remain Germans, for a revision of that thousand-year process which has robbed us of our hereditary culture and forced us into a straight-jacket which cripples the most noble members of our body....

And then comes the assertion that, among the Germanic tribes, Christianity destroyed more moral values that it introduced.[2]

Again, take the following statements from *Der Polizeibeamte* (*The Police Official*), No. 6, 1935:

> In the massacre at Verden on the Aller, four thousand Saxons were murdered with the executioner's axe by the Semitico-Roman hirelings.

---
[1] *Cf. Berlin Diocesan Gazette*, September 4th, 1935.
[2] Quoted in *Nordland*, No. 3, April 28th, 1935.

"Become a Christian or I shall strike you dead." The Germanic tribes, however, remained faithful to their thousands of years old sun worship, and for them, with their heroic outlook, the unheroic Christian faith with all its miracles can have no meaning.

4. *The National Socialist Teachers' Union*

This Union, whose members are in close contact with the rising generation, is one of the most effective in imbuing youth with anti-Christian ideas. Its attitude is characterised by a questionnaire sent to all its members, one of the questions on which was:

Are you willing to put your entire strength at the service of the National Socialist Movement and hence at the service of our country, even, should the occasion arise, regardless of situation and denomination?

The feeling behind this question was given sharper expression when, on September 29th, 1936, the national headquarters of the Union issued a circular instruction which stated that " members of the National Socialist Teachers' Union may not at the same time be members of denominational associations," and that therefore " members of the Union who at the same time belong to a denominational Teachers' Society must choose either the one or the other." In many cases membership of the Sodality of Our Lady and membership of the Union was looked upon as double membership. Finally, in autumn, 1936, the National Administration of the National Socialist Teachers' Union insisted that teachers, both men and women, should break their connections with Catholic associations by making the following statement:

Statement

I hereby declare in conformity with a decree of the National Administration of the National Socialist Teachers' Union and considering my oath of loyalty to the Führer, Adolf Hitler, that I, etc.

Certain circles of the National Socialist Teachers' Union advanced a proposal for the reform of religious instruction which the headquarters of the same Union declared excellent. Among other things the reader finds the following:

Religious instruction should aim at giving the young German the ultimate grounds of his outlook as a German, and this can only be National Socialism. In the foreground is the German conception of God and the heroic struggle of Jesus. . . .[1]

St. Paul, of course, is not accepted.

In April, 1935, the Ministry of Education approved the appointment of Dr. Steffes, a Catholic priest and a University professor, as director of the German Institute for Scientific Pedagogy in Münster, Westphalia. In the same month the District Director of the National Socialist Teachers' Union forbade all teachers to attend this institute.

---

[1] Quoted in the *Korrespondenzblatt* of the Evangelical-Lutheran clergy in Bavaria, January 7th, 1936.

He even went so far as to make ill-mannered intrusions into the institute to cause a disturbance during the lectures.

In the *Nationalsozialistischer Erzieher*,[1] the regional publication of the Hessen-Nassau section of the Teachers' Union, one may read the following statements in the article " Alfred Rosenberg's Answer: To the Obscurantists of our Time ":

> The only point at issue is that Rosenberg has laid bare the temporal power of the Latin racialism organised within the Catholic Church, as well as its destructive activities against the national strength of the Germans. Rosenberg has, in his " Myth of the Twentieth Century," put into the hands of Germans a weapon with which to regain their honour and spiritual self-determination. In his fight Rosenberg is not concerned with religion as such or with Christianity as such. . . . The Catholic Church has no intention of allowing the causes and problems of the defections from the Church with all its priestly domination to be discussed freely from the point of view of German nationalism. The point of Rosenberg's fight, therefore, is the opposition between a cultural and political ideology and the " Latinism " of the Catholic Church. . . . And in consequence it is the duty of every German fighting for freedom of mind and soul to make himself familiar with Rosenberg's " Myth of the Twentieth Century " and his struggle against the obscurantists. In this matter there is no question of tampering with the religious peace which every human being has made with his God.

The same paper published in its number for September 7th, 1935, the following report of a congress of school inspectors and the area directors of the Teachers' Union:

> The District Director gave a sketch of the various groups, divided among themselves, which are opposed to our National Socialist work of reconstruction. Certain groups, particularly the political clergy, take up a negative attitude and depreciate everything. The political clergy (see the latest Pastoral Letter !) maintain that they have no ambition for political power, while at the same time they lay claim to the use of the street and the right to enjoy publicity. It is because the political clergy realise quite well that in this fight for temporal power the active portion of the population is turning its back on them that they raise such a loud cry of " persecution." The first concern of these agitators is not the well-being of the country, but the right to parade the streets. They think first of the Church and that Centre Party type of temporal power which their position in the Church affords them; it is only then that Germany gets a look in. The accusations levelled against the Civil Servants of the National Socialist Government in the Pastoral Letter issued by the Bishops' Conference at Fulda (namely, that these officials are unprincipled) are so monstrous that it is a wonder the Government tolerates such irresponsible conduct. . . . If Churches are turned into places for anti-Government demonstrations, the clergy will discover that those Churches are shunned by the people and, above all, by their leaders.

And so the bishops, too, were classed with " political clerics," for they had dared to publish a Pastoral Letter in which they claimed that Christianity ought to be able to manifest itself publicly in Germany.

In many parts of Germany teachers have been obliged since 1935 " to apply their united forces to the business of attracting all children over ten years of age to the Hitler Youth." They were forbidden in

[1] May 13th, 1935.

any way to recruit new members for denominational movements, or to play any part in their affairs. There is, moreover, abundant evidence to show that the training given in many Teachers' Training Colleges was deliberately given an anti-Christian bias and was conducted in the spirit of Rosenberg's philosophy.

At a provincial assembly of the Nazi Teachers' Union held at Bielefeld in 1936 Principal Stricker delivered a propaganda speech in favour of the National Socialist community school, and stated in the course of it that, whereas German schools were today divided between Catholic and Protestant sects, the schools of the future would necessarily be community schools, and the Teachers' Union should keep that aim steadily in view. There would be no question of depriving German children of their belief in God, for complete religious freedom would be observed in such schools. Since they were united in the same blood, German citizens were no longer to be the victims of denominational divisions.

At an educational course for teachers in 1936 it was stated that teachers must seek to rectify in their charges the daily perversions instilled by an alien religion; they might give lessons in Church History, but the " dark side " was not to be omitted. The Church and National Socialism were said to be utterly incompatible. In a speech delivered to teachers in Franconia, District Leader Streicher urged them to become officially " believers in God "—*i.e.*, neo-pagan—and so become all the more suitable for their profession. They ought to register themselves as such.[1]

On April 13th, 1937, the Vienna *Reichspost* published an account by an eye-witness at a Congress of the Nazi Teachers' Union held in Kleve. The speaker was Herr Hamacher, Head of the Personnel Department of the Essen district. Attendance was compulsory, and, contrary to custom, the Area School Inspector had issued invitations to the Congress, a fact which gave special importance to the occasion.

The speaker began by observing that he had received explicit orders to speak to these representatives of the Kleve district on the subject of " political denominationalism." He then referred to the troubles in Spain, and regretted that Spain had become the scene of such sacrifices. It was true that the Reds had not spared themselves in hatred against the Church, but it was also a fact that the Spanish Church had received but its due deserts. Catholicism had ruled there for 300 years without giving the Spaniards the necessaries of life. So long as Spaniards live in underground caves, Spanish Cathedrals must be regarded as a crying injustice.

The speaker went on to characterise the nature of " political denominationalism " by means of two quotations from *Der Deutsche Weg*, a periodical " edited by that traitor to his country, Fr. Muckermann, who escaped the attentions of the State attorney by flight." The paper was dealing with an allocution by the Pope to Spanish fugitives, in which he urged the necessity of prayer in order to overcome Bolshevism by means of an apostolate of prayer. " Prayer, prayer ! An old man's delusion ! Do you really think

[1] Quoted in *Reichszeitung der deutschen Erzieher*, No. 4, April, 1937

Franco would arm his soldiers with prayer leaflets, with bottles of holy water and a profusion of rosaries in order that they might escape alive from this Hell ? We, too, pray daily: ' Lord, preserve our Führer, that Germany may live.' That is National Socialist prayer. Just as the Pope in Rome demands belief in his dogmas and the Confessional Evangelical Church obedience to its laws, so National Socialism demands unconditional obedience to the Führer. The old fellow on the other side of the Alps has no say whatever in the matter." (Feeble applause.)

The speaker then informed them that 95 per cent. of the leading people had already severed all connection with the Church. "We refuse to allow those people who brought Germany to ruin to prate to us about love of one's neighbour. We have created the greatest charitable organisation the world has ever seen, the Winter Relief Work. And now I'm going to tell you the latest ! Just listen to this ! By spring everyone who holds a responsible position in the Party will have to decide between membership of the Church and membership of the Party. Hitler Youth leaders are also included in this category. No one who has made up his mind that he cannot break with the Church will suffer harm, but there is no longer any position of leadership for him in the Party. It is the man who cannot support the Party programme who will suffer harm. Those who still belong today to a denominational Union of any kind thereby espouse the cause of Catholic Action, which is nothing but the continuation in disguise of the happily deceased Centre Party (under different leaders).

"Such people, therefore, must be rigorously punished, no matter whether the Unions to which they belong are protected by the Concordat or not. It was the State that made the Concordat, but we are the Party Movement with our own laws." With reference to this Church Apostasy movement he informed them that it was based on instructions from the National Training Centre, Vogelsang, and had been communicated by authoritative quarters. "We National Socialists have no need of priests to mediate between our people and God. We reject such mediators who, following their basest instincts themselves, and leading dirty lives, outwardly screened by their wonderful celibacy, sit with their fat paunches in their confessional boxes passing judgement on other swine. Then out they come with their sanctimonious faces and get down to it again. We're more respectable than that." (The audience is getting very restless and many go out; cries of " Shame !" mingle with the applause. There are loud murmurings and a good deal of tension in the room.) The speaker: " I'm well aware that I'm saying something with which many will not agree, but we National Socialists of the revolutionary period realise that things have got to be said even though they don't suit everybody. Many will certainly find it hard to break with the Church. I'm in the same boat as you are and have a lot of trouble with my relatives who are Catholics. But, then, they're all half cracked !" (This insult is not tolerated by the assembly and a large number leave the room in indignation.)

Cries of indignation were heard: " That's the limit ! Shame ! Dirty !" The speaker: " I stand by what I have said; for all I care you can make complaints about me !" But he could not stop people walking out of the room. One could hear the audience loudly giving vent to its indignation. Suddenly the cry rang out, " Rebellion !" but no one took any notice of it. In the general disturbance the speaker endeavoured to explain himself: " By ' half cracked ' I mean only those who combat the Sterilisation Law and want to obstruct the hygienic improvement of the German people." His further observations were drowned in the general uproar. The speaker also attempted to explain the decree of the Reichsminister (concerning the designations " believing," " Catholic," " Evangelical," " godless," etc.). The chairman took up this point in his concluding speech and said: " We must be believers, but also act as believers." These words were drowned in tumult. At the Sieg-Heil many who had left the room in protest came back. They crowded to the speaker's table and demanded that he take back his insults and give further explanations. The speaker had to defend himself on all sides and nothing could be heard but expressions of lively indignation. All over the room groups of people were still arguing with those who had applauded everything the speaker had said.

The Silesian Educator, the periodical of the National Socialist Teachers' Union of Silesia, published on September 5th, 1937, a special number, *Religious Education in the Schools*. The articles in this number deal in a very significant way with the place which religious instruction occupies in the German schools and with the duties of teachers in regard to the ideological education of children. The introductory article states that the educator may shirk, much less than other people, questions of an ideological and religious nature, for every day his work in the classroom compels him to take sides.

A teacher cannot simply say: " In the matter of religion there are no new regulations, textbooks or curricula as yet, so the old regulations still apply for us." Such a thing is simply impossible. We know that the majority of teachers nowadays, inspired by the feeling of their personal responsibility to the people, instruct and educate the children entrusted to them in the National Socialist spirit without heeding the antiquated regulations and prescriptions. This feeling of personal responsibility towards the children of our people must also spur on the National Socialist teacher to acquire for himself the necessary clarity of ideas in the religious field.

This concerns not only every teacher of religion, but every teacher, male and female, since religious education in our schools should not only be a subject in the school curriculum, but must accompany and permeate the wole work of the school. We cannot rest satisfied with handing over to the Churches the responsibility for the way in which religious education is given in the schools, especially as the various Church groups do not really know what they want themselves, and because some of these groups advocate and teach ideas which must be considered today to be disruptive and dangerous to the unity of the State.

It is not the Churches, nor the clergy of any denomination whatsoever, who are responsible for the education of our youth in the schools, but we German teachers, and we alone, bear this responsibility to the State and to the people, to our consciences and also to God.

Catholic teachers have repeatedly informed the diocesan authority concerned that they refused to give further religious instruction in the schools, since they rejected the Old Testament as a matter of principle. It was reported on November 25th, 1938, in the Press Agency of the National Socialist Teachers' Union for the district of Franconia that the teaching body of the urban area of Nürnberg refused to give any more religious instruction because it entailed the holding up of Jews as models to the children and so on.[1] On June 2nd, 1939, the National Socialist District Department for Teachers in Upper Bavaria sent a confidential circular to the leaders of the Schools' Supervision Department in Upper Bavaria, requesting them to fill up a list of questions. Part of the information required was the names of the teachers in the district under their jurisdiction who still took part in religious processions. They were also asked to give their opinion about the

Quoted in the *Allgemeine Evangelische Kirchenzeitung* of November 25th, 1938.

aim and diffusion of the Third Order of St. Francis and to give a list of the teachers who belonged to it. There can, of course, be no doubt as to the purpose of such a questionnaire.

5. *The National Socialist German Undergraduates' Union*

At a Fortnightly Training Camp that took place at the beginning of September, 1935, in a town in Central Germany, the head of the District Training Department gave vent to the following views: "National Socialism is an ideology, and that ideology is to be found in Rosenberg's ' Myth of the Twentieth Century.' . . . People who do not possess our faith, or cannot possess it on account of their racial inferiority, must be eliminated, a process which in part is already being effected by sterilisation. . . ." The speaker pointed out that in the National Socialist German Undergraduates' Union camps a shock-troop had to be welded together for Rosenberg in view of the future battle for the German soul. He then went on: " A fight with the denominations has got to come, not, of course, a fight with weapons, for the denominations will die in any case. . . ." He kept on emphasising that these thoughts were not his personal opinions, but represented the official attitude of the Party and the Führer. (These heads of training departments are personally trained in camps by the leading men of the Party.)

It was quite clear, asserted the speaker, that the Führer stood behind Rosenberg, for he had entrusted to him the ideological training of the Party. It was often permissible not to tell the whole truth to a man who was grievously ill lest his will to live be destroyed. The people were not yet sufficiently mature for the new ideology and would hardly survive a religious war.

The camp was also visited by Derichsweiler, at that time Reich Leader of the National Socialist Undergraduates' Union, who developed a similar train of thought in his speech. The time would come when many Party members, who had believed that they had fought for a political movement, would note with disappointment that they had fought for a new ideology. Such people must make their decision now.

In the *Frankfurter Zeitung*[1] there is the report of a speech of Dr. Scheel, Reich Leader of the National Socialist Undergraduates' Union, at the Würzburg University Students' Meeting:

A solid phalanx of National Socialist leaders is necessary. Dr. Scheel enumerated the exacting qualifications required in its members from Group Leaders upwards. He demanded from everyone an uncompromising National Socialist attitude and complete freedom from denominational or, indeed, any other ideological connections.

In the *Bewegung*,[2] the central organ of the National Socialist Undergraduates' Union, a watchword for this 1939 Würzburg meeting was drawn up in these terms:

During the Würzburg meeting German undergraduates will show to the advocates of political Catholicism that they are inflexibly determined to uphold National Socialist ideals.

[1] 268-9, May 28th, 1939. [2] May 23rd, 1939

There then follows a description of the most important task of German scholarship:

There is another fight to the finish which we have to carry on in the midst of our people—namely, the elimination of political agitation and sabotage, and of the exploitation of religious institutions, ideas, feelings and submissiveness in the interest of brutal international and antinational powers. In short, it is the elimination of the *political influence of the priesthood* (italicised in the original). This priestly power has definite strongholds in Germany, and one of them is Würzburg.

The last sentence of this article reads:

The watchword of the Würzburg meeting is: to create a body of soldiers of the spirit to fight against the international power of the clergy, the enemy of the people. We want all leaders of the National Socialist German Undergraduates' Union to be obsessed with this aim.

The *Bewegung* published on February 10th, 1934, the following characteristic article against the use of the word *Volk* in referring to Church congregations:

We recognise but one German *Volk*, which as such is religious-minded and prepared to allow everyone to work out his own salvation in his own way. We do not recognise a *Kirchenvolk*. It goes against the grain for German people to be ordered by denominationalists and clericals to take up arms against freedom of conscience in favour of intolerance. If the priests want to fight, let them do so among themselves. The German people feel more clearly than ever that the primary thing is not the Churches, but religion.

"Christ has left us . . . a creed and a religious teaching which of its very nature cannot be compressed into theological dogmas. It is time for us to give ear to this religious teaching." Let these words of Houston Stuart Chamberlain be taken to heart at this juncture.

The Catholic Church, too, which is about to wreck the Concordat by the insidious use of Catholic Action, ought to beware of the " independent conscience, the sun of our moral day " (Goethe). An attack on that is in our opinion treason against Germany.

" God's SA-men " (a Protestant clergyman used this phrase of himself and his confrères) should stop talking to us about the " United Front of those who are bound together solely by their common faith in the Bible and in the Confessions." Nor do we want to have excluded from Christianity those who, no longer seeking their " living union with God " in the Bible or in Christian dogma, " dare to approach the living God along the insecure path of their personal beliefs." Each man has his own God. There are as many revelations of God as there are God-believing men. It is also unnecessary to relegate to the camp of the godless the members of the German Faith in whose hearts a Saviour is beginning to speak in tones which seem to come from the very depths of the soul of the German people; nor, again, is it necessary, in deliberate opposition to the decree of Hess, to brand as blasphemers those Germans who give themselves up freely and generously to their Germanic Faith.

The great and believing German people which has awakened to a new life yearns for a kindly God of Light, common to all Germans. Sooner than many expect, it will strip off the vile mask of the Church people (*Kirchenvolk*), and those who are seeking to rob it of its precious possession—purity and freedom of conscience—will be confronted with a countenance on which the features of all great Germans—Thinkers, Seers, Reformers and Poets—are impressed: a Gorgon's head for all those who " make a trade out of what is holy."

ERNST PISTOR.

The *Bewegung* of March 11th, 1936, under the heading, "An Episcopal Greeting in a Time of Confusion," dealt with the message which the President of the Fulda Bishops' Conference, Cardinal Archbishop Bertram, sent in his pastoral solicitude to those who were finishing their course at the secondary schools. The central organ of the National Socialist Undergraduates' Union described this message of the Cardinal in the following terms: "A cheap tract, sob-stuff, a piece of bad taste, camouflaged atrocity propaganda, and sly digs at German cultural achievements." Catholic Students' Unions are characterised as more injurious to the people than any other activity that goes on in German Universities. The fact that the Cardinal extols the merits of these Catholic Students' Unions is considered scarcely compatible with his personal good faith. The condemnation by the Church on moral grounds of duelling and its preparatory practice (*Mensur*), and the consequences which necessarily follow from this condemnation, are represented as "opportunist measures of clerics mixing in politics" which are contrary to common sense. Moreover, the Cardinal is reproached for his "black Centre Party sentiments."

On April 1st, 1936, the same periodical under the heading "Spiritual Vitamin from Joseph's Shop" makes unbridled attacks on the religious periodical of Professor Joseph Wurm, *Die Seele*, as also against Catholic brochures and Church newspapers.

No. 31 of the year 1936 contains a leading article entitled "Pastoral Letters that were not Delivered to Us," which is an abusive attack on the German bishops. It reads as follows:

Pastoral Letters! A holy awe lays hold of us. There is an atmosphere around us of a good ten thousand votive candles and hundreds of thousands of litanies. And now the bishop begins to speak. Oh, it is not always piety that drips from their lips. Forgive our modest layman's opinion when we say that we are reminded all too clearly of the abominable procedure of the prelates of the Centre Party. It really is a "pious" practice: a solemn peal is rung from the steeple in order to put the people in a religious frame of mind and direct their thoughts to God; then get them to kneel down . . . and then read out the Pastoral Letter. It's Jesuit stuff! With a cunning beyond compare the "Catholic people" is talked out of its senses. . . . An organ prelude from Palestrina, a pious church choir . . . and then the consecrated priest stands before the congregation. The Bible remains unopened. He reads a letter, the Pastoral Letter, the song of hate against National Socialism. He has just taken it out of his drawer, where it was locked away in strict secrecy. His cultured priestly voice gives out a string of vile attacks in the presence of the "Church people." For a Pastoral Letter is read out in the best professional manner. The faithful who had come to pray are amazed. Amen! The letter is ended. The organ strikes up. What a magnificent framework for this filthy scrap of paper that lies before us on our table. This disgusting document, this abominable screed only fit for a third-rate comedy, has been read out by priestly lips in the house of God.

That is what it is in reality, this noble document, this Pastoral Letter. Names count for nothing. The same authors are at work as of old when we fought to drive the Centre Party from power. They heaped insults and slanders on us against all the precepts of Christianity; they banished our colours from the churches and refused "Christian burial" to Catholic members of the Party. The Centre Party Press has been silenced; the Pastoral Letter is the oral newspaper of political Catholicism.

In its issue of October 19th, 1937, the same paper attacks the Catholic *Karitasverband*. It asserted that Christian charity was not spiritual work for souls, but pure politics, a cloak for Rome's political struggle, a cunningly planned attempt to falsify National Socialist ideas by charitable activity.

Under the heading " Scatter the Idols " the same periodical, in its issue of November 1st, 1938, says:

> . . . The Catholic Church today is simply an international party pursuing purely earthly objectives, with its problems of eternity and an after-life. . . . The Vatican is concerned to uphold, not any particular belief in God, but (with an eye on the profits) the destructive, international machinations of Jewry, Freemasonry and Bolshevism, which are being more and more hard pressed . . . .
>
> Today the young national Powers of Europe are confronted by a solid front of adversaries: World Jewry, World Freemasonry, a World Church and World Bolshevism. Those are the idols of an age that is past.

The periodical considers, in a tone of triumph, that National Socialism has conquered Bolshevism, Jewry and Freemasonry.

> The last international idol will also fall and must fall under the iron hand of National Socialist politics. The States of the new Europe cannot tolerate any disruptive institutions in their midst. But the determination of the Roman Church is not to build up but to tear down. Clericalism—we must not mince our words today—is our enemy. It is alien to the people, without a Fatherland ! . . . The Vatican has not yet understood the beacons of the new age. Papal diplomacy thinks it can check a development which builds on blood and soil. But no Lord God will help the Pope and the wire-pullers he has got among all nations and peoples out of the crisis into which the Vatican diplomatists have manœuvred them. We fight the clerical wire-pullers and their politics in order that true religion and belief in God may flourish, and that the new Europe, the National Socialist Europe, may be built up. Shatter the idols ! . . .

In the first issue of the Freiburg Students' paper of April 15th, 1935, the following is found in the column entitled " Have you Heard this One ?":

> Did you know that the Jew David in the Old Testament already had the secret hope of building an aeroplane'? We read in No. 13 of the *Freiburg Catholic Parish Magazine* of March 31st, 1935, in an article on " The Liturgy of the Blessing of an Aeroplane": For fifteen years, therefore, at the head of the liturgical blessing of an aeroplane stands the 103rd Psalm of David: " Who maketh the clouds his chariot; who walketh upon the wings of the wind."

In the *Heidelberg Student* of May 4th, 1935, the periodical of the Heidelberg University Group of the National Socialist Undergraduates' Union, there is a picture representing a Freemason, a Jew and a Jesuit sitting together at a table in amity. The words " They are unmasked " stand under the picture. Someone is tearing aside the curtain behind which the three are sitting. The game is up. At the conclusion of the article entitled " Popular Front opposed to National Powers " which accompanies the satirical cartoon we read:

> Today, however, we know where our enemies are, and will know how to deal with them to prevent the flower of the world's manhood from going down in their millions to an early grave.

The *Dietwart*,[1] official periodical of the Reich Athletic Union, inveighs against Christianity as " an alien imposition on German national life," " negative asceticism," " the subversion of the life of the people," etc.

6. *Camps and Courses for the Different Social Classes*

Here we can mention only a few of the camps and courses, chosen at random from the great number organised at regular intervals by the German National Socialist Workers' Party for the training of all groups and classes of the people.

According to the Reich Regulations for the Appointment of University Professors issued by Dr. Rust on December 13th, 1934, all the future professors are to pass through what is called the Professors' Academy. *Germania*[2] commenting on this measure, says among other things: " After their academic studies proper they have to prove their ability in a two months' Military Athletics Camp or in the Labour Service as a condition of being received in the Professors' Academy." The newspaper then cites an article by Kurt Uterman in *Deutsches Wollen*[3] as follows:

> The Academy for Professors brings all the different faculties together. . . . On the basis of the doctrine of biological heredity there will be built a new order, founded on the nature of the body, general ability and man's fighting powers. The central idea of the training will be the National Socialist notion of race, which is a biological and historico-political concept.

Since 1934 there have been also " Short Courses in National Politics " for the pupils of secondary schools, lasting usually for three weeks. In a regulation of the Bavarian Ministry of Education of July 31st, 1935, we read: " There should be a careful selection of the teachers accompanying the pupils. For the work in the national political lectures only those teachers are considered suitable who avow themselves enthusiastic Nazis and who are not bound by any other ideological ties."

In the camp of the Junior Barristers at Jüterbog a speech was delivered in 1936 by a SS officer, who accused the Catholic Church of being an " enemy of life and of regarding the body as a mere ulcer, whereas National Socialism advocated and stressed its unhindered development."

In October, 1937, a camp for medical students was held in the Vogelsang *Ordensburg*. From the *Kölnische Volkszeitung* report[4] we take the following:

> The students as well as those professors of German Universities who, as guests, were assisting at our proceedings were looking forward with great interest to the speeches of the Chief of Central Training Department of the Party, SA-Commander Schmidt, who was to expound the mission of National Socialism from the historical and racial point of view. In connection with the Nürnberg Days, the speaker remarked that everybody in Germany today

---

[1] No. 11, September 5th, 1937.
[2] No. 147 of March 29th, 1935.
[3] May 12th, 1935, No. 132 (3 Beilage).
[4] No. 275, October 6th, 1937.

felt that the National Socialist ideology was not merely a Party affair, but that its ideas were the necessary and inevitable outcome of the development of the last century and were the harbingers of a revolutionary historical epoch of the greatest dimensions. . . .

Referring to the great questions involved in the education of our people, the speaker pointed out that the main task was to prepare the young man for the service of his people. The struggle for the people's existence, he went on, and the tasks that face a warlike youth were issues that belong to the world in which we live, and that is why everyone was at a loss to imagine what function a denominational education, utterly bound up as it was with a world to come, sought to perform in any German educational institution. The introduction of a German school was a necessity for the State. It was no good teaching German history in a Protestant or a Catholic sense, for it was the history of the German people and nothing else.

The whole field of medicine, as well, was far too much under the influence of the religious denominations. A hospital was not the place to prepare a man for a world to come, but the place to make him healthy and fit for working for his people. And for that reason all denominational ties and associations which were still prevalent in the clinics should be severed. The doctor by profession and the family doctor would be the National Socialist doctors of the future.

Although the Führer was accustomed to conclude his great speeches with words addressed to divine Providence, they (the National Socialists) could not allow certain quarters to put such words down to mere opportunism: the words of the greatest German must not be misinterpreted. The search for God was not an occult science for which only theologians were competent, but was a common German virtue, and it was no crime to seek God in the perpetual laws of nature and of our people and to bring Him into harmony with them. Dogma was a man-made product of the Councils. For centuries the dogma of the Catholic Church had rejected the teaching about the revolution of the earth round the sun, and yet the earth *did* revolve on its own axis and round the sun.

The man who, as an isolated individual, was compelled to walk alone through this earthly vale of tears would never be able to achieve great deeds for his people. We should make it clear to him that he came from eternity and was going to eternity, and by this new knowledge we should rid him of the unfounded fear of death and at long last banish for ever the conceptions of Heaven, Hell and Purgatory. We all should become again believing men, with belief in the Providence that had given life and origin to our Führer. . . .

In general it can truthfully be asserted that the purpose of all these courses, camps, etc., is to saturate those who take part in them with the ideas of the National Socialist ideology, and especially with contempt for the Christian Faith and the Christian life. With the most obsolete catch-words, already outworn in the days of the free-thinkers, they set people against everything that is sacred to a loyal Catholic.

CHAPTER III

ORGANISATIONS FOR YOUTH AND THEIR PUBLICATIONS

"The child is father of the man." This saying is more fully recognised in Germany, Russia and Italy than it is, apparently, elsewhere, and in all these three countries every effort is made to saturate youth with the ideas that the dominant Party is trying to establish.

In Germany, where organisation is more of a fine art than elsewhere, youth is so marshalled that, almost without exception, every boy and girl is brought by some device or another under the influence of the Party and, once there, the child cannot altogether escape being tainted. Many, indeed, in spite of the restraining influence of religion and home, caught in their most impressionable years when they are most open to be inflamed with ideals whose true value they are as yet unable to assess (witness the tendencies to Communism among undergraduates in English Universities), become enthusiasts for the exaggerated, even idolatrous, patriotism that is for ever being put before them. Such, even more than the older generation, are already the embodiment of the spirit of the new Germany.

In the following pages we give an outline of the organisations of German youth and a brief account of the publications designed to direct and stabilise the growth of National Socialism in their young hearts.

1. *The Hitler Youth*

The comprehensive and systematic character of the training carried out year by year by the gigantic organisation of the Hitler Youth is brought home to the reader by the programme of ideological training for the winter months (1937-38) which was published by the *Nationalzeitung*[1] of Essen:

> In every region, education in *Weltanschauung* is supervised by a special Hitler Youth leader called the "Sectional Leader for Instruction in *Weltanschauung*." He appoints a number of boys as "local instructional leaders." The first general training, what is called "group training," takes place during weekly meetings which are held separately for every single unit or troop. Directives are issued by the National Headquarters of the Hitler Youth in the *Blätter für Heimabendgestaltung* (Suggestions for Programmes of Meetings) which have the sub-titles *Die Kameradschaft* (Comradeship) for the Hitler Youth and *Die Jungenschaft* (Boyhood) for the Junior Section respectively. Annual programmes for the training of the Junior Section are to be published as from the next year. The training of officers of the lowest rank in the Hitler Youth will be carried out during week-end courses,

[1] No. 304, 1937.

which contain lectures and addresses by members of the National Headquarters of the Hitler Youth, Party leaders, and high officials of the State and the Army, and leading business men. The high ranks of the Hitler Youth and of the German Girls' League and their junior sections are trained for several weeks in special regional schools and monthly Leaders' Meetings. There is a plan afoot to institute a *Führerschulungswerk* (Special School for Leaders) of the Hitler Youth, which is to acquaint the Hitler Youth leaders with the results of German research work in those branches of learning—history, prehistory and racial biology—which are the basis of any deeper knowledge of the vital laws that govern the destiny of the German nation. The periodicals recommended for this training are *Wille und Macht* (Will and Power), edited by Baldur von Schirach for the Hitler Youth Leaders; the weekly *H.J.* and the *Führerblätter* (Training Outlines) published by the different regions and generally known as *Führerdienst* (The Leader's Task).

The following facts and quotations will suffice to characterise the basic attitude adopted towards Christianity in this training of the Hitler Youth:

On November 5, 1934, Baldur von Schirach, Supreme Leader of the Hitler Youth, declared in an address in Berlin: " Rosenberg's way is the way of the German Youth."

On February 26, 1935, the Weimar newspapers published a decree of Günther Blum, Regional Leader of Thuringia, with instructions for the ideological training of the Hitler Youth. This task is to be entrusted only to such Party members and comrades " as took an immediate and passionate part in our struggle and who were already in our ranks before the ultimate triumph of National Socialism." Special permission will be necessary for any exceptions. " This decree is to prevent any adulteration and falsification of National Socialistic ideas, a process easily initiated by those imbued with the obsolete theories of the intelligentsia."

Paragraph 7 of this decree reads as follows:

The training of the Hitler Youth must under no circumstances whatever be carried out by ministers of any denomination, since the purpose of this training is political education, whereas the clergy is concerned with the cure of souls. A combination of these two aims is bound to lead to grave interior conflicts, as the minister of religion who takes his vocation seriously would be bound of necessity to let his denominational opinions insinuate themselves in the training he gave.

Of course, the authorities give the usual promises that there shall be no interference with religion. So the DNB published the following announcement on June 26th, 1937:

Two new enactments of the Reich Youth Leader in line with the recently decreed Service Plan regulate the relations between the Hitler Youth and the denominations. The Service Plan itself determined that the members of the Hitler Youth should enjoy all facilities for the fulfilment of their religious duties. Accordingly one of the enactments, recognising that the Churches and other religious corporations have pastoral duties which lie outside the scope of this Service Plan, enjoins upon the Hitler Youth authorities the obligation of granting, on request, leave of absence for special religious functions in exceptional cases. Such religious activities as the following are more especially envisaged: Retreats and other religious practices that take up several days, such, for instance, as pilgrimages, religious exercises, periods of special preparation, missions to the people, courses in Aryanism, preparation for ecclesiastical examinations, instruction for Confirmation, etc. All Hitler Youth officials are forbidden to refuse, on any sort of sectarian or religious ground, the granting of such requests, or to discriminate in this matter between one religious body and another, or to allow the fact of the request to tell in any way against the petitioner's service record. Where such requests are not contrary to the civil laws or regulations it is only official or disciplinary reasons that can justify a refusal. The other enactment recapitulates all the regulations hitherto laid down concerning the question of double membership—*i.e.*, membership at one and the same time of the Hitler Youth and of one of the denominational Youth Associations.

We shall see later how these " enactments " are carried out in practice.

On every occasion when representative leaders of the Hitler Youth enumerated the educative factors which should influence German youth no mention was made of the Church or of religion in general. In a very true sense the Hitler Youth monopolises the education of youth in the Third Reich. It was laid down, for example, by the Chief of the Social Bureau of the Reich Youth Headquarters that the Hitler Youth was in charge of the training in the Apprentices' Homes—*i.e.*, the hostels where young workers are boarded. There is already a large number of such institutions, especially in Westphalia, Saxony and Silesia. The " People's Car " enterprise alone has caused the erection of eight of these Apprentices' Homes in which 500 youths are lodged. According to the Reich Youth Press Bureau, in future the directors of such homes are to be taken exclusively from the leaders of the Hitler Youth and the German Girls' League. We learn from a statement made in Bad Hersfeld on June 26th, 1939, by Regional Leader Petter, head of the Academy for the Training of Youth and inspector of the Adolf Hitler Schools, that the school and the parent were charged with a part of the education of youth, while the Hitler Youth, the most important factor, was entrusted with their character formation.[1] It is not, therefore, to be wondered at that young people in the Hitler Youth and German Girls' League quite commonly despise their parents and steadily resist their influence.

Education in the Hitler Youth is deliberately anti-Christian, yet when the *Essen Parish Magazine* in 1935 (No. 10) quoted the statement of the Evangelical divine, Dr. Kübel of Frankfurt, to the effect that German Youth was being systematically deprived of Christianity, it was confiscated. Nevertheless the truth of the statement is borne out by numerous facts.

As reported by the *Germania* of May 25th, 1935 (No. 145), Günther Blum, Regional Leader of Thuringia, published a proclamation in which he forbade members of the Hitler Youth, the German Girls' League, and their corresponding junior sections to take any active or leading part in the propaganda of any religious denomination. Those who

---

[1] *Cf.* North German edition of the *Völkischer Beobachter*, June 27th, 1939.

acted contrary to this prohibition were threatened with expulsion from the Hitler Youth.

Since 1935 it has been almost a common custom in the Hitler Youth groups to practise and sing in public songs ridiculing the Church, the Pope, etc. The complaints of parents and ecclesiastical authorities have been, as a general rule, quite unavailing.

In the meeting-place of a Hitler Youth group in Baden two candles were kept lit before a picture of Rosenberg, the whole arrangement being regarded as a shrine.

The programme of training for the winter months 1936-37 in a certain Hitler Youth region contains *inter alia* the following sketch of a lecture on Rome:

First the usual historical lies—*e.g.*, that the Roman Church was to be blamed for the devastation of Germany in the Thirty Years' War. Then Catholic Action is the continuation of political parties. And (verbatim): " Look at the means by which the peoples were kept in a state of subjection (that is, by Rome)!" Confession, the doctrine of Heaven, reward in an after-life, the doctrine of Hell, etc., . . . camouflaged politics—*i.e.*, love of one's neighbour. Methods of brutal force in the bringing of Christianity to Germany. The religious Orders of the Roman Church are contrary to nature. The General Staff of Rome consists of the Jesuits. Rome and Bolshevism. . . . General conclusion: " When Germany is united and strong, Rome comes on the scene to destroy her." Our view of life as contrasted with that of Rome: Honour, truth, bravery as opposed to oppression, cowardice, and whining fear. Pride and responsibility as opposed to the enslavement of souls.

The *Bayerische Volkszeitung* of February 26th, 1937 (No. 48), gives the following information:

Throughout the Reich the Hitler Youth is carrying out extensive work in the training of leaders. . . . It is divided into four study circles devoted to the following subjects: Political Racial Biology, Political Economy, Strategical Geography and Foreign Policy, and Rosenberg's " Myth of the Twentieth Century."

To members of the Hitler Youth it was insinuated that they were not allowed to act as altar servers, yet nothing is known of an official decree to that effect. Although it sounds incredible, a special department for spying on religious instruction was set up in many troops; so, too, for the meetings of Catholic Associations, Bible Evenings, etc. The groups charged with this work of espionage were for the most part called " packs " (*Bubenrudel*). They were told, in addition, to counteract religious instruction by forming story-telling groups, etc.

That the Hitler Youth leaders in their meetings, training courses and the like refer offensively to Catholic priests as " black dogs," and make fun of belief in the after-life and other doctrines, is placed out of all dispute by an abundance of evidence.

What has been said above about the anti-religious bias that the Youth

Movement imparts in its training is expressly confirmed by the Pastoral Letter of the Bavarian Bishops of December 13th, 1936. We read there:

> In recent times members of Party organisations, even of Youth Associations,[1] have been announcing their official withdrawal from the Church in ever increasing numbers. . . . When have the Pastoral Letters of bishops ever been so contemned and derided as they are today—even in papers intended for the young? One is thoroughly ashamed of that ignorant and uneducated writer who describes Pastoral Letters as vile and obscure tracts, scraps of dirty paper, full of frivolity and vulgarity. And that, mind you, in the journals of the Hitler Youth leaders in August, 1936! Recently, what are called " packs " were secretly formed to keep an unobtrusive watch on classes for religious instruction and Bible reading, and to note in both the tendencies of each day's lesson. These packs have also to counteract the influence of religious instruction by the telling of relevant anecdotes, sagas and short stories. In order to offset the influence of religion the members of these packs are to assume an air of authority when treating with the parents of the Hitler Youth boys. According to the instructions of a district leader of the Junior Section of the Hitler Youth, the greatest care is to be taken in the selection of boys and teachers for this work of espionage. . . . Everything that they observe, even the smallest thing, concerning the work of Catholic Action is to be reported to this leader. Is not this the total destruction of all authority? Is it not to train youth in lack of faith and lack of character? Is it not to cause the deepest divisions in families?

The Hitler Youth and attendance at religious services.

Complaints were heard on this score as early as the beginning of 1934. The *Church Gazette for the Archdiocese of Cologne*[2] published a decree of the Vicariate-General in which it was recalled that the leader of the Western Regional Organisation of the Hitler Youth had laid it down

> that under all circumstances all members of both denominations must be given facilities to fulfil their Church obligations on Sundays and holidays of obligation.

The Vicariate-General decree adds the significant remark:

> Taking this order into account, we hope that certain people, especially Catholic priests and teachers, will cease in the future to blame the Church authorities for the fact that the boys at some large Youth Meetings had missed Mass. Such complaints are not based on a knowledge of the true facts: the Church has made convenient and ample provision for sufficient services.

In the *Church Magazine for the Catholic City Parishes of Ulm-Neu-Ulm*[3] we read the following very significant complaints:

> On Sunday the Hitler Youth, the German Girls' League and the affiliated Youths' Athletic Union were marched in a body, Catholic members and all, to divine service in the Protestant Cathedral. Consequently a large number of Catholic young people not only attended a non-Catholic religious service—a thing strictly forbidden for a Catholic—but also, another thing strictly forbidden, neglected to fulfil their obligation to hear Sunday Mass.
> The Catholic clergy is obliged in conscience to call this procedure an infringement of vital rights guaranteed by treaty and an encroachment on

---

[1] *I.e.*, The Hitler Youth and German Girls' League.   [2] January 1st, 1934.
[3] March 11th, 1934.

the claims of the Catholic Church that are down in black and white. No one can relieve us of our responsibility in this matter, and consequently no one can forbid us to carry out our duty of protesting against this occurrence. The judgement as to whether or not an essential duty of a Catholic is here at stake belongs to the Church authorities and to no one else.

However, the parish authorities are never officially informed in good time that a Hitler Youth Camp is being held in their district, but, at best, they acquire this information from the daily press and the like. Enquiries from the competent parish authorities about arrangements for the holding of religious services are generally answered in such a dilatory way by the leaders of the Hitler Youth Camps that many an opportunity is thereby lost. Moreover, the people who take part in excursions, camps, training courses, etc., are either given no information or insufficient information as to where and when they have an opportunity to attend religious service.

Here is another device. In a large number of cases the attendance at religious service is made impossible by the prohibition to attend it in uniform or camp attire. Nearly all departments of the Party and officials of such Nazi organisations as the SS, SA, Hitler Youth and Labour Service have passed a decree of this nature, knowing full well that in most cases the people in question have either no civilian dress with them, or have no time to change their clothes before going to church. Again, take the following case, which is of frequent occurrence: Members of the Hitler Youth are not permitted to attend religious service at school in uniform. But immediately after the service the hoisting of the colours takes place in the school yard and all must attend this function in uniform. The result is that attendance at the school service is impossible. In one town the Hitler Youth fixed 10 to 11 a.m. on Sundays as their cinema hours for 1937. Since some of the boys had to be on duty as early as seven or half-past seven, and on the other hand were not allowed to go to church in uniform, the majority of them did not get to Mass Sunday after Sunday.

Frequently, too, the prohibition to attend religious service in uniform is first made known in the camp itself, when, for the most part, it is too late. The following enactment in the *Official Gazette of the National Headquarters of the Hitler Youth*[1] is of interest: " Attention is drawn to the fact that members of the Hitler Youth are not forbidden to attend in uniform the religious services of the Evangelical Church, the Free Church and the Old Catholic Church." It is patent, therefore, that it is only the Catholic Church which is excluded from this privilege.

Then, too, as if to make a farce of the provisions of the Reich Concordat and of the assurances of the higher authorities of the Hitler Youth, roll-calls, route marches, rifle practices and fêtes are arranged precisely for Sundays and Holidays of Obligation, and so render attendance at religious services impossible.

Take, for example, the " Neumeier Memorial Cross-Country Race "

[1] No. II, 11, August 18th, 1934.

of the Hitler Youth. One has only to read the *Völkischer Beobachter*[1] to see that there was not a single moment available for any religious service, and so, on that Sunday, 900 members of the Hitler Youth went without divine service.

The roll-call for the Hitler Youth is often fixed so early on Sunday mornings that attendance at even an early religious service is rendered practically impossible if we take into account the journey that has to be made and the necessity of a change of clothes. In a certain district in South Germany the officials of the Junior Section of the Hitler Youth fixed the time for falling in on Heroes' Memorial Day, Sunday, March 8th, 1936, at the same hour at which the parish religious service took place; the boys had then to march to the cemetery, so that none of them could attend Mass. It frequently happens in camps that singing practices, games, propaganda marches through the village, etc., are put precisely on Sunday mornings. Often, too, a "national service" takes place at meetings of the Hitler Youth on Sundays and almost always at the time of the religious service. Many young people then feel that a second religious service is too much, especially as often enough these are immediately after this "national service." In one case a leader of the German Girls' League asked explicitly: "Does anyone really need now to go to Mass after this beautiful service we have had?" Again, in a BDM camp in 1937 the girls were ordered to listen in to the speech of Minister of State Wagner just at the time when they should have gone to Mass.

Route marches and map-reading expeditions during the night of Saturday to Sunday are very popular, and these so fatigue the boys that they oversleep and miss the religious service on Sunday morning. Special religious functions for young people in the parish churches, such as devotions for solemn feasts and seasons like Advent and Passiontide, Youth Weeks and the like, are very frequently impeded by the Hitler Youth arranging official duties for the same hour. Young Catholics were prevented over and over again from taking part in Corpus Christi processions by having official duties assigned them at the time of the procession.

Another way of keeping the boys away from church is that those who apply to go to religious services are derided. In a camp during the summer of 1935, for example, the Catholic boys were told by the officials: "You don't need to go to Mass on Sundays, for the only thing you see there is the parish priest swigging his wine." In another camp in 1937 a Hitler Youth official, without giving any reason, refused permission to go to Mass and adhered to his refusal even when a fairly large number—once as many as fifty boys—asked for permission. People who took part in the camp at Oberbach (Franconia) in 1935 report that the boys who had sent in their names for religious service on Sunday had to get up before the others and go through some especially fatiguing physical drill. Those who still held to their resolve were publicly derided and finally allowed to go with the

[1] No. 79, March 19th, 1936, and No. 83, March 23rd, 1936.

remark: " All right, then, clear off; and sing the Currency ditty to the old scoundrel to buck him up !" One of the leaders in the camp boasted quite openly that he had succeeded in keeping the majority of the boys back from Mass.

During a Whitsuntide excursion of one of the Hitler Youth groups in 1937 the boys who had given in their names to go to divine service were told by a leader: " Comrades, here we are not shut up in a monastery, but are free in the midst of Nature. We can best serve our God and our religion where we are." Drill, the hoisting of flags and so on filled up the time that should have been given to the religious service.

At a Whitsuntide camp of the Hitler Youth in Bavaria a leader proclaimed at morning roll-call: " Anyone who wants to go to Mass please stand forward." When the majority stepped forward, he ordered a map-reading expedition which lasted till the time for Mass was over.

In nearly all the camps the boys who give their names for Mass can, with impunity, become the butts of their comrades, and often of their leaders, and be called cowards, blockheads, parsons' boys and the like. (This, we know, is what happened in the *Hochland* Camp near Lenggries in 1935.) At the best, the participation of Catholic Youth in religious functions is tolerated, a thing which the boys themselves, of course, realise, and consequently they fight shy of asking explicitly for permission. Often, too, the names of those who attend religious services are taken down, and this creates the impression that they are being put on the black list, a circumstance which naturally causes many to hold back.

The same complaint is made in the official report of the Freiburg diocesan authorities of which we have already made so much use:

> Numerous complaints have been made that, contrary to the guarantee given in Article 31, Section 4 of the Reich Concordat to the effect that members of sport organisations and other civil organisations for youth should be given regular facilities for the fulfilment of their religious duties on Sundays and Holidays of Obligation, attendance at Mass on these days has been rendered difficult and not infrequently impossible by the fault of subordinate officials in Training Camps, Recreation Camps and Labour Service Camps.

The anti-Christian tone of the Hitler Youth celebrations.

On July 7th, 1935, all German radio stations relayed a Hitler Youth morning programme from Breslau. With Rosenberg's well-known brochure of the same title in mind, the speaker chose the " Obscurantists " as the butt for his provocative remarks. Speaking of the Catholic priests, for instance, he said:

> For centuries we have to put up with the situation that priestly hypocrisy is free to infect our whole life. It is power alone that they want; not God, but themselves. . . . We want to see our country in the clear light of eternity, not in the dark shadows of the Church.

The same feeling may be detected in " The New Creed," an " oratorio " which was repeatedly performed among Hitler Youth (*e.g.*, in Osterode in the Harz in the winter of 1935). It speaks of the experience and understanding of God enjoyed by the new youth. This work—which is poor stuff—says in one place:

> They shut up God in chapel-dark seclusion
>   And drink His blood from goblets gold and bright:
> They rant about the holy blood's effusion
>   And how it washes them so pure and white.
>
> The ancient order will not stay;
> The ancient faith's in swift decay;
>   We'll gladly let it crumble.
> From all that's worthless free us, Lord,
> And give us strength with fire and sword
>   The things of yore to tumble.
>
> O God, how young Thou art and bright!
> O prove Thyself more full of might
>   Than to our petty fathers.
> The passing age Thou dost away:
> We face the new, the dawning day—
>   And Thou dost bear the colours.[1]

From the *Church Gazette for the Archdiocese of Cologne*, No. 6, 1937, we take the following information about the programme in the meetings of Hitler Youth and German Girls' League. *Die Mädelschaft* (the magazine which suggests programmes for German Girls' League meetings) in the number for January, 1937 (pp. 7, 11 and following), gives arguments to show how the piety and morality of Holy Scripture are at variance with the piety and morality of the German people. The words with which St. Paul urges obedience to secular authorities in the thirteenth chapter of Romans are represented as exhibiting a typically Jewish " fear of punishment." The words with which God pronounces the punishment of Adam and Eve are interpreted as the outcome of a typically Jewish " contempt of the soil " and a typically Jewish conception of " work as a curse." St. Paul's injunction that women are to be silent in church is brought under the heading: " Contempt for women. For the Jew, woman is merely something which serves to satisfy his sexual instincts." The words of St. Peter, " But you are a chosen race, a royal priesthood, a holy nation . . .," are taken to prove, together with passages of the Old Testament and the Talmud, that the Jews have plans to dominate the world.

On the last page (p. 32) it is stated that this number is a selection from various works including Wulf Sörensen's *Die Stimme der Ahnen*. The characteristic feature of this latter is its insistent demand for a severance from the " poison of Sinai " and the " poison of Nazareth."

The *Nationalzeitung* (Essen) in No. 304 of 1937 gives details of a morning service organised by the Hitler Youth and German Girls' League in the Mülheim-Ruhr area and broadcast by the Cologne Radio Station. The leit-motif of the service was:

" All that we have must be put to service." A high leader gave a speech in which the following turgid phrases occurred: " We know that this life

---

[1] Quoted in *Deutscher Glaube*, a monthly periodical of the German Faith Movement, November, 1935.

has no meaning for us without Germany. . . . But we constantly feel that the past times must have been dark and gloomy, to represent our service and work as the curse of an angry God. . . . We serve because behind this service we see a great and eternal goal: the life that we call Germany. . . . This law (the law of service) is our life. God has appointed it. We recognise this God and therefore recognise His law. Our people, our Reich, our Germany owes its existence to this law, to this will of God. . . . But if you, my comrades, possess this happiness (the happiness of service) in your life, then you always radiate light and strength and security because you stand in the law of the divine Will, because you serve Germany. . . . We have a great law above us. It is called Germany. We have before us the greatest of Leaders. But Adolf Hitler is Germany."

At the end of February, 1938, a Hitler Youth morning service was broadcast by the Königsberg Radio Station and relayed by Cologne, Vienna, Hamburg, Stuttgart, Leipzig and Saarbrücken. On this occasion the speaker tried to belittle the Christian faith in immortality. With passionate words he turned against " those who here on earth distribute claims to a better life in the hereafter," and opposed the National Socialist belief in the immortality of blood to the belief in the immortality of the individual soul: " We believe in a continued existence after death—namely, the continued existence in our people, in our sons and grandsons."

The neo-pagan " religion " of the Hitler Youth.

In *Volk im Werden*, a periodical edited by Professor Ernst Krieck, there appeared on September 1st, 1935, an essay written by the Berlin University student and Hitler Youth leader, Martin Hieronimi, which was entitled "The Religious Attitude of German Youth." In this essay he says of the Hitler Youth:

In addition to the denominational youth and the relatively small group of liberal Christians, a third Front is now coming into existence which in these days is becoming stronger and ever more clearly defined. This Front refuses to call itself Christian. It presents itself especially to the German youth as the German Faith Front and claims that the knowledge of God based on Blood and Race is the only form which is truly suited to the German people. From the very fact that they feel that it is something essentially new and young and that the future belongs to it, large numbers of young Germans show an eager readiness to accept the doctrines of this German Faith. But it must be stated quite openly that their expectations are disappointed time and time again. It can be observed, especially at the Universities, political training schools, etc., that convinced young National Socialists in particular undoubtedly see the political expediency of the German Faith Front, but only realise to a small extent its religious possibilities. The fault lies quite clearly with the German Faith Front itself. For the supposition on which it is mainly based—namely, that by reason of their common blood all Germans have a common religious feeling which merely needs purging of its alien infiltrations—is not borne out by the facts, nor in view of the increasing differentiation in individuals and peoples can it possibly be. But if this is the case, then the German Faith, which has no sort of fixed system to offer, must of its very nature lead to religious individualism, to private religion in the most liberal meaning of the term. Everyone will call a different faith (to wit, his own) the German Faith. The best proof of that is the presence of countless fragmentary sects in the German Faith Front already endangering its unity. Youth is aware of this. It looks with a spirit of criticism at the Germanomania which is breaking out here and there, at curious ceremonies which are more well-intentioned than seriously meant, at the crass disproportion between claims and intrinsic possibilities. It is aware that the religious unity of the German people is more difficult to attain in this way than through a Christian national Church. It feels much sympathy, but looks elsewhere for its perfect substitute.

Hieronimi characterises this third Youth as a " youth looking for its religious bearings " which here and there has proceeded to "proclaim the National Socialist idea as ' a substitute for religion.' " " Their ' I work for work's sake ' is more than the escape of resignation, it is the religious feeling of a time of transition, the religion of service."

In his numerous speeches, which were often broadcast, the Reich Youth Leader, Baldur von Schirach, laid great stress on representing the Hitler Youth as " religious " and " believing." This " belief," to be sure, was interpreted in a new heathen Nazi sense. In any case Baldur von Schirach, according to the report of the German News Agency, turned his attention in the first place to those circles which were said to have slandered the Hitler Youth as godless iconoclasts and heretics. Such attacks, however, he said, could not touch the pure conscience of the Hitler Youth.

" We share too intimately in the true religious experience of the present age," he continued, " to be able to be insulted by people who, despite all pretences, remain outside this experience. We all believe in an all-powerful God. For all of us, even the youngest, are witnesses of the wonderful transformation which our people has experienced by His help, the transformation from impotence and disruption to strength and unity. The purpose of the Hitler Youth is nothing else than to safeguard this strength and unity for all future time. By working for the unification of youth, and thus overcoming all divisions in its all-embracing unity, the Hitler Youth enables even the smallest members to become an instrument of the divine will. The experience of comradeship and union is for us not only a political experience, but also a religious experience. No one has the right to soil such an experience with vulgar abuse, least of all those who use religious things for political ends. It is our opinion that we are serving the Almighty when with our young strength we strive to make Germany once again united and great. This service on behalf of eternal Germany seems to us to be a real and honest service of God."

Baldur von Schirach concluded with the assertion that the Hitler Youth was united with God as no other Youth was, that it would not allow anyone to contest its religious attitude, and that it would permit no one to outstrip it in its loyalty to God, to the Führer and to Germany.[1]

There were even cases of Hitler Youth leaders publicly officiating at marriages. The *Thüringer Allgemeine Zeitung* of September 11th, 1935, writes as follows under the heading: " Günther Blum performs the Marriage Service of a Jungbannführer ":

The National Socialist District Service of Thuringia reports: " On Saturday, September 7th, Regional Leader Günther Blum conducted in the presence of a large gathering of local leaders of Hitler Youth and the German Girls'

[1] Quoted from *Germania*, No. 174, June 3rd, 1935.

PRIGS AND HUMBUGS.

"If also our singing and revelry does not please the prigs and humbugs——"

[*Die H. J.*

THE CARDINAL'S JOURNEY TO FRANCE.

"She is certainly not pretty, but she **can** cook."

[*Das Schwarze Korps*, July 22nd, 1937.

League the marriage service of Camillo Gärdtner, leader of the Junior Sections of the Hitler Youth 1/32, 2/32, 3/32, in the chapel of the thousand-year-old imperial residence of Allstedt. With impressive solemnity the notes of the National Socialist hymn ' Earth creates the new,' played by the organ, resounded through the room. The walls were draped with Hitler Youth colours. The Regional Leader conveyed to the bridal pair the good wishes and congratulations of the Reich Youth Leader and then proceeded to solemnise the marriage. Kark Seele, Regional Leader of the Junior Sections of the Hitler Youth, presented the married couple with a copy of Adolf Hitler's *Mein Kampf*."

According to a report in the *Völkischer Beobachter* of February 24th, 1936, Baldur von Schirach, at a meeting of Hitler Youth leaders in Berlin, referred to the charge of godlessness and heresy brought against the Hitler Youth:

If it is heresy for us to love our German people above all else, then we are glad to be heretics. We have given proof of real faith by bringing the Protestant and Catholic youth together again and teaching them that there is one big thing in which we are all united—the people!

In April, 1939, on the occasion of the opening of a Youth Hostel, Baldur von Schirach made a speech in which he described the religious position of the Hitler Youth as follows:

I know that the people who live here around Fulda, and in particular the young people who are growing up here, no longer think in terms of denominations, but pre-eminently in terms of Germany. Each one of us should believe what the dictates of conscience prescribe and serve that belief.

But everyone should clearly recognise and take to heart that the service of Germany, which is also a service of God, stands above the service of any denomination, and among our youth there must be no one who does not belong unconditionally to Germany. Our present age inspires a true and profound religious feeling. None of us would be here unless these thoughts were a living reality for us. And the Führer's Youth Movement itself would not have had such a tremendous success unless the whole of the young generation had not overcome the discord, the arrogance and the denominational separatism of old. That does not mean that we are an anti-religious Youth Movement. On the contrary, all of us who have gone through the period of struggle which this movement has had to face, and now experience the miracle which confronts us in the Germany of today are imbued with this religious feeling. How could we deny God today since we daily experience in our people the miracle of His goodness? We see and recognise how He blesses this people and in it our Führer. We serve God by being loyal to our Führer and fulfilling our duty towards the Fatherland. We are a God-believing youth, since we serve the divine law which is Germany.

In July, 1939, at a demonstration of the Mittelelbe district of the Hitler Youth, the Reich Youth leader delivered a speech before 45,000 members on the Cathedral square in Magdeburg in which he expatiated on the " holy emblem " of the Hitler Youth:

The banner which the Hitler Youth follows is a holy emblem; for the Youth of Adolf Hitler it is the true sign of a joyful faith. When people assert that the Hitler Youth is a youth without religion and without God, then the Hitler Youth replies: This service of ours for Germany is also a service of God! If the Hitler Youth loyally and bravely fulfils its duty to the people and is obedient to its Führer sent by God, then it is also acting in agreement with the Almighty.

Not without reason have the bishops repeatedly protested against the anti-clerical spirit of the Hitler Youth and called the attention of parents to the fact that they will have to answer to God if they hand their children over to the guidance of such people whose convictions, words and actions are moulded by anti-Christian ideals. How this spirit expresses itself in action we have already shown in our description of the many acts of violence of the Hitler Youth against Catholic Youth organisations and their widespread campaign of desecration.[1]

The periodicals of the Hitler Youth.

The periodicals of the Hitler Youth are guided by the same anti-Christian tendencies as the utterances of its leaders. Those tendencies display themselves chiefly in two currents of ideas that run through these publications: old prejudices and calumnies against the Church are uncritically accepted and Rosenberg's vague ideas are enthusiastically propagated as though they contained a new Gospel.

To convey some idea of the extent and quality of this anti-Christian spirit it will be sufficient to place before the reader a number of brief references together with representative extracts from the papers themselves.

We begin with *Die HJ*,[2] the magazine of the Hitler Youth:

There they all are: Widukind rides once again as in the past; he rides forth for the freedom of the *Volk* and allows no one to dictate the path he shall follow. Today he has fighters and to spare ! Is he to bow the neck once again ? And that emperor who was once forced to his knee, is he once again to take the bitter road to Canossa ? There, too, are the bands of the Stedinger peasants striding forth lustily to guard their rights and freedom. The Lion (*i.e.*, Henry the Guelph) is with us. He fights for Saxony and Germany. He is ever alive in the nation, and of it he is ever mindful. And that utterance of Herr Walther comes to mind: the German spirit is awake and is more feared than arms and fire and sword. From the Rhine there comes another whose word is no less mighty, Meister Eckehart, who wellnigh perished in the flames for freedom of belief. And greater and greater grows the number of those who flock to the army, to that army that fought and died; for never could it allow a foreign power to determine its own innermost conscience. It had to think, believe and act as by birth it was fated to do. But it was not all in vain ! Its fight is our fight. Its spirit is about us and in us, we who are now massed thick and close around a mighty Führer, ready to fight not only for our country and our might, but also for the spiritual deliverance of every single German, for the emancipation of German scholarship and German art, for the emancipation of belief and of the German conscience, which desires to find its own proper home within itself, proud in its own deep thoughts and in its own strength.

The number for July 6th, 1935, makes an attack on Christian missionary activity and on the morning devotions of a Students' Hostel, while in No. 35 (1935) the booklet " Youth to Christ " of Dr. Gröber, Archbishop of Freiburg, is attacked. It taxes the Archbishop with wishing to reintroduce the mediæval Inquisition. The article is headed: " Long Live the Inquisition !"

The number for August 10th, 1935, pokes fun at belief in Heaven

---

[1] *Cf.* Part II, chaps 3 and 9.   [2] *Hochland* edition, No. 20, 1935, p. 15.

and Purgatory in a way that would do honour to Communist freethinkers. Here are the actual words:

> For a small contribution—some 50,000 marks, let us say—the temperature of Purgatory is lowered. On request, the candidates for Eternal Bliss may enjoy breaks for shower-baths in the course of the roasting process.
> Is there a good view of the joys of Heaven also from the cheaper seats?
> Is Heaven in telephonic communication with Hell, where in all probability most of my comrades will be roasting?

Some reflections on the Feast of Christmas provoke the following:

> It has caused us no surprise that the witch doctors of the supra-national Roman system, with all its appetite for power, have sought to retaliate upon the totalitarian claims which National Socialism has made good, by intrigue and dirty work on a large and small scale. We know to whom we must ascribe all the boycotting and the mischief-making, all the misunderstanding and bad will.[1]

In the number for January 18th of the same year there was an article: "More Peter's Pence!" Here are the actual words of the conclusion of this article:

> In any case it is certain that the disastrous falling-off of its revenues provides the Vatican with one more motive for continuing its efforts at reconciliation. . . . True it is that the ways of God are ever wonderful and extraordinarily intricate. Are at long last the sanctions that have held the steady drip of Peter's pence in their icy grasp to have the result of reminding the successor and representative of Christ of the peace message of Christ? Then, ye heavens, send the thaw and make them flow again!

In the number for the following week we read the following sentence, which occurs under the heading: "Crozier, Commune, and Imperial Crown":

> At the moment there is a black broth being prepared for the peoples of Europe in the witches' cauldrons of Paris and Moscow under the ever more apparent supervision of the most distinguished witch doctors of Rome. This being so, it is the rising generation of these peoples, and especially of the German people, which sooner or later will have to swallow it. . . .[2]

Here is a quotation from *Die HJ* of April 4th, 1936:

> "Infallible Film Criticism! An unfortunate mistake! The Vatican paper mistakes an Austrian film for a German film and bespatters it with filth as Nazi balderdash." Thus far the title. In the article itself we find this: "But here the infallible Film Censor has made an unfortunate blunder. The furious critic made one blind onslaught on two films. To the superficial observer both of them seemed to be of German origin and they both received the full (and infallible) charge of His Holiness's liquid-manure squirt. The two films in question were *Hohe Schule* and *Nur ein Komödiant*. . . ."

From an article entitled "Our Führer will not have it!"[3] we take this:

> We don't want political parsons to degrade the Churches of their creed to the level of markets for the wholesale dissemination of their unclean political ideas. We don't want convents and houses consecrated to God

---
[1] January 11th, 1936.   [2] January 25th, 1936.
[3] National edition, July 4th, 1936, pp. 1 and 2.

to be made dens of vice and a source of general moral contamination. ...
We don't want a priest of high ecclesiastical rank in a Munich church to throw mud at our Party comrade Rosenberg or to deride him. We don't want fat-paunched " Christians " to fill the pews and applaud and approve with their " well-said's " and " bravo's."

Turning now to other papers, in the *Catholic Parish Magazine of Cologne* of July 21st, 1935, we read a noteworthy extract from the *Kameradschaftliche Blätter für Heimabendgestaltung in der HJ*, Berlin:

Now, when they need have no further anxiety about their jobs and can no longer carry on their haggling in the interests of their repellent power politics, these same gentlemen come along and claim in the name of Christ the right to bring up the young in their own spirit. With unctuous language on their lips they blow clouds of incense like poison gas among the young. They compose their features to an expression of humility and then strive, by the misuse of choir and organ, to drown the song of the German Revolution.

Dr. Gröber, Archbishop of Freiburg, is then mentioned by name as a horrible example of this despicable type.

Die Fanfare, the Hitler Youth magazine, presents on the title-page of the number for June, 1935, a full-page picture of a Vincentian nun. Underneath the picture we find this: " A blasphemy of a unique type. ' For me, imprisonment is one long Communion '—saying of Sister Wernera, the notorious currency smuggler in religious garb." There is a prominent reference to an article entitled " Currency Smugglers in Religious Habits." This occupies two pages and most of the space is taken up by provocative illustrations. There is a photo of Sister Wernera's convent—no abode of luxury, this, to be sure. Above this there leers the ugly face of a Sister who is busy counting money. The letterpress under this picture runs: " General view of the convent from which the widespread currency smuggling through Holland has been effected." Sister Wernera, who was condemned to five years' imprisonment, is photographed in three different garbs. Alongside two pictures of the convent there are the words: " Spiritual refuge. The Sisters have renounced the world with all its temptations in order to lead in the seclusion of the convent a life pleasing to God. No one would have dreamed of finding currency racketeers among those who sought spiritual retirement behind convent walls." " Do not possess gold, nor silver, nor money in your purses " (Matt. x, 9). " The Two-Faced Catholic Religious Order "—that is the large-type heading of the article itself, of which we give the following extract:

Convent life with all its peace and self-renunciation is held in high esteem, especially in the Catholic districts of Germany. ... And hence Catholic nuns are often referred to as the " Brides of Christ." It is therefore only natural that there should have been a wave of indignation and disgust when it came to light that quite a number of Religious Orders were involved in grave violations of the currency laws carried out under the cloak of the religious habit. More than fifty criminal prosecutions have been instituted against members of these Congregations. Already, by the cases tried by the Moabit District Court, a strong light has been thrown on the two-faced policy of these Catholic Religious Orders, which, like wolves in sheep's clothing, conceal their true features beneath the cloak of their pseudo-pious activities. The case of Sister Wernera in particular . . . exhibits a degree of moral depravity that is deeply shocking to decent folk. . . . When in the Women's Prison she had to lay aside her religious habit—which was not quite in the fashion in her new surroundings—she consoled her Sisters in religion with the reflection that Christ, too, was despoiled of His garments. Sister Wernera's counsel pleaded, as a mitigating circumstance, that the Catholic Orders had deserved well of the country in the World War. The authorities of the Diocese of Breslau have considered it necessary to associate themselves with this plea. Now what did Christ say of the Pharisees? " But ye do all your works that ye may be seen by the people. . . ." We have no hesitation in agreeing heartily with the plea of the diocesan authorities: the merits of the Orders are the merits of a Pharisaism that does good works as an excuse for evil deeds to come. . . .

The *Führerblätter der Hitler-Jugend* in the edition of July, 1935, writes:

Today every little chap stands at his post in the midst of the barrage. Day by day and hour by hour he is subjected to a vast and unprecedented campaign of spiritual intimidation. With their house-to-house visiting, with their Conferences for Parents, by their misuse of the pulpit and the confessional, with the courses of pedagogy, their so-called Spiritual Exercises and every kind of piously camouflaged publicity and propaganda, with all the wiles of a thousand years' experience in influencing the masses, they set to work upon the young comrade; he, this little fellow, his Führer's youngest soldier, has to reply to a thousand calumnies, rectify a thousand lies, fortify a thousand doubters. The Church calls him godless; at his place of work they require him to explain and justify his conduct; his teachers talk away the things that he holds sacred; in his own home he is misunderstood. This is a fight indeed, a fight that demands tremendous things from men, from quite young men. In very truth, this is the " hour of struggle." . . .

Open your eyes ! See for yourselves ! They reject absolutely the world and nature. Nor have they ever attained unity among themselves. Councils have to be for ever settling their differences; over the whole of Europe the bonfires for heretics have to be for ever a-burning. They have hundreds of different Orders, each one of which has its own ideal of perfection. There are Franciscan, Dominican, Benedictine and Jesuit " ways"; a Molinistic and a Thomistic theology, a school that accepts the world and a school that rejects it—and so on and so forth. For a thousand years they have had all power in their hands and yet they have never been able to effect real unity.

In another passage of this article we are told by the author, O. W. v. Vacano, that the Church is in no way a " world outlook," but merely a " next-world outlook "; that we Catholics regard ourselves here on earth merely as " poor, banished children of Eve "; that according to the teaching of the Church, " work " is God's punishment for the Fall; that the Church has never originated anything, but has always followed the fashion of the time, etc.

From the same paper,[1] we take this: " The Vatican as a Political Power ":

1. The resumption of the mediæval power politics of the Vatican.
2. The Vatican, the only power that got anything out of the war.
3. The Vatican, the most influential political structure.
4. Effect on the political world surrounding Germany.

KARL ROSENFELDER.

[1] *HJ* issue, December, 1935, pp. 17-27.

The following passage is among a number tacked on at the end:

We must learn to think of world Catholicism as a political world power which is run from the Vatican on international lines. From the time of Widukind the activity of this world power has been directed chiefly against Germany as the champion of the Nordic protest against the political pretensions of the Papacy and the Vatican.

The same article also appeared in the *Führerinnenblätter* of the German Girls' League. This and all the articles like it in leaders' papers must be read by all boy and girl leaders of the Hitler Youth and the German Girls' League at their meetings, and they, in their turn, have to examine those under them to see whether they are sufficiently instructed in these subjects.

In his *Diocesan Gazette* of March 4th, 1937, Bishop Michael Buchberger of Regensburg published the following declaration:

The Pastoral Letter read on the first Sunday of Lent contained this sentence: "The *Führerblätter der HJ* writes: The communities of Orders in which we see nothing but a negation of life and which are a great danger to the morality of the German people must disappear."

It has been said that this assertion is a lie. That is untrue, and therefore I reaffirm that this sentence is to be found in the *Führerblätter der HJ, Ausgabe HJ*, July, 1936, at the top of page 31.

It goes without saying that every quotation in a Pastoral Letter has been checked. The allegation, therefore, that Pastoral Letters contain lies is itself a lie and at the same time an insult, and I flatly deny it.

MICHAEL, *Bishop of Regensburg.*

The *Reichssturmfahne*,[1] the organ of the Württemberg Hitler Youth, indulged in an attack on the Foreign Mission activity of the Church.

Germans abroad ! Germans in need !
German children abroad without German schools in danger of losing their Mother country.
Germans abroad starving and destitute because they love their Motherland more than a foreign country, because they want to remain German even when the result is hunger and want.
Black children, born in light and sun, grow like the plants and fruit of their own country. They have not to struggle for their nationality; they know no destitution.
Aunt Eulalia knits stockings and makes shirts for " the poor little heathen children," she collects silver paper and stamps in order to "rescue" the little negroes. She is all zeal in her efforts to bring to the little blacks the blessings of a civilisation that they do not understand and do not need.
" Oh, the poor little black children !" How kind she is, Aunt Eulalia !
" A penny for the Germans abroad ! What again—already ?" said Aunt Eulalia and pulled a face. " Germans abroad ? What's that got to do with me ? They can stop at home ! I've got no money for that ! I've got to collect for the black children." . . .

Here is a selection from the number for December, 1935, of *Kämpfertum*, the organ of the promoters of the Land Youth, which is brought out by Wilhelm Kohlmeyer, the Regional Leader, and has Wilhelm

---

[1] Quoted in the *Reichsbote*, No. 36, June 8th, 1935.

Baeyer as its editor-in-chief. On the subject of the Warrior Spirit we read:

The man who lives loyally, the man who lives honourably, who fights to the death for a good cause is certain of Valhalla. . . . Such a man has no need to quake, to tremble and cry out. Such a man needs no knowledge of the after-life. He marches on joyfully into the Great Unknown. . . .

In the paragraph " The Religion of our Ancestors " we read of the Germanic man that:

He lives free from any feeling of guilt and knows nought of the idea of Original Sin. . . . He knows nought of Purgatory nor yet of an eternity of bliss spent in doing nothing.

Under the heading " Meister Eckehart: a Fighter for the German Faith " there is a little study in contrasts which has reference to Rosenberg's conclusion that Eckehart was " a priest who cut out the clericals ":

The God of Eckehart's religious teaching is an up-to-date God; he did not believe in God on the strength of fables nor on account of the miracles that He is supposed to have worked. While the Apostle Paul declared, " If Christ be not risen, then is our faith and our preaching vain," Eckehart's religion is absolutely unaffected by such considerations. Eckehart does not build up his religion, like a house of cards, out of any old dogmas: he takes his stand on the forces of the Race, the Soul and of Nature. . . .

The tune is now taken up by a set of verses. They are all about the German soldier who fell at Kemmel, and tell how, driven to his knees by fear, he started to pray, beseech and implore a God who lived above the clouds for grace and succour.

But this is how *I* see him: There he is, a crouching figure who springs up with a cry of exultation and hurls his hand grenades at the machine gun. Then, going forward at full tilt, he gets his bullet and sinks down with " Germany must have the best," as his dying thought. . . . This hero took the bitter cup with a great laugh of pride and drained it at a draught. To the very dregs he drained it with scarcely a wince. He did not beg that the cup might pass from him. He reached out for it himself, knowing full well that: " Whatever must be, is good !" . . .

Then there is some philosophising about destiny:

Men on whom the sun of life has shone think that high above the stars there is a kind and gracious God and that all is in His hands. They think that with their childish pleadings they can influence the course of events. But men who have grown great in need and obscurity, who have witnessed misery and suffering, who have met with injustice in a thousand ways, have their doubts about such a God. . . .

While on the subject of the hard and inexorable law that governs " human life as well as nature," the writer glances aside rapidly at the " Consolation of Wotan ": " Nought but the All is eternal. For only the One is eternal; and nought but the All is one," etc. And so the reader is left with " the Hero's Trust " before the " Unknown God ":

For us God is the eternal riddle, for us He is the idea that sums up everything that is good and noble. But what He is ultimately we do not know. But we *do* know what the meaning of life is ! It is to be fighters for God !

Along with all this sheer agnosticism there are not wanting a number of sly digs at a notion of God which quite obviously is meant to represent the Biblical conception.

And thus they have thought of God as a man with a white beard and other human traits: a God who can smell and see and hear. It is in human colours, too, that they have depicted life after death ! Eternal bliss, the resurrection of the body, Hell fire and Purgatory." (Quoted by Bishop Tügel, an Evangelical, in the *Hamburgische Kirchenzeitung*, No. 2, of February 15th, 1936, under the heading: " That's not the Way ! A Candid Word to the Hitler Youth Headquarters in Hamburg !")

The following quotations are from the *Führerinnenbrief* (25/26, 1936) of the Department for Ideological Instruction. These *Führerinnenbriefe* (Notes for Girl Leaders), it should be noted, are issued to serve as the foundation of instruction for leaders of the German Girls' League.

The fact is, moral depravity goes hand in hand with the conversion of the German tribes to Christianity. . . . Otto I. received a letter from the Roman people, which reported that under the vicious eighteen-year-old Pope John the women of all nations refused to go on pilgrimage to the tombs of the Apostles because they had heard that, some days before, the Pope had violated wives, widows and virgins. . . . Is not the dogma of the Immaculate Conception a degradation of the whole idea of matrimony, of child-birth ? . . .

The paper of the Hitler Youth National Headquarters, *Wille und Macht* (editor: Baldur von Schirach), praises in the issue of October 1st, 1937, No. 19, Jam's book, " The Catholic Church a Danger to the State." It calls it a successful work that can easily be understood by everybody, and adds: " Most important and indisputable from both the historical and the ideological points of view are the two sections: ' The Danger of the Catholic Church to the State ' and ' The Ultramontane Parties and their Subordinate Organisations.' "

In the Christmas number (1937) of the same magazine we read in a leading article by Günther Kaufmann, member of the National Headquarters of the Hitler Youth:

So we need no Holy Scriptures, no parables and stories of the Apostles, no confessional and no celibacy, none of the threats of Purgatory, and no moral teaching on the part of the Church to lend support to such as feel doubt about moral questions. . . .

That is why the political Church is not afraid of demonstrations in the *Sportpalast* when the subject is, *e.g.*, the violence of the Czech policy, but it scents a danger to its influence in the ever-increasing number of the Youth Movement's impressive and solemn celebrations which aim not at tackling what is external, but at influencing every single youth, his character and moral attitude, as the manifestation of his inmost self. How different is the priest who does not draw his teaching from a Church's dogma-ridden faith, but from the depths of his own religious convictions. Such a religious teacher, his mind attuned to the religious outlook of those under him, will give his full approval to the political education that is offered nowadays to the young. If we strip this so-called " Christian morality " of its supernatural threats and promises, expressed in the " Thou shalt not's " of the Decalogue and the apostolic writings, we shall realise that every religion contains a moral order and a moral law, and that no one of them possesses a special monopoly of moral teaching. . . . How unfortunate for a nation if its priesthood has destroyed the moral ties of its traditional faith by an antinational attitude. . . .

In the same paper[1] we read the following recommendation of a book of K. H. Faber with the characteristic title: " Political Catholicism, the Work of the Jesuits and the Ultramontanes, an Enemy of Every State."

This brochure of Faber is an interesting contribution to the history of political Catholicism. In a few pages the author gives a résumé of the history of the Jesuit Order (Foundation, Spread, Morals).

There is, too, a criticism of the Catholic doctrine and its practical influence. Many well-selected examples taken from the Catholic moral theologian St. Alphonsus Maria Liguori, whose books are standard works today, show the dangers of this " moral theology " for the morality of nations. The evils inherent in auricular confession and in celibacy, with all the ill-effects that have resulted from it in the history of the Church, are indicated: the immorality and sins of priests with their penitents, as well as Liguori's attitude to these questions, are treated in a clear, objective way. There are in this work of controversy a few, slight mistakes of quite minor importance, but they in no way derogate from its value, nor will they diminish the interest it will arouse in all men of keen intelligence, and so we give it a warm recommendation.

The results which this incessant anti-Christian barrage of the Hitler Youth periodicals is bound to produce in the minds of the young are clearly set forth by the *Catholic Parish Magazine of Cologne*.[2]

Day after day a large proportion of our young people is subjected to an agitation that aims at the revival of pre-Christian usages, not merely as something national, but also as a form of religion openly hostile to Christianity. Here is one example of many:

Jungvolk vom Bau (The Youth magazine of the Reich Corporation of the Building Trade, 14th Annual, No. 1, Berlin, 1935) takes up a whole number with an illustrated article on " Primitive Worship and Customs." Round the vague pantheism of Baldur von Schirach's verse there is drawn an idealised version of the old Germanic religious life from which everything brutal, sombre and demoniacal is carefully excluded. Across this golden Germanic background there falls the dark shadow of the Roman priest who extinguishes the sacred fire, brings the sacred horse into contempt and leads the German away from the eternal youth of Nature into dank and lifeless temples. With his teaching on humility and resignation he kills the proud, free soul of the German, burns his Wise Women as witches, and inoculates him with the doctrine of Original Sin and Redemption by the *priest* (!). In a word, Christianity appears all along the line as a force of negation and destruction.

Nietzsche, Goethe, Baldur von Schirach and, of course, Rosenberg with his " nine million heretics burnt " are extolled as the heralds of the Revival. In high indignation a Catholic young man sends us this production and asks us to castigate publicly this lying and unscrupulous attempt to work up anti-Christian feeling. Well, we have brought things before the public in this way times without number ! And have things grown better ? Baldur von Schirach simply declares that it is a calumny to suggest that he is not a good Christian—and that's that ! In the Hitler Youth one is not allowed to hurt the religious feelings of denominational members, and so everything in the garden is lovely ! If anyone cites an example to the contrary, he is merely generalising. They refuse to admit that it is possible to draw conclusions about the whole from a large number of particular cases. Despite

[1] December 15th, 1938. [2] February 17th, 1935.

every protest, the anti-Christian shower splashes down day after day on a large section of our young people. Of course, not everything that is printed is read, and not everything that is read is believed. Gradually a good stout oilskin is formed against the rain. But, in the last resort, what is to be got out of all this for the formation of a real community spirit ? Instead of a spirit of comradeship, there is embitterment; instead of youthful straightforwardness, we have insincerity and a feeling of inferiority. Anyone who understands anything at all about the young and about our own people beholds this development with deep concern. It is high time that a sincere and honest peace was concluded and put into effect without reserve. Failing this, we have the gravest fears both for our youth and for Germany. . . .

2. *The Reich Labour Service (RAD)*

Among the other institutions for the instruction and training of the German people the Reich Labour Service occupies a very important position. In its camps the greatest stress is laid on the ideological training of the young men and women in order to alienate them from the Church. At first, of course, the usual reassuring promises were given that the practice of religion would in no way be interfered with. Thus we read in the " Suggestions for the Spiritual Care of the Young in the Voluntary Labour Service," published in the *Gazette of the Archdiocese of Breslau*:[1]

Above all it is necessary that Catholic workers in the camps should get enough time on Sundays and feast days to enable them to attend Catholic divine service and that, if the Catholic church is some distance away, the day before should not be filled up with heavy camp work and exercises in such a way as to render devout participation in the service impossible. This latter point has been a source of widespread complaint. It may be stressed, too, that the administration of the Labour Service attaches great importance to the maintenance of friendly relations with the clergy and to the meeting of their wishes in this matter.

So, too, the notice published in the *Diocesan Gazette*[2] of Münster would seem to indicate that the authorities were ready to act up to their professions:

In answer to a complaint sent to the authorities that the Catholic members of a Labour Camp were forbidden by the director to receive their parish magazines we have received the following reply: " I have given personal instructions to the director of the camp not to hinder Catholic members from possessing or reading periodicals of a religious content and I shall instruct the subordinate officials to the same effect.

For this reason we request parish priests and rectors of churches to continue to send regularly their parish magazines to the workers in the camps.

THE VICAR-GENERAL.

Münster, *March 28th*, 1934.

This seemingly conciliatory attitude could not, however, allay the anxiety of the bishops. On the feast of Christ the King, 1933, Cardinal Bertram of Breslau made a speech from which we quote some characteristic sentences:[3]

And now a reminder of importance today. I turn my gaze to the Labour Camps. I know and praise the noble intentions of those who planned them.

---

[1] *Cf. Köln. Volkszeitung*, August 29th, 1933.   [2] March 28th, 1934.
[3] *Junge Front*, No. 46 of November 12th, 1933.

But we all know that these intentions will bring good results only if a religious atmosphere and the care of the purity of both body and soul lend their aid to protect this life in common. This cannot be done by external compulsion. " It is the Spirit that gives life." I am acting according to the mind of the parents and also according to that of the leaders of the Reich and of the State when I bid the noblest of our youth in the Labour Camps: Keep together, that the chaste mind and the religious character may reign in your comradeship. Nothing is more needed at the present day than this warning. And you parents, claim your rights as parents. It cannot be a matter of indifference to you how your children return home from the Labour Camps. . . .

In the Instructions of the bishops about the spiritual care of those in the Labour Service,[1] we can perceive clearly some of the difficulties to be faced. We quote some lines:

At the request of the Church the National Headquarters emphasised that every member should be given the possibility of attending divine service on Sundays and feast days as long as he is in the Labour Service. The instructions speak of the practice in some camps of conducting their members in a body to divine service and say that in many the Catholics succeeded in getting leave for such attendance. But as this was not the case everywhere, the young and their parents should claim their rights, guaranteed by the law.

We are sorry to say that the National Headquarters have refused a request for suitable rooms for divine service on Sundays in cases where the nearest church is too far away, " this being impossible for local reasons." Nevertheless they were inclined in such cases to offer whatever vehicles were available. Indeed, in some places there were for a time bicycles for the church-goers, but later on this facility was withheld " for fear of losing the bicycles." The camp authorities make no direct provision for promoting religious life and activities within the camps, in many of which, as these instructions point out, the official attitude to religion is at the least doubtful and there is even a tendency to introduce a National Church.

To another petition asking that the Catholic members of the Labour Service should, if possible, be sent to places with a church in the vicinity, and that, as far as possible, members of the different denominations should be drafted into different camps, the answer was returned that this could not be done " for technical reasons."

The request that capable clergymen should be admitted to the camps to give instruction on important moral questions was refused as well, on the grounds that " the teaching staff of the camp is sufficient. The church is the proper place for the clergyman." The Bishops' Instructions, therefore, in view of the impossibility of caring for the spiritual welfare of those in the Labour Camps by direct contact, advise priests to avail themselves of the few indirect methods still left for helping young Catholics to go through their six months of camp life without suffering harm to their faith, and suggest that the easiest of these ways is to provide the camps with good religious literature, especially periodicals, as in most camps these are still allowed.

The Instructions treat also of a special difficulty—namely, the interdenominational religious service held on such special occasions as the harvest festival and services for the dead. " We emphasise that wherever such services take the place of the Mass of obligation on Sundays or holidays, Catholic members are not allowed to attend."

[1] *Gazette of the Archdiocese of Breslau*, No. 5, 1935.

It is a fact that since 1936 books like "The Myth of the Twentieth Century," "To the Obscurantists of our Time," "The Mirror of Priestcraft," have been officially sent to the leaders of the Labour Service Camps to be used for the ideological instruction of the inmates. Often directors put difficulties in the way of attendance at divine service. This is what happened, for instance, in a Labour Camp for young girls in 1937. Among the thirty members of the camp, five of the girls were Catholics. One of these asked leave to go to Mass one Sunday, and she cycled to the nearest church, $7\frac{1}{2}$ miles away. When she came back a number of her comrades (some of them prostitutes, by the way) stood at the door armed with sticks and made her run the gauntlet. The same thing happened on the second and third Sundays. At last the leader of the camp declared: "We don't want to make martyrs." And from that time on the girl was given the dirtiest work to do, and had to put up with all the mean tricks they could think of. Repeatedly work is done in the camps on great feast days like Corpus Christi, and there are often complaints not only about the immoral behaviour of the members of the Labour Service in places outside their camps, but also of their deliberate irreverence.

Songs full of hatred of Christianity and of the Church are practised and sung in the camps—*e.g.*, "Stick the Jews and the black-coated priests against the wall." The official administration of the Labour Service expressly refuses any support for Catholic ministrations to the members of the camps.

3. *The Land Year*

In the Land Year children of the ages of fourteen to fifteen years who have left school are brought together in hostels for about nine months to be given education in common in a National Socialist atmosphere. One of the most important elements of this scheme is that the children should be removed as far as possible from their parents, who not only have no choice in their going, but are, in fact, prosecuted if they fail to send them. It is equally important that each hostel should house children of all denominations, and no priest is allowed within its walls nor is any divine service conducted there. As the Catholic children are often, indeed usually, sent to hostels very far removed from a Catholic church, it is practically impossible for them for the whole of the nine months to attend Mass on Sunday, for it is very rarely that a priest can manage to organise near the hostel a special service for the children to attend. The Diocesan Administration of Berlin has issued directions to help the children to keep the faith of their parents during the many months which, in the uniform of the Hitler Youth, they spend in these State homes—without Holy Mass, without organised morning and night prayers, without grace at meals—and expresses the wish that before their departure for the camps they should be given an opportunity of experiencing the strength and greatness of the corporate unity of the Church.

The difficulties in the way of any spiritual influence being exercised on the children in the Land Year may be seen in an account issued from the office of the Vicar-General of Münster. The *Diocesan Gazette of Münster*[1] says:

> Several hundreds of Catholic children from the towns of the diocese are to be sent for a ninth school year on a so-called Land Year to the agricultural districts in the east of Germany. As we have learned from reliable persons, there is no guarantee that the groups of Land Year children will be separated according to denomination or sex. The accommodation of exclusively Catholic units in Catholic Homes of the West has been refused. We ask the priests to notify such parents as have entered their children for the Land Year of these facts and to remind them of their responsibility for the spiritual welfare of their children. The parents are responsible in the sight of God for having their children brought up in a moral and religious way of life according to Catholic principles, and for ensuring that they do not omit their daily prayers, that they attend Holy Mass on Sundays and feast days, and that they receive the Sacraments regularly.
>
> We ask the priests to communicate as far as possible with priests in whose parishes the children are accommodated and to remain in touch with the children themselves by correspondence and by sending them periodicals from home, etc.
>
> The Vicar-General.
>
> Münster, *March 28th*, 1934.

In May, 1935, we read the following notice in the Press:

> Reichsminister Rust, in reply to a request of the Head of the Evangelical Youth, declared that a series of untoward events had caused him to forbid the distribution in the Youth Hostels of denominational newspapers as well as of parish and Youth magazines. There existed the danger that not only different Christian but also different ideological organisations might try to influence the youth of the Land Year, and he could not allow any danger to the religious convictions of the young people.

Another difficulty is that the children are not allowed to attend church in the costume of the camp, the Hitler Youth uniform. A petition of the diocesan authorities of Berlin to the Minister of Education to cancel that prohibition was refused, so the priests were instructed by the bishops to tell the parents that their children should take also their ordinary clothes with them.

There are, alas! too many testimonies from the parents of the Land Year children for there to be any doubt of the sad fact that the Land Year is extremely dangerous to the faith of Catholic children and that the moral harm resulting from it is serious in the extreme.

In the preceding pages we have enumerated only the largest and most important of the National Socialist organisations, and we have pointed out that they all disseminate (especially through their lecture courses and writings) that National Socialist ideology which is to be found in the books of Alfred Rosenberg, the Reich Leader of the Ideological Training of the Party, particularly in his " Myth of the Twentieth Century."

We have not mentioned the many groups for particular occupations

[1] March 28th, 1934.

that are linked together in the Labour Front, nor yet again the associations that are co-ordinated with the Hitler Youth or form part of it (*e.g.*, the German Girls' League, the Junior Section of the Hitler Youth). There are, finally, all the institutions for general welfare work, like the Strength through Joy Organisation, the National Socialist Public Welfare Service, etc. But what we have said above applies with equal truth to these, too: they all convey to every rank and class of the people the National Socialist outlook, with all that it implies in the way of hatred for everything that is Christian and truly religious.

CHAPTER IV

OFFICIAL SUPPORT LENT TO OTHER ATTACKS ON THE CHURCH

IN the last few chapters we have described the complexity and thoroughness of the machine which the National Socialist Party, as the controlling power in the Third Reich, has come to possess. This machine, with its massive organisation and its publications so lavishly distributed by means of subscriptions which are, in practice, obligatory, is consciously and systematically devoted to the destruction of Christianity.

Up to the present year, 1940, this official attack, always more or less camouflaged, has come more and more into the open. Side by side with it, though somewhat less prominently as official attacks became increasingly brazen, private anti-clerical circles have waged a continuous campaign against Christianity. For this, too, the National Socialist Party must be held responsible in view of its all-powerful position and its directing and regulating function in a totalitarian State. The slightest sign from a Party leader or from any of his subordinates would suffice to stifle any anti-Christian outburst, printed or spoken. Herr Hitler himself promised expressly to act in this way; but the promise remained unfulfilled.

In autumn, 1934, the Bishop of Münster made a speech at Recklinghausen in which he dealt in passing with " the propaganda for an ostensibly ' Teutonic Paganism.' " Later he said:

> I have good reason to hope that they (*i.e.*, neo-pagan movements) will not remain unpunished for long. Our Führer and Reich Chancellor, Adolf Hitler, in an audience given to several German bishops on June 27th, 1934, promised that he would give explicit orders to the Party and to national organisations for the suppression of all neo-pagan propaganda in the future.

No such orders were ever given. On the contrary, it became increasingly clear that the Party was keenly interested in assisting philosophical and political campaigns against the Christian Faith and the Church with all the means in its power and on as wide and varied a front as possible: indeed, by the mere fact of its acquiescence in them, the Party must be held responsible for anti-Christian activities. The simplest German citizen cannot fail to note a benevolent approval —often an active encouragement—of anti-Christian movements on the part of leaders in the Third Reich, and the immediate frustration of any attempt by the Church to employ similar methods in its own defence.

It would be easy to select many examples of support given by members of the Party to unofficial anti-clerical forces. It is not, however, our intention to describe here the various anti-Christian movements and organisations existing in modern Germany, which, in any case, are for ever transforming and rearranging themselves. We shall be content to indicate the way in which books, periodicals, newspapers and public meetings, all officially sanctioned by the Party, are made the vehicle of bitter attacks on Christian belief and on the Catholic Church; and in this way to establish the responsibility of the Party which not merely tolerates but frequently encourages and aids them.

1. *The Campaign against the Church in Books and Pamphlets*

Not even in the so-called " Free-thought Period " (*Freidenkerzeit*) was the German people so overwhelmed with anti-Christian books and pamphlets of every kind as during the seven years of Nazi rule. Particularly striking are the high publication figures attained by a yellow-press type of writing wholly devoid of literary value. For example:

	Total.
Otto von Corvin: " Mirror of Priestcraft " (*November*, 1938)	2,000,000
Otto von Corvin: " The Floggers "	500,000
B. Emil Koenig: " Witch Trials "	230,000
K. Revetzlow: " The Priest and the Woman in the Confessional " (7th edition)	20,000
B. Assmus: " Mirror of Jesuits: Startling Revelations of Jesuit Infamies "	60,000
B. Assmus: " The Fate of Nuns: Startling Revelation from Monastic Documents "	76,000-80,000
B. Assmus: " Life in the Cloister: Revelations of Immorality in Monasteries and Convents "	106,000-115,000
J. Leutheuser: " Towards a German National Church " (6-7th edition)	
E. and M. Ludendorff: " The Secret Aims and Power of the Jesuits "	46,000-50,000
E. and M. Ludendorff: " The Bible not the Word of God "	281,000-290,000
E. and M. Ludendorff: " A Retort to Clerical Babblings "	21,000-30,000
M. Ludendorff: " Salvation from Jesus Christ "	48,000-52,000
E. Ludendorff: " News of the Great War of 1914 "	121,000-130,000
E. Ludendorff: " The Instigators of War and Slaughter "	91,000-93,000
Gangler: " Catholic Action attacks Germany "	21,000-30,000
Mohring: " The Pope as a War Chief "	16,000-20,000
Griese: " A Priest's Call: 'Away from Rome and Christ' "	28,000-32,000
Griese: " Christianity's Great Mistake: Explanation by a Priest "	17,000-21,000
Loehde: " The Pope enjoys Himself "	11,000-17,000
Murawski: " The ' Political Church ': its Sources in the Bible "	21,000-30,000
Gottschling: " Two Years in a Monastery "	38,000-42,000
Kaempfer: " Political Catholicism "	9,000-13,000

Any reader of these or similar publications cannot but feel disgusted at the thought of such high figures achieved by an arid array of outworn clichés and exploded calumnies, unadorned by any pretence of good writing.

In order to appeal to popular love of sensation this type of " literature " is shamelessly advertised in publishers' blurb. Typical is that of Rugel's " A Trappist breaks Silence." In some 240 lines of print the book's twenty chapters are analysed, sometimes page by page. Thus, for example:

> P. 29: The author's struggle to find the Truth.
> P. 31: A word to troubled souls.
> P. 32: Ought one to leave the Church ?

From a chapter headed: " What is a Monk ?"—" Under Skull and Crossbones." From another: " I become a Trappist "—" Frustrated Love." From another, " Trappist Silence," is taken the following sub-title: " The Sinful World and Sham ' Saints.' "

The chapter " Beyond the World " has attractive contents—*e.g.*, p. 72, " Lady Visitors to the Monastery "; and p. 73, " Underground Passages."

Further on the prospectus gives for p. 163, " What Paul the Jew has to say about Marriage "; and later, " How Celibacy can be got round and Nothing Said."

The responsibility of the Nazi Party.

Recommendations of the Reich Department for the Promotion of German Literature:

This department, created by the Nazi Party, considers its function to be the pushing of all " books which ought to be encouraged so that they may have the place of honour over all other books in public notice." (Thus Dr. Wiesmann in the periodical *Die Literatur*, September, 1936.) In this way newly-issued books and pamphlets receive an official judgement from the Party, and the attitude of the Reich Department may be gauged by the fact that worthless propaganda publications against the Church frequently receive flattering reviews. A review of " The Sins of Rome," for example, reads as follows:

Reich Department for the Promotion of German Literature

Wilhelm Glasenapp: " The Sins of Rome." Published by Giordano Bruno-Verlag, Leipzig.

Sectarian history labours industriously to hush up the vices and horrors by which the Papacy has offended against humanity and in particular against the German people. Moreover, " objective historical investigation " provides so many loopholes for touching up, that a clear, undistorted picture of Papal history is seldom forthcoming. A review of Papal history from the Aryan standpoint would be timely; and such a revelation of the true nature of the " Pope-King " should no longer be withheld from the public.

Wilhelm Glasenapp's " The Sins of Rome " supplies this need very competently. Neither too extensive nor too brief, written in an easy, flowing style, with clear, straightforward chapter divisions, it fully meets all the requirements of a German guide to the Papacy, and does so all the more perfectly by virtue of the author's purely German outlook throughout his sketch. Inspired with an incorruptible love of truth, Glasenapp traces the careers and activities of the Popes throughout the centuries. Against all the wordy propaganda about the " blessings " bestowed by the Papacy on German culture, the author shows how little such " blessings " count in comparison with all the mischief perpetrated by the Papacy against the

German people, and goes on to show the unwavering loyalty of the Papacy to its own peculiar arrogance and superstition. We heartily recommend Glasenapp's book for information about the Papacy.[1]

The Reich Department for the Promotion of German Literature sees as one of its main functions the regular supply of what may be called " expert opinions," which, according to Dr. Wiesmann, are intended for internal consumption only. Thus: " From time to time we shall supply publishers of newspapers and periodicals, as well as the radio, with the titles of books selected by us, and we beg you to give them unstinted recommendation."

The department in its recommendations classifies books as " positive," " restricted " or " negative." We give below an example of the type of work which receives the label " positive "—*i.e.*, which receives the Department's warm commendation.

In 1936 there appeared from the press of the *Nationale Verlagsgesellschaft*, Leipzig, a book entitled " The Catholic Church a Menace to the State," by Dr. Jam, a work consisting of endless slanders, spiteful untruths and misrepresentations. This concoction, from which we shall quote a few sentences, earned the official classification " positive."

The Catholic Church is a power which employs a brutally compulsory attendance at services and the use of auricular confession, and paints lurid pictures of the tortures of Hell, tortures which spineless devotees come to think can be inflicted by the priests on all who are not blindly obedient— and all this in order to establish an unrestricted sway over the souls of its faithful sheep. It is a power which has learnt how to use its *Index Librorum Prohibitorum* (a mere heretic tribunal, not indeed against " heretical " individuals, but for the fiery destruction of all books dangerous to the popish system) with such prudent care that none of its devotees can have access to any written or spoken enlightenment from which he might learn the truth or come to know something of the true nature of his Roman idol. Such a power is intolerable !

The passage continues in an even more bombastic style:

This longing for world domination on the part of the Catholic Church presents us with an arrogant challenge of the most shocking kind, if we but realise the true nature of this edifice built on lies and trickery and doctored history—a stale, reactionary, supremely intolerant system, the mortal enemy of freedom, spiritual activity and culture; if we realise, too, the insane and accursed career of this Catholic Church which exhibits a record soiled, more than any other in the world, with corruption, vice and blood. Can there exist any race or any human institution which wallows in its private bog of vice and crime as much as the Catholic Church, so that moral corruption and a repulsive criminality seem stamped, an indelible token, on the features of that Church !

Literature thus calculated to damage Christianity is regularly recommended, however low its literary value may be.

The epithet " restricted " is applied to works such as Papal Encyclicals, the writings of St. Thomas Aquinas and those of St. Augustine. Books issuing from Catholic publishing firms are usually labelled

---

[1] Printed in *Börsenblatt für den deutschen Buchhandel*, No. 267, November 16th, 1935.

"negative"—for example, Archbishop Gröber's One is your Teacher, Christ; Alois Dempf's *Meister Eckehardt*; Hermann Muckermann's *Grundriss der Rassenkunde*; Alfons Erb's "Thomas More and John Fisher"; Jacob Kneips' *Das Reich Christi*.

In 1937 a violent propaganda work, A. W. Rose's *Rom mordet, mordet Seelen, Menschen, Völker!* ("Rome, Murderer of Souls, of Men and of Peoples"), formerly banned as dangerous and undesirable, was removed from the forbidden list, and now enjoys an unrestricted sale.

Recommendations of anti-Christian works in Nazi publications:

It is only necessary to scan the advertisements of books in Nazi papers and periodicals to realise how consistently Nazi literature consists of writings against the Church, writings which could never have hoped to obtain such high sales' figures without constant pressing recommendation in widely circulated Nazi publications. A few examples will suffice.

Otto Bangert's "The Earthly God: A German Breviary," a work dedicated to "The Martyrs of Untrammelled Worship," teaches complete paganism. In the *Völkischer Beobachter*[1] the book is thus commended:

> The longing for God of northern mankind, a race free, pure and great, unadulterated and unsullied by foreign strains, rings out harmoniously in these songs. In them the reader senses that struggle of the true believer for a right concept of God, which the best and noblest representatives of the Teutonic race have carried on for centuries.

A pamphlet called "The Pope's Men" first appeared as a series of articles in the *Angriff*, the official paper of the German Labour Front. From this pamphlet, overflowing with spite directed against Pius XI and his *curia*, two passages are worth quoting:

> The Vatican again! And what about it? Why so much fuss about this miserable scrap of earth hidden away in the capital of the Roman Empire? Many readers of the National Socialist Press are asking this question. Roosevelt, Ibn Saud, Chamberlain, Dimitroff, Herriot and above all Mussolini—these are men of our time who determine the politics of their own countries and of the world. But these Roman prelates, these gliding Nuncios and incense-laden Cardinals—what a set they are!
> These men of rustling silk and red birettas, whose every step claims genuflections from clergy and people seek—blessings, and receive—politics!

Other types of official support:

A little work which we mentioned above, "Two Years in a Monastery," by Gottschling (a former Dominican novice), received in 1935 the Art and Literature Prize of the University of Jena. Gustav Frenssen (once a Protestant pastor) was awarded the Goethe medal in 1937 by Herr Hitler for his services to art and science, and the Nazi press made it clear that this pioneer of the neo-pagan movement received this public honour as a reward for his most recent work, "The Faith of the Nordmark." This work, a passionate rejection

[1] June 9th, 1939.

of Christianity, was sheer propaganda for a " Germanic " or Teutonic Faith, and enjoyed the fullest official aid of the Party to ensure the widest possible circulation. We quote a few typical passages:

The Christian religion, like all religions, is a human creation and therefore mortal; after the manner of such things, it becomes outworn and withered. The eternal Creative Force ever demands something new—ever, and in all spheres. He is indeed blind who cannot see that. It was God's wish, therefore, that something new should see the light. . . .

And what of the Pope, the head of the Catholic Faith, the representative of Christ? An unreliable, timid but cunning politician! Just one of those innumerable men who have led others, first up to the clouds, then down to the mire ! . . .

In our time Germany has seen a new kind of religion—indeed, a new form of belief in God and a new piety—develop and come into power through the efforts of one ardent soul, and within fifteen years it has won over more than three-quarters of our great race. Once it had gained strength, this religion, through its special type of piety, did more in four years to assist interests dear to the German heart—*e.g.*, physical health and hygiene, genuine education and learning, early marriages, beauty and true happiness, honourable dealing between men, chivalry and bravery—than the Catholic Church has done in 1,400 years or the Protestant Church in 400. . . .

The God of the New Testament, with His unnatural miracles—turning water into wine, sending evil spirits into swine, reviving rotting corpses—this is not *our* God !

A passionately anti-Christian work, " Illusion or Reality," was published by Dr. M. Ziegler, a high official working under Alfred Rosenberg, the editor of the *Nationalsozialistische Monatshefte*. The author states that his work proposes to deal with matter " about which I have had to express myself repeatedly—*i.e.*, with matter which he, as a recognised official of the Party, had sought to impress on the hearers of special training courses and lectures. The book is a mass of attacks on Christianity and the Church. On page 8, for example, the concept of a personal God is condemned as Jewish and oriental. The priesthood, he considers, depends for its existence on " keeping the superstitious masses in a state of fear and trembling at the thought of the devil." Chapter II is headed: " The Jewish Basis of the Christian Churches." The Papacy is an " imperial power-house employing religious devices on a world-wide scale in the service of Jewish world domination." The immortality of the soul is denied and contrasted with the true immortality of blood. " Nordic mankind knows nothing of the oriental antithesis of Here and Hereafter, of this world as a sinful vale of tears and of life after death as a state of eternal reward and punishment," nor does it recognise any " oriental duality of the natural and the supernatural."

Christian morality is condemned as a matter of course. " The sole, supreme touchstone of moral conduct for racial philosophy is the People."

Official support of the *Pfaffenspiegel* (" Mirror of Priestcraft "):

The *Pfaffenspiegel*, a high-water mark in anti-Christian invective, was confiscated in 1934 (January 29th), but released within four months (May 8th). Since then this unique work has received the fullest support from National Socialism. The following extract is taken from the official *Börsenblatt für den deutschen Buchhandel*.[1] " The unexpurgated issue of the *Pfaffenspiegel*, released by the police, has topped a sales-figure of 1¼ millions. This well-known work has a special significance nowadays. See that it appears in your windows. . . ." On the advertisement sheet issued by the *Pfaffenspiegel's* publisher one reads: " This well-known work is as opportune today as when first issued, and the widest possible circulation is desirable in the interests of the political and ideological aims of National Socialism, and for a right understanding of the German National Movement."

In many parts of Bavaria Catholics found this propaganda work delivered to them unasked, and large numbers were sent to various post offices. By order of the Archbishop of Munich the following notice was read from all pulpits of the diocese on February 28th, 1937: " We understand from many reports that a publishing firm is delivering unordered copies of the notorious *Pfaffenspiegel*. We wish therefore to state:

1. The *Pfaffenspiegel* is one of the most deplorable concoctions of scandalous stories directed against the Church, a collection of gross calumnies against Church and priesthood.

2. Otto von Corvin-Wierzbitzki, who, some ninety years ago, compiled this book from anti-clerical sources of every kind, was an adventurer and a revolutionary (he fought at the barricades in Paris), a Freemason and an enemy of Germany, a friend of Jews, Marxists and Communists. Jews did good business with his books; Marxists and Communists favoured and circulated them as suitable propaganda for their pernicious theories.

3. On account of its worthlessness, its untruthful and provocative nature, this book has been confiscated no less than eight times, and is still forbidden by the Church to all Catholics, since it is both harmful to morals and damaging to proper respect towards the Church, the clergy and to all respect for authority.

Support given to the works of Rosenberg:

On February 7th, 1934, Alfred Rosenberg's " The Myth of the Twentieth Century " was officially included in the Index of Forbidden Books by the Pope. To an appeal of the Bishop of Trier, arising from the scruples of conscience caused amongst teachers by the official order to recommend the book and to place it in school libraries, the Prussian Ministry of Education replied as follows:

In reply to your communication of September 14th, 1934, may I beg to point out that the work " The Myth of the Twentieth Century," by Alfred Rosenberg, merely appears on the list of books deemed suitable for inclusion in school libraries. No obligation to read it arises; nor, therefore, does the question of scruples of conscience arise for those Catholic members of the teaching profession to whom your communication refers.

To similar queries from Catholic quarters, official replies constantly stated that the contents of Rosenberg's books were " the outcome of the author's private investigations, as he himself, in the preface to the ' Myth,' had expressly stated." That his writings were, nevertheless,

[1] May 22nd, 1935.

deliberate propaganda appears clearly in the light of the following facts:

1. Rosenberg writes not as a private individual, but as one specially commissioned by the Führer to be the ideological pedagogue, the official professor of politics and philosophy for the Party and, by virtue of the Party's key position in Germany, for all responsible German citizens. Even his " private " findings necessarily receive a special authority; and how can any German citizen distinguish clearly between what he puts forward as a private investigator and what he professes as the educational deputy of the Führer?

2. In countless speeches delivered at training courses, etc., in his official capacity Rosenberg puts forward precisely the same views as he holds in the " Myth."

3. At the Reich Party Congress held in Nürnberg in 1937, Herr Hitler publicly distinguished Rosenberg as his Deputy for the Ideological Instruction of the Party by making him the first recipient of the new State Prize for Art and Science. The official document accompanying this award expressly praises Rosenberg as the person who " has in a scientific and penetrating manner laid the firm foundations for an understanding of the ideological bases of National Socialism."

This can only mean that Rosenberg is regarded in the highest quarters as one whose works, of which the " Myth " is the most outstanding, expound the ideology of National Socialism, and not mere private speculations.

4. Rosenberg's books are encouraged by profuse recognition in Nazi Party propaganda.

5. The whole Nazi press seeks to propagate the " Myth " and other works by Rosenberg. Thus, for example, the " Training Letter " for May, 1935, recommends his *An die Dunkelmänner*, a work previously praised in the April issue of the *NS Monatshefte*, which stated that on the rejection or acceptance of Rosenberg's propositions hung the very possibility of the National Socialist position. The *SA-Mann* of January 15th, 1938, praises Rosenberg unreservedly, singling him out as an " indispensable teacher for National Socialism and for Germany." In the *Schwarze Korps* of May 1st, 1935, an illustrated front-page article was devoted to praise of Rosenberg's writings. Other examples are issues of the *NS Beamtenzeitung*[1] and the *Hitler Youth*.[2] *Wille und Macht*,[3] the organ of the National Youth Leaders, invited all Hitler Youth Leaders to make a study of the " Myth." In another issue[4] the *HJ* puffed the " Myth " and styled it " The Book of German Honour."

The *Schwarze Korps*, official organ of the SS, treats the " Myth " as anything but mere private speculations of its author. We cite a short notice concerning the condemnation of Mgr. Leffers of Rostock:[5]

[1] May 26th, 1935. [2] May 18th, 1935. [3] May 1st, 1937.
[4] June 27th, 1936. [5] May 1st, 1935.

A special court in Rostock has had occasion to condemn the priest of the Rostock Catholic Church to imprisonment for one and a half years for a breach of § 1 of the law for the Preservation of State and Party. This priest had expressed decidedly strange views on the subject of Alfred Rosenberg's "Myth of the Twentieth Century" to certain students at Rostock University. These remarks, consisting of bitter attacks on the authority of the State and the good name of the Party, obliged the court to make an example of this remarkable "pastor of souls." He will have opportunity enough, in the solitude of his cell, to reflect on the fact that the days of a "cure of souls," which was downright treason to the State, are now over. A year and a half will suffice to teach Herr Leffers that the new law of the German people takes precedence over any canon law; and self-examination in a lonely prison cell will be altogether wholesome. This case should be a warning to all clerical gentlemen, whether tonsured or not.

6. The "Myth" is to be found on official lists of books recommended to teachers and is often to be found in school libraries throughout Germany.

7. In innumerable training courses, in Labour Camps, and Students' Camps, Rosenberg's "Myth" is made the basis of instruction and openly proclaimed as an exposition of National Socialist ideology. The thing has gone so far that teachers taking part in Nazi training courses are requested to bring a copy of the "Myth" with them "as a fundamental work on National Socialism."

8. By an order of the Ministry of Justice junior barristers preparing for the examination which will make them "assessors" are obliged to study the "Myth" and become acquainted with its fundamental ideological doctrines.

9. The Saxon Ministry of Public Education recommended the book for official use in schools.[1]

10. All popular rejoinders to the "Myth" have been confiscated and forbidden by the authorities.

2. *The Campaign against the Church in Newspapers and Periodicals*

As early as 1934 the *Kölnische Volkszeitung*[2] quoted the following sentences from the *Archdiocesan Gazette of Cologne*.

The increase in literature both anti-Christian and likely to stir up sectarian prejudice made us decide to try a little experiment. On one day, in Cologne, we found openly displayed on a single newspaper-stand seven anti-Christian papers or periodicals, adorned in some cases with headlines deeply distressing to Catholic feelings. We would request other parish priests to make the same experiment and send in their findings.

With the sole exception of official Church magazines, all newspapers and periodicals must open their columns for the Party to use in its ideological struggle—*i.e.*, in its struggle against Christianity. Even papers formerly Catholic—so far as they have survived—are obliged to print the attacks of Rosenberg and the vulgarities of District Leader Streicher in their reports of public meetings. German bishops have not failed to make protests and compose memorials; but all in vain. Anything which lowers esteem for Christianity or the Church, anything

---

[1] *Cf.* the Ministry's *Verordnungsblatt*, October 15th, 1935.   [2] December 4th, 1934.

which upholds the new " myth " of blood and race, may be printed without the slightest interference by the press of the Third Reich. Sentences such as the following:[1] "The Catholic Church is outstanding in its continual opposition to what is meant by true, Christian brotherly love," are to be found by the hundred in the German daily press.

We may make a reference to the anti-Jewish propaganda paper, *Der Stürmer*, a weekly of incredibly low literary standard, which vilifies Catholics no less willingly than Jews. (*Der Stürmer*. German Weekly in the Fight for Truth. Ed. Julius Streicher, District Leader of Nürnberg.)

In a November number of 1936 was printed the following letter under the heading: " A Priest Writes to the *Stürmer* ":

DEAR STÜRMER,

I have the greatest pleasure in informing you that dawn is beginning to break amongst the Catholic clergy. For long I tried in vain to direct attention to opposition to the Jews at clerical conferences and gatherings, but now I frequently meet with agreement and interest.

Dear *Stürmer*, why should I, a Catholic priest, be an open enemy of the Jews ? Why do I read *Der Stürmer* ? Why do I welcome and support your cause ? For the following reasons: Jews are members of a race which was rejected and cursed by God, and I see the hand of this divine curse in the fact that Jews seem destined for all time to work at the beck and call of the devil. Were I not to fight these colleagues and hirelings of the devil in every way I can, I should have sadly misunderstood my vocation and my mission of one who is to lead men to God.

Yours, etc.,

FRANZ STEIGERWALD, *Curate.*

With regard to this the *Catholic Church Magazine*[2] of the Bishopric of Berlin published the following notice of the Diocesan Administration:

Concerning Curate Franz Steigerwald

In answer to a circular of the 15th inst. concerning a supposed curate named Franz Steigerwald, whose letter appeared in *Der Stürmer* in November, the replies from all German Archbishops and Bishops, as well as from the Prelate of Schneidemühl and the Vicars-General of Braunitz and Mittelwald, are all negative, and enable us to assert that a curate named Franz Steigerwald, or indeed any priest of that name, is unknown to any religious superior in Germany.

In 1936 a November number of *Der Stürmer* published caricatures of preachers, and mockery of the confessional as a school of immorality.[3]

At Easter, 1937, appeared a special number of *Der Stürmer*, reiterating the well-known anti-Semite teaching about the " Aryan Jesus Christ, Forerunner of Adolf Hitler." Thus, Jesus Christ was not only not a Jew, he was the opponent of Jews. He was one of the greatest, most genuine and most courageous of their opponents throughout the ages. Moreover, the religion which he founded, Christianity, was and still is essentially a religion and a movement against Judaism,

---

[1] *Berliner 12-Uhr Blatt*, April 17th, 1937   [2] January 17th, 1937.
[3] *Cf., e.g.,* p. 443.

and is one of the greatest anti-Semite movements of all time. Christ's followers, too, were Aryans. (Proof? They were fishermen and manual workers.) Judas was an exception, a half-Jew, in whose case Jesus had abandoned his strict anti-Semite instinct. " Christ's crucifixion was the greatest ritual murder of all time," for " today everybody understands how Jews are accustomed, in connection with the Feast of Purim and the Passover, to kill non-Jews and use their blood for ritual purposes." The paper goes on to give a sketch of a " Jewish world revolution " in post-Christian days, in which Nero receives special notice. " He gave a command which crushed the first Jewish world revolution, and ordered the destruction of Jerusalem. He was thus responsible for one of the greatest deeds of history."

This type of text is usually accompanied by pictures which satisfy the pornographic standards of the paper.

Where Christ failed and Christianity has bungled, Adolf Hitler has succeeded, and National Socialism has reached perfection.

The German people, made up of 65,000,000 men of racially sound stock, would be snuffed out but for Adolf Hitler. Thus it is that Hitler has brought about not only the greatest event in Germany history, but the greatest event in Christian history as well. It is a matter of God and religion. A matter of life or death for non-Jewish mankind. All who join in this struggle are at once both Germans and Christians. But all who hold aloof, or work against National Socialism secretly, are traitors, servants of Bolshevism, Judases. Two thousand years ago Christ climbed Calvary and breathed out His life on the Cross amidst the scornful laughter of the Jews. Things are different today. Germany celebrates her resurrection, and the whole non-Jewish world wakes with her. Soon, very soon, we shall be celebrating a true Easter.

On March 15th, 1936, the parish priest of St. Matthias' in Berlin had the following notice read at every Mass:

In January the *Stürmer* published photographic facsimiles of two official communications of this parish on the subject of the reception of members of the Jewish religion into the Catholic Church. The parish priest then requested the police authorities in writing to explain how these came into the possession of the *Stürmer*. There was no reply. The episcopal authorities then took similar steps, with no result. Suddenly the *Stürmer* again publishes an official communication of this ecclesiastical district, in consequence of which the parish authorities will not, in future, supply the police with copies of their notices. Your priest is not going to allow his daily activities to be dictated by the *Stürmer*, but by his own conscience; and, following it, he will not hesitate to receive unbelievers of any race whatsoever into the Church which Christ founded for all men, so long as he has no reason to suspect dishonourable intentions on their part. Indeed, so long as no such suspicion existed, your priest would be willing, if asked, to receive even people of the *Stürmer* type.

To remove a possible misconception we would add that what has here been stated in no way implies commendation of marriages between Aryans and non-Aryans.

It is in the periodicals of the neo-pagan movements, of the " German Faith Movement," and of variations of these, that the war on Christianity is waged with least restraint, so that this literature will always be a stain on German culture. A few examples may be given.

The *Durchbruch*, " a periodical fighting for German belief, German race and German nationality," excels all other types of literature in the Third Reich for malice towards Christianity. In its issue for January 30th, 1936, appeared the following paragraphs:

All tension which arises between Catholicism and the State has its origin in a mistaken and outworn bid for power on the part of the Roman court. The Concordat is a treaty which creates discord, not harmony, for it seeks to unite forcibly two incompatible kinds of belief, two incompatible culture strains. . . .

Those who are accustomed to judge by Jewish and oriental standards will necessarily depreciate Nordic standards of value. Since, however, the German " Will to Unity " has overcome thirty parties and 300 minor principalities, it will easily deal with two or three denominations. We should otherwise be unworthy of the name of German warriors ! From the religious standpoint Germany has no firm ground under her feet; all this imported Jordan water has turned the land of Germany into a swamp ! We have to think of " drainage," and one of the preliminaries essential to efficient drainage will be the separation of Church and State.

Not Faulhaber and Muckermann, not Meiser and Wurm,[1] not little monks and nuns, will direct the future of Germany, but the triumphant, clear-thinking German man, the type in whom real German blood flows and whose feet tread a land with which he feels deep spiritual and religious sympathy.

In another 1936 issue the Holy See is accused, without the faintest pretence of any proof, of having staged the Abyssinian war

" as a means of destroying opponents of the Lord Pope and his most holy followers—*i.e.*, of destroying the Coptic Christian Church !" The passage continues: " We are horrified by the cold, calculating nature of this organisation which throughout the centuries has sacrificed whole peoples and races and men of the finest type to its folly. Only seventeen years after the last holocaust in Europe this organisation does not shrink from kindling the flame afresh—in the name of God, as representative of God on earth !"

Elsewhere the paper stigmatises Christian prayer as " a pitiful crawling before wooden representations, a lamentable crying to plaster statues."

Our race does not need to lie whining on the ground while its priestly leaders beg their dear Lord for salvation from present miseries. The Führer has taught us that unsuspected powers slumber within our race, that a truly holy blood flows in our veins.

It would seem that the " Bride of Christ " has grown a little old and unpresentable, and that is easily understood since she chooses nowadays to offer her failing charms to the unpretentious Abyssinians, offering episcopal trinkets to warriors who will draw dusky children by force to her virgin bosom. Yes, the " Bride of Christ " has undertaken no easy task in trying to win over Black and White, Yellow and Red, at one and the same time ! How the poor Bride's face must suffer from such daily changes of cosmetics; and in spite of the tenacity with which she clings to life she seems to be withering within, for she can never make up her mind to consummate a marriage with any of her suitors, but constantly pursues passionate love affairs with new ones. The German race is at long last tiring of this international flirting, and now seeks to bring about the fulfilment of love in its own land.

Perhaps the " Bride of Christ " will score a success with these Moorish children of Africa for whom she still begs our pennies and for whose sake she allows quantities of German possessions to be withdrawn from our

---
[1] Evangelical bishops.—*Translator's note.*

country. We would see her withdraw altogether from our northern land without regret. But we know how dangerous the oriental temperament can be, we know what insidious poisons these southern beauties possess. And we know, too, that German men—truly strong and royal men—need never fear the hatred of " Christ's Bride " so long as " Little Snow-white's eyes "—the soul of Germany—watches over them.

In a later number (No. 10) for 1936 occurred the following:

We Nordic men now oppose the glistening shield of our honour like a firm wall against *that* Jewish orientalism which would trample the honour of German womanhood in the dirt. Our clarion call rings out for the defence of the honour of German womanhood, and we ignore all attempts to wash it away with Catholic or Protestant baptismal waters.

There are still mothers who kneel before the Madonna's altars, blinded by the glimmer of candles and the gilded glitter of paint to the murky gloom which lies behind the plaster. Future generations, however, will not bow in the dust before a " spotless Mother," nor will they attribute their sinfulness to the Original Sin of mankind. Let these Christian pastors in Fulda " earnestly beg and warn our dear Youth to avoid all friendships which may lead to mixed marriages and ever in such matters to put the question of religion in the first place"; our German maidens will mock to their hearts' content at the enticing promises of these chaste ancients who never tire of preaching national unity, yet unceasingly dare openly to sabotage the Führer's labours for unity, and aim only at creating artificial sectarian divisions in a race already one in blood.

You, German maidens, should never offer your hand to a German husband merely to prevent that prostitution which is, quite literally, the conception in the mind of the Christian arch-Jew, Paul. No child of German blood will say to you, as Christ once said to His mother, " Woman, what is it to Me and to thee ?" No malicious parson will be able, when you are a mother, to cast anguish into your soul by questions in the confessional about the " infidelity " of your children.

In the 25th issue of 1936 appeared the following:

Now that we see in the courts depraved sexual criminals dressed in the habits of monks and priests, we can understand how men of this nature, their wills undermined and their moral sense shattered, slaves of a powerful and well-organised system which aims at priestly domination, can still today, as in the Middle Ages, do endless damage if they feel themselves to be dealing with a weakened race. Those who refuse the world and scorn natural strength and natural beauty can only act as unbalanced trouble-makers, mortal enemies of life, of the human community and of all true innate good dispositions.

In order to decide " in the name of God " what precisely is unchaste, what is mortal and what is but venial sin, these " holy " celibates have put together weighty volumes of " Moral Theology," and in them with undisguised lasciviousness have evolved a collection of filth such as no specimen of pornographic literature can equal. The " Moral Theology " of these monkish and priestly perverts can therefore safely be styled " Instruction in the Art of Sinning " or " Sexual Vice Systematised," and all such books should be classified as " Manuals of Sin."

Neither historical examples nor the cases recently completed in German Law Courts suffice to give a complete picture of the depravity of the Roman organisation, even though we strive to give publicity to individual cases which accidentally come to light.

The following passage appeared in the 31st issue for 1936:

German people ! Whenever you meet, in German streets or on German mountain peaks, the figure of the Cross, reflect that it is not Christ who hangs there. It is our people whom they have hung there; our people degraded to be slaves of the Asiatic-Semitic lust for power, slaves and playthings of a world-wide priestcraft. There hangs the soul of Germany! Look carefully; is it not a German face, German features? It is no son of the Jewish race, this Christ, but a true German such as you and I. That face cries out accusingly for a race which has once believed in the Cross and has itself been crucified for it. German citizens, be on your guard; this cross is falling. See that it is completely cast down, that German men once again may be strong and powerful and never again succumb to this disease! May the power of German life and joy, of German morals and faith reign once again on German ground! German mankind has arisen from the tomb, bearing still the marks of torture! Never allow them to be forgotten!

The cross must fall if Germany is to live!

Farther on the passage continues:

Our point of view stands in clear opposition to that of those who do homage to Asiatic conceptions of humility and self-degradation; to that of all those who gobble angrily in their benefices like swollen turkey-cocks, because German people feel no desire to let themselves be kneaded into shape with the aid of such a " wisdom." Now we realise well enough that our race was supplied in the past with the spiritual treasures of Moses, Paul, Marx and Rathenau in order that it might the more easily be dominated—a preliminary to that battlefield of robbery and exploitation with which the monstrous Weimar Government presented our people.

In the issue for November 19th, 1936, appeared the following verse:

> Citizens of Germany, beware!
> Citizens of Germany, take care!
> A Jewish race to fight against
> Our unity of Faith and Blood is sworn,
> Abetted by the power of Rome,
> Which laughs our noble German faith to scorn.
> German citizens, be brave nor ever retreat:
> We are shaking the German conscience out of its sleep.
> Our forefathers bid us take care,
> And of traitors from Rome to beware.

In the issue for January 28th, 1937, appeared the following passage:

In modern Germany thinking men no longer feel any need to reckon with Christianity. They simply give up their sect as one would give up an old and crumbling building, and return to their paternal home, casting no backward glance at a Sodom and Gomorrah cursed by God.... Their one wish is to be *free*, and to that end they break through Heaven and Hell with true German strength and tenacity. If any Church stands in the way, it is simply crushed. In this way our stolen primitive holiness, our freedom of faith and conscience, have been won back....

National Socialism caused the last prison walls to collapse and free the German soul. It was no collection of fanatics, devoid of political experience and subservient to Rome, such as peasant nature developed at the time of the Reformation, which grew up with National Socialism. Rather was it a group of men hardened by the horrors of the Great War, men whose minds were newly orientated by growing acquaintance with German thought and learning; and the orientation was not towards the East, but towards fundamental values inherent in our own blood and land. The final disappearance of the Church from the Reich can now only be a matter of time.

Here is another passage, from the issue of October 10th, 1936.

With the growth of National Socialist ideology there has come to life in the breasts of our leaders a new value, a new concept expressed in the words *Ewiges Deutschland* (Eternal Germany) !

The aim of their struggle, the content of their almost unconscious desire, can be found summed up in those two words. A dim intuition of a lost, buried world which must once have been theirs struggles upwards from the depths of consciousness, slowly imprinting on their hearts and minds the knowledge that a new " value " has been found, a value previously unknown in the history of the West. Eternal Germany ! The intuition grows less dim, becomes real knowledge, takes first place over all other knowledge, and rises like sunlight after a long night to welcome a joyful future in an era of our history almost devoid of true knowledge. Eternal Germany !—this knowledge of you is our new revelation, our new religion !

In this central point, whence flows the power of our race, lies our " supreme value," our " God." And now all painfully laboured philosophy and theology must collapse, for whoever has achieved this " race consciousness " has gained God.

Eternal Germany ! To this formula of our faith clings no odour of Christian decay; from it arises no pathological flight from reality, no rejection of life's foundations as Nature has laid them down.

Eternal Germany ! This supreme " value," this spiritual concept, the source of strength in the life of our soul, this tangible reality, this *fact*, is now creating a new conception of the universe, is heralding a new era.

> Why religion ?
> Why the Church ?
> You are all in all to us—
> Eternal Germany !

As soon as Teutonic man turns away from Christianity and hears the true God speaking to him in the mystery of his blood, as soon as he experiences Heaven and Earth, Time and Eternity, the Here and the Hereafter as a divine pattern contained within himself, as his forefathers once experienced these things, then has his salvation become a reality, then is all childish fear of the devil quenched, and German man has truly found himself in the fulness of his being, found his Paradise in the consciousness of his own purity and his own divine nature. Behind him he has left a land of horror overshadowed by the Cross, that sign of death, a land darkened by funeral pyres and troubled by religious strife. A new generation is growing up in which Catholicism and Protestantism, its younger brother, have no power to instil their poison and produce lifelong cripples; for their poison is more than neutralised by the powerful antidotes which the cleansing strength of our native earth and the experience of our comradeship in blood have provided.

In this connection the *Durchbruch* for September 2nd, 1937, may be quoted as containing attacks on original sin, Catholic theology and the Catholic Church, on the Christian view of private property, on the Holy Ghost, on Christ and the Immaculate Conception.

A similar paper, *Der Blitz*, strives to excel even the *Durchbruch*. The following passage appeared in its issue for January 19th, 1936.

After the political victory of National Socialism has been won, the final triumph will be gained in the ideological sphere. Daily experience teaches us that it is inevitable. Ultramontanism, Sectarianism and Talmud-ridden Judaism must, after their political defeat, receive a moral and ideological death-blow. The time for skirmishing is past; the whole front line is engaged and the decisive battle has begun. It is all or nothing. . . . The dogmatic Christianity of the Churches was the greatest misfortune which the long history of the Nordic race has had to bear, and a brief consideration of its "blessings" is enough to arouse horror in our minds. Without Judæo-Christianity it is inconceivable that the German race could have been thus betrayed and martyred. One could make an almost endless catalogue of the monstrous crimes which Christianity has committed in the name of its Founder. Terrible has been the moral destruction which this foreign, Christian-oriental teaching has created amongst Nordic peoples; and it is this same dogmatic Christianity which seeks today to turn all its forces against the newly-created German State. The times are indeed ripe for a decisive conflict. We do not merely accept the challenge, we seek it out and welcome it, for here no compromise is possible, here exists no possible bridge between Christianity and our racial ideals. . . . Thus, for example, the preservation of the mentally defective is, in the eyes of Catholic theologians, one of the most meritorious labours of Christian brotherly love, whereas in our view such a thing is no service to the race, but a dogmatic infamy perpetrated against the race. Only when dogmatic Christianity has been crushed shall we make rapid and easy progress towards the perfection of National Socialist ideology and become truly united !

On January 12th, 1936, the *Blitz* published the following:

The German people is no longer blinded by illusions as at the time of the Reformation. It has come to recognise not only Judaism, but Christianity too, as foreign to its genius. The cloud of Roman magic and superstition is dissolving.

The Roman Church prides itself on having, up to now, weathered all storms victoriously. Yet she was only victorious when treachery and dissension went hand in hand among the people as her allies. Now the soul of Germany has come into its own, and the clock cannot be put back. Rome must be overcome ! The Nordic giant braces himself and shakes off the fetters with which these sons of the South bound him. The star of Juda-Rome is sinking !

The following passage appeared in the *Blitz* for August 2nd, 1936:

The Franciscans may be taken as representative of Monasticism, and on that account we take it upon ourselves to speak to them. You monks have so exalted the unnatural as a law in place of nature, that nature has taken revenge on you, and *we* have to expiate the fact in the shape of those of our children who have fallen into your hands. You are only able to carry on with your monkery, in spite of all the harm you have done to the community, because you have managed to persuade people that mankind needs you as intermediaries with God, and that in spite of the fact that you have merely done the devil's work and prepared those who trusted you for Hell. No, neither God nor man has need of *you* that they may come together. We need only give ourselves, our hearts, to God, not our bodies to you ! You are nothing but an obstacle, and a very evil one ! You have taken on this work unasked; have fattened on it like petty commission agents; have made it your "vocation," though nobody has "called" you. You have made it a going concern, a trades union with branches throughout the country, haunts of the unnatural hidden behind walls and bars. You have done violence to nature and have in return become filthy and spreaders of filth beneath your "holy" habits. All these places must be destroyed in which men believe that they can only serve the Creator by dint of doing violence to His creation, places in which what is holy is degraded and what is pure is besmirched. Away with these un-Nordic, un-German places ! They have their origin in the East, where hot blood finds its standards only in the senses, where asceticism and mortification are practised as a remedy for degradation.

In other numbers of the *Blitz*, Nos. 38, 39, 40, for 1935, the following attacks on Christianity and the Church were made:

Two attacks on denominational schools,
Two articles calumniating the Jesuits,
Three articles insulting to the Papacy,
Three propaganda articles for the neo-pagan " German Faith Movement."

In these three numbers Catholic Faith and Catholic views were scoffed at at least ten times.

Die Stimme is an " Independent Popular Weekly," published in Berlin. In its issue for May 31st, 1936, it criticised sharply the " Sunday for the Sick " which the Pope had ordered for Whitsuntide. The paper published a vulgar cartoon entitled, " Can Faith make Whole ?" and the article ended thus: " We, as Germans, need healthy citizens in order to live as a race; and we need that type of ' health ' [N.B.—There is a play on words, *Gesundheit* and *Sündhaftigkeit*, healthiness and sinfulness], which takes a pagan joy in its physical ' sinfulness,' in order to do service to the life of the German people rather than to do homage to the suffering of a ' Saviour ' from the near East."

In its issue for August 2nd, 1936, the same paper published the following:

The Christian Churches find themselves unable to refrain from the vulgarity always evoked by the excitements of the Olympic Games, and an Evangelical Olympic Committee has actually been formed and has set up a Christian pavilion. This pavilion is meant to give some idea of the work done by various branches of the Christian Church. What is more, they hope that 2,000 people will be crowded into this tent, to be soft-soaped in an Olympic style. We are at a loss to understand how such an " Evangelical Olympic Board " ever came to be formed, and we should be glad to presume, for the sake of the good name of the German Olympia, 1936, that we have here something that really will go by the *board* !

Their Catholic colleagues, in their papers, are only slightly less emphatic in their insistence that the Olympic idea was always Christian. We can understand that easily enough if only we think of Jesus, as He went about preaching, as the first Long-Distance Walker.

After the *Stimme* had poured scorn on the Swiss competitors who attended Sunday Mass before winning their bobsleigh events at Garmisch-Partenkirchen, the article went on:

So, sportsmen of the world, Unite ! and, if you want to win, become Catholics ! It is only the Catholic javelin-thrower who overcomes his opponent; only a Catholic jump can outdistance poor heathens trammelled by Satan, etc. According to this recipe, we can only be sure of winning if, before every event, we have relays of Masses celebrated *à la* endless conveyor. It is enough to make anyone sick.

We could fill many pages with similar examples of malice. A large number of neo-pagan publications compete, as it were, with those already cited. The *Flammenzeichen*,[1] for example (a Stuttgart weekly), wrote on the occasion of a speech by the Bishop of Münster: " The mitre is no protection against stupidity and vulgarity." The

[1] No. 43, 1936.

whole number is characterised by attacks on Church, Pope, bishops, priests, etc. The leading article, for example, is headed " When will Rome show her True Colours ?" The paper considers that Rome has not yet spoken out clearly enough against Bolshevism: " Political Catholicism is still not far removed from Bolshevism, and Rome counts on Bolshevism." Other articles are entitled: " He's Going the Pace !" (concerning a priest who dared to collect money for the *Kindheit-Jesu-Verein* and to distribute missionary magazines); " Parson Kottmann Seeks for Martyrs "; " Church turned Cinema "; " Provocation in Grünmettstetten " (by the parish priest, of course !); " A Clerical Front-line is set up "; " Life must be hard !" (referring to the Catholic *Karitasverband*, which was reproached with making a little income for itself in a perfectly legitimate way out of Winter Relief Work takings). There were, in addition, some articles against the Jews.

From the *Reichswart*[1] a single quotation will suffice. The Catholic Church is described as a " heartless power-organisation caring nothing for the happiness or misery of whole nations and ruthlessly sacrificing the prosperity and good order of States to its own lust for power. . . ."

The reader will perceive that the " Down with God " movement of Bolshevism, even though National Socialism proclaims its eagerness to destroy it utterly, lives on sturdily in a thin disguise. The almost limitless range of expression afforded to this hatred of Christianity and of the Church in the press of the Third Reich could give even Bolshevism a stimulus to emulation.

Nevertheless, any Catholic periodical which so much as mentions the existence of a " Down with God " movement in Germany finds itself in trouble, and several Catholic papers have actually been confiscated for this " crime."

3. *The Campaign waged against the Church in Public Meetings*

Since 1935, when Catholics were forbidden to hold public meetings even for purely religious purposes, the German Faith Movement and similar organisations have been allowed to hold meetings frequently in public halls. Under National Socialism, just as during the " Free thought " period which succeeded the Great War, unfrocked priests have been allowed to vilify all that they once held sacred, and former members of religious Orders to wage war on the élite to which they once belonged. Propaganda agents of neo-paganism have joined forces with such people to calumniate the Church at public meetings, hoping to undermine the official standing of the Church's representatives by exposing carefully collected scandals.

At a training course sponsored by the German Faith Movement in Munich a lecture[2] was given entitled " Has Christianity Helped or Harmed the German People ?" The sole aim of this lecture was a gross calumniation of Christianity under a superficial disguise of historical exposition.

[1] May 1st, 1937. [2] February 24th, 1937.

In the same Movement's own hall in Munich a lecture[1] was given in which a newly-elected local organiser styled Christianity " Public Enemy No. 2." He sneered at the Catholic teaching about Hell, the Immaculate Conception, the Trinity, the Resurrection, etc., and coined the phrase " Christ's Ascension from the Olivet Aerodrome." To call Christ God was, he said, to defile God. We should be a disgrace to posterity were we still to adhere to Christianity in this era of Adolf Hitler. It must be a daily, constant task with us to bring Christianity to an end.

In the Mannheim *Ballhaus* the German Faith Movement held a meeting at which a speaker described " that world religion which calls itself Catholic " as satanic, dangerous, fraudulent. Christ was a Jewish reformer. The German Faith Movement acknowledges only one Lord, Adolf Hitler. One must be either Christian or German. Parsons are parasites and criminals. The Paradise of National Socialism is, warfare ! " We desire no Jewish Heaven with Halleluias and Hosannas." The Pope has nothing to offer, and still less has the Bible. The Führer is " the spiritual director of the whole nation."

These are a few examples of propaganda at meetings, for which National Socialism must take full responsibility. The orators of the German Faith Movement have always been allowed to act as though they had behind them the backing of responsible authorities in the Third Reich. Thus the handbills and notices advertising these gatherings were frequently adorned with the Swastika—*e.g.*, the bill announcing a German Faith Movement lecture,[2] " Christianity Sets the Pace for Bolshevism." At the meeting referred to above,[3] the " local organiser " was able to announce that the new meeting-room was open for the use of Nazi organisations and a desire was expressed for smooth co-operation with officials of the Party and of the State. In the case of the German Faith Movement the police winked at the decree forbidding public assemblies, and allowed plain cards to be issued on which any who wished could register their names. These cards were posted in thousands at the very same time that parochial authorities were forbidden to send even religious announcements to members of Catholic associations. Moreover, at meetings of the German Faith Movement, uniformed members of Nazi organisations constantly appeared. In Eichstätt,[4] for example, a priest named Münchmayer gave an address full of attacks on the Church: " The Church has failed . . . it's your income that counts with the clergy . . . look at your bishop decked in silk and velvet," etc. His hearers were almost all in uniform. Members of the Hitler Youth, aged from sixteen to twenty, applauded him wildly, and afterwards an organised demonstration was made in front of the residence of Fr. Kraus, the chief cleric of the Cathedral.

[1] March 3rd, 1937.
[3] In Munich.
[2] January 18th, 1937.
[4] March 1st, 1937.

CHAPTER V

ATTACKS ON THE CHURCH AND HER REPRESENTATIVES

THE war which National Socialism is waging against the Catholic Church is a *total* war. Every organ of power or means of influence belonging to the State or Party is exploited against the Church with uninterrupted thoroughness. The aim is to stifle all outward manifestations of the Church's life, and at the same time to inflict mortal injury on the principles vital to the Church, her hierarchical organisation and her doctrine.

In this total warfare, the Church's enemies shrink from no lie, misrepresentation, calumny or insinuation, no matter how mean and petty, wildly improbable or even untenable it may be. Thus the Church is reproached with being *anti-national*, and of having close associations with Bolshevism, world Jewry and Freemasonry, and history is distorted and falsified to lend support to the charge. It is alleged against the Church that she is *anti-social*, that she has " fabulous " riches at her disposal and possesses extensive landed property, and yet does not employ these resources for the general good of the nation. Both these reproaches are made with the obvious intention of suggesting that the Church is in opposition to modern tendencies and movements, and thus of representing her in the worst light possible to the eyes of the easily influenced masses. This succeeds all the more easily, because the Church is deprived of almost every possibility of defending herself against these attacks or of issuing public statements or corrections to stem the flood of falsehood and calumny. Meanwhile, the attack is pressed unceasingly, on the principle that " Constant dripping wears away a stone," and " If you throw enough mud, some of it is bound to stick." Out of the vast complexity of these attacks, we can deal here with only a few characteristic examples, some of which (*e.g.*, those immediately following) were employed only for a time, and have now been given up in favour of methods more suited to the later developments of the struggle.

1. *The Church is Anti-National*

National Socialism, till it found another policy more convenient, professed itself to be the sworn foe of Communism. Other enemies were the Jews and the Freemasons. To persuade men, therefore, that the Church was anti-national, it would be enough to make her out to be the friend of Germany's enemies. So according to the *Völkischer*

THE CHURCH IS ANTI-NATIONAL

Beobachter,[1] the " Catholic Congress " held in Prague on June 30th, 1935, was made the occasion for arranging a closer co-operation between Catholicism and Bolshevism, and on July 31st, 1935, the same paper announced that the Holy See was negotiating with Russia for a Concordat, news which the *Osservatore Romano* described on August 4th, 1935, as " a triumph of journalistic invention." Similarly the Hitler Youth magazine for January 25th, 1936, in a leading article headed " Crosier, Communist Commune, and Imperial Throne," asserted close co-operation between the Church and Bolshevism.

In the first section of the anti-Bolshevist Exhibition, held in Munich in 1936, a notice was to be seen: " Priests, too, unfortunately, fight under the Red Flag," an assertion made also in the *Völkischer Beobachter*.[2] The exhibition showed pictures of a priest working under Communism, a Fr. Kremers, of whom the episcopal authorities in Munich later stated that he had never had any relations either with individual Communists or with the Communist party, and that he had never expressed Communist opinions either publicly or privately.

The *Schwarze Korps*[3] wrote as follows in an article entitled " Dear Vatican, We Beg a Little Greater Indignation !"

For us Westerners it is difficult to understand the tolerance which Rome shows towards a Bolshevism which disseminates universal destruction from the Kremlin. . . . They march separately in order to strike down, together, the real enemy of their theories, National Socialism. . . . Catholic Action has never been more closely in line with Bolshevism than today. . . . It does not matter whether one is Indian, Hottentot or Anglo-Saxon so long as all acknowledge the Church of Rome; all are equal and equally worthy of Heaven, to which a democratically elected Pope claims the keys. . . .

Bolshevists may shoot priests ignominiously; they are, after all, only soldiers who must be sacrificed. As for posters depicting the Pope as a *souteneur*, a criminal, a ravisher of women, the Vatican merely smiles at them. . . .

(The article was illustrated with anti-papal propaganda pictures from Bolshevist sources.)

At the beginning of the Spanish Civil War the same paper[4] wrote as follows:

Today we see French and Czech aeroplanes raining bombs on the enemies of Bolshevism and the defenders of the Church. That is not an accident. Those who know of the links which bind Rome with Paris and Prague, and reach out to Moscow, will well understand the Vatican's reticence.

This assertion of a Vatican-Moscow pact may also be found in *Die Bewegung*,[5] the organ of the National Socialist Undergraduates' Union, under the title " Crusade against Moscow."

The *Schwarze Korps*[6] again, this time under the heading " Clerical Stabs in the Back," accuses the Church, because of its leanings towards a Bolshevist pact, of an ambiguous attitude towards Communism and political assistance to the Reds. Much is made of the peculiar circumstances of the Spanish war, in which a section of the Catholic

---

[1] July 14th, 1935, cited in *Die HJ*, January 25th, 1936, p. 1.
[2] No. 32, 1936.
[3] April 23rd, 1936.
[4] August 20th, 1936.
[5] October 21st, 1936.
[6] February 25th, 1937.

Basques, with political leanings towards Federalism, supported the Reds against the centralising aims of General Franco. From this fact the *Schwarze Korps* deduced that the Catholic Church must be incapable of genuine opposition to Communism; that a theoretical opposition might exist, while practical co-operation could take place at any time. " The Catholic standard of moral conduct is such that it can allow even priests and monks to fight on the side of Communism, as today in Spain." The article closes thus: " We cannot believe a word you utter about warfare on Bolshevism. . . . Such hypocrisy will not deceive us. We can see the facts, the reality, and we learn our lesson from them."[1]

In the *Schwarze Korps*,[2] Catholicism is identified also with Judaism, and later[3] the Church is accused of an alliance with Judaism and Marxism. In the *Angriff*[4] the question is asked, " Has the Vatican decided, in the light of this reasoning, to revise its curious alliance with Judaism ?" The same accusation of a Jewish alliance is repeated in the *Völkischer Beobachter*.[5]

That the whole history of the Papacy had been affected by the spirit of Judaism was insinuated, for example, in a list of " Jewish Popes," given in the *SA-Mann*.[6] A pamphlet, also, entitled " The Pope Prostrate before the Throne of the Dragon,"[7] let itself go in abuse of the Papacy—*e.g.*, " As with the devil, so with the Catholic Church; give him your little finger and he will take the whole hand." (This was not an original work, but a resuscitation of a pamphlet published at Briasson, near Paris, in 1739.)[8]

That the Church is allied also with Freemasonry is alleged—*e.g.*, by the *Angriff*.[9] Under the title " Cardinal and Master of Masonic Lodge," it wrote:

The whole world sees . . . what a terrible burden the policy of the Vatican, wantonly bound up with French Freemasonry, has imposed on the conscience of the Austrian Episcopate. . . .

In the autumn of 1933 appeared a pamphlet by Otto Helmut, " Our People in Danger. The Decline in the Birth-rate, and its Meaning for the Future of Germany."[10] In an appendix to this work Dr. Gütt, an official of the Ministry of the Interior, accused the Catholic Church of an anti-German attitude:

All " internationalism," whether Jewish or clerical, considers the ideal condition of any country to be a peace-loving intermingling of racial strains which knows nothing of Race or Fatherland or national Honour, a community which worships the golden calf by a life devoted to pleasure and personal

---

[1] The same accusation was repeated in *Das Schwarze Korps*, April 1st, 1937, in a leading article entitled " More Clerical Stabs in the Back." For the sake of completeness we record some other articles of the same kind in the same paper; April 8th, 1937, p. 8; April 15th, 1937, p. 7; April 22nd, 1937, p. 7; May 6th, 1937, p. 1 and cartoon 1 (*cf*. p. 64); June 24th, 1937, p. 2; January 6th, 1938, cartoons 2 and 3; May 19th, 1938, p. 2; *cf*. also the *SA-Mann*, February 19th, 1938, p. 4; the *Völk. Beobachter*, August 14th, 1938, an article entitled " St. Peter and the Star of Moscow."
[2] June 11th, 1936.   [3] October 29th, 1936.   [4] November 19th, 1937.
[5] March 17th, 1938.   [6] June 12th, 1936.   [7] P. 8.
[8] The same type of abuse may be found in *Die HJ*, June 13th, 1936, p. 11; *Schwarze Korps*, December 30th, 1937, *Wille und Macht*, February 1st, 1938, p. 10, etc.
[9] June 21st, 1938.   [10] Published by I. F. Lehmann, Munich.

prosperity, and which blindly digs its own suicide's grave. This wretched fate is in no way hindered by certain groups in the community which call themselves national, but in reality consider only the interest value of their capital; nor by those others who profess idealism and a belief in supernatural forces and cognate ideals, while in reality they merely exploit the people in the interests of their own selfish desire for supreme power. It matters little that these groups fight amongst themselves for the first place; on one point they are in full agreement—the uprooting of racial consciousness amongst the people. They care nothing for the physical or spiritual welfare of the people or for the happiness of future generations; they care solely for an international domination of which the foundations were laid centuries ago. With their outlook thus orientated, these groups despise all racial or national political views or theories which may lead, through internal purity and stability, to the higher development and improvement of any given race.

It is clear from the context that the writer refers exclusively to Judaism and the Catholic Church.

The *Schwarze Korps*[1] wrote in the same vein:

We are not surprised to find that representatives of political Catholicism have allowed their aims and forces to be subordinated to the criminal international ideals which inspire Jews and Marxists in their lust for murder, even though the co-operation may be comparatively recent; for they have indulged for many a decade Jewish-democratic and Marxist parties, breeding grounds of criminality. The Catholic press of foreign countries, under the patronage of the Pope, has continually emulated the efforts of the Marxist, Communist and Jewish press in spreading poisonous calumnies against the new Germany. The *Osservatore Romano* stands out as a leading example of such publications.

One wonders why responsible Catholic circles in Germany remain silent about this campaign of slander. . . .

Political Catholicism, which is willing to work together with Bolshevism, international Freemasonry and similar anti-German organisations, has come into line with the professed ideals of such international propaganda cliques, and, like them, aims at the death of its political opponents. . . .

In the history of Roman factions murder is, unhappily, by no means uncommon.

A *Schwarze Korps*[2] leading article, entitled "The Pope and Versailles," engaged to show that the papal attitude to Germany was hostile, by proving that the Pope was partly responsible for the Treaty of Versailles. The value of this demonstration may be gauged from the following sentence: " The Pope gave his blessing to the initial stages of the peace moves, and was therefore responsible for their outcome." In its issue for December 30th, 1937, the same paper described the papal Encyclical *Mit brennender Sorge* as a propaganda pamphlet against Germany.

In its issue for October 15th, 1936, the same paper indicated Catholic action as the political weapon selected for the destruction of National Socialism, and on other occasions[3] attacked the Church for its rejection of National Socialist racial teaching.

On November 17th, 1938, it published a full-page attack on the Catholic Church. It asserted, for example, that the intention of

[1] May 21st, 1936.
[2] January 23rd, 1936; *cf.* also the same paper, September 15th, 1938, p. 16; January 26th, 1939, p. 2.
[3] February 4th, 1937; August 4th, 1938.

politically-minded Catholic clerics " to lead the faithful into a spiritual, cultural and ideological ' splendid isolation ' " had been repeatedly demonstrated.

From the Pope, who by proclaiming " a universal Catholic race " typifies his denial of the divinely-willed existence of independent races, down to the smallest propaganda parson proclaiming to half-witted old women the earthly " leadership " of Christ, Catholics seek to build their own type of world—a lonely island, a noxious foreign body in the midst of the German people.

The Church was abused for its attitude to racial questions also by Dr. Wagner, Leader of German doctors, at the Nürnberg *Parteitag*, 1935, and by the *Schwarze Korps*.[1] On November 12th, 1938, the *Angriff* stigmatised the Vatican as " Legal Defender of Racial Pollution," and the *Schwarze Korps*, on November 24th, 1938, ridiculed Pius XI's " ignorance of racial questions."

The *Schwarze Korps* for February 9th, 1939, dealt with the enormous sums devoted by the National Socialist State to ecclesiastical purposes. The article concluded:

" Nothing shows up better the utter corruptness of these clerical apostles of propaganda ! They quietly allow themselves to be maintained by a State to which they wish nothing but evil, in order the better to calumniate it. . . . The Churches act well enough as cash-counters over which the German State may pay, while responsible clerical leaders inveigh against it or remain silent when foreign enemies of Germany agitate against ' Godless Germany.' " The article then threatens separation of Church and State as a solution. " This state of affairs must end, for one cannot be expected to swell perpetually the propaganda funds of the very person who slanders one's good name and seeks to end one's very life." The article describes clearly enough the nature of such a separation—viz., a subordination of the Church to the State and an enforced approximation to a Germanic code of moral conduct. " Then could no Church be a State within the State, such as has existed in the past, a group possessing its own schools and other organisations unconnected with purely religious purposes. . . . The Churches would be allowed to exist only so long as they did nothing to impair the welfare of the State, or to undermine the moral sensibilities of the German race. . . . Positive Christianity must not be embodied in traditional types of sectarian organisations, but must show itself in the readiness of individuals or of religious communities to preserve and harmonise with the supreme community of the race."

The *Mainfränkische Zeitung*[2] wrote under the heading " To Us, German Children are More Vital " against financial support given to the Holy See by German Catholics—Peter's Pence, etc.

From 1916 to 1918—*i.e.*, during the hardest of the war years—when Germany knew hunger and emaciation, German Catholics paid twenty million marks into the Roman banking account, as if making up for the diminished generosity of France, Belgium, the U.S.A., etc. Amongst those who conducted this transfer we may cite Matthias Erzberger, who stated in a circular that German Catholics should regard it as a duty and an honour to save the financial independence of the Roman See.

Twenty million marks were sacrificed; and in gratitude the Holy See proclaims the Treaty of Versailles to be a device for maintaining peace in

---
[1] August 11th, 1938; September 15th, 1938.   [2] August 25th, 1937.

the world ! Will people ever learn that, while National Socialism and the Third Reich are constantly inveighed against from the pulpits, the pulpits have to thank National Socialism for the privilege of remaining open to preachers. Had the Storm Troopers whom they curse never existed, the Bolshevists would no doubt have spoken as mockingly of " freedom of religion " over the ruins of German churches as they have done in Red Spain.

That financial contribution to the " Roman bank " during Germany's hardest war years was high treason !

Despite all the solemn promises and assurances for the preservation of Catholicism and its activities given in the Reich Concordat, National Socialism soon began to find it an impediment to its complete domination of the German nation. The Concordat, therefore, was " anti-national " and the German people must be brought to see it. So began a long series of attacks on it in periodicals of all kinds. Here are some examples.

The *Schwarze Korps*,[1] under the heading " What must we think of the Concordat ?" wrote:

" A long series of Concordat agreements have fallen into decay. . . . New agreements cannot hope to be maintained for long . . ." and the writer asks: " Is a Concordat really expedient in view of modern conditions in Germany ? . . . The question arises, Should the Concordat be rescinded ?"

More openly the *SA-Mann*[2] stigmatised the Concordat as Pacelli's chosen instrument for waging war on National Socialism, and the *Berliner Tageblatt*[3] similarly described it as a means chosen to serve the Church's lust for power. The *Durchbruch*[4] renamed the Concordat " Treaty of Disgrace with the Vatican."

An official propaganda monthly, *Unser Wille und Weg*,[5] posed the question, " Is a Concordat opportune in the spiritual and ideological atmosphere of the new Germany ?" Similarly the official *NS Monatshefte*[6] explained " that the Reich Concordat in its legal aspect was not proposed from the side of National Socialism, but, at least so far as many of its provisions are concerned, was conceived in a spiritual atmosphere both previous and foreign to that of our times." The article ended:

Values and ideas native to the Weimar constitution live on in the Reich Concordat and in the sphere of ecclesiastical politics, whereas in all other spheres of public life since 1933 a fundamental alteration of national conceptions has taken place and both national law and domestic politics have developed by leaps and bounds. The clerical partner in the Concordat, hampered by excessively formalistic legal conceptions, can scarcely comprehend developments in Germany, and imagines that it can stand firm on the narrow ground of clerical politics or the bygone conditions of the Weimar era.

Hence it is that we hear of " breaches of faith " on the part of the secular partner, when the root of the matter is to be found in a tension which inevitably arises between a party whose whole mental outlook is grounded in the static conditions of a former age and a party vitally interested in the

[1] February 17th, 1938. [2] November 20th, 1937. [3] June 20th, 1937.
[4] September 9th, 1937. [5] No. 9, September 1938. [6] No. 107 1939.

dynamic conditions attached to a living, present development pregnant with tasks and problems for the future. This tension will last so long as a Reich Concordat, which is a feeble reflection of the Weimar constitution, is allowed to remain as a petrifying element in the stream of time.

A different type of periodical, the *Zeitschrift der Akademie für deutsches Recht*,[1] published an essay by Professor Dr. W. Weber, entitled " The Reich Concordat in the Light of the Development of German Law," and in it developed the strange view that the official Concordat had, as it were, shrivelled up with the appearance of National Socialist State law, since the Concordat conformed too closely to the concept of law current under the Weimar constitution.

Under the title " The Programme of the Party and the Concordat with the Reich " a long essay was published by A. Richter, a high Government official, in *Deutschlands Erneuerung*[2] (a monthly journal), in the course of which he stated:

> The Concordat is only valid in so far as it does not oppose the inner development of our people and the decrees of the National Socialist State.

This last quotation sums up fairly the National Socialist attitude and explains all the opposition to the just implementation of the provisions of the solemnly enacted, bilateral agreement between two sovereign States—the Concordat.

Attacks based on the history of the Church constitute another favourite means of representing Catholicism as alien and anti-German. Speeches at meetings and articles in the Party Press, drawn from avowedly anti-Catholic and usually unscholarly sources, serve up time and time again every unsavoury episode of the Church's history and also countless fancies that never found a place there. No attempt is made to sift the evidence or to give an objective account of the facts, and the long catalogue of the Church's great achievements and her benefits to mankind are passed over in silence or even changed into the exact opposite. From the vast range of such examples we have chosen a few.

In December, 1935, Professor Baümler addressed the National Socialist Teachers' Union in Berlin in the following way:

> The unedifying struggle between Popes and Emperors, the wars of religion, and the attempted domination of the Catholic priesthood appear to be essential features of the Middle Ages. Only with the rise to power of Adolf Hitler has Germany been able to free herself from the spirit of Rome and to inaugurate a new era in her history. One can only consider Mediævalism as conquered and ended from the moment that a radical change took place in the relations between Christianity and the Nordic, Germanic race. What used to be called " modern times " was merely a continuation of the Middle Ages.

On April 23rd, 1936, the *Schwarze Korps* published a cartoon of " Pope Joan," with explanatory script which not only wholly ignored the fact that the fable has long been rejected by all serious historians, but added, " Political Catholicism remains silent about this !"

[1] No. 15, August 1st, 1938.   [2] No. 8, 1936, p. 464.

On November 26th, 1936, the same paper set forth a false account of the medieval relationship between Christianity and the Empire, it grossly misrepresented the history of the Papacy in its issue for December 17th, 1936, and later[1] selected Alexander VI as typical of the depravity common amongst the Popes. Later still,[2] it attacked the labours of the Papacy for civilisation in past centuries; on May 6th, 1937, it wrote against political Catholicism as depicted in history, and on May 27th, 1937, it published an article and a cartoon against clerical lasciviousness. The *SA-Mann*,[3] quoted and generalised cases of immorality taken from the history of the Papacy; and on November 13th, 1937, represented the 1855 Concordat between the Vatican and Austria as an attempt on the part of the Papacy to gain domination over Austria. History has been similarly used as an armoury against the Church by the Nazi Teachers' periodical, *Bewegung und Staat*.[4]

As for the warped and tendentious accounts of historical events put forward against Christianity by Alfred Rosenberg, we shall be content merely to mention their existence.[5]

2. *The Church is Anti-Social*

In its issue of March 17th, 1938, the *Schwarze Korps*, in an article with the title " Can Heaven be Bought ?" delivered a violent attack on the " crass materialism which underlies the teaching of Rome ":

Can we hope to reconcile the incalculable riches of Rome, her immense estates scattered throughout the world, her heaped-up gold, silver and precious stones, her papal and episcopal palaces, the huge incomes of her religious Orders—can we reconcile such things with the example of Christ, who said He had not where to lay His head ? How reconcile clerical love of power, all the bloodshed of centuries of fanaticism, with that love which is the essence of Christ's teaching ? Or, again, how reconcile oriental ceremonial, all the kissing of hands and feet, the display of incense, of gold and silver, and silk of every colour for different church ranks, the receptions, banquets and rich honours—honours even for those who prepared the way for Communist atheism—with the words of Christ, " I am a worm and no man "?

Similarly the ever-shifting game of diplomacy carried on with the great ones of this world squares ill with the life of one who sat at table with publicans and cursed the mighty as a brood of vipers ! How can we explain away the fact that Renaissance Popes rewarded their officials with entrance tickets to brothels, in the light of the teaching of another Pope that a pure life (*i.e.*, according to their teaching, abstention from women) is the highest stage of perfection ?

Under the heading " The Chink of Money-Boxes " the *Schwarze Korps* continues:

The more the agents of the Vatican strive to vindicate their system, the more they experience the meaning of the ancient tag, *Mundus vult decipi* ! The secret motive of their conduct is becoming steadily clearer to a race arousing itself from torpor, the inner materialism on which Catholic teaching, by reason of its origins, is based !

Paul, that oriental carpet-maker, understood clearly that in order to

---
[1] January 21st, 1937.   [2] April 9th, 1937.   [3] June 26th, 1937.
[4] *E.g.*, September 11th, 1938; September 18th, 1938; October 16th, 1938; October 30th, 1938.
[5] *Cf. Völk. Beobachter*, April 27th, 1939.

enslave a man one should employ the potent weapons of mental and moral bondage. To this end he had to evolve a system in which this tendency was carefully concealed; hence his sharp division of the cosmos into two sections, one a world of sin, the other the life to come, a wholly unknown but wholly desirable world . . . hence, too, the assertion of corruption latent in all things of this world, and more especially in man—the assertion of original sin, of a radical sinfulness, leading to the necessity of a Saviour whose death should expiate sin and whose sacrifice should be perpetually renewed in a bloodless manner in the sacrifice of the Mass. From this followed the magical power of the priesthood to bring God down to earth under the forms of bread and wine, the notion of grace in the sense of an arbitrary choice of the elect, the distribution of the means of grace by the priesthood in the shape of sacraments; and, finally, the conception of a judgement not of this world, which men can avoid by means of " good works "—*i.e.*, in practice by paying for indulgences, by heavy stole fees and contributions to Church extension lotteries—and by an unconditional surrender to priestly power as the sole channel of grace.

The *Völkischer Beobachter*[1] drew the contrast " Rich Churches—Poor People."

Millions of marks lie hoarded in the vaults of churches and monasteries. On the one hand we see these millions of " dead " capital—jewellery, monastery buildings, palaces, estates and other lucrative sources of income; and, on the other hand, in every diocese of the Church we meet thousands of poor wretches who know the meaning of hunger and cold and get no relief from Churches and parsons. Some relief, perhaps ! Yes, a little praying and begging—prayer to the pity of the Saints in celestial bliss, and begging which plays on the pity of poor unsanctified men with the promise of bliss to come. . . . Meanwhile these earthly agents who guard divine riches live in splendid palaces and draw rich revenues from their business dealings. . . .

Thoughts such as these are stimulated nowadays by the sight of street collections for the Winter Relief Work, a national charity to which all, even the poorest, give freely what they can to fulfil their duty towards the poor and to relieve them during the coming winter. In this way the German people obey Christ's precept: " Feed the hungry, clothe the naked," etc. Think how much more such help could be given if those who preach this also practised it ! Think of the rich resources at their disposal !

In its issue of December 9th, 1937, the *Schwarze Korps* developed the thesis that Church property belonged, not to the Church, but to the German people, and on November 17th, 1938, demanded its confiscation:

If clerical property owners retain their liberalistic commercial tendencies, if they feel themselves under no obligation to the people, if they withhold large areas of German land from cultivation merely in virtue of their ownership or because circumstances make them independent of labour, then they are depriving the German people of part of their economic resources. . . . We cannot endure this selfish isolation of German land by the Church; let it restrict its selfishness to the next world !

The *Schwarze Korps* would like to see this " State within the State "[2] confiscated for the benefit of the German nation. To this end the economic and moral conditions prevalent in Catholic monasteries and convents are painted in the blackest colours, and headlines such as

[1] October 16th, 1938.   [2] *Cf.* p. 418.

" Conditions which cry to Heaven for Vengeance," " Robbery and Rape," " Unspeakable Filth," etc., are freely employed. The paper concludes its suggestions thus:

If these examples are not convincing, others are still forthcoming. In general they all point to this fact—a morally corrupt and treasonable clerical set, indifferent to the welfare of the nation, is neither willing nor able to exploit profitably or to administer German resources. If its property is confiscated, it merely gives up something to which it has no colourable claim. What pious donors have given was received to be used for the nation's welfare, not for its destruction, and still less for the maintenance of an unchristian life of unbridled luxury. Such a " State within the State " must no longer exist in Germany.

The *Schwarze Korps*[1] argued on the same lines, that the maintenance of the Church should be the responsibility of its members, and demanded that all State assistance should be withdrawn. Aid given to parishes and all State bounties to the Church should cease.[2] In an April issue[3] it was stated:

Times have changed. Now that the respective spheres of Church and State are clearly understood, the former can claim no aid as of right from the latter, just as the State never dreams of claiming financial aid from the Church. In this connection we will quote the judgement of the courts given in the Arnsberg case: " Claims made by parish authorities who do not see eye to eye with the State should be quashed in the courts, since there is no danger of total collapse in such cases, a collapse which might follow were State aid in general to be withdrawn from the Church."

On May 21st, 1939, the *Völkischer Beobachter* announced the confiscation of estates belonging to a religious house at Klosterneuburg under the headline " Monastic Property for Vienna Mothers." The report stated:

To a Catholic religious community at Klosterneuburg was entrusted a lease which now, thanks to the intervention of the Party, benefits mothers in Vienna. Nothing " Christian " was done with the proceeds of that lease by a Church which preaches, as one of God's commandments, that mothers should be honoured. " Honour thy father and thy mother, that thou mayst be long-lived upon the land " runs the fourth commandment, the only one of the ten which promises an earthly reward from the divine gratitude. The very people who preached that command held it cheap themselves and thought only of their own welfare on earth. . . .

3. *Attacks on the Church's Representatives*

The Papacy, of course, is a target for constant attacks, and Pope Pius XI, on account of his intrepid defence of the persecuted German Catholics, was subjected to a torrent of odious vilifications and calumnies, without any consideration being given to his position as an independent sovereign.

According to the *SA-Mann*,[4] for example, Pope Pius was of Jewish birth.

Pope Pius's name was Achille Ratti; and, as a Redemptorist Father once said to a reader of our paper, Achille Ratti is of Jewish descent. At the

---

[1] March 16th, 1939. [2] February 2nd, 1939; April 6th, 1939.
[3] April 6th, 1939.   [4] September 9th, 1938.

same time (1935) the periodical *Judenkenner* pointed out that Achille Ratti was half-Jew; and, strange to say, an English paper, *The Fascist*, being asked by a high Italian authority to investigate this statement, reported from Italy that various documents relating to the Pope's genealogy had been destroyed to save his face. . . .

This assertion, which was made public not only in the Nazi press but also at training courses, meetings, etc., sponsored by the Party, was refuted in April, 1936, by an official episcopal declaration issued from Paderborn.

Pius XI's ancestors for many generations back were peasants. His father, Francesco Ratti, was a peasant who later became a worker in a textile factory. Industry and prudence helped him till he became a director and partner in the Galli textile factory in Fertusella. The Pope's mother was a member of the Galli family, and Pius XI, the fourth son of her marriage to Francesco Ratti, was born at Desio in the province of Milan and immediately christened Ambrosio Demiano Achille. His genealogical papers are wholly irreproachable.

Under the heading " The Pope Instructs the Newly Married," the *Schwarze Korps*[1] sneered at the *Catholic Church Magazine of the Münster Diocese* for reproducing the Papal Encyclical on marriage.

" What a lot is expected and demanded from the Holy Father ! He must even know all that is required for the holy state of matrimony—knowledge for which celibacy seems to us an unsuitable preparation." . . .

Some quotations of the Encyclical follow, and the article proceeds:

" These assertions need no commentary. They illustrate what we have often pointed out, and throw light on the diminishing birth-rate amongst ' good ' Catholic families. They prove the Holy Father to be unsuitable as a teacher on matrimonial questions. We hope that nobody will accuse us of lack of reverence towards the great Roman sovereign, for we here refer to him solely as a teacher on marriage, in which capacity we consider him incompetent, and not a ' sovereign.' "

In the issue for May, 1937, of Baldur von Schirach's periodical, *Wille und Macht*, appeared an article entitled " The Protestant Cecilia and the Catholic Pius," which opens as follows:

It was indeed no joyful Easter message that the ancient representative of Christ sent to the Third Reich a few weeks ago in his Encyclical. The national and racial formulas of the Reich do not square altogether with the dogmas of the Catholic Church, and this sickly wearer of the mitre went so far as to address his holy letter " even," as he said " to prison cells and Concentration Camps in gratitude to those there suffering for loyalty to the Church, and with the assurance of his fatherly recognition." We mention this matter not because we consider that any fruitful discussion can arise from a consideration of something which is most certainly the affair of the people and the State alone, but in order to depict, in the light of these choice, spring buds from the Vatican garden, the sort of atmosphere in which the Protestant Crown Princess of Prussia lately paid her respects to the Pope.

(N.B.—This " crime " was committed by the former Crown Princess Cäcilie, who attended the Pope's Easter Mass in St. Peter's.)

[1] February 11th, 1937.

ATTACKS ON THE CHURCH'S REPRESENTATIVES 425

The *Schwarze Korps*[1] accused Pius XI of lying. In a leading article under the heading " Holy Father ' Objectively ' Untruthful," exception was taken to a papal address of May 19th, 1937, in which the Pope referred to the existence of " a bitter and wicked war made on religious conscience, on God and divine Faith." The article stated:

> We shall be tireless in making the truth known to the " faithful," a truth which their " Holy Father " unhappily hides from them. Let them call us enemies of the Church because we protect our countrymen against criminals in clerical dress. We will risk being dubbed enemies of Christianity for showing up the utter corruption of an international gang which is for ever prating of another world in order to mask its aims in this. We are content to leave the question undecided, whether the old " Father " indulges in " objective " untruth because his flock and its official shepherds have deceived him, or because he wishes to ratify the lies uttered by his dependents from their pulpits as a weapon in his fight against the National Socialist Government.
>
> Truth has always proved the best device, better than any argument trumped up to hide one's tracks. And truth is on our side in spite of the " Holy Father's " assertions to the contrary.

On June 12th, 1937, the *Völkischer Beobachter* sneered at the Pope's " tearful voice," " his tear ducts moved to action by the false, lying accounts of pious pilgrims."

On the grounds of his Encyclical *Mit brennender Sorge* and his address to pilgrims at Castel Gandolfo, the *Schwarze Korps*[2] accused the Pope of meddling in politics; and about a month later,[3] under the headline " The Liars," accused him of lying.

In a leading article entitled " The Puppets of Pius XI " published in the *Angriff*,[4] an address by the Pope to members of an international Archæological Congress[5] was attacked.

> It was formerly typical of Papal methods of warfare to discredit so-called enemies of the Church by means of distorted historical descriptions and comparisons. The puppet shows of Roman prelates are richly supplied with characters with which to present little historical fictions, edifying their audiences with saints and heretics.
>
> One of the puppet villains which gives a thrill of horror to these grown-up children represents the Roman Emperor Julian, a descendant of Constantine the Great.

The *Angriff* went on to describe Julian the Apostate as a tolerant ruler and praised his anti-clerical edicts. The article went on:

> " We have briefly sketched the history of the Emperor Julian because Pius XI has recently included him amongst his puppets. In his above-mentioned address to scholars gathered together in the interests of archæology the Pope was pleased to compare what he called the restriction of the Catholic Church's activities by the Third Reich with the ' bloodless but not less terrible persecution of Christianity ' by the Emperor Julian.' . . . The Roman Curia would like Germany to be seen only through the historical distorting-mirror of the Roman puppet theatre. The Vatican will stop at nothing to prevent the world knowing the plain truth." St. Ambrose was also dealt with in passing as a half-wit who merely plagiarised and adapted to Christian tastes the teaching on duty of the pagan Cicero. " Today, for lack of any personal views on politics and philosophy, St. Ambrose

[1] May 27th, 1937. [2] May 19th, 1938. [3] June 10th, 1938.
[4] October 27th, 1938. [5] *Cf.* p. 11.

would probably steal his thunder from the political ideology of Fascism or of National Socialist racial doctrines—unless, indeed, the Popes had managed to evolve other political notions and formulas from the various ideologies worked out during the intervening centuries.

The article concluded:

Our quarrel is neither with Christianity nor with the Church, but with the latter's arrogance, an arrogance which dates from the time of Constantine the Great, who used the Church as a political tool and gave it official privileges. Above all, our quarrel is with the political betrayal of the nation's unity for the sake of the Church's private ends. It is a fact that the Catholic hierarchy has always and consistently stood in the way of German unity.

Let the Pope play as much as he likes with his historical puppets, with Julian the Apostate or even with Nero. That has nothing to do with us. He will not succeed in sabotaging the unity of the German nation or in weakening its power of resistance by means of hostile encirclement.

This same address gave offence also to the *Schwarze Korps*,[1] which a little later[2] accused the Pope of differing radically in his attitude to the Jewish question from the Gospels, the Fathers of the Church and the Councils:

This " senile champion " of " a Catholic universal race " has nothing better to offer them than a manifestation of old age.

Vatican policy at one time had the reputation of being extremely astute. It was famous for its great sensitiveness to spiritual and intellectual developments and for realising their future importance. Its skill in adapting itself to contemporary movements was once regarded as unsurpassable. Once! In those days Vatican politics were directed by young men. Today these are lacking. At the Vatican old men, sometimes extremely old men, think that they can influence world politics, and nothing will convince them of their error. . . . The Vatican well illustrates a saying of Alfred Rosenberg: " Many old people hold so fast to traditions and customs dating from before 1914 that the sight of our modern world disconcerts them." Thus the ancient fathers of the Vatican do not understand the signs of the times, which demand a radical and thorough-going solution of the Jewish problem. By means of radio and press they set themselves against a development which is merely fulfilling the demands of the early Christian Church. It has come about that all those who really put their hearts into the solution of the Jewish problem are better Catholics than His Holiness and all his underlings. . . .

This same *Schwarze Korps*[3] excelled itself in insults against the aged Pope in a poem published under the title " The Chief Rabbi of all Christians." This effort sneered at the " Firm of Juda-Rome " and the labours of the old " Chief Rabbi " to judaise his flock of mingled nationalities and colours.

> Go bury the delusive hope
> About His Holiness the Pope.
> For all he knows concerning Race
> Would get a schoolboy in disgrace.
> Old, muddled-headed, doddering, ill,
> His knowledge is precisely nil.

[1] November 3rd, 1938, p. 16. [2] November 24th, 1938.
[3] January 19th, 1939.

And, gone in years, he can but keep
His motley flock of piebald sheep;
Since he regards both Blacks and Whites
As children all with equal rights,
As Christians all (whate'er their hues),
They're " spiritually " nought but Jews.
The Vatican (e'en blockheads know)
With verdigris is covered so,
And wants, no doubt, the faithful band
Of Christians who around it stand—
As far as " ghostly welfare " goes—
To lead 'em by the (hooked) nose.
A pretty picture all men know—
The firm of " Juda-Rome and Co."
An " Old Man " e'er can tell the tale
And, sure, his pity will not fail.
The banner is at last unfurled:
" Chief Rabbi of the Christian world."

Even after the Pope's death, the *Schwarze Korps* went on with similar attacks[1] and with accusations of his having waged a political campaign against Germany,[2] even in the mocking obituary notice[3] it dedicated to him.

The most intimate collaborator of Pope Pius XI, Cardinal Pacelli, now *Pope Pius XII*, is attacked wtih the same implacable hatred. During the last few years, when he was Secretary of State,[4] the Nazi press has indulged in vulgar cartoons against him. In the summer of 1937 all Nazi organs read a political meaning into his visit to France for the consecration of the Basilica of Lisieux, and waxed indignant over his alleged attempt to favour a " moral encirclement " of Germany. The way in which his election to the Papacy was welcomed may be judged from the *Schwarze Korps* for March 9th, 1939.

On the occasion of the last Conclave, the *Angriff*[5] published a report from its Roman correspondent about the Sacred College. This article, entitled " Cardinals on Parade," tried to assume an ironical and sarcastic tone, but in reality only achieved a criticism of the Princes of the Church in the language of a guttersnipe. Describing the procession of Cardinals going to pay their last respects to the dead Pope, the correspondent wrote as follows:

First came a solemn, aristocratic old man, Cardinal Granito di Belmonte, and then Ascalesi of Naples . . . then Faulhaber, strong as a butcher, much stared at by all who wish to damage the Third Reich. (He will help the French and tell the Italians, " You must elect Pacelli "). . . . Then come two more—first the tiny Spaniard, Vidal of Tarragona, who knows well who saved his bishopric for him from the hands of the Reds; then Dougherty of Philadelphia, who measures about 6 feet round by 5 feet 2 inches high. What must the graceful Mikado have thought when this giant visited him in February, 1936, as bearer of the Pope's greetings ? . . .

[1] February 23rd, 1939; *cf.* also a satirical poem of January 12th, 1939, and issue of January 26th, 1939. [2] February 16th, 1939. [3] February 23rd, 1939.
[4] *E.g., Schwarze Korps*, June 10th, 1937, p. 1; *Brennessel*, August 3rd, 1937, *cf.* p. 279.
[5] February 23rd, 1939.

Next to him, an imposing and stately matron with a nose like a radish, walked Cardinal Mundelein," King George," the ruler of millions in Chicago and the intimate friend of President Roosevelt. The Romans paid no attention to him. Yet if only they knew of his fatal influence in the Conclave ! The final new Papal buildings on the Gianicolo were his work. From " King George," moreover, they will learn when the American fleet will join forces with the British and French in the Mediterranean, and how many planes President Roosevelt will send to his dear friends in London and Paris, and how all this favours the Church. . . .

Next came Van Roey, the Belgian, who thunders against all national movements in his own country and seeks to perpetuate the union of Catholics with Liberals and Marxists, a man who adheres to the French and is certain to vote for Pacelli. Then Hlond of Poland, who would be elected Pope if only he were not a Pole. He loved Schuschnigg and hated the Germans, a man who joined in the Cardinals' song of hate against " Racism." He would gladly march against Moscow and dedicate a rescued Russia to the " Sacred Heart of Jesus."

After these came two dressed in black, Benedictine Cardinals. The one, Seredi of Hungary, who is for ever casting furtive glances to right and left to see if enough attention is being paid to him; the other—ah, for him the crowd surges and whispers excitedly, " Look, Schuster of Milan, a *papabile*; he has a good chance of the Papacy." A gaunt little man with the face of an ascetic, whose lips murmur prayers behind his stiffly folded hands. It that is not a Saint, all holy pictures are worthless ! That is the man who used to frighten his hearers from his pulpit in Milan with threats of invasion by northern barbarians, and whose Catholic Action organisation attracted the attention of the police. And then Pacelli, THE Cardinal, murmuring prayers, his eyes cast down, and gracefully picking his steps. . . . Then Cardinals of the *Curia*, many of them so old and deformed that you would think that under those clothes they were all old women. . . .

Next, Innitzer, who always looks tearful here. Then little dalla Costa of Florence, with a pale " Saint's " face and the eyes of a fanatical dreamer. He, too, is praying, and one can well believe that he really fears the tiara which all who desire a *papa santo* would like to impose on him. Then Marmaggi, a former Nuntio in Poland, who knows the East well and who also awaits the hour of deliverance from Moscow. . . . Then Kaspar of Prague, who smiles as prettily as ever, as if he had never lost his friend and master, Benes. . . .

The Cardinals gathered together in Rome for the election of a new Pope were described by the *Schwarze Korps*[1] as a " Meeting of Crown Princes."

Clerical papers inform us that the business of electing a new Pope to the See of Peter does not afford the Cardinal electors any opportunities of indulging in unwonted pleasures. Articles and pictures describe skilled tailors employed in making clothes for the new Holy Father, and show us the sleeping quarters whither the Cardinals may retire, after the strain of electioneering, to seek a comfortless renewal of strength on humble beds. Comfort is represented only by a soft, upholstered prie-dieu, and by a variety of artistic exhibits.

Other pictures show us the humble, wooden tables provided for the Cardinals' meals, and do not omit to include the modest amenities of the kitchen, amenities which are not calculated to foster undue luxury. If, indeed, the sessions prove negative and black smoke pours forth from the chimney to signify the fact, it is in accordance with ancient custom that the food should become more restricted and the beds more uncomfortable. It is clear that the inventor of this device knew his comfort-loving electors well ! They all love high living, and would regard it as tactless in the highest

[1] March 2nd, 1939.

ATTACKS ON THE CHURCH'S REPRESENTATIVES 429

degree should any of the competitors cause immoderate delay. We do not in the least intend to indulge in criticism of these intimate circumstances. We are not really interested to know whether they fulfil their duties with the aid of ordinary food or order in a little manna for the purpose; whether they aim at giving an impression of Spartan endurance, while actually shortening their days in an atmosphere of Grecian luxury, . . . whether they repose on swelling cushions or pillows of iron. We are concerned with but one thing—the man who, as the new Pope, will scatter his blessings. Is it to be a true shepherd of souls or a clerical politician? We have not long to wait; soon the white smoke will go out from the Vatican flues as a sign that the choir of Cardinals has sung *Papam habemus* (" We have a Pope!").

Coinciding with the Papal election, the *Angriff* published its serial feature " The Men who Surround the Pope " as a pamphlet, and sold more than 100,000 copies. The frontispiece shows the present Pope, Pius XII, stretching out his hand for the Fisherman's ring to be kissed. The pamphlet itself consists of a mass of insinuations and insulting attacks against clerical dignitaries.

The Nazi campaign of vilification embraces all ranks of the Church's hierarchy. Non-German **bishops** are insulted and attacked when they rise in defence of their brethren in the Faith of the Third Reich, but the brunt of the attack is naturally borne by the German Episcopate, as we have repeatedly seen already in the course of this book.

In 1935 a Nazi political magazine, the *Deutsche Volkskirche*,[1] published by Dr. Dinter, described the Episcopal Conference at Fulda for 1935 as " a devilish beginning," " treasonable activities," " these Jewish-Roman Jehovah priests," etc. The following passage is worthy of note:

We choose one incident as truly typical of events at Fulda. According to the press here and abroad, Cardinal Prince-Bishop Bertram performed the following ceremony. With a supposed bone of the supposedly holy Boniface he touched each bishop on the forehead and exhorted each to imitate that first German bishop by offering his life for his Faith. The sole object of this ceremonial mischief perpetrated at the grave of that servant of Rome in Fulda was to arouse the greatest possible fanatical resistance to the National Socialist State amongst the clergy. All accommodation between the Roman Church and National Socialism is impossible; there can only be a struggle for victory or defeat.

The April number of *Die Fanfare*, 1934 (a Hitler Youth publication), attacked Cardinal Faulhaber's Advent sermons in its leading article, under the headline " Herr Cardinal, we shall Defend Ourselves." " We shall not allow you to besmirch the blood and honour of our race," etc.

On March 5th, 1936, the *Schwarze Korps* accused Cardinal Faulhaber of maintaining connections with Bolshevism in an article entitled " Who is Lying, Herr Cardinal?" and a week later *Die Bewegung*,[2] the official organ of the Nazi Students' Union, accused Archbishop Gröber, on account of his book " The Christian Man," of indulging in " political Catholicism."

[1] No. 36.   [2] March 11th, 1936.

On April 22nd, 1937, the *Schwarze Korps* sought to ascribe a double standard of morality to Cardinal Faulhaber, in view of certain evaluations of the Old Testament which the Cardinal had put forward in sermons. Studied in their relations with one another, they show, according to the Nazi paper, " a certain alarming characteristic of what is fundamental to the Christian outlook." They justify the oft-asserted " double-sided morality and the practical contradiction between theory and practice in the Roman communion." (N.B.—No thinking man could read any such meaning into the passages which were cited.)

On June 24th, 1937, the same paper once again violently attacked Cardinal Faulhaber under the headline " Really, Herr Cardinal !" because he had remarked that in France, as compared with Germany, Catholic schools could be maintained. The article ended as follows: " We wish once again to point out to German people the demagogic principles of a Roman Cardinal who may say ' Germany ' with his lips, but means in his heart only Rome and its political supporters."

One of the most insulting Nazi cartoons appeared in the *Schwarze Korps* for May 6th, 1937,[1] where a Catholic bishop is represented in the midst of a herd of labelled swine, under the title " Go and Feed my Lambs." Again, on July 8th, 1937, the same paper referred to bishops in general in a cartoon entitled " Your Power is Slipping from You." On September 1st, 1938, it styled the Pastoral Letter issued by the Bishops' Conference at Fulda a " propaganda letter," and, amongst other falsehoods, once more asserted that the Catholic Church maintains secret relations with Bolshevism. In the following month,[2] the Bishops' Joint Pastoral was described as " the high-water mark of episcopal mendacity," and the accusation was made against the " political " priesthood of having stood on the side of the enemies of the German people in its hour of need. On November 10th the bishops were named " deserters."

A large proportion of German bishops regarded those days of political tension merely as an opportunity to stab the State in the back . . . they are permanently branded as November men, and are cut off for ever from our ranks. We have nothing further to do with them; they are deserters, and as deserters we are bound to regard them.

The **priests** who loyally stand by their ecclesiastical Superiors—and they, thank God, include the whole of the German clergy, with very few exceptions—are exposed, if that is possible, to even more brutal and vile assaults on their honour and their liberty. One could, indeed, fill a large book by merely naming the places in Nazi literature where remarks detrimental to the Catholic priesthood are to be found. Bishop Buchberger of Regensburg did not exaggerate when he said in a sermon:[3]

It is sad indeed that the priesthood should be mocked and despised on notice boards set up in every village, even before the eyes of children. In a recent issue of a certain paper a whole page is devoted to pictures of which

---

[1] P. 2, *cf.* p. 64.   [2] October 27th, 1938.   [3] November 15th, 1936.

ATTACKS ON THE CHURCH'S REPRESENTATIVES 431

the sole aim is to lower respect for the priesthood and damage trust in its labours. There is in particular a cartoon of St. Paul which has scarcely been equalled by the most openly anti-Christian periodicals. Now that such hatred of priests has become the hall-mark of Bolshevism, one would seek such pictures in an anti-Communist exhibition rather than on public placards. In Russia and Spain priests suffer the loss of their lives, but here in Germany the enemies of the Church seek to take away their honour and all trust in them, and there are many priests who would rather lose their lives than their good name.

A few years ago there appeared, under the title " The Parson-rogue," a whole volume of satirical verse, illustrated with caricatures, ridiculing the priestly vocation.

In 1936, No. 46 of Julius Streicher's *Stürmer* printed the following passage:

Priests know well how thankful they should be to National Socialist Germany. They know that they have to thank God for the gift of a man who has swept away the Jewish-Bolshevist underworld. Yet what do the priests do? They hold up sheltering hands before corrupters of our race in Franciscan habits. They stand up for the descendants of that race which martyred Christ and nailed Him to His cross. They are not troubled by the thought that certain Popes were anti-Semites and hated the Jews; our modern priests want nothing of that. They misuse religious instruction and the pulpit in the most despicable way. . . .

Nevertheless, even the priests cannot turn back the wheel of history. The day will come when a cleansing process will emerge from within the priesthood itself, without any external stimulus, and the chaff will be sifted from the wheat. The devil will take his own, and only those priests will labour who love their people and in whom the people repose an unshakeable trust.

In a similar style the *SA-Mann* stated on August 14th, 1937,[1] that priests are " deeply grieved . . . not on account of the good estate of our souls, however, for they have never concerned themselves with that."

On June 3rd, 1937, the *Schwarze Korps* expressed indignation because a Catholic dean had recorded his grief at the ruthless and unjustifiable suppression of a Catholic hospital in his parish. The article ended with the following remarks, printed in heavy type:

The methods adopted are always the same, and we shall never tire of drawing attention to them. It does not matter whether the crime is immorality or murder or homicide or smuggling out currency—whatever it may be and however revolting it may be, these Roman communities always seek to hide it or to distort it with all the means of pressure or falsification in their power. Any clerical offender, however infamous and sub-human, must be decked out with his little martyr's crown to serve as a decoration for honourable service in the campaign against the State and the peace of the nation.

On February 29th, 1936, and again on October 17th of the same year, *Die HJ* published cartoons of Catholic priests. On April 9th, 1936, the *Schwarze Korps*, under the title " At the Gates of Death," accused priests of misusing their pastoral office, and throughout the

[1] P. 12.

whole of the following year no issue of this paper appeared without articles or illustrations designed to belittle the priesthood.[1]

One of its favourite allegations against priests was that they were avaricious. For example, on May 7th, 1936, it asserted that they exploit the hour of death to squeeze money out of penitents, and on May 13th, 1937, and again on June 24th, it attacked their " thirst for money." Base accusations of engaging in business transactions in connection with " stole fees " received from the faithful were made in the *SA-Mann* for December 18th, 1937, and on May 29th, 1937, the *Arbeitsmann* published a cartoon of a bishop with an indignant article on the gluttonous lives of priests.

Another line of attack consisted in accusations against priests of being mixed up in political plots against their country. In an article published on July 24th, 1935, the *Schwarze Korps* spoke of a whole series of crimes without any shadow of proof, and invented epithets such as " clerical assassins," " traitors in priestly cowls," etc. Other articles libelled " parsons who have been killjoys in the life of Germany "[2] and attacked a priest who stood out for the just rights of the Church.[3] The Munich edition of the *Völkischer Beobachter* for April 29th, 1936, published an article by Herr Heydrich, a Chief of the Secret Police, describing priests as " enemies of the State " and " sanctimonious hypocrites." The *Stürmer* for November, 1936 (No. 46), complained that priests misused their pulpits in order to carry on a campaign against German ideological principles, and the *SA-Mann*[4] made similar accusations of clerical misuse of spiritual functions for the sake of political aims.

Accusations of immorality against the priesthood were repeated endlessly in Nazi publications. On June 12th, 1937, for example, the *SA-Mann* discussed moral offences of a certain priest at great length, and in conclusion made the following general accusation:

The question naturally arises as to the desirability of reform in the whole system, since it appears to lack the vigour required to combat sin and evil conditions.

Another periodical, *Stimme der deutschen Weltanschauung*,[5] was allowed to publish the following " Cry of Distress from a German Mother " without any official interference:

As German mothers are responsible for bringing up the coming generation, we demand the castration of all Catholic priests whatsoever.

---

[1] Some of its cartoons are reproduced in this book. *Cf*. pp 52, 64, 338, 427.
To support the general assertion just made we offer the following references to outstanding examples: January 7th (cartoons); January 21st (against a priest who had objected to the distribution in his parish of Rosenberg's " Myth "); February 11th; April 8th (cartoons and articles); April 22nd (cartoons); May 6th (front page cartoon); May 20th, p. 17 (articles); May 27th, p. 9; June 10th, p. 14; July 1st, pp. 1-2, etc.; *cf*. also March 10th p. 11; September 15th, p. 7 of 1938; and January 5th, p. 6; March 2nd, p. 21; March 9th, p. 12, etc., of 1939. *Cf*. also, *e.g.*, the *SA-Mann* of June 12th, 1936, and June 26th, 1937.
[2] December 30th, 1937. [3] January 28th, 1937, p. 14. [4] February 19th 1938.
[5] July 19th, 1936. Examples can be multiplied. *Cf*., *e.g.*, the *Schwarze Korps*, May 22nd and June 26th (under the title " Spicy Stories from the Confessional "), 1935; May 11th, June 18th, 25th, July 9th, 1936; January 7th, April 14th, May 13th, 20th, June 3rd, July 1st, 8th, November 4th, 11th, 1937; February 17th, 1938; August 3rd, 1939. The *HJ*, February 1st, 1936; the *Bewegung*, June 17th, 1936; the *Wille und Macht*, February 1st, 1938 ,which accused the whole body of Catholic priests of homosexual practices.

ATTACKS ON THE CHURCH'S REPRESENTATIVES

A special virulence was reserved by the Nazi press for material dealing with **priestly celibacy**.

On February 5th, 1937, there appeared in *Der öffentliche Gesundheitsdienst*[1] an article by Dr. Pfotenhauer entitled " The Duty of Propagation; Another Aspect of the Law for the Prevention of Unfit Offspring," from which we select the following passage:

> We must take into consideration the fact that a not inconsiderable section of the community, drawn in part from the best stock of the nation—I mean the priesthood and members of religious Congregations in Germany—is impeded from propagating the race by the enforcement of ecclesiastical laws. It should be obvious that these regulations for such a class of people have a far more radical effect than the harmless process of sterilisation, which has no particular after-effects. The loss to the race of generations of a high quality throughout past centuries cannot be measured, for it had no connection with racial hygiene. On the contrary, this limitation inherent in celibacy affects a specially select section of the community, and in the future the general welfare of the German people will not be able to permit it. (*Cf.* the exposition of the matter in *Volk und Rasse*, 1935, No. 8, p. 253.) One need only consider for a moment the vast quantity of valuable racial material which has come into existence through the medium of Protestant clerical families, an inheritance which has been transmitted.

On June 26th, 1937, the *SA-Mann* asserted on its front page, " The courts have established the fact that priestly celibacy played a leading part in filling these sewers." (The reference is to the " immorality " trials.) In July, 1937, the *Training Letter* (No. 7) attacked celibacy, and in the same month the *Schwarze Korps* made wild general insinuations against the Catholic priesthood. The latter article opened as follows:

> The alarming bulk of " immorality " trials in which priests have figured has once more drawn the attention of the general public to moral conditions prevalent in Roman congregations for men. Many who know little or nothing of the nature of Catholicism or of Catholic moral tenets will be astounded at the large number of so-called " individual lapses " which have suddenly come to light. The courts have rightly stressed the fact that the blame for this repulsive large-scale revelation should not be placed upon the frailty or natural tendencies of the persons accused, but upon the system adopted by the Catholic Church, and more especially upon its monastic life.
> The so-called vows of chastity which Catholic priests and monks are obliged to take, at an age when they are in no position to estimate their real significance, drive a large proportion of the priesthood into sexual aberrations, simply because a natural mode of satisfying natural instincts is impossible for them. Catholic moral teaching actually regards those relations between the sexes which nature has ordained as fundamentally sinful, and puts them on much the same level as the unnatural vices practised by so many of its representatives. It is scarcely a matter for surprise that a priest or a monk, living in a state of enforced celibacy, should choose the " easier way " of satisfying his sexual instincts.

Much was also written against the study of theology and against ecclesiastical measures for ensuring a steady supply of priests. A good example of this line of attack is supplied by the *Schwarze Korps* for February 2nd, 1939, under the headline " We still have Unemployed !"

---

[1] P. 607.

It was recently computed that Germany lacks more than 17,600 engineers.
... Yet one Faculty is 100 per cent. full; one, and one alone, is anything but short of numbers; one has no fears for a steady supply of students. That Faculty is the Faculty of Theology !

There are in Germany some 4,500 students who wish to become engineers. Yet clerical seminaries have some 9,000 students on their books preparing for the ministry. That means that those callings which possess the least value for Germany's political development, and which can be most easily dispensed with from the standpoint of the economic strengthening of the Reich, are the best supplied with candidates. . . .

It is quite true that parishes are in need of pastors of souls; but we have already more than enough unemployed " political " priests, priestly propaganda agents. The supply will last for many years to come !

The Churches represent the only aspect of social life in which Germany is still radically infected with unemployment. From the unemployed of former days these differ only in that they receive money from the State. We cannot endure such things much longer—neither the unemployed nor the State support !

On March 16th, 1939, the *Schwarze Korps* drew attention to the list of matriculants for Borken, in Westphalia, and pointed out indignantly that it included ten *Theologen* (students destined for the Church).

It is incredible that, out of seventeen presumably healthy, sensible and grown-up youths, so many as ten should, of their own free will, show an inclination towards exclusively theological studies.

The provision of future generations for the most fruitful types of vocation is decisive for the future of the nation. And yet, in face of this burning need which occupies our nation and its leaders, there are those who dare to offer to ten out of the seventeen matriculants from one class a calling which ignores all care for future generations, which does, however, offer young men, studying in a Catholic Faculty, the opportunity of avoiding military service.

What are we to think of institutions which regularly turn out youths with a training and characteristics in no way suited to the generations which are to inherit the National Socialist State ?

What sort of parents are these who are so devoid of any sense of responsibility towards the nation that they send their children like sheep to the clerical slaughter, simply in order to ensure, by means of a sacrifice which causes them no pain, a safe place in Heaven !

One question remains. What is to be done ? It will be answered in due time. The German people shows little inclination to allow those who do nothing and those who sabotage its labours to receive their education at its expense in secondary schools or Universities; nor does the nation show any further inclination to allow these same drones to escape their two years of national service. Some few may have imagined that high ideals played a part in this attraction to theological studies. This information must shatter all such illusions.

In the same way the *Schwarze Korps* for July 6th, 1939, denied that a young Catholic could give himself to the study of theology on purely idealistic grounds. Under the title " Idealism—for What ?" the article ran:

What is the idealism of a seminary student ? In modern Germany and in view of the tasks which face us, can anybody become a seminarist on idealistic grounds ? The sole " wherefore " for " idealistic " living, fighting and dying today, the sole criterion which counts, is the German People. No German has any right to call himself an idealist, unless that people is the sole content of his ideals.

At a Congress of the National Socialist Undergraduates' Union held in Würzburg in May, 1939, Dr. Heinz Franz (head of the Students' Economic and Social Bureau) demanded a limitation of the former subsidies granted for Catholic theological studies. He argued that the flow of students in that direction was determined precisely by the system of subsidies. He demanded that responsible national authorities should divert bursaries, scholarships, etc., which were at present being automatically received by students of theology, to technical and science students. The original foundation clauses of such moneys should be disregarded. He also demanded that all Catholic seminarists should be obliged to complete their term of service in the Labour Camps and in the Army before beginning a regular course of theology. So far, the reception of the subdiaconate had served as a dispensation from military service.

A base and wholly unfounded insinuation (on the same lines as that dealt with in the " Schülle case ")[1] was made by the *Schwarze Korps*,[1] that men who had committed incest were permitted to take up a priestly vocation.

As in the Bismarckian *Kulturkampf*, so now, it has been one of the chief aims to discredit the **religious Orders.** Their schools have been closed, their good name besmirched in the currency and " immorality " trials, but they still survive. Below we give one or two other ways of attack.

Accusations which concerned only individual members of such Orders were commonly generalised with no justification.[2] In the *Schwarze Korps*,[3] Catholic nuns in general were accused of a lack of piety. The *SA-Mann*[4] published accounts of scandals involving a nun who had left her Order, and whose " revelations " were fully set forth. On October 16th, 1937, the same paper published an article concerning a whole series of crimes which an Order was supposed to have committed during the conquest of America.

The Nazi press specialised in attacks directed against the Jesuits. On May 4th, 1935, the *Heidelberger Student*, a students' magazine, published a violent article, illustrated by a cartoon, against the Jesuits, under the title " A National Front against Supra-national Riff-raff," and an essay, by Erich Ludendorff, entitled " Jesuitry: the Enslavement of Conscience."[5]

On March 2nd, 1939, there appeared in the *Schwarze Korps* a satirical poem on the Capuchins, introduced as follows:

In its fifth issue the *Catholic Magazine for the Diocese of Augsburg* published the following advertisement: " Are you about to choose your career ? In the habit and after the manner of St. Francis of Assisi, Capuchins work both at home and on the foreign missions for the welfare of their fellow-men. Boys (from ten to twelve years of age) who are healthy, have courage and talent, and feel inclined to this way of life, should apply to . . .''

[1] January 21st, 1937, p. 1.
[2] *Cf. Völk. Beobachter*, July 31st, 1935.   [3] June 11th, 1936.   [4] October 9th, 1937.
[5] Examples of the use made against religious Orders of the " immorality " trials were given in Part II, Chap. 11. Further references are found earlier in this chapter (p. 432).

This introduction was made the occasion of a piece of doggerel verse, based on the fact that the advertisement required boys to be *erbgesund*—*i.e.*, healthy subjects.

> The Vatican infallibly
>   Vouchsafes the truth to state,
> That race a mere delusion is
>   Of heathens incarnate.
>
> The Capuchins are said, indeed,
>   To preach the self-same truths;
> And yet, remarkably, they seek
>   For " sound and healthy youths."
>
> They seek to give the loving God
>   An offspring healthy, pure;
> But such all join the Hitler Youth—
>   Much healthier, to be sure !
>
> The Vatican infallible,
>   Alarmed for its supplies
> Of fitting youngsters, now to take
>   Our " race-delusion " tries.
>
> Inclined to do the generous thing,
>   With young " deludeds " free—
> Yet flatly we refuse to give
>   On tick to a monast'ry.
>
> Unmasked in all our courts of law—
>   Their " pure !" young men, in sooth !—
> It's manifest they are not fit
>   To meet our German Youth !

The account presented in this chapter is a mere synopsis, but it must suffice to give an idea of Nazi methods. The Nazis determined to discredit the Church and her representatives, and any old lie would serve the purpose—told often enough, part of it at any rate would be believed by many. They could tell it as often as they liked, for they alone had newspapers and all Germans are *bound* to buy them, at least those of their organisation; they controlled broadcasts and every other means of spreading news; whereas the Church, with her newspapers suppressed and her parish magazines censored, had no way left of answering, except the pulpit and Pastorals—the former spied on, the latter often confiscated before being read.

CHAPTER VI

ATTACKS ON CATHOLIC FAITH AND PRACTICES

It is not only the Church as an institution that, to the Nazi mind, stands in the way of National Socialism's taking complete possession of the German, body and soul, but also what the Church stands for, what is indeed her whole *raison d'être*—the Faith and the moral teaching that she preserves and promulgates. These, therefore, are attacked, ridiculed and jeered at continually in all the Party publications. Here, once again, from such abundant material, we can offer only a small selection.

1. *Attacks on Catholic Beliefs*

During September and October, 1936, the *SA-Mann* issued a series of articles on faith, "What is meant by Faith?" In the first article the " living ideology " and the faith of " true human beings "—*i.e.*, the National Socialist ideology and National Socialist teaching—were compared with Christianity.

> In this connection the following two features of Christianity should be noted—namely, faith does not arise spontaneously from man's nature, but consists in something revealed to man by God; and, secondly, faith is referred to an act performed by God, and not to actions and tasks of men. Both conceptions represent a passive element in Christianity, rather than that dynamic element which is characteristic of real life. Our National Socialist *Weltanschauung* ranks amongst dynamic " life-regarding " ideologies, and has nothing in common with " revealed " faith that implies its own unescapable ideology. Still less can there be compromise between the two. . . . If Blood and Race are the very essence of our being, ideology and faith must also be rooted in Blood and Race. Hence we must speak of a National Socialist faith, a faith which reacts upon life as life and which, regarded from the National Socialist point of view, demands. . . . Christianity conceives two types of life: earthly in this world, and heavenly in a world to come. Christian faith is something announced by God and ultimately is concerned, not with this earthly life, but with life in Heaven. . . . National Socialist ideology proclaims that body, soul and spirit are one unity—that is to say, there is but one life, a life concerned purely with the Here and Now, not with something " Beyond," although, indeed, this life is a tangible realisation of a world " Beyond," and has eternal value. . . .
>
> Do you now understand what is meant by faith in our eternal Germany? The Eternal is revealed in this Germany of ours and in its history; no mere passing earthly development, but a divine Becoming. The Eternal reveals itself and is worked out within each one of us. Reality has once more taken on the radiance of " holiness," of the miraculous. How often has the Führer expressed this from his own experience; through us, and in our very midst, a miracle has become real, the miracle of faith. Our " political " faith, a faith in this life, is a faith which reaches out to the Eternal, the Divine, a faith which has blossomed forth into glory through the driving power of our ideology.

Another attack on the divine revelation appeared in the *Schwarze Korps* on November 4th, 1937 (p. 11):

> Since these uncertain and for the most part spurious documentary sources, these "divine revelations," have formed the tottering foundations of Christian faith and of the Christian Church, it is small wonder that Christianity has had such a deplorable history since the first fine fervour died down, about a century after the death of Christ.

On November 18th, 1937, the *Schwarze Korps* printed the following remarks:

> Dogma is the product of completely unbalanced minds, but the true Christian way of life was discovered by Jesus Christ. The essence of Christ's teaching is contained in two phrases: " et homo factus est " (" and He became man ") and " et incarnatus est " (" the Word became flesh ")—*i.e.*, the Logos, the Word, the Spirit took on a human form. The literal-minded clique of Pharisees, however, understood these truths only in the light of certain words added by the Church—viz., " ex Maria Virgine " (" of the Virgin Mary "). That addition blotted out the very nature of primitive Christianity, a nature which met so-called " Paganism " on its own ground, identified itself, indeed, with that Paganism; and thus was the one creative factor which Christianity contained nullified.

The same firm which had published Rosenberg's " Myth " issued in spring, 1939, a booklet entitled " Illusion or Reality," by Dr. Ziegler, editor of the *NS Monatshefte*. The work was intended to provide material for Nazi training colleges and educational camps. In his preface the author assured his readers that his sole object was " to point out the theoretical presuppositions of the Church in its teaching on racialism, and its essentially Jewish-oriental structure." According to him, belief in revelation is an oriental characteristic, an oriental quality arising from a sense of inferiority and of " unfitness," with " lack of unity and stability," " inner infirmity " and " lack of all capacity for regulated form and order." Out of such a " dualistic view of the world and of life " the " apocalyptic type of desert dweller " excogitates his notion of a personal God.

> The idea of perpetually waiting and listening for salvation, for a resolution of dualistic tension, is typically oriental. Such an attitude is responsible for oriental teachings about revelation and personal conversion. It is the key to those hallucinations which mark the history of Churches and sects. The concepts of salvation and revelation constitute the grand self-deception of all orientals. . . .

Teutons do not believe in a personal God. " For them God is but the concept innate in all Life, is the very force and power of Life. . . ." " Christian theology stands in complete and exclusive contrast to this Germanic faith, for the Christian ideology is pervaded with the rigidity and the empty coldness of a scorn for Life and a denial of all Life's values." The Teuton " despises the oriental dualism of Nature and the Supernatural," and, as a result, dispenses with the doctrine of grace. Germanic morality is determined solely " by obedience to the eternal laws of Life," and has but one motto—viz., " The strongest must be victors, and the victors must rule." Such a motto involves the rejection of all doctrines of sin and salvation such as the Church holds, for those doctrines indicate the " Jewish-oriental origin of Christian morality " and its " correspondence with the anti-civilising spirit of the desert. . . ."

We must accustom ourselves to the fact that our warriors, our fighters, and they alone, proclaim divine mysteries to the German race, not an official priesthood—warriors who hearken to the commandments and the laws of life through their deeds and through the harmonious unity of their own lives.

Since we believe in life, death has no terrors for us. Since we find the meaning of life in life itself, and not somewhere beyond life, we are indifferent to all supposed punishments in Hell or rewards in Heaven. We are wholly content to know that we live on in the blood of our children, in the consciousness of our comrades, and perhaps, indeed, in the memory of the whole race. Such fame and such honour seem to us the true reward of our active and joyful way of life.

On June 8th, 1939, the *Schwarze Korps* published the following reflections on religion under the title " The Nature of God."

We have long considered the problem: Which Christian doctrines are repugnant to the moral dispositions of the German race, and must be regarded, according to the clear teaching of Article 24 of the Party Programme of the NSDAP, as incompatible with racial conceptions ? We have come to the conclusion that a host of Christian conceptions are, indeed, incompatible with our own. . . .

Those of us who travel through the German countryside and suddenly, in the midst of some view of snow-covered Alpine peaks or on some solemn Westphalian moorland, meet with the figure of the Crucified must feel deep down in our hearts—if we have any true blood-consciousness at all—a strange, enduring sense of shame. The Gods of our forefathers were not like that. They were true men, men with weapons in their hands, typifying the innate view of life and the dynamic realisation of personal responsibility of our race. How different is this pale crucified one ! His attitude of passivity, the deeply-engraven sorrow of His features, expressing humility and complete self-abandonment—these are all qualities which contradict the heroic, fundamental presuppositions of our blood-consciousness.

And now, let us view the panorama of history through the medium of blood and race, and we light upon the most incredible and degrading of all historical attacks upon rights, upon the destruction of all that our ancestors held sacred. The pure, clear, proud faith of Nordic man in his own power and the inerrancy native to clean, manly living have been destroyed by zealous " faith " preachers, whose ways of thought were alien, and who proclaimed to our race the terrifying bogy of belief in sin.

That " evil," which our forefathers, men of fine, sound blood, were wont to encounter with unsheathed arms, became an overwhelming power even amongst us. The Devil, that convenient necessity for a priestly caste whose ambition was money and power, coiled his blood-stained lash over a world degraded and cowed, robbed of its true virile might, a world of which we, too, were members.

And more fundamental still:

The mythological formulas of Christian theology depend for the most part on Jewish-Asiatic theories of salvation dating from the Hellenistic period. It is well known that the figure of the Saviour Himself—from the theological point of view—is a most complicated construction, arising from sources in the near East and in Babylonia, and later radically affected by the Aryan cult of Mithra.[1]

[1] *Schwarze Korps*, June 29th, 1939, p. 11.

To illustrate attacks on Sin, the Fall, etc., we quote the *Schwarze Korps* for June 15th, 1939 (p. 13):

For over a thousand years the emissaries of an alien system of thought have preached to our race that all its theories and views, regarded as worthy and true for some ten thousand years, were false and corrupt. The concept of " heroism," which formed the standard of all ethical values in Aryan thought, was battered and twisted for so long by clerical pundits that it eventually took on quite another form, namely—" heroism of faith," the hero of faith whose humility and self-abnegation led him to offer the other cheek after receiving a blow.

Thus we read in Luther's General Confession: " Poor miserable, sinful man that I am, I acknowledge before You all my sins and misdeeds with which I have provoked You, and whereby I have earned punishment both in this world and in the next. For them I am truly sorry, and repent most heartily." . . . Why, precisely do the followers of Christianity adopt such an attitude of complete self-degradation ? Why is it demanded of them ? It arises from the strange doctrine of Original Sin, elaborated in the early Middle Ages by a priestly caste itching for power, in order to carry through its political aims. For this the priests found it necessary to set forth the figure of a Saviour who takes away sin. . . .

To us the whole notion of sin appears warped and foreign to our nature. . . .

No wrong or evil deed can be atoned for from outside, by any species of grace or through any intermediary, even though he be a priest, but only from within, through the power of a pure heart and pure intentions. . . .

We need say nothing here of the fact that political Catholicism often exploits the obligation of Confession (resting, as it does, on the doctrine of sin) in order to produce a ghastly and permanent violation of personal freedom. That particular perversion of a purely religious institution, as it is regularly practised today, is being constantly sought out and attacked by us.

Here we are only concerned to establish the fact that this Christian sin-complex is daily and hourly poisoning hundreds and thousands of young people in Germany, poisoning them for the whole of their lives. Upright and honourable young souls are being constantly impressed with the idea that they are evil through and through, hopelessly corrupt, so that only the agency of a priest can preserve them from eternal damnation.

Such an outlook does not correspond with the outlook of our modern State. Our religious conscience demands no intermediary between God and man and so needs kindly help, not priestly ministrations, in its struggle. Hence we cannot permit under any circumstances an anonymous and, moreover, a political power to insinuate itself in between the personal responsibility of the individual and the standard of ethical values. . . .

For centuries the Church has degraded and slandered bodily health and all its outward manifestations. Such an execrable distortion of reality represents the precise opposite of Aryan evaluations of such things. . . .

We may sum up thus: Christianity has frequently been a kind of soul malady, not only paralysing all natural psychical powers, but finally causing a vast number of German people, as a result of its depreciation of the body, to become pitiable wretches.

On January 7th, 1937, the *Schwarze Korps* wrote as follows:

For us all morality which is dictated from above and forced on the Race is to be rejected with as much execration as that hypocritical behaviour whereby, for example, ordinary human failings on the part of unsophisticated youngsters are exploited for the sake of political domination through the mystery of the Confessional.

The abstruse doctrine of Original Sin, whence the need of salvation is said to arise; the Fall—and, indeed, the whole notion of sin as set forth by the

Church, involving reward or punishment in a world beyond—is something intolerable to Nordic man, since it is incompatible with the " heroic " ideology of our Blood.

For us, over and above all sectarian squabbles—and discussions on religions can never be anything more than that in modern Germany—one unshakeable fact stands out—namely, that it is of primary importance for the future of our Race that Religion, as a servant of the Race, should shape new spiritual formulas calculated to assist in realising the heroic " life-ideals " of our Race.

On January 28th, 1937, the *Schwarze Korps* published an article entitled " Original Sin: Popular Version."

A certain young mother's first walk after her confinement was to the church, but on arriving she was not permitted to enter the consecrated part, but had to wait in the unconsecrated vestibule until she had been " purified." That is what Catholic usage demands. The fundamental postulate of Catholicism and the kernel of its teaching on Original Sin may be summed up in the words " Life itself is sin, and Death signifies Salvation." That this doctrine enshrines the whole of oriental depreciation of women is not admitted from the Roman side, at least with regard to German women; for German women regard the hour in which they are privileged to give birth to a child as the proudest hour of their lives; they know that the meaning of womanly existence has found its fulfilment, and thank God with joyful hearts for the grace He has shown them.

Attacks on the **Sacraments** follow as a matter of course. On November 4th, 1937 (p. 12), for instance, the *Schwarze Korps* published an article entitled " Touch me not and kiss me not."

Parents and doctors who interest themselves in the welfare of children are outdone by Catholic priests, who expend great energy in seeing to it that the souls of newborn babes should be washed free of Original Sin in **Baptism**. The reverend gentleman puts his finger in his mouth and wipes the spittle on the nose and ears of the child, after he has blown in its face. Should the infant begin to bellow, he crumbles a pinch of salt between its lower lip and the gum in order to soothe it. In most cases, however, that does not work, and he then pours cold baptismal water on the back of its head. Nurse then has her hands full with the business of calming the excited child and putting it back in its cradle, over which a placard hangs informing the world, " Touch me not and kiss me not "; and the delighted father must view it from behind glass, since ordinary mortals have spittle laden with germs, unlike the spittle of his reverence, which wipes away original sin !

Now Baptism is supposed to be a sacrament instituted by Christ, although it was Saint John who first practised it, baptising Jesus in the Jordan. Neither he nor Christ licked their fingers or swallowed salt, and, indeed, Christ was too old to be in danger of infant mortality. The priesthood adopted " symbolic " acts, acts neither ordained nor desirable. . . . Doctors in maternity homes should see to it that baptism does not take place before the father is able to approach his child with no intervening pane of glass.

Episcopal regulations, too, with regard to the baptism of Jews were ridiculed in the Nazi press.[1]

On July 27th, 1939, the *Schwarze Korps* reported the following case from Essen. The wife of a man who had left the Church some years before bore a child which its grandmother had secretly baptised. The

---

[1] *Cf.* the regulations laid down by Cardinal Seredi of Hungary, dealt with in the *Schwarze Korps*, January 5th, 1939, p. 2.

father then formally notified the local authorities that the child also was not a member of the Church. Since, however, the mother of the child refused to give her sanction, as the law demanded, the local authorities repudiated the notification. The Nazi paper then expressed its indignation:

The law appears to be distinctly faulty on this point. Either, as ought to be the case, the father alone decides the denominational adherence of his children as long as they are too young to express their own wills, and in that case the Church can presume nothing against his will and the secret baptismal sprinklings were a farce, void in the eyes of the law: or both parties, acting together, decide the nature of such adherence, in which case the baptism may rightly be regarded as not having taken place at all.

If this were not the legal position, zealous priests could creep secretly into all maternity homes and carry out mass-baptisms of all new-born children, without any liberty being left to the father to raise objections.

Such methods are, no doubt, employed in the African bush on poor naked negro children. There the missionaries have exposed themselves to the danger of reaching Heaven in the shape of crisply-baked martyrs. We have no wish, however, that such methods should gain ground in Germany.

On June 3rd, 1937 (p. 10), the *Schwarze Korps* wrote concerning the **Blessed Sacrament:**

The feast of Corpus Christi did not arise from childlike simplicity or from the desire to set aside one day in the year on which the Body of the Lord should receive special reverence. This feast was given to the Church in 1264, and merely represents the triumph of the Roman Catholic Church over heresy. Only in 1215 did men find themselves obliged to believe in transubstantiation, in the transformation of wheaten bread into the real and true Body of the Lord, and all who did not so believe were *ipso facto* heretics. Such a one had to step very warily in order to avoid ending up on a red-hot grill, burnt for heresy. Such was the upshot of the campaign against the Albigensians under Pope Innocent III, when thousands of people were mutilated, burnt or condemned to wholesale executions. This Roman Catholic species of mass-murder was only made possible by the Lateran Council which, in 1215, carried through the doctrine of the mystery of transubstantiation. And in just the same way later ages have seen every inhuman barbarity, which the Catholic Church has instituted, justified and decked out for polite consumption through some mystery intimately connected with it.

The same paper,[1] in a disrespectful dig at the Feast of Corpus Christi, starts off by quoting the mystical vision of St. Juliana of Liège:

Then did she behold a bright and radiant moon, and in the midst thereof a dark spot as though a piece had been broken off. The moon was a symbol of the liturgical year. The meaning of the dark spot was that there was one feast still wanting, a feast to venerate the Most Sacred Body of Our Lord.

The *Schwarze Korps* then continues:

That is a good and likely interpretation for there are even today quite a number of people who see dark spots in the moon. Only, let us be glad that when this happens nowadays it is not taken as an occasion that calls for a public holiday; otherwise we should have more than 365 of them and Hermann Göring would have to look out for the completion of his Five Years' Plan.

[1] June 29th, 1939, p. 7.

THE CONFESSIONAL.

"But, Father, I don't even know the meaning of the sins you are asking me about."

[*Der Stürmer*, No. 31, 1936.

GERMAN CHRISTMAS.

The Sacrament of **Penance** is an especially favourite object of Nazi attacks. In E. Thomassin's " I was a Catholic. Letters to a Friend," occurs this passage: " One who is not and never has been a Catholic simply cannot grasp what auricular confession means for an upright German citizen," etc., and the whole booklet is an example of psychological distortion and disgusting malice.

On February 11th, 1937, a book review in the *Schwarze Korps* opened as follows:

Confession as prescribed by the Roman Catholic Church has changed radically in nature. The reverend fathers no longer wish to hear of contrition and gnashing of teeth on the part of seekers after penance. They now disregard such things. No longer is anybody to beat his brow against hard, altar steps and bemoan his sinful body. A booklet has appeared, published by the Genesius Company at Warendorf, in Westphalia, and written by Fr. Andreas Wittmann, O.S.B., a work adorned with the very highest Imprimaturs—*e.g.*, *Schyrae, die* 7 *Julii* 1936, ✝ *Simon, O.S.B., Abbas . . . Monasterii, die* 30 *Septembris,* 1936. *No. L.* 2360 *Meis Vicarius Episcopi Generalis.*

Whoever reads it will find a stumbling-block removed from his path! Father Andreas has discovered a solution which we may summarise in the phrase, " Sin made easy !"

The same paper[1] produced articles on the subject of the seal of Confession which, at any rate in their lack of respect, were paralleled by others in the *SA-Mann*.[2] In one of the latter, **Extreme Unction** was made the object of a virulent attack. The paper stated that it objected to Extreme Unction because " we do not wish to see the sick and the mentally afflicted tortured to death," and a little farther on referred to the holy oils as " salad oil."

On June 30th, 1938, the *Schwarze Korps* published an article entitled " Death-bed Coercion," dealing with priestly attendance at death-beds and the priestly duty of adjusting defective marriage relationships. (The case concerned a particular hospital in Cologne-Niehl.)

The works of piety carried on in this house are by no means what one would expect. The Chaplain who has been called to attend a dying person finds himself unable to insult his God by sending this soul before Him armed with the Last Sacraments, for this sinful soul made a second marriage with a Protestant ! A marriage ? According to the priestly view, the person is living in the accursed state of concubinage, and the priest strives to force the dying woman to renounce her husband, until the husband himself arrives and the repulsive scene draws to a close. After that the wife dies, happy in the knowledge that she has remained true to her husband in spite of all temptations, and no doubt this spiritual greatness which she displays in death will stand her in better stead than the Extreme Unction which has been denied her.

Another case, in which the priest concerned had acted with absolute correctness according to the regulations of the Church, was commented upon as follows by the *Schwarze Korps*[3] under a headline which ran "Must This Go On ?"

The bonds of clerical coercion at death-beds will not slacken or be broken until such breaches of the elementary laws of decency and of honourable

---

[1] January 16th and October 15th, 1936.
[2] June 26th, 1937, and January 15th, 1938.   [3] February 16th, 1939.

living are made the subject of stringent punishment. We now present the Reverend Peter Balleis, parish priest of the Sacred Heart Church, Augsburg, as an example of such soul-masseurs and angel-manufacturers. . . .

Only an unnatural and conscienceless extortioner, intent on collecting data against the marriage laws of the State and sabotaging the National Socialist view of marriage rights, could have put together this particular declaration made by a sick person—viz., that he repents of marrying a divorced woman, he himself being divorced. This interesting document bears the name of two witnesses: Sister M. Annunciata and Sister M. Gonzaga. These two were present at the clerical massaging operations, and acted as attendants.

On February 2nd, 1939, the *Schwarze Korps*, under the heading " Extortioners at Death-beds once More," returned to the charge:

These two nuns were working as nurses in the municipal hospital at Augsburg—that is to say, in an institution in no way connected with the Church. What has the management to say to the fact that two members of the staff countenanced an act of coercion, an abuse of their patients' liberty ?

Such cases are constantly arising in public institutions. Measures must be taken to ensure that patients who seek care and protection in municipal or State institutions do not become victims, through their helplessness, of mean, malicious attacks.

Bitter attacks on **Indulgences** appeared in the *Schwarze Korps* for July 13th, 1939 (p. 7), and the same paper wrote as follows on January 25th, 1940, in an article directed against Church patronage:

When the most High Count Warensbach of Tschischkowitz near Lobositz was nearing his end, he reflected on his sins and found them by no means few. We write of days following the Thirty Years' War, a time of extreme need, when sins were viewed lightly. Nevertheless the Count found his indulgences dear, for in the deaneries, the presbyteries and the monasteries round about people were saying that the Count was revolving in his mind the possibility of putting his eternal salvation on a sound money basis. The clerical gentry turned up at the death-bed of the gouty sinner and made their bids. There was no question of balancing up credits and debits for every individual lapse, and, on account of his many sins, they agreed on a lump sum in settlement. Otherwise, indeed, there would not have been enough Masses going in the whole kingdom of Bohemia to make satisfaction ! So they simplified matters.

The count received a plenary indulgence, and in recognition of this took over the patronage of churches in Tschischkowitz, Schirschowitz, Trebnitz and Wellemin; he conferred an easement on the Capuchin monastery in Leitmeritz; and, since he was one who appreciated good liquor, he granted the monastery in perpetuity a gift of 2,000 kilos. of grain and 800 litres of wine in return for Requiem Masses—and from this one may calculate something of the superabundance of his sins. . . .

In the *SA-Mann* for August 14th, 1937 (p. 11), an article adorned with cartoons described **Hell** as " a device for terrifying old women and children," and on June 22nd, 1939, the *Schwarze Korps* also dealt with " this alien eternity," commenting on Catholic belief in eternal life as follows:

It is a fact that the promise of " Abraham's bosom " has aroused but little instinctive pleasurable anticipation, and that continuous singing of Halleluias to the sound of harps does not greatly attract even the musically-minded. That would seem to indicate that the positive aspect of eternity in the Jewish-Christian myth of the next world has not been sufficiently developed, either in literature or philosophy, to counteract innate Nordic conceptions.

These latter fought valiantly against late-Jewish and Alexandrian theological formulas of a resurrection of the body and eternal life for the psycho-physical composite which every individual presents.

Such an artificial prolongation of man's nature beyond death appeared to Nordic man as a blow struck at nature. The human soul is too intimately bound up with the phenomenological process implied in its union with the body to relapse into an eternal fixation when once the natural course of childhood, youth, maturity and old age has been run. The theory implies that all these things are resolved into a state of perpetual youth, independent of time.

Because it is static and not engaged in development into higher categories, this heavenly condition must, on mature reflection, appear unspeakably revolting.

Since Christian theology was not in a postition to set aside that doctrine of " eternalisation of the individual " which had been set forth, one might say, by mistake, it thought out in cold blood an alternative and opposite to its unappetizing eternal happiness. That opposite extreme was Hell. Its crudely painted horrors—hairy devils with horns and claws, tweaking victims according to the extent of their sins with red-hot pincers, basting them in boiling oil, roasting, broiling, cooking them in every imaginable way—these things had but one object, to keep the " faithful " submissive to the lust for power of a priestly caste.

Then appeared a singularly effective device, the notorious Indulgence racket which enabled men to be saved from the sadistic punishments of Hell through the priests, and mightily enriched the pastoral salvation-bureau with chinking coins.

On the one hand the horrors of Hell served to drive pious souls into that somewhat unattractive Heaven, and, as we saw, gave scope to certain purely mercantile considerations; on the other hand, the whole device betrays an excessively skilful camouflaging of the real views entertained by Christian theology.

As a result all Nordic races, including the Germans, were overwhelmed in the early Middle Ages with a veritable terror of death. Yet none whose life has been clean and upright need ever die with fear and trembling, and the whole hocus-pocus, with which the over-businesslike methods of theologians even today surround the simple and natural event of dying, arouses feelings of revulsion in any healthy-minded German. . . .

The fact that Catholic handling of this annoyance (viz., prayers for the dying) is sometimes turned into a source of income—by announcing that the expiatory Extreme Unction depends upon previous payment of Church taxes—is but a charming refinement of the whole procedure. . . .

Instead of looking death manfully in the eye and going forth, after a worthy life, into the peace of an eternal sleep, many of our citizens are obliged to endure a spiritual torment which reeks of the torture-chambers instituted in the name of Faith in the Middle Ages. And all this arises purely through the overweening lust for esteem on the part of a priestly caste which, to say the very least of the matter, belies its pastoral intentions by turning death, the harmonious climax of life, into a threshold of horror.

2. *The Attack on Catholic Morality*

On April 1st, 1937, the *Schwarze Korps* wrote as follows, in connection with an account of punishments commonly meted out by Nordic peoples for homosexuality:

The entry of Christianity led gradually to a change of view. The death penalty was certainly retained, but no longer for offenders against the race, but for sinners against God's commands—*i.e.*, heretics. The harm caused by this type of morality is plain. Offences against the race cannot be expiated, yet for sin there is absolution.

The following passage appeared in the *Schwarze Korps* for May 11th, 1939:

> Today we witness the increasing collapse of a principle of leadership and power which for more than a thousand years was in a position to mould the destiny of the West and of the whole civilised world. We see Christian Churches no longer in a position to do justice to their tasks, since their belief in the miraculous has made them fall between two stools in the realm of reality. This is not the place to discuss the fact that this dissension, or dualism, was present in their systems from the very beginning. We come up against the fact whenever the moral demands of Christianity do not square with reality, as has, indeed, very frequently happened. . . .
>
> We have given more than enough information about those who preach love but whose sole aim is self-interest; about those who demand purity whilst their deepest conviction is of their own Original Sin; who demand sacrifices whilst for themselves they desire only a sure income and the comforts of life. . . .
>
> We know that the dogmatic rigidity of alien, non-Germanic moral teaching has broken more men than it has ever helped. . . .
>
> Priests who really work for their flocks must eventually throw overboard many things thought out in the past by Jewish and half-caste Fathers of the Church. . . .

On June 8th, 1939, the same Nazi paper accused Christianity of "violating" Germanic moral feelings.

> Since our Fatherland became infected with Christianity the innate sense of honour and morality of our race has been overshadowed by alien theories, has been falsified and stained. . . . We should like to state plainly now that we are less interested in the historical inevitability of this warping of race-consciousness than in the certainty that our times must set aside the dire confusion resulting from the influx of alien concepts into the life of our soul.

On October 22nd, 1936, the same paper described Catholic, charitable work as a device of political Catholicism, and on May 13th, 1937, ridiculed the various requirements of Christian love of one's neighbour under the headline "Mortgaged Piety." On June 20th, 1939, it described Christian teaching on charity as *artfremd*, alien to the Germanic nature:

> "Love your enemies, do good to them that hate you, and pray for them that persecute and calumniate you." This fundamental law of Christianity completely contradicts our moral conscience, contradicts above all the warrior-like nature peculiar to the soul of our race. "If a man will . . . take away thy coat, let go thy cloak also unto him"; such a command is on the one hand a direct invitation to theft and on the other constitutes a shameless inducement to be cowardly and humble.

Similar sneers at Christian teaching about patience, meekness, etc., appeared in *Die Bewegung* for October 21st, 1936.

On July 1st, 1937, the *Schwarze Korps* wrote indignantly on the immorality of Catholic moralists, and in particular of St. Alphonsus Liguori. On September 15th, 1938, it described Catholic applications of moral principles to athletics for girls, bathing costumes, etc., as an undermining of true morality: " It is not morality that runs risks through bathing dresses, etc., but moral theology." Catholic principles with regard to women's dress, mixed bathing, etc., were violently attacked by means of cartoons in its issue for July 1st, 1937 (p. 8).[1]

Attacks on the Christian view of **marriage** formed another phase of the general assault on the Church's moral teaching. We can but give a very brief sketch of some of the forms it took.

The following references are to the *Schwarze Korps*. On February 11th, 1937 (p. 6), it attacked the Papal Encyclical on marriage. On the 4th of the same month it asserted that the Church is incapable of raising the birth-rate. On April 1st, 1937, and on February 17th, 1938, it attacked Catholic teaching on marriage, and in particular the use of dispensations. On March 23rd, 1939, it expressed indignation at " the battle, arising from the rigid persistence of the Church, waged by her against mixed marriages," and on August 26th, 1937 (p. 12), it attacked bishops and priests who defended the discouragement of mixed marriages. On March 5th, 1936, it summarised Christian principles with regard to the sixth commandment as " Bygone Morality."

In February, 1937, the *Training Letter* completely distorted the position accorded to women in the moral teaching of the Church, by means of many quotations taken for the most part from mediæval authors. Similar misrepresentations appeared in the *Schwarze Korps* on February 18th, 1937 (p. 12). For example:

We refer to the position accorded to God's " mother " Mary, to the theory of convent life, to celibacy, and so on, simply in order to draw attention to the peculiar attitude towards women in Catholic teaching. . . .

The celibacy to which a priest binds himself, the vows of chastity taken by monks and brothers, are, in the last analysis, really acknowledgements of the respect due to women. But one can well understand how men living solely with their own kind and cutting themselves off for ever from women must continually seek after new arguments to justify their unnatural condition. Such a conclusion could only be reached by diseased minds, or by men who view women as repulsive creatures created by God merely as a substitute for Lucifer whom he condemned to Hell.

These men in cowls and soutanes say nothing of all this—yet this view obsesses them, and always has done. . . .

In the same way the *SA-Mann*[2] published an article in which every conceivable quotation from the Bible was produced in order to prove that Christianity has degraded women.

3. *Attacks on Various other Catholic Practices*

Faith needs to be supported by **education** and Christian practice, and in Catholic Germany that was done and done well. On the other hand, any power attacking the Faith must needs, if it hope for success,

---

[1] Some of these are reproduced on p. 338. *Cf.* also *SA-Mann*, May 8th, 1937; *Schwarze Korps*, April 1st, 1937, and June 8th, 1939.
[2] December 11th, 1937, p. 4 *seq.*

attack, too, what goes with it. We have already dealt at length with the Government campaign against Catholic schools, associations and devotional manifestations. Here we shall give a brief indication of the support the Party gave, and gives, to that attack.

On October 3rd, 1936, the *SA-Mann* wrote under an insulting title against a Pastoral Letter issued by the bishops at Fulda on the subject of Catholic schools.

We wish to state soberly the following facts. These schools are financed by the State, their teaching staffs are paid by the State, and this same National Socialist State is an organism created by the will of the nation, an organism representing national interests. Did it not do so—were it, for example, to represent sectarian interests—it would offend against the will of the people. That is and must be our starting-point in dealing with the question of denominational schools. Any other presupposition is illusory, unfounded in solid reality, and can but resemble some product of Jesuit dialectic.

Schools are necessarily a concern of the State, for they serve primarily to educate the coming generation of citizens, and to prepare them for life. And what kind of a life? Life in this world, life within the bosom of the race! To prepare them completely for carrying on the struggle inherent in life. These are purely earthly concerns, concerns of this world, concerns from which a sober consideration must exclude all question of other possible allegiances.

The claim made by the Pastoral—viz., that our curricula should be in accord with the Christian spirit—seems to us a most odd appeal. We never knew before that Mathematics, Geography or Chemistry had points of contact with the Christian spirit. We have never heard of a " Catholic " decimal-system, or of " Protestant " orthography! Do they think, perhaps, that " Catholic " gymnastics would lead to specially successful results!

Truly, it is no question of denominations, but of Race. It is not the Church which is primarily interested in the mental and physical education of German children, in its excellence or lack of it, but the State, which represents the Nation.

The State, moreover, is concerned with impregnating young people with the realisation of national unity, the realisation that they belong by ties of blood to a unity arising from those ties. How can it, therefore, favour a denominational separation of Catholics from Protestants? It is not our appointed task to point out to boys and girls those sectarian differences which divide them. Rather we aim at showing them in the course of their education that the great community of the German people stands out over and above all such divisions and oppositions, and that they belong to it, come what may. That is the true meaning of German community schools.

The Church has its own institutions, apart from these, in which she can prepare men for the world to come.

Another publication, *Jugend und Recht*, produced an essay written from the standpoint of political philosophy, which was quoted as follows by the Essen *Nationalzeitung* on March 31st, 1937. The exclusion, it stated, of denominational and other organisations for the education of youth

indicates that a generation is in charge of the State which follows the Führer in acknowledging obligations, not to any denomination or to any class, but solely to Germany. It is inspired by a faith which Baldur von Schirach formulated as follows: " He who serves Adolf Hitler, our Führer, serves Germany, and he who serves Germany, serves God."

On April 29th, 1937, the *Schwarze Korps* objected to State patronage of religious instruction:

We do not regard Religion as a " subject " which must be mastered before one may qualify for higher education. Religion is the private concern of the individual and has nothing to do with educational courses as such. Everybody has the right to see that his children receive religious instruction, but nobody is under an obligation to do so. We must recognise the fact that those who nowadays belong to no Church, belong to no Church; how, then, can their children possibly be excluded from higher education, since they are absolutely unable to take any examination in religion ?

On May 13th, 1937, the *Schwarze Korps* wrote as follows: " The Catholic Church has always adopted the trick of talking about danger to religion and the Church whenever Roman religious Congregations have been excluded from the public affairs of the State." The article then proceeded to attack a leaflet issued by the parish of St. Mary's, Berlin, in defence of denominational schools. Later it stated: " There is downright impudence and duplicity involved in the accusation made against our community schools, that they endanger faith and morals." The article concluded with the citation of a memorial presented by German patriots at Frankfurt, 1848, in favour of the abolition of denominational schools.

On July 8th, 1937, the same paper quoted the following short exposition of the aims of Catholic education by Canon Thielemann of Fulda:

Education which aims at producing German citizens is not the highest kind known to us. The very highest aims, in our view, are represented by an education which has in view man's natural and supernatural status, which treats him as a child of God, and aims at leading God's children, with the aid of His grace, to an eternal union with God. Education to citizenship is contained within this framework, and will be achieved the more surely, the greater the value attributed to religious motives as the most supreme and fundamental envisaged by education. Those who, contrariwise, remove purely human values, based on the nature of human society and, indeed, vital and worthy of all honour upon the purely terrestrial plane, from their human and terrestrial setting, and make them the supreme norm of all values, including religious values—such men do nothing less than make idols of them, and warp and falsify the divinely-instituted order of things.

Having given this quotation, the writer showed by his attacks against this clear and conclusive exposition that the standpoints adopted by Catholicism and National Socialism are incompatible, and at the same time indulged in the following deplorable calumnies against Catholic education:

Emerging from this significant bombast came a demand to the State by this representative of the Episcopacy for all children who are dependent on public care to be given over to Catholic charitable organizations. This would mean that they are to be handed over to criminals.

This demand and, still more, its theoretical foundation constitute a terrible revelation of the views current in ecclesiastical circles with regard to so-called charitable work. Only the underlying theory can explain the fact that in such institutions orphans, waifs, anti-social and mentally defective cases are lumped together; for these pious educators are concerned primarily with achieving record totals of pious deeds, and not with the educational welfare of individual lives.

What Rev. Dr. Thielemann has written reveals the chasm which separates two standpoints. " Education which aims at producing German citizens is not the highest kind known to us," says this pious fellow, and with that statement all argument ceases. The rest of his remarks are but mendacious babblings. We know only too well what " education which aims at forming children of God " has come to mean in such Catholic institutions. The " immorality " trials utter their own awful speech against Catholic " educators."

The essay from which the above quotations are taken bore the title " No More Spiritual Slave Traffic."

Attacks on **Christian missionary work** are also frequent. Adolf Hitler wrote in *Mein Kampf*[1] that both Catholics and Protestants were burdening negroes with Missions which they neither desired nor understood. " Devout missionaries wander through Central Africa, setting up Missions for the negroes, until our own ' higher culture ' has acted upon those healthy, long-established primitive peoples, and produced once more a putrid bastard brood." Alfred Rosenberg, the Third Reich's special professor of Ideology, wrote on the same lines in his " Myth of the Twentieth Century,"[2] setting missionaries on the same level as opium traffickers and dubious adventurers, and expressing the hope that all missionaries would depart from China.

The *Schwarze Korps* wrote on September 26th, 1935:

American negroes must have gone half-crazy with the feeling of being courted so ardently ! First came Jewish Communism, with its strenuous efforts to win these blacks; then the sects got going with equal zeal, striving to present the prospect of Heaven to the children of Africa.
In St. Louis, U.S.A., they are now training lay-people to secure black souls. A society has been founded whose members aim at transforming black into white, and whose duty it is to instruct in the Catholic Faith, in biblical history and hymn-singing, all negroes whom they can get into their clutches. It would seem that unemployment in the U.S.A. is even greater than official statistics allow, for otherwise how could so much valuable time possibly be squandered ?

In the same paper for January 7th, 1937, appeared an article entitled " German Girls for India ":

If it were not plain to read in black and white, one would scarcely believe that our title represents the contents of an invitation appearing in churches, clubs and clerical papers. It would seem that our " race-conscious " and " patriotic " clerical circles are prepared to deprive healthy German girls of their duty of motherhood within the race, and to tear them away from their home-country.
Perhaps the Catholic Lord God in his Heaven will forgive us poor heretics for entertaining views, with regard to the tasks appropriate to German girls and women, wholly different from those of His representative on earth. To be precise, we consider that German womenfolk must first fulfil their duty towards their own race, and only after that be free to rove abroad. One may suitably leave such foreign excursions to over-prolific nations !

On February 18th, 1937, the *Schwarze Korps* attacked the practice of making collections for Catholic missions:

In the eyes of the pious, the most pitiable of all creatures are undoubtedly those little negro children who have never come into contact with either calico or the waters of baptism. Missionary societies have therefore set

[1] P. 446. [2] P. 653.

to work collecting corks, tin-foil, silver paper, and the like, in order to save heathens from eternal damnation. Old jewellery is received, of course, with a hearty " May God reward you ! " and serves for the manufacture of chalices, etc., for Missions in the darkest parts of the earth.

On August 25th, 1937, the *Mainfränkische Zeitung* published the following remarks under the headline " German Children Count More for Us ":

> All these so-called " Offertory-boxes for Pagan Children " must be smashed. German children mean infinitely more to us than pagan children. We remind our readers of this nuisance because the season is rapidly approaching at which the German Winter Relief Work calls to every member of the German nation, the season when its collecting-boxes appeal for alms in every shop. How absurd are these continual appeals for pagan children at a time when all German citizens are bound to relieve the rigours of winter !
> We would even style it treason to the race ! May the Winter Relief collecting-boxes appear with no such rivals, lest righteous anger should chance to speak its own plain language !

On October 14th, 1938, the *Völkischer Beobachter* announced with the greatest satisfaction that

> Vatican circles show dissatisfaction with the progress of Catholic missions. Whereas non-Christian populations in general are multiplying rapidly, the figures for conversions in Catholic missions show no proportionate increase; and a relative decrease in the Catholic population of the world is becoming more and more noticeable.
> Possibly this indicates that there is no solid foundation for the Vatican doctrine of " one, universal, Catholic race." Possibly, too, those " heretics " are correct who maintain that every race seeks to acknowledge God according to its own peculiar laws. Judging by reports from Catholic missions, there would seem to be much truth in this.

In connection with a Congress of the " German Society for Racial Research " (March, 1939), many representatives of the State and the Party, and amongst them the Director of the Party's Department for Racial Policy, listened to a paper by a Professor Rodenwaldt on " Racial-Biological Problems in Colonial Countries," in which a violent attack was made on Christian missions in pagan countries. The report in the *Völkischer Beobachter* for March 31st reads as follows:

> The lecturer next dealt with the effects of Christian missions, which, he said, making all allowances for the personal achievements of individual missionaries, must be regarded as altogether unhealthy. Such an uprooting of natives from a traditional and long-tried attachment to tribal and clan-laws, and from a type of religion which answers to their very nature, produces men who are drifters, men with no firm attachments, given over to every passing temptation. The very fact that European missions are obliged to present God in the guise of a white man deranges the minds of natives. Acting in an altogether contrary way, while gradually educating natives so that they may master the technical achievements of European civilisation, we must strive to retain unspoilt as much as possible of all that is peculiar to their make-up. Professor Rodenwaldt maintained that doctors, officers and lawyers are better suited to act as ambassadors from Europe than are missionaries. In the future the National Socialist State will shape its colonial policy on those lines. Legislation for the protection of the race will be obliged to prevent, not merely the intermingling of coloured and white races, but also intermarriage between different coloured races.

On May 18th, 1939, the *Schwarze Korps* made the following observation in the course of an article entitled " Pious Theft ":

It is an open secret that missionary activity, and more especially that of the Catholic Church, is often directed to the production of an anti-German propaganda which closely resembles the unbridled outburst of a mendacious, world-wide press.

The same paper published a series of articles under the general heading " White for Black," in the course of which it objected to Christian missionary work. We quote a few passages, the first from the issue for June 8th, 1939 (p. 8):

The missionary, too, has come up to date. He visits his black flock in a luxury car in no point inferior to its European equivalent; and should a coloured woman in Stellenbosch wish to have her youngest child baptised, she must first put two shillings on the font, otherwise there is nothing doing. Grace has to be paid for ! Moreover the little nigger babies must have even white names—and preferably taken from the Old Testament !

The article goes on to speak of

a man from the Bantu tribe of the Xosa who had married four wives, a concession which the Mission had been obliged regretfully to grant, lest such an excellent member of the Christian community should be lost.

The article ended as follows:

There is no longer any need to ask whether it was wise to make Christians of negroes, for nothing suits them so ill as the Christian religion. Negroes inherited no little sense of order and discipline from their home-life and tribal conditions; but the Mission wrenched them from their roots in the tribe and deprived them of all independence. What has the Mission offered them ? Nothing more than the privilege of being tolerated amidst the white community as a species of half-men ! Even if negroes do not fully comprehend the " Christian " gulf which separates them from white men, and hope to meet the white man in Heaven—still, baptism has not been able to change their nature.

The next article of the series argued that Christianity corrupts the characters of natives. It described " the outstanding characteristics of God's grenadiers "—*i.e.*, the missionaries—as " perseverance and diplomacy," and then presented two pictures of Kaffir chiefs. Under the first stood this sentence: " A Christian Kaffir Chief . . . and yet he possesses a dozen wives, a secretary and a telephone. He has learnt how to combine tradition with modernity to the best advantage." Under the second picture was printed: " A Pagan Kaffir Chief; pagan, but uncorrupted, healthy in both thought and action."

The third article in the series aimed at proving that Christian missionaries are, in practice, paving the way for the spread of Communism amongst coloured peoples. Under certain circumstances the results of education given by missionaries must be catastrophic. Indirectly, at least, Christian missionaries encourage the emancipation of coloured races, and foster their longing for equal treatment and their hatred of Europeans.

ATTACKS ON CATHOLIC DEVOTIONS 453

Catholic devotional practices, too, come in for their share of ridicule. On February 16th, 1936, for instance, the *Schwarze Korps* directed its scorn against the adoption of St. Christopher as the patron of car owners.

Catholic Action has turned graciously to the motor industry and has provided the new Germany with the use of one of its finest saints. No doubt pilgrimage shrines will be set up in various districts whither car owners may go to have their cars, from simple " baby " cars to luxury limousines of all makes, German and foreign, dedicated to St. Christopher. Moreover little shields are being sold so that all may know that horse-power is now in the service of higher things. . . .

St. Christopher is numbered amongst the fourteen Helpers in Need, and people have resort to him on the most varied occasions. He puts his abilities, for the whole day, at the service of all who look upon his picture early in the morning. True, he must find it a little difficult to help those who are suffering from a certain courtly and contagious disease, but a single little prayer does the trick. At the same time he will act as a poor man's solicitor in criminal affairs; he looks after sailors and bargees, pilgrims and travellers, porters and gardeners, and, even so, finds time to protect the harvests of English peasants against storm and hail. Any spare time he has he employs in keeping an eye on French fortifications. The fortress of Belfort has long been his chief residence.

In view of his adaptability and gifts it is not surprising that he has now been made the protector of the motor industry. Yet it is, perhaps, a little surprising, in view of the magnitude of his burdens, that he should now have been called upon to watch over the *Hanomagwerke*. Every car turned out of that factory now bears a picture of him as far as his knees, the rest of him being in the water.

We are against all two-job men. We may let Christopher exercise his powers in the service of Insurance Companies against storm and hail; let him enter into competition with solicitors; even let him watch over tulips in greenhouses. But the motor-car industry he must leave to others, for, in the first place, he knows nothing about it, and would only get in the way of the teams at races; and in any case . . .

Saints who hawk their blessing and their portrait remind us too vividly of globetrotters with their photographs . . .

However, let him carry on guarding the French fortifications and giving advice to the recruits within them, whenever Venus gives them a box on the ear.

On May 28th, 1936, the same paper satirised the practice of praying to the saints, and illustrated its article with cartoons. On June 24th, 1937, it wrote as follows under the title " Sancta Hysteria " on the occasion of a service on the feast of St. Catherine of Sienna:

St. Catherine was a completely neurotic subject. She maintained that Jesus Christ associated Himself personally with her, had betrothed her, exchanged His Heart with hers, and allowed her to drink His Blood. Nowadays we should waste no time in consigning her to the nearest asylum. The majority of milliners will refrain from striving to imitate her example, particularly as this saint has done nothing professionally for their calling, and has not become famous on account of any special " creation." Viennese milliners are reputed to be as practical as they are gay, and it speaks much for their sound good sense that they manage, after this ecclesiastical function, to wash down the oppressive claims of this hysterical model with a hearty draught of lager.

On May 18th, 1939, the *Schwarze Korps* published the following satire on the subject of votive tablets in Catholic churches, referring in particular to one inscribed: " In gratitude to the Mother of God for releasing us from unemployment."

> Again the nation has its bread;
> At joiner's bench the lathe-shaft clanks.
> On festive days rings overhead
> The cry " Thanks to our Führer, thanks."
>
> The chimneys smoke, machines revolve,
> No unemployed need tear their hair.
> Who can indeed the question solve—
> How came about this change so fair ?
>
> To God's own Mother should we utter
> Our thanks (or should it be the Pope ?)
> For Friday's wage—our bread and butter—
> Put in a little envelope.
>
> Believe it ? No, the folks don't dare;
> And yet it stands the acid test.
> The folded arms of pious prayer
> Help factory economics best !

The same paper published satirical verses about a piece of silk, on which the Holy Coat of Trier had rested till 1933 and which had been given, on April 21st, 1937, to a lady by the Vicar-General of Trier. The letter which accompanied the gift was reproduced in facsimile and the verses followed.

> Those who with truly pious soul
> Become involved in business feats,
> Can spin such yarns as ne'er unroll
> On pagan printed sheets.
>
> The pious will believe the lot.
> The clerics then exploit their faith,
> And touch rock-bottom—and the slot
> Of a Christian fire-proof safe.
>
> These oracles ne'er hesitate,
> To mar the face of truth afraid,
> And so come business deals in spate—
> The " relic " retail trade.
>
> The carpenter with awe removes
> The shavings from his heaped-up bench—
> The cry of " True Cross Splinters " proves
> A fair, alluring wench.
>
> For pale hen's bones demand 's no less,
> And buyer's tastes the markets meet;
> They long for genuine " holiness,"
> With bishop's seal complete.
>
> A special joy for bleary eyes
> Of pious lambs, they then present
> Whole bales of silk in first-class dyes
> For uses reverent.
>
> The " faithful " clothier and dyer
> Comes here on special business bent;
> On every 100 yards gets Trier
> Reduction 5 per cent.

In 1937 the *Berlin Catholic Magazine* contained a report of a petition in favour of the beatification of Martin de Porres, O.P., a holy negro who was famous as a doctor some 300 years ago. In its issue for November 4th, 1937, the *Schwarze Korps* commented on this in verses which we translate as follows:

> Rejoice, you pious Christian band,
>   Both erudite and rude;
> From you the black-skins now demand
>   A reverent attitude.
>
> Now Brother Martin's negro lips,
>   (Unless the Pope has more),
> Will find a place in Christmas cribs—
>   On sale at the church door.
>
> They'll sell like fresh cakes offered hot
>   —Black plaster statuettes—
> For hard cash down paid on the spot
>   A good reduction gets.
>
> Now, in the Maori style perhaps,
>   With organ stops at swell,
> They'll ask the pious canting saps
>   The " Wumba " hymn to yell.
>
> 'Tis sure the good God's love so vast
>   Includes the negro host,
> Though many a Hottentot's grand repast
>   Is missionary boiled or roast.

On December 18th, 1937, the *SA-Mann* published a gross attack on the Catholic custom of venerating relics. A cartoon represented a priest with a hammer in one hand, smashing idols, while with the other he presented a garment, labelled the Holy Coat of Trier, to be kissed by a woman.[1]

The *Schwarze Korps*,[2] too, published a disgusting article entitled " Sacred Germ-carrier," in which the veneration of relics was alleged to be a horrible crime and a deliberate attack on public hygiene. St. Aldegund, for example, was described as a lady probably no less dirty than devout, and under a sub-heading " A Bone to Kiss " she was ridiculed in the following way:

It appears to be an indubitable fact that Aldegund had, during her life, the importance of a whole chemical trust, for her scanty remnants—a medium-sized fragment of cranial bone—exert a germicidal power equal to the needs of a large hospital. It is only on this tacit supposition that the parish priest of Arzheim can have taken upon himself a grave responsibility for the health of a whole parish by exposing once more for public veneration this cranial bone of his competent patroness.

Much more distressing to Catholics is an article of the *Schwarze Korps*[3] which sneers cynically at the Devotion to the Sacred Heart of Jesus. We give the beginning and the end:

In the Convent of the Visitation at Koblenz-Moselweiss, the Heart of the Saviour has transformed itself into a clock-face which has gone on " ticking " now for something like nine years without arousing much

---

[1] *Cf.* also the *SA-Mann*, February 26th, 1938. A quotation is given on p. 346.
[2] March 30th, 1939, p. 7.
[3] April 30th, 1936, p. 2.

attention in the public. In the summer of 1927, the Holy Father gave the Superior General of the Convent permission to set up, so to speak, as a clock-maker. As a result of this permission " The Archconfraternity of the Guard of Honour " came into existence—a queer sort of concern whose associates have their names inscribed round the " wounded Heart of Jesus," which sends forth its beams from the centre of a clock-face.

The members of the Confraternity pledge themselves to " an hour's watching "—*i.e.*, " without interfering with their ordinary occupations," they watch in spirit at their post of love before the Tabernacle, devote their thoughts to the Saviour and present Him with " a small offering." The " small offering " (in large print) seems to be the chief feature of this remarkable " Guard of Honour "—a bit of mischievous mediævalism at which one can only shake one's head. All this " tick-tock " with the heart of the Saviour which is in such appalling taste is further proof of how ingenious and unscrupulous a certain section of the clergy can be where " small offerings " are concerned—for which, to be sure, there is an enormous demand. And there actually are mugs who do " keep guard in spirit at the post of love without interfering with their ordinary occupations. . . ."

" May the Sacred Heart of Jesus be everywhere loved "—with this ejaculation 100 days Indulgence can be gained ! Just like 400 years ago !

A propos of an article in the periodical *Im Reich des Herzens Jesu*, the *SA-Mann* of June 26th, 1937 (p. 5), makes merry over the veneration of the Heart of Jesus and speaks of " Sacred Heart Germans," priestcraft and the like.

Devotion to the Guardian Angels is also held up to ridicule. Thus we have this from the *Schwarze Korps* of May 8th, 1939 (p. 16) :

The person who is diligent in going to Church and to Confession, who joins his hands nicely in prayer and does not overlook the Poor-Box, has a Guardian Angel told off for him by the Celestial Watch and Ward Society. Such a person needs no A.R.P.[1]

An outspoken Pastoral Letter of the Bishop of Berlin, which was read in all the churches of the diocese on July 11th, 1937, sums up the facts mentioned above in a clear and impressive manner:

Dear Children in Christ ! What has specially moved me to write to you is the fact that the attack on Faith and Morals, on the Church, the Pope, bishops, priests and faithful, has broken out in the Press, magazine articles and cartoons in a way that is unprecedented. This attack is launched not, as might be thought, by those papers alone which at all times have been given up to open warfare with Christianity. No, it is official Party organs enjoying the widest circulation, papers directed and promoted by those in high places, that are in the forefront of this attack on the Faith and on the Church, an attack that is carried on with weapons of every kind (including poisoned ones)—with slander, mockery, scorn, falsehood and misrepresentation.

The attack deplored by the Bishop was against all that is most fundamental in Catholic life. It aimed at destroying, but destruction alone could not achieve its purpose. A gap, a vacuum, must be filled, and so the place of Christian Faith and religion was given an *Ersatz*, a substitute—Germany, the new faith.

[1] *Cf.* the *Schwarze Korps*, August 17th, 1939, for a similar gibe.

CHAPTER VII

THE NEW MORALITY

ONE might perhaps be inclined to regard the indirect war against the Church as less harmful and effective than the direct, but in reality it is by far the more dangerous, for all the innumerable means of influencing public and private opinion which are at the disposal of National Socialism are continually employed in pursuance of its declared and consistent policy of supplanting Christianity and of setting up in its place its own pagan ideology.

It would be a fatal misunderstanding of the true nature of National Socialism to consider it a political system pure and simple. It is an ideology, and as such totalitarian—*i.e.*, uncompromising and intolerant. Its supreme values have been made absolute. All views and ideas, including the dogmas of the Christian religion, all human activities of the community and the individual, have to give up their own existence to become subordinate and subservient to this one all-embracing system.

National Socialist writers and speakers never weary of proclaiming this fact, that National Socialism is an ideology—*e.g.*, the *NS Lehrerzeitung* (*National Socialist Educational Journal*) emphasised as early as in 1934 that the National Socialist Movement alone has the right of re-forming and re-shaping the nation, and that it claims the *whole of man*. The claims of this ideology, the official exponent of which is Alfred Rosenberg, are thus outlined by Herr Friedrich Schmidt, director of the Central Training Department of the NSDAP:

> Instruction in ideology and political science, in short, in every branch of education, is one of the sovereign rights of the Party. . . . Consequently, there can be only one body responsible and competent for the education and training of the German people in the ideology of National Socialism.

In his speech at Reichenberg in March, 1939, Alfred Rosenberg declared, *inter alia*:

> We make no distinction between our State and our ideology, not even for the benefit of those who are willing to recognise our State and refuse to accept only our ideology. We did not fight to gain control of a police-state and a bureaucracy devoid of any ideology. We have been fighting for an idea, and we are not going to yield an inch of our claims.

In 1937, Rosenberg had said at Detmold: " National Socialism has always claimed the whole of man and his entire personality."[1] High Party officials are consistent in declaring that nothing is to be left to the Churches but the Beyond; life on earth in its entirety is to be subject to the National Socialist ideology.

---
[1] *Cf.* the *Frankfurter Zeitung*, No. 32, January 18th, 1937.

In consequence, life, to a very large extent, has become pagan in Germany, and the moral principles of paganism contained in this new philosophy are more and more gaining ground in the nation and the family. Neither, of course, is the individual conscience allowed any right of formulating or following its own decisions. The Führer alone " receives orders " from God, as was asserted by a scientist, Professor Wetzel of Tübingen, at a meeting of the National Socialist University Professors' Union. The *Frankfurter Zeitung*[1] summarises his lecture as follows:

> Another scientist, Professor Wetzel of Tübingen, outlined a realistically uniform plan of organic nature including Man. There was, he said, a hierarchy of living beings, starting from the cell and ending in the nation, each of them endowed with the instinct of self-preservation and service—*i.e.*, carrying out orders: thus the cell carries out the orders of its organism, the individual those of his nation and his Führer. The cell and the individual are mortal. The nation is immortal. It is not a part, but a unity and a whole; properly speaking, only the nation can be called God's creature.

The last conclusion drawn from this conception, which is of supreme political significance, emphasises

> that it would be an inversion of the right order for the individual to assume that he might receive immediate orders from God; there is only one who receives such orders: the Führer of the Nation.

In a letter to the editor of *Die Bewegung*,[2] a student had declared that, on account of the excesses committed against the Jews, which were a concession to savage mob instincts, his conscience and his membership in a Christian church would no longer allow him to remain in the SA (which, together with the SS, had been ordered to carry them out—*Translator*). The editor replied:

> His (the letter-writer's) conscience and his membership of a Christian Church impel him to take this step since, as a Christian, he alleges that he cannot subscribe to the National Socialist conception of right and justice. He manufactures his own conception of justice, a Christian, not a National Socialist conception. He holds himself responsible not to his Nation and his Führer, but, personally and individually, to his own conscience and to the Christian Church—*i.e.*, only to a section of the Nation. . . . This sort of theological student has no right to attend a German University; such are to be expelled.

Any considerations of a higher life, a personal and eternal existence after death, are resented as obstructions in the way of co-ordinating and subordinating the individual to the dynamism and totalitarianism of the National Socialist Movement.

It is only natural, therefore, that National Socialism, based as it is on such fundamental principles, should attempt to introduce in Germany a new pagan morality, which is bound to prove not only essentially antagonistic to Christian ethics but also destructive of the best vital energies of the nation, especially with regard to marriage, family and sexual life.

[1] No. 314, June 23rd, 1939. [2] No. 6, February 7th, 1939.

1. *The Fundamental Features of National Socialist Morality*

These are outlined with all desirable clarity in the *Schwarze Korps*[1] in an article entitled " Racial Morality." The views expressed there are, in our opinion, so important and instructive in elucidating the frankly pagan and anti-Christian character of this morality that, if space allowed, we would reproduce it unabridged. We quote the most important passages:

For nearly two thousand years the German people have been brought up in the belief that moral principles are not fundamentally derived from blood and racial characteristics, but from a revealed religion alone which claims to be valid for all nations and all races. Consequently, the German personality was outrageously raped in its spiritual and racial elements; its soul was deflected to follow alien laws; above all, its morality was forcibly based on a Beyond which was totally unknown, abstract, and thus continually clashing with the realities of life. This violation of the wonderful vitality of our forbears was slowly destroying the very essence of our people. The well-known expression of a deputy of the Centre Party " There is no such thing as a Germanic morality " is highly significant of the progress which this process of violation has made in the course of twenty centuries.

But it was not completely successful. It is a most gratifying proof of the racial superiority of the German people that it was able to produce a Führer and once again a racial ideology of its own. For National Socialism is nothing else. Nay, it is even more than an ideology in the traditional sense.

Its aim is not only to derive from the consideration of things certain practical rules of life, but it presupposes a *totally different* conception of the universe or philosophy of life. It is fundamentally a complete re-orientation of all former philosophical ideas. National Socialism introduces a new fundamental value which constitutes the basis of every being, which exists always and is always valid, which has been since the first beginnings and will be for all times to come. This supreme fundamental value is *Life*. This philosophy of life presupposes a re-orientation of all religious ideas by removing them from the intellectual sphere into the interior of man and transforming them into a perception of the Divine in the unceasing creative movement of Life. Thus a completely new morality becomes necessary.

It will only be possible to lead our people back to its true religion and morality by taking up an absolutely positive attitude towards Life. If man affirms Life, its heights and its depths, if he allows it to penetrate his whole being, he will again become conscious of the Divine. This Life, however, is to be regarded neither as a vegetative existence nor as the craving after all the sensual pleasures of the so-called *bon vivant*, but as a continual struggle, an unceasing forming, conquering, and suffering.

After misrepresenting the Christian doctrine about suffering, the article continues under the sub-title " Our Chief Aim is the Increase of Vitality."

A morality based on the demands of life is unable to set up an unchangeable moral code, because the eternal flux of life necessitates a progressive internal readjustment. The ethics of the Life-philosophy cannot and will not provide anything but an orientation, an attitude towards these problems. It is of little avail to educate man according to rigid, preconceived rules; the one important thing is to open his mind and to penetrate every fibre of his being with the current of life. Increase of vitality, that is the supreme demand of the Life-philosophy.

[1] May 6th, 1937, p. 6.

Of what kind is the morality growing out of this new Life-religion ? It is life, immediately lived, in contrast to life subjected to rigid moral rules. A man of a noble and superior cast of mind said once: " All theories, even those set up by the young, are bad, foolish, and harmful." Spiritual vitality is the foundation of every moral existence; he that is devoid of such vitality is worth nothing, even if he possesses the youthful strength of all mankind.

A morality that extols vitality, light, strength, love and joy will, under certain circumstances, be able to approve of many things that are contrary to traditional standards. Only one thing is contrary to this new morality—asceticism, the enemy of vitality.

The following paragraph is entitled " Everything that is Strong and Beautiful is Good."

Therefore we say: " Everything is good that promotes vitality—in short, everything great, strong, and beautiful; everything is wrong and immoral that sets up walls and barriers around the centre of vitality. This view comes at once into collision with a great number of ecclesiastical moral laws—*e.g.*, the attitude of the Church towards the eugenic legislation of the State.

A morality that justifies the unchecked procreation of stock by heredity and therefore also morally inferior, a morality that destroys the work of the Creator by the breeding of racially degenerate offspring, cannot claim to correspond to the moral order willed by the Creator, and is therefore devoid of any absolute value.

Everything that serves the preservation of the nation is morally good; everything that in the slightest degree threatens its vitality is wrong and abominable.

The moral man can neither approve the attitude of weak-kneed cowards who excuse everything on the plea of being determined by fate, nor the attitude of those who replace their own personal responsibility, wholly or partly, by the expiation of another man or of God Himself. True human dignity is impossible without the consciousness of the most exacting personal responsibility.

Another similar summary of the principles of this new morality is found in the *NS Monatshefte*[1] (*National Socialist Monthly*). The article treats at first of the Catholic doctrine of moral freedom and moral responsibility.

Properly speaking, although from a scientific point of view a discussion of this attitude might be dispensed with, it is inevitable, for Catholicism wields among the German people great influence and power of which it must be deprived because it is a danger to the national community.

The problem of compatibility of heredity and moral responsibility does not exist for National Socialist philosophy; it is already " a thing of the past " for the Party, and the same will soon be true for the German people.

Even the question as to the morality of human actions is irrelevant because

there can be no other moral standard than our will to safeguard the eternal life of our nation. This means . . . that we wish to have the greatest possible number of large families whose stock is sound and racially valuable to the German nation. It is by this standard that we judge man and his actions. What is all this talk about Christian morality ? It is enough for us to state here that it is based on oriental values which, in spite of all assertions to the contrary, are expressive of a racial mentality essentially alien to our own and which therefore were never really adopted by the Nordic Race. This contrast between racial and Christian standards should be sufficient to demonstrate that a morality based on the life of the nation is far superior to that of the Jewish or Christian religions.

[1] November, 1937.

FUNDAMENTAL FEATURES OF NS MORALITY

The moral code of National Socialism could be expressed in the one fundamental maxim: "The interests of the community override those of the individual." Whoever has understood this fact, whoever has felt that he is a German and thus part of that tremendous current of Life and Blood, has acquired an unassailable standard of action. For such a man the problem of moral freedom is no longer bound up with preliminary questions about moral responsibility.

2. Pagan Marriage Morality. The Significance of the New Marriage Law, published on July 8th, 1938

The New Marriage Law is, in the fullest meaning of the word, National Socialist, and characterized by all the relevant principles of its ideology. It excludes all Christian or religious views about matrimony and makes the marriage contract or the continuation of married life dependent on the vital laws of the nation, the race and the community. Matrimony is no more regarded as a Divine institution, but as the germ-cell of the State and the community.

It is then no longer an intimately personal and vital relationship, essentially based on the consent of husband and wife, but a public act related to the State and the community and legally valid only if performed by the State Registrar. The preconditions of the contract of marriage and of its continuation are fulfilled if and as long as its political and racial aims are accomplished and, therefore, the chief impediments of matrimony will be difference of blood and unfitness for marriage according to the National Socialist Eugenic Laws. Thus there will no longer be any nullity of matrimony in itself (*e.g.*, on account of the lack of consent of the parties), but only those marriages will in future be considered null and void that have been contracted in violation of the racial and eugenic laws, and any other defective marriages will have to be dissolved by the State that had performed them. Such a dissolution, however, is to have no retroactive force even if the parties withheld their consent at the civil marriage.

Consequently the only aim pursued by the new National Socialist morality is the racial benefit accruing to the national community.

A necessary corollary of this thesis is that this racial benefit which is good in itself and to be accomplished by all possible means must not be judged by the means necessary for its accomplishment but only by itself. This racial benefit alone is the standard of morality.

This morality proclaims that the end of matrimony is neither natural nor divine, but political; it is the procreation of children for the State.

Whenever this end is not achieved, such a marriage is morally evil and wrong and is to be dissolved, whereas, whenever it is accomplished, even if the bond of matrimony was concluded without legal formalities, the moral commandment has been fulfilled.

The *Schwarze Korps*[1] comments on this law as follows:

The value of this new law consists in the fact that the liberal thesis which looked upon marriage as a private contract has been done away with, whereas the interests of the national community have been given due prominence, Useless and barren marriages, and those whose continuation is morally unjustified, are to be dissolved. In this way healthy and strong partners.

---

[1] July 28th, 1938, p. 1.

bound by a meaningless and exasperating marriage, are to be given an opportunity of finding happiness in a new marriage and of fulfilling the national duty of procreation. This idea is made abundantly clear in the new law in spite of all the ifs and buts and concessions and reservations.

On September 29th, 1938, the same periodical is even more outspoken:

Unhealthy, unreal and purely formal marriages are of no avail to the State. It had and has to insist on healthy partners who may form a harmonious whole in a healthy marriage, on healthy children and a healthy family life! This is the sense of the reform achieved by the new Marriage and Divorce Law.

Naturally the new law provides greater facilities and more reasons for divorce.

A new and additional reason for divorce is sterility, or refusal to co-operate in the procreation and conception of progeny. Hitler himself has decided that marriages may be dissolved on the plea of sterility if one party has become prematurely sterile. There is, however, another clause that will be most frequently applied, which sanctions the dissolution of a marriage after a separation of three years, and in this case even the guilty party is allowed to claim the benefit.

The *Schwarze Korps*[1] wrote the following gloss on this clause:

The principle of guiltless disintegration of marriage, for which a demand had been most energetically advanced, has been realised—*i.e.*, a marriage in which the parties have drifted away from each other and which is of no value to the national community, may be dissolved even if, properly speaking, no guilt has been established. But it need not be dissolved, if one of the parties protests and attributes to the other the responsibility for the disintegration of the marriage.

Accordingly, by the decision of a County Court, a divorce is justified by the fact that the wife of a National Socialist had made purchases in Jewish shops. This Court dissolved the marriage, attributing the guilt solely to the wife, and based its decision on the following reason:

If the wife of a National Socialist, especially of a National Socialist official, makes purchases in Jewish stores and shops, in spite of the explicit veto of her husband, he cannot be blamed for growing cold in his matrimonial feelings.

The necessity of reasons for divorce has been retained, but their number has been increased. A sufficient reason for divorce, for instance, is quarrelsome conduct or hysteria in one partner.[2]

In a decision of the County Court of Halberstadt, the following principle was laid down:

" A marriage can become disintegrated by the continual nagging of an individual at the collaboration of his wife in the National Socialist movement. For years on end the defendant had made life intolerable for his wife by incessantly sneering at her being a member of the Union of National Socialist Women." The defendant had also expressed his indignation at his son giving the salute " Heil Hitler." On account of this guilt of the husband the marriage was dissolved. A further reason for divorce is announced in the periodical *Die Rechts-*

---

[1] July 28th, 1938.   [2] The *Schwarze Korps*, July 28th, 1938.

sprechung des Reichsgerichts auf dem Gebiete des Zivilrechtes[1] (*Decisions of the Supreme Court of the Reich in Cases of Civil Law*), edited by Dr. Otto Warneyer, Counsellor of the Supreme Court: " Disparagement of the Führer by a wife entitles her husband to claim a divorce."

Since its publication, paragraph 55 of the new Marriage Law has frequently been discussed in the Party Press. This paragraph laid down that a party can petition for a divorce if there has been a separation for at least three years and if the marriage itself is irremediably disintegrated so that it would be impossible to bring about a true matrimonial reunion. This paragraph, however, contains a clause according to which a party may not petition for divorce if he or she is wholly or preponderantly responsible for the disintegration of the marriage. In that case the other party can oppose the divorce.

The *Schwarze Korps* has repeatedly and bitterly criticised decisions of Courts which, based on this restriction, had dismissed petitions for divorce; there was even a public clash of opinion between the SS periodical and an official organ of the German Judicature.[2]

In March, 1939, however, this clear restrictive clause was rejected as irrelevant by an official commentary, and so the long-drawn-out controversy between the National Socialist Press, especially the *Schwarze Korps*, on the one side and professional juridical writers on the other, was decided in favour of the former. This new decision was published in the *Völkischer Beobachter*[3] as an authentic commentary on paragraph 55 of the Marriage Law. It says, *inter alia*:

> The allegation, based on paragraph 55, that the fact of issue excludes a petition for divorce, is completely unjustified. Disintegrated marriages are to be dissolved if such a petition is made after a separation of three years. The law " orders the dismissal of the opposing plea of the party if, in view of the true essence of matrimony, the preservation of the marriage bond cannot be regarded as morally justifiable." According to the National Socialist view of the essence of matrimony, a disintegrated marriage (of which disintegration a three years' separation is to be considered a sufficient criterion) is " unprofitable and, furthermore, deprives the partners of any opportunity to make full use of their energies for the benefit of the community." According to this commentary, the question as to the personal responsibility of either party is to be ruled out when judging whether a marriage is morally valuable or not. Thus the law-giver, in a commentary to his law, has sanctioned the principle put forward by the Party that it is " morally justifiable " to sacrifice an old marriage in favour of a new which is of greater value " in its racial and political aspects."

3. *Conclusions Drawn from this Marriage Morality*

Equal status of illegitimate children.

National Socialism, it is true, emphatically proclaims that it esteems highly and protects the family as the germ-cell of the nation, but it is only a logical deduction from the above-mentioned thesis to place illegitimate and legitimate motherhood more and more on the same level. This view, then, is often encountered in National Socialist writings.

[1] No. 2, 1935, p. 50   [2] *Cf.* issue of February 9th, 1939, p. 16.   [3] March 29th, 1939.

The *Reichswart* wrote as early as April 21st, 1935 (No. 16):

The State can only justify its claim to these (illegitimate) children if it prevents the illegitimate mother and child from being regarded and treated as second class individuals and second class members of the national community, and from being branded as such by pharisaical minds. National Socialism places honour first and foremost in national as well as in individual life. It will not allow millions of illegitimate mothers and children to be treated or regarded as Germans of inferior honour.

The equal status of the illegitimate child is also advocated by the *SA-Mann*.[1] The *Schwarze Korps*[2] writes in an article entitled " Every Mother of Good Blood is Sacred to Us " as follows:

In many cases the fact that the union is not legitimate is due to reasons which do not impair the human qualities of the parents.

The main reason, it would appear, is the material impossibility of young marriages. Between the time of sexual maturity and the material possibility of marrying, there is introduced too long an interval for the young people to expect them to pass through it in strict observance of chastity in the Christian sense. Another reason is the surplus of women. Hundreds of thousands of women are unable to marry because the men are lacking, especially those fallen in the Great War. A cruel fate prevents them from fulfilling their natural destiny. Many of them, nevertheless, snatch that destiny by force. They prefer to be illegitimate mothers rather than acid old spinsters. . . .

One cannot impose unnatural chastity on young people, but one can tell them that racial hygiene does not begin at marriage. In the same degree as our age champions a healthy sensuousness and rejects the evil spirit of bourgeois pseudo-morality, it will have to propagate the doctrine that it is dishonourable for a person of superior and valuable qualities to enter into a union with one of inferior qualities. " Tell me with whom you go and I will tell you what I think of you." That alone is the standard for the national community by which to judge legitimate as well as illegitimate unions.

According to this standard, however, we shall have to regard as valuable even the illegitimate union concluded between persons of valuable qualities; and that for two reasons: First, because it is the fault of our own social order and our own shortcomings that they are forced into that illegitimate union instead of into a legitimate one; and secondly, because the German nation cannot afford to lose millions of children of sound stock that are and will be the issue of illegitimate unions. We cannot and will not lose the children of parents who otherwise would have to waste the most prolific years of their existence, because their material earnings are not sufficient for marriage; we cannot afford to lose the children of those women who, belonging to the " surplus," can become mothers but not wives. This does not affect our fundamental maxim that marriage is and shall be the ideal union between persons of first-rate racial qualities. The education and future of children is best safeguarded in the marriage-union.

If we waited until this bourgeois morality had changed and all moralising elder aunts had died out, generations and generations of illegitimate mothers would have to pass through their purgatory on earth. No, we must not wait. Nor did those men wait who last year founded the *Lebensborn* (Source of Life), an association which makes the first practical attempt at treating illegitimate mothers in conformity with the moral standards that ought to be applied to them and their children.

The Homes of the *Lebensborn* are to provide for expectant mothers accommodation in a family atmosphere; these great families are open to them as soon as they wish to escape from the harshness of their surroundings.

[1] August 14th, 1937, p. 4. [2] December 30th, 1937, pp. 3 and 9.

They are allowed to enter the Home in the fourth month of their pregnancy and remain there for eight weeks after their delivery. . . .

" Every mother of good blood is to be sacred to us," thus the Reich Führer has written in the guest-book of one of the Homes of the *Lebensborn*. That is our maxim.

The *Lebensborn* receives every mother of good German blood, if it is to be expected that her child, too, will be of good blood. The racial and eugenic qualities of the mother and the father are therefore enquired into before her reception. . . .

The *Lebensborn* safeguards the private and public secrecy of pregnancy and delivery. The Homes have their own Registration Offices. The *Lebensborn* takes official charge of the unborn child and is the guardian of all children born in its Homes. By assuming this guardianship it safeguards the future of mother and child.

The *Schwarze Korps*[1] expresses great indignation at the term " begotten in dishonour." It writes as follows:

A man requests the Protestant parson in Limbach near Oschatz (Saxony) to forward to him the baptismal certificate of his grandmother. The parson sends him an extract from the baptismal register; the man on receiving it scarcely trusts the evidence of his senses when he reads " Baptised, etc., on March 20th, 1839, begotten in dishonour." We don't mind at all going through life with a grandma born out of legitimate wedlock and certified as such in our official pedigree, if in all other respects she was worth her salt. We are also quite willing to overlook great-grandma's " trespass," if the result was good; in any case, she most probably had good reasons for it.

But we are not going to accept the aspersion that grandma, that good old lady, should have been " begotten in dishonour." We have our own views about honour and dishonour different from those of the pious parson who, a century ago, had the living of Limbach and poured out the vials of his wrath in true Old Testament fashion. . . .

Since, however, such degrading and idiotic notices, due to the sense of the decencies of the parson then in charge, are found in many old church registers, it would be appropriate to grant express leave to the church authorities to rectify these entries. For it is not necessary that, according to the precepts of the Bible, the sentiments of wrath felt by those ancient parsons should pursue the grandchildren even unto the seventh generation.[2]

On June 1st, 1939, the *Schwarze Korps* wrote:

Compromises only produce confusion. Illegitimate mothers have to bear the same burdens and undergo the same perils as legitimate mothers. Every healthy motherhood is sacred ! So-called moral considerations are to have no say in this matter.

Single persons are asked to become mothers.

The principles which we have described above lead, when consistently acted upon, to another terrible consequence. Unmarried women are asked to bear children. We refer in this connection to what the *Schwarze Korps* wrote on December 30th, 1937: " We cannot afford to lose the children of those women who, belonging to the ' surplus,' can become mothers but not wives."

A proclamation by the Mayor of Wattenscheid (in Westphalia), which was explicitly approved and praised by the *Schwarze Korps*, the official " Organ of the Élite of the Party," makes it clear that National

[1] February 16th, 1939.   [2] *Cf.* also *Schwarze Korps*, March 2nd, 1939, p. 21.

Socialism is determined to draw this fatal conclusion. We read thus in its edition of April 6th, 1939:

The city of Wattenscheid is suffering from a deplorable scarcity of births. . . .

The Mayor has now decreed that measures are to be taken at once to remedy this calamity, measures *worthy of all praise and imitation.* As from January 1st, 1940, the Corporation is going to grant to every eugenically sound family which will produce a fourth, fifth, or further child after January 1st, 1940, the necessary capital to acquire a house of its own or to rent a modern and healthy four-roomed flat at a maximum monthly rent of thirty-four marks.

For every third, fourth or further child born after April 1st, 1939, the Corporation will pay the mother a bonus of one hundred marks.

All these grants, however, will be made dependent on the written intimation, made known to the Corporation beforehand, that there is an intention of establishing a large family and of procreating more children.

Thus for the first time in history stress is laid on the difference between " intentional " and " haphazard " children. Only the intentional child can be regarded as the fulfilment of one's national duty, and gives its parents the right to put forward greater claims on the national community.

The same grants, this proclamation continues, are due already, at the birth of the first or second child, to all women born before 1910 who, through no fault of their own, have remained unmarried for the sole reason that the men destined for them by nature have fallen in the War, if only they can overcome traditional prejudices and bear children to their people. The city of Wattenscheid will take the place of honorary sponsors to all such children honourably born. The godchildren of the city receive as a birthday present a savings certificate of five hundred marks and may rest assured that special care will be devoted to them by their home city until they come of age.

In this way vital reserves of our nation will be mobilised, which up to the present have remained unused because whole generations of German women were condemned to sterility by ignorance and stupidity, by the moralising mediocrity of philistines and by the anti-national whisperings of the guardians of the confessionals.

Although moralising, maudlin, old maids had decreed that, to the two millions of men sacrificed in the War, the corresponding two millions of women should be added by mummifying them into old spinsters, they are now called upon to follow their natural destiny as women.

The clause, that the child to be begotten is to be brought beforehand to the notice of the authorities, ensures that no child begotten without serious intention should be regarded as a voluntary contribution to the common weal. At the same time, this clause will induce those unmarried women that are willing to bring forth children, to examine the prospective fathers of the children to see whether they are worthy of that dignity. For the national community cares only for such children as are eugenically and racially first-rate, not for those that will only prove a burden and increase our stock of inferior humanity.

The Mayor of Wattenscheid emphasises that these clauses cannot be applied for the benefit of antisocial and eugenically inferior persons. This presupposes, of course, that the authorities, too, have subjected the prospective fathers to a close scrutiny.

The institutions established by the *Lebensborn* are also in this respect perfect. The Homes of the *Lebensborn* receive only those expectant mothers that are in themselves eugenically first-rate and can prove the like of the fathers. Since the maternity homes of the *Lebensborn* possess Registration Offices of their own, the origin of the children can be discovered only by those concerned, not by the prying guardians of morality.

How much this is necessary is clearly shown by a letter received from Wattenscheid by the *Schwarze Korps.* This reader of our periodical, a man,

SINGLE PERSONS ASKED TO BECOME MOTHERS

writes: " The demographic policy of our Mayor is, in my opinion, contrary not only to the sane sense and feelings of the people, but also to the eugenic principles proclaimed by the National Socialist State. Such a policy is bound, in the long run, to create conditions which up to the present have been vigorously condemned by the Government. Quite apart from that, however, every German woman and girl considers her honour insulted by this degradation, and the publication of your article has roused a real storm of indignation. . . ."

Those that sympathise with such " storms of indignation " have apparently not yet realised that the wedding ring does not constitute a biological hallmark, and that it is scarcely honourable for a German woman to look down on those whose prospective husbands, destined for them by nature, fell on the battlefields of the War.

This language is not ambiguous; yet up to the summer of 1939 there were only found sporadic measures or tentative projects of this kind. The war, however, gave the National Socialists a very welcome opportunity of brutally pushing to the fore their crude biological point of view. They opened a nation-wide campaign in order to induce the German people of its own freewill to abandon the most elementary moral principles. Since Christmas, 1939, the National Socialist Party and the State have started a systematic propaganda in favour of their motto, " More children at any cost, if necessary out of wedlock !" a motto that debases woman to the function of a child-bearing machine and degrades the whole national life to the level of a stud farm. The Party and its different sections have made liberal promises to promote the welfare of illegitimate children and their mothers. We quote two documents illustrative of this policy.

In its Christmas edition of 1939, the *Völkischer Beobachter* published in large type two letters entitled " Rudolf Hess to an Unmarried Mother." The first letter is that of a young woman who expects a child by her fiancé fallen in Poland, and has in her distress sought the help of the Representative of the Führer. The second letter is Minister Hess's answer to this mother; he expresses his willingness to take charge of the mother and the child, as its sponsor. The mother and the child would be treated by the Party in exactly the same way as if the marriage had been concluded beforehand. Similar provision would be made for all young mothers of the same category. He writes:

Every new life is of the greatest importance to the nation, especially in time of war, which demands the sacrifice of so many young men. Therefore if young men of unimpeachable racial and biological qualities are called to the colours and leave behind to hand on their blood to coming generations children borne by women of corresponding age and similar qualities, with whom marriage for some reason or other is not immediately possible, steps will be taken to preserve this valuable national inheritance. Considerations to the contrary, justified in normal times, have to take second place in this matter.

The Minister declares himself convinced that within a short period his point of view will be shared by the whole German people. The letter concludes with these words:

" The common weal—*i.e.*, the life of the nation—takes precedence over any principles reasoned out by men, over any customs which may be the expression of acknowledged usages but not of morality itself and, above all, over any preconceived ideas. The highest service a woman can render to the community is to contribute to the preservation of the nation by giving life to children of racially sound stock. You ought to be thankful that the man you love is living on in your child.

Heil Hitler !
RUDOLF HESS."

This correspondence takes up nearly the whole of page 10 of No. 358 of the *Völkischer Beobachter*. The editor remarks in his comments: " The Representative of the Führer has invested the expression of the National Socialist point of view with high dignity." These two letters were reprinted by the greater part of the German Press. Almost simultaneously, a leader appeared in the *Schwarze Korps*[1] entitled " A Serious Question and a Serious Answer." It dealt with the same question and advocated the same solution. In its following numbers, too, the same paper repeatedly inculcated the necessity of bringing about a radical change of heart in the obsolete bourgeois attitude towards unmarried mothers and their children ; *e.g.*, on January 4th, 1940, under the headline " The Victory of the Women "; on January 25th, 1940, under the title " . . . And What will Happen Later ?"

The second official document is an order issued by the Reichsführer of the SS, Himmler.

THE REICHSFÜHRER OF THE SS AND CHIEF OF THE GERMAN POLICE IN THE REICH MINISTRY OF THE INTERIOR

BERLIN,
October 28th, 1939.

SS Order to the whole SS and Police Force

Every war causes the loss of most valuable blood. Many a victory gained by its armies actually meant for a nation a crushing defeat of its vitality and blood. It is, however, not the death of the best, necessary and regrettable as it is, that is to be deplored most, but the lack of those children that during the war ought to have been begotten by the living soldiers and after the war will never be begotten by the fallen.

The old wise saying that only he may die peacefully who leaves sons and children behind must find its application in this war, especially in the case of the SS. He may die peacefully who knows that his " clan " and family, his own aims and aspirations as well as those of his forbears, are to live on in his children. The greatest gift to the widow of a fallen soldier is invariably the child of the beloved.

Beyond the pale of civil laws and customs, which in other circumstances are perhaps necessary, it will be possible for German women and girls of good blood to take upon themselves the high privilege of becoming, even out of wedlock, mothers to children of soldiers called to the colours, of whom fate alone knows whether they will return or die for Germany.

Those men and women also who are ordered by the State to fill their place on the home front, are, especially during this time, reminded of their sacred obligation of creating new life.

Let us never forget that the victory, gained by the sword and the blood of our soldiers, would be illusory if it were not supplemented by the victory of the child and the colonisation of the newly-won territories.

During the last war, many a soldier, conscious of his responsibility as a husband, had decided to beget no more children for the duration of that conflict, because in case of his death he did not wish to add another burden

[1] December 21st, 1939.

to the heavy cares of his wife. You, men of the SS, need not entertain such fears and doubts: they have been removed by the following decree:

1. The Reichsführer of the SS will personally appoint guardians for all legitimate and illegitimate children of good blood whose fathers have fallen in the war. We will take special care of these mothers by charging ourselves with the upbringing and education of their children until these come of age, so that no mother or widow need suffer any distress.

2. In case of need or misfortune all expectant mothers and all children, legitimate and illegitimate, who are born during this war, will be provided for by the SS. After the war, the SS are ready to grant additional material aids in a liberal way to any fathers who have returned from the front, and are able to substantiate their claims to these grants.

Men of the SS and you, mothers of those children that Germany expects from you, prove that, inspired by your faith in the Führer and your determination to safeguard the eternal life of our Blood and our Nation, you are resolved to hand on your life for the good of Germany with the same courage as you are willing to sacrifice it for Germany.

The Reichsführer of the SS,
Signed: H. Himmler.

Taking into account that this decree and the above quoted articles are not isolated facts but supported by the all-embracing and powerful propaganda of the Third Reich, we are able to realise to what an abyss of moral perversity National Socialism is dragging the German people.

Another consequence : Divorce.

In the annual statistics published by the City of Essen, we come across some instructive figures of marriages and divorces which may be taken as the average of the industrial district of Western Germany. These statistics show that since National Socialism has come into power the number of marriages (which have been encouraged in every possible way) has considerably increased, but that in the same degree the number of divorces has risen. In the course of 1935, 6,683 marriages were concluded in Essen, while during the same period 714 marriages were dissolved. Compared with 1925, the number of divorces shows an increase of nearly 100 per cent.

The following are the figures for the whole Reich:

According to the statement of the Statistical Department of the Reich, 50,377 marriages were dissolved in 1936—*i.e.*, 32·5 divorces out of every 1,000 marriages in 1936, compared with 33 in 1935, and 15·2 in 1913. By far the largest relative number of divorces is found in Berlin, where there are 227·9 divorces out of every 100,000 inhabitants. The smallest relative number of divorces is found in Lippe, the frontier province Posen, Western Prussia and Upper Silesia. In Bavaria, too, where in 1936 3,545 marriages were dissolved and 94 declared null and void, the frequency of divorce (45·2 out of every 100,000 inhabitants) is considerably below the average for the Reich (74·7). Among the reasons for divorce the most frequent are: violation of matrimonial duties and dishonourable or immoral conduct. In 1936, 30,720 men and 18,091 women in Germany were found guilty of these delinquencies; 8,665 men and 7,488 women were found guilty of adultery.

It is worth while to note the increase in divorces since 1880. According to the periodical *Volk und Rasse*[1] (*Nation and Race*), the number of divorces in the Reich (pre-war and post-war territory) was as follows:

    1880: 62,221—*i.e.*, 0·14 per cent. of the total population.
    1890: 74,872—*i.e.*, 0·15 per cent. of the total population.
    1900: 92,017—*i.e.*, 0·16 per cent. of the total population.
    1910: 128,578—*i.e.*, 0·22 per cent. of the total population.
    1925: 283,139—*i.e.*, 0·45 per cent. of the total population.
    1933: 494,522—*i.e.*, 0·76 per cent. of the total population.
    1937: approximately 1 per cent. of the total population.

The introduction of the Racial Laws led to an astounding increase of divorces. In 1933, the year of the decisive victory of National Socialism, 37 marriages out of every 10,000 were dissolved—*i.e.*, 54,402 from a total of 15,317,000. Since then this number has decreased a little; but the annual average of 50,000 divorces, or 33 out of every 10,000 marriages, is more than double the average of 1913 (16,657 divorces from 10,923,000 marriages, or 15·2 out of every 10,000). The periodical *Wirtschaft und Statistik* (*Economics and Statistics*) supplements these figures with instructive comparisons about the duration of divorced marriages. The year 1934 had already witnessed an increase in the number of " life unions" dissolved after one year only; yet in 1935 it was 18 per cent. higher than in 1934, and in 1936 14 per cent. higher than in 1935. It would seem that the encouragement and aid now given to marriage lead to the union of many couples who after the lapse of a few months realise that they are not suited to one another. In regard to marriages concluded before 1933, it usually took a long time for the parties to resolve definitely to end their disharmonious union by divorce. Thus out of 50,337 couples divorced in 1936, 1,537 had celebrated the silver jubilee of their marriage, and more than 20,000 had been married over ten years.

Increase of mixed marriages.

In 1936, 19·14 per cent. of all Catholics who married concluded mixed marriages—*i.e.*, nearly one out of every five. Add to this the sad fact that in the last ten years only 37·94 per cent. of these mixed couples were married in the Catholic Church, and that of these only 58·15 per cent.—*i.e.*, little more than half—had their children baptised by a Catholic priest.

The testimony of these few figures is unequivocal. Tens of thousands of Catholics and their descendants are annually lost to the Church by these mixed marriages.

4. *Pagan Sexual Morality*

The *Schwarze Korps* in commenting on a word of advice against moral dangers, addressed to recruits by the *Parish Magazine of Lage* (Lippe), takes the opportunity to protest against the repression of healthy instincts:

[1] No. 4, 1938.

It is not he who after reaching marriageable age represses his healthy instincts for other worldly reasons that is, to our eyes, a man, but he is a man indeed that affirms his instincts joyfully and on account of this affirmation forces himself to observe the necessary restrictions, conscious as he is of his own responsibility to the national community. We cannot admit into our ranks one who, trusting in the promise of an eternal life, believes that he may despise this earthly life whose supreme perfection we consider to consist in the eternal re-birth of human life.

Puberty is a period of transition during which the young man, on account of his inner experiences, is more than usually susceptible to all exterior stimuli. A sensible education, however, can easily avert all difficulties and dangers which, despite their delicate nature, certain old-fashioned moralists deem it necessary to discuss with the young. Since this subject has been broached we are going to give our own opinion on it. Presupposing, as we may, that the greater part of our youth takes a sensible view of life, we are of the opinion that those young women, who are generally classed together as frivolous and dissolute and whose attractions are said to be heightened in the eyes of young men under the influence of drink, are of less importance in this matter than youthful homosexual delinquencies which, if not discovered in time, may do great damage to the interests of the national community; and that these evil tendencies are essentially furthered by the above-mentioned moral theories which, from our modern point of view, cannot but be regarded as cranky. The healthy instincts which begin to agitate the young man are condemned by them as base and immoral, instead of being directed into their natural channels. Consequently the young man, unless he has sufficient strength of mind to ignore these warnings, takes up the fight against the supposed foe in his own heart, but often enough he is led to aberrations which cannot be termed healthy, let alone normal. And all this happens because the attempt has been made not to aid a natural development but to deflect it by an education which is biological nonsense.

Imbued with such principles, the Party press derides as prudish cant any admonitions to preserve modesty, reserve and moral self-control.

A sensation was caused by the decree against prudish cant issued by Röhm, Chief of Staff of the SA (shot on July 1st, 1934). We quote it from the *Hamburger Fremdenblatt*:[1]

The Chief of Staff of the SA, Röhm, issues the following decree:

It is evidently for want of some other productive occupation that certain individuals and associations have taken upon themselves the task of carrying out the " moral " reform of the German people.

These reformers may be left to themselves as long as they merely proclaim their ideal aims privately in pamphlets or in such periodicals as agree with them. But real damage is done as soon as such persons, claiming to act on the authority of the State or the Party, proceed to put this pastime into practice. It cannot be denied that this is the case and that a very orgy of reforming is being indulged in by these prudish hypocrites.

E.g., the most stupid regulations have been made regarding bathing costumes and conduct in public baths.

German women have been forbidden to use face powder, or to smoke in restaurants; in the large cities all places of amusement not in keeping with narrow bourgeois standards are to be banned; a campaign is being waged against so-called prostitution, a campaign as hypocritical in its nature as it is brutal in its execution and fatal in its consequences to public health and hygiene.

All this activity is inspired, it is alleged, by a sentiment of sacred responsibility for the good of the nation; in reality it is nothing else but

[1] No. 263, September 23rd, 1933.

attempts at satisfying repressed complexes which for centuries have repeatedly been made by hypocrites and prudes.

It is clear from evidence at my disposal that there exists a great gulf between theory and practice in the lives of many who in this respect have come to the fore as moral reformers.

More recently I have received new information that even SS- and SA-leaders and men have publicly set themselves up as moral censors, and on these grounds have subjected women to molestations, insults and even maltreatment, in public baths, restaurants and in the streets.

The growing number of such excesses of prudery and worse, which often, too, are of a ridiculous nature, provides me with a welcome opportunity of stating in unequivocal terms that the German Revolution was won, not by philistines and canting morality preachers, but by revolutionary fighters. These alone will safeguard its rights.

It is not the task of the SA to watch over the costume, facial culture and chastity of other persons, but to rouse Germany by their free and revolutionary fighting spirit.

I, therefore, forbid all leaders and members of the SA to lend any active assistance in this direction to those cracked, moral æsthetes. This prohibition finds a special application in the case of those members of the SA and SS who have been placed by me at the disposal of the Government as Commissioners of Police or other State Officials.

The Chief of Staff.
Signed: Röhm.

As a matter of fact, the campaign against immoral and trashy literature, which had been initiated in 1933 with a great show of energy and propaganda, has long since been abandoned and has even given way to a large degree of toleration and encouragement. The exaggerated cult of the body, the abetting of nudist tendencies and shameless performances, not least the advertisements for contraceptives—all these facts go a long way to prove that there exists no longer any danger of reproaching National Socialism with too great a care of purity. The war cry of the Minister for Propaganda, Dr. Göbbels, " Stop those self-appointed censors and lying moralisers," but most of all the unrestricted and detailed publicity given to immoral crimes in the whole Press of the Third Reich, have been undermining the morals of the people, especially of the younger generation, to a horrifying extent.

5. *Glorification of the Nude*

In its edition of December 17th, 1936, the *Schwarze Korps* in an article entitled " Is the Care of the Body a Private Concern of the Individual ?" explains the National Socialist principles in this matter. This article refers explicitly to the directives given by Adolf Hitler in *Mein Kampf*:[1] " The aim of the entire educational activity of the racial State is not so much the dinning-in of mere knowledge but the training of first-rate bodies." The article then proceeds to extol a book by Major Surén, entitled *Mensch und Sonne* (Man and Sun), which is praised for its exposition of the fundamental principles of the whole question and warmly championed as inspiring a new Aryan attitude to the body. We shall have to concern ourselves with

[1] P. 452.

this work later on, a work which openly advocates the Cult of the Nude.

The article of the *Schwarze Korps* continues:

The fostering of this new attitude to the body is in large measure due to the *Freikörperkultur* (Cult of the Free Body), which was founded by Major Surén and frequently recognised by all competent authorities as highly conducive to better national hygiene.

We consider it, however, still necessary to take up the cudgels in defence of Major Surén's theories and especially of the practical measures recommended by him, because of the insults heaped on his great moral work by those hypocrites and moralisers whom we have sufficiently branded elsewhere. They are not ashamed of giving free vent to their licentious imaginations . . . only because their obsolete mentality considers nudity indecent or even immoral, whereas it is the natural prerequisite for any care of the body. It is against these attacks that we state: The naked body as such can never under any circumstances whatsoever conduce to immorality, unless the onlooker, degraded in his sensual life, approaches it with indecent thoughts.

We learn in the same article that Herr Darré, Minister of Agriculture, is also an outspoken champion of the Cult of the Nude.

SS-Commander and Minister Darré has stated his fundamental views on this subject as follows: Since it is possible to learn how to judge and appreciate a body only by education and gradual and continual practice exercised on the living individual, the Nordic Race made it their principle to give their members an opportunity of becoming acquainted with each other in the state in which God had created them. This was the case not only in regard to individuals of the same sex, but also of both sexes for the purpose of learning how to judge each other.

The true aim of every Cult of the Body is the selection of mates on racial principles for the benefit of future generations. For us town-bred people the absence of clothes, effected for a short time but on principle, means the determined and wholehearted abandonment of the dualistic body-soul philosophy, and thus a deliberate attack on the anti-national and anti-racial tendencies of medieval ecclesiasticism; nakedness also signifies the victorious ascendency of our racial ideas which have again saved our people on the very threshold of destruction. In this respect, the racial consciousness of our nation is of supreme importance. We demand a healthy existence on earth, and for that reason we emphasise the body.

The next passage is directed against those who identify the new Cult of the Free Body with the Cult of the Nude which had been propagated by the Marxists.

It is a great merit of Major Surén's courageous book to have rescued the " Cult of the Free Body " from the dangerous influence of those petty, decadent minds who prated about sun and health, and debased the good cause to the dreamings of romanticists. We are, like Surén and his book, opposed to this tendency and demand a strong and joyful affirmation of this new attitude towards the things of the body, because we need it for the creation of a strong and self-possessed race. Only in that case will the coming generations be able, in their exterior form and appearance too, to live up to the high demands which nowadays, as during the time of Greek culture, are the indispensable prerequisites for great achievements.

What, then, is the truth about this much advertised book of Surén's?

It is entitled "Man and Sun: The new Cult of the Nude in Germany," published by Scherl, Berlin. By the beginning of 1936, 85,000 copies had been sold. The author introduces himself as a Major (retired), Director of Physical Training for the members of the *Reichsnährstand* (Agricultural Corporation of the Reich), late Inspector of Physical Training of the Labour Service, and Director of the School for Physical Training of the former Reichswehr.

Three facts prove that this book represents the official views of National Socialism.

1. The author emphasises his position as Director of Physical Training for the members of the *Reichsnährstand*.

2. Representatives of the Third Reich, such as Hitler, Rosenberg, Göbbels, Darré (especially the last-named), are quoted in support of his claims.

3. On February 27th, 1936, the official Reich Department for the Promotion of German Literature approved this book in a very laudatory testimonial, some passages of which follow:

The author lays special and reiterated stress on the fact that promiscuous bathing and play of the sexes in a nude state leads to the routing of any false and hypersensitive eroticism, and thus provides a remedy essential for the establishing of healthy sexual feelings and relations. The book, in explicit and emphatic terms, dissociates itself altogether from the Cult of the Nude as advocated by Marxist associations under the old régime. It bases its demands completely on the racial and national aims and ideals of National Socialism, quotes long passages from speeches or works of the Führer, Dr. Darré, and Dr. Göbbels, and vigorously emphasises the great importance which the execution of these demands will have in furthering the racial aims of National Socialism. *Viewed from a racial and political angle, the tendency of this book is to be approved and encouraged on principle.* Such ideas as breeding and upbringing, which presuppose a renewal of the natural and original esteem of the family as a means of living on in one's children, can and will, in the long run, only be realised if the human body, the foundation of all earthly life and racial perpetuity, is redeemed from the defamation attached to it even today by many as a result of ascetical beliefs. We welcome on principle, from our National Socialist point of view, every work which helps to see natural things naturally, and thus to regard the naked human body as something as pure and valuable in itself as the human mind and soul.

The author, it is true, tries to prove an essential difference between his views and those of the Marxist champions of the nude, by emphatically rejecting the phrase "Cult of the Nude," and replacing it by "Cult of the Free Body" and "Aryan-Olympian Spirit"; but, as a matter of fact, the vigorously stressed difference exists only in his imagination, for:

1. The same book was issued before in 1924 and hailed by the Nudist Movement of the Socialists and Communists as a pioneer work of their own ideas.

2. The methods of propaganda are exactly the same as those used under the old régime—*i.e.*, pictures, slogans against prudery, cant, hypocrisy, and, above all, the passionate campaign of insults and calumnies against the Catholic Church.

Just to demonstrate what kind of extremist ideas are propagated in the book, we quote the introductory sentence of a longer paragraph: " It is of primary importance from a hygienic point of view, to set free the privy parts. . . ." Eighty-five nude pictures illustrate the ridiculous campaign which in the name of Nordic racial morality is waged against the " un-Germanic bathing costume " and the last scanty remnants of clothing worn at games, athletic sports and bathing.

The following facts, concerning the " Movement of the Cult of the Free Body," will be of interest. The Prussian Minister of the Interior, in a decree issued on March 3rd, 1933, had forbidden the former Nudist associations to hold any public meetings, a prohibition which reduced them to insignificance. But as early as towards the end of that same year, new groups were formed which called themselves the *Freikörperkulturbewegung* (Movement for the Cult of the Free Body), and which, organised in the *Bund für deutsche Leibeszucht* (German Union for Physical Training), come under the direction of the Department for Mountaineering and Excursions, a subdivision of the National German Union for Physical Training. These groups issue a periodical, entitled *Gesetz und Freiheit* (*Law and Freedom*), which in the summer of 1936 averaged 4,000 copies. In the April number of this periodical, a decision of the County Court of Appeal of Stettin is printed which in its main lines is equivalent to a cancellation of the above-mentioned decree of the Prussian Minister of the Interior. The copies of this monthly are filled with illustrations which, exactly as before the triumph of National Socialism, show groups of naked men and women.

The *Bund für d. Leibeszucht* issues a periodical, *Deutsche Leibeszucht* (*German Physical Training*), the first number of which (January, 1938) advocates and defends the joy felt at the sight of a well-developed, noble and healthy human body. In the May edition (A) of 1938, we read the following: " We are of the opinion that a healthy human being may in suitable places openly enjoy the free play of his limbs and the uncovered beauty of his body, even in the presence of the other sex."

Exactly the same principles are propagated in National Socialist writings; *e.g.*, the *NS Monatshefte*[1] extols Lucas Cranach, that, daring to advance much farther than the Italian Renaissance and Dürer or the Dutch painters, he restored to her proper place in life the German woman and mother who had been debased as an instrument of concupiscence by medieval asceticism, and placed " her slender, naked body in its tree-like beauty as a symbol of grace and fertility amidst the budding and growing life of the German landscape." (This article is illustrated with pictures of naked women by Cranach.) The *Schwarze Korps*, too, on October 20th, 1938, advocated true and noble nakedness.[2]

---

[1] No. 87, 1937, p. 523.

[2] The fact that the National Socialist Press has no inhibitions in reproducing obscene nude pictures, can be evidenced by the following references: The *HJ*, February 1st, 1936, p. 3; the *SA-Mann*, June 26th, 1937, p. 10; the *Schwarze Korps*, May 27th, 1937 (poem *Verliebtes Gemecker*); and the following issues: February 17th, 1938, p. 13; April 14th, 1938, p. 15; August 18th, 1938, p. 1; January 19th, 1939, p. 10; March 9th, 1939, p. 13; July 6th, 1939, p. 10; July 13th, 1939, p. 5; *Völk. Beobachter*, No. 146, of May 26th, 1939, p. 4.

We need only refer to the speeches of the notorious Gauleiter Streicher to characterise the obscene way in which high officials of the Third Reich address even the young. Isolated voices of disapproval may sometimes be heard, even in the National Socialist press, which call attention to the fatal consequences inherent in these activities. Thus the October edition, 1935, of the periodical of National Socialist Women *Die deutsche Kämpferin* (*The German Woman's Fight*) wrote, *inter alia*:

It is necessary to ask oneself with all seriousness whether the minds of the young are not in danger of suffering vital harm from the extremely crude representation of sexual crimes and other sub-human abominations which are publicly displayed everywhere in print and pictures. One cannot but notice that these posters and periodicals are regularly surrounded by children of every age asking each other: " I'd like to know what that is, criminal assault and murder ?" or " Do you know what racial violators do ?" or " How does one take advantage of a girl ?" or " What is rape ?" Is it, further, a sign of a moralising philistine to object to the frequent transmissions of rhymes and of more or less indecent couplets which sufficiently characterised a past age whose artistic tastes were unrivalled for their liberal toleration of the obscene ?

Terrible consequences of these tendencies.

It is, then, small wonder to find that the last years have brought a tremendous increase in the number of people suffering from venereal diseases, and of criminals under the legal age. According to the *Schwarze Korps*,[1] 75 per cent. of all men in Germany are said to be infected with venereal diseases.

The *Statistical Annual of the German Reich* publishes the following figures concerning the increase of cases dealt with by the Juvenile Courts. In 1934, 1,058; in 1938, 3,374. This figure shows an increase of 300 per cent. due to the influence of the National Socialist philosophy. In estimating the significance of these figures one has to take into account the fact that nowadays in the Third Reich prosecutions are frequently dropped if the accused are members of National Socialist associations. Moreover, numerous decrees were issued which gave explicit and far-reaching orders in this respect.

Another significant increase of 258 per cent. during this period is that of abortions procured by girls under age; next in order come vagrancy (increase of 150 per cent.), murder (increase of 129 per cent.), arson, grave bodily injuries, fraud, theft, blackmail, robbery, etc. An extraordinary increase is noticed, too, in the category of immoral crimes, such as rape, incest, etc. In 1934 the Reformatories housed about 54,000 youthful inmates; in 1938 about 78,000.

619 young persons under age were found guilty of immoral delinquencies in 1932, 612 in 1933, 779 in 1934, 1,058 in 1935, 1,465 in 1936, 2,374 in 1937. The statistics, however, deal only with immoral crimes in the strict sense. In 1937, two and a half times as many juveniles as in 1934 were sentenced on account of damaging other people's property. In 1934, 6,947 young persons under age were found guilty of theft by the German Courts; in 1937, 12,475.

[1] May 11th, 1939.

6. *Other Pagan Moral Principles*

The frankly pagan principles advocated by the National Socialist press regarding honour, suicide, consideration due to the dignity of the human person, etc., are a consequence of the neo-pagan morality which we have outlined above. In the *Völkischer Beobachter*[1] duelling is defended in an article entitled " Vindication of Honour by a Court of Justice or by a Duel ?" The duel, although endeavours are made to restrict its use to the gravest cases, is regarded as the primary and appropriate means of vindicating one's honour, and, as we have mentioned above, all members of National Socialist associations have to declare their readiness to fight if necessary. The following comment is added to the word " honour " in the new German *Allbuch*, formerly " Mayer's Encyclopedia ":

> "*Honour*": A man is honourable only if the idea of German honour is inseparably bound up with his whole being. The entire new German universe is based on this new conception of honour. The Christian idea of charity is radically opposed to this conception of honour as entertained by the German people.

In the monthly *National Socialist Education of Girls*[2] we find the following remarks about " Blood Feuds ":

> The law of Blood Revenge underlies all Germanic life. Blood Revenge, vengeance for clan-blood which has been shed, vengeance for the honour of a woman who has been violated ! Blood Revenge leads us into the very depths of the Germanic religious sense; it is not, as was alleged, a relic of barbaric primitive periods. It was only considered sinful when the blood of the clan had been deprived of its sacredness.

No comments need be made on the well-known fact that, in its treatment of the Jews, the National Socialist State excludes all considerations of the dignity of human personality, justice, etc.

Though the *Schwarze Korps*[3] in an article on suicide rejects it in general, it nevertheless admits the following reservation:

> In some exceptional cases we may consider suicide a just expiation of grave crimes, but only if the perpetrator is absolutely unable to recover his honour in the life of the community.

The obituary notice dedicated to Captain Langsdorff by the High Command of the German Navy[4] is also significant in this respect:

> The Commander of the armoured cruiser *Graf Spee*, Naval Captain Hans Langsdorff, refused to survive the loss of his ship. He took his resolve in accordance with the tradition and training of the calling to which he had belonged for nearly thirty years. After he had assured the safety of his crew he considered his task achieved and followed his ship.
> The navy understands and appreciates his deed. Captain Langsdorff has thus in a soldierly and heroic way lived up to the expectations placed in him by his Führer, the German nation and the navy.

[1] South German edition, No. 184, July 3rd, 1937. [2] April, 1937.
[3] April 6th, 1939. [4] *Völk. Beobachter*, No. 356, December 22nd, 1939.

This account of Germany's " new morality " makes sad reading, for the mind turns naturally to the thought of the young who, inoculated with the virus, cannot help but succumb to the disease. Indeed the course of the war so far bears that out only too well. No consideration of what others would call honour, mercy or chivalry is allowed to stand in the way. The standard is—Germany: what is deemed to advance Germany is good; anything that impedes her is evil. The outstanding example is the fate of Poland, where horrors and excesses took place that beggar description—nor are they all yet known. There, so said an eyewitness of some of those atrocities, it was the young National Socialists who were the worst, the most brutal, the most barbarous; the older men, who had not yet, despite all the propaganda of the Party, forgotten the Christian tradition in which they were brought up, were, by comparison, angels of mercy—they dared not interfere with the others, but they did little themselves to torture and destroy the conquered.

How long will it take to root out of the German people all traces of this " morality "? God alone knows. It will, doubtless, need the passing of this generation and the rise of a new and then, perhaps ——. It is far and away more difficult to get rid of evil, too much in harmony with the lowest tendencies of human nature, than to build up good.

CHAPTER VIII

THE *ERSATZ* RELIGION

ERSATZ means substitute, and in latter years, so as to limit as much as possible its dependence on other countries for raw materials and to " waste " as little as possible of its native resources and its imports on non-military objects, Germany has been developing a host of " substitutes." To the Nazi way of thinking, however, the greatest obstacle to the fulfilment of the National Socialist programme is not the lack of materials but the Christian religion, because this proposes a loyalty to Someone who transcends even the nation and inculcates standards by which that, too, should be judged. The Christian religion, therefore, must go, and with it the ideals and aims that it embodies and which have been for centuries the inspiration of the German as of so many other peoples.

Man, however, is a creature with a positive attitude of mind; he will toil, suffer privation and even death itself for a positive, though perhaps extremely indefinite, ideal but not for mere destruction, unless that appears to him to be a step towards the attainment of his aims. This is true of Germany today. In the Third Reich the Christian religion is being relentlessly destroyed; Christian ideas are being ousted by the thoroughly pagan conceptions which National Socialists proclaim about God, Man, the universe, and the eternity and divinity of Blood and Race. This is not destruction merely for destruction's sake, but to leave the field clear for something else, something positive that will furnish ideals in conformity with the spirit of the " new Germany." National Socialism amid the ruins of Christianity is investing itself with the nimbus of a religion; a new religious mentality is being advocated, a liturgical language of its own is being introduced, and the Christian sacraments and symbols are being replaced by pagan ceremonies, symbols, and services. National Socialism is not only combating the old Church but also constituting itself into a church of its own, by taking advantage for its own purposes of the religious yearning and desire of service in modern man, of the religious energies that had been released by the reaction against Rationalism and the superficiality of our mechanical age.

Such a programme, carried out day by day with relentless insistence and indifference to opposition, and supported by the huge array of the forces of a totalitarian State, is bound, in the long run, to undermine the very existence of the Church.

1. *National Socialism sets itself up as a Religion*

The *Westdeutscher Beobachter*[1] commenting on a public administration of the Oath of Allegiance, wrote as follows:

> Yesterday witnessed the profession of the religion of the Blood in all its imposing reality. Yesterday saw the triumphant and decisive beginning of our fight to make National Socialism the only racial religion of the German people. Whoever has sworn his oath of allegiance to Hitler has pledged himself until death to this sublime idea. There is no more room for doubts and uncertainties, no room for retreat.

Dr. Schnabel, Professor in the University of Halle, wrote in the *Mitteldeutsche Nationalzeitung*:[2]

> In a certain sense National Socialism is a religion because it asks its followers not to become convinced of the truth of its doctrine (!), but to believe in it. Like any other religion, National Socialism possesses its own teaching on moral questions, and its own ethics, the classical expositions of which are, first, what the Führer wrote in his book *Mein Kampf* about the Aryan; and then the work of Alfred Rosenberg, " The Myth of the Twentieth Century."

In a speech delivered at Fulda[3] about " *Weltanschauung* and Religion " Herr Kerrl, Minister of the Reich for Ecclesiastical Affairs, dealt with what he called " the Babylonian confusion of tongues " which in our times had invaded religion and ideology. He protested against the attempts at playing off *Weltanschauung* and religion against each other and stated that National Socialism is " a Movement which not only acknowledges but lives the obligations due to God and the divine order." He continued:

> All the actions of the National Socialist State in the past four and a half years have been nothing but absolutely and positively Christian in their character. National Socialist positive Christianity translated its faith into practice; not only was it able to move mountains, but it actually did move them. We heard, it is true, the Churches proclaiming such a faith able to move mountains, but we never saw the corresponding deeds. . . . Then *he* came to us who restored to these words a wondrous meaning: it was he who told us: " Believe in the mission that God Himself has written in your hearts ! Be convinced that it is deeds, not words that matter. Be assured that God placed you in this world that being Germans you should devote yourselves to the service of Germany. Then you will live to see a miracle, a miracle not worked by intervention from above but by our active faith !"

Shortly afterwards, on November 30th, 1937, in a speech delivered at Hagen in Westphalia, Herr Kerrl said:

> Religion and our ideology converge in as far as they represent the sum total of human attempts to find an answer to the problem of right action. We have succeeded in finding the right answer. We have found it clearly and unmistakably by means of our reason; it is: " You are to act according to the strength that lives in you, according to your knowledge and your duty. Only politics can be the basis of true human freedom. There is a complement to this moral norm which we owe to our Führer. He taught us. . . . ' You must do your duty, you must act according to your conscience

[1] March 28th, 1934.   [2] July 4th, 1935.   [3] November 23rd, 1937.

—*i.e.*, the voice of your blood, that God has poured into your veins.'" Our blood is our conscience. Deep in our blood God has impressed the order that all who are of one blood should belong together and should grow together into the great organism of one national community. The Führer has transformed the conception of conscience in a socialistic sense by saying: " We have to fulfil God's orders by our deeds and our actions. Become positive Christians in deeds."

Even more outspoken is a lecture given by Minister Kerrl in the *Lessing-Hochschule* in Berlin on January 15th, 1938, which was thus summarised by the *Frankfurter Zeitung*:[1]

A comprehensive and uniting ideology would not be able to strike deep roots in a fertile soil unless, like a religion, it gave the people a certain and determined belief. . . . The principles of National Socialism are the principles of an eternal and unchangeable religion which consists in the development and achievement of the topical, national and socialistic tasks of the State.

In a book entitled *Rechtsgrundlegung des NS-Führerstaates* (Juridical Foundations of the National Socialist Aristocratic State), issued by the Central Publishing House of the Party, Dr. Frank, Minister of the Reich, writes, *inter alia*:

National Socialism is no denomination; it is, however, a doctrine which professes its faith in the divine vocation of the nations and especially in the great mission of the German nation. . . . Service given to one's own nation is a consecration and a service offered to God.

We may in this context recall Rosenberg's words which concluded his speech at Weimar in November, 1938: " To be a Nation, that is the religion of our age."

At intervals during the last few years Baldur von Schirach, leader of the Youth of the Reich, has expressed in slightly varied form the same idea, which he formulated, *e.g.*, at the inauguration of the Youth Hostel of Fulda in the spring of 1939 as follows:

All of us who have taken part in the fighting period of our Movement and now are seeing the wonder of Germany's resurrection are inspired by the same religious feeling. . . . We serve God by being loyal to our Führer and doing our national duty. We are, therefore, a youth that believes in God, because we serve the Divine Law that is called Germany.

This attitude frequently invests the absolute allegiance given to the person of the Führer with a distinctly religious halo. Leading officials of the Party speak of Adolf Hitler as if he were a Divinity, and by elevating his qualities into a superhuman sphere they proclaim a kind of pseudo-religious worship of his person.

At a meeting of the Hitler Youth in the Frankfurt Hippodrome, the chief speaker, Herr Willi Becker, Leader of the German Labour Front of the Province of Hessen-Nassau, said that " National Socialism was not to be compared with any former Party. Only future generations would recognise that fact. When in centuries to come mankind would see the present events in their true proportions they would say: ' Christ was great, but Adolf Hitler was greater !' " . . .

[1] No. 28, January 16th, 1938.

The *Kölnische Volkszeitung*[1] quotes the following sentences from a speech delivered at Kiel by Dr. Ley, Leader of the German Labour Front:

We owe everything that has been accomplished to Adolf Hitler alone. Our efficacy is derived from his strength, his mind, and his will. "*I am with you and you are with me*," the Führer said at a roll-call a year ago. This consciousness of a personal relationship between the Führer and ourselves is always present to us.

After three thousand years the teaching of Adolf Hitler will be as clear and unadulterated as today; it is the task of the Party organisation to safeguard its purity. Every official has to live his life according to his precepts and ask himself before every action: " Would Adolf Hitler approve of this ?" The word of the Führer must always be in all hearts.

At the conclusion of a demonstration of the Hitler Youth and the German Girls' League at Freiburg (in Breisgau) which had been ordered as a counter-move to a solemn profession of Faith organised by the Catholic Youth on the Feast of St. Boniface, the Hitler Youth proclaimed their loyalty to the Führer in these words: " Adolf Hitler, yesterday, today and the same for ever ! Heil !"

The *Nationalzeitung*, Essen, published on September 13th, 1938, the following poem by Baldur von Schirach, Leader of the German Youth:

HITLER

In serried ranks ye follow me,
And ye are I, and I am ye.

I've never lived a single thought
That in your hearts was not first wrought.

And forming words I know of none
That is not with your wills at one.

For ye are I, and I am ye,
And all our faith is Germany.

The echo awakened in the hearts of the people by such speeches of their responsible leaders is clearly shown by a number of letters to the editor of the *Schwarze Korps*,[2] who had asked certain readers to testify what " the Führer meant to them, and what part he played in their spiritual and material existence, their personal thoughts, impressions and aspirations." The answers which were sent in are very instructive.

To a father of seven children, Adolf Hitler

is all, he is my faith, my support and my hope . . . to my children the Führer is the visible personal expression of what in our youth was represented as God.

A mother confesses that the Führer has given aim and direction to her life.

Today I need not trouble myself to ask how to educate my children. The Führer in his crystal-clear words has wonderfully defined all ideas. He has uncovered all the sources of German life to which I need only lead my children. . . . They say that we Germans have become atheists. I have never felt the Divine Power as near as in the greatness of our Führer.

[1] June 7th, 1937. [2] April 20th, 1939.

NATIONAL SOCIALISM—A RELIGION

An Austrian woman writes:

What the Führer has given me is not only a political ideology, but also a religion. He has given me a faith, which, in its true form, I never before possessed, not even when I was young. This faith is the belief in ourselves, in our strength, in our greatness; the belief in the mysterious power of the Blood, of the soil of our Country, and of the German Nation.

Another cannot express in words what the Führer means to him. " He is my fate, as also that of all true Germans. Can a man describe his fate in words ? I deem it arrogance !"

To another it appears a profanation to think a personal relationship with the Führer possible ! " There are things of such a nature that by trying to explain them, they are divested of their Divine character."

The greatest emphasis is laid by all writers on the fact that the Führer constitutes the ideal that supports their whole life.

Once we were educated in a religious spirit. That attitude did not make us better, it scarcely deepened our souls; it led us, rather, to discouragement (*i.e.*, " humility ") and passivity. Since I entered the Party, the words and deeds of the Führer have always accompanied me, and they are becoming more and more the essence of my own wishes and actions.

Another letter confesses: " *Whatever he says is true; whatever he thinks is good; howsoever he acts, it is for the best.*"

In another testimony we read the following passages:

To me the Führer is the essence of all the virtues of the German people. He is my model in everything. He is my father who has redeemed me from the pressure and the dross that weighed upon my soul. As a matter of fact, I am not devout in the Christian sense; on the contrary, I have left the Church. But I consider the racial community of the blood to be a community much more in accordance with God's Will than the confessional community of all the denominations of this world, constructed as it is by men. This is my service to God: every day, an hour of quiet interior recollection and reflection. I do not, however, attribute to my father and Führer, Adolf Hitler, any Divine qualities in the meaning of the Christian doctrine of Redemption, but my Führer is the standard of my conscience.

Another letter:

How shall I put in words what I feel for my Führer and what part he plays in my existence ? I look up to him now as I prayed to God in my childhood, when I was deeply imbued with His kindness and omnipotence.

A woman, who, as she says, had been " spiritually famished " before the National Revolution, calls the Führer

the bread of which the soul stands in need. I would like to say openly that the high teaching of the Führer is to me a religion, the German religion ! I cannot think of a more beautiful explanation.

But it is not only hysterical women who write in this vein ! To one Adolf R., from Frankfurt, " Adolf Hitler means the same as the word, God, means to a fanatical and orthodox Christian."

To another who " in his early youth turned his back on the Catholic ideology " the Führer by his ideology gave a firm support.

Arthur L., from Hessenthal, compares the spiritual experience that the Führer means to him with that of his First Communion. But whereas the latter disappointed him because he did not feel any influx of Divine virtue, the Führer now takes the place occupied " in his youth by the good God."

One Hans W., from Munich, reveals that the portrait of the Führer " as my creator hangs in my office as well as in my drawing-room at home." Every glance at it releases in me " the feelings that devout people allege they experience in earnest prayer."

Quite consistently National Socialism has created a new piety, a new " National Socialist Faith "; moreover, the Party authorities do all in their power to replace Christian usages by pagan pseudo-religious customs. Baptism is imitated by a solemn " Conferring of the Name "; marriages and funerals are surrounded with a pagan religious ceremonial; the meaning of Christian feast days is changed in a pagan sense, and National Socialist services are provided with a neo-pagan cult and a pseudo-religious liturgy.

But National Socialism is not therefore in any way endeavouring to found a new Church; it does not aim at establishing a third denomination among the German people. On the contrary: while National Socialist leaders unceasingly proclaim " the Divine Mission " of National Socialism, though the immediate aim they have in view is to reduce the Christian Churches to the existence of poor, negligible sects, their ultimate aim is to make National Socialism itself a religion, and the loose ends, so to speak, of these aims are neatly spliced by the often quoted " positive Christianity " of the Party programme. Since the German people has been Christian in the past, the terminology of the new National Socialist creed will be moulded on Christian models— its terminology, but not its theology. As heretofore, men will speak of God, Faith, Sacrifice, Resurrection, Eternity, and Immortality, and the ceremonies celebrated in the course of the last few years at the Cult Places of the Party in Munich and Nürnberg and at the " Thing " Places " (*Thingstatt*) in the country will, perhaps, later be performed in former churches. State ceremonies and religious acts are to become identified. There will be neither a National Church nor a State Church in the accepted sense of the word, but a *Cult State*, the Political Church of National Socialism.

2. *The Neo-Pagan Cult*

Neo-pagan cult places instead of Christian churches.

According to the *Reichspost*[1] a question was asked at a meeting of the German Faith Movement in Hanover: " What is to become of the numerous churches when the present generation which still clings to Christianity has died out ? " The lecturer, Provincial Leader Dr. Hammerbacher, replied:

Churches of artistic and historic value will, of course, be preserved; they will be used for the solemn festivals of the German people, but naturally only after removing all Christian symbols. Many second and third rate churches, however, will be demolished. . . .

[1] April 2nd, 1937.

The same tune is played by the *Schwarze Korps*[1] in an article entitled "Things not Mentioned by the Priest-Agitators."

In our eyes the church buildings with their innumerable and unique works of art are not productions of the denominations but are due to the inspiration of the German spirit. The creations in stone in lofty cathedrals as well as in lowly village churches will for all times be regarded by our nation as the supreme achievements of the Masters of the Golden Age of Art: even he who never bent his knee before the wood-carving of a Madonna will gaze with reverent awe at the wonder created out of a piece of linden-tree by the inspired hand of the artist. The National Socialist State will, as hitherto, do all in its power to preserve these treasures of the past, be it the masterpiece of a genius or the work of a sensitive country artisan, whose simple name has long since been buried with his ashes. The interior of many churches will even be re-decorated so that men in search of beauty may the better enjoy their artistic attractions, and architects and builders find models for their future creations....

We know very well that there exists a clear distinction between an organisation, the clergy, on the one hand, and its possessions, the ecclesiastical property, on the other. Whatever those denominational officials deem necessary is of no interest to the State unless they trespass on its own natural competencies. If, however, the Churches in spite of sufficient means do not keep in a worthy condition works of German culture committed to their care, they must be made to fulfil their duty of preserving these valuable creations which were produced by the people, and therefore belong to the people.

History has proved in more than one instance that, priests being mortal, the religious doctrines preached by them are transitory. The peoples, however, that are conscious of their racial character, defy the ages. On October 17th, 1937, the *Alltagskirche* in Torgau was consecrated *a National Socialist* "Cult Place" by Reichsleiter Rosenberg; in the district of Mecklenburg three former chapels have been transformed into "Ancestral Halls," and many deserted buildings that once served ecclesiastical purposes will be given back to life in our youthful age.

It is too often the case that churches are left unused and do not fulfil their purpose. Other monumental buildings, often of exceedingly great artistic value, are still used as storerooms because the means at the disposal of the authorities are not sufficient to provide for all necessary repairs at once. The Party Associations, on the other hand, lack rooms that would captivate the heart by the attractions of their wonderful architecture, and are obliged to meet in village public houses and dance halls.

May the prophecy soon be fulfilled which Gustav Frenssen expressed in his work *Glauben der Nordmark* (The Faith of the Nordmark): " By the same church door where once the Catholic Faith, then the Evangelical entered, the new—no, the original—faith will enter, slowly, gently, naturally and without noise."

Since the triumph of National Socialism, a great number of so-called " Thing Places " have been built which are to become the Cult Places of National Socialist beliefs and aspirations—*e.g.*, near Heidelberg on the *Heiliger Berg* (Holy Mountain), where had been in succession a German shrine of Wotan, a Roman temple of Mercury, and later a Christian monastery dedicated to St. Michael. There is another, the *Sachsenhain* (Grove of the Saxons), near Verden (province of Hanover), and in October, 1937, still another was opened at Parsewalk in Pomerania by Reichsminister Hess in remembrance of the time spent in hospital there towards the end of the Great War by Adolf Hitler.

[1] February 16th, 1939, p. 6.

Neo-pagan perversion of the meaning of Christian festivals.

Christian feasts are gradually undergoing a metamorphosis of their meaning, to be replaced in the end by neo-pagan celebrations. There exists already a large literature working towards that end.

At the beginning of April, 1939, a certain Dr. Karl Ruprecht gave a lecture over the Austrian wireless on " The Church and Popular Customs." He alleged that the Church had misappropriated all popular Germanic customs; consequently Christmas, Easter, and other festivals would have to be divested of their artificial Christian character to be reinstated in their original dignity as racial and Nordic feasts of the German nation.

Christmastide Festivals.

In a course of political training, the Christmastide festivals were given a neo-pagan meaning. We summarise the outlines of this attempt.

This period covers the time from November 25th until January 6th. Important days are November 25th (St. Catherine's Day); December 4th (St. Barbara); December 6th (St. Nicholas); December 13th (St. Lucia); December 24th and 25th (Christmas); December 28th (Holy Innocents); December 31st (New Year's Eve); January 5th and 6th (Twelfth Night and Epiphany).

St. Nicholas, *e.g.*, is traced to Wotan; St. Catherine, St. Barbara, and St. Lucia, to the Three Fates, which in the north were called *Norns*, in ancient Greece *Moirai*, and in Italy *Parcae*.

The Nativity was for the first time celebrated at Rome on December 25th, 354, to replace the feast of *Sol Invictus*, or the Persian *Mithras*.

" In Germany the ecclesiastical Christmas festivity was first heard of in 813; it was introduced to supplant the native midwinter feast. Two names of this feast are mentioned: *Modraneght* in Anglo-Saxon and *Yule* in the Scandinavian languages. There are, moreover, two traditions about a child, *Nornagest* or *Helgi*, which was born at this time and endowed by the Fates."

The Magi are said to represent Male Fates, either the three brother-smiths Odin, Hönir, and Loki, or Slagfid, Egil, and Wieland.

The *Schwarze Korps*[1] alleges that

Christmas is not a spiritual property of the Christian denominations. They have taken this day without so much as saying " by your leave." . . . This Festival is so deeply rooted in the essence of our German being, . . . it is so exclusively the property of the German race that once and for all it is placed beyond the reach of hair-splitting theological and historical controversies.

The article then urges Germans living abroad to assemble round the loudspeakers and listen to the message of the Representative of the Führer because at this hour and at this German feast it is irrelevant whether they style themselves Catholics or Protestants, Christians or *Gottgläubige*.

[1] December 16th, 1937.

Another instance of these attempts to deprive Christmas of its Christian character is quoted by the *Osservatore Romano*.[1] The article in question is taken from the November issue of the monthly *Die neue Gemeinschaft* (*The New Community*), with the sub-title *Parteiarchiv für nationalsozialistische Feier- und Freizeitgestaltung im Auftrag der Reichspropagandaleitung* (*Party Instructions and Suggestions, issued by the Supreme Council for Propaganda, concerning Amateur Theatricals and Other Leisure Time Amusements*).

In this issue a new kind of celebration of the " Holy Night " is described, that night which heretofore has been kept as the Night of the Birth of Jesus Christ. The National Socialist celebration of Christmas is to avoid all reminiscences of denominational Christianity; because it is a profession of faith (in the Party of course). . . . The new programme for Christmas contains three principal items: first, Christmas as it once was; secondly, the German " religious " vision of Christmas; thirdly, Christmas as a profession of faith (in National Socialism). The *Osservatore Romano* goes on to quote at length a " sermon " published in the above periodical which explains the meaning of the new German Christmas. We read there, *e.g.*, that many Germans abroad, although they lived only a few yards from the church, were no longer satisfied with an ecclesiastical celebration of Christmas. Many preferred " The German Christmas " with the Fire, the Tree, and the Swastika as its symbols. While the fanatical " Church Christians " set up their cribs, those Germans who were insultingly described as pagans, decorated with the same joy their Tree.

Among the symbols of Christmas, every German ought to remember, come, first and foremost, all the Sacred Things of the nation, those fallen in the War, but above all the Third Reich which will exist for many thousand years. . . . Most of all we ought to remember him who has rescued the German people from poverty and distress. . . . His faith is also our faith. . . . Adolf Hitler ! Sieg Hiel !

The periodical *NS Erziehung*[2] (*National Socialist Education*), official organ of the National Socialist Teachers' Union, Berlin, gives suggestions how to invest school celebrations of Christmas with a racial character. A model racial celebration is outlined. Instead of the traditional ecclesiastical pattern which starts with the Bible story and is full of Judaisms such as " Jerusalem," " Bethlehem," " City of David,"" Alleluia," etc., names repulsive to a racially-minded German, " the headmaster emphasised in his address that they had no intention of travelling to a Jewish country. He dwelt on the strong sense of national unity and community as evidenced by the work of ' Winter Relief,' and urged all to be loyal to their Blood, their traditions and their Nation." The " German " Christmas Play that followed contained no ecclesiastical hymns, but in their place Praises of the Sacred Fire by Baldur von Schirach, Leader of the Hitler Youth.

The Bishop of Trier, Mgr. Bornewasser, in his sermon on New Year's Eve, 1937, characterises the attempts made to supplant Christmas by the so-called Winter Solstice celebrations:

You have heard of the so-called Winter Solstice celebrations. A few years ago I said: " I am not sure whether there lies therein a hidden danger for our youth." Today I am sure. *This artificially stirred-up old Germanic*

[1] February 9th, 1938. [2] December 4th, 1937.

pagan Consecration of Fire is meant as a direct challenge to the highest mystery of our religion, the Incarnation of Jesus Christ on the Holy Night of Bethlehem.

I leave it to you to judge for yourselves. What I am going to read is taken from the periodical *Führerdienst* (The Leader's Task) of the *Jungvolk* (Junior Section of the Hitler Youth), 12th Number, December, 1937, page 6: " At another meeting the Winter Solstice will be celebrated. We have to train our young members in order to enable them to celebrate this Christmas, stripped of all the parasitical excrescences which were implanted in the hearts and minds of the German people by the Christian denominations."

What is the meaning of this blasphemous remark ? Our young children are told that they have to get rid of all parasitical excrescences implanted in the hearts and minds of the German people by the Christian denominations. What are these ? The mystery of the Incarnation of Jesus Christ on the Holy Night. From the hearts of the young, the memory that Christmas is the day of the birth of our Saviour is to be eradicated, and an old Germanic pagan Consecration of Fire is to take its place. . . .

Christian Fathers and Mothers ! Now you know the real meaning of the celebration of the Winter Solstice. Up to now it had been concealed behind a mask, but today this mask has been dropped. We know now that all this talk about the German Winter Solstice is in reality directed against the most sublime mystery of Christmas, the Incarnation of Jesus Christ the Son of God. . . .

Der Arbeitsmann (*The Labour Service Man*), the official organ of the Labour Service of the Reich, gives on December 31st, 1938, an account of the Christmas celebrations of the Battalion *Ehrwald*, District Ostmark of the German Labour Services. It is entitled " The First Christmas of the Labour Service in Austria."

A high fir tree has been erected on a hill that looks towards the East; by its side a great stack of wood has been piled up. . . . The Battalion has taken up its position; they surround the fir tree and the pile in a wide circle. Dawn is slowly advancing, but the sun is still hidden behind the near mountain ridge. Suddenly its first rays cross the crest. The pile blazes up; the outstretched arms of the Labour Service Man salute the rising light: Winter Solstice! Silhouetted against the dawning sky and the background of mountains which are gradually lighted up, the Labour Service Men stand in solemn silence, saluting the light. The District Leader of the Labour Service is also present. He explains the meaning of the ceremony, the long night and the coming light. The contours of the men outlined against the sky form the symbol of the Rune of Life.[1] Head and trunk represent the vertical stroke, the outstretched arms the transversal.

For Christmas, 1938, the National Headquarters of the National Socialist Teachers' Union, Department for Popular Customs and School Celebrations, issued to all schools a decree that was clearly intended to deprive Christmas of its Christian character. Christmas was to be celebrated in the schools as a " People's Christmas, born of German Racial consciousness." The custom of hanging up the " Yule wreath " was to symbolise the old Germanic yearnings for the light during the winter.

In 1938 the Party organisations too, more than in preceding years, have celebrated in place of Christmas the pre-Christian Yule Feast and the Winter Solstice. The formations of the Party assembled in towns and villages around blazing piles of wood and followed nearly

[1] The Rune of Life is the sign placed by Party members over Press announcements of births of their children.

NEO-PAGAN "CHRISTMAS"—NAZIS CELEBRATE THE WINTER SOLSTICE.

[*Das Schwarze Korps*, Jan. 22nd, 1936.]

NAZI DEMAGOGY.

"Yes, indeed, brother; and yet they say that in Germany every man can live happily *in his own way*."

[*Das Schwarze Korps*, April 11th, 1936.

everywhere exactly the same ceremonial: hymns were sung, poems couched in the language of worship recited, an address on the Sacred Fire given, and wreaths thrown into the flames. In Berlin, *e.g.*, a SS-Leader threw into the fire six fir wreaths, dedicated to " the Heroes of the Great War," " the Dead Soldiers of the Führer," " the Earners of Our Daily Bread," " the Mothers of Our People," " the Youth, our Standard-bearers of tomorrow " and " the Holy German Fatherland." Every one of the six sentences recited by the SS-Leader was repeated by the Guards of the Fire and the surrounding formations. In one place twelve young men symbolising the twelve months of the year stood round the fire.

The celebrations of the SS are especially marked by their pagan character. The Reich Leader of the SS, Himmler, celebrated the Winter Solstice of 1938 in the Sudetenland. His personal staff took part in the Yule Feast celebrated by detachments of the Hitler Youth in the forests of the Mark Brandenburg. Fanfares of the Hitler Youth inaugurated the ceremony, and after the Fire address, delivered by an SS-man, an SS Group Leader lighted the pile of wood. Twelve men of Hitler's Bodyguard thrust their brands into the pile, while the hymn *Flamme empor* (Soar upwards, flame) was intoned. A gentle beat of drums, fanfares, and another hymn followed. Then the Group Leader kindled a torch at the blazing pile, and with some appropriate words delivered it to a Hitler Youth Leader who promised faithfully to guard the Fire.

Whereas National Socialists keep on reproaching Christianity for having adopted ancient Germanic customs and transformed their meaning, they themselves frequently adopt and de-Christianise traditional Christian customs. Well-known Christmas hymns have been changed to a National Socialist sense—*e.g.* (according to a report from Berlin of the *Neue Züricher Zeitung*):

> Oh, thy happiness ! Oh, thy holiness !
> Homely German Christmastide.
> No innovations,
> No latinisations;
> German, German,
> Shall be our belief.

The Christmas tree, too, is given another function; its top is no longer crowned with a star, but with a Swastika.

The following substitute for the well-known hymn *Stille Nacht* was widely propagated:

> Vault of the night, thou starlit dome,
> Soaring on high to bridge the deep,
> Over your arch our warm hearts roam
>   In far-distant lands to sleep.
>
> Vault of the night with its glowing fires,
> Kindled on mountain summits wild !
> The earth today has its young desires,
>   Like a lusty new-born child.

> Mothers, for you they are all aflame,
> All of the stars and all the fires:
> Deep in your hearts there beats again
> The heart of the Universe.

Easter.

In the small, old-world town of Lügde, situated on the Altenbeken-Hameln railway line, processions in honour of the Holy Eucharist used to be held several times a year until National Socialism came into power. The commemoration of Christ's Passion, too, has been celebrated there in moving ceremonies since times immemorial. On Good Friday the whole population, praying and singing hymns, go the Way of the Cross, which stretches for hours over hills and dales and is adorned with shrines and crucifixes.

These facts are, of course, not mentioned by the *Völkischer Beobachter*, but it relates that the little town has kept the ancient custom of the Easter Fire and the Easter Wheels. On Easter Sunday at nightfall the Easter Fire is lighted on the Osterberg (Easter Mountain), (formerly also on the Kirchberg), and huge wheels, of diameter about two yards, the spokes of which are plaited with straw, are set alight and rolled downhill. Only a few years ago the Christian population of the town had erected a huge Cross on the top of the mountain. When the wheels have all been rolled down the hill the people are assembled and greet them with Resurrection hymns, usually the ancient Easter Hymn the first verse of which reads:

> Let us acclaim with joyous glee
> Our Saviour's Resurrection.
> The shame and anguish of the Tree
> Are changed to benediction.
> Lift up your hearts, with love afire
> Sing with th'exultant angel-choir
> Triumph to the Victor.

National Socialism has Germanised this festival; and since this is a typical instance of the methods employed in the Third Reich, we quote the passage taken from the *Völkischer Beobachter*[1] in full:

> Even today, Easter, the spring festival of our forbears, in spite of all attempts to falsify it, has preserved its original meaning as the Feast of Victory, the celebration of the Resurrection of Life and the Victory of the Sun over the forces of Winter!
> Of the many and various Easter customs of our ancestors, the Easter Fire is most conspicuous in our country; it is part of the Germanic worship of the Sun.
> The purpose of this Spring Fire was not, as is alleged, to dispel " evil Winter Demons," or to influence the returning Sun with magical incantations; but to the ancient Germans the Fire was the symbol of the Sun, as the Edda has it: " Fire is the face of the Sun." Thus the lighting of the Easter Fires is the culminating point of the Germanic Easter celebrations.
> Never did our German peasants give up the custom of the Easter Fire although it was branded as " pagan." The most beautiful and outstanding

[1] April 7th, 1939.

form of the Easter Fire is found in some districts of our country, where lighted wheels are rolled down the mountain slopes.

This custom is immemorial and the most typical expression of the ancient pagan Sun worship. It has been kept alive in spite of all prohibitions, decrees, transformations and falsifications. It has been preserved especially in a small town of the district Westfalen-Nord, in Lügde, Kreis Höxter, near Bad Pyrmont.

Following ancient Germanic custom, on the night of Easter Sunday the blazing, heavy, oaken wheels roll down the slopes of the Holy (!) Osterberg; thus proclaiming that throughout the centuries our people has faithfully preserved the customs and usages of its forefathers. . . .

This year, too, preparations are being made for this celebration. During the last years of the decadence of our people, the number of those who cared for this old custom had considerably dwindled; but now, after the victory of National Socialism, a radical change has taken place. The SS have taken upon themselves the task of preserving the ancient custom of Easter Wheels, and in close union and collaboration with the Hitler Youth have given this Easter ceremony a new and worthy form. . . .

The SS, co-operating with the *Ahnenerbe* (Preservation of the National Heritage) of the Reich Leader of the SS, considered it to be incumbent on them to purge this ancient tradition of all alien, parasitical excrescences grown up during an age of indifference to the true National spirit, and to cultivate in its original meaning this custom which had been preserved essentially intact. It may be that someone or other misses some ceremonies which had grown dear to him, and that some alien additions have been removed which, like so many other things, had to give way to the true conception of Germanic freedom, but as the years roll on it will become more manifest that, in taking up the original Easter custom, our people has returned to the true, old traditions of its forefathers.

The Month of May and Whitsuntide.

Die Spielschar[1] contains an article by Karl Hayding, entitled "May Customs":

Whitsuntide customs are in complete harmony with other May customs. They were originally ancient popular traditions, which the Church laboriously transformed and to which it gave some kind of external connection with its new Feast.

On the eve of May 1st a tall fir tree is fetched from the woods and set up in the village. It is carefully watched, as the young men from neighbouring villages will try to remove it. The May Ride is performed around it, a custom which the Church in some places attempted to transfer to Corpus Christi.

The meaning of the usages of this season is indicated by the fact that a couple, the May King and May Queen, lead a Festive Procession. In Carinthia a highly significant race is run on every Whitsunday. Three lads compete, and the victor is welcomed by the "Whitsun Bride." A legend relates that in a pestilence only one young maid, and three young men had been spared. All three courted the young maid, and she consented to take as her husband the victor in a race. This story, which tries to trace the origin of this custom back to a historical event, points clearly to similar fairy tales where the bride is won after a contest. Shooting at a bird, running in a race, and other demonstrations of strength and agility are meant to prove the manliness of the wooing swain. Similarly Siegfried takes Günther's place in fighting for Brünhild.

The meaning of the climbing of the May Pole and of the Meetings of Marksmen, too, can be deduced from fairy tales. The danger of hasty and far-fetched interpretations is clearly seen in this matter—*e.g.*, some take

[1] XI., No. 4, April, 1938.

the bird as a symbol of the Summer Sun and thus bar the way to the true explanation, while, on the other hand, they leave to the Church a field for investigation which by right belongs to us. The Associations of Marksmen, which hold their meetings principally at Whitsuntide or in May, can be traced back to very ancient times. An essential feature of all of them is the shooting at a bird, which is either alive or carved in wood or sometimes only painted on a target. The victor is proclaimed " King of the Marksmen." These Associations often possess valuable cups, which are filled with wine and offered to the victorious " King." Some cups in the form of birds, which are rare nowadays, point to the original sense of the drinking. The Aryan peoples have a story about a wonderful beverage, the Water of Life or of Wisdom, which is stolen by a bird and carried off into the Other World. The hero of the fairy tale shoots at the bird, pursues it until he captures it, and at the same time wins the bride and the Water of Life. Thus we find in this festive custom the same fundamental idea of the renovation of all life that must be won by a struggle. This idea provides also an explanation for the " Miracle of Pentecost " as related in the New Testament. " The pouring out of the Holy Ghost " who filled all the Apostles is equivalent to the winning of the Water of Wisdom. The New Testament story has been borrowed from ancient Aryan sources which, however, were transformed out of all recognition. The Descent of the Holy Ghost makes the disciples suddenly speak with divers tongues which astonishes the devout Jews. That this trait is originally derived from the same source is clearly shown by the legend (!) of the Annunciation (!) where the Holy Ghost descends in a bodily shape as a dove (!) At Pentecost, too, the Holy Ghost descends in the shape of a dove (!) as is implied by certain popular customs. Until a short time ago, for instance, it was the practice in some churches for the Verger to let down from the " Holy Ghost Window " a wooden dove which he made circle round, or sometimes even a living dove was released from the roof of the church. . . .

Neo-pagan services.

In his *Eiserne Blätter*[1] the well-known Protestant divine D. Traub, writes as follows:

On Good Friday we listened in to the Munich radio which transmitted until 10.20 a Catholic Service, and at 10.30 a service of the Hitler Youth. We listened with great attention, recalling meanwhile the word of the Führer that the German National Socialist Workers' Party takes its stand on positive Christianity. But what did we hear ? A service dedicated to Baldur and words like these: " We achieve our own salvation," " our own strength leads us to the freeing Light," but not a single word about the meaning of Good Friday. So this was what the German Youth on the highest Christian Feast day of the year was offered in a solemn morning service ! In the evening we were given Johann Sebastian Bach—music acceptable to the rest of the world too. At Bari as well as at Toulouse the same notes were heard as at Leipzig, and, if we are not mistaken, they were relayed by South American stations. Anyhow, we rejoiced deeply at such a conclusion of Good Friday. We are, however, the more surprised that the morning service for the German Youth completely disregarded the character of the day's Feast.

It is, of course, our duty as Christians to ask the grave question: " Which is the real decisive factor in Germany, the National Socialist Programme with its profession of positive Christianity, or the Germanic education ? Are, perhaps, those right who mockingly proclaim that the old generation will be left their Christianity, but that the young, the future generation, will be trained in an anti-Christian and neo-pagan spirit ? *This latter fact seems to be proved with scarcely any possibility of doubt* by the morning service on Good Friday, which was, it was said, relayed by all German stations. On

---

[1] No. 17, April 26th, 1935.

Good Friday the German Hitler Youth is only told about Baldur. What, then, is the meaning and value of the Christian schools ? Is it to be wondered at that we should speak out quite plainly that theory and practice are not the same ? *Or is it perhaps intentional* that they should not be the same ?

On Sunday, September 29th, 1935, all German stations transmitted at 10 o'clock a morning service from Leipzig, which was dedicated to the coming Harvest Thanksgiving. Near the end of the service a poem was recited from which we quote the beginning and two other verses:

> We never learnt our knee to lower
> Or lift our hands in suppliant prayer.
> The God within us, life-bestower,
> Bears silent witness He is there.
> His will it is that we be scattered
> As seeds upon the fields of earth,
> His name we bear, in death though shattered. . . .
>
> To a fabled God we make no supplication,
> Who on the first man's fields his curses sent;
> God smiles from out His vegetation,
> And stretches forth His hand in benediction
> On rend'ring fruitful all our crops intent.
>
> For us lives God in cornfield mellow,
> And incense find we in smoking-furrow
> On which He bids His smiling Heavens rain.
> We learnt to bend no knee for heav'nly vision,
> Nor drones there from our lips a litany;
> In silence to His breath within we listen,
> We cannot flee our God-commanded mission.
> We serve His country—yet we still are free.

The conclusion of this service was a kind of " Confession of Faith ":

I believe in the land of all the Germans, in a life of service to this land I believe in the revelation of the divine creative power in the pure blood shed in war and peace by the sons of the German national community, buried in the soil thereby sanctified, risen and living in all for whom it was immolated. I believe in an eternal life on earth of this blood, that was poured out and rose again in all who have recognised the meaning of the sacrifices and are ready to submit to them. . . . Thus I believe in an eternal God, an eternal Germany, and an eternal Life.

The annual commemoration of Hitler's and his followers' abortive *Putsch* on November 9th is celebrated with pseudo-religious forms. The official reports speak of a Resurrection of the Dead, and that night is officially proclaimed sacred; but not a single word savouring of Christianity is pronounced at the annual funeral celebrations of the men fallen in that *Putsch* and declared national heroes; no cross surmounts their tombs, which are said to be the unifying symbol of the German people.

An anonymous pamphlet, entitled *Entkonfessionalisierung* (De-denominationalisation—*i.e.*, De-Christianisation) and printed by C. Blech, Mülheim-Ruhr, contains on pages 23-24 the following " official suggestions of the *Reichspropagandaleitung* (the Supreme Council of Propaganda) concerning a National Socialist Ritual or Ceremonial,"

(There is a notice on the back cover: " Published on the instruction of the *Reichspropagandaleitung* as a private circular of the German National Socialist Workers' Party by the Central Publishing House of the Party, Franz Eher, Munich; copies can be ordered only by Party authorities from the *Propagandaleitung* of the districts.")

We give a verbatim extract:

In future a permanent rite will be prescribed for all National Socialist celebrations. Only by fixing certain fundamental features of our programmes shall we gradually succeed in developing forms of celebrations of a liturgical character which shall be valid for centuries. The principal items of a National Socialist celebration are to be: the *Verkündung* (Announcement), a solemn address of fifteen to twenty minutes in poetical language, followed by the *Bekenntnis* (Confession of Faith) recited by the congregation, and the *Lied der Verpflichtung* (Hymn of Duty) which, to the accompaniment of the organ, is to be sung in unison by all present. The ceremony is to close with the " Salute to the Führer " (" Sieg Heil "), and one verse of each of the National Anthems.

The following sentences, taken from the " Announcement " on November 9th, are very significant and informative:

On these steps leading to the *Feldherrnhalle*,
To which today great men come as pilgrims,
The Sacrament of our Struggle was once born.
To this unique Minster which is called Germany, only those are admitted
Who have expressed their wills in hard deeds.
You are true pilgrims if you esteem the glory of our Nation
Higher than the revelation of all religions !
You feel the sacred atmosphere of the *Feldherrnhalle*;
What are hymns and Mass prayers and the swinging of glittering censers
Compared to the rhythm of our muffled drums
When our Führer ascends these steps ?
Those that behold him stand with bated breath;
The earth vibrating with our steps is silent;
Noise has withdrawn to the ends of the world.
The Führer stands on high;
The Führer lifts his hand in an eternal salute.
His heart beats at one with that of his people.
Today his ascent is prayer. . . .
He ascends and stops, invested with wonder;
He is inflamed by the faith of his comrades.
No priestly consecration ascends with greater power
Than this prayer, silent and hewn in stone,
Of that one man
Whose heart throbs with the heartbeat of a whole nation.
The oath of the *Feldherrnhalle* is the prayer of all of us to our Creator.
Let fire, smoke and death surround us,
We will rejoice if only the flag . . .
Our flag, keeps flying. . . .
Touch the steps of the *Feldherrnhalle*,
Lift the flag up higher, the Germans' sublimest symbol,
Steeped in the blood of western battles and proclaiming our faith.
And all our standards joyfully exclaim:
What is death, if thou demandest our lives,
O Germany ?

It is rather remarkable that Hitler in his speech on Culture at the Party Rally of 1938 vigorously protested against the identification

NEO-PAGAN SERVICES

of his Party with a Cultic Movement or cultic acts, even though there exists an official ritual for these cultic acts, as we have just shown.

As another instance of the growth of neo-pagan religious scenes in the German National Socialist Workers' Party, we quote a passage from the *Weihespiel* (*Sacred Play*), *Die Losung* (*The Watchword*), by H. Böhne. The scenario gives the following directions:

Three heralds of the SA with trumpets march over the stage from right to left and take their stand in the foreground towards the spectators. They give three short blasts in quick succession. At the third an echo of unseen trumpets answers, and a large flag is brought in, which will be later hoisted on the flag-staff in the centre of the foreground.

Over the hill in the background the drummer appears, accompanied by two heralds with trumpets. All three wear the forbidden SA uniforms of the period of the revolutionary struggle.

Drummer: Sanctify this place by our flag.
Flag-guards: The watchword !
Drummer: " Struggle " is the watchword !

(Citizens, peasants and workmen appear; the drummer is not satisfied with the expressions on their faces.)

Drummer:

> You are not the Order which I called;
> Self-sacrificing, you do not mount the sacred steps
> That lead to our true country, as bids the oath
> That keeps us, though betrayed, faithful to our flag.

Knights of the Teutonic Order ride in, asking the workmen, peasants and citizens whether they have risked their lives in the winning of the German Eastern Provinces. (The Giant Mountains in Silesia are specially mentioned.) Their only answer is that they work and till their fields. Another rider who appears at this moment, a member of the German Baltic Free Corps, wearing the same uniform as the drummer, claims to have taken over the sacred torch of German patriotism from the Knights of the Order and to have carried it on. He expresses his contempt for the workers, peasants and citizens, who do nothing else but work and go to church.

Rider:

> I see you, I hear you, but you leave me cold.
> What has become of the Sacred Fire
> Of the German faith ?
> Where is your Order ?
> Attack the portals of those heavy monstrous buildings
> Wherein man gives grace to man.
> You must be more than servants,
> You must be blood on the sacred altar
> Of the Fatherland; and your flags shall soar upwards
> Like flames of fire born of God.

(The workers, peasants and citizens are won over.)

Citizens:

> We will escape the vain belief
> That has entangled us.
> Each one must, as best he can,
> Find his way to the Order. . . .

(They join the ranks of the approaching SA.)

Drummer: "Struggle" is the watchword !
Choir: " Struggle " is the watchword !

Rider:
>A plough, a sword, the strength of our German Faith,
>And an inflexible brotherhood—
>That is the Order, proclaimed by our blood.

Knight: That is the Order faithful to God.
Flag-bearer: Flag of our Soil, our Faith and our Blood!
Drummer: Under this Flag we Germans praise God.
Choir: Under this Flag we Germans praise God.
Drummer:
>Let us proclaim our loyal allegiance to it:
>We fight and believe!

Choir: We fight and believe!
Drummer:
>We believe in the mission of the Führer,
>In the purity of light,
>In the fertility of its blessing rays
>Which are the immense sword of our Eternal God.

Choir: We believe.
Drummer: We believe in the strength of our Blood.
Choir: We believe.

At the end:

Flag-bearer (lifting up the flag): May God bless the Reich through our Führer!

>Adolf Hitler: Sieg Heil!

The Director of the "Department for Ideological and Cultural Development" in the Supreme Command of the SA has himself arranged the text of a morning service entitled "Men, Fighters and Soldiers." The actors are: A Military Band, A Choir of Men, Three Speakers: The Believer, The Doubter, the Caller. The parts of these three speakers are indicated by their names.

The text is an arrangement of historical quotations and songs; the Doubter enumerates the defeats of Germany, which are, however, every time contrasted with a German victory—*e.g.*, the Thirty Years' War and Frederick the Great.

The climax of this contrast is reached in a passage where the Caller recites a quotation from Schopenhauer about death. The Doubter rejoins:

Doubter: You speak of death, but I want life!
Caller: Thou shalt not simply live, but rise living!

>(FRIEDR. NIETZSCHE.)

The Doubter is convinced; he remains silent until at the end he joins in the loud and solemn words of the Believer:

Believer:
>Through us, ourselves, the current of blood sweeps on its way,
>Driving and compelling us, Men and Soldiers!

Doubter: Eternal Germany!
Believer: We hammer ourselves into thy Immortality!

On May 21st, 1939, the Vienna National Socialist Organisation, Strength through Joy, Section for Leisure-time Amusements, arranged a German morning service for the Viennese mothers. The Director of this service explained its meaning, stating at the same time that it would become a regular feature in the wireless programme:[1]

> German morning service: These words mean to us all that we can imagine of beautiful and lofty joys. Morning is the time of rising to one's task; it means new ideas, youth and growing strength. The trumpet-note of youth rouses what has been slumbering in the blood and is now trying to express itself in new forms. The magnificent streams of our cultural achievements which up to now have flowed on in smooth waves, as in the large and open stretches of our symphonies, have to concentrate their current in a deep, narrow channel so that their power may rouse the hearts of all. Thus the fanfare's blended notes will call in simple harmonies to men to open their hearts, until at last the whole community of the people answers, as it were, in the mighty rushing floods of the organ. Thus the Choir of our age will come into being. As the sacred flame of the Eternal Growth of our people is soaring up to new heights, as the German mother, the Sacred Root of this Growth, is receiving her due glory, Art will come into her own, ascending from simple family music to the Master, Wagner, and to the full strength of the orchestra, until it finds its perfection in the all-embracing choir of men and women who join in a community of true lovers of music.

The Song Book of the German National Socialist Workers' Party had reached a circulation of two million copies in the summer of 1939. In this small brown volume, rearranged several times during these last years, the trashiest and crudest " Fighting Songs " have been omitted to be replaced by neo-pagan and pseudo-religious hymns, etc.

On p. 26 of the latest edition we find the hymn *In unsern Fahnen lodert Gott* (God reveals Himself in our flaming flags), one verse of which reads:

> Who bides at home when out we plod,
> His love has not requited:
> Who wills us ill, in him has God
> No holy fire ignited:
> To victory leads his flaming rod
> Which all the land has lighted.
> God wants no roof, no home, the day
> We sally from our homesteads;
> He marches with us to the fray
> And blesses all our hatreds;
> Within the strife to Him we pray,
> By clutching firm our standards.

The next hymn is entitled *Heilig ist unser Schwur* (Our oath is sacred), and in it the Swastika flag is thus addressed:

> Rise then our flag; firm take thy stand,
> Rousing, avenging and judging our land,
> Rise then our flag !
> For who offends against thy light,
> Who takes no part in thy just fight,
> Is dead as dust, forgotten by all.
> Immortal is he who is prompt to thy call,
> Germany's eternal Race.

[1] *Cf. Völkischer Beobachter,* Vienna Edition.

Two pages later follows the hymn *Führer, wir rufen dich an!* (Führer, we call upon thee), the second verse of which we quote:

> Ever when we are marching,
> Ever when the standards are praying,
> To glory and feast, for honour and right,
> Calls thee the whole of Germany's might.
> Führer, thy name we acclaim;
> Führer, bear on our banners to fame.
> To clouds, yea, and sun, and to Freedom's renown,
> For our Banners for us are sanctity's crown.
> Führer, lead ever on.

On p. 42 is the hymn:

> Faith creates the new, Faith destroys the old.
> Holy German faith, ne'er in us grow cold,
> Out of murky gloom reborn for German men.
> Flying flags proclaim "Our country free again."
> Faithful, face uplifted, we, the youthful band,
> Are a sacred power of our German land.

This Song Book also contains three neo-pagan Christmas hymns.

It would seem, however, that a new Ancestor-worship is to be introduced and promoted in German families. The *Schwarze Korps*[1] in an article entitled " Veneration of Ancestors in Former Times and Today " openly urges the giving of a deliberately sacred character to the Cult of the Race and of the Family.

Not only the National Socialist State but also the whole future of our people is, for better or worse, inseparably bound up with the racial idea. . . . If this idea of the eternity of our people is to become an efficient instrument in our fight against powers that even in the eyes of modern man are still invested with transcendental demoniacal horrors, this conception will have to be gradually elevated to the sphere of a myth. We are fully aware of all that is implied when we say that the belief in Germany and its future, as it is understood and realised by us, constitutes a source of spiritual strength, because this belief is related to eternal and supernatural things.

If we are to specify what would lend itself most readily to an external expression of our faith in our people and our country, it is the cult of the blood, expressed in practical measures. . . .

In the course of the last thousand years, Christianity, as we have mentioned above, has put an end to the customs of our forefathers by replacing and assimilating them in a very superficial way. One might rejoin that this very fact proves how little vitality was left in those customs. But this would be a false conclusion because the Germanic Ancestor-Worship did not die out at once even in those districts where the Church applied the strongest pressure to eradicate it. As a matter of fact, it took centuries of the severest persecution to destroy these customs. We urge, therefore, as a matter of supreme importance to the individual as well as to the State, the removal of the cult of the race and the blood from the sphere of everyday life, and its elevation to a sacred plane. . . .

We remember a custom, still prevalent among certain ancient German families, of lighting candles before the portraits of their ancestors on certain commemorative days. Moderns as we are, we may place the few relics of our ancestors in a shrine which by that very fact becomes an ancestral shrine. Finally, portraits of ancestors and the " genealogical trees," which have become an established feature in Germany, may, if put up in

[1] February 18th, 1937, p. 6.

the right place, grow quite naturally into centres of future customs which, however, will develop only gradually in the course of very long periods.

Thus the newly aroused national consciousness of the sacred character of our ancestors will slowly produce a form worthy of the mythical value of the family idea.

3. *Neo-pagan Substitutes for Christian Customs and Symbols*

Substitutes for Christian names.

The *Almanac of German Labour*, 1934 (published by the German Labour Front, Berlin), urges German parents not to give their children just any names they like, but the names of those assassinated during the struggle for the liberation of Germany. The Almanac itself records on their respective days the names of the Heroes of the Movement.

The *NS Monatshefte*[1] in a longer article entitled " Alien Names Introduced by the Church into Germany," deals with the historical development in Germany of the conferring of Christian names at baptism. The author asserts that the custom of the ancient Germans of giving appropriate names to their children was more and more abolished by the intervention of the Church; that native names had mostly been converted into names of Saints and thus deprived of their original meaning and degraded into instruments of ecclesiastical policy.

The periodical *Neues Volk* (*The New People*), edited by the Department for Racial Policy of the German National Socialist Workers' Party and published by the Central Publishing House of the Party, investigates in its September edition, 1938, the origin of the most common German Christian names and arrives at the conclusion that many Germans and National Socialists even today carry about with them " relics of Judaism as if they had inherited them like original sin." The great majority of them bear Christian names of " Jewish origin."

The name John, for instance, has " as little meaning for a German " as Balthasar or Cyprian or Joseph. National Socialist prospective parents are given a list of names of Jewish provenance which are no longer to be conferred on children of racially-minded Germans: " *e.g.*, Anna, Elizabeth, Eve, Jacob, Joachim, Mary, Michael, George, and Paul."

In the *Normalkalender*, published by the Minister of the Interior, German parents are notified that the names of biblical Saints, Angels, Apostles, Martyrs, etc., are no longer to be used.

Use of Christian terms.

The uninitiated are astonished to meet again and again Christian expressions in the National Socialist press, the speeches of the Party leaders, and especially at Party festivals. Scrutinising them more closely, however, we discover that all these Christian terms have been

[1] February, 1938.

emptied of their original content and falsified in a neo-pagan sense. All the National Socialist writings and the speeches of the high Party officials are literally teeming with expressions taken from religious and Christian terminology. To mention only a few, there are: the " Order " of the SS; the training places of the élite of the Party which are called *Ordensburgen* (Castles of the Order); the Party leaders are styled " Apostles " of the Führer, and the officials of the German National Socialist Workers' Party are often referred to as the "Pastors " of the German people. National Socialism is proclaimed as the " only saving faith "; Nürnberg is " The Shrine and Place of Pilgrimage " of the New Germany, " The City of the Temple of the Movement "; Hitler's *Mein Kampf* is the " Bible of the Movement," out of which passages are read at training courses. Adolf Hitler is called " Our Redeemer," and everyone is obliged " to believe in him."

For Christian prayers.

Even Grace before and after meals is being transformed in a neo-pagan sense. At a free dinner given by the National Socialist Welfare Committee of Cologne to poor children of that city, the children, almost exclusively Catholics, had to say the following " Grace ":

Before Dinner

Führer, my Führer, on me by God bestowed,
My life in times to come, protect and hold;
Our of deepest distress thou hast Germany led,
To thee I owe, alone, my daily bread:
Abandon thou me never, with me for e'er abide,
Führer, my Führer, my Faith and my Light,
    Heil, my Führer.

After Dinner

For this food, my Führer, my thanks I render,
Protector of age as of childhood tender.
Thou hast cares, I know, but be not afright,
My heart is with thee by day and by night.
Place thy head on my lap and quietly rest,
Thou alone art my Führer, for thou art best,
    Heil, my Führer.

In a seaside Home for Children on the Island of Sylt (in the North Sea) instead of Grace the following verse was recited:

Earth that did this food bestow,
Sun that made it riper grow;
Dearest Sun and dearest Earth,
Ne'er will I forget your worth.

We must mention the " Grace " said by the Guard of the SA of the *Feldherrnhalle*:[1]

The " Sturmbannführer " pronounces the word *Der Führer*, and all answer in solemn and subdued tones *Der Führer*. This word expresses everything to them, everything.

[1] *Cf. Völkischer Beobachter*, November 15th, 1936.

Substitutes for different Christian symbols.

The following notice was put up in 1936 in the Munich Public Health Institution:

> *Grüass di Gott* ! (God be with you !)
> Thou shalt not take the name of the Lord in vain !
> Therefore say:
> *Heil Hitler* !

The Seal of the University of Munich used to contain a beautiful engraving of Our Lady. This Seal was therefore abolished and replaced by a Swastika.

The National Socialist press has frequently affirmed that, at the planning or re-planning of towns, the German National Socialist Workers' Party insists that an important Party building should form the centre of the locality, a place hitherto occupied by the church, situated as it usually was in the middle of the town and prominent by its spire. It is, for example, well known that at the re-planning of the German capital special care was taken that, in the same way as in Vienna the spires of St. Stephen's Cathedral can be seen from all streets converging on to the St. Stephen's Platz, so the turrets of the new *Versammlungshaus* (Assembly Hall) in Berlin should be visible for a distance of several miles.

The *Frankfurter Zeitung*[1] reports:

> In Gladbeck several elementary schools have been re-named—*e.g.*, St. Aloysius' School is now known as " Horst-Wessel School," St. Lambert's School as " Schlageter School," St. John's School as " Richthofen School," St. Joseph's School as " Weddingen School," St. Anthony's School as " Herbert-Norkus School," and the former " Overberg School " as " Hans-Schemm School."

In January, 1939, the Austrian Ministry of the Interior ordered that all crucifixes should be removed from the wards and rooms of the Austrian hospitals and replaced by portraits of Hitler.

The town of Alfeld near Hanover was given a new coat-of-arms. The former representation of a bishop was replaced by a town gate, flanked by massive towers.

The neo-pagan periodical *Nordland*[2] urges that " Eagle trees " should be erected in the place of wayside crucifixes. After stating that in every village the National Socialist emblems have been given the predominant place of honour, the article continues:

> And then one comes into the open country, passes along the fields, climbs over the hills and skirts the fringes of the woods; if one is only a little " awake " and keeps one's eyes opened, one will find there that we have " forgotten " our countryside. There nothing reminds us of the fact that Germany has become a National Socialist State. On the contrary, one discovers there other symbols—*e.g.*, one, that somehow or other is connected with the Thirty Years' War, even though it is evidently only six months old, and its wood, of course, has not become darkened by age.

[1] No. 305/6, June 18th, 1939.   [2] September 2nd, 1939.

(This refers, as one can easily see, to the Christian crucifix.) The article goes on to attack this Christian symbol:

In our countryside . . . we find a symbol holding undisputed sway, that recalls that suicidal war of three hundred years ago which was waged to the Glory of God, to the advancement of the Pope and to the detriment of our people. We ought, therefore, not to be indifferent as to what kind of symbols are predominant in our countryside." The erection of " Eagle-trees " is advocated by the writer instead of the wayside crucifixes. Such a " Silver Eagle " " ought to grow out of its natural surroundings as part of them; it ought to be in harmony with them by being a kind of tree itself. It ought to be very impressive by its size and its clear-cut contours."

Some sketches of such " Eagle Symbols " are given.

Substitutes for Christian burial.

The neo-pagan periodical *Der Blitz*[1] (*The Lightning*) gives an account of a German *Totenweihe* (Consecration of the Dead) at Limburg:

A member of our community, who had expressed the wish to be buried in her home town of Limburg, had met with a fatal accident at Lübeck. While representatives of the Party and of the German Faith Movement surrounded the open grave, the funeral oration was delivered by the President of the Lübeck Group of the German Faith Movement. He took as his text the following words of Fichte: " You ought to act as if on you and your actions alone depended the fate of Germany, and as if all responsibility were yours." In plain but convincing words he extolled the excellent German qualities of the deceased, her readiness for sacrifice, her loyal fulfilment of duty, her kind, unobtrusive manner, and the deep conviction of her German faith. All present were deeply moved by these touching words.

The writer asserts in the following paragraph that this funeral had left a deep and lasting impression which would not fail to influence the Catholic population especially, but on another page of the same issue of the *Blitz* there is another notice about the *Totenweihe* of Limburg.

The deep impression made by this ceremony, even on simple minds, is evidenced by the following incident. A comrade met at the cemetery gate a good old lady of his acquaintance, sixty-five years old. " Well, how did you like it ?" he asked her. She answered candidly, " Oh ! it was very beautiful. But I missed one thing: they ought to have said the ' Our Father ' at the end."

We are surprised that the *Blitz* published the comment of this good old lady, for her simple words contain a trenchant and decisive criticism; that it was a funeral without prayers and without uplifting the mind to the Lord of life and death.

The *Schwarze Korps*[2] writes in an article entitled " A Civil Funeral is Needed ":

To whom belong the cemeteries ? To the Churches ? If the Church, with regard to her secular possessions, is only the trustee of the property of the people, she is the same in a higher degree concerning the administration of cemeteries which belong to all, we think, who at some time are to find their resting-place there. In small towns and villages there are often only

[1] No. 25, August 18th, 1935.   [2] March 9th, 1939.

ecclesiastical cemeteries. Are those who do not happen to be members of this particular church to be buried like carrion in a knacker's yard because such is the pleasure of the parson ? Is the parson to have the right to prescribe to the relatives of the deceased how to adorn the graves of their dead ? Such was not the intention of our forefathers when they left the cemetery grounds for the use or the administration of the Church, because at their time there was no distinction between the civil and the ecclesiastical parish.

The living want to know not only if and where they will be buried but also in what manner.

This is a deficiency that ought to be remedied.

German men and women who have done their duty as members of the national community and died an honourable death have a right to demand that we, the representatives of the national community, should be allowed to bid them farewell in the manner they deserve. Their deaths must not be allowed to become occasions for haggling over their bodies either for those who in their lifetime were only interested in their church rates, or for undertakers in partnership with death. Since we have elevated civil marriage from the plane of a mere official act to that of a solemn celebration, why should we not have a civil burial too ? (This expression, we grant, sounds horrible, but it only serves for purposes of distinction.)

4. *Neo-Pagan Substitutes for the Sacraments of the Church*

For Baptism.

The *Ostseebote* of Doberan (Mecklenburg-Schwerin) published on November 11th, 1937, an account of a solemn National Socialist baptism, the so-called *Namensweihe* (Solemn Conferring of the Name), which took place in the " Ancestral Hall " of Güstrow (formerly a Catholic Church).

Last Sunday ten parents of Güstrow met in the " Ancestral Hall " in the cemetery of St. Gertrude in order to proclaim solemnly their willingness to educate their children for a life dedicated to the service of the German national community and fortified by a belief in God and in the eternity of the German Blood. The ceremony was inaugurated by Handel's " Largo." Thereupon the Mayor, Party Comrade Lemm, in the name of the Party received the profession of faith of the parents. After the address of the Mayor all present joined hands, and Party Comrade Lemm pronounced the solemn vow on behalf of all. The ceremony was concluded with the hymn " Holy Fatherland." The parents were given certificates of the Solemn Conferring of Names.

In June, 1938, a National Socialist Solemn Conferring of the Name took place at Linz (on the Danube), which was presided over by the Cultural Adviser of the SA Group 14. The " Baptismal Act " was performed on a dais in front of a bust of Hitler. The Cultural Adviser thus addressed the infant:

You, little life, are the next step of our race into the future. The darkness of innumerable past centuries obscures the way our nation has come. You are not a being of today nor of tomorrow. You are a being of a thousand years past and of a thousand years to come. For a thousand years generations have guarded their blood that you might become what you are, for you are the living current of blood that unites our forbears to the future ages of Germany. Guard, therefore, your soul and your blood in order that those that will come after you may thank you. For this is the meaning of the life that God awakes in the blood; but God is only in pure blood ! Your current of blood is still small. But it shall yet flow in deep and mighty ways, sweeping away all alien constructions imposed on spirit and soul, for only he who carries a living, flaming soul in his breast is a free and independent being. Listen to the voice of your ancestors that whispers in your soul, and guard against the hand of strangers the flower that grows out of your own being. In you is slumbering the wisdom of a thousand generations. Awaken it and you will have found the key of the gate that opens the way to your deepest yearnings, the gate leading to God who is in you and to your People, unique and holy.

The Cultural Adviser then asked the sponsor, a Brigade Leader, what the boy should be called.

He shall be called Horst. He shall become like our model Horst Wessel!

Then the mystagogue addressed the parents:

Mother, may your courage help him to find his way; Father, be you to him a strong comrade on his path in life. And you, boy, bear your name with pride, not with lowly humility. May your will find its highest aim in our ideal: " Everything for Germany !"

The National Socialist Press reported that in November, 1938, the National Socialist Solemnity of the Conferring of the Name on the son of Hess took place in the house of the Representative of the Führer. Only the nearest relatives and Adolf Hitler were invited. The child received the names Wolf Rüdiger.

As from January 1st, 1939, the Solemn Conferring of the Name and the issue of a corresponding certificate have been made obligatory in Austria. This measure was decreed in connection with the introduction of the German Registration Laws of November 3rd, 1937, and is to replace the Christian Baptism as is openly admitted by the National Socialist press of Vienna. The *Wiener Kleine Volkszeitung* announced this innovation in the following terms:

For months young couples have had to present themselves at the Registry Offices to conclude their German (!) marriages; with the beginning of the New Year the new-born children, too, are to be registered with the State Authorities who in the name of the national community take cognizance of their arrival. The Registrar of a district has to be notified of a birth within a week. If the child is still-born, its birth has to be communicated on the next day. A month's interval is allowed for the conferring of the name; within that period the parents can decide on a nice name. The Solemn Conferring of the Name and the issue of the corresponding certificate are to replace the former ceremony of Baptism. Ecclesiastical Baptism may be conferred later, but it is not obligatory since it has no longer any legal consequences.

For the Christian marriage ceremony.

The *Mitteilungsblatt*[1] (*Notices*) issued by the National Socialist authorities of Munich published a detailed and glowing article about " German Marriage." It represented as a model the " German Wedding " which took place on August 4th, 1935, in front of the Shrine of Our Lady of Altötting.

As early as in September, 1935, Leaders of the Hitler Youth performed public marriages, using a neo-pagan ceremonial of their own

[1] No. 32, August 8th, 1935.

making. (*Cf.* the Report quoted above on page 380 : " Günther Blum marries leader of the Junior Section of the Hitler Youth.")

In December, 1936, the local National Socialist Leader of Sohlingen-Nord submitted to the Town Council of Sohlingen a motion to reform the Civil Marriage Ceremony, in which he advocated the substitution of a new formula for the one drawn up in 1876 and still in use.

Although up to the present no official changes have been introduced, it is, nevertheless, possible to surround the prescribed legal act with a certain solemnity. As it frequently happens that parties omit the ecclesiastical marriage, we should do all in our power to transform the civil marriage into a solemn National Socialist ceremony, since marriage is of such tremendous importance in the National Socialist State.

What this " certain solemnity " is like can be seen from the *Durchbruch*,[1] which published the following account by an eye-witness of the " Consecration of Marriage " of the Junker Karl Steeb, performed in the *Ordensburg* Vogelsang, according to the NS Neo-pagan Rite, in the spring of 1937.

The " Consecration of Marriage " took place in the imposing hall of the Castle, and was performed exclusively in the spirit and according to the rite of National Socialism. On either side of the hall were seated the " clans " of the bridegroom and the bride, and between them the wedding ceremony was celebrated. It was inaugurated by fanfares and drums of the *Jungvolk*; then, to the accompaniment of marches played by the Band of the Castle, the standard-bearers escorted by guards marched through the hall into the adjoining " Room of Honour." The marriage was performed by Dr. Breuer, Mayor of Gemünd. Adolf Hitler's Book, *Mein Kampf*, was presented as a gift to the newly-married couple. After the marriage ceremony, Bereitschaftsführer Bruhn of the Castle received the solemn profession of loyalty of the couple. He had previously explained to them the attitude and the duties essential to their life and the cardinal virtues of a National Socialist marriage, which were to be belief and love, readiness for sacrifice and loyalty. He defined as the most important points of life: the hour of birth, of marriage, the growth of the family as a link in the chain of eternal life, and, if life had been rightly lived according to National Socialist principles, even death, which had no horror for a National Socialist who had done his duty by his " clan " and his nation. Then followed the solemn profession of loyalty of the National Socialist couple to the ideas of the Führer, and the exchanging of rings in the presence of the Commander of the Castle as the representative of the Führer and of the witnesses as representatives of their " clans " and the community, a ceremony doubly solemn, as the speaker explained, because performed in the Holy of Holies, the " Room of Honour " of the Castle, which was the symbol of the National Socialist Fight and Belief and in which were enshrined in brilliant letters the names of the fourteen heroes fallen on November 9th (1923) who had been called on by the Führer to mount " Eternal Guard " for the protection of the new German nation. At the end of the ceremony the standards were escorted out of the hall, followed by the marriage procession.

The administrator of the Rhein-Wied Area issued the following decree to the Mayors of places under his jurisdiction (as reported by the *Reichspost* of April 8th, 1937):

Civil marriages are to be concluded in a dignified way with all possible solemnity. The Registrar is to wear a dark suit (or his Party uniform), but on no account a sports suit; the room is to be decorated with the symbols

[1] April 15th, 1937.

of the National Socialist State and with other permanent adornments. The young couple will be offered by the town as a wedding present that most valuable German book, *Mein Kampf*, by Adolf Hitler. In a short address inspired by the National Socialist ideals, the Registrar is to point out the great importance of marriage in our National Socialist State. A great number of people have drifted away from the denominations; many, and not the worst, have left the Churches, although they still believe in God. In the eyes of these, as well as of such as are still bound by denominational ties, the civil marriage is to stand out as the most impressive ceremony connected with their marriage.

The following episode was reported to the *Reichspost* from Munich on June 13th, 1937.

A short time ago the local leader of the German Girls' League, Hilde Königsbauer, married the local president of the Red Cross, Gotthold Dziewas. After the civil marriage the couple was " married " by the District Leader, Wagner, in the main room of the Munich Town Hall, in the middle of which a bust of the Führer had been placed. At this solemn ceremony the District Leader called upon the following witnesses: " The BDM Girls, the Comrades of the bridegroom, our Standards, and the gigantic faith given to us by Adolf Hitler."

Afterwards the District Leader placed the rings on the fingers of the newly-wed and wished them all happiness in their married life.

The *Spielschar*[1] (*The Touring Company*), *Zeitschrift für Feier-und Freizeitgestaltung* (a periodical containing suggestions for amateur theatricals and other leisure-time amusements), which is edited by the National Headquarters of the Hitler Youth, gives *inter alia* outlines of ceremonies of National Socialist marriages, and the Conferring of the Name (as a substitute for baptism).

The *Schwarze Korps* wrote on February 9th, 1939, page 9:

A new regulation of the Minister of the Interior, which was welcomed on all sides, has ordered the Registrars and the competent authorities, the Town Councils, to have marriage ceremonies performed in a dignified and solemn form as befits the great importance of matrimony.

Thus a long cherished wish of many Germans and of the *Schwarze Korps* has at long last been fulfilled. Up to the present the civil marriage ceremony was scarcely distinguishable from an audience with an awe-inspiring collector of taxes. No large rooms were provided for the purpose, they were not adorned and were not even allowed to be adorned, and the presence at this most important act of a large circle of relations or friends was strictly forbidden. All this is to be changed and, of course, the official dress of the Registrar too.

Several proposals, however, to introduce as official dress a kind of ecclesiastical gown are scornfully and indignantly repudiated in the same issue. In the issue of February 23rd, 1939, the same subject is again taken up, and one such suggestion is thus criticised:

This suggestion, as its illustration shows, has fully succeeded in effecting a cross between the gaberdine of a Chief Rabbi and the robe of a Catholic Cardinal. The skull-cap is not lacking, nor the penitent's girdle which was not contained in the first suggestion; it is, however, not girded round the loins, but used as a kind of trimming.

This periodical, it is true, asserts with all possible emphasis that these new forms are not meant as a substitute for the ecclesiastical

[1] *E.g.*, September 6th, 1938.

solemnisation of marriage: " The idea has been mooted that in Catholic regions the customary pomp of the Church ought to be met by something equivalent. Such projects would remove the essence of civil marriage to another and alien plane."

Civil marriage is no substitute for the ecclesiastical solemnisation of marriage; it is something radically different. Neither is it a religious act; no mystical forces are set in motion by the ceremony performed by the Registrar. He does not conjure down on bride and bridegroom supernatural sacraments; he is neither a magician nor a medicine man, nor a priest of the State-idea, let alone of the National Socialist ideology interpreted as a system of religious doctrines.

In reality, however, this is just the aim of nearly all those circles that advocate a more solemn form of civil marriage; for they have discovered that even tepid or apostate Christians are not satisfied with the bare and prosaic performance of the Registry Office marriage, and crave for a kind of sentimental substitute for the religious ceremony.

This need is more clearly recognised by the periodical *NS Gemeinde* (*National Socialist Community*). In its July/August edition, 1939, the suggestions made by Party District Official Dr. Förg for a reform of civil marriage repudiate any participation of the Party authorities in the marriage ceremony, because the conclusion of marriage is regarded as an exclusive right of the State which cannot be shared with any other authorities; but, on the other hand, the Party has the task of ensuring that the State marriage is performed according to National Socialist ideas and principles. It is in the interest of the unity of Party and State that there should be only one marriage, that performed by the State, which ought to have for all Germans the same solemn dignity.

With regard to the exterior setting of the State marriage ceremony, it is suggested that the room where the ceremony takes place should be large enough to accommodate the relatives, friends and acquaintances of the bridal couple. A special place of honour is to be reserved for the portrait or bust of the Führer and the Flag of the National Socialist Reich. Only the very best National Socialists ought to be appointed as Registrars, and they should wear the Party uniform at the marriage. Essential parts of every marriage ceremony should be: a musical introduction, an address and, as conclusion, the salute to the Führer.

For the First Communion and Confirmation.

The German Faith Movement advocates the introduction of *Gottgläubige Jugendleiten* (approximately: Religious or Neo-Christian —i.e., in reality Neo-pagan—Consecrations of Youth) as a substitute for Communion and Confirmation. The *Siegrune* (*The Victory Rune*), a periodical for Nordic culture, publishes in its June issue, 1939, page 1, a photograph of such a ceremony. A point worthy of notice is the fact that nearly all the boys and girls present wear HJ or BDM uniforms, which means that, in view of the very strict regulations issued by the German National Socialist Workers' Party about the wearing of

Party uniform, such celebrations are officially sanctioned by the Party. The *Siegrune* thus comments on the *Jugendleiten*:

> In all German districts " Religious Consecrations of Youth " took place so as to prevent the impression from gaining ground that we have nothing to substitute for Communion or Confirmation. In the future development of National Socialist popular education, the place of the " Religious Consecration of Youth " will be taken by the solemn reception of our German boys and girls into the Hitler Youth. We are convinced that the " Religious Consecrations of Youth " are stepping-stones to a great future reorganisation of our life.

Similar pagan celebrations connected with puberty are held by other neo-pagan sects. In the *Gemeinschaft Deutscher Volksreligion* (Community of the German People's Religion), founded by Professor Bergmann, these celebrations are called *Jugendweihen* (Dedications of Youth). The periodical of this sect *Deutsches Werden* (*German Growth*) describes them as follows in its May issue, 1939:

> It goes without saying that the rooms chosen for these dedications were decorated in the best style, that the music and the hymns expressed true German feelings, and that the moving address urged parents and children to be loyal and faithful to their Führer, their people, their Fatherland, and to the ideals of a truly national community. . . . At this " Dedication of Youth " our children do not profess any denominational creed; but they pledge themselves joyfully to strengthen their German religion, which is a natural one and has nothing to do with Christianity, and to defend it later as members of the " Community of the German People's Religion." The " Dedication of Youth " is no ecclesiastical Confirmation. At the end of this important period of life we offer to the young our heartiest congratulations, and welcome them to our ranks as future comrades in the fight for the supreme cultural ideals of our German nation.
>
> The slogan " Give up Ecclesiastical Confirmation " must be vigorously propagated outside our community. That is our duty.
>
> Parents and children, it is true, want a solemn celebration, and because many believe that only the Church can offer this, thousands of children flock to the priests although they feel no interior attraction. The " Dedications of Youth " of our German religion will certainly have won many new followers and friends for our community.

Significant in this respect is a letter of congratulation written to a boy on his Confirmation by a man with a University education from Frankfurt-on-Main, who had left the Church; it is published by the periodical *Kommende Kirche*[1] (*The Church to Come*):

> DEAR L.,
>   On the occasion of your feast we wish you everything beautiful and good—in spite of the ecclesiastical ceremony to which you had to submit. May you celebrate it in a sense similar to that in which our pagan children will celebrate it next year, as a feast of youth and of spring, and as a feast of joy, but also of sacred determination to live a life of sincere comradeship and loyalty, for these are the ideals of German men and women, but not of Old Testament characters.
>   We offer our best congratulations also to your parents.
>
> Heil Hitler !
>
> DR. D. AND FAMILY.

[1] June 18th, 1939.

5. National Socialism the Only Religion

The meaning of the new racial piety is revealed by the *Schwarze Korps*.[1] We quote a significant passage:

> The All, or that mysterious power which permeates the Universe, now in vast, roaring waves, now in gentle, tender ripples, is not loved by the thoughtless, the superficial, the foolish and the insincere; but by those whose minds are deep, serious and sincere, and who cherish and preserve inviolate the sanctuary of their inner being with fidelity and determination.
>
> It is only thus that men and women will attain the full bloom of their being and their abilities. The eternal power loves such men and women who again and again to the very day of their death derive strength, graces and blessings from the sanctuary of the All. Such men we call devout. . . . This, in our eyes, is true piety. Churches are superfluous, but piety is indispensable. . . .
>
> It is not to be tolerated that the Nordmark (the Northern Marches—*i.e.*, Northern Germany) should go to men of a different nation and of a different race to receive from them their faith. All nations have their own faith and their own specific form of belief, moulded by their own blood and soil, and the sun and the winds that move over them, and the fate that they have experienced.
>
> Yes, these are the three determining factors. The Arabs and the Indians, the Chinese and the Japanese, the Jews and the Europeans, they all have different souls and different beliefs. Even the Christian Faith is different in Spain and in Abyssinia; different in Berlin and in Chicago. Thus the Nordmark, too, is to have its own faith. . . . The Nordmark has given up the Christian Faith; the past gives no answer, nor does nature. . . .

The fundamental emotional experience found in the act of believing occupies a particularly important place in this pseudo-religion. Under the title "What is Believing?" the *SA-Mann*[2] explains the essence of National Socialist belief.

In the first article of this series, the living *Weltanschauung* of the "real man"—*i.e.*, the National Socialist ideology and the National Socialist belief—are contrasted with Christianity:

> Two things are different in the Christian religion: first, the Christian belief does not grow out of the essence of man, but has been revealed by God; and secondly, this belief has no relation to human tasks, but only to an action performed by God. In both cases Christianity evidences a passive relationship; real life, however, is characterised by an active relationship. The National Socialist ideology is living and true; it can never be compared, let alone reconciled, with a revealed belief which contains an ideology imposed from outside. . . . If the essence of Being is rendered visible in Blood and Race, Ideology and Belief are to be based on Blood and Race. . . . Consequently we are, willy-nilly, obliged to use the expression National Socialist Belief, which means that life has to be shaped according to the National Socialist vision. . . . In the Christian belief there are two lives—one earthly in this world, and the other transcendental in Heaven. The Christian belief has been announced by God and is not concerned with this earthly life, but with the transcendental life in Heaven. . . . In the National Socialist philosophy, spirit, soul and body are one—*i.e.*, there is only one life, but this life, by reason of its very this-worldliness which is only a visible form of the Transcendental, has an eternal value. . . . Do you understand now, comrades, what it means to believe in the eternal Germany? The eternal is being revealed in our Germany and in its history; it is a Divine progress,

---

[1] November 18th, 1937, p. 11.   [2] August 12th, 1938.

not only an earthly one. The eternal is being revealed and is active in every one of us. Reality is again being invested with the halo of the " Holy " and the " Miraculous." How often has the Führer given expression to this experience: " It is a miracle that has been worked before our eyes and through us; the miracle of faith has created a miracle in the reality of facts. . . ." Our " political " belief, our belief in this earthly life is a belief in eternal and divine things, it is a belief grown out of our ideology with the beauty of a blossom and the swiftness of a flame.

The nation in its racial and communal aspect has been constituted the supreme and final norm directing the whole life of the community and of the individual. Thus, in the hierarchy of values it is not the Transcendental and Divine that reigns supreme but the purely earthly and human.

In his speech at Münster on July 6th, 1935 (as also on many other occasions), Rosenberg affirmed the " eternal and creative life of the nation," " the eternity of the Blood," etc. He said that it was a " divine commandment " to protect this Blood.

In the *Völkischer Beobachter*[1] we come across the following sentences in an article by Eghard Stegmann, entitled " To the Young ":

The more ardently the educationalist is inspired by National Socialist conceptions, the greater will be his power to train a youth of iron determination and fanatical allegiance to its Germanhood, a youth that will recognise the Divine in its own faith in the eternal existence of the nation.

Everything is to be subordinated to the idolised race. There is no moral right nor justice founded on the Divine Will; whatever benefits the nation (or the race) is right, whatever is contrary to its interests is wrong; that is the official and public standard of morality. There is no room for a morality independent of racial conceptions. People whose progeny, from a racial and biological point of view, would not constitute an asset for the community, are to be sterilised, thus violating the natural right of every person to found a family.

The Christian denominations themselves, according to Rosenberg (1935), are " only useful in so far as they protect the ethical (understand: racial) values of the nation."

The *Schwarze Korps*[2] is " only prepared to tolerate the Christian Churches if and as long as they do not run counter to the ethical and moral sensibilities of the Germanic race." Positive Christianity " would have to prove its value by its readiness to give absolute service and undivided allegiance to the great national community."

In consistent pursuance of these ideas, Dr. Gross, director of Department of Racial Policy of the German National Socialist Workers' Party, demands that dogmas should be put in their right place and subordinated to the Race, the supreme value. He writes:

We take in this respect the hard and uncompromising point of view that the national fundamental principle of the National Socialist movement, the racial principle, should be kept absolutely inviolate in its entirety. If you do not like that, if it is not in harmony with your forms, laws and dogmas,

[1] No. 61, March 2nd, 1939, p. 5.   [2] February 9th, 1939, p. 6.

well, change your forms, laws, and dogmas until they fit life as it is. . . . We shall never cease to proclaim that culture and spirit, art, learning and science . . . are and have to be based and dependent on Race and Blood.[1]

In a leader, commenting on a meeting of the National Socialist University Professors' Union, *Die Bewegung*[2] the periodical of the National Socialist Undergraduates' Union, affirms that the National Socialist belief is to regulate all learning and science.

We students subscribe wholeheartedly to the words addressed to the professors by the District Leader and Minister of State, Herr Adolf Wagner: " it is the task of scholars to examine how they can best serve the nation, for only by doing that can they truly fulfil their *raison d'être*. Belief is better than knowledge, therefore learning and science have to be subordinated to our belief. Our belief is the belief of National Socialism; it is also the belief of our National Socialist professors."

Thus scientific scholarship, deprived of its essential character as investigation of objective truth, and art, as well as every other cultural activity, have to be subservient to the absolute claims of the racial conception.

The same view is expressed by the *Schwarze Korps*.[3] Under the title " This was Correct Forty Years Ago," this weekly concludes a review of a book by Hermann Sauer, *Die Stunde des Offiziers* (*The Hour of the Officer*), with the following remarks:

The religious attitude of the soldier is so deeply influenced and moulded by the supreme ideas of nation, Führer and Reich, which constitute for him real revelations of the Divine Will, that the private reservations of dogmatic theories cease to be of any importance. Every member of the national community has to give up his entire personality in undivided and absolute allegiance to the supreme national value (which is represented by the Führer).

It does not matter whether this idol is one time called Nation or Race, another time Germany or National Socialism or even Adolf Hitler himself, since the Party is regarded as the protector of the cult of the Race, and the Führer as the interpreter of the racial will. Thus, *e.g.*, one Schulz, SS-commander, said in 1935: " National Socialism puts forward this claim in real earnest: ' I am the Lord, thy God; thou shalt have no other Gods before me.' " Baldur von Schirach defines the same attitude as follows: " He who is not prepared to say that Germany comes first and foremost before everything else will no longer be tolerated in our German house."[4]

In the *Schwarze Korps*,[5] a young member of a National Socialist political training centre thus expresses the aims of the new German youth:

We demand a national community. We desire the eternal Reich—all German blood united in one nation, in one Reich. We must be penetrated to the core of our hearts by the irresistible force of that allegiance, the only one we recognise. This must become our belief, our fanatical creed: Germany alone is our faith ! (And if this is pagan and atheist, then I am proud of being a " pagan.") This belief has welded together our young community.

[1] *Frankfurter Völksblatt*, January 24th, 1935.
[2] No. 25, June 20th, 1939.
[3] March 16th, 1939.
[4] *Führerblätter der HJ*, edition *DJ*, June, 1936, p. 9 ff.
[5] November 5th, 1936, p. 3.

This community is to be the élite of the youth of our nation. We are no longer Protestants, Catholics, Old-Lutherans, ... we are only Germans.

This chapter cannot have a better conclusion than the " creed " already quoted, which, modelled on the most universal and ancient Christian formula of Faith, the Apostles' Creed, puts into a few words the whole aim and content of the new *ersatz* religion.

I believe in the land of all the Germans, in a life of service to this land; I believe in the revelation of the Divine creative power in the pure Blood shed in war and peace by the sons of the German National Community, buried in the soil thereby sanctified, risen and living in all for whom it was immolated. I believe in an eternal life on earth of this Blood, that was poured out and rose again in all who have recognised the meaning of the sacrifices and are ready to submit to them. . . . Thus I believe in an eternal God, an eternal Germany, and an eternal Life.

CONCLUSION

IN surveying once more the persecution of the Church as it reveals itself in the preceding documents, we are brought up against two characteristics of the National Socialist procedure: First, the diabolically thorough and systematic method of the war waged against the Church; and second, but not of less importance, the almost perfect camouflaging of the religious persecution.

1. *Determination to Destroy the Church*

The religious persecution in Germany is not restricted to any one part of the Church; the whole of Christendom, the Church in all her activities and departments, is threatened with extermination by National Socialism. The real aim of the attacks is not some particular aspect of German Catholicism—*e.g.*, the supra-national union with Rome— or some point of Catholic dogma or morals; nor is National Socialism satisfied, as were former persecutors, to curb the influence of the Church in public life and to destroy the strong positions she held in the schools, the press, education, etc. The claims of National Socialism are insatiable and not moderated by any willingness of the other side to meet them half-way or even most of the way. No concession, however painful on the part of the Church, made her opponents slacken their fierce assaults; no position gained, however important it might seem, caused them to defer for a single moment their ruthless and determined attack on the next. The true aim of National Socialism is the complete destruction and extermination of Christianity: it attacks the smallest and most insignificant religious customs and symbols and does not even stop at the Christian conscience of the individual.

The diabolical hatred of National Socialism against the Church reveals itself especially in the thorough and systematic plan of its campaign which may, without exaggeration, be called a real strategy. Christianity and the Church are beleaguered and attacked like an enemy fortress. Today even the most superficial observer will admit that in the first years of the struggle National Socialism proceeded methodically to occupy the key positions. First, Christian officials in all important departments were replaced by safe men—*i.e.*, " such as had no denominational ties." Then, National Socialism seized all the means of influencing public opinion, especially the press, and took over the whole educational system so as to be able to educate the future generation exclusively in its own ideals. As a next step all the forces and means at the disposal of a modern civilised, but totalitarian, State were simultaneously set in motion against its victim. In this persecution National Socialism not only makes use of laws, decrees and regulations, but also employs slanderous propaganda, terror and economic pressure varied with diversions and dissimulations; in short, it is absolutely unscrupulous in the choice of the means to secure its aims.

2. *The Camouflaging of the Persecution*

The second characteristic of the religious persecution in the Third Reich is the perfect camouflaging and falsification of the facts. Although the widespread ruin due to its anti-religious measures is only too manifest, even today, after seven years of systematic religious persecution, National Socialism considers it necessary to camouflage its attacks and to launch them under false pretences. After arresting and imprisoning Catholic priests by the hundreds, the persecutors keep on alleging at every new arrest of a priest that this step had to be taken on account of " incredible attacks on the present State " and unjustifiable " encroachments on the political sphere." Even after annihilating the whole Catholic Daily Press, every penalty inflicted on the most insignificant parish magazine is vindicated by the plea of " subversive propaganda against the Third Reich." Now that the flourishing private schools of Religious Orders and all the denominational schools have been cunningly and brutally destroyed—and that in total disregard of the will of the parents—these same parents are being intimidated and deterred from sending their children to religious instructions organised by the Church or even to their First Holy Communion—not, as might be thought by the simple, from anti-religious motives, but because " malicious attacks are made against the State during these services." And if Civil Servants who, even in 1939, had the courage to take part in the Corpus Christi Procession are threatened with dismissal, that is, of course, only because National Socialism has found out that these processions are " demonstrations of political Catholicism." Although the National Socialists have broken the Concordat of 1933 more than a thousand times, they are too astute to renounce it, because they prefer to go on sailing under a false flag. As late as in 1939,[1] National Socialism indignantly repudiated the reproach of being hostile to the Church. Even today these gentry are never at a loss to discover new catchwords to disguise and falsify patent facts—*e.g.*, " We have to defend ourselves against the infringements of political Catholicism "; or " These are isolated cases of encroachments by subordinate State officials "; or " The difficulties complained of are typical of a period of transition and will cease as soon as State and Church have found their relative bearings," etc.

The reader of this book will have found out for himself that the documents and facts contained in it are in themselves a striking refutation of such subterfuges. It is not merely a case of political priests that have to be " relegated to their religious sphere of influence "; it is

---

[1] *E.g.*, the leader of the *Schwarze Korps*, January 19th, 1939, entitled " Our Answer to the Vatican "; *ibid.*, February 9th, 1939, p. 6, etc.

the Church herself that is persecuted in all her activities and even in her most vital religious and pastoral spheres. It is not merely a case of trifling incidents which are, as is alleged, laboriously garnered and garbled by the opponents of National Socialism, but of systematic and methodical wholesale attacks on the Church. It is not merely a case of encroachments on the part of subordinate State officials, but it is the Party as such and the total array of the forces of the State that have been mobilised against the Church. It is not merely a case of isolated phenomena, typical of a period of transition, but it is a war of extermination waged against the Church by a system whose ideology is completely and fundamentally opposed to hers.

Of the above assertion there can be no doubt whatsoever, and it is essential that those who see this truth clearly should give their knowledge to others, if not only the Catholic Church and her civilising influence are to be saved from complete destruction in Germany, but also all Christianity there, since all the Churches have a very great deal in common. The danger is not confined to Germany alone. A disease can become an epidemic, and National Socialist ideology, or something like it, can cross the German frontiers and invade other countries too.

Thus we think we have given a clear and satisfying answer to the question that is so often raised: Is the religious persecution in Germany only a tactical manœuvre, and if not, what is the real motive of the National Socialist campaign against the Church? The answer is: The religious persecution is determined and actuated by the *very nature and essence of the National Socialist totalitarian system.*

In examining the preceding documents, again and again we dug down in our search into deeper and, as it were, more responsible strata, and we found that underneath the State lies the Party, and underneath the Party with all its organisations, literature, periodicals, training courses, etc., lies the National Socialist pagan theology, a fact we have endeavoured to establish in the last section of this book. This is the root and ultimate reason of the religious persecution: National Socialism represents a totalitarian ideology which uncompromisingly claims the homage and subordination of all human activities and spheres, even of the last and most intimate, man's soul ! Therefore National Socialism becomes by its very nature the rival and mortal enemy of every genuine religion.

It may be that many members of the so-called elite of the Party leaders look upon the religious paraphernalia of their own system merely as a bait and a sop thrown to the masses. Be that so, yet the fact remains: a fundamental reconciliation between National Socialism and Christianity is only possible if National Socialism gives up its absolute claims, if it is no longer totalitarian—in one word, if it gives up its very essence and nature and ceases to be itself.

APPENDIX I

CONCORDAT BETWEEN THE HOLY SEE AND THE GERMAN REICH

His Holiness Pope Pius XI and the President of the German Reich, moved by a common desire to consolidate and enhance the friendly relations existing between the Holy See and the German Reich, wish to regulate the relations between the Catholic Church and the State for the whole territory of the German Reich in a permanent manner and on a basis acceptable to both parties. They have decided to conclude a solemn agreement, which will supplement the Concordats already concluded with certain individual German states, and will ensure for the remaining States fundamentally uniform treatment of their respective problems.

For this purpose:

His Holiness Pope Pius XI has appointed as his Plenipotentiary His Eminence the Most Reverend Lord Cardinal Eugenio Pacelli, his Secretary of State.

The President of the German Reich has appointed as Plenipotentiary the Vice-Chancellor of the German Reich, Herr Franz von Papen.

Who, having exchanged their respective credentials and found them to be in due and proper form, have agreed to the following articles:

Article 1.—The German Reich guarantees freedom of profession and public practice of the Catholic religion.

It acknowledges the right of the Catholic Church, within the limit of those laws which are applicable to all, to manage and regulate her own affairs independently, and, within the framework of her own competence, to publish laws and ordinances binding on her members.

Article 2.—The Concordats concluded with Bavaria (1924), Prussia (1929) and Baden (1932) remain in force, and the rights and privileges of the Catholic Church recognised therein are secured unchanged within the territories of the States concerned. For the remaining States the agreements entered into in the present Concordat come into force in their entirety. These last are also binding for those States named above in so far as they affect matters not regulated by the regional Concordats or are complementary to the settlement already made.

In future, regional Concordats with States of the German Reich will be concluded only with the agreement of the Reich Government.

Article 3.—In order to foster good relations between the Holy See and the German Reich, an Apostolic Nuncio will reside in the capital of the German Reich and an Ambassador of the German Reich at the Holy See, as heretofore.

Article 4.—In its relations and correspondence with the bishops, clergy and other members of the Catholic Church in Germany, the Holy See enjoys full freedom. The same applies to the bishops and other diocesan officials in their dealings with the faithful in all matters belonging to their pastoral office.

Instructions, ordinances, Pastoral Letters, official diocesan gazettes, and other enactments regarding the spiritual direction of the faithful issued by the ecclesiastical authorities within the framework of their competence (Art. 1, Sect. 2) may be published without hindrance and brought to the notice of the faithful in the form hitherto usual.

Article 5.—In the exercise of their spiritual activities the clergy enjoy the protection of the State in the same way as State officials. The State will take proceedings in accordance with the general provisions of State law against any outrage offered to the clergy personally or directed against their ecclesiastical character, or any interference with the duties of their office, and in case of need will provide official protection.

Article 6.—Clerics and Religious are freed from any obligation to undertake official offices and such obligations as, according to the provisions of Canon Law, are incompatible with the clerical or religious state. This applies particularly to the office of magistrate, juryman, member of Taxation Committee or member of the Fiscal Tribunal.

Article 7.—The acceptance of an appointment or office in the State, or in any publicly constituted corporation dependent on the State, requires, in the case of the clergy, the *nihil obstat* of the Diocesan Ordinary of the individual concerned, as well as that of the Ordinary of the place in which the publicly constituted corporation is situated. The *nihil obstat* may be withdrawn at any time for grave reasons affecting ecclesiastical interests.

Article 8.—The official income of the clergy is immune from distraint to the same extent as is the official salary of officials of the Reich and State.

Article 9.—The clergy may not be required by judicial and other officials to give information concerning matters which have been entrusted to them while exercising the care of souls, and which therefore come within the obligation of pastoral secrecy.

Article 10.—The wearing of clerical dress or of a religious habit on the part of lay folk, or of clerics or religious who have been forbidden to wear them by a final and valid injunction made by the competent ecclesiastical authority and officially communicated to the State authority, is liable to the same penalty on the part of the State as the misuse of military uniform.

Article 11.—The present organisation and demarcation of dioceses of the Catholic Church in the German Reich remains in force. Such rearrangements of a bishopric or of an ecclesiastical province or of other diocesan demarcations as shall seem advisable in the future, so far as they involve changes within the boundaries of a German State, remain subject to the agreement of the Government of the State concerned.

Rearrangements and alterations which extend beyond the boundaries of a German State require the agreement of the Reich Government, to whom it shall be left to secure the consent of the regional Government in question. The same applies to rearrangements or alterations of ecclesiastical Provinces involving several German States. The foregoing conditions do not apply to such ecclesiastical boundaries as are laid down merely in the interests of local pastoral care.

In the case of any territorial reorganisation within the German Reich, the Reich Government will communicate with the Holy See with a view to rearrangement of the organisation and demarcation of dioceses.

Article 12.—Without prejudice to the provisions of Article 11, ecclesiastical offices may be freely constituted and changed, unless the expenditure of State funds is involved. The creation and alteration of parishes shall be carried out according to principles with which the diocesan bishops are agreed, and for which the Reich Government will endeavour to secure uniform treatment as far as possible from the State Governments.

Article 13.—Catholic parishes, parish and diocesan societies, episcopal sees, bishoprics and chapters, religious Orders and Congregations, as well as institutions, foundations and property which are under the administration of ecclesiastical authority, shall retain or acquire respectively legal competence in the civil domain according to the general prescriptions of civil law. They shall remain publicly recognised corporations in so far as they have been such hitherto; similar rights may be granted to the remainder in accordance with those provisions of the law which apply to all.

Article 14.—As a matter of principle the Church retains the right to appoint freely to all Church offices and benefices without the co-operation of the State or of civil communities, in so far as other provisions have not been made in previous Concordats mentioned in Article 2. The regulation made for appointment to the Metropolitan See of Freiburg (the Ecclesiastical Province of the Upper Rhine) is to be duly applied to the two suffragan bishoprics of Rottenburg and Mainz, as well as to the bishopric of Meissen. With regard to Rottenburg and Mainz the same regulation holds for appointments to the Cathedral Chapter, and for the administration of the right of patronage. Furthermore, there is accord on the following points:

1. Catholic clerics who hold an ecclesiastical office in Germany or who exercise pastoral or educational functions must:

   (*a*) Be German citizens.
   (*b*) Have matriculated from a German secondary school.
   (*c*) Have studied philosophy and theology for at least three years at a German State University, a German ecclesiastical college, or a papal college in Rome.

2. The Bull nominating Archbishops, Coadjutors *cum jure successionis*, or appointing a *Praelatus nullius*, will not be issued until the name of the appointee has been submitted to the representative of the National Government in the territory concerned, and until it has been ascertained that no objections of a general political nature exist.

By agreement between Church and State, Paragraph 1, sections (*a*) (*b*) and (*c*) may be disregarded or set aside.

Article 15.—Religious Orders and Congregations are not subject to any special restrictions on the part of the State, either as regards their foundation, the erection of their various establishments, their number, the selection of members (save for the special provisions of paragraph 2 of this article), pastoral activity, education, care of the sick and charitable work, or as regards the management of their affairs and the administration of their property.

Religious Superiors whose headquarters are within Germany must be German citizens. Provincials and other Superiors of Orders, whose headquarters lie outside Germany, have the right of visitation of those of their establishments which lie within Germany.

The Holy See will endeavour to ensure that the provincial organisation of conventual establishments within the German Reich shall be such that, as far as possible, German establishments do not fall under the jurisdiction of foreign provincials. Agreements may be made with the Reich Government in cases where the small number of houses makes a special German province impracticable, or where special grounds exist for the retention of a provincial organisation which is firmly established and has acquired an historic nature.

Article 16.—Before bishops take possession of their dioceses they are to take an oath of fealty either to the Reich Representative of the State concerned, or to the President of the Reich, according to the following formula:

" Before God and on the Holy Gospels I swear and promise, as becomes a bishop, loyalty to the German Reich and to the State of. . . . I swear and promise to honour the legally constituted Government and to cause the clergy of my diocese to honour it. In the performance of my spiritual office and in my solicitude for the welfare and the interests of the German Reich, I will endeavour to avoid all detrimental acts which might endanger it."

Article 17.—The property and other rights of public corporations, institutions, foundations and associations of the Catholic Church regarding their vested interests, are guaranteed according to the common law of the land.

No building dedicated to public worship may be destroyed for any reason whatsoever without the previous consent of the ecclesiastical authorities concerned.

Article 18.—Should it become necessary to abrogate the performance of obligations undertaken by the State towards the Church, whether based on law, agreement or special charter, the Holy See and the Reich will elaborate in amicable agreement the principles according to which the abrogation is to be carried out.

Legitimate traditional rights are to be considered as titles in law.

Such abrogation of obligations must be compensated by an equivalent in favour of the claimant.

Article 19.—Catholic Theological Faculties in State Universities are to be maintained. Their relation to ecclesiastical authorities will be governed by the respective Concordats and by special Protocols attached to the same, and with due regard to the laws of the Church in their regard. The Reich Government will endeavour to secure for all these Catholic Faculties in Germany a uniformity of practical administration corresponding to the general spirit and tenor of the various agreements concerned.

Article 20.—Where other agreements do not exist, the Church has the right to establish theological and philosophical colleges for the training of its clergy, which institutions are to be wholly dependent on the ecclesiastical authorities if no State subsidies are sought.

The establishment, management and administration of theological seminaries and hostels for clerical students, within the limits of the law applicable to all, is exclusively the prerogative of the ecclesiastical authorities.

Article 21.—Catholic religious instruction in elementary, senior, secondary and vocational schools constitutes a regular portion of the curriculum, and is to be taught in accordance with the principles of the Catholic Church. In religious instruction, special care will be taken to inculcate patriotic, civic and social consciousness and sense of duty in the spirit of the Christian Faith and the moral code, precisely as in the case of other subjects. The syllabus and the selection of textbooks for religious instruction will be arranged by consultative agreement with the ecclesiastical authorities, and these latter have the right to investigate whether pupils are receiving religious instruction in accordance with the teachings and requirements of the Church. Opportunities for such investigation will be agreed upon with the school authorities.

Article 22.—With regard to the appointment of Catholic religious instructors, agreement will be arrived at as a result of mutual consultation on the part of the bishop and the Government of the State concerned. Teachers who have been declared by the bishop unfit for the further exercise of their teaching functions, either on pedagogical grounds or by reason of their moral conduct, may not be employed for religious instruction so long as the obstacle remains.

Article 23.—The retention of Catholic denominational schools and the establishment of new ones, is guaranteed. In all parishes in which parents or guardians request it, Catholic elementary schools will be established, provided that the number of pupils available appears to be sufficient for a school managed and administered in accordance with the standards prescribed by the State, due regard being had to the local conditions of school organisations.

Article 24.—In all Catholic elementary schools only such teachers are to be employed as are members of the Catholic Church, and who guarantee to fulfil the special requirements of a Catholic school.

Within the frame-work of the general professional training of teachers, arrangements will be made which will secure the formation and training of Catholic teachers in accordance with the special requirements of Catholic denominational schools.

Article 25.—Religious Orders and Congregations are entitled to establish and conduct private schools, subject to the general laws and ordinances governing education. In so far as these schools follow the curriculum prescribed for State schools, those attending them acquire the same qualifications as those attending State schools.

The admission of members of religious Orders or Congregations to the teaching office, and their appointment to elementary, secondary or senior schools, are subject to the general conditions applicable to all.

Article 26.—With certain reservations pending a later comprehensive regulation of the marriage laws, it is undertood that, apart from cases of critical illness of one member of an engaged couple which does not permit of a postponement, and in cases of great moral emergency (the presence of which must be confirmed by the proper ecclesiastical authority), the ecclesiastical marriage ceremony should precede the civil ceremony. In such cases the pastor is in duty bound to notify the matter immediately at the Registrar's office.

Article 27.—The Church will accord provision to the German army for the spiritual guidance of its Catholic officers, personnel and other officials, as well as for the families of the same.

The administration of such pastoral care for the army is to be vested in the army bishop. The latter's ecclesiastical appointment is to be made by the Holy See after contact has been made with the Reich Government in order to select a suitable candidate who is agreeable to both parties.

The ecclesiastical appointment of military chaplains and other military clergy will be made after previous consultations with the appropriate authorities of the Reich by the army bishop. The army bishop may appoint only such chaplains as receive permission from their diocesan bishop to engage on military pastoral work, together with a certificate of suitability. Military chaplains have the rights of parish priests with regard to the troops and other army personnel assigned to them.

Detailed regulations for the organisation of pastoral work by chaplains will be supplied by an Apostolic Brief. Regulations for official aspects of the same work will be drawn up by the Reich Government.

Article 28.—In hospitals, prisons, and similar public institutions the Church is to retain the right of visitation and of holding divine service, subject to the rules of the said institutions. If regular pastoral care is provided for such institutions, and if pastors be appointed as State or other public officials, such appointments will be made by agreement with the ecclesiastical authorities.

Article 29.—Catholic members of a non-German minority living within the Reich, in matters concerning the use of their mother tongue in church services, religious instruction and the conduct of church societies, will be accorded no less favourable treatment than that which is actually and in accordance with law permitted to individuals of German origin and speech living within the boundaries of the correspondnig foreign States.

Article 30.—On Sundays and Holy days, special prayers, conforming to the Liturgy, will be offered during the principal Mass for the welfare of the German Reich and its people in all episcopal, parish and conventual churches and chapels of the German Reich.

Article 31.—Those Catholic organisations and societies which pursue exclusively charitable, cultural or religious ends, and, as such, are placed under the ecclesiastical authorities, will be protected in their institutions and activities.

Those Catholic organisations which to their religious, cultural and charitable pursuits add others, such as social or professional interests, even though they may be brought into national organisations, are to enjoy the protection of Article 31, Section 1, provided they guarantee to develop their activities outside all political parties.

It is reserved to the central Government and the German episcopate, in joint agreement, to determine which organisations and associations come within the scope of this article.

In so far as the Reich and its constituent States take charge of sport and other youth organisations, care will be taken that it shall be possible for the members of the same regularly to practise their religious duties on Sundays and feast days, and that they shall not be required to do anything not in harmony with their religious and moral convictions and obligations.

Article 32.—In view of the special situation existing in Germany, and in view of the guarantee provided through this Concordat of legislation directed to safeguard the rights and privileges of the Roman Catholic Church in the Reich and its component States, the Holy See will prescribe regulations for the exclusion of clergy and members of religious Orders from membership of political parties, and from engaging in work on their behalf.

Article 33.—All matters relating to clerical persons or ecclesiastical affairs, which have not been treated of in the foregoing articles, will be regulated for the ecclesiastical sphere according to current Canon Law.

Should differences of opinion arise regarding the interpretation or execution of any of the articles of this Concordat, the Holy See and the German Reich will reach a friendly solution by mutual agreement.

Article 34.—This Concordat, whose German and Italian texts shall have equal binding force, shall be ratified, and the certificates of ratification shall be exchanged, as soon as possible. It will be in force from the day of such exchange.

In witness hereof, the plenipotentiaries have signed this Concordat.

Signed in two original exemplars, in the Vatican City, July 20th, 1933.

Signed: EUGENIO, CARDINAL PACELLI.
Signed: FRANZ VON PAPEN.

The Supplementary Protocol.

At the signing of the Concordat concluded today between the Holy See and the German Reich, the undersigned, being regularly thereto empowered, have adjoined the following explanations which form an integral part of the Concordat itself.

In re: **Article 3.**—The Apostolic Nuncio to the German Reich, in accordance with the exchange of notes between the Apostolic Nunciature in Berlin and the Reich Foreign Office on the 11th and the 27th of March respectively, shall be the Doyen of the Diplomatic Corps thereto accredited.

Article 13.—It is understood that the Church retains the right to levy Church taxes.

Article 14, Par. 2.—It is understood that when objections of a general political nature exist, they shall be presented within the shortest possible time. If after twenty days such representations have not been made, the Holy See may be justified in assuming that no objections exist to the candidate in question. The names of the persons concerned will be kept confidential until the announcement of the appointment. No right of the State to assert a veto is to be derived from this article.

Article 17.—In so far as public buildings or properties are devoted to ecclesiastical purposes, these are to be retained as before, subject to existing agreements.

Article 19, Par. 2.—This clause is based, at the time of signature of this Concordat, especially on the Apostolic Constitution, *Deus Scientiarum Dominus* of May 24th, 1931, and the Instruction of July 7th, 1932.

Article 20.—Hostels which are administered by the Church in connection with certain Universities and secondary schools, will be recognised, from the point of view of taxation, as essentially ecclesiastical institutions in the proper sense of the word, and as integral parts of diocesan organisation.

Article 24.—In so far as private institutions are able to meet the requirements of the new educational code with regard to the training of teachers, all existing establishments of religious Orders and Congregations will be given due consideration in the accordance of recognition.

Article 26.—A severe moral emergency is taken to exist when there are insuperable or disproportionately difficult and costly obstacles impeding the procuring of documents necessary for the marriage at the proper time.

Article 27, Par. 1.—Catholic officers, officials and personnel, their families included, do not belong to local parishes, and are not to contribute to their maintenance.

Par. 4.—The publication of the Apostolic Brief will take place after consultation with the Reich Government.

Article 28.—In cases of urgency entry of the clergy is guaranteed at all times.

Article 29.—Since the Reich Government has seen its way to come to an agreement regarding non-German minorities, the Holy See declares—in accordance with the principles it has constantly maintained regarding the right to employ the vernacular in Church services, religious instruction and the conduct of Church societies—that it will bear in mind similar clauses protective of German minorities when establishing Concordats with other countries.

Article 31, Par. 4.—The principles laid down in Article 31, § 4 hold good also for the Labour Service.

Article 32.—It is understood that similar provisions regarding activity in Party politics will be introduced by the Reich Government for members of non-Catholic denominations. The conduct, which has been made obligatory for the clergy and members of religious Orders in Germany in virtue of Article 32, does not involve any sort of limitation of official and prescribed preaching and interpretation of the dogmatic and moral teachings and principles of the Church.

Signed: EUGENIO, CARDINAL PACELLI.
Signed: FRANZ VON PAPEN.

At the Vatican City, *July 20th*, 1933.

APPENDIX II

THE PAPAL ENCYCLICAL "MIT BRENNENDER SORGE"

ENCYCLICAL LETTER

TO THE VENERABLE ARCHBISHOPS AND BISHOPS AND OTHER ORDINARIES IN PEACE AND COMMUNION WITH THE APOSTOLIC SEE: ON THE SITUATION OF THE CATHOLIC CHURCH IN GERMANY

POPE PIUS XI

VENERABLE BRETHREN, GREETING AND APOSTOLIC BENEDICTION

WITH deep anxiety and with ever growing dismay We have for a considerable time watched the Church treading the Way of the Cross and the gradually increasing oppression of the men and women who have remained devoted to her in thought and in act in that country and among that people to whom St. Boniface once brought the light of the Gospel of Christ and of the Kingdom of God.

This anxiety of Ours has not been lessened by the reports which the representatives of the reverend Episcopate dutifully and truthfully brought to Us on Our sick-bed. Besides much that is consoling and comforting in the struggle for religion the faithful are now making, they could not, in spite of their love for their people and country and their care to express a balanced judgement, pass silently over too much that is bitter and sad. When We heard their reports We could exclaim with the Apostle of Love in the deepest gratitude to God: "I have no greater grace than this, to hear that my children walk in truth" (3 John i. 4). But the outspokenness which befits the responsibility of Our Apostolic office and the determination to lay before you and the whole Christian world the real truth in all its gravity require Us to add: We have no greater concern and no heavier pastoral anxiety than when We hear: many forsake the way of truth (*cf.* 2 Pet. ii. 2).

When in the summer of 1933, Venerable Brethren, at the request of the German Government We resumed negotiations for a Concordat on the basis of the proposals worked out several years before, and to the satisfaction of you all concluded a solemn agreement, We were moved by the solicitude that is incumbent on Us to safeguard the liberty of the Church in her mission of salvation in Germany and the salvation of the souls entrusted to her—and at the same time by the sincere desire to render an essential service to the peaceful development and welfare of the German people.

In spite of many serious misgivings We then brought Ourselves to decide not to withhold Our consent. We wished to spare Our loyal sons and daughters in Germany, as far as was humanly possible, the strain and the suffering which otherwise at that time and in those circumstances must certainly have been expected. By Our act We wished to show to all that, seeking only Christ and the things that are Christ's, We refuse to none who does not himself reject it the hand of peace of Mother Church.

If the tree of peace planted by Us with pure intention in German soil has not borne the fruit We desired in the interests of your people, no one in the whole world who has eyes to see or ears to hear can say today that the fault lies with the Church and with her Supreme Head. The experience of the past years fixes the responsibility. It discloses intrigues which from the beginning had no other aim than a war of extermination. In the furrows in which We had laboured to sow the seeds of true peace, others—like the enemy in Holy Scripture (Matt. xiii. 25)—sowed the tares of suspicion, discord, hatred, calumny, of secret and open fundamental hostility to Christ and His Church, fed from a thousand different sources and making use of every available means. On them and on them alone and on their silent and vocal protectors rests the responsibility that now on the horizon of Germany there is to be seen not the rainbow of peace but the threatening storm-clouds of destructive religious wars.

Venerable Brethren, We have not grown weary of presenting to the rulers who guide the destinies of your nation the inevitable consequences of tolerating or worse still of favouring such tendencies. We have done all We could to defend the sanctity of the solemn pledges, the inviolability of obligations freely entered into, against theories and practices which, if officially approved, must destroy all confidence and render intrinsically worthless every future pledge. When the time comes to place before the eyes of the world these endeavours of Ours, all right-minded persons will know where to look for the peace-makers and where to look for the peace-breakers. Anyone who has any sense of truth left in his mind and even a shadow of the feeling of justice left in his heart will have to admit that, in the difficult and eventful years which followed the Concordat, every word and every action of Ours was ruled by loyalty to the terms of the agreement; but also he will have to recognise with surprise and deep disgust that the unwritten law of the other party has been arbitrary misinterpretation of agreements, evasion of agreements, evacuation of the meaning of agreements, and finally more or less open violation of agreements.

Our moderation in spite of all this was not suggested by considerations of human expediency, still less by weakness, but simply by the wish not to root out with the tares any good plant, by the intention not to pronounce a public verdict before minds were ready to recognise its inevitability, by the determination not to deny definitely the loyalty of others to their pledged word, before the iron language of facts had torn away the veil which by deliberate camouflage covered and still covers the attack on the Church. Even today when the open war against the confessional schools, which were guaranteed by the Concordat, and the nullification of the freedom of ballot for those entitled to a Catholic education, show the tragic seriousness of the situation in a field which is a vital interest of the Church and an oppression of the conscience of the faithful such as has never before been witnessed, Our paternal solicitude for the well-being of souls counsels Us not to leave out of consideration any prospects however slight which may still exist of a return to the faithful observance of the pacts and to an agreement permitted by Our conscience. In accordance with the prayers of the most reverend members of the episcopate, we shall not weary in the future of defending violated right before the rulers of your people, unconcerned with temporary success or failure and obedient only to Our conscience and to Our pastoral office, and We shall not cease to oppose an attitude of mind which seeks with open or secret violence to stifle a chartered right.

However, the purpose of the present letter, Venerable Brethren, is different. As you have kindly visited Our sickbed We now turn to you and through you to the faithful Catholics of Germany, who, like all suffering and persecuted children, are very near to the heart of the Common Father. In this hour in which their faith is being tried like true gold in the fire of tribulation, and of secret and open persecution, when they are surrounded by a thousand forms of organised religious bondage, when the lack of truthful news and of normal means of defence weighs heavily upon them, they have a double claim to a word of truth and of spiritual encouragement from him to whose first predecessor Our Saviour addressed these deeply significant words: " But I have prayed for thee, that thy faith fail not; and thou being once converted, confirm thy brethren " (Luke xxii. 32).

True Belief in God

Before all else, Venerable Brethren, see that belief in God, the first and irreplaceable foundation of all religion, remains pure and uncorrupted in German lands. He cannot be considered a believer in God who uses the name of God rhetorically, but he only who unites to that sacred word a true and worthy idea of God. Whoever with pantheistic vagueness identifies God with the universe, and materialises God in the world and deifies the world in God, cannot be reckoned a believer in God. Whoever according to an alleged primitive German pre-Christian conception substitutes a gloomy and impersonal fate for a personal God, denying God's wisdom and providence which " reacheth from end to end mightily and ordereth all things sweetly " (Wisdom viii. 1), cannot claim to be numbered among believers in God.

Whoever transposes Race or People, the State or Constitution, the executive or other fundamental elements of human society (which in the natural order have an essential and honourable place), from the scale of earthly values and makes them the ultimate norm of all things, even of religious values, and deifies them with an idolatrous cult, perverts and falsifies the divinely created and appointed order of things. Such a man is far from true belief in God and from a conception of life in conformity to it.

Direct your attention, Venerable Brethren, to the growing abuse shown in speech and in writing of using the thrice holy name of God as a meaningless label for a more or less arbitrary product of human research or aspiration, and labour amongst your faithful that such an error may be as vigilantly repelled as it deserves. Our God is the personal, transcendent, omnipotent, infinitely perfect God, one in the Trinity of persons and threefold in the unity of the divine essence, Creator of the universe, Lord, King and ultimate end of world-history, who does not and cannot suffer any other gods beside Himself.

This God has given His commandments in the manner of a sovereign. They are independent of time, space, country, or nation. As God's sun shines on all the human race without distinction, so His law knows no privileges, no exceptions. Rulers and ruled, crowned and uncrowned, great and small, rich and poor, depend equally on His word. An essential consequence of the fullness of His rights as Creator is His claim to absolute obedience from individuals in whatsoever society they be. Such a claim to obedience extends to every sphere of life in which moral questions have to be settled in accordance with divine law and therefore with the adjustment of mutable human laws to the structure of the immutable laws of God.

Only superficial minds can fall into the error of speaking of a national God, of a national religion, and of making a mad attempt to imprison within the frontiers of a single people, within the pedigree of one single race, God, the Creator of the world, the King, and lawgiver of the peoples before whose greatness the nations are as small as drops in a bucket of water (Isaias xl. 15).

The Bishops of the Church of Christ " ordained in the things that appertain to God " (Heb. v. 1) must watch that such pernicious errors which usually bring in their train even more pernicious practices find no support among the faithful. It belongs to their sacred office to do all in their power to see that the commandments of God are regarded and obeyed as a necessary foundation of a moral and ordered life whether private or public; that the rights of the divine majesty, the name and the word of God, be not blasphemed (Titus ii. 5); that blasphemies against God in speech, in writing, or in pictures, as countless at times as the sand of the sea, be silenced; and that against the defiant Prometheus-like spirit of those who deny, outrage, and hate God, the propitiatory prayer of the faithful may never falter, for it rises every hour like incense to the Almighty and stays His hand of punishment.

We thank you, Venerable Brethren, your priests, and all the faithful who have done and are doing their duty as Christians in defending the rights of the divine Majesty against an aggressive neo-paganism which only too often is supported by influential persons. Our thanks are doubly heartfelt and are combined with a recognition and admiration for those who in doing this duty were thought worthy of enduring temporal sacrifices and temporal sufferings for the cause of God.

True Belief in Christ

No belief in God will long be maintained pure and uncorrupted if it is not supported by belief in Christ. " No one knoweth the Son but the Father: neither doth anyone know the Father, but the Son and he to whom it shall please the Son to reveal him " (Matt. xi. 27). " This is eternal life: That they may know thee, the only true God, and Jesus Christ, whom thou hast sent " (John xvii. 3). Therefore no one can say: I believe in God, and that is enough religion for me. The word of Our Saviour allows no room for evasions of this kind. " Whosoever denieth the Son the same hath not the Father. He that confesseth the Son hath the Father also " (1 John ii. 23).

The fullness of divine revelation has appeared in Jesus Christ, the Son of God made man. " God, who at sundry times and in divers manners spoke in times past to the fathers by the prophets, in these days has spoken to us by his Son " (Heb. i. 1, 2). The sacred books of the Old Testament are all God's word, an organic part of His revelation. Corresponding to the gradual unfolding of revelation there hangs over them the darkness of the time of preparation for the full noonday of the redemption. As is inevitable with books of history and law, they reflect in many details human imperfection, weakness, and sin. Besides much that is great and noble they relate the materialism and worldliness which appeared again and again in the people of the old covenant, who received the revelation and the promise of God.

But for every eye not blinded by prejudice or passion, in spite of the human weakness of which Bible history speaks, the divine light of the way of salvation, finally triumphant over all error and sin, shines all the clearer. " The Law was our pedagogue in Christ " (Gal. iii. 24) and the saving tutelage of the Eternal God opens out on just such a background, often it is true a gloomy background, into perspectives which at one and the same time direct, warn, excite, cheer and bring happiness. Only blindness and self-will can close men's eyes to the treasure of instruction for salvation hidden in the Old Testament. He who wishes to see Bible history and the wisdom of the Old Testament banished from church and school blasphemes the word of God, blasphemes the Almighty's plan of salvation and sets up narrow and limited human thought as the judge of God's plans. He denies faith in Christ who truly appeared in the flesh, and who took His human nature from the people which was afterwards to nail Him to a Cross. He fails completely to understand the world-drama of the Son of God who as high priest set the divine action of His redeeming death in opposition to the evil deeds of those who crucified Him and thus made the Old Testament find in the New its fulfilment, its end, and that by which it is superseded.

The culmination of revelation in the Gospel of Jesus Christ is definitive and obligatory for all time; it admits no additions at the hands of men, and acknowledges no substitute whatever, and no replacement by the arbitrary " revelations " that certain contemporary prophets try to extract from the so-called myth of blood and race. Since Christ, the Messias, fulfilled the work of redemption, broke the dominion of sin, and merited for us the grace to become the sons of God, " there is no other name under heaven given to men, whereby we must be saved " (Acts iv. 12) but the name of Jesus. Thus though a man should embody in himself all wisdom, all might, all the material power of the world, he can lay no other foundation than that which is already laid in Christ (1 Cor. iii. 11). He who sacrilegiously misunderstands the abyss between God and creation, between the God-Man and the children of men, and dares to place beside Christ, or worse still, above Him and against Him, any mortal, even the greatest of all times, must endure to be told that he is a false prophet to whom the words of Scripture find a terrible application: " He that dwelleth in heaven shall laugh at them " (Ps. ii. 4).

True Belief in the Church

Belief in Christ will not remain pure and uncorrupted if it is not supported and defended by faith in the Church, " the pillar and ground of the truth " (1 Tim. iii. 15). Christ Himself, God blessed for ever, erected this pillar of the faith. His command to hear the Church (Matt. xviii. 17) and to hear through the words and commands of the Church His own words and His own commands (Luke x. 16) is obligatory on men of all times and of all countries. The Church founded by the Redeemer is one for all peoples and for all nations; and under its dome, which like the firmament of God stretches over the whole universe, there is a place and home for all peoples and all tongues, and there can be developed all the qualities, aptitudes, tasks and vocations with which God the Creator and Redeemer has endowed individuals and societies. The mother-love of the Church is wide enough to see in the divinely planned development of such special gifts and callings rather the richness of variety than the danger of divisions; she rejoices in the spiritual advancement of individuals and peoples; with a mother's joy and pride she perceives in their real achievements the fruits of education and of progress which she blesses and promotes whenever in conscience she can. But she knows, too, that limits are set to this freedom by the majesty of divine law that has willed and founded this Church as an indivisible unity in all its essential parts. He who violates this indivisible unity takes from the Bride of Christ one of the diadems with which God Himself has crowned her; he subjects the divine building that rests on eternal foundations to re-examination and remodelling by architects on whom the heavenly Father has bestowed no power.

APPENDIX II

The divine mission which the Church fulfils among men and must fulfil by means of men, may be grievously obscured by the human—sometimes all-too-human—element which in certain times appears like tares among the wheat of the kingdom of God. He who knows the word of our Saviour about scandals and those who give them knows in what way the Church and each individual has to judge what was sin and is sin. But whoever bases his arguments on these reprehensible discrepancies between faith and life, between words and actions, between the exterior conduct and the interior attitude of individuals—even though they be many—and forgets, or even deliberately ignores, the vast sum of genuine effort for virtue, of self-sacrifice, of brotherly love, the heroic striving for sanctity in so many members of the Church, displays a lamentable blindness and injustice. And when it becomes obvious that the rigid standard with which he judged the Church he hates is put aside, the moment he discusses other societies akin to him in sentiment or interests, then it becomes evident that in his alleged outraged respect for purity he is akin to those who, in the incisive words of our Saviour, observe the mote in their brother's eye, but do not see the beam in their own eye. But however far from pure may be the intention of those who make a career—often a despicable profession—out of occupying themselves with the human element in the Church, and though it be true that the power of the ecclesiastical official, resting as it does on God, is not dependent on his human or moral level, yet no epoch of time, no individual, no society, is free from the duty of an honest examination of conscience, of unrelenting purification, and of thorough renovation of mind and action. In Our encyclical on the priesthood, and in Our letters on Catholic Action, We have pointed out with earnest insistence the sacred duty of all members of the Church, especially members of the priesthood, of religious Orders, and of the lay apostolate, to bring faith and conduct into that harmony required by the law of God and demanded with untiring emphasis by the Church. And today, too, We repeat with the deepest seriousness: it is not sufficient to be numbered with the Church of Christ: men must be living members of that Church—in spirit and in truth. And only they are such who are in the grace of the Lord and walk always in His presence, whether in innocence or in sincere and efficacious penance. If the Apostle of the Gentiles, " the vessel of election," kept his body under the rod of mortification in order that, having preached to others, he might not himself become a castaway (1 Cor. ix. 27), can there be for others any way but that of the closest union of the apostolate and of personal sanctification, for in their hands is placed the guardianship and the increase of the kingdom of God ? Only so can men of today, and especially the adversaries of the Church, be shown that the salt of the earth and the leaven of Christianity has not lost its power, but is able and ready to bring to our contemporaries in doubt and error, in indifference and in spiritual bewilderment, weariness of faith, and separation from God, the spiritual renewal and rejuvenation of which—whether they admit it or not—they more than ever stand in need. A Christianity in which all its members keep watch over themselves, that casts aside every tendency to what is merely material and worldly, that takes the commandments of God and of the Church seriously, and that keeps itself in the love of God and in active love of one's neighbour, can and must be a pattern and guide to a world sick to its very heart, which looks for support and guidance if it is not to be overwhelmed in unspeakable ruin, in a catastrophe that surpasses everything imaginable.

All true and permanent reform has in the last resort originated in sanctity, from men who were inflamed and urged on by the love of God and of their neighbour; who by their great generosity in answering every call from God, and in making it real first of all in themselves, grew in humility and the conviction that they were called by God, and have enlightened and renewed the times in which they lived. When zeal for reform has not sprung from the pure source of personal singleness of heart, but has been the expression and explosion of passionate force, it has brought darkness instead of light, it has pulled down instead of building up, and has often been a starting-point for errors still more disastrous than the evils which it desired or claimed that it desired to correct. It is true the spirit of God breatheth where He will (John iii. 8); He can raise up from stones those who are to fulfil His designs (Matt. iii. 9; Luke iii. 8); He chooses the instruments of His will according to His plans and not according to the plans of men. But He who founded the Church and called it to life in the Pentecostal fire does not break in pieces the foundation of the institution for salvation He Himself planned. He who is moved by the spirit of God has for that very reason both outwardly and inwardly a respectful attitude towards the Church, that precious fruit of the tree of the Cross, the Pentecostal gift to a world in need of guidance.

In your territories, Venerable Brethren, voices are raised in an ever louder chorus, urging men to leave the Church, and preachers arise who from their official position try to create the impression that such a departure from the Church and the consequent infidelity to Christ the King is a particularly convincing and meritorious proof of their loyalty to the present régime. By disguised and by open methods of coercion, by intimidation, by holding out prospects of economic, professional, civil or other kinds of advantages, the loyalty of Catholics to their faith, and especially of certain classes of Catholic officials, is subjected to a violence which is as unlawful as it is inhuman. With the feelings of a father We are moved and suffer profoundly with those who have paid such a price for their fidelity to Christ and to the Church; but the point has been reached where it is a question of the last and ultimate end, salvation or perdition, and here the only way of salvation for the believer lies in heroic fortitude. When the tempter or the oppressor approaches with the traitorous suggestion that he should leave the Church, then he can only answer, even at the price of the heaviest earthly sacrifices, in the words of our Saviour: " Begone, Satan: for it is written: The Lord thy God shalt thou adore, and Him only shalt thou serve " (Matt. iv. 10; Luke iv. 8). But to the Church he will speak these words: " O thou who art my mother from the earliest days of my childhood, my comfort in life, my advocate in death, may my tongue cleave to the roof of my mouth if I, yielding to earthly persuasions or threats, should turn traitor to my baptismal vow." Then to those who flatter themselves that they can reconcile with outward abandonment of the Church an interior loyalty to her, let the words of the Redeemer be a severe rebuke: " He that shall deny me before men, I will also deny him before my Father who is in heaven " (Luke xii. 9; Matt. x. 33).

True Belief in the Primacy

Belief in the Church will not be kept pure and uncorrupted if it is not supported by belief in the primacy of the Bishop of Rome. At the very moment when Peter anticipated the other Apostles and disciples and professed his faith in Christ, the Son of the living God, came the answer of Christ, the announcement of the foundation of His Church, of the one Church on Peter the rock (Matt. xvi. 18), rewarding him for his faith and for his confession. Belief in Christ, in the Church, and in the primacy are thus joined in a consecrated interdependence. Real and lawful authority is everywhere a bond of unity, a source of strength, a security against disruption and disintegration and a guarantee for the future, and in the highest and noblest sense when in the unique instance of the Church such an authority has given to it the promise of the supernatural help of the Holy Spirit and His assistance, against which nothing can prevail. When persons who are not even united in faith in Christ entice you and flatter you with the picture of a " German national church," know that that is nothing but a denial of the one Church of Christ, manifest apostasy from the command of Christ to preach the gospel to the whole world, which can alone be accomplished by a universal Church. The historical development of other national churches, their spiritual torpor, their stifling by, or subservience to, lay power show the hopeless sterility which inevitably attacks the branch that separates itself from the living vine-stem of the Church. Whoever on principle gives to these false developments a watching and unflinching " No " is rendering a service not only to the purity of his own faith, but also to the welfare and vitality of his people.

No Transformation of the Meaning of Sacred Words and Ideas

You must have a specially watchful eye, Venerable Brethren, when religious ideas are emptied of their real content and are transformed into a profane meaning.

Revelation in the Christian sense means the word of God to man. To use this same word for the " subconscious tendencies " which come from blood and from race, for the " inspirations " of the history of a people, is in every case a cause of confusion. Such false coinage does not deserve to be received into the treasury of a faithful Christian.

Faith consists in holding as true what God has revealed and through His Church lays down for our belief: it is " the evidence of things that appear not " (Heb. xi. 1). Joyous and proud confidence in the future of one's own people which everyone holds dear means something very different from faith in a religious sense. To employ one for the other, to substitute one for the other and on that ground to claim to be regarded as a " believer " by a convinced Christian, is an empty play on words, a deliberate confusion of terms, or even worse.

Immortality in the Christian sense is the survival of man after temporal death as a personal individual for eternal reward or punishment. Whoever uses the word immortality to mean only collective survival in the continuity of one's own people for an undetermined length of time in the future perverts and falsifies one of the fundamental verities of the Christian faith and shakes the foundations of every religious outlook which demands a moral ordering of the universe. Whoever does not wish to be a Christian ought at least to renounce the desire to enrich the vocabulary of his unbelief with the heritage of Christian ideas.

Original sin is the inherited, though not the personal, guilt of each one of the sons of Adam who have sinned in him (Rom. v. 12) and lost grace and consequently eternal life, together with the propensity to evil which each one has to subdue and overcome by means of grace, penance, effort, and moral endeavour. The passion and death of the Son of God redeemed the world from the inherited curse of sin and of death. Faith in these truths, which are today made a target for the vulgar scorn of the enemies of Christ in your country, belongs to the inalienable substance of the Christian religion.

The Cross of Christ, though its very name may have for many become a stumbling block and foolishness (1 Cor. i. 23), remains for the Christian the hallowed sign of redemption, the standard of moral greatness and strength. In its shadow we live: we kiss it in death: on our graves it will stand to proclaim our faith, to testify to our hope which reaches out towards eternal life.

Humility in the spirit of the Gospel and prayer for God's help are compatible with self-respect, self-confidence and heroism. The Church of Christ, which in all ages up to those which are nearest to us counts more heroic confessors and martyrs than any other moral society, certainly does not need to receive instruction from such quarters about heroic sentiment and action. By foolishly representing Christian humility as a self-degradation and an unheroic attitude, the repulsive pride of these innovators only makes itself an object for ridicule.

Grace in a wide sense can be said to be everything which comes to the creature from the Creator. Grace in the proper and Christian sense of the word includes, however, the supernatural gifts of divine charity, the loving-kindness and the work of God whereby He raises man to that intimate communion in His own life which the New Testament calls sonship of God. "Behold what manner of charity the Father hath bestowed upon us, that we should be called and should be the sons of God" (1 John iii. 1). The repudiation of this supernatural elevation to grace because of the alleged particular nature of the German character is an error, an open declaration of war on a fundamental truth of Christianity. To put supernatural grace on a level with the gifts of nature is to do violence to the language created and sanctified by religion. The pastors and guardians of the people of God will do well to oppose this spoliation of sacred things and this work of leading minds astray.

Moral Doctrine and Moral Order

The morality of the human race is grounded on faith in God kept true and pure. All attempts to detach the doctrine of moral law from the granite base of the faith in order to build it up again on the shifting sands of human regulations sooner or later bring individuals and nations to moral decadence. The fool who says in his heart "there is no God" will tread the path of moral corruption (Ps. xiii. 1). The number of such fools who presume to separate morality from religion has today become legion. They do not perceive, or they do not wish to perceive, that by banishing confessional (*i.e.*, clear and definite) teaching from instruction and education, by preventing its co-operation in the formation of social and of public life, they are treading the paths of moral impoverishment and decadence. No coercive power of the State, no purely earthly ideal, however great and noble, can in the long run replace the ultimate and decisive motives which come from faith in God and in Christ. Take the moral support which comes from what is eternal and divine from the elevating and consoling belief in Him who rewards all good and punishes all evil, away from anyone who is called to make the hardest sacrifices, the surrender of his own petty self to the common good; the result will be that innumerable men will not do their duty but will shirk it. The conscientious observance of the ten commandments of God and of the precepts of the Church—and these latter are only regulations derived from standards laid down in the Gospels—is for every individual an incomparable school of systematic discipline, moral strength, and character-formation. It is a school that asks much but not too much. The God of mercy, when He as lawgiver declares " thou shalt," gives in His grace the power to do and to make perfect. To leave moral forces of such profound strength unused or deliberately to exclude them from the field of popular education is irresponsible co-operation in the religious starvation of a community. To hand over moral teaching to subjective and temporary human opinions instead of anchoring it to the holy will of the everlasting God and to His commandments means opening wide the doors to the forces of destruction. Thus to encourage the abandonment of the eternal principles of the objective moral law in the formation of consciences, in the ennobling of all the spheres of life and of all its ordinances, is a sin against the future of a people, and its bitter fruit will have to be tasted by future generations.

Recognition of the Natural Law

It is a trend of the present day to dissociate more and more, not only moral teaching, but also the foundations of law and justice from true faith in God and from the revealed commandments of God. Here We have in mind especially what is usually called natural law, written by the finger of the Creator Himself on the tables of man's heart (Rom. ii. 14, etc.), which sound human reason not blinded by sins and passions can read on these tables. By the commandments of this natural law every positive law, whoever may be the lawgiver, can be tested as to its moral content and consequently as to the lawfulness of its authority and as to its obligation in conscience. Those human laws which are irreconcilably opposed to natural law have an innate defect which can be cured neither by compulsion nor by any external display of force. By this standard we must judge also the fundamental principle: " Right is what is advantageous to the people." It is true a right meaning may be given to this principle if it is understood to mean that what is morally illicit can never be to the true advantage of the people. Even ancient paganism recognised that the maxim to be perfectly accurate should be inverted and should read: " Nothing is ever advantageous if at the same time it is not morally good, and it is not because it is useful that it is morally good, but because it is morally good it is also useful " (Cicero, *De Officiis* iii. 30). This fundamental principle, cut off from moral law, would mean in relations between states a perpetual state of war amongst the various nations; in the life of the state it confuses advantage and right, and refuses to recognise the fundamental fact that man as a person possesses rights given him by God which must be preserved from every attempt by the community to deny, suppress, or hinder their exercise. To overlook this truth is to lose sight of the fact that the true common good is ultimately defined and discovered from the nature of man with its harmonious co-ordination of personal rights and social obligations, as well as from the purpose of society which is determined by the same human nature. Society is willed by the Creator as a means to the full development of the faculties of the individual, and a man has to make use of society, now giving and again taking for his own good and for the good of others. Nay more, those higher and more universal values which cannot be realised by individuals but only by society are intended by the Creator ultimately for the sake of the ultimate end of man, for his natural and supernatural development and perfection. Whoever transgresses this order shakes the pillars of society and imperils its tranquillity, security, and even its existence.

The believer has an inalienable right to profess his faith and to practise it in the manner suited to him. Laws which suppress or render difficult the profession and practice of this faith are contrary to natural law.

Conscientious parents, aware of their duty in education, have a primary and original God-given right to determine the education of the children given them by God in the spirit of the true faith and in accordance with its fundamental principles and precepts. Laws or other regulations concerning schools, which take no account of the rights of the parents given them by natural law, or which by threats or violence nullify them, contradict the natural law and are essentially immoral.

The Church, the chosen guardian and interpreter of the natural law, cannot do otherwise than declare that the enrolments of pupils which have just taken place in circumstances of notorious coercion are the effects of violence and void of all legality.

To Youth

As the representative of Him who said to a young man in the Gospel: " If thou wilt enter into life keep the commandments " (Matt. xix. 17) We direct especially fatherly words to youth.

By a thousand tongues today there is preached in your ears a gospel which has not been revealed by the heavenly Father: a thousand pens write in the service of a sham Christianity which is not the Christianity of Christ. The printing-press and the radio flood you daily with productions the contents of which are hostile to faith and to Church, and unscrupulously and irreverently attack what, for you, must be sacred and holy.

We know that many, many amongst you, because of your attachment to faith and Church, and because you belong to religious associations guaranteed by the Concordat, have had to endure, and must still endure, unhappy days of misunderstanding, of suspicion, of disgrace, of denial of your patriotic loyalty, of manifold injury to your professional and social life. We know well how many an unknown soldier of Christ is to be found in your ranks, who, with broken heart, but with head erect, bears his lot and finds comfort solely in the thought that he suffers reproach for the name of Jesus (Acts v. 41).

And today when new perils and trials threaten, We say to this youth: " If anyone preach to you a gospel besides that which you have received " at the knees of a pious mother, from the lips of a believing father, from the lessons of a teacher faithful to God and to His Church, " let him be anathema " (Gal. i. 9). If the State organises a national youth association which is compulsory for all, then—without prejudice to the rights of religious associations—it is an obvious and inalienable right of the young, and also of their parents who are responsible before God for them, to demand that that association be cleansed from all activities hostile in spirit to Christian faith and to the Church, activities which up to the most recent times, and even at the present moment, place believing parents in a state of insoluble perplexity of conscience, since they cannot give the State what is demanded from them in the name of the State without taking from God what belongs to God.

No one has any idea of putting stumbling-blocks on the way leading German youth to the realisation of true national unity, to the fostering of a noble love of liberty and steadfast loyalty to their country. What We attack and what We must attack is the intentional and systematically inspired opposition set up between these educational aims and the aims of religion. Therefore We say to this youth: sing your songs of liberty, but do not forget in them the liberty of the children of God. Do not allow the nobility of this irreplaceable liberty to pine away in the slave-chains of sin and sensuality. He who sings the song of loyalty to his earthly country must not become a deserter and traitor in disloyalty to his God, his Church, and his heavenly country. You are told much about heroic greatness, intentionally and falsely contrasted with the humility and patience of the Gospel; but why are you not told that there is a heroism in the moral struggle, that to keep baptismal innocence is a heroic act which ought to be appreciated as it deserves whether in the religious or the natural sphere? You are told much of human weaknesses in the history of the Church, but why are you not told of the great deeds which have accompanied her path across the centuries, the saints she has produced, the blessing which came to Western civilisation from the living union between that Church and your people? You are told a great deal about athletic sports. Practised in moderation and discretion, physical training is beneficial to youth. But often today so much time is devoted to it that no account is taken of the complete and harmonious development of body and spirit, nor of the fitting care of family life, nor of the commandment of Sunday observance. With a disregard bordering on indifference the sacred character and peace of the Lord's Day, which are in the best German tradition, are taken away. We confidently expect from believing Catholic youth that in the difficult atmosphere of compulsory State organisations they will unflinchingly insist on their right to keep holy the Christian Sunday, that the care of physical fitness will not make them forget their immortal souls, that they will not allow themselves to be overcome by evil, but will strive to overcome evil by good (Rom. xii. 21), that their highest aim will be to obtain the crown of victory in the race for eternal life (1 Cor. ix. 24).

To Priests and Religious

We address a word of special recognition, encouragement, and exhortation to the priests of Germany, on whom, under their bishops, rests the task of showing the flock of Christ in difficult times and in trying circumstances the right paths by daily sacrifice and apostolic patience. Be not weary, beloved sons and sharers in the divine mysteries, in following the eternal High Priest, Jesus Christ, in His love and in His care, like the good Samaritan. Go on every hour in conduct undefiled before God, in untiring self-discipline and zeal for perfection, in merciful love for all entrusted to you, especially for those in danger, the weak, and the wavering. Be leaders of the faithful, supports of those who stumble, teachers of those in doubt, consolers of those who mourn, unselfish helpers and counsellors of all. The trials and sufferings through which your people has passed since the war have not been endured without leaving marks on its soul. They have left behind strain and bitterness which can be healed only slowly, and can be overcome only in the spirit of unselfish and active charity. This charity which is the indispensable armour of the apostle, especially in the contemporary world in its restlessness and confusion, We pray and beg God to bestow on you in abundant measure. This apostolic charity will make you, if not forget, at least forgive the many undeserved trials that are strewn more plentifully than ever before in your path as priests and pastors of souls. This understanding and merciful charity towards the erring and even towards the contemptuous does not, however, mean and can never mean that you should cease proclaiming, insisting on, and courageously defending the truth and applying it freely to the realities which surround you. The first and the most obvious gift of love which the priest has for the world is the service of truth, truth whole and entire, the unmasking and confutation of error whatever be its form or disguise. To renounce this task is not only to act as traitors to God and to your holy vocation, but a crime against the true welfare of your people and of your country. To all those who have maintained towards their bishops the loyalty they promised at ordination, to those who in the fulfilment of their pastoral office have had to bear and still have to bear sorrows and persecutions—some even to bear imprisonment and condemnation to concentration camps—goes forth the thanks and praise of the Father of Christendom.

Our paternal thanks are extended likewise to the religious of both sexes, and with Our thanks, Our deepest sympathy, in the fate that in consequence of measures taken against religious Orders and Congregations has taken many away from their beneficent and loved activities. If some have failed and shown themselves unworthy of their vocation, their misdeeds, condemned also by the Church, do not lessen the merits of the overwhelming majority of those who with unselfishness and in voluntary poverty have striven to serve their God and their people with complete self-renunciation. Their zeal, loyalty, and struggle for perfection, the active charity towards their neighbour, and the readiness to render help on the part of those religious whose activities were centred in pastoral work, in hospitals, and in schools, are and remain a glorious contribution to private and public welfare to which a later and more tranquil time will render more justice than does the troubled present. We feel confident that the superiors of religious communities will take occasion from their present trials and difficulties to implore from the Almighty an increase of growth and fruitfulness on their hard field of labour, through redoubled zeal, through a deepened spiritual life, through a holy earnestness in their vocation, and through true discipline according to their rule.

To the Faithful among the Laity

Before Our eyes stand the countless host of Our beloved sons and daughters for whom the suffering of the Church in Germany and their own suffering has in no way affected their devotion to the cause of God, their tender love towards the Father of Christendom, their obedience to their bishops and priests, their joyful readiness to remain in future, come what may, faithful to what they have believed and what they have received as a precious heritage from their forefathers. From a heart deeply moved We send them Our paternal greeting.

In the first place We send it to the members of the Catholic associations who steadfastly, and at the cost of sacrifices that have often been grievous, have kept themselves true to Christ and have never been disposed to give up those rights which a solemn agreement had freely guaranteed to the Church and to themselves.

We address a particularly heartfelt greeting to Catholic parents. Their rights and their duties in the education of the children God has given them are at the present moment at a crucial point in a struggle than which none graver could scarcely be imagined. The Church of Christ cannot wait to begin to mourn and weep until her altars have been despoiled and sacrilegious hands have destroyed the houses of God in smoke and fire. When the attempt is made to desecrate the tabernacle of a child's soul, sanctified by baptism, by an antichristian education, when from this living temple of God the flame of belief is cast out and in its place is put the false light of a substitute for faith which has nothing in common with zeal for the Cross, then the spiritual profanation of the temple is at hand, and it is the duty of every believer to separate clearly his responsibility from that of the other side, and to keep his conscience clear from any sinful collaboration in such unhallowed destruction. The more adversaries strive to deny or gloss over their dark designs, the more necessary is a vigilant distrust and distrustful vigilance stimulated by bitter experience. The nominal maintenance of religious instruction, especially when controlled and fettered by incompetent people in the atmosphere of a school which in other branches of instruction works systematically and invidiously against this same religion, can never justify a faithful Christian in accepting freely such an antireligious educational system. We know, beloved Catholic parents, that there can be no question on your part of such a consent. We know that a free and secret ballot would mean for you an overwhelming majority in favour of the confessional school. Therefore in future We shall not grow weary of frankly reproaching those in responsible positions with the illegality of the coercive measures hitherto adopted and of demanding the right to allow a free manifestation of the people's will. Meanwhile do not forget this: no power on earth can free you from the bond of responsibility imposed by God that binds you to your children. No one of those who today are obstructing your educational rights, and who claim to take on themselves your educational duties, can answer for you to the eternal Judge when He puts to you the question: " Where are those I have given you ?" May each one of you be able to reply: " Of them whom Thou hast given me, I have not lost any one " (John xviii. 9).

Venerable Brethren, We are certain that the words which We in this decisive hour address through you to the Catholics of Germany will awaken in the hearts and in the actions of Our loyal children an echo answering the loving solicitude of their Common Father. If there is anything that We beseech of the Lord with special fervour it is that Our words may also reach the ears and the hearts and move to reflection those who have already begun to let themselves be beguiled by the flatteries and threats of the enemies of Christ and of His holy Gospel.

We have weighed every word of this Encyclical in the balance of truth and also of love. Neither did We wish by inopportune silence to be guilty of not having made the situation clear, nor by excessive severity to harden the hearts of those who since they are placed under Our pastoral responsibility are no less the objects of Our pastoral charity because they are now wandering in the paths of error and estrangement. Though many of these who have adapted themselves to the customs of their new surroundings have for their Father's house they have left and for the Father Himself only words of disloyalty, ingratitude, and even insult, even if they forget what they have thrown away, the day will come when the horror they will feel at their estrangement from God and at their spiritual desolation will weigh down these prodigal sons, and homesickness will bring them back to " God who rejoiced their youth " and to the Church whose maternal hand taught them the way to the heavenly Father. To hasten this hour is the object of Our unceasing prayers.

Just as in other times of the Church, this time too will be the harbinger

APPENDIX II

of new progress and inward purification, when determination to profess the faith and readiness to endure sacrifices on the part of Christ's faithful is strong enough to oppose to the physical force of the oppressors of the Church an invincibility of interior faith, the inexhaustibility of hope anchored in eternity, and the compelling omnipotence of active charity. May the holy season of Lent and Easter, which preaches recollection and penance and directs the eyes of the Christian more than at any other time to the Cross, but at the same time to the splendour of the Risen Christ, be for each and every one of you an occasion you will welcome with joy and eagerly use to fill the whole mind with the spirit of heroism, patience and victory which shines forth from the Cross of Christ. Then the enemies of Christ— and of this We are certain—who imagine that the hour of the Church has come will recognise that they rejoiced too soon and were too hasty to dig her grave. Then the day will come when, instead of the premature hymns of triumph sung by the enemies of Christ, there will rise from the hearts and from the lips of the faithful the Te Deum of liberation: a Te Deum of thanks to the Almighty, a Te Deum of joy that the German people, even its members who today are in error, has trod again the homeward path of religion with a faith purified by suffering, that it has again bent the knee before the King of time and of eternity, Jesus Christ, and has girt itself in harmony with all men of good will of other nations to fulfil the mission assigned to it in the designs of the Eternal God for the struggle against those who renounce and destroy the Christian West.

He who searches the hearts and the reins (Ps. vii. 10) is Our witness that We have no more heartfelt wish than the restoration of a true peace between Church and State in Germany. But if through no fault of Ours there is not to be peace, the Church of God will defend her rights and her liberties in the name of the Almighty whose arm even today is not shortened. Full of trust in Him " we cease not to pray and to beg " (Col. i. 9) for you, the children of the Church, that the days of tribulation may be shortened and that you may be found faithful in the day of trial; and also for the persecutors and the oppressors that the Father of all light and all mercy may grant to them and to all who with them have erred, and are erring, an hour of enlightenment like that given to Saul on the way to Damascus.

With this prayer of supplication in Our heart and on Our lips, as a pledge of divine assistance and as a support in your difficult and responsible decisions, as an aid in the struggle, a comfort in sorrow to your bishops, pastors of your faithful people, to the priests, to the religious, to the lay apostles of Catholic Action and to all your diocesans and not least to those who are sick and those in prison, We impart with fatherly love the Apostolic Blessing.

Given at the Vatican on Passion Sunday, March 14th, 1937.

Pius PP. XI.

APPENDIX III

SERMON PREACHED BY CARDINAL FAULHABER TO THE MEN'S SODALITY IN ST. MICHAEL'S, MUNICH, ON SUNDAY, JULY 4TH, 1937.

Dear Catholic men, I have broken my confirmation journey, and, though tired after a consecration ceremony of almost five hours' duration at the Rosary Church of Rosenheim-Furstatt, I have returned to Munich to be with you at this chief meeting of the men's sodality. For the first time Fr. Rupert Mayer, the president of the sodality, is not preaching. I profit by this solemn occasion to give public utterance to the surprise, the indignation and bitterness felt by the Catholic men of Munich on hearing of Fr. Rupert Mayer's arrest on June 5th, and the weight of sorrow caused by its continuance. The time has now come for plain speech.

Fr. Rupert Mayer, of the Society of Jesus, went to the battlefield a healthy man. As chaplain in the army he risked his life a thousand times to bring to his brethren in the danger zone the comforts of our holy religion, and after being severely wounded in barrage-fire he returned to his Fatherland in broken health. Now he has received the thanks of the Fatherland.

As an apostle among the men of Munich Fr. Mayer has lived the words of the evangelist St. Matthew and set his light—the guiding flame of Christianity—on a candlestick that it might shine before men. He has led the way in practising Faith in daily life and always urged the men to render to the State the things that are the State's and to God and His Church those things that are their due. At the same time, as a true son of the people, Fr. Mayer has exposed religious impostors and challenged Communism in meetings and speeches, and explained in private the blessings of the true political and social order. With the courage of St. John the Baptist, Fr. Mayer has propounded the truth before the faces of the great ones of this world. Had he bound himself by his signature not to preach outside Munich he might have been freed long ago, but as an upright man, he scorned to repudiate the Catholic principle that " the Word of God is not bound " (2 Tim. ii. 9), declaring that he would rather remain in prison than sign.

The men's sodality, though deeply affected by Fr. Mayer's arrest, has maintained order in accordance with my request. I urged you, through my Vicar-General, in spite of your reverence and enthusiasm for your president and in spite of your grief at his arrest, to avoid street demonstrations. No greater service could we do the police than to furnish them with means to bring action with cudgels and arrests, with lock-outs and dismissals against the odious Catholics, nowadays more hated and persecuted than the Bolsheviks. You have obeyed Fr. Mayer's wishes in keeping order and refraining from thoughtless words and deeds. There is a time to be silent.

My dear Catholic men, continue to maintain the peace. Make a promise in spirit before your bishop that today you will not interrupt my address, nor will you disturb any future sermon by shouting or by other demonstrations of agreement or indignation, for it must be remembered that we are in church. Instead you will pray for your imprisoned president by attending in an orderly manner the evening devotions here at St. Michael's and by offering this meeting as a prayer, for the time has now come to speak to God. For this purpose we should consider three prayer intentions: first, that Fr. Rupert Mayer may preserve the peace and composure of his soul. It is not easy on a sudden to be sent into the lonely desert after an active life. Remember that he has preached every Sunday three or four times and that many a one has been broken by the silence of the grave-like prison; secondly, that the time of affliction may be shortened and the gates of the prison soon opened—we realise now the significance of the Church's prayer on Good Friday that " the Lord may open the gates of the prisons "; thirdly, that Divine Providence may once more transmute evil into good.

Before Fr. Mayer's imprisonment, I sent a protest to the Reichsminister for Ecclesiastical Affairs against the veto of May 28th, forbidding him to preach. My appeal was, as was to be expected, rejected and the veto was not repealed, so I turn today to the Catholic men of Munich; there is a time for silence and a time for speech. On the 9th of June, a few days after the arrest, with my consent the Vicar-General sent to the Reichsminister of the Interior, to the Foreign Office, to the Minister for Ecclesiastical Affairs, to the Secret Police in Munich, to the Reich Representative with the Government of Bavaria and to the Bavarian Premier the following thoroughly justified protest against the arrest:

" Fr. R. Mayer has no need to prove his patriotism. His exemplary conduct, recognised on all sides, both in the war and in the revolution of 1918, his grave wound, his numberless patriotic speeches at post-war military commemorations, his undaunted attacks at hundreds of meetings on Communism and Marxism—one, indeed, of which took place in the presence of the Führer and was acknowledged by him in a special letter for his Silver Jubilee—all speak for his loyalty. Wherever he appeared, whether it was in the trenches or in the military hospital, in the pulpit or on the platform, he proved his rare priestly character, that of a man's apostle of commanding and captivating qualities. He was a promoter of courage and conscientiousness, a champion of religion and morality, of authority and loyalty, of order and public spirit."

This true-born German who, like the Führer, wears the Iron Cross, first class, and side by side with him has striven against the Communists of Munich and received from him an appreciative personal letter, is now consigned to prison. Fortunately the sermon which Fr. Mayer preached before you, my dear sodalists, on May 23rd, was written. You are witnesses of what he then so courageously said, " We do not allow ourselves to be forced from our loyalty to the State. We refuse any self-defence of a revolutionary character." These are the words of the man who is today charged with enmity against the State !

His accusers will say that Fr. Mayer preached politics—on the contrary he has, whilst denouncing the use of the slanderous slogan " Political Catholicism," wielded " the sword of the Spirit," as the Word of God is called in the Epistle to the Ephesians, against those powerful influences which, contrary to the word of the Führer, are at work to change the political movement into a second reformation. The Führer still maintains what is reiterated in his book again and again: that he has no wish to be a religious reformer, and declares: " Christianity has been united with the German people for a thousand years. This fact cannot be denied." To this I add, that what has been so closely interwoven for a thousand years,

540 APPENDIX III

as Christianity and the German people, cannot be torn asunder without inflicting deep wounds on both sides. He, therefore, who defends Christian faith and morality in national life serves the community and the State; in this respect the work of Fr. Rupert Mayer has been, not only religious, but national.

Speaking as a Bishop I pronounce this formal judgement on the imprisonment of Fr. Mayer: The State has no right to forbid a priest who complies with the requirements of the Concordat and who has received jurisdiction from his Bishop, or as a Religious from his superior, the right to preach within the precincts of the Church. Preaching is one of the essential duties of the clergy and those duties are the Church's concern only, for Article 32 of the Reich Concordat, while stating that " clergymen are debarred from activity on behalf of any party," yet concedes that no infringement of the teaching and explanation of the Church's doctrines, dogmatic or moral, incumbent on the clergy is to be made. It is evident that the State has no right to forbid the authorised preaching of any priest nor, on his refusal to comply with their orders, to arrest him.

In the Acts of the Apostles, chapters 4 and 5, we read that, when the Apostles were put into prison for the first time because they had announced the Word of God, the High Council of the Jews gathered together, " And setting them in the midst, they asked: By what power or by what name have you done this ?" The Apostles answered: " By the name of the Lord Jesus of Nazareth whom you have crucified, whom God hath raised from the dead." Then " they charged them not to speak at all nor teach in the name of Jesus." But the Apostles answered: " If it be just in the sight of God to hear you rather than God, judge ye." When they had been set free, they went on preaching, were again arrested, brought before the Council and told: " Commanding we commanded you that you should not teach in this name." But Peter and the Apostles answering said: " We ought to obey God rather than men."

With the arrest of Fr. Rupert Mayer, my dear brethren, the record in the Acts of the Apostles of early Christian times comes to life again. May God grant His grace to the persecuted that the spirit of the holy confessors and martyrs of early Christian times may also revive.

Last Wednesday, June 30th, thanks to the kindness of the officers of the law, I visited Fr. Mayer at Stadelheim. In accordance with the usual regulations an officer was present at the talk, which was limited to ten minutes. I wished to reassure our dear president that his Bishop and the Catholic men and people of Munich have not forgotten him, for it is a work of mercy to visit the imprisoned. Fr. Mayer is in good spiritual and bodily health (his easy conscience serving him in good stead). He has a private cell, a comparatively spacious room, which normally serves for a sick-room and is lighted by two upper windows and furnished plainly like the cell of a prophet (4 Kings iv. 10). Fr. Mayer bears his involuntary absence with the iron courage with which he went through the barrage-fire to his soldiers. He endures this time of silence with the stoic calmness with which he waited on the operating table before his leg was amputated at the military hospital on the Eastern front. He even remarked with a hearty laugh that in the past twenty-five years he had never had such an opportunity of going for a daily walk as he did now in " the house of contemplatives," and when free he had not had such unbroken time for study as the gaol afforded. To silence absurd rumours not set in circulation by the golden-hearted citizens of Munich—for example, that he had been taken to Coblenz—I will tell you how he passes his days; not in brooding over his fate, but in prayer, in study and making his retreat. After my visit I wrote a reassuring letter to Fr. Mayer's eighty-three-year-old mother, telling her that her son is well and bears himself with courage, and preserves that holy indifference which St. Ignatius emphasised so strongly in his Exercises.

Dear Catholic men, the imprisonment of Fr. Mayer has a supra-personal significance over and above its personal one. This arrest marks the entrance upon a new phase of the *Kulturkampf* for the destruction of the Catholic Church. The decisive hour is at hand; the Son of Man has taken the fan into His Hand to separate the wheat from the chaff. Beacons are being fired and one is the arrest of the apostle of the men of Munich.

In the notorious speech of Fürstenfeldbruck, Fr. Mayer's imprisonment was mentioned in the survey of the existing status of the Church. The speaker announced, " I must state with regret that one power and authority, namely that of the Churches, still molests national life." Is it credible that not the Freemasons, not the Communists, nor the Bolsheviks, till recently regarded as " Public Enemy No. 1," are stigmatised as the last power hostile to the State and the public good, but the Churches ? In a flash our position has been made plain.

Though challenged, I do not intend to discuss the Fürstenfeldbruck speech in detail; one or two remarks will suffice. Additional supplies by the State to the Church and the salaries of bishops were mentioned. These controversies, familiar themes in Marxist days and in Communist newspapers, even when raised, do not win the eager support of the people, especially of the working people. It is regrettable, moreover, that in this connection, the figures of the salaries and secret funds of the universities were not made known, and that the people who are to be incited against the Church were not informed that the subventions of the Bavarian State to the Catholic Church and the salaries accorded to the bishops by the Concordat are but a part payment for the wealth seized by the Bavarian Government from the ecclesiastical principalities and monasteries at the time of the secularisation. Let the Bavarian State restore to the Church the real estates and buildings, especially the extensive forests it took from her in the secularisation, and we will renounce all State salaries.

The speaker at Fürstenfeldbruck in an access of devotion declared all men to be equal before God and the law. Who can recognise this equality in the public reports on the offences of clergymen on the one hand and of Party members on the other ? Or who can consider the defence of the Christian denominations through the press and radio to be in any way equal to the attacks themselves ?

Be warned, my dear Catholic men, by the signs given week by week in German newspapers and periodicals wherein Catholic bishops are subjected to the vilest slanders and calumnies, both in words and pictures. The wireless, correspondence bureaus, even parish magazines—the means by which we could reveal the false teaching against the institutions of the Church—are withheld from us. We who are bound in conscience to respect the authority of the State must support that authority whilst the Church's is disregarded and trodden in the dust. Some newspaper articles,and speeches are tantamount to a summons to remove by violence the " Roman mischief makers " and " the State's enemies." One newspaper was allowed to declare the German Bishops, as a body, guilty of high treason; the Corpus Christi procession, a purely religious public profession of belief in the dearest mystery of our Faith, was represented as a celebration inimical to the State, and, what is worse, the *Durchbruch*, allowed to publish slanderous articles on the close of this year's Corpus Christi procession, produced as a proof and gave out as photographs of this year's procession two pictures of a previous procession.

Yesterday I received from Holland a letter in a disguised hand purporting to reveal to the frontier and post-office police a plot between Catholics and Jewish Bolshevism and a conspiracy of Catholic assassins. " We listened with great interest," runs this libel, " to the verbal report of Fr. Elpidius. . . . We shall inform you of the next steps in the Jewish German union. We can easily obtain from India the necessary poison, a small dose of which causes at least madness. We are unanimous in dissuading you from this course. . . . We can easily get hold of him in Berlin without it . . . besides, a determined man who has no more interest in this vale of tears has put himself at our disposal. Our common plan will and must succeed." A clumsily drawn swastika serves for a signature to this palpable forgery which many, even here in Munich, will be ready to credit.

These proofs of the Church's precarious position justify the significance I attach to Fr. Mayer's arrest. I formally state that as long as he was forbidden to address meetings outside the church he obeyed the law, but when he was forbidden to preach in a church he obeyed the dictates of his conscience, for there is a time for speech as well as for silence and the law of God must come before that of men.

Government circles were indignant at the report in foreign newspapers of Fr. Mayer's arrest and at the allusion, found in these, to my letter to the Reichsminister for Ecclesiastical Affairs. On principle I never give information on Church matters to foreign papers. Only recently I have refused to answer a phoned enquiry from London and requests to interview me. I cannot suppress, however, my great amazement that it is not the facts themselves, in this case Fr. Mayer's arrest, but foreign reports of undeniable truths that give rise to indignation; this, in the words of the Gospel, is straining at gnats and swallowing camels. It is obvious that the report concerning Fr. Mayer's arrest was not sent abroad by any ecclesiastical official in Munich as it contains data known by every citizen of Munich to be false, such as the announcement by the Strasbourg wireless that Fr. Mayer had been discharged from prison. Not only was the arrest on June 5th openly discussed everywhere in Munich, but a declaration was read by order of the Vicar-General in every church that everything was being done by the Church authorities for Fr. Mayer's release, and that a letter had been sent by me to the Reich Government—measures taken to prevent public demonstrations by the embittered people. Though reporters for the foreign press must be blind and deaf if they had not learned these things, no special foreign correspondents are necessary when the daily and weekly papers of the Reich provide ample material on which foreign papers can base their judgements on the state of the Catholic Church in Germany.

Dear Catholic men ! At this most critical time it is essential that we should understand the Mystery of the Cross; it is the law and secret of God's Kingdom whose Church always bears the signs that she is the Mystical Body of Christ, His true Church, namely, the stigmata of her Divine Master. Let us not desert this Church when, like her Divine Founder, she is made to bear the purple cloak, the Crown of Thorns and the Cross, and when we too have to suffer personally for our Faith:

" When the beacons blaze away,
The hour will need men.
They are formed only on the Cross."

That hour has come. Every one of us will have to answer the question, " Are you a ' believer in God ' ?"[1] or a believer in Christ and His Church ? According to today's religious tenets, a " believer in God " need believe no more than what a Turk or a Hottentot might believe; he denounces Christ and His Church. Anyone, therefore, who calls himself a mere " believer in God " betrays Christ and declares his apostasy from the Church. When you individually are faced with this question, without hesitation or compromise you must boldly confess, if necessary in writing: I am a Catholic; I not only believe in God, I believe also in Christ and in my Church. Yes, I am a Catholic, I am a Catholic. Amen.

[1] Gottgläubig—*i.e.*, an adherent of the German neo-pagan cult.

APPENDIX IV

DIOCESAN REPORTS ON THE DESECRATION OF
CRUCIFIXES, ETC.

IN the Archdiocese of **Munich-Freising**, in the summer of 1935, the parish priest of Lenggries had erected an altar in the open air in order to enable the Catholic members of the Hitler Youth in the adjacent *Hochland* camp to hear their Sunday Mass. One day the altar was found scrawled all over with inscriptions. One of these on the epistle side of the altar ran: There should be a shit-heap here. In Erding in the night of October 21st, 1937, four of the open-air Stations of the Cross were smashed and ruined by some malicious hand. During the same night the notice-board with the wall-newspaper on the parish church was destroyed.

The Munich Vicariate-General made the following survey of the outrages committed in summer, 1937:

Whit Monday night, May 17th-18th, 1937, in the parish of Glonn near Grafing a 130-years-old wayside crucifix was pulled down and a plough set on it.

On the night of July 12th, a wayside cross in the parish of Hohenkammer was pulled down and apparently taken away in a motor-car.

On the night of July 24th from a large, 14-feet high crucifix opposite the entrance to the church in Lustheim, parish of Oberschleissheim, the figure was torn down, smashed into fragments and thrown into the castle-moat.

On the night of July 27th the figure was again torn down from a crucifix, this time in Teisendorf near Traunstein, and dragged off to some unknown place.

The archiepiscopal authorities of Munich ordered that in the parishes where such outrages on crucifixes had taken place, there was to be a solemn service of reparation with sermon and Stations of the Cross. On such occasion all crosses in the church were to be decorated and also, as far as possible, all wayside-crosses in the parish.

In the Archdiocese of **Cologne**: In connection with the conferences given by Professor Muckermann in Duisberg, August, 1935, and the disturbances consequent on them, the Hitler Youth smashed the crosses and the pictures of saints in the meeting-house of the parish youth.[1]

In 1939 crosses, statues and similar objects in the open in the Archdiocese of Cologne were damaged or destroyed. In many places people did not dare to bring such blasphemous outrages to official notice, obviously for fear of violence and persecution. The ecclesiastical authorities ordered therefore that in all such instances a reliable report was to be forwarded to the archiepiscopal Vicariate-General.

In the diocese of **Rottenburg** a Pastoral Letter of the Bishop was read on Rogation Sunday, 1936, in which the following outrages committed on wayside crosses were enumerated:

On one and the same night of May 8th the following outrages took place:

---

[1] Another outrage contained in this report was described on p. 241.

APPENDIX IV

1. Three wayside crucifixes were thrown down, destroyed and scattered on the highway between Hohenmühringen and Nordstetten in the Horb district.
2. A statue over 6 feet high on the main road from Bühl to Kiebingen in the Rottenburg district was pulled down and broken and a similar attempt was made on a wayside crucifix in the vicinity.
3. A stone crucifix on the road leading to Haigerloch in the Rottenburg district was pulled down and completely destroyed.
4. An attempt was made with the help of ropes to pull down the statue of St. John Nepomucene which stood at the entrance to the village of Hemmendorf, Rottenburg district. It would appear that the culprits were disturbed and made off in a motor-car which stood ready.
5. In several neighbouring parishes in Hohenzollern similar outrages were committed on wayside crosses.

On the following night of May 9th the heavy ferro-concrete cross above Deggingen on the North Alp was torn out, thrown down and destroyed. This cross was put up by a Christian soldier of the Great War in consequence of a vow. Its concrete foundation went down almost 3 feet into the solid rock. The Bishop called attention to a certain statement which had been published to the effect that to tolerate the image of the crucified Saviour in every field and at every corner was no longer worthy of the Nordic man.

In the diocese of **Regensburg**, on the night of August 16th, 1936, between two and five in the morning, all the windows of a Catholic youth house were broken, the iron bars in front of them bent apart, and an entry forced. The crucifix and the pictures of Our Lady were broken and scattered on the floor. No police action about the matter ever matured.

In the diocese of **Augsburg** in spring, 1939, a further case of desecration of sacred places occurred at Oberstdorf in Allgäu. On the main street of the village there is a chapel, with artistically wrought iron gates, in which there is a life-size statue of the suffering Christ. One day in the week before the Ascension, 1939, a farmer found the statue on his dung-heap completely destroyed amongst the twisted remains of the iron gates. A solemn triduum of reparation was held, to which large crowds came and which finished with a great procession to the desecrated spot.

In the **Saar** territory, summer, 1935, the much frequented shrine, *Maria Waldrast*, which had been erected by the Catholic young men in the form of a Lourdes grotto, was desecrated and destroyed under cover of darkness. According to the report of the *Westpfälzische Zeitung*, the evil-doers removed the wrought-iron cross from the entrance to the grotto, smashed the statues of Our Lady and of St. Bernadette and threw them into the pond. The same thing happened to the statue of St. Anthony, of which the head was first cut off. The cross at all the Stations of the Cross was knocked off; the same was done at all the collecting boxes. Traces left showed that an attempt had been made to pull down the 33-foot high crucifix of the Calvary. In Bous, in 1938, the rope of the church-bell was cut to pieces. At a place in the vicinity a chapel was desecrated and in Warnsdorf a large mission cross was destroyed.

In the diocese of **Münster** in Westphalia a crucifix was desecrated in May, 1939, at Harkebrügge in Oldenburg. The parish priest went to the church in the morning and found that he could not get the church door open. He got into the church by another way and found on the floor a crucifix in pieces. The figure was missing and was later found hanging by a rope from a tree. As far as is known the matter was never cleared up.

APPENDIX IV

In the diocese of **Limburg**[1] the following desecrations of crucifixes took place in 1939:

On the night of April 25th, nine outdoor Stations of the Cross at Wirzenborn near Montabaur were overthrown and completely destroyed. The miscreants were detected and assurance was given that they would be punished and the damage made good.

On the night of May 12th the crucifix at the crossing of the main roads from Wallmerod to Nenterhausen and Steinefrenz to Weroth was desecrated and destroyed.

The figure from the large wooden crucifix on the Limburg main-road was found to be missing and was later discovered in the ditch.

On the night of May 5th a crucifix on the outside of a small chapel at Allmannshausen near Montabaur was desecrated. The cross itself was dragged some distance from the spot, while the figure had disappeared.

On the night of May 22nd, the figure of a crucifix belonging to Count Schmiesing was stolen, and during the same night a crucifix near Horressen was desecrated.

On the day after Whit Monday, 1939, a crucifix and the statues on the May-month altar together with a statue of St. Joseph were demolished at Frankfurt am Main. On May 31st, 1939, in the same town a cross and a statue of Our Lady were destroyed.

In the diocese of **Aachen** no less than seven wayside crosses were destroyed at night-time during the month of June, 1939, in the parish of Würselen. It would appear that the miscreants did their work by travelling round from one place to another on a motor-bicycle. They have not yet been discovered and probably never will be. The broken fragments of the crosses were found everywhere by passers-by in the early morning hours. These sacrileges aroused the greatest indignation among the people.

On July 16th, 1939, a Pastoral Letter was read from the Bishop of **Speyer** from all pulpits. It is dated July 13th, 1939, and is as follows:

" Dearly beloved Brethren,

" It is with the deepest sorrow that I narrate to you the following brief account of a number of fearful sacrileges which have recently taken place in churches in the frontier districts.

" On the afternoon of July 12th this year the beautiful Church of Our Lady in Landau presented a terrible picture of destruction. It happened during the midday hour without anybody noticing the perpetrators. Three of the six large statues which are near the high altar had been thrown down and lay on the floor. The remaining three statues, of which all are bigger than life-size, had been so twisted round as to be in great danger of falling. At an altar in the side-aisle the artistic Pietà had been thrown to the ground and broken, likewise the statues of St. Anthony, St. Conrad and eight Stations of the Cross.

" That was the second time this sort of destruction had happened in this very beautiful church. On Sunday, July 2nd, the statue of the Sacred Heart, as well as two other statues, were pushed over. There was the greatest consternation among the people of the parish, and many viewed the desolating scene in tears.

" In other places, too, the house of God was desecrated, for instance in Bergzabern and Rheinzabern. In Rheinzabern the head of the figure was knocked off from the old and venerated cross in the church square. On

---

[1] *Cf.* the *Ecclesiastical Gazette*, No. 11, June 1st, 1939.

APPENDIX IV

July 8th in Bergzabern seven statues were thrown down from their places. The iron crucifix which stands on the road from Simten to Vinningen was pulled down. It had been erected many years ago in memory of a fatal accident which had occurred on the spot. The relatives erected it again, and then it was badly bent. This damage was made good, and then quite recently it was again bent, this time so badly that it must have needed very savage force to do it. To these must be added the damage done to a Calvary group at the entrance to the village of Kleinsteinfeld, where the statue of Our Lady was thrown down and damaged.

" We order, therefore, that on one of the coming Sundays a general Communion of reparation shall take place and in the afternoon or evening a service of reparation with exposition of the Blessed Sacrament, in order to give expression to our sorrow and sympathy with these afflicted parishes. The parish priests are to exhort the faithful earnestly to take part in these services and urge the parents to send their children to them. It will also be prudent to keep the doors of the churches closed for some time to come, except at certain hours, when the parish priests can arrange for a number of worshippers to be always present.

" The police have indeed promised to do all in their power in order to arrest the guilty persons. To know that these had been brought to justice would, indeed, be a comfort to us in our overwhelming sorrow, when we see that in a time which is already filled with so many trials and difficulties, our own most sacred convictions should be singled out for such brutal onslaughts.

" Let us therefore join in earnest prayer with the Church and say: ' O Lord, hear the prayer of Thy Church, and grant that, protected from all danger, she may serve Thee in safety and freedom.'

Signed: LUDWIG,
Bishop of Speyer."

SPEYER, *July* 13*th*, 1939.

In the Archdiocese of Freiburg in Breisgau an open letter from Archbishop Gröber to various parishes enumerates the sacrileges committed in the course of 1936.

On the night of April 19th, the eve of Hitler's birthday, a heavy stone cross was destroyed on the road to Steinhofen in the parish of Zimmern. The arms of the cross were torn apart and, together with the top piece, were found on the ground while the left arm of the cast-iron figure was broken off. On the night of May 8th, two wayside crosses were broken in the parish of Rangendingen. In the parish of Stein, on the night of May 15th, a wayside cross was destroyed. Appearances pointed to its having been pulled over with ropes to which great force had been applied, for even the iron supports and the heavy stone base were overturned. The figure itself was shattered into small pieces. In the parish of Steinhofen, on the night of April 19th, two stone crosses were destroyed.

It was announced from the diocese of Rottenburg that three crosses were destroyed there.

In December of the same year crosses were destroyed in Hohenzollern, Mittelbad and on Lake Constance. In the report which has already been mentioned of Archbishop Gröber of 1938 concerning the effect of the National Socialist fight against the Church in the archdiocese of Freiburg there occurs the following section on the profanation of crosses:

The fight against the symbol of our Redemption, the crucifix which Rosenberg, in his " Myth of the Twentieth Century," would like to see replaced by other images, is a still more unmistakable sign of the hostile attitude towards the Church and towards Christianity which is developing in our time. The Mayor of Waibstadt, in 1936, caused all the crucifixes to be taken out of the school and in spite of the protests of the inhabitants and the ecclesiastical authorities they have not yet been replaced. In the lower secondary school at Säckingen, and in the school at Dielheim the same occurred in 1937 and, in 1938, for a short period in the school at Bötzingen. In various places, as, for instance, in 1936 at Ketsch, the crucifixes were removed to inconspicuous positions. The removal of crucifixes from town-halls was reported in 1936 and 1937 from Kirchhofen and Oestringen respectively. In 1936 a fourteen-year-old BDM-leader in Bleibach removed the crucifix from a room in the town-hall which had been allocated to her organisation, putting it first in the waste-paper basket and then hiding it up in the loft. In the same year the crucifix in a school at Neckarhausen was bombarded with rotten apples. In 1936 in Dogern the glass in front of a picture of the crucifixion was broken, obviously by youths, and an obscene remark written across the picture. In February, 1937, one of the pupils burnt the very fine cross in the continuation school in Ofen. It was reported from Dettingen, Constance district, that in October, 1937, a customs official took the cross from a wall in an inn and mockingly carried it between his legs to a rubbish-room.

Since 1935 the desecration of crucifixes in open fields increased in a terrible way and in very few cases could the perpetrators be found.

On the night of August 19th, 1935, a wayside cross near Castle Helmsdorf, in the parish of Immenstadt, was pulled down and destroyed; at the same time a similar act took place on the road from Oberuhldingen to Ueberlingen.

In the parish of Prinzbach a crucifix on the main road Schönberg-Reichenbach was found with broken legs, while the picture of Our Lady underneath it had been destroyed, on September 14th, 1935. The perpetrator, a stable-hand, was sentenced to eight month's imprisonment.

On the night of April 10th, 1936, a crucifix was destroyed in the parish of Urloffen by two local youths.

In the parish of Wöschenbach a wayside crucifix was badly damaged on May 1st, 1936, the nose, hands and feet of the figure having been cut off.

On the night of May 8th two wayside crosses were pulled down in the parish of Rangendingen, and the culprits seem then to have gone on to another cross in the neighbouring parish of Stein, where the figure from the cross was broken into pieces.

On the night of May 19th, 1936, three wayside crosses in the parish of Steinhofen were demolished.

On the night of August 2nd, 1936, a wayside cross on the main road to Kirchberg in the parish of Immenstadt was pulled down.

On September 28th, 1936, the plot in front of a wayside cross in Spessart was defiled and the arms knocked off a Lady-statue.

On the night of February 4th, 1937, a wayside cross in the parish of Winterspüren was pulled down.

On May 30th, 1937, a wayside cross, again in Wöschenbach, was damaged, and the head struck off the Lady-statue.

On the night of June 28th, 1937, a wayside cross in the parish of Hausen in Taunus was pulled out of the ground and 300 yards further on erected again head downwards.

APPENDIX IV 549

On July 29th, 1937, the large Sacred Heart statue behind the sanatorium was broken and, together with its shrine, thrown down the hill.

In December, 1937, the valuable crucifix in the cemetery at Dossenheim was removed and the figure destroyed.

On the night of January 29th, 1938, the figure was wrenched from a cross in the parish of Markelfingen and hung on a near-by fence.[1]

[1] The report of the Archdiocese of Paderborn has already been given on p. 242.

APPENDIX V

NATIONAL SOCIALIST ORGANISATIONS

A word of explanation about the administrative division of Germany will perhaps explain why there are so many different titles of officials. About a century ago what is now Germany was a number of separate kingdoms or States, which on their union retained their independence to a very large degree (something like the U.S.A.). After the Great War the Weimar Constitution did nothing to alter this and later National Socialism promised to preserve the arrangement, though in practice it has persistently centralised the administration of all functions of importance.

At present, therefore, there is the central Government—*i.e.*, the Reich Government, with all its Ministries and Departments, the personnel of which is composed of Reich Ministers, Reich officials, etc. It has, also, an official representative at each State (now called *Land*) Government. This hierarchy of officials extends over the whole of Germany. Parallel to these and, in part, identical with them are the officials of the Party—again a hierarchy covering the whole country. Besides these, each separate State has its Government with Ministries and Departments, whose jurisdiction, in so far as it has not been taken over by the Reich Government, is limited to its own territory. The personnel of any State Government is composed of State Ministers, State officials, etc.

After this brief explanation, the following classification and description will enable the reader to steer his way through the maze of highly specialised organisations which National Socialism has called into being.

A. Organisations Reserved for Members of the Party

1. General

On the whole the Party organisation follows the divisions of the civil administration. Thus, the *Gau* (district) corresponds more or less to a *Regierungsbezirk* or *Provinz*, a Government district about the size of an average English county. The next subdivision is the *Kreis* (Urban or Rural Area) which is made up of *Ortsgruppen* (local groups) in towns and villages, the number of these local groups varying according to the size of the locality. Smaller places with fewer than 500 inhabitants are called *Stützpunkte* (bases), while larger local groups in cities and towns are subdivided into " blocks."

The heads or political leaders of these divisions are called:

Blockwart	Block Warden.
Stützpunktleiter	Base Leader.
Ortsgruppenleiter	Local Leader.
Kreisleiter	Area Leader.
Gauleiter	District Leader.

The *Kreisleitungen* and *Gauleitungen* (Area and District Headquarters) contain several *Ämter* (departments)—*e.g.*:

APPENDIX V

Personalamt	Personnel Department.
Presseamt	Press Department.
Kulturamt	Cultural Department.

2. The SS—i e.., "*Schutzstaffel*" (*Protective Guards*)

A military body with ranks similar to those in the SA.[1]

B. ORGANISATIONS IN WHICH PARTY-MEMBERSHIP IS NOT NECESSARY—GROUPED ACCORDING TO NATURAL OR OCCUPATIONAL DIVISIONS

1. Groups based on Natural Divisions

(a) **Youth Organisations.**

Boys: *HJ* (The Hitler Youth); age: fourteen to eighteen. Girls: *BDM* (German Girls' League); each of which has a Junior Section: *Jungvolk* (age: ten to fourteen).

Different ranks:

Rottenführer	(approx.) Patrol Leader.
Scharführer	Troop Leader.
Bannführer	Area Leader.
Gauführer	District Leader.
Gebietsführer	Regional Leader.
Obergebietsführer	Leader for several regions.
Reichsjugendführer	Reich Youth Leader.

As with the political organisation, the headquarters of the different divisions includes a number of departments.

The *Landjahr* (Land Year) is a year of agricultural work for boys and girls after they have left the elementary schools at the age of fourteen.

The *Reichsarbeitsdienst* (Labour Service) becomes obligatory for young men and women when they attain the age of nineteen years. It lasts six months. After leaving the Hitler Youth, the young men are expected to join the SA (Stormtroopers); the senior section of the German Girls' League is called *Glaube und Schönheit* (Faith and Beauty).

(b) **Adult Organisations.**

NS Frauenschaft (NS Women's Union).

The SA—*i.e., Sturmabteilungen* (Stormtroopers). This body is organised on military lines, the names of its various divisions being taken from old German expressions:

Rotte	Patrol.
Schar	Band.
Trupp	Troop.
Sturm	Company (roughly).
Sturmbann	Battalion.
Standarte	Regiment.
Untergruppe	Several regiments.
Brigade	Brigade.
Gruppe	Division.
Obergruppe	Army Corps.
Oberste SA Führung	SA Headquarters.

[1] *Cf.* below B. 1 (b).

2. *Groups based on Occupational and other Divisions*

(a) **Die Deutsche Arbeitsfront (German Labour Front).**

This is organised along the same lines as the Party and membership is obligatory for all employers and employees. Its head is *Reichsorganisationsleiter* Dr. Ley. A *DAF* official is called *Walter* (administrator) and his office or administrational division *Waltung*—e.g.:

> *Ortswaltung* (local administration).
> *Kreiswaltung* (area administration).
> *Gauwaltung* (district administration).

These divisions consist of various departments, the best known of which is the *Kraft durch Freude* (Strength through Joy) organisation which is modelled on the lines of the Italian *Dopolavoro*: its aim is to provide free-time amusements, cheap excursions and holidays for the workers.

The smallest unit of the Labour Front is the *Betriebszelle* (business cell, works cell, business staff cell) which takes in the staff of a firm which employs twenty-eight hands or more—or one of the branches of such a firm.

(b) **The Liberal Professions:**

> *NS Deutscher Studentenbund* (NSDSTB)—NS Undergraduates' Union.
> *NS Deutscher Dozentenbund*—NS University Professors' Union.
> *NS Lehrerbund* (NSLB)—NS Teachers' Union.
> *NS Ärztebund*—NS Doctors' Union.
> *NS Rechtswahrerebund*—NS Jurists' Union.
> *Reichsbund Deutscher Beamter*—Reich Union of German Civil Servants.
> *Reichskulturkammer*—Organisation of German artists.
> *Reichsschriftumskammer*—Organisation of German writers and newspaper editors.

(c) **Other Organisations:**

> *NS Kraftfahrerkorps* (NSKK)—NS Motor Corps.
> *NS Frontkämpferorganisation* (NSFK)—NS Ex-Servicemen's Organisation.
> *NS Kriegsopferorganisation*—NS Union of Disabled Soldiers.
> *NS Schwesternschaft*—NS Nurses' Union.
> *NS Volkswohlfahrt* (NSV)—NS Public Welfare Service with the *Winterhilfwerk* (WHW) Winter Relief Work as its chief feature.
> *NS Reichsbund fur Leibesübungen*—NS Reich Union for Physical Training.

INDEX

IN the references that follow, figures connected by a hyphen (*e.g.*, 20-25) indicate continuous treatment over the interval mentioned; f. after a figure (*e.g.*, 20 f.) indicates *passim* mention on that and the following page; ff. after a figure (*e.g.*, 20 ff.) indicates *passim* mention on that and two or more following pages.

(P) = Periodical.
(N) = Newspaper.
(n) = footnote.

AACHEN, 42, 212, 216; Bishop of, *see* Sträter
" Abuse of Pulpit," 63-9, 291-2, 432
Abyssinian War, 406
Ackermann, Fr., 302-3
Adelheim, 245
Admont, 46
Adolf Hitler Schools, 174, 348 f.
Agents Provocateurs, 67, 237
Aigner, Fr., C.S.S.R., 296
Albertus Magnus Union, 198
Aldegund, St., 455
Alemanne, Der (N), 298
Alexian Brothers, 303, 308, 320
Algermissen, Dr., 79
Almanacs, 269, 355-6, 499
Altenberg, 109 f.
Altinger, Fr., 262
Altötting, 240, 284
Alzey, 316
Amann, Max, Pres. of Reich Press Bureau, 70, 72 f.
Amberg, 101, 134
Ancestor-worship, 498-9
Anders, Frau, 270
Angriff, Der (N), 189-90, 253-4, 425 ff.
Anhalt, 172, 181-2
Anheier, Mgr., 92
Anrath, 210
Apostasy Movement, 17, 24, 29, 51 f., 226-33, 329, 336, 338, 342, 344 f., 350 ff., 362; statistics, 336-7
Arbeitsmann, Der (N), 488
" Aryan," 74, 167, 177, 404-5, 440. *See also* Racialism
Associations: Catholic Adult, guaranteed, 187-8; decree against Double Membership, 188-94; restrictions, 190-1; violence against, 195; compulsory resignation, 192-4; dissolution, 195-9. *See also* names of individual associations. Catholic Youth, 1 ff., 4, 236, 358; guaranteed, 83-6; threatened, 86-90; limitation of activity, 89 f., 98; defamation of, 91-4, 104, 366; school propaganda against, 95-8; economic pressure against, 98-102; violence against, 102-8, 239; dissolution of, 108-11. NS., compulsory membership, 327-8. *See also* names of individual associations, Double Membership, and App. V
Augsburg, 444
Augsburger Nationalzeitung, Die (N), 290
Augustinian Hermits, 298
Austria, 6, 9 f., 30 f., 38 f., 42, 45-51, 54 f., 57, 72, 76, 80, 110, 132, 135 ff., 158, 166 ff., 170-1, 173, 194, 198-9, 205, 207, 210, 216, 222-3, 225, 227, 231-2, 250, 260, 262, 278, 501, 504
Austrian Bishops, 9 f., 37 f., 138

Backofen, 252
Bad Aibling, 285
Baden, 1, 56, 62 f., 79, 81, 109 ff., 158, 166, 170-1, 215, 306
Baden Administrational Gazette, The, 215
Bad Gastein, 176
Badisch-Laufenburg, 243
Bad Reichenhall, 299
Bad Segeberg, 274 n.
Bad Tölz, 264
Balleis, Fr. Peter, 444
Balve, 242

Banasch, Mgr., 42
Bangert, 190
Baptism, attacks on, 441-2; refusal of, 343; NS. substitute for. See "Conferring of the Name"
Baris, Bp. of Berlin, 189
Baronovski, 291
Baudrillard, Cardinal, 10
Bauer, Munich City School Inspector, 117, 148, 164, 252, 283
Bäumler, Prof., 174, 420
Bavaria, 1, 54, 64 f., 96, 101, 110, 128 f., 131, 140-2, 147, 158, 166, 167, 191, 194, 201, 207, 210, 212, 231, 298, 306-7, 313, 368, 469, 541
Bavarian Bishops, 54, 61, 62; pastorals, 14, 22, 112, 133, 140-2, 172, 293-4, 319, 374
Bavarian Government Gazette, The, 98, 129
Bayerische Anzeiger, Der (N), 316
Bayerische Volkszeitung, Die (N), 373
Beck, 324
Becker, Willi, 481
Believer-in-God (*Gottgläubig*), 184, 227-8, 276, 361, 365, 543
Benedictines, 135, 304
Berchtesgaden, 214
Berlin, 42, 107, 159, 172-3, 196, 202, 208, 218, 469; Bishop of, *see* Baris and Preysing
Berning, Wilhelm, Bp. of Osnabrück, 16, 28
Bertram, Cardinal Adolf, Archbp. of Breslau, attacks on, 366, 429; pastorals, 26, 29; protests, 15, 19, 189, 223; speeches, 390-1
Best, Dr., 283
Bevölkerungspolitischen Blätter, Die (P), 334
Bewegung, Die (P), 292, 364 ff., 458, 511
Biberach, 303-4
Birnau, 212
Bislich, 126
Bismarck, 133
Blitz, Der (P), 409-11, 502
Block Wardens, 145, 161
Blum, Günther, 371 f., 380-1
Boepple, 132
Bohemia, 46
Bohne, 495
Bohrmann, 230
Bojunga, 118
Bolshevism, 5, 6, 22 f., 61, 74, 78, 92-3, 122 f., 142, 164, 275, 283, 287, 290, 333, 343, 347, 367, 412, 415 ff., 474

Bonn, 102
Bonus for illegitimate children, 466
Books, anti-Catholic, 288-9, 396-403; Catholic, 64 f., 79-80
Börger, Prof., 282 (n. 3)
Borken-i-W., 344
Bornewasser, Franz Rudolf, Bp. of Trier, 319, 401; attacks on, 252-3; pastorals, 27, 150-1, 159-62, 166; protests, 240, 355-6; sermons, 15, 487-8
Borromäus Verein, 81
Bottrop, 159
Bregenz, 136
Brennessel, Die (N), 292-3
Breslau, 66, 218, 312; Archbishop of, *see* Bertram
Broadcasting, ban on Catholic services, 218-9; NS. propaganda, 94, 305; NS. religious, 377 ff., 492-3, 496-7. *See also* Vatican Radio
Bromberg, 222
Brothers of Christian Schools, 298
Brothers of Mercy, 312
"Brown Sisters," 203 f., 316
Bubenrudel, 373 f.
Buchberger, Michael, Bp. of Regensburg, 22, 63, 155, 430-1
Buchsheim, 22
Budapest, 211
Buer, 20
Bund für deutsche Leibeszucht, 475
Bundeshaus (Düsseldorf), 110
Bürckel, Reichskommissar, 45, 46, 150, 163, 170, 207, 210, 260-1
Burckmühl, 285
Burgenland, 232
Buttmann, Dr., 85

Calendars, 80
Camouflage of persecution, 53, 112-13, 227 f., 514-15
Canisianum (Innsbruck), 49-50
Capuchins, 435-6
Caricatures and Cartoons, 284-6, 293 ff., 340 f., 367, 384, 404, 420-21, 430 ff., 435, 447, 455
Carinthia, 232
Castellaun, 126, 247-8
Catherine of Sienna, St., 453
Catholic Action, 11, 346, 362, 415, 417
Catholic Schools, guaranteed, 116; threatened, 116-18; preliminary attacks on, 119-20; destruction of Christian character of, 121-30; State imposition of textbooks, 128-9; withdrawal of State subsidies, 131; closing of, 134 ff.; resulting effect on taxation, 138-9,

INDEX 555

141. *See also* Elementary, Kindergarten, Mission, Secondary, Vocational Schools; Crucifixes, Religious Instruction
Celibacy, Clerical, 321, 334-5, 433-4, 447
Censorship, 61, 76-7
Centre Party, 116, 190, 274, 276, 345 f., 360, 362, 366, 459
Ceremonial, NS. Religious, 487, 495-6
Chamberlain, H. S., 332, 365
Chiemsee, 349
Christmastide, 486-90
Christopher, St., 453
Church Buildings, Destiny of, 484-5
Cistercian Nuns, 133
Cistercians, 45, 136
Civil Servants, propaganda amongst, 99 ff., 131, 191, 213, 215 ff., 228, 357-8; economic pressure on, 161, 192, 223 f.; apostasy, 230 f.; Catholic Unions of, 190; NS. League of, 100, 357-9. *See also* Associations, Catholic Adult
Clarissian Nuns, 133
Cluny, 176-7
Coblenz, 15, 298, 305, 311
Cologne, 41, 86, 106 f., 127, 159, 209, 230-1; Archbishop of, *see* Schulte.
Commonweal, The (P), 48
Communism. *See* Bolshevism
Community Schools, 115 ff., 128, 144 ff., 369, 448 f.; propaganda for, 119-20, 361; restrictions on religious instruction, 163-6, 168-73; exclusion of clergy, 166-8; spirit of, 173 ff.; spread of NS. ideology in, 178-86
Concentration Camps, 158, 222, 237 f., 313
Conclave of 1939, 427-9
Concordats, with Bavaria (1924), 516, 541; with Prussia (1929), 516; with Baden (1932), 170, 516; with Austria (1934), 173; with the Reich (1933), *see* Reichconcordat
" Conferring of the Name," 503-4
" Confession of Faith," NS., 493, 512
Confirmation, Sacrament of, NS. substitutes for, 507-8
Congregation for Seminaries and Universities, Sacred, 10
Congress, Archæological (Rome), 11 f., 425; Eucharistic (Budapest), 74, 211, 218. *See also* Party Congress

Constance, 34, 106, 212
Corpus Christi, 213, 216, 237, 442; processions, 37, 191, 209 f.,212 ff., 217, 541-2
Cörrenzig, 210
Corvin-Wierzbitzki, Otto von, 401
Cranach, Lucas, 475
Crosinsee, 348
Crucifix, 407 ff., 501-2; removed from schools, 121-7, 247-8. *See also* Desecrations
Crusades, 177
Cüppers, Urban dean of Duisburg, 48
Currency Ditty, 108, 221, 252, 265 ff.
Currency Trials (Devisenprozesse), 243, 279, 282, 295-7, 384-5

Dachau, 68, 291
Dahl, 79
Damian, Bp. of Fulda, 157
Danzig, 243
Darré, Walter, Reichsminister of Agriculture, 356, 473
" Death-bed Coercions," 443-4
Decree against Communists (February 28th, 1933), 66, 106, 111, 194, 197, 208, 236
Derichsweiler, 364
Desecrations, 36, 108, 241-3, 259, App. IV
Dettinger, Fr., 300
Deutsche in Polen, Der (N), 216-17, 247, 258
Deutsche Jugendkraft, 109 f.
Deutsche Justiz, Die (P), 309
Deutsche Kämpferin, Die (P), 476
Deutsche Leibeszucht (P), 475
Deutsche Volkskirche, Die (P), 429
Deutsche Weg, Der (P), 361
Deutsche Wissenschaft, Erziehung und Volksbildung (P), 131
Deutscher Glaube (P), 378
Deutsches Werden (P), 508
Deutschlands Erneuerung (P), 420
Dhunen, Felix, 270
Dibelius, Dr. Otto, 275
Dietrichswalde, 15
Dinkelsbühl, 193
Diocesan Administrations, interference with, 41 f., 62 f.; declarations and protests of, Berlin, 404; Cologne, 94, 103, 544; Freiburg, 253-4, 256, 300. *See also* Report. Munich, 68, 173, 239-40, 544; Münster, 213-4; Paderborn, 273, 424
Diocesan Gazettes: Breslau, 390 f.; Cologne, 374, 403; Ermland, 61; Freiburg, 61, 74, 76; Linz, 198;

Munich, 75 f., 239-40; Münster, 117, 122, 188, 390, 393; Regensburg, 386; Trier, 355-6
Divorce, 462-3; statistics, 469-70
Dogma, Catholic, 347, 369, 438, 510-11
Dollfuss, Dr. Engelbert, 169
Dominican Nuns, 133, 136
Donat, Fr., S. J., 50
Dortmund, 192
" Double Membership," 22, 89, 98, 188-90, 359, 372
Dramatic performances, anti-Catholic, 270-2, NS. religious, 378
Dresden, 180-1
Drewitz, 333
Druck, Württemberg Chief State Councillor, 159
Duelling, 335, 366, 477
Duisburg, 48, 65, 98, 244
Dunkelmänner unserer Zeit, An die, 331 f., 357-8, 392, 402
Durchbruch, Der (P), 124, 292, 321, 406-9, 505
Düsseldorf, 77, 95, 109, 159, 190, 197

Easter, 490-1
Echternach, 214
Eckehart, Meister, 382, 387
Eden, Anthony, 178
Education, Catholic ideal of, 141, 449; Nazi ideal of, 146, 159, 163, 173 ff., 185-6, 369, 447, 457, 472, 510; Nazification of, 146, 176-8; NS. Syllabus of, 178 ff. *See also* Schools, Religious Instruction
Eggenberg, 45
Ehede, 344
Ehrenfried, Matthias, Bp. of Würzburg, 14, 16, 35, 42
Eichstätt, 17, 44, 68, 283, 413; Bishop of, *see* Rackl
Eiserne Blätter (P), 492-3
Elections, political, 20, 42 f., 60, 241, 245; school, *see* Schools, Catholic Elementary
Elementary Schools, Catholic, conversion by election, 132, 143-57; pressure on electors, 150, 152-5, 160 f.; falsification of results, 153-4; free elections, 156; conversion by decree, 157-9; statistics, 159
Ellgering, 98
Ellwangen, 304
Elsässische Kurier, Der (N), 64
Emmerich, 126, 248
Encyclicals, *Divini Illius Magistri*, Dec. 31st, 1929 (On the Christian Education of Youth), 59; *Casti Connubii*, Dec. 31st, 1930 (On Christian Marriage), 424, 447; *Mit brennender Sorge*, March 14th, 1937 (On the Situation of the Church in Germany), 7, 25, 29, 59, 80, 183, 248, 309, 323, 417, 424 f. For text, see App. II.; *Divini Redemptoris*, March 19th, 1937 (On Atheistic Communism), 30; *Ingravescentibus Malis*, Sept. 29th, 1937 (On the Holy Rosary), 8, 25, 30, 74; *Summi Pontificatus*, Oct. 20th, 1939 (Darkness over the Earth), 59
Engel, Dr., 252
Engelzell, 46
" English Ladies," 133 f.
Entkonfessionalisierung (pamphlet), 493-4
Epp, Ritter von, 258
Erding, 544
Erwitte, 242, 351
Erzberger, 418
Espionage, 66, 160, 224, 373 f. *See also* Preaching
Essen, 93, 104 f., 208, 237, 441, 469
Essener Nationalzeitung, Die (N), 104, 334, 370-1, 482
Essen-Steele-Horst, 290
Esser, Hermann, 315
Eucharist, The Holy, 274, 283, 286, 422, 442
Evangelical Church, The, 231 f., 275, 277, 411
Exhibitions, anti-Bolshevist (Munich) 415; Catholic Press (Rome), 5-6, 71; German Book (Budapest), 269-70; *Grüne Woche*, 268-9, 357
Extreme Unction, Sacrament of, 443, 445
Eysele, 336

Faber, H. K., 389
Faith, NS., 437, 509
Fanfare, Die (N), 91, 92, 107, 384-5
" Fascist, The," 424
Faulhaber, Michael, Cardinal von, Archbp. of Munich, attacks on, 252, 254, 258, 261-2, 264, 427, 429 f.; protests, 116, 289, 304; sermons and statements, 6, 22 ff., 27, 29, 34, 51, 63, 132-3, 143, 149, 229-30, 320, 401, App. III.
Feast Days, Catholic, 129, 206-9; NS., 179, 208, 210, 355
Feierstätte, 274
Feldkirch, 136
Feldkirchen bei Klagenfurth, 46
Fellbach, 245
Films, 218, 272-3

INDEX

First Holy Communion, NS. substitutes for, 507-8
Fischer, Dr. Pius, 80
Flags, display of, 207, 209-10, 213, 246
Flammenzeichen, Das (P), 411-2
Florian, 230, 329
Foreign Missions, 219, 282, 386, 406, 450-2
Förg, Dr., 507
Forstenried, 264
Franciscan Brothers, Congregation of, 310, 319
Franciscans, 45, 410
Franconia, 361, 363
Frank, Dr., Reichsminister, 275, 481
Frankfurt, 52, 153, 159, 217
Frankfurter Zeitung, Die (N), 56, 67, 173-4, 357 f., 364, 458, 481, 501
Franz Joseph, Archduke, 355
Frauenberg, 264
Freemasonry, 100, 290, 355, 367, 416 f.
Freiburg i. B., 41, 51, 212, 214 f., 231, 243, 256, 285, 307, 482; Archbishop of, see Gröber
Freiheit und Brot (P), 192
Freikörperkultur, see Nudism
Freimann, 245
Freising, 51, 267
Frenssen, Gustav, 399-400, 485
Frères de la Charité, 301
Frick, Dr., Reichsminister of the Interior, 5, 48, 98, 206; regulations, 46, 51 f., 131, 194, 202, 207, 209, 215, 227, 506; statements, 88, 190, 192, 274, 305, 318
Fritsch, Dr., 256
Führer, Der (N), 290
Führerblätter der HJ. (P), 385-6
Führerdienst (P), 488
Fulda, 53, 429 f; Bishop of, see Damian
Fulda, German Bishops' Conference of, attacks on, 60, 61, 62, 264, 360, 448; communications, 174; joint Pastorals, 17, 19, 21 f., 30, 108, 121, 173 (n. 1), 319
Funerals, substitutes for, 502-3
Fürstenfeldbruck, 54, 168

Gaesdonk, 137
Galen, Clemens August, Count von, Bp. of Münster, 48, 129, 167, 253, 275; attacks on, 246, 261; pastorals, 27, 34, 43 f., 61, 124 f., 128 f., 156 ff., 164 f.; protests, 62, 111-12, 117; sermons and statements, 19 f., 24, 26, 151, 167, 172, 183, 238, 247, 319, 395

Gangelt, 246
Gars, 261
Gelderlander, De (N), 211
Gelsenkirchen, 159
Gensert, 79
Gerichtssaal, Der (P), 235
Gerlich, Dr., 324
German Faith Movement (*Deutsche Glaubensbewegung*), 66, 120, 178, 218, 240, 254, 310, 329, 336, 338, 365, 379, 400, 405, 412-3, 484, 502, 507
German Girls' League (BDM), 45, 96, 315 f., 371 f., 374, 376, 378, 386, 388, 482, 506
German Labour Front (DAF), 188 ff., 193, 317, 331, 552. See also " Double Membership," Ley, Dr.
German News Agency (DNB), 67, 117, 290, 300 f., 309, 371-2
Germania (N), 72, 105, 189-90, 271-2, 368, 380
Geseke, 242
Gesetz und Freiheit (P), 475
Gestapo, 13, 41, 43, 46, 49 f., 59, 61, 64, 66, 77, 79, 125, 158, 196 f., 199, 209 f., 213, 215, 221, 236-7, 244, 246, 248 f., 251, 255, 312-3
Giesing, 254
Glasemapp, Wilhelm, 397-8
Gleiwitz, 209, 218
Glöckel Decree, 169
Gnesen, 221, 250-1
Göbbels, Dr. Joseph, Reichsminister of Propaganda, 61, 274, 305, 308, 314, 318
Goch, 214
God, NS. conception of, 33, 35, 179 f., 337, 357, 365, 369, 379 ff., 387, 400, 409, 438, 481 ff., 493
Godesberg, 102, 137
Goldenstedt, 158, 238
Good Friday, 492-3
Göring, Field-Marshal Hermann, 5, 208, 324
Görlitz, 218
Göttweig, 46
Götz, Curt, 272
Graduates' Union, Catholic, 197. See also Associations, Catholic Adult.
Graf von Spee, The, 477
Graz, 46, 51, 216, 232
Grenzach, 316
Grevenbrück, 242
Gröber, Konrad, Archbp. of Freiburg, 18, 37, 289-90, 306; attacks on, 61, 256, 281, 292, 302, 382, 429; pastorals, 16, 23, 28, 36,

37, 202; protests, 13, 285, 311-12; sermons and statements, 34, 36, 203, 547
Grohé, 230, 280
Gross, Dr. Walter, Director of Dept. of Racial Policy, 334, 510-11
Gruber, 168
Grüne Woche, see Exhibitions
Guardian Angels, 456
Guillot, R., 93
Gumppenberg, Baroness von, 157
Gürtner, Dr., Reichsminister of Justice, 309, 325
Güstrow, 503
Gutsfeld, 341
Gütt, Dr., 416

Hadamar, 45
Haeckel, Ernst, 330
Hagen, 236
Haidn, 102
Halberstadt, 462
Hamacher, 361-3
Hamburg, 218, 286
Hamburger Fremdenblatt, Das (N), 471-2
Hamburger Kirchenzeitung, Die (N), 218
Hamm, 252 f.
Hammerbacher, Dr., 484
Hastenrade, 246
Hattingen, 321
Hauer, Prof. Wilhelm, Director of German Faith Movement, 336, 338
Hayding, Karl, 491-2
Heaven, 277, 279, 283, 369, 383, 387, 439, 444-5
Heckel, Dr., 136
Heidelberger Student, Der (P), 435
Heines, Edmund, 325
Heinz, Dr. Franz, 435
Heisig, Canon, 296
Held, 276
Hell, 276, 279, 283, 369, 398, 439, 444-5
Hellefeld, 242
Herberisch, Fr., 171
Hermsdorf, 51
Hess, Rudolf, representative of Führer, 97, 193, 197, 338, 467-8, 504 ff.
Hessen, 221
Heydrich, leading Police official, 60, 290, 330, 432
Hieronimi, Martin, 379-80
Hildesheim, 194
Hilfrich, Anton, Bp. of Limburg, 154
Hilgenfeldt, 201
Hiltrup, Fathers, 297
Himmler, Heinrich, Reich Leader of SS., 223, 335 ff., 468-9, 489

History, NS. treatment of, 179
Hitler, Adolf, Führer and Reich Chancellor, 11, 14, 164, 314, 315 324 f., 369, 402, 465, 539; and the Church, 18, 20 f., 24, 43, 53, 84, 112, 116 ff., 188, 235, 250, 273 ff., 309, 364, 395, 420, 450, 539; and the Concordat, 85, 88, 241; cult of, 170, 175-6, 257, 280, 284, 341, 350, 357, 362, 379, 381, 405, 413, 448, 458, 481-4, 494 ff., 500, 511; honour paid to his picture, 121, 125 f., 248, 270, 353, 501, 507.
See also *Mein Kampf*
Hitler Youth, 86-89, 212, 358, 551; difficulties for Catholics in, 225, 240, 375-6; immorality in, 314 ff., 317, 325; periodicals, 292, 382-390; propaganda for, 95 ff., 360; religion and HJ., 221, 248, 264, 272, 284 f., 371-2, 373-82, 482, 489, 491; training, 370-1, 373; violence of, 93, 103 ff., 212, 237, 241, 244, 252, 259, 544
HJ., Die (N), 292, 321, 382-4
Hochland Camp, 221, 265, 285, 377
Hoffmann, 198
Hofius, Dr., 296 f.
Hohenzollern, 56, 171
Holtz, 230
Holy Cross Sisters, 137
Holz, 281-2
Holzschuher, Baron von, President of Lower Bavaria and Palatinate, 99
Holzweber, 262
Holzwickede, 242
Hospitals, 48, 222-3, 369, 443-4, 501
Hottingen, 316
Hümmer, Frau, 345
Hunsrück, 253
Hymns, Catholic, 129, 490; NS., 129, 489-90, 493, 497-8

Ibbenbürener Volkszeitung, Die (N), 92
Ideology, NS. (*Weltanschauung*), 21, 22, 173, 178-82, 236, 344, 364, 409, 437, 457 ff., 509 ff.
Illegitimate children, 463-9
Immorality in NS. Party, 313-18, 324-5
" Immorality " Trials (*Sittlichkeitsprozesse*), 209, 298-313, 318-25, 343, 407, 433; NS. accounts and facts, 298-308; NS. use of, 308-13, 321-22; attitude of Bishops to, 318-21, 343. See also Open Letter to Dr. Göbbels

INDEX 559

Immortality, attacks on Catholic doctrine of, 279, 400, 445; NS. conceptions of, 34, 176, 183, 379, 439, 458 f., 509-10
Indulgences, 444 f.
Informationsdienst, Der (P), 190
Ingolstadt, 21
Innitzer, Theodor, Cardinal Archbp. of Vienna, attacks on, 259, 262; statements, 10, 169-70
Innsbruck, 47 ff.
Inquisition, 278

Jam, Dr., 398
Jesuits, 49 f., 64 f., 177, 293, 355, 367
Jesus Christ, 36, 181 f., 241, 275, 279 f., 282, 404-5, 407 f., 413, 439, 481, 488
Jews and Judaism, 36, 49 f., 62, 177, 179, 219, 241, 246, 251, 260, 275 ff., 279-80, 283, 287, 290, 296, 333, 347, 354 f., 367, 378, 404-5, 416, 426-7, 431, 458, 462, 499
Johannis, Fr. Franz, 311
Journeymen's Association, Catholic, 188 ff., 193, 195 f. See also Associations, Catholic Adult
Jud, Fr. Adelheim, 66
Judges, position of, in Third Reich, 234-6
Jugendlust, 303
Jugend und Recht (P), 448
Juliana of Liège, St., 442
Jung, Edgar, 324
Jungführer, Der (P), 91
Jungvolk vom Bau (P), 389
Jüterbog, 368

Kaas, Prelate, 280
Kahr, 289
Kahr, Dr. von, 324
Kaller, Maximilian, Bp. of Ermland, attacks on, 60, 61; pastorals, 20, 24; sermons, 15
Kämpfertum (P), 386
Karitasverband, 22, 200-5, 243, 367; achievements in 1935, 200; limitation of activity, 202-5; limitation of collections, 52, 200-1, 243
Karlsruhe, 224.
Kaufman, Günther, 317, 349, 38 ;- 9
Kelheim, 45
Keller, Dr. Erich, 178
Keminski, 248
Kenn on the Moselle, 125
Kern, Anderl, 271
Kern, Prof. Eduard, 235
Kerrl, Dr. Hans, Reichsminister for Ecclesiastical Affairs, 30, 43 f., 51, 61, 66; declarations, 53, 118, 163, 220, 274-5, 305, 480 f.; regulations, 25, 51, 199
Ketteler, Bp. W. E. von, 77
Kevelaer, 211, 214
Kindergartens, Catholic, 159-60
Kirchensteuer. See Taxes.
Kirchheim, 178
Kislau, 301
Klausner, Dr. Hans, 324
Klein, Kaspar, Archbp. of Paderborn, attacks on, 252; protests, 287-8; sermons, 242
Kloppenburg, 123
Klosterneuburg, 46, 423
Knapp, 270
Koblenz-Moselweiss, 455
Koblenz-Neuendorf, 65
Koblenzer Volkszeitung, Die (N), 309-10
Koch, Fr. Anton, S.J., 79
Kolbermoor, 285
Kölnische Volkszeitung, Die (N), 116, 118, 159, 270, 276 f., 368-9, 482
Kommende Kirche (P), 508
Königsbrunn, 262
Körbecke, 242
Kraus, Canon, 44, 68 f., 284 (n.), 290-2, 300-1, 313-4
Kravarnik, Fr., 259
Krebs, Dr., 66
Kremers, Fr., 415
Kreuz, Dr., 201
Kreuzberg, 45 f.
Kreuzlschreiber, Die, 270
Kreuznach, 240, 253
Krieger, Karl, 303
Kriegsgräber Fürsorge (P), 341
Krone, Dr. Heinrich, 64
Kübel, Dr., 372

Labour Camps, 225, 390-2, 403
Lammers, Dr. Heinrich, Reichsminister, 43 f.
Landersdorfer, Bp. of Passau, 28
Land Year (Landjahr), 237, 392-3
Langsdorff, Capt. Hans, 477
Lateran, Council of (1215), 442
Laufen, 191-2
Lauterbacher, 86, 94
Laws, Against malicious attacks on State and Party, 63, 66; Associations', 46; Austrian, of Church Taxes, 55; Authorisation, 116; Collections, 52-3, 204; Currency, 297; Editors', 69; Educational Committee, 118; Hereditary Farm, 269 (n.); Kongrua, 55 (n.), 57; Land, 56; Marriage, 32, 38, 461-3; Officials, 235; Party Leaders,

interrogation of, 317, 325; Registration, 504; Wills and Testaments of, 57
Lebensborn, 464 ff.
Leffers, Mgr., 67, 402-3
Leibbrandt, Georg, 92
Lemke, A. D., 341
Lemm, 503
Lenggries, 221, 265, 285, 544
Leo III, 287
Leovigil, Fr., 321
Ley, Dr., Leader of German Labour Front, 188 ff., 321, 331, 350, 482
Libraries, Catholic, 81
Liebesbeicht, Die, 270
Life, value of earthly, 33, 437, 439, 509
Liguori, St. Alphonsus, 389, 446
Limbach, 214, 465
Limburg, 42, 105, 110, 502; Bishop of, *see* Hilfrich.
Linz, 51, 503
Lippe, 469
Literary Chamber of the Reich (Reichsschriftumskammer), 69
Löningen, 238
Losung, Die, 495-6
Ludendorff Book Company, 264
Ludendorff, General von, 180
Ludwig, Brother, 299
Ludwigshafen, 97, 196
Lügde, 490 f.
Luther, Martin, 177, 283
Lutz, 299
Lutze, Victor, Head of SA., 230, 342-4
Luxemburger Wort (N), 214

Magdeburg, 381
Mainfranken, 158, 208
Mainfränkische Zeitung, Die (N), 108, 418, 451
Mainzer Anzeiger, Der (N), 90
Maising, 107
Manage Case, The 301, 323
Mannheim, 65, 316
Mariaschein, 51
Maria-Sorg, 46
Maria-Tann, 302
Mariazell, 45
Marienburg, 348 f.
Mariensäule, 249
Marienthal, 211
Marist Brothers, 298-9
Marriage, NS., 461-3; mixed, 407, 447, 470
Marxism, 28, 33, 169, 275, 417, 473 f.
Mass Stipends, 54
Materna, 120
Matrimony, Sacrament of, attacks on, 447; NS. substitutes for, 504-7

Mayen, 65
Mayer, Fr. Rupert, S.J., 25, 67 f., 217, 538 ff.
Mecklenburg, 342
Meetings, Public, attacks on Church in, 412-3
Mehrerau, 45, 136
Mein Kampf, 323, 472, 480, 500, 505 f.
Meissen, 307
Membership Lists, 90, 194, 240
Mensch und Sonne, 472-4
Mensink, 344
Mergenthaler, 144
Metten, 135
" Michael Germanicus," 322-5
Miesbach, 345
Mindelheim, 299
Mirror of Priestcraft, The (*Pfaffenspiegel*), 272, 283, 392, 400-1
Mission Schools, Catholic, 135
Missions, Parish, 220 f.
Mitteldeutsche Nationalzeitung, Die (N), 480
Morales, Juan Garcia, 341
Morality: Catholic, attacks on, 445-7, 460. NS., 400, 446, 510; principles, 457-61; results, 476-8. *See also under* Marriage, Illegitimate Children, Divorce, Sex, Nudism
Moral Theology, 389, 407, 446-7
Moschner, Canon, 66 f.
Muckermann, Fr. Friedrich, S. J.,361
Muckermann, Prof. Hermann, 65, 244
Mühldorf on the Inn, 262
Mühlheim-Styrum, 104
Münchener Neueste Nachrichten, Die (N), 193, 275, 303
Münchener Tagblatt, Das (N), 119
München-Sendling, 108
Mundelein, Cardinal, 178, 322 ff., 428
Münder on the Deister, 221
Munich, 22, 25, 42, 51, 65, 119, 132-3, 143 f., 145-50, 173, 212, 216 f., 220, 231, 243-4, 249, 259, 304, 501; Archbishop of, *see* Faulhaber
Münnerstadt, 137
Münster, 44, 109, 159, 172, 191, 196, 246 f., 274, 306; Bishop of, *see* Galen
Münsterische Zeitung, Die (N), 91
Münsterscher Anzeiger, Der (N), 72, 188
Mussolini, Benito, 354
Mutschmann, 230
Myth of the 20th Century, The, 29, 67, 124, 332, 360, 364, 392, 401 ff., 480; *Studien zum Mythus*, 79, 332

INDEX

Names, Christian, 499
Naumberg, Uta von, 270
Neheim, 242
Neresheim, 304
Neudeutschland, 3, 109 ff.
Neue Freie Presse, Die (N), 181-2
Neue Münchener Tageblatt, Das (N), 71, 191
Neues Volk (P), 499
Neunkirchen, 210
Neustadt, 312
Niederdeutsche Beobachter, Der (N), 120
Nieder-Russbach, 262
Niermann, Fr., 249
Nordland (P), 501
NSDAP (*NS. Deutsche Arbeiterpartei*), 100, 197, 219, 329 ff., 351, 353-5, 501
NS. Erziehung (P), 487
NS. Gemeinde (P), 507
NS. Monatshefte, Die (P), 330 f., 402, 419, 460-1, 475, 499
NS. Parteikorrespondenz (P), 190
Nudism, 472-6
Nuns, 39, 133, 138 ff., 159-60, 200, 202, 204, 279, 285, 293, 295, 444
Nürnberg, 145, 231, 278

Oath, Civil Servants', 358
Oberbach, 376
Odal Right, 269, 269 n.
Oeventrop, 242
Offenburg, 300, 316
Offenstein, Dr., 194
Öffentliche Gesundheitsdienst, Der (P), 433
Old Catholics, 66, 232, 321
Oldenburg, 43, 59, 61, 122-5, 157-8, 238, 248
Old Testament, 128, 168, 171 f., 181-2, 184, 256, 363, 367, 378, 430
Olympic Games (1936), 411
Open Letter to Dr. Göbbels, 317, 322-5
Oppeln, 209
Ordensburgen, 348-51
Ordinariates, *see* Diocesan Administrations
Organisations, see Associations
Original Sin, 282, 387, 421-2, 440 f.
O'Rourke, Edward, Bp. of Danzig, 243
Osnabrück, 196; Bishop of, *see* Berning
Osservatore Romano (N), 1, 5, 7, 9 f., 11, 38, 43, 75, 197, 276, 286, 306, 331, 417, 487
Ostschweiz, Die (N), 170, 257
Ostseebote, Der (N), 503

Our Lady, 36, 279, 407, 454; Immaculate Conception, 282, 338, 339; Virgin Birth, 283
Our Lady of Czenstochau, 211
Our Lady of Fatima, 210, 285

Pacelli, Cardinal Eugenio, 2 f., 6, 264, 313-4, 427. *See also* Pius XII.
Paderborn, 286-8; Archbishop of, *see* Klein
Paffrath, 79
Pageants, anti-Catholic, 287
Palling, 126
Papacy, 176 f., 265, 293, 367, 383, 385 f., 388, 397-8, 399 f., 406, 416, 420-1, 423-9
Papen, Franz von, 214
Parish Magazines, Berlin, 66 f., 74, 94, 191, 268-9, 271, 273, 311; Cologne, 389; Essen, 75 f., 372; Munich, 74, 94, 292; Münster, 76 f., Ulm-Neu-Ulm, 374-5
Parodies, NS., of Catholic rites, 286, 287, 337
Party Congress, Nürnberg, 342, 350, 402, 494-5
Passau, 90, 212, 239, 264
Pastoral Letters, attacks on, 60-2, 264, 333, 341, 360, 366. *See also* under individual Bishops
Paul, St., 172, 332, 378, 407, 421-2
Pauly, 43, 122, 158
Pawlikowski, Ferdinand, Bp. of Graz, 42
Penance, Sacrament of, 281, 398, 404, 440, 443
Periodicals, Catholic, 77-8, 197; NS., 329 ff., 403-12
Petter, 372
Pflanzelt, Fr., 291
Pforzheim, 316
Pfotenhauer, Dr., 433
Pietrowski, 249
Pilchowitz, 312
Pilgrimages, 5, 7, 219; obstruction and suppression of, 90, 210-12; attacks on, 5, 105-6
Pistor, Ernst, 365
Pius II, 265
Pius XI, statements of, 1-11 *passim*; attacks on, 354, 361-2, 423-7. *See also* Encyclicals
Pius XII, 12, 429. *See also* Encyclicals, *Summi Pontificatus*; Pacelli, Cardinal Eugenio
Planetta, 262
Poland, 8, 221-2, 250-1, 478
Police, methods, 247 ff., 261, 313; partiality of, 105, 195, 201, 237, 239, 244, 246, 259, 413

INDEX

Political Catholicism, 9, 18, 27, 29, 35, 65, 179, 216 f., 260, 262, 274, 276, 284, 286, 290 f., 341, 347, 360, 365 f., 389, 412, 417, 440
Polizeibeamte, Der (P), 358-9
Poor Sisters of the Schools, 133
Porres, Martin de, O. P., 455
Posen, 221 f., 251
Positive Christianity, 16, 418, 480, 510
Posters, 238-9, 253, 260 ff., 264-5, 284 f., 311
Potempa, 325
Prayer, 279, 283, 361-2, 387, 406, 493
Prayers, abolition of, in schools, 129, 175; substitutes for, 175-6, 500
Preaching: confiscation of sermons, 63; espionage, 64, 219. *See also* "Abuse of Pulpit"
Premer, 96
Press, Catholic, 14, 17, 35, 219, 274; measures against, 30, 69-81, 197-8, 292, 311, 320; International Exhibition (Rome), *see* Exhibitions; NS. 16, 20, 25, 35, 288-94, 329-35, 403-12, 456, 541
Preysing, Konrad, Count von, Bp. of Berlin, pastorals, 26, 28, 155, 163, 167, 183, 311, 320, 456; sermons and statements, 17, 25, 320
Pribilla, Fr. Max, S.J., 79
Prien, 286
Priesthood, attacks on, 271 ff., 279, 281, 284 f., 287, 291, 293, 295, 362, 365, 377, 384, 400, 422, 430-33, 439, 445
Priests, 132, 225-6, 246; expulsion of, 43-4, 68, 220, 238; violence against, 107, 195, 244-5, 250 f., 259, 290. *See also* Religious instruction, Community schools
Processions, religious, 208, 247; interference with, 212-18; Reich regulation of, 213. *See also* Corpus Christi
Professors' Academy, 368
Propaganda, Ministry of, 300, 305, 308 ff., 323
Protective custody, 19, 64, 66, 105, 126, 239
Prussia, 1, 56, 101, 158
Public Welfare Service, NS. (*Volkswohlfahrt*-NSV), 52, 159, 192, 201, 203 ff., 274
Publishers, Catholic, 59, 80
Purgatory, 369, 383, 387

Quedlinburg, 337
Questionnaires, 100, 168, 191, 228-9, 359

Racialism, 11, 180 f., 184, 219, 256, 275 ff., 318, 334, 350, 418, 498-9; Department of Racial Policy, 334-5
Rackl, Michael, Bp. of Eichstätt, 21 f., 44
Rainer, 45
Ratibor-Altendorf, 66
Raupp, Walter, 303
Recklinghausen, 159, 342
Regensburg, 154 f.; Bishop of, *see* Buchberger
Reich Agricultural Corporation, The, 355-357
Reichconcordat, 1 f., 6-7, 18, 24-5, 29 f., 42, 59 68, 82, 84-5, 87 f., 108, 112, 116, 123, 128, 133, 142, 151, 154 f., 160 ff., 164 f., 188, 192, 209, 240, 293-4, 362, 540; attacks on, 406, 419-20; text of, App. I
Reichenheim, Dr., J. O., 269 (n.)
Reich Department for Promotion of German Literature, 397-9, 474
Reich Labour Service (RAD), 390-2
Reichling, 297
Reich Press Bureau (*Reichspressekammer*), 70, 72, 309
Reichspost, Die (N), 37, 72, 269-70, 275, 303, 307 f., 310, 316, 349, 361-3, 484, 505 f.
Reichssturmfahne, Die (P), 386
Reichsverwaltungsblatt, Das (P), 87
Reichswart (N), 336, 412, 464
Reinhardt, 99
Relics, Holy, 454 f.
Religious instruction, 30, 146, 449; guarantees, 147, 163; pressure on teachers, 168 ff.; exclusion of clergy, 30, 129, 165 ff., 170 f.; prohibition of textbooks, 165, 171; restrictions, 63, 95 f., 127-130, 163-6, 168-73; substitution of NS. ideology, 30, 178-186; withdrawal of pupils facilitated, 168 ff.; suppression of, 172-3
Religious services, disturbance of, 221-2; attempts to keep Catholics from attendance at, 224-5, 375-7. *See also* Apostasy Movement
Remigius, Brother, 299
Report of Freiburg Ordinariate to Holy See, 52-3, 56, 66, 110-11, 170-1, 203-4, 211-12, 215, 231, 377
Retreats, 219-23
Revelation, Divine, 438, 511
Reventlow, Count, 336, 338
Rhede, 195
Rheingönnheim, 107
Rheinische Landeszeitung, Die (N), 104

INDEX 563

Ribbentrop, Joachim von, Reichsminister for Foreign Affairs, 230
Richter, A., 420
Rittweger, 282
Rodenwaldt, Prof., 451
Roder, 282
Röhm, Ernst, 314, 324 f., 471-2
Ronay, Mgr. von, 250
Roosevelt, President, 428
Rösch, 254
Rose, A. W., 399
Rosenberg, Alfred, Reich Leader of ideological training, 124, 180, 241, 243, 270, 274 f., 332, 349, 360, 364, 373, 401-3, 450, 481, 485; speeches, 83, 276-8, 352, 457. See also Myth of the Twentieth Century, The; *Dunkelmänner unserer Zeit, An die*
Rosenfelder, Dr., 352
Rosenheim, 240
Rostock, 67, 403
Roth, Albert, 283
Rottenburg, 167, 254-6; Bishop of, see Sproll
Röver, 230
Rübenach, Elz von, Reichsminister of Transport, 214
Ruhr, 103
Rupertinum, 51, 137
Ruprecht, Dr. Karl, 486
Russia, see Bolshevism
Rust, Dr., Reichsminister of Education, regulations of, 51, 83, 96, 127, 131, 137, 165-6, 171, 182, 358, 368, 393; speeches, 116, 118, 136, 151, 275, 322
Rutha, Heinz, 315

SA. (*Sturmabteilung*), 225, 257, 264, 284 f., 325, 342-7, 472, 500, 551; violence of, 107, 195, 214, 239, 244 ff., 248, 258 f., 344.
Saarbrücken, 211
Saarland, 90, 150 f., 158
Säckingen, 36
Sacred Heart, 341, 455-6
Sacred Heart nuns, 137
Saints, veneration of, 346, 442, 453-5
Salaries, clerical, 27, 53 ff., 418
Salesians, 135
Salzburg, 42, 44 f., 45, 50 f., 136 f., 170, 232, 286; Archbishop of, see Waitz
SA-Mann, Der (N), 119-20, 207-8, 344-7, 402, 421, 423-4, 431, 433, 435, 437, 444-5, 455 f., 509-10
Sassbach, 298
Sauerland, 224, 273
Saxony, 158, 180-1

Schaffhausener Zeitung, Die (N), 245
Scheel, Dr., 364
Schenzinger, 176
Schirach, Baldur von, Reich Youth Leader, regulations, 89, 349; speeches, 83, 86-9, 94, 371, 380 f., 448, 481 f., 511
Schlegel, Fr. Leo, 79
Schleissheim, 344
Schlipf, 304
Schmidt, Dr., 289-90
Schmidt, Friedrich, Head of Central Training Dept. of NSDAP, 279, 457
" Schmidt, Friedrich," 303
Schmidt, Willy, 324
Schmitthenner, Dr. Paul, 176-7
Schmutz, Fr. Stephan, 66
Schnabel, Prof., 480
Schools, see Adolf Hitler, Catholic, Community Schools
Schöpfer, Mgr., 80
Schoot, Dr., 254, 282
Schülle Case, the, 68, 300-1
Schulte, Karl, Cardinal Archbp. of Cologne, pastorals, 16, 28, 165; statements, 69, 155
Schulungsbrief, Der (P), 331-3
Schulz, 511
Schumann, Gerhard, 292-3
Schürmann, 189-90
Schuschnigg, Dr. Kurt von, 169, 260
" Schwab, Fr. Otto," 304
Schwäbe, 304
Schwäbische Mercur, Der (N), 182-3
Schwäbische Rundschau, Die (P), 333-4
Schwarz, Dr., 282
Schwarz, Dieter, 53
Schwarze Korps, Das (N), 120, 157, 178, 265-6, 272 f., 292 f., 295, 300 f., 310, 314, 322, 337 ff., 402-3, 415 ff., 421 ff., 438 ff., 445 ff., 452 ff., 459 ff., 470 ff., 476 f., 482-4, 485 f., 498-9, 502, 506-7, 509 ff.
Schwarzer, Dr., 299
Schwede-Koburg, 129
Schweinfurt, 108
Schwippbogen (P), 355
Sebastian, Ludwig, Bp. of Speyer, pastorals, 150-1, 152-3, 154 f., 546-7; protests, 134
Seckau, 42
Secondary Schools, Catholic, 39, 170; dismissal of teachers, 48, 134-42; closing of, 47, 130-42
Seele, Die (P), 366
Seelgerat, 269
Seewald, Dr., 290-2

Seifried, Fr., 170
Serajevo, 355
Services, NS. Neo-pagan, 492-7
Servite Nuns, 133
Servites, 47
Sex, NS. theories of, 282, 470-2
Siegrune, Die (P), 507-8
Sigmaringen, 66, 111, 171
Silesia, 110, 206, 209, 211, 216 f.
Silesian Educator, The (P), 363
Simon, Canon, 79
Sin, 440 f.
Sion, 50
Sisters of the Holy Cross, 46
Sisters of Mercy, 24, 295, 297
Society of Christ the King, 45-6
Sodalities of our Lady, 111 f., 193, 197 f., 212, 217, 359
Sohlingen-Nord, 505
Songs, NS. abusive, 221, 265-8, 285-6, 342, 373, 392
Sonthofen, 348, 350, 352
Sörensen, Wulf, 378
Spain, 334, 340, 361; Spanish War, 5 f., 122 f., 283, 415 f.
Spielschar, Die (P), 491-2, 506
Sportpalast (Berlin), 208, 338, 354
Springenschmid, 136
Sproll, Johannes Bapt., Bp. of Rottenburg, attacks on, 42, 254-7; pastorals, 29, 544-5; sermon, 25
SS (Schutzstaffel), 285 f., 314-5, 325, 335-8, 472, 489, 491; violence of, 107, 195, 245 f., 250, 252
Stähle, Dr. 282 (n. 2)
St. Annaberg, 211
Statistical Year Book, The Reich, 317-8
St. Blasien, 137
Steeb, Karl, 505
Steffes, Dr., 359
Stegmann, Eghard, 510
Steigerwald, Franz, 68, 404
Stella Matutina, 137
Sterilization, 219
Sterkrade, 261
Stimme der deutschen Weltanschauung (P), 432
Stimme, Die (P), 411
Stimmen der Zeit (P), 77
St. Lamprecht, 45-6
St. Matthias Church (Berlin), 221, 405
Stohr, Albert, Bp. of Mainz, attacks on, 286; pastorals, 29, 35, 184
St. Ottilien, 135
Sträter, Hermann, Auxiliary Bp. of Aachen, attack on, 246; pastoral, 28, 127

Straubing, 47
Streicher, Julius, editor of *Der Stürmer*, 279-81, 306, 322, 476. *See also Stürmer, Der*
"Strength through Joy" (*Kraft durch Freude*), 211, 270, 496-7
Stricker, Principal, 361
Students of Theology, 433-5
Sturm, Fr., 245
Stürmer, Der (N), 68, 212, 264, 311, 404-5, 431
Styria, 232
Sudetenland, 55, 205, 489
Suicide, 477
Suren, Major, 472 ff.
Swastika, 11, 100, 209 f., 257. *See also* Flags, Display of

Tablet, The, 269 (n.)
Tauberbischofsheim, 171, 289-90
Taxes, Church, 51 (n.), 54-7; withdrawal of exemption, 54, 56, 132, 204; Bachelors', 56
Teachers: Catholic, 127 f., 130 f., 174-5; dismissal of, 48, 134 ff., 139; forced to support NS., 95-6, 215, 363. *See also* Catholic Schools and Religious Instruction. NS., 146, 183; Union of, 168, 174 f., 196, 359-64, 488
Telgte, 90
Terboven, Pres. of Rhine Province, 98, 131
Terminology, Christian, 499-500
Theological Faculties, 48-51
Thielemann, Canon, 449 f.
"Thing-places," 211, 484 f.
Thomassin, Erich, 443
Thüringer Allgemeine Zeitung (N) 380-1
Thuringia, 158, 182
Tiburtia, Sister, 134
Tiengen, 316
Tisis, 136
Torgau, 485
Training Camps, 124, 368-9
Training Courses, 124, 175, 368-9, 403
Traub, D., 492-3
Traunstein, 239, 299
Trier, 167; Bishop of, *see* Bornewasser
Trier Clergy Communications, 125 f., 151, 196
Troppau, 277
"Truths of the Catechism," 62 f., 79, 171
Tügel, Bp. (Evangelical), 218, 388
Tyrol, 49, 232
't-Zand, 210

Undergraduates' Union, The NS. German (NSDSTB), 193, 197, 364-8
Uniforms, Regulations for, 335, 375, 393
Universe, The (N), 49 f.
Unterspiessheim, 239
Upper Palatinate, 101
Ursulines, 47, 133
Uterman, Kurt, 368

Vaals, 223
Vaterland, Das (N), 305-6, 317-8
Vatican radio, 10, 243
Vechta, 43
Versailles, Treaty of, 417 ff.
Victor Emmanuel, King of Italy, 354
Vienna, 42, 47, 135, 166, 216, 231 f., 259, 497; Archbishop of, *see* Innitzer
Villingen, 302
Visbek, 238
Vocational Schools, 164-5, 170
Vogelsang, 225, 348, 368
Vogt, 316
Volk im Werden (P), 379-80
Völkische Beobachter, Der (N), 102, 120, 139, 158, 185 f., 273-4, 290, 303, 311, 315 f., 321, 330, 349, 399, 422 f., 451, 463, 467-8, 490-1, 500, 510
Volk und Russe (P), 470
Vorarlberg, 232
Vorstoss, Der (P), 178
Vorwerk, Mgr., 43 f., 122 ff., 158
Vreden, 26

Wächtler, 83, 230
Wagner, Leader of German Doctors, 278, 418
Wagner, Adolf, Bavarian State Minister, 54, 117-8, 146-7, 158, 225, 244, 258, 511
Wagner, Robert, Reich Governor of Baden and district leader, 224, 230, 309
Wagner, Robert, Bavarian State Minister, 184
Waitz, Sigismund, Archbp. of Salzburg, 286
Waldbreitbach, 319
Waldmann, Württemberg Secretary of State, 276
Wallwey, 86
Walter, Ernst, 303
Waltrop, 193
Wang, 261
Wangler, Fr. Elzear, O.S.F., 66
Warensbach, Count, 444

Wattenscheid, 465-6
Weber, Dr. W., 420
Weidling, 108
Weingarten, 25
Weltanschauung. *See* Ideology
Wemding, 210
Wernera, Sister, 384-5
Wesermünde, 221
Westdeutsche Beobachter, Der (N), 333, 480
Westernkoten, 242
Westphalia, 62, 90
Wetzel, Prof., 458
Wewelsburg, 242
Whitsuntide, 491-2
Wichart, 287
Wick, Dr., 317-8
Widukind, 382
Wiener Kleine Volkszeitung (N), 504
Willebadessen, 242
Wille und Macht (P), 289, 388-9, 424
Willi, 73
Wilson, Woodrow, 342
Winsen on the Lahe, 221
Winter Relief Work (*Winterhilfwerk*-WHW), 52, 200, 204, 274, 325, 422, 451
Winter Solstice, 487-8
Wirtschaft und Statistik (P), 470
Wittmann, Fr. Andreas, O.S.B., 443
Wohlmuth, 276
Wolfratshausen, 195, 240
Wolsfeld, 125
Women Teachers' Union, Catholic, 196-7. *See* Associations, Catholic Adult
Women's Union, NS, 100, 192
Workers' Association, Catholic, 188 ff., 195 f. *See* Associations, Catholic Adult
Worlitscheck, 79
Wuppertal, 241
Wurm, Prof. Joseph, 366
Württemberg, 42, 54, 109 f., 144, 158, 172, 178
Würzburg, 51, 99, 196, 231, 239, 264, 307, 364 f., 435; Bishop of, *see* Ehrenfried
Wüstrow, 349

Xanten, 19

Young Men's Association, Catholic, 109 ff. *See* Associations, Catholic Youth

Zeitschrift der Akademie für deutsches Recht (P), 420
Ziersdorf, 262
Zöllner, Dr., 275

*Printed in Great Britain
by
Billing and Sons Ltd., Guildford and Esher*

www.ingramcontent.com/pod-product-compliance
Lightning Source LLC
Chambersburg PA
CBHW030328240426
43661CB00052B/1563